KB151546

고대영어
OLD ENGLISH

전 상 범

한국문화사

어머님께

고대영어 Old English

1판 1쇄 발행 2006년 5월 20일
1판 2쇄 발행 2007년 7월 19일
1판 3쇄 발행 2021년 11월 10일

지 은 이 | 전상범
펴 낸 이 | 김진수
펴 낸 곳 | 한국문화사
등   록 | 제1994-9호
주   소 | 서울시 성동구 아차산로49, 404호(성수동1가, 서울숲코오롱디지털타워3차)
전   화 | 02-464-7708
팩   스 | 02-499-0846
이 메 일 | hkm7708@daum.net
홈페이지 | http://hph.co.kr

ISBN 978-89-5726-376-1 93740

• 이 책의 내용은 저작권법에 따라 보호받고 있습니다.
• 잘못된 책은 구매처에서 바꾸어 드립니다.
• 책값은 뒤표지에 있습니다.

오류를 발견하셨다면 이메일이나 홈페이지를 통해 제보해주세요.
소중한 의견을 모아 더 좋은 책을 만들겠습니다.

책머리에

고대영어는 1100년까지 영국에서 사용된 언어이다. 영어의 과학적 연구를 위해 가장 기본적이고 기초적인 준비 단계가 고대영어와 중세영어에 대한 초보적 지식을 갖는 것이다. 이것은 국어의 본격적 연구를 위해서는 옛 글에 대한 지식이 필수적인 것과 같다.

영어에 대한 우리의 학습 열기는 극에 달한 느낌이 있다. 열기 그 자체가 나쁠 것은 없다. 그러나 그 열기의 대부분은 회화 하나만에 국한 된 느낌이다. 생각이 있는 축구 코치라면 어린이들에게 공을 다루는 발 재주부터 가르치지 않는다. 우선 뜀박질부터 가르쳐야 한다. 육상이 모든 경기의 기본이기 때문이다. 마찬가지로 그림만 잘 그린다고 디자이너가 되는 것이 아니다. 제대로 된 한 명의 디자이너를 키우기 위해서는 색의 배합에 대한 물리학 공부는 말할 것도 없고 동서양의 미술사부터 시작해서 사회학이나 심리학에 이르기까지 폭넓은 공부를 시켜야 한다. 과학에서 기초과학의 중요성을 역설하는 것도 같은 이유에서이다. 세계적으로 유명한 게임기 제작 회사에서 가장 많은 보수를 받는 이는 우리가 흔히 생각하듯이 프로그래머가 아니라 극작가라고 하지 않는가.

고대영어는 그 중요성에도 불구하고 관심만 있다고 해서 쉽사리 배울 수 없는 것이 현실이다. 고대영어에 관한 연구서의 출판은 주로 영, 미국에서 이루어지고 있는데, 많은 경우 이들 출판물들은 고대영어 그 자체에 대한 학습을 목적으로 한 다기보다는 고대 영국의 문물을 소개하는 하나의 방편으로 고대영어를 소개하는가 하면 고대영어의 학습을 목적으로 하는 책들도 경우에 따라서는 원문의 소개는 없이 문법 설명에만 시종 한다든지, 아니면 원문만을 모아 놓은 경우가 많아 초보자들이 접근하기 쉽지 않은 경우가 허다하다. 이들 외의 다른 나라들에서 본격적인 고대영어 학술서를 발견하기는 쉽지 않다.

본서는 고대영어에 관심을 갖는 한국 독자들을 위해 이와 같은 결점을 보완하고 누구든지 쉽게 고대영어에 접근할 수 있도록 계획되었다. '세계에서 가장 고대영어를 쉽게 배울 수 있는 책', 이것이 본서를 집필하는 동안 필자가 잊지 않고 마음에 새겨두었던 구호이다. 그러기 위해 우선 필수적인 고대영어 문법에 대한 소개부터 시작하여 난이도에 따라 배열된 본문에 상세한 발음 설명과 주석을 달았을 뿐만 아니라 모든 원문에는 번역을 곁들였으며, 권말에는 상세한 어휘사전을 첨가하였다. 대개의 사전이 원형만을 제시하여 초보자들이 이용하기 불편했던 점을 감안하여 본서에서는 대표적인 변화형도 표제어로 제시하여 초보자들도 학습하기 편하게 하였다.

Sweet는 입버릇처럼 고대영어를 공부하려는 학생들에게 문법책과 사전을 주고 난 뒤에 선생이 할 일이 무엇이 있느냐고 말했다고 전해진다. 머리 좋은 사람들을 위한 책은 본서가 아니더라도 많이 있다.

우리가 갓을 쓰는 것은 반드시 머리가 시려서만이 아니다. 이 정도의 영어 인구가 있는 나라에 고대, 중세영어 책 한두 권이 없다면 제대로 된 모양새라고 할 수 없다. 그렇다고 하더라도 찾는 사람이 많지 않을 이와 같은 책을 찍는다는 것은 용기를 필요로 한다. 출판을 쾌히 맡아준 한국문화사에 깊은 사의를 표하는 바이다.

끝으로 고대영어에 종사하는 사람들의 오랜 숙원이었던 thorn의 자형(7a)을 여러 번의 시행착오를 마다 않고 예쁘게 도안해주신 포항공과대학교 전기과 허중관 님에게 고마운 마음을 전하고자 한다.

2006년 초여름에

vi

차례

일러두기

발음 표시를 위해 종전의 IPA 표기 중 다음 다섯 기호를 위해 다음과 같은 새로운 기호를 사용하였다.

[ʃ]	→ [š]	예: ship	[ʃip]	→	[šip]
[ʒ]	→ [ž]	pleasure	[plézə]	→	[plézə]
[ʧ]	→ [č]	church	[tʃə : tʃ]	→	[čə : č]
[ʤ]	→ [ǰ]	judge	[dʒʌdʒ]	→	[ǰʌǰ]
[j]	→ [y]	yeast	[ji : st]	→	[yi : st]

새로운 음성기호를 사용해야 할 몇 가지 이유가 있다.

첫째, 새로운 기호는 하나의 음에 하나의 기호를 부여한다는 원칙에 맞는다.

둘째, 간결하다. [tʃə : tʃ]와 [čə : č], [dʒʌdʒ]와 [ǰʌǰ]를 비교해보면 그 차이는 분명하다.

셋째, 종전의 기호는 종종 오해를 가져온다. 예를 들어 adjust를 종전의 [ədǰʌst]로 표기하는 경우 이것을 [어쟈스트]가 아니라 [어드쟈스트]로 잘못 발음하는 경우가 생긴다.

넷째, 종전의 발음기호로서는 정확한 발음을 알 수 없는 경우가 있다. 예를 들어 courtship(구애)를 [kɔrtʃip]로 표기하는 경우 이것을 [kɔrt ʃip]로 발음해야 하는 것인지, 아니면 [kɔr tʃip]로 발음해야 하는지 분명치 않다.

다섯째, 현재의 독자들은 대개 영어를 주 외국어로 사용하므로 yes를 [yes]로 표기하는 것이 독일어를 근거로 만들어진 IPA의 [jes]보다 읽기가 쉽다.

여섯째, 새로이 사용하는 위의 다섯 기호는 현대 음운론에서 널리 사용되는 기호이다.

이와 같은 여러 가지 이유 때문에 본서에서는 새로운 음성표기를 사용하였다.

Grammar
문 법

1. 자모와 발음

1.1 고대영어의 기원과 방언

영어의 역사는 관례적으로 다음과 같은 세 단계로 분류된다.

고대영어 (Old English: OE)　　　　　450　—　1100
중세영어 (Middle English: ME)　　　1100　—　1500
현대영어 (Modern English: ModE/MnE)　1500　—

고대영어의 시작을 450년으로 못박은 것은 현재의 영어가 본래 영국에 살던 종족의 언어가 아니라 구라파 대륙에서 이주해 온 게르만족의 언어이기 때문이며, 최초의 이민이 449년에 시작되었기 때문이다. 게르만족이 이주해 오기 전의 영국에는 켈트족에 속하는 브리튼인들(Celtic Britons)이 살고 있었다. 앵글로색슨족이 영국으로 이주해 와 눌러앉게 된 사정은 본서의 다음 글에서 그 편린을 엿볼 수 있다.

The Settlement of the Angles, Saxons and Jutes (214쪽)

고대영어에는 다음 지도에서 보듯 네 개의 대표적인 방언이 있었다.

Northumbrian과 Mercian은 Angles족이 사용하던 방언이고, 따라서 그들 사이의 차이가 크지 않았었다는 점을 고려하면 고대영어는 세 개의 방언으로 이루어져 있다고 할 수 있다.

영국으로 이주해 온 Angles, Saxons, Jutes의 세 종족 가운데서 가장 강력한 종족은 Angles족이었다. England라는 단어가 Engla-land(Angles' land)에서 나왔다든지

English가 Englisc([éŋgliš])에서 비롯했다는 사실이 당시의 Angles족의 세력을 말해 준다.

고대영어 방언

그러나 9세기에 들어와 Viking족의 침략을 받게 되면서 특히 피해가 심했던 Angles족의 문화는 거의 말살되고 말았다. 풍전등화와 같았던 영국의 운명은 이들과 용감히 맞서 싸운 West Saxon의 Alfred 대왕에 의해 부지하게 되었으며, 영어도 그 명맥을 유지하게 되었다. 당시의 처참했던 사정은 본서에 실린 다음과 같은 글들에서 엿볼 수 있다.

침입자들과 강화를 맺은 Alfred 대왕은 Wessex의 재건에 힘쓰는 한편 문화의 창달에 남다른 노력을 기울이게 된다. 스스로가 라틴어 문헌들을 번역하는 한편(본서의 Alfred's Preface to *Pastoral Care*도 그와 같은 노력의 일환이다) Northumbria와 Mercia의 작품들도 West-Saxon 방언으로 기록해두는 일에 정열을 기울였다. 오늘날 전해지는 고대영어 문헌의 대부분이 West Saxon 방언에 의한 것은 이와 같은 사정 때문이다.

1.2 고대영어의 자모

아래에 고대영어와 현대영어의 자모를 열거해놓았다. 비교해보기 바란다.

고대영어: a æ b c d e f ʒ h i (k) l m n o p r s t a/ð u Þ x y (z)
현대영어: a b c d e f g h i j k l m n o p q r s t   u v w x y z

위에서 보다시피 고대영어에서는 g, j, q, v, w가 사용되지 않았으며, k와 z는 드물게 사용되었다. 한편 고대영어에는 현대영어에 없는 æ(ash), ʒ(yogh), a(thorn), ð(eth), Þ(wynn)의 다섯 글자가 사용되었다. æ는 [æ]의 음가를 가지며, ʒ와 Þ는 인쇄의 편의상 현대의 고대영어 문헌에서는 각기 g와 w로 표기된다. 한편 a는 고대 게르만인들이 사용하던 Rune문자에서 가져온 것이며, ð는 d에 작대기를 그어만든 것으로서 이들은 상호 교체 사용이 가능하다. 예를 들어 since라는 뜻의 단어는 siaaan, siððan, siðaan 등의 여러 모습으로 나타난다. a와 ð의 대문자는 각기 7와 Ð이다. 이들도 상호 교체 사용이 가능하다.

1.3 고대영어의 구두점

초기의 고대영어 문헌에는 거의 구두점이 사용되지 않았다. 후대에 오면서 마침표부터 사용되기 시작하였다. 현재 우리가 대하는 고대영어 문헌에 표시된 마침표(,)나 따옴표 (" "), 콜론(:)이나 세미콜론(;)은 모두 편집자의 판단에 의한 것이다. 뿐만 아니라 모음의 장음을 나타내기 위한 장음표시(macron)도 사용되지 않았다. 다음 원고를 참고하기 바란다. 처음 몇 줄은 통상적인 고대영어 철자로 옮겨 놓았다.

(Algeo, J. 1993. *Problems in the Origins and Development of the English Language*, 77.)

(ic næfre ain wif. forðan ae ic sylfwylles eom criste ge
halgod. ne ic aam hæaenum godum lac ne geoffrige.
forðan ae ic on crist gelyfe. 7a hēt se arleasa flaccus. aa
femnan gebringan on aysterfullum cwearterne. & cwæa.
aæt man ne sceolde ænigne bigleofan hire dōn binnon seo
fon nihton.)

이와 같은 관행은 경우에 따라 혼란을 가져오거나 해석상의 차이를 가져올 수 있다. 편집자의 역량이 발휘되는 것은 이 부분에서이다. 후기에 오면서 현대와 같은 구두점이 사용되기 시작한다.

1.4 고대영어의 발음 : 모음과 2중모음

고대영어는 거의 쓴 대로 읽힌다고 해도 과언이 아니다. 다음을 보자.

단모음

    a [a]   assa (=ass), nama (=name), habban (=to have)

    ā [a：] twā (=two), stān (=stone), hām (=home)

    æ [æ] fæder (=father), æfter (=after), hæt (=hat)

    ǣ [ε：] sǣd (=seed), dǣl (=deal), mǣdenn (=maiden)

    e [e]   beran (=to bear), etan (=to eat), settan (=to set)

    ē [e：] cwēn (=queen), hē (=he), grēne (=green)

    i [i]   sittan (=to sit), wind (=wind), cwic (=quick)

    ī [i：] fīf (=five), wīn (=wine), wrītan (=to write)

    o [o]   oxa (=ox), oft (=often), god (=god)

    ō [o：] sōna (=soon), cōl (=coal), gōd (=good)

    u [u]   cuman (=to come), duru (=door), sunu (=son)

    ū [u：] mūs (=moue), cū (=cow), nū (=now)

    y [ü]   yfel (=evil), fyrst (=first), synn (=sin)

    ȳ [ü：] mȳs (=mice), brȳd (=bride), dȳstiġ (=dusty)

[ü]는 독일어나 프랑스어에서 들을 수 있는 원순의 전설고모음으로서 [i]를 발음하면서 입술을 둥글게 해서 얻는 음이다.

2중모음

    ie [ie]   ieldra (=elder), ġiefan (=to give), ġiest (=guest)

    īe [i：e] hīeran (=to hear), nīewe (=new), ġelīefan (=to believe)

    ea [εə]   heard (=heard), eall (=all), beard (=beard)

    ēa [ε：ə] ēast (=east), drēam (=dream), hlēapan (=to leap)

    eo [eo]   weorc (=work), eorðe (=earth), sweostor (=sister)

    ēo [e：o] dēop (=deep), dēor (=animal), ċēosan (=to choose)

이상에서 알 수 있는 것은 고대영어에서는 현대영어와는 달리 모음의 장단이 변별적이었다는 사실이다. 따라서 고대영어는 /a, e, i, o, u, y/의 일곱 개의 단순모음 (simple vowel)과 /ie, ea, eo/의 세 개의 2중단모음(short diphthong)에 더하여 이들 각각의 장모음을 가지고 있었다.

1.5 고대영어의 발음 : 자음

고대영어의 자음은 원칙적으로는 하나의 음가를 갖는다. 그러나 다음에서 보듯 약간의 변이형이 있다. 현대영어와 동일한 b, d, l, m, n, p, t의 발음은 생략하고 c, f, g, h, r, s, a, ð, w, x 등의 발음에 대해 알아보자. 첫째, s, f, a/ð의 세 마찰음은 유성음 사이에서는 각기 [z], [v], [ð]의 유성음으로 발음되며 그 밖의 위치에서는 본래의 음가대로 발음된다.

> s, f, a/ð
> s [s]   hūs (=house), sunu (=son), singan (=to sing)
>   [z]   ·cēosan (=to choose), ārīsan (=to rise), hæsl (=hazel)
> f [f]   folc (=people), līf (=life), full (=full)
>   [v]   lufian (=to love), heofon (=heaven), healfe (=half)
> a/ð [Ɵ]   aīn (=thy), mūa (=mouth), wora (=worth)
>   [ð]   swīae (=very), brōaor (=brother), hǣðen (=heathen)

단 이들이 유성음과 형태소 경계를 사이에 두고 인접하거나 중복자음(geminate consonant)으로 사용될 때에는 유성음화하지 않는다.

> s [s]   ġe-sæt (=sat), ā-sittan (=to dwell together)
>   cyssan (=to kiss), blissian (=to bliss)
> f [f]   of-ġiefan (=to abandon) ā-faran (=to travel).
>   offrian (=to ofer), offerian (=to carry off)
> a/ð [Ɵ]   oð-lǣdan (=to lead away), oa-beran (=to bear away)
>   siaaan (=since), oððe (=or)

둘째, c와 g는 앞뒤에 /i. e/ 등의 전설모음이 올 때 각기 [č]와 [y]로 발음되며, 그 밖의 위치에서는 [k]와 [g]로 발음된다. 초학자들을 위한 교재에서 [č]의 음가를 갖는 c는 ċ로, 그리고 [y]의 음가를 갖는 g는 ġ처럼 해당 글자 위에 점을 찍어 표기한다. 본서에서는 주에서는 모든 경우에, 그리고 본문을 위해서는 IX장까지 이 관행을 따르기로 한다.

c, g

c [k] cnēo (=knee), cōl (=cool), catt (=cat)

ċ [č] iċ (=I), ċild (=child), bēċe (=beech), diċ (=ditch), streċċan (=to stretch), tǣċan (=to teach), sēċan (=to seek, cf. beseech), ċirċe (=church), benċ (=bench), aenċan (=to think)

       예외 : cēne (=keen), cynn (=kin), wrecan (=to wreak), bæc (=back), cearu (=care)

g [g] gān (=to go), god (=god), dragan (=to draw), boga (=bow), lagu (=law), fugol (=fowl), dagas (days)

ġ [y] ġiefan (=to give), ġēar (=year), weġ (=way), ġeoc (=yoke), hāliġ (=holy), dæġ (=day), weġ (=way), twēġen (=two)

       예외 : gīgant [gi : gant] (=giant)

위에서 보듯 c의 경우는 [k]와 [č] 가운데 어느 쪽 발음인지 결정하기 쉽지 않은 경우가 많다. 한가지 단서는 고대영어의 c는 현대영어의 발음을 비교적 충실히 반영하고 있으므로 현대영어의 발음에서 고대영어의 발음을 추측할 수 있다. 다음 예를 보자.

c [č] ǣlċ (=each), benċ (=bench), drenċan (=to drench), swelċ (=such)

    [k] drincan (=to drink), prician (=to prick), sincan (=to sink)

셋째, h는 위치에 따라 다음과 같은 세 가지 상이한 발음을 갖는다. 첫째, h는 모음 앞에서는 [h]로 발음되지만 둘째, 음절 말에 오거나 뒤에 자음이 오는 경우, 또는 그 앞에 후설모음이 오는 경우에는 [x]로, 그리고 셋째, 앞에 전설모음이 오는 경우에는 [ç]로 발음된다. [x]는 독일어의 Nacht([naxt])에서, 그리고 [ç]는 역시 독일어의 nicht([niçt]) 등에서 들을 수 있는 음이다. [x]는 한국어의 '흐'를 강하게, 그리고 [ç]는 한국어의 '히'를 강하게 발음할 때와 비슷한 음이다.

h

[h]   hand (=hand), habban (=to have), hīera (=to hear)

[x]   aēah (=though), lēoht (=light), hwæt (=what)

[c]   riht (=right), niht (=night), miht (=power)

넷째, w는 항시 발음된다.

       wrītan (=to write), nīwe (=new), grōwan (=to grow), grēow (=grew)

다섯째, x는 weaxan [weaksan]에서 보듯 [ks]로 발음된다.

여섯째, cg는 [ǰ]로, sc는 [š]로 발음된다. 초학자들을 위한 책에서는 편의상 cg
와 sc를 각기 cġ와 sċ로 표기하기도 하나 거의 예외가 없으므로 본서에서는 본래
대로의 모습으로 표기한다. 단 sc가 [sk]로 발음되는 예외적인 경우에는 따로 발음
을 표시해 놓았다.

       cg, sc
       cg [ǰ]   ecg (=edge), brycg (=bridge), licgan (=to lie), secgan (=to say)
       sc [š]   scip (=ship), fisc (=fish), sceal (=shall), scēotan (=to shoot)
              예외 : ascian [askian] (=to ask), scōl [sko : l](=school)

일곱째, 자음군은 모든 경우에 발음된다.

       cn   [kn]   cnāwan (=to know), cniht (=boy)
       cw   [kw]   cweaan (=to say), cwēn (=queen)
       gn   [gn]   gnagan (=to gnaw), gnorn (=sad)
       hl   [hl]   hlāf (=bread), hlūde (=loudly)
       hw [xw]   hwæt (=what), hwǣr (=where)
       hr   [xr]   hring (=ring), hrēosan (=collapse)
       hn   [hn]   hnappian (=to doze), hnīgan (=to bend down)
       wr   [wr]   wrītan (=to write), wræc (=misery)
       wl   [wl]   wlanc (=proud), wlite (=face)
       fn   [fn]   fnǣst (=breath), fnēosan (=to sneeze)
       ng [ng]   bringan (=to bring), lang (=long), singan (=to sing)

여덟째, 중복자음은 현대영어와는 달리 중첩자음으로 발음해야 한다.

       habban (=to have), frogga (=frog), offrian (=to offer), sunne (=sun), siaaan (=since),
       cyssan (=to kiss), ierre (=anger), sittan (=to sit), willan (=to wish)

영어나 독일어를 비롯한 게르만어에서는 중복자음은 하나의 자음으로 발음된다. 다음이 그 예들이다.

영어
ammonia [əmóunyə], pepper [pépər]
독일어
Zimmer [tsímər] (=room), besser [bɛ́sər] (=better)

단 고대영어에서도 중첩자음이 어말에 오는 경우에는 탈락한 것으로 보인다. 그 증거는 mann~man(=people), spell~spel(=story), wild-dēor~wildēor(=wild beast) 와 같은 변이형의 존재에서 찾아볼 수 있다.

아홉째, g는 n 뒤에 오는 경우 흔히 [j]로 발음된다.

g [j] :　　sengan (=to singe), sprangan (=to scatter)

끝으로 r은 현대영어의 r과는 달리 혀끝을 진동시켜서 내는 연탄음(trill)이다. 현대영어에서는 스코틀랜드와 아일랜드에서 들을 수 있으며, 영어 이외의 경우에는 러시아나 서반아어에서 들을 수 있다.

1.6 고대영어의 강세

고대영어에서는 여타의 게르만어들에서 그렇듯이 강세는 어간의 첫 번째 음절에 놓인다. 따라서 접두사로 시작되는 단어의 경우에는 접두사 바로 뒤의 음절에, 그렇지 않은 경우에는 첫 번째 음절에 강세가 놓인다. 대표적인 접두사로는 ā-, be-, for, ge-, on-, tō- 등이 있다. 다음 예 중 (a)는 어간으로 시작되는 경우이며 (b)는 접두사로 시작되는 경우이다.

(a) éndelēas 　　(=endless)
　　ándswarian (=to answer)

(b) betwéonan 　(=between)
　　forġíetan 　　(=to forget)

onmíddan　(=amid)

1.7 i-변환

소리는 상호 영향은 주고받기 마련이다. 게르만어에 널리 퍼져있던 음변화 가운데 하나가 i-변환(i-mutation)으로서 독일어로 umlaut라고 부르는 것이다. 이것은 한마디로 말해 후속하는 음절의 i 모음 때문에 주어진 모음이 i에 가까워지는 현상을 말한다. 고대영어에서는 기록이 나타나기 이전에 이미 i-변환이 완료되었다.

i-변환은 아래에서 보듯 한국어에서도 볼 수 있다.

[a]…[æ]　잡히다 /caphita/　　…　잽히다 /cæphita/
[u]…[ü]　눕히다 /nuphita/　　…　닙히다 /nüphita/
[ə]…[e]　먹히다 /məkhita/　　…　멕히다 /mekhita/

고대영어의 경우 i-변환을 가져오게 한 원인인 i가 i-변환이 일어난 뒤에 사라져서 현재로서는 변화는 보이지만 그 원인은 알 수 없게 되었다. 이것은 현대 독일어의 복수형에 나타나는 움라우트의 경우와 같다. 많은 명사들의 복수형에서 후설모음에 i-변환이 일어나는데 정작 어미의 i가 사라짐으로써 i-변환이 일어난 음성학적 근거가 사라지게 된 것이다.

i-변환을 정리하면 다음과 같다. 여기서는 동사의 경우만을 다루고 명사의 i-변형은 뒤에서 다시 다루겠다.

			Inf	Ind 3 Sg	
[a]	…	[æ]	faran	færa	(=to go)
[ā]	…	[æ]	hātan	hǣtt	(=to call)
[an]	…	[en]	standan	stent	(=to stand)
[ō]	…	[ē]	grōwan	grēwa	(=to grow)
[ū]	…	[ü]	lūcan	l̄yca	(=to lock)
[e]	…	[i]	cweaan	cwiaa	(=to say)
[ea]	…	[ie]	healdan	hielf	(=to hold)
[ēa]	…	[īe]	hēawan	hīewa	(=to hew)
[eo]	…	[ie]	feohtan	fieht	(=to fight)

[ēo] … [īe]　ċēosan　ċīest　(=to choose)

: Inf=Infinitive, Sg=Singular, 3=3rd person

위의 관계를 모음4각도로 나타내면 다음과 같다.

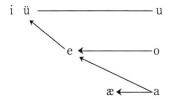

ea…ie는 e와 a가 각기 i와 e가 된 경우이며, eo…ie는 e와 o가 각기 i와 e가 된 경우이다.

　i-변환은 다음과 같은 경우에 나타난다. 첫째 i-변환은 앞서 예시한 것과 같이 직설법 현재형 동사의 2, 3인칭형에서 나타난다. faran…færa(=to go)가 그 예이다. 두 번째 i-변환을 볼 수 있는 것은 명사의 격변화형에서이다. dohtor…dehter (Dative Sg) (=daughter)가 그 예이다. 세 번째로 i-변환은 동사나 형용사에서 파생된 명사형에서 볼 수 있다. dēman(=to judge)…dōm(=judgment)이 그 예이다. 네 번째는 형용사나 부사의 비교급이다. eald(=old)…ieldra(=older)가 그 예이다. 다섯 번째로 i-변환이 나타나는 것은 명사의 단, 복수형에서이다. fōt(=foot)…fēt(feet)가 그 예이다. fōt의 본래의 복수형은 fōt-i였던 것으로 알려져 있다. 복수 어미 i가 선행하는 모음 ō를 ē로 바꾼 뒤 스스로는 사라짐으로써 i-변환의 원인이 소멸된 것이다.

1.8 대모음추이

　중세영어가 현대영어로 넘어오면서 대모음추이(The Great Vowel Shift)라는 큰 음운변화를 겪게 된다. Chaucer와 Shakespeare의 영어를 구별하는 것은 대모음추이의 적용여부이다. 간단히 말해 고대영어나 중세영어의 장모음이 한 단계씩 상승했고, 가장 높은 위치에 있던 /ī/와 /ū/는 각기 [aɪ]와 [aʊ]라는 2중모음이 되었다. 이 관계를 도표로 나타내면 다음과 같다.

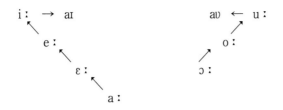

다음이 그 예이다.

			OE	ME		Mod E
(a)	[i :]	> [aɪ]	rīdan	ride	>	ride
(b)	[e :]	> [i :]	dēd	deed	>	deed
(c)	[ɛ :]	> [e :]	dǣl	deel	>	deal
(d)	[a :]	> [ɛ :]	nama	name	>	[nɛ : mə] > name
(e)	[u :]	> [aʊ]	hūs	hous	>	house
(f)	[o :]	> [u :]	mōn	mone	>	moon
(g)	[ɔ :]	> [o :]	stōn	stoon	>	stone

대모음추이에 대한 지식은 고대영어를 해독하는데 큰 도움이 된다. 고대영어의 많은 단어들은 대모음추이규칙을 적용하면 별다른 노력 없이 현대영어로 바꿀 수 있기 때문이다.

OE   MnE

[i :] > [aɪ]   wīn(=wine), rīdan(=to ride), drīfan(=to drive), aīn(=thine),

[u :] > [aʊ]   hūs(=house), ūt(=out), ūre(=our), aū(=thou)

[e :] > [i :]   mē(=me), hē(=he), wē(=we), gēs(=geese)

[o :] > [u :]   gōs(=goose), tōl(=tool), sōna(=soon), mōr(=moor)

2. 어형론

2.1 명사

2.1.1 성, 수, 격

고대영어의 명사는 현대 독일어나 프랑스어, 러시아에서처럼 남성(Masculine), 여성(Feminine), 중성(Neuter)의 세 가지 성 중 어느 하나로 분류된다. 더러는 사물의 자연성(sex)과 문법성(gender)이 일치하는 경우가 있었으나 그것은 우연의 수준을 넘어서지 못한다. 다음의 예들이 그 사정을 말해준다. 각각의 예에서 (a)는 자연성과 문법성이 일치하는 경우이고, (b)는 반대되는 경우이며, (c)는 양자가 무관한 경우이다.

M   (a)   se mann(=the man), se brōaor (=the brother)

      (b)   se wīfmann(=the woman), se mōna (=the moon)

      (c)   se stān (=the stone), se mūð (=the mouth)

F   (a)   sēo sweostor (=the sister), sēo dohtor (=the daughter)

      (b)   sēo sunne (=the sun), sēo smiððe (=smithy)

      (c)   sēo ġiefu (=the gift), sēo tunge (=the tongue)

N   (a)   aæt scip (=the ship), aæt ēage (=the eye)

      (b)   aæt wīf (=the woman), aæt mæġden (=the maiden)

      (c)   aæt ċild (=the child), aæt bearn (=child)

합성어에서는 마지막 명사의 성이 전체의 성을 결정한다.

M   se wīf-mann(=the woman)=ðæt wīf(=the wife)+se mann(=the man)

N   ðæt burg-ġeat(=the city gate)=sēo burg(=the city)+ðæt ġeat(=the gate)

이처럼 자연성과 문법성이 일치하지 않으므로 초학자들은 현대영어의 the에 해당하는 se(M), sēo(F), aæt(N)를 명사와 함께 외우는 것이 좋다. 그러나 많은 경우에 다음에서 보듯 어미가 명사의 성에 대한 정보를 제공해주는 경우가 있다.

(a) 남성
-a   se mōna (=the moon)
-dōm   se wīsdom (the wisdom)
-hād   se ċildhād (=the childhood)
-scipe   se frēondscipe (the friendship)

(b) 여성
-nes   sēo hwītnes (=the whiteness)
-ung   sēo scotung (=the shooting)
-u   sēo strenġu (=the strength)
-du   sēo bieldu (=the boldness)

우리가 대하게 될 고대 명사의 45%는 남성명사이다. 이들 중 대부분은 강변화명사로서 단수 속격에서 -es를, 그리고 복수 주격/대격에서 -as를 갖는다. 각기 현대영어의 -'s와 -(e)s에 해당한다. 나머지는 약변화명사로서 위의 두 경우 모두에서 -an을 갖는다.

한편 명사의 30%는 중성명사이며, 이들 중 대부분은 단수 속격에 -e, 복수 주격/대격에 -a나 -e를 갖는다. 나머지는 약변화명사로서 위의 두 경우 모두에서 -an을 갖는다.

마지막 25%가 여성명사로서 이들은 단수 속격에 -e, 복수 주격/대격에 -u가 붙거나 아무 것도 붙지 않는다.

거의 모든 명사는 복수형의 주격과 대격의 모양이 같으며, 단수형에서도 남성과 중성명사에서는 주격과 대격형이 같다. 한편 복수 속격의 어미는 -a이며, 모든 명사의 복수 여격형은 -um이다.

고대영어의 명사는 단수, 복수로 구분되며, 대명사의 경우에는 양수(dual number)의 구별이 있다. 양수란 '우리 둘'처럼 두 개의 수를 나타낸다. 1, 2칭에서만 있다가 곧 사라져버렸다.

명사의 경우 복수형은 그 변화에 있어 남성, 여성, 중성이 모두 동일한 모양을 갖는다.

2.1.2 강변화

한편 고대영어의 명사들은 네 개의 격을 갖는다. 현대 독일어의 경우와 같다. 주격(Nominative)은 주로 주어나 보어로 사용되며, 대격(Accusative)은 주로 목적어를 나타내기 위한 것이다. 한편 속격(Genitive)은 소유를 나타내며, 여격(Dative)는 간접목적어로 사용되는 것이다.

고대영어에서 명사나 형용사, 동사의 변화를 말할 때 강변화/약변화(weak/strong declension)라는 표현을 사용하는데, 명사와 형용사의 약변화란 전에 있던 격변화의 차이가 어미 상실에 의해 -n이라는 단일 어미로 약화된 경우를 말하며, 동사의 경우 약변화는 시제의 차이를 singan(=to sing)—sang(=sang)에서처럼 동사의 어간 모음의 변화에 의해 나타내는 대신 -de(=-ed) 따위의 어미의 도움에 의하는 경우를 말한다.

현대적 감각으로 볼 때 불규칙 명사라고 할 수 있는 강변화 명사도 나름대로 몇 가지 부류로 나눌 수 있다. 우선 강변화를 일으키는 남성명사에 대해 알아볼 것인데, 자음으로 끝나는 남성명사들이 여기에 속한다. 강변화 남성명사의 대표 주자라고 할 수 있는 se stān(=the stone)과 engel(=angel)의 변화를 아래에 제시해놓았다.

(a) stān (=stone)			(b) engel (=angel)		
	Sg	Pl		Sg	Pl
N/A	stān	stān-as	N/A	engel	engl-as
G	stān-es	stān-a	G	engl-es	engl-a
D	stān-e	stān-um	D	engl-e	engl-um

(a)와 (b)의 차이는 engel의 경우 어미의 첨가와 동시에 어간의 모음이 탈락했다는 점이다. 이와 같은 모음의 탈락은 engel처럼 어간의 모음이 단모음인 경우에 흔히 일어나는 현상이다.

아래에 이들과 동일한 변화를 하는 명사들을 열거해 놓았다.

(a) stān 형

cniht (=youth), cyning (=king), dǣl (=part), dōm (=judgement), eard (=country), eorl (=nobleman), fisċ (=fish), gāst (=spirit), hām (=home), hlāf (=loaf), hlāford (=lord), hund (=dog), mūa (=mouth), prēost (=priest), rāp (=rope), ēow (=sheep), wer (=man), weġ (=way), wīsdōm (=wisdom), ċeorl (=churl)

(b) engel 형

ēael (=native land), dēafol (=devil), drihten (=lord), ealdor (=prince), fugol (=bird), næġel (=nail)

중성명사의 강변화형은 다음과 같다.

(a) scip (=ship)

	Sg	Pl
N/A	scip	scip-u
G	scip-es	scip-a
D	scip-e	scip-um

(b) hūs (=house)

	Sg	Pl
N/A	hūs	hūs
G	hūs-es	hūs-a
D	hūs-e	hūs-um

(a)와 (b)의 차이는 hūs는 주격과 대격의 단수, 복수형이 동일하다는 점인데, 이것은 scip의 경우는 어간이 경음절(단모음과 하나의 자음)인데 비해 hūs는 중음절(장모음, 이중모음, 혹은 어말에 두 개의 자음이 있는 경우)이라는 차이에서 비롯된다.

아래에 이들과 동일한 변화를 하는 명사들을 열거해 놓았다.

(a) scip 형

fæt (=vessel), god (=god), ġeat (=gate), ġebed (=prayer), ġewrit (=writing)

(b) hūs 형

bān (=bone), bearn (=child), dēor (=wild beast), flōd (=flood), mōd (=mind), scēap (=sheep), wīf (=woman)

끝으로 여성명사의 강변화형은 다음과 같다.

	(a) ġiefe (=gift)			(b) sprǣċ (=speech)	
	Sg	Pl		Sg	Pl
N	ġief-u	ġief-a	N	sprǣċ	sprǣc-a
A	ġief-e	ġief-e	A	sprǣċ-e	sprǣc-a
G	ġief-e	ġief-a	G	sprǣċ-e	sprǣc-a
D	ġief-e	ġief-um	D	sprǣċ-e	sprǣc-um

양자의 차이는 단수주격형에서의 어미의 유무의 차이이며, 여기서도 이 차이는 어간음절의 경중의 차이에서 비롯된다.

아래에 이들과 동일한 변화를 하는 명사들을 열거해 놓았다.

(a) ġiefu 형

lufu (=love), talu (=tale)

(b) sprǣċ 형

feorm (=food), healf (=half), heall (=hall), hwīl (=time), lār (=learning), scīr (=shire), sorg (=sorrow), stōw (=place), strǣt (=street), wund (=wound)

2.1.3 약변화

강변화의 경우와는 달리 약변화에서는 대개의 격어미가 -an의 모양을 갖는다. -a 로 끝나는 남성명사와 -e로 끝나는 중성, 여성명사가 여기에 속한다. 남성명사의 약 변화형은 다음과 같다.

nama (=name)

	Sg	Pl
N	nama	nama-n
A	nama-n	nama-n
G	nama-n	nam-ena
D	nama-n	nam-um

-a로 끝나는 모든 남성명사는 nama와 동일한 변화를 한다. 아래에 몇 개의 예를 열거해놓았다.

nama 형

cnapa (=boy), flota (=fleet), fōda (=food), ġelēafa (=belief), guma (=man), mōna (=moon), mūaa (=mouth of river), oxas (=ox), steorra (=star), tīma (=time), aēowa (=servant), wita (=wise man)

중성명사의 약변화형은 다음과 같다.

	Sg	Pl
N/A	ēag-e	ēag-an
G	ēag-an	ēag-ena
D	ēag-an	ēag-um

이 밖에 동일한 변화를 하는 명사로는 ēare(=ear)만이 있다.

여성명사의 약변화형은 다음과 같다.

sunne (=sun)

	Sg	Pl
N	sunne	sunn-an
A	sunn-an	sunn-an
G	sunn-an	sunn-ena
D	sunn-an	sunn-um

동일한 변화를 하는 명사 가운데는 다음과 같은 것들이 있다.

sunne 형

ċirċe (=church), eorðe (=earth), fǣmne (=virgin), heorte (=heart), hlǣfdīġe (=lady), nǣdre (=snake), tunge (=tongue), wīse (=manner)

2.1.4 군소 변화형

고대영어를 비롯한 많은 언어에서 모음변이(mutation) 현상이 관찰된다. 흔히 움라우트(umlaut)라고 부르는 것이다. 간단히 말해서 주어진 모음이 후속하는 모음 i의 영향을 받아 i모음 쪽으로 이동하는 변화를 말한다. 고대영어에서는 주어진 명사형에 복수 어미 -i가 첨가되는 경우에 움라우트 현상이 일어나는데, 복수 어미 그 자체는 뒤에 없어지거나 e로 변했다. 다음이 모음변이의 모습이다. 모음변이는 품사와 상관없이 일어난다.

(a) a → e   mann (=man)   —   menn (=men)
(b) ā → ǣ   lār (=learning)   —   lǣran (=to teach)
(c) ō → ē   dōm (=judgement) —   dēma (=judge)
(d) u → y   full (=full)   —   fyllan (=to fill)
(e) ū → ȳ   tūn (=enclosure) —   tȳnan (=to enclose)
(f) ea → ie eald (=old)   —   ieldra (=older)
(g) ēa → īe hēan (=despised) —   hīenan (=to humiliate)
(h) eo → ie ġeorn (=eager)   —   ġiernan (=eager)
(i) ēo → īe stēor (=star)   —   stīeran (=to steer a (ship))

다음에 몇몇 대표적인 변화형을 제시하였다.

(a) mann (=man)

	Sg	Pl
N/A	mann	menn
G	menn-es	mann-a
D	menn	mann-um

(b) fōt (=foot)

	Sg	Pl
N/A	fōt	fēt
G	fōt-es	fōt-a
D	fēt	fōt-um

(c) bōc (=book)

	Sg	Pl
N/A	bōc	bēċ
G	bēċ	bōc-a
D	bēċ	bōc-um

(d) burg (=city)

	Sg	Pl
N/A	burg	byriġ
G	byriġ, burg-e	burg-a
D	byriġ	burg-um

모음변이에 의한 변화형을 갖는 명사들 가운데는 이 밖에도 다음과 같은 것들이 있다.

gōs (=goose) — gēs (=geese)
mūs (=mouse) — mȳs (=mice)

tōa (=tooth) — tēa (=teeth)

lūs (=louse) — līys (=lice)

군소 변이형 가운데 두 번째로 중요한 변이형은 현재분사에서 온 -nd형의 명사들이다.

freond (=friend)

	Sg	Pl
N/A	freond	frīend, freond-as
G	freond-es	freond-a
D	frīend, freond-e	freond-um

fēond(=enemy)도 동일한 변화를 한다.

세 번째로 언급해야 할 변이형은 sun-u(=son)처럼 단수 주격/대격형에 -u를 갖는 명사들이다.

sunu (=son)

	Sg	Pl
N/A	sun-u	sun-a
G	sun-a	sun-a
D	sun-a	sun-um

이와 동일한 변화형을 갖는 명사에는 wudu(=wood), duru(=door) 등이 있다.

마지막으로 언급해야 할 변화형은 fæder(=father), mōdor(=mother), dohtor(=daughter), brōaor(=brother), sweostor(=sister)처럼 가족관계를 나타내는 말들로서 이들은 다음과 같이 변화한다.

brōaor (=brother)

	Sg	Pl
N/A	brōaor	brōaor, brōar-u
G	brōaor	brōar-a
D	brēaer	brōar-um

2.2 형용사

2.2.1 강변화

명사와 마찬가지로 형용사도 성, 수, 격의 구별이 있다. 그러나 명사와는 달리 단수형에 도구격(instrumental case)의 구별이 있다. 한편 명사와 마찬가지로 강변화와 약변화의 두 가지 변화형을 가지고 있다. 그러나 명사의 경우는 주어진 명사가 강, 약변화 중 어느 하나의 변화형만을 갖는데 비해 형용사의 경우에는 통사적 상황에 따라 강,약변화의 어느 하나를 택하게 된다.

형용사의 약변화는 명사 앞에 형용사가 있고, 그 앞에 다시 정관사 se(=the, that)나 지시사 ðēs(=this), 혹은 소유대명사 등의 한정사(determiner)가 오는 경우에 나타난다. 한편 강변화는 명사 앞에 형용사만이 있을 때 나타난다. 형용사 앞에 한정사가 오면 명사의 성, 수, 격을 나타내는 일은 한정사에게 맡기고 대신 형용사는 거의 모든 경우에 -a나 -an이라는 단순한 격어미로 편한 자세를 취한다.

다음의 두 경우를 보자.

    (a) 강변화

        Iċ eom gōd   hierde.

        I am a good shepherd.

        earla   witena   ġemōt

        all   wise men's meeting

    (b) 약변화

        se   gōda   hierde

        the   good   shepherd

        aisses hālgan cyninges

        of this holy   king

(b)에서는 형용사 앞에 se나 aisses라는 한정사가 있어 형용사는 약변화형이 사용되고 있다.

다음이 대표적인 강변화형이다.

cwic (=alive)

	Sg		
	M	N	F
N	cwic	cwic	cwic-u
A	cwic-ne	cwic	cwic-e
G	cwic-es	cwic-es	cwic-re
D	cwic-um	cwic-um	cwic-re
I	cwic-e	cwic-e	(cwic-re)

	Pl		
	M	N	F
N/A	cwic-e	cwic-u	cwic-a(-e)
G		cwic-ra	
D		cwic-um	

2.2.2 약변화

다음이 대표적인 약변화형이다.

gōd (=good)

	Sg			Pl
	M	N	F	
N	gōd-a	gōd-e	gōd-e	gōd-an
A	gōd-an	gōd-e	gōd-an	gōd-an
G	gōd-an	gōd-an	gōd-an	gōd-ra (-ena)
D	gōd-an	gōd-an	gōd-an	gōd-um

형용사가 성이 다른 두 개 이상의 명사를 수식할 때에는 중성의 어미변화형을 갖는다.

His song and his lēoð wǣron wynsumu tō ġehīerenne.
his song and his poem were agreeable to hear.

여기서 song(M)과 lēoð(N)라는 성이 다른 두 명사에 대해 중성 복수형의 wynsumu

가 사용되고 있다.

2.2.3 비교급

현대영어에서는 형용사에 따라 -er이나 -est의 어미를 부쳐 비교급을 나타내는 것과 형용사 앞에 more나 most를 곁들어 비교급을 나타내는 두 방법이 있다. 그러나 고대영어에서는 모든 형용사의 비교급에서는 -ra를, 그리고 최상급에서는 -ost를 첨가하여 비교형을 만들었다. 다음 예를 보자.

원급	비교급	최상급	
earm	earm-ra	eamr-ost	(=poor)
heard	heard-ra	heard-ost	(=hard)
lēof	lēof-ra	lēof-ost	(=dear)

이들은 모두 약변화형을 갖는다. 예를 들어 lēof-ra는 여성형이 lēof-re, 복수형은 lēof-ran이 된다.

형용사의 경우에도 다른 품사에서와 마찬가지로 비교급에서 모음변이(mutation)를 동반하는 경우가 있다. 다음이 그 대표적인 경우이다.

원급	비교급	최상급	
brād	brǣdre	brǣdest	(=broad)
eald	ieldra	ieldest	(=old)
feorr	fyrra	fyrrest	(=far)
ġeong	ġiengra	ġiengest	(=young)
hēah	hīerra	hīehst	(=high)
lang	lengra	lengest	(=long)
sceort	scyrtra	scyrtest	(=short)
strang	strengra	strengest	(=strong)

대개의 변화형에서 그렇듯이 형용사의 변화형에도 어간과 변화형이 상이한 보충법(suppletion)이 사용되는 경우가 있다. 이들은 현대영어에서도 동일한 변화형을 갖는다.

원급		비교급		최상급	
gōd	(=good)	betera	(=better)	betst	(=best)
yfel	(=evil)	wiersa	(=worse)	wierrest	(=worst)
miċel	(=great)	māra	(=more)	mǣst	(=most)
lȳtel	(little)	lǣssa	(=less)	lǣst	(=least)

2.2.4. 부사의 비교급

부사는 비교급과 최상급을 위해 각각 -or과 -ost의 어미를 첨가한다.

원급	비교급	최상급	
hraðe	hraðor	hraðost	(=quickly)
luflīċe	luflīcor	luflīcost	(=lovingly)
oft	oftor	oftost	(=often)
swīae	swīaor	swīaost	(=greatly)

2.3 수사

고대영어의 수사는 다음과 같다.

	기수	서수
1	ān	forma
2	twā	ōaer
3	arēo	aridda
4	fēower	fēoraa
5	fīf	fīfta
6	siex, six	siexta, sixta
7	seofon	seofoaa
8	eahta	eahtoaa
9	nigon	nigoaa
10	tīen	tēoaa
11	endleofon	endleofta
12	twelf	twelfta

13	arēotīene	arēotēoaa
14	fēowertīene	fēowertēoaa
20	twentiġ	twentigoaa
21	ān and twentiġ	ān and twentigoaa
30	arītiġ	arītigoaa
40	fēowertiġ	feowertigoaa
50	fīftiġ	fīftigoaa
60	siextiġ	siextigoaa
70	hundseofontiġ	hundseofontigoaa
80	hundeahtatiġ	hundeahtatigoaa
90	hundnigontiġ	hundnigontigoaa
100	hund, hundred hundtēontiġ	hundtēontigoaa
110	hundendleofontiġ	hundendleoftigoaa
120	hundtwelftiġ	hundtwelftigoaa
200	tū hund, tū hundred	
300	arēo hund, arēo hundred	
1000	aūsend	

20에서 90까지의 기수 어말의 tiġ는 현대영어의 -ty에 해당하며, 서수 어말의 -ta 나 -aa는 현대영어의 -th에 해당한다.

70에서 120까지는 주의를 요한다. 70, 80, 90을 각각 seofontiġ나 eahtatiġ, nigontiġ 로 하지 않고 그 앞에 hund를 첨가한 이유는 분명치 않다. 짐작컨대 게르만족의 12 진법의 관례와 관계가 있는 듯 하다. 본래는 120을 hund라고 하던 것을 뒤에 기독 교의 영향으로 100을 hund라고 하면서 이런 혼란이 생긴 것 같다. 110이나 120도 각 기 111이나 112로 오해하기 쉽다.

1000 이상의 수를 고유의 영어로 셀 수 있는 길은 없으며, 100 이상의 서수도 없 다. 가령 200th(200번째)를 굳이 표현하려면 æftemest on aæm twām hundredum (=last in the two hundred (200 중 마지막 것))이라고 해야 한다.

21을 ān and twentiġ라고 하는 것은 ein und Zwanzig와 같은 독일어식의 표현이 다.

기수의 처음 세 수만 정상적인 변화를 하며 4에서 19까지는 변화하지 않는다. 서 수는 ōaer(=second)를 제외하고는 약변화형을 갖는다. ōaer는 현대영어의 every other line에 그 잔재가 남아있다. aridda(=third)는 r과 i의 음위전환(metathesis)에 의해 현대영어의 third가 되었다. 이와 같은 예는 고대영어의 bridd가 현대영어의 bird가 된 경우에서도 찾아볼 수 있다. 한편 tēoaa는 현대영어의 tithe(십일조)에 그 잔재가 남아있다.

수사 뒤의 명사는 속격이 원칙이다.

    (a) fíftiġ wintra
          fifty (of) winters(=years)
    (b) eahta hund mīla
          eight hundred (of) miles

2.4 대명사

2.4.1 인칭대명사

고대영어의 인칭대명사는 비교적 그 모습이 온전하게 현대영어에 보존된 경우이다. 다음이 고대영어의 인칭대명사이다.

(a) 1인칭

	Sg	Dual	Pl
N	iċ (=i)	wit (=we two)	wē (=we)
A	mē	unc	ūs
G	mīn	uncer	ūre
D	mē	unc	ūs

(b) 2인칭

	Sg	Dual	Pl
N	aū (=thou)	ġit (=ye two)	ġe (=ye)
A	aē	inc	ēow
G	aīn	incer	ēower
D	aē	inc	ēow

(c)   3인칭

Sg	M	F	N	Pl
N	he (=hē)	heo (=she)	hit (=it)	hīe (=they)
A	hine	hīe	hit	hīe
G	his	hiere	his	hiera
D	him	hiere	him	him

iċ는 라틴어 ego의 동족어로서 중세영어에서는 어말의 ċ가 탈락하고 대신 앞의 모음이 ī로 장음화했다가 현대영어로 넘어오면서 [ai]로 변하게 된다. 그 사이 i만으로서는 너무 빈약하다고 생각한 나머지 대문자의 I로 바뀌었다.

한편 iċ의 나머지 세 격인 mē, mīn, mē는 모두 iċ와는 상관없는 단어에 의한 보충법(suppletion)의 경우이며, 이것은 3인칭 복수의 wē, ūs, ūre, ūs의 경우도 마찬가지이다. ūs는 정상적으로 변했다면 [aus]가 되었을 터이지만 이 단어는 통상적으로 강세가 없는 위치에 나타나기 마련이어서 현재의 [ʌs]가 되었다가 현재는 보다 약화되어 [əs]가 되었다.

고대영어에서 특이한 점은 1인칭과 2인칭에서 양수(dual number)가 있다는 사실이다. 예를 들면 다음과 같다.

Ġemiltsa *unc*, Davīdes sunu!
(=Have mercy upon us two, David's son!)

이 용법은 곧 사라지게 되며 고대영어에서도 3인칭에는 양수가 없다.

ġe는 1611년에 나온 성경의 흠정판(Authorized Version)에서 주격과 대격에서 ye의 모습으로 여전히 사용되고 있으나 그 뒤 그 밖의 격에서는 you가 사용되다가 나중에는 이것이 단수에서도 사용하게 되어 현대영어에서는 you가 단수와 복수를 겸하게 되었다.

3인칭 단수의 hit는 뒤에 어두의 h가 떨어져 it가 되고, 한편 속격을 위해서는 its가 사용되게 된다. 그러나 성경에서는 여전히 the tree is known by his fruit. (Matt., xii, 33)에서 보듯 its대신 his가 사용되고 있다.

3인칭 단수 여성형의 hēo는 중세영어에서는 [hi :]가 되어 남성형과 혼동하게 되어 그것을 피하기 위해 지시대명사의 여성형 sēo를 가져다 쓰기 시작한 것이 현대영어의 she가 되었다. 한편 3인칭 복수형이 모두 th-로 시작하는 것은 바이킹족의 침략

이후 영어에 미치게 되는 스칸디나비아어의 영향의 결과이다.

전체적으로 보아 3인칭 중성을 제외하고는 모든 경우에서 여격이 대격형을 대신하게 되었다. 3인칭 중성형에서는 이와는 반대로 대격형이 여격형을 대신하고 있다. 이치카와 교수(1955 : 23)는 이것은 인간과 사물의 차이에서 비롯하는 것 같다고 말하고 있다. 인간의 경우에는 이해관계를 나타내는 여격의 용법이 많고, 반대로 사물의 경우에는 목적어로 사용하는 경우가 많기 때문일 것이라는 것이 그의 추측이다.

2.4.2 소유대명사

대명사의 속격이 그대로 소유대명사가 된다. 다시 정리하면 다음과 같다.

    (a) 1인칭   mīn   (=my)
                      uncer   (=of us two)
                      ūre   (=our)

    (b) 2인칭   aīn   (=thy)
                      incer   (=of you two)
                      ēower   (=your)

    (c) 3인칭   his   (=his)
                      hiere   (=her)
                      his   (=its)
                      hiera   (=their)

1, 2칭은 형용사의 강변화와 동일한 변화를 하며, 3인칭은 변화하지 않는다.

mīn이나 aīn의 n은 중세영어에서는 탈락하나, 모음이나 h 앞에서는 그대로 쓰였다. mine host 따위가 그 예이다. 이들 용법은 Shakespeare 등에서 흔히 볼 수 있다. 이것은 현대영어 부정관사에 a와 an의 두 변이형이 있는 경우와 같다. 다음 예를 보자.

Give every man *thine* ear ; but few *thy* voice.
                          - *Hamlet*, I, iii, 68.

(여러 사람이 말하는 것은 잘 듣되 자기 의견은 말하지 않는 것이 좋다.)

2.4.3 지시대명사

대표적인 고대영어의 지시대명사에는 se(=that, the)와 aes(=that)가 있다.

se, sē (=that, the)

	M	F	N	Pl
N	se, sē	sēo	aæt	aā
A	aone	aū	aæt	aā
G	aæs	aære	aæs	aāra
D	aæm	aære	aæm	aæm
I	ay		ay	

지시대명사는 동시에 정관사로도 쓰인다. 지시대명사로 사용될 때에는 sē로 길게 발음된다.

도구격의 ay는 thy[ðai]로 변했어야 하나 통상 강세가 없는 자리에 나타나는 관계로 the[ðə]가 되었다. the more, the better 등의 구문에서 볼 수 있는 the가 도구격의 잔재이다. 여기서 the는 by that much(그만큼 더)의 뜻을 갖는다.

다음이 aes의 변화형이다.

aes (=this)

	M	F	N	Pl
N	aes	aēos	ais	aās
A	aisne	aās	ais	aās
G	aisses	aisse	aisses	aissa
D	aissum	aisse	aissum	aissum
I	ay	(aisse)	ays	

2.4.4 의문대명사

대표적인 의문대명사로서 hwā(=who)와 hwæt(=what)가 있다. 다음이 그 변화형이다.

```
        hwā (=who)    hwæt (=what)
        M/F           N
N    hwā              hwæt
A    hwone            hwæt
G    hwæs             hwæs
D    hwǣm             hwǣm
I    hwȳ
```

의문대명사의 남성형과 여성형이 동일한 것은 당연한 귀추이다. 누군지 알지 못
하는 상황에서는 성별도 알 수 없기 때문이다. 도구격의 hwȳ는 by what의 뜻으로
서 현대영어의 why가 되었다.

현대영어의 which는 고대영어에서는 hwelċ였다.

2.4.5 관계대명사

고대영어에서는 ae나 지시대명사(sē, sēo, aæt)가 관계대명사로 쓰인다. 관계대명
사는 다음 네 가지 중 어느 하나로 나타낸다.

    (a) ae의 경우
      (i) ae 단독으로
          se stān, *ae* aā wyrhtan āwurpon
            (=the stone, which the workers threw away)
          ǣlċ aāra *ae* aās mīn word ġehiera
            (=everyone who hears these words of mine)
      (ii) sē, sēo, aæt + ae
          se stān, *aone ae* aā wyrhtan āwurpon
            (=the stone, which the workers threw away)
          Augustinum *aone ae* hī ġecoren hæfdon
            (=Augustine, whom they had chosen)
      (iii) 인칭대명사 + ae
          Fæder ūre, aū *ae* eart on heofonum

(Our Father, who art in heaven)

(iv) ae + 인칭대명사

　　se stān, *ae hine* aā wyrhtan āwurpon

　　　(=the stone, which the workers threw away)

(b) sē, sēo, aæt의 경우

　　se stān, *aone* aā wyrhtan āwurpon

　　　(=the stone, which the workers threw away)

　　hīe aā hine āwurpon intō ānum sēaae, on *ǣm* wǣron seofon lēon

　　　(=they then threw him into a pit, in which were seven lions)

　　hēr aū hæfst *æt* aīn is

　　　(=here thou hast that which is thine)

2.4.6 재귀대명사와 부정대명사

재귀대명사가 따로 없는 고대영어에서는 통상적인 대명사가 재귀대명사 구실을 한다. 다음이 그 예이다.

　(a) hīe ġesemmodon *hīe*

　　　(=they collected themselves, assembled)

　(b) wit *unc* ⋯ werian aōhton

　　　(=we-two intended to defend ourselves)

때로 강조를 위해 self가 사용되기도 한다.

　　swā swā hīe w̄yscoton *himselfum*

　　　(=as they wished for themselves)

고대영어의 대표적 부정대명사(indefinite pronoun)는 다음과 같다.

　　ǣlċ (=each), ǣniġ (=any), man (=one, people), nǣniġ (=none), sum (=some), swā hwā swā (=whoever), swā hwelċ swā (=whichever), swā hwæt swā (=whatever)

man은 부정대명사이지만 mann은 man의 뜻을 갖는 명사이다. 이것은 독일어의 Man(=man)과 man(=people)의 관계와 같다. 부정대명사로 쓰인 man의 예를 들면 다음과 같다.

> his brōaor Horsan man ofslōg
> (=they killed his brother Horsa)

2.5 동사

2.5.1 강변화 동사

고대영어의 동사는 강변화동사(strong verb)와 약변화동사(weak verb)로 나누어진다. 강변화동사는 bindan(=to bind)—band(=bound)처럼 어간의 모음이 변하면서 굴절(inflection)을 일으키는 동사이고, 한편 약변화동사는 hīeran(=to hear)—hīerde(=herd)처럼 현대영어의 -ed에 해당하는 -de, ede, -ode 따위의 어미를 첨가해서 굴절형을 만드는 부류의 동사를 말한다. 강변화동사는 대부분 현대영어의 불규칙동사와 일치하며 약변화동사는 규칙동사와 일치한다. 그러나 고대영어에는 별도의 불규칙동사가 있으며 강변화동사는 그 수가 많지는 않지만 어디까지나 규칙동사이다.

고대영어 동사의 약 4분의 3은 약변화동사이며 나머지 4분의 1이 강변화동사이다. 그러나 그 사용빈도에 있어서는 양자는 거의 동등하다. 이 이외에 몇 개의 불규칙동사(irregular verb)가 있다.

고대영어에는 여타의 게르만언어들과 마찬가지로 현재(Present : Pr)와 과거(Past, Preterite : Pt)의 두 시제의 구별이 있었으며, 각 인칭에 따라 어미가 구별되었다. 부정형(infinitive)은 강약의 구별 없이 -an으로 끝난다.

설명의 편의를 위해 우선 대표적인 강변화동사의 변화형을 아래에 제시해놓았다.

bindan (=to bind)

		Ind			Sbj
Pr sg	iċ	bind-e		iċ	bind-e
	aū	bind-est,	bintst	aū	bind-e
	hē	bind-ea,	bint	hē	bind-e

Pr pl	wē	bind-aa		wē	bind-en
Pt sg	iċ	band		iċ	bund-e
	aū	bund-e		aū	bund-e
	hē	band		hē	bund-e
Pt pl	wē	bund-on		wē	bund-en
Imp sg		bind			
pl		bind-aa			
Inf		bind-an	Inflected Inf	tō bind-enne	
Prp		bind-ende	Pp	(ġe)bunden	

Ind=Indicative (직설법), Sbj=Subjunctive (가정법), Pr=Present (현재), Pt=Preterite (과거), sg=singular (단수), pl=plural (복수), Imp=Imperative (명령법), Prp= Present participle (현재분사), Pp=Past participle (과거분사)

위의 변화표에 대해 몇 가지 지적해둘 사항들이 있다. 첫째, 인칭에 따른 어미의 차이는 직설법 현재 단수형에서만 나타난다. 복수형은 인칭에 상관없이 동일한 어미를 가지며, 가정법은 수에 따른 어미의 차이는 있지만 인칭에 따른 어미의 차이는 없다. 단수형은 모두 -e로 끝나며 복수형은 -en으로 끝난다. 그렇기는 해도 고대영어는 현대영어에 비해 가정법 어미가 많이 남아있는 셈이다. 둘째, 직설법 과거의 단수형(band)과 복수형(bundon)은 상이한 어간모음을 갖는다. 그러나 직설법 과거 단수 2인칭형(bunde)의 어간은 직설법과거 복수형(bundon) 및 가정법 과거(bunde) 와 동일한 모음을 갖는다. 셋째, 명령형은 수에 따라 두 가지 형태로 나타난다. 넷째, 현재분사와 과거분사는 형용사와 동일한 변화를 한다. 한편 과거분사에는 ġe-를 첨가하는데 이미 다른 접두사가 있을 때에는 생략한다. 예를 들어 forġiefan(=to forgive)의 과거분사는 forġiefen이다.

위의 변화표에서 진하게 표시한 부정형과 직설법 과거단수 1인칭형, 직설법 과거 복수 1인칭형, 과거분사형을 네 개의 중요한 형태(Four Principal Parts)라고 부르는데, 그 까닭은 이들의 모양만 알고 있으면 나머지 형태들을 도출할 수 있기 때문이다. 첫째, 부정형(bindan)의 모양에 의해 현재형의 모양 전체와 명령형, 동명사의 굴절부정형(inflected infinitive)의 모양을 알 수 있다. 둘째, 직설법 과거 단수형(band) 에 의해 직설법 과거 단수 3인칭형의 모양을 알 수 있다. 셋째, 직설법 과거 복수 1 인칭형(bundon)에 의해 직설법 과거 단수 2인칭형과 과거분사 및 가정법 과거형 전체의 모양을 알 수 있다. 넷째, 과거분사형((ġe)bunden)으로부터 주어진 동사가 habban(=have) 동사나 bōon(=be), weoraan(=become) 등의 동사들과 결합하였을 때의 완료형과 수동형의 모양을 알 수 있다.

따라서 bindan은 bindan-band-bundon-ġebunden으로만 표시하게 되며, 이 때 이들 어간의 모음의 대응인 i-a-u-u를 모음전환(Ablaut, Gradation)이라고 부른다. 어찌하여 이와 같은 특정한 모음의 대응을 일으키는가에 대해서는 알려진 바 없다.

어미의 자음들은 직설법 현재 단수의 2, 3인칭형에서 아래에서 보듯 발음하기 편하도록 축약되는 경우가 있다.

-test, tea → -tst, -tt	l͞ætst, l͞ætt	l͞ætan	(=to let)
-dest, -dea → -tst, -tt	bītst, bītt	bīdan	(=to wait)
-ddest, -ddea → -tst, -tt	bitst, bitt	biddan	(=to pray)
-aest, -aea → -(a)st, -aa	cwi(a)st, cwiaa	cweaan	(=to say)
-sest, -sea → -st, -st	čīest, čīest	čēosan	(=to choose)
-ndest, -ndea → -ntst, -nt	bintst, bint	bindan	(=to bind)

Sweet는 강변화동사들을 모음전환의 모양에 따라 일곱 가지로 분류하였다. 예시하면 다음과 같다.

Class	inf	inf	pr3	pt sg	pp
I	drīfan	ī	ī	ā	i
II	čēosan	ēo/ū	īe	ēa	u
III	bindan	i	a	u	u
	ġieldan	e/ie	ea	u	o
	weorpan	eo	ea	u	o
IV	beran	e	æ(a)	ǣ(ō)	o(u)
V	ġiefan	e/ie	æ(ea)	ǣ(ēa)	e(ie)
VI	scacan	a	ō	ō	a(æ)
VII	feallan	ie	ēo	ēo	ea
	hātan	ǣ	ē	ē	ā

　　　　: pr3=3인칭 현재

각 부류에 속하는 대표적인 동사들을 아래에 예시해놓았다.

I 형 (drive 형)

inf	pr3	pt sg	pt pl	pp
(ā)rīsan (=to rise)	(ā)rīst	(ā)rās	(ā)rison	(ā)risen
bīdan (=to wait)	bītt	bād	bidon	biden
bītan (=bite)	bītt	bāt	biton	biten
drīfan (=to drive)	drīfa	drāf	drifon	drifen
rīpan (=to reap)	rīpa	rāp	ripon	ripen
scīaan (=to cut)	snīaa	snāa	snidon	sniden
scīnan (=to shine)	scīna	scān	scīnan	scīnen

II 형(choose 형)은 부정형의 모음에 따라 다음 두 가지로 분류된다.

(a) 어간모음이 ēo인 경우

inf	pr3	pt sg	pt pl	pp
bēodan (=to offer)	bīett	bēad	budon	boden
brēotan (=to break)	rīett	brēat	bruton	broten
ċēosan (=to choose)	ċīest	ċēas	curon	coren
flēogan (=to fly)	flīeha	flēag	flugon	flogen
tēon (=to pull)	tīeha	tēah	tugon	togen
flēon (=to flee)	flīeha	flēah	flugon	flogen

(b) 어간모음이 ū인 경우

inf	pr3	pt sg	pt pl	pp
brūcan (=to enjoy)	brȳca	brēac	brucon	brocen
būgan (=to bow)	bȳha	bēag	bugon	bogen
lūtan (=to bow)	lȳtt	lēat	luton	loten
scūfan (=shove)	scȳfa	scēaf	scufon	scofen

III 형(bind 형)은 그 환경에 따라 다음 세 가지로 분류된다.

(a) __nC

inf	pr3	pt sg	pt pl	pp
(on)ġinnan (=to begin)	(on)ġina	(on)gann	(on)gunnon	(on)gunnen

bindan (=to bind)	bint	band	bundon	bunden
drincan (=to drink)	drinca	dranc	druncon	druncen
findan (=to find)	fint	fand	fundon	funden
ġelimpan (=to happen)	ġelimpa	ġelamp	ġelumpon	ġelumpen
springan (=to spring)	springa	sprang	sprungon	sprungen
swimman (=to swim)	swim	swamm	swummon	swummen

(b) _lC

inf	pr3	pt sg	pt pl	ppl
delfan (=to dig)	dilfa	dealf	dulfon	dolfen
ġieldan (=to pay)	ġielt	ġeald	guldon	golden
helpan (=to help)	hilpa	healp	hulpon	holpen
sweltan (=to die)	swilt	swealt	swulton	swolten

(c) _rC

inf	pr3	pt sg	pt pl	ppl
beorgan (=to protect)	bierha	bearg	burgon	borgen
ċeorfan (=to cut)	ċierfa	ċearf	curfon	corfen
weorpan (=to throw)	wierpa	wearp	wurpon	worpen
weoraan (=to become)	wiera	weara	wurdon	worden

IV 형 (bear 형)

inf	pr3	pt sg	pt pl	pp
beran (=to bear)	bi(e)ra	bær	bǣron	boren
brecan (=to break)	brica	bræc	brǣcon	brocen
scieran (=to cut)	sciera	scear	scēaron	scoren
stelan (=to steal)	stila	stæl	stǣlon	stolen
teran (=tear)	bi(e)ra	tær	tǣron	toren

V 형 (give 형)

inf	pr3	pt sg	pt pl	pp
(on)ġietan (=to know)	(on)ġiett	(on)ġeat	(on)ġēaton	(on)ġieten
biddan (=to pray)	bitt	bæd	bǣdon	beden
cweaan (=to say)	cwiaa	cwæa	cwǣdon	cweden
etan (=to eat)	itt	ǣt	ǣton	eten

licgan (=to lie)	līa	læġ	lǣgon	leġen
sittan (=to sit)	sitt	sæt	sǣton	seten
sprecan (=to speak)	sprica	spræc	sprǣon	sprecen
ġiefan (=to give)	ġiefa	ġeaf	ġēafon	ġiefen

IV형과 V형은 과거분사의 모음만이 다르다.

VI 형 (shake 형)

inf	3 pr	pt sg	pt pl	pt ppl
faran (=to go)	færa	fōr	fōron	faren
sacan (=to quarrel)	sæca	sōc	sōcon	sacen
scacan (=to shake)	scæca	scōc	scōcon	scacen
scieppan (=to create)	sciepa	scōp	scōpon	scapen
slēan (=to strike)	slieha	slōg	slōgon	slæġen
standan (=to stand)	stent	stōd	stōd	standen

VII 형 (fall 형)

(a) 과거형이 ēo인 경우

과거형은 단수, 복수형의 어간모음이 같으며, 부정사와 과거분사의 어간모음도 같다.

inf	3 pr	pt sg	pt pl	pt ppl
blāwan (=to blow)	blēow	blēowon	blāwen	blāwen
cnāwan (=to know)	cnǣwa	cnēow	cnēowon	cnāwen
feallan (=to fall)	fiela	fēoll	fēollon	feallen
grōwan (=to grow)	grēwa	grēow	grēowon	grōwen
healdan (=to hold)	hielt	hēold	hēoldon	healden
hlēapan (=to leap)	hlīepa	hlēop	hlēopon	hlēapen
sāwan (=to sow)	sǣwa	sēow	sēowon	sāwen
weaxan (=to grow)	wiext	wēox	wēoxon	weaxen
wēpan (=to weep)	wepa	wēop	wēopon	wōpen

(b) 과거형이 ē인 경우

inf	3 pr	pt sg	pt pl	pt ppl
fōn (=to catch)	fēha	fēng	fēngon	fangen
hātan (=to command)	hǣtt	hēt	hēton	hāten

lǣtan (=to let)	lǣtt	lēt	lēton	lǣten
slǣpan (=to sleep)	slǣpa	slēp	slēpon	slǣpen
(on)drǣdan (=to fear)	(on)drǣtt	(on)drēd	(on)drdon	(on)drǣden
hōn (=to hang)	hēha	hēng	hēngon	hangen

2.5.2 약변화 동사

약변화동사는 현대영어의 규칙동사에 해당한다. 그러나 현대영어의 불규칙동사 가운데서도 -d나 -t로 끝나는 것들 가운데는 약변화에 속했던 것들이 있다.

약변화는 현대영어로 말하자면 -(e)d의 어미를 첨가하여 과거형을 만드는 경우인데, 보다 자세히 분류하는 경우 다음 세 가지로 나눌 수 있다.

    (a) 1형 (femman형) 어미가 -an으로 끝나는 것
       (i) $\breve{V}C_iC_i$ (단모음 뒤에 중첩자음이 오는 경우) : fremman(=to perform)
       (ii) _r (어간이 r로 끝나는 경우에는 어미가 -ian) : nerian(=to save)
       (iii) $\bar{V}$ (어간이 장모음인 경우) : hīeran(=to hear)
          VC_iC_j (단모음과 두 개의 상이한 자음이 오는 경우) : sendan(=to send)
    (b) 2형 (lufian형) 어미가 -ian으로 끝나는 것
    (c) 3형 (불규칙동사)

이들에 대해 차례로 알아볼 것인데, 우선 (ai)의 경우 과거와 과거분사의 어미는 각기 -ede와 -ed이다. 다음에 대표적인 두 동사의 변화표를 제시해놓았다.

<table>
<tr><td colspan="6" align="center">fremman (=to perform)</td></tr>
<tr><td></td><td></td><td>Ind</td><td></td><td>Sbj</td></tr>
<tr><td>Pr sg</td><td>iċ</td><td>fremm-e</td><td>iċ</td><td>fremm-e</td></tr>
<tr><td></td><td>aū</td><td>fremm-est</td><td>aū</td><td>fremm-e</td></tr>
<tr><td></td><td>hē</td><td>fremm-ea</td><td>hē</td><td>fremm-e</td></tr>
<tr><td>Pr pl</td><td>wē</td><td>fremm-aa</td><td>wē</td><td>fremm-en</td></tr>
<tr><td>Pt sg</td><td>iċ</td><td>frem-ede</td><td>iċ</td><td>frem-ede</td></tr>
<tr><td></td><td>aū</td><td>frem-edest</td><td>aū</td><td>frem-ede</td></tr>
<tr><td></td><td>hē</td><td>frem-ede</td><td>hē</td><td>frem-ede</td></tr>
<tr><td>Pt pl</td><td>wē</td><td>frem-edon</td><td>wē</td><td>frem-eden</td></tr>
</table>

Imp sg	freme		
pl	fremm-aa		
Iinf	fremm-an	Inflected Inf	tō fremm-enne
Prp	fremm-ende	Pp	frem-ed

fremman과 동일한 변화형을 갖는 동사들 가운데는 다음과 같은 것들이 있다.

gremman(=to irritate), lecgan(=to lay), settan(=to set), trymman(=to strengthen)

다음은 어간이 -r로 끝나면서 부정형의 어미가 -ian인 (aii)의 경우이다. 과거와 과거분사의 어미는 역시 -ede와 -ed이다.

nerian(=to save)

		Ind		Sub
Pr sg	iċ	ner-i(ġ)e	iċ	ner-i(ġ)e
	aū	ner-est	aū	ner-i(ġ)e
	hē	ner-ea	hē	ner-i(ġ)e
Pr pl	wē	ner-iaa	wē	ner-ien
Pt sg	iċ	ner-ede	iċ	ner-ede
	aū	ner-edest	aū	ner-ede
	hē	ner-ede	hē	ner-ede
Pt pl	wē	ner-edon	wē	ner-eden
Imp sg		ner-e		
pl		ner-iaa		
Inf		ner-ian	Inflected Inf	tō ner-ienne
Pr ppl		ner-iende	Pt Prt	ner-ed

nerian과 동일한 변화형을 갖는 동사들 가운데는 다음과 같은 것들이 있다.

ferian(=to carry), herian(=to praise), spyrian(=to investigate), werian(=to defend)

다음은 (aiii)의 대표적인 동사 hīeran(=to hear)의 변화형이다. 과거와 과거분사의 어미는 -de와 -(e)d이다.

hīeran(=to hear)

		Ind		Sub
Pr sg	iċ	hīer-e	iċ	hīer-e
	aū	hīer-st	aū	hīer-e
	hē	hīer-a	hē	hīer-e
Pr pl	wē	hīer-aa	wē	hīer-en
Pt sg	iċ	hīer-de	iċ	hīer-de
	aū	hīer-dest	aū	hīer-de
	hē	hīer-de	hē	hīer-de
Pt pl	wē	hīer-don	wē	hīer-den
Imp sg		hīer		
pl		hīer-aa		
Inf		hīer-an	Inflected Inf	tō hīer-enne
Pr ppl		hīer-ende	Pt Prt	hīer-ed

hīeran과 동일한 변화형은 갖는 동사들 가운데는 다음과 같은 것들이 있다.

(ā)līesan(=to release), lǣdan(=to lead), ġelīefan(=to believe), sendan(=to send), tǣċan(=to teach), wendan(=to turn)

2형은 어미가 -ian으로 끝나는 것들로서 아래에 그 대표적인 동사 lufian(=to love)의 변화표를 제시해놓았다. 과거와 과거분사의 어미는 -ode와 -od이다.

lufian(=to love)

		Ind		Sub
Pr sg	iċ	luf-i(ġ)e	iċ	luf-i(ġ)e
	aū	luf-ast	aū	luf-i(ġ)e
	hē	luf-aa	hē	luf-i(ġ)e
Pr pl	wē	luf-iaa	wē	luf-ien
Pt sg	iċ	luf-ode	iċ	luf-ede
	aū	luf-odest	aū	luf-ede
	hē	luf-ode	hē	luf-ede
Pt pl	wē	luf-odon	wē	luf-eden
Imp sg		luf-a		

		pl	luf-iaa		
Inf			luf-ian	Inflected Inf	tō luf-ienne
Pr ppl			luf-iende	Pt Prt	luf-od

lufian과 동일한 변화형은 갖는 동사들 가운데는 다음과 같은 것들이 있다.

āscian(=to ask), bodian(=to proclaim), blissian(=to rejoice), clipian(=to call), endian(=to end), folġian(=to follow), gadrian(=to gather), leornian(=to learn), macian(=to make), timbrian(=to build), wunian(=to dwell), wundrian(=to wonder)

2.5.3 불규칙 동사

3형은 불규칙 동사로서 다음의 세 부류로 나누어 설명하는 것이 편하다.

(a) habban (=to have), libban (=to live), secgan (=to say), hycgan (=to think)
(b) 과거형 현재 동사 (Preterite-Present verb)
(c) wesan/bēon (=to be), willan (=to wish), dōn (=to do), gān (=to go)

　(a)형은 1형과 2형의 혼합형으로서 habban(=to have), libban(=to live), secgan(=to say), hycgan(=to think)의 네 동사가 여기에 속한다. 아래에 이들 변화형을 제시해 놓았다.

			habban	libban	secgan	hycgan
Pr Ind	sg		hæbbe	libbe	secge	hycge
			hæfst	leofast	sæġst	hyġest/hogast
			hæfa	leofaa	sæġa	hyġea/hogaa
	pl		habbaa	libbaa	secgaa	hycgaa
Pr Sub	sg		hæbbe	libbe	secge	hycge
Pt sg			hæfde	lifde/leofode	sæġde	hogode
Imp	sg		hafa	leofa	sæġe	hyġe/hoga
	pl		habbaa	libbaa	secgaa	hycgaa
Pr ppl			hæbbende	libbende	secgende	hycgende
Pt ppl			hæfd	lifd/leofod	sæġd	hogod

(b)형은 이른바 과거형 현재동사(preterite-present verb)로써 주어진 동사의 과거형이 새로운 뜻을 갖게 되면서 새로운 현재형 동사가 형성된 경우이다. 예를 들어 wāt라는 동사는 본래 witan(=to see cf. Lt. vidēre)이라는 동사의 과거형으로서 'I have seen'의 뜻이었었는데, 이것이 어느덧 'I know'라는 뜻을 갖게 되면서 wiste(=I knew)라는 새로운 과거형이 생기게 된다. 그 밖에 witan(=to know), sculan(=to have to, be obliged to), cunnan(=to know, be able), magan(=be able), aurfan(=to need) 등의 예가 있다. 아래에 witan(=to know), sculan(=to have to), magan(=to be able), mōtan (=must)의 변화표와 대표적인 witan의 변화형을 제시해 놓았다.

			witan	sculan	magan	cunnan	mōtan
Pr	sg	iċ	wāt	sceal	mæġ	cann	mōt
		aū	wāst	scealt	meaht	canst	mōst
		hē	wāt	sceal	mæġ	cann	mōt
	pl		witon	sculon	magon	cunnon	mōton
Pt			wiste	sceolde	meahte	cūae	mōste
Pr	Sub	sg	wite	scyle	mæġe	cunne	mōte

witan (=to know)

			Present	Past
Pr	sg	iċ	wāt	wiste
		aū	wāst	wistest
		hē	wāt	wiste
	pl	wē	witon	wiston
Pr Sub	sg		wite	wiste
	pl		witen	wisten
Imp	sg		wite	
	pl		witað	
Pr ppl			witende	ġewiten

마지막으로 (c)형의 동사들은 문자 그대로 불규칙 동사이면서 많이 쓰이는 것들이므로 잘 암기해둘 필요가 있다. 우선 현대영어의 be동사에 해당하는 wesan과 bēon의 변화형에 대해 알아보자.

wesan/bēon

			Present		Past
Pr	sg	iċ	eom	bēo	wæs
		aū	eart	bist	w̄ære
		hē	is	bia	wæs
	pl	wē	sind(on)	bēoa	w̄æron
Pr	Sub sg		sīe	bēo	w̄ære
	pl		sīen	bēon	w̄æren
Imp	sg		wes	bēo	
	pl		wesaa	bēoa	
Pr	ppl		wesende		

wesan과 bēon은 그 쓰임에 있어 별 차이가 없어 보인다. 구태여 구별하자면 wesan이 현재의 계속적인 상태를 나타낸다면 bēon은 미래나 진리를 나타낸다. 다음이 그 예들이다.

(a) wesan

iċ *eom* ġeanwyrde munuc (=I am a professed monk)

ðēos worold *is* on ofste (=this world is in haste)

(b) bēon

aū *bið* wel (=you will be well)

winter *byð* ċealdost (=winter is coldest)

아래에 나머지 세 동사의 변화형을 제시해놓았다.

			dōn	gān	willan
Pr Ind	sg	iċ	dō	gā	wille
		aū	dēst	gǣst	wilt
		hē	dēa	gǣa	wille
	pl	wē	dōa	gāa	willaa
Pr Sub	sg		dō	gā	wille
	pl		dōn	gān	willen
Pt sg			dyde	ēode	wolde
Imp	sg		dō	gā	

	pl	dōa	gāa
Pr ppl		dōnde	(gangende)
Pt ppl		ġedōn	ġegān

2.6 단어형성

2.6.1 합성어

고대영어에서의 새로운 단어형성은 차용(borrowing), 합성(compounding), 파생(derivation)의 세 가지 방법에 의해 이루어졌다.

고대영어의 차용은 그 수가 미미하나 그 중 가장 비중이 큰 것은 라틴어와 희랍어였고, 그밖에도 약간의 켈틱어나 스칸디나비아어, 프랑스어 등의 차용어가 있었다.

합성에 의한 새로운 단어의 형성은 현대독일어 못지 않게 왕성하였다. 아래에 몇몇 예를 제시할 것인데, 한 가지 지적해두어야 할 점은 합성어나 파생어를 막론하고 새로이 생성된 단어의 문법적 범주는 항상 마지막 구성요소의 특성에 의해 결정된다는 사실이다. 이것은 형태론에서 우변핵심어규칙(Righhand Head Rule)이라는 이름으로 잘 알려진 사실이다. (자세한 것은 전상범 (1995),『형태론』§9.4를 참조하기 바란다.) 그런 이유 때문에 접두사가 첨가되는 경우에는 생성된 파생어(예 : counterattack)의 문법범주가 항상 어간(attack)의 그것과 동일하며, 파생어(예 : teacher)의 경우에는 가장 오른 쪽에 놓이게되는 접미사(-er)의 특성이 생성된 단어 전체의 문법범주를 결정하게 된다. 따라서 다음 합성어의 경우에도 생성된 단어 전체의 범주는 마지막(오른쪽) 요소의 그것과 동일하게 된다. 우선 합성명사의 예부터 제시하겠다.

합성명사
(a) 명사+명사
dēaddæġ(=day of death) dēad(=dead)+dæġ(=day)
folclagu(=law of the people) folc(=people)+lagu(=law)
hellewīte(=torment of hell) helle(=hell)+wīte(=torture)
storm-s̄æ(=stormy sea) storm(=storm)+s̄æ(=sea)

Sunnandæġ(=Sunday) Sunnan(=sun)+dæġ(=day)

(b) 형용사+명사

eallwealda(=the Almighty) eall(=all)+wealda(=power)

godspel(=gospel) gōd(=good)+spell(=message)

hēahburg(=capital) hēah(=high)+burg(=city)

wīdsǣ(=ocean) wīd(=wide)+sǣ(=sea)

(c) 부사+명사

ǣrdæġ(=first dawn) ǣr(=early)+dæġ(=day)

eftsīa(=return) eft(=again)+sīa(=journey)

ingang(=entrance) in(=in)+gang(=going)

다음은 합성형용사의 예들이다. 우변핵심어규칙에 의해 합성형용사의 마지막 요소는 항상 형용사이다.

합성형용사

(a) 명사+형용사

ælmesġeorn(=charitable) ælmes(=alms)+ġeorn(=eager)

beadurōf(=bold in battle) beadu(=battle)+rōf(=brave)

dōmġeorn(=ambitious) dōm(=glory)+ġeorn(=eager)

merewēriġ(=sea-weary) mere(=lake)+wēriġ(=weary)

형용사+형용사

efeneald(=of equal age) efen(=even)+eald(=old)

glēawhȳdiġ(=wise-minded) glēaw(=wise)+hȳdiġ(=thoughtful)

scīrmǣled(=brightly adorned) scīr(=glittering)+mǣled(=ornamented)

wīdcūa(=widely known) wīd(=wide)+cua(=known)

(b) 부사+형용사

ǣrwacol(=early awake) ǣr(=early)+wacol(=awake)

felamōdiġ(=very brave) fela(=much)+mōdiġ(=brave)

foraġeorn(=eager to advance) fora(=forth)+ġeorn(=eager)

welwillended(=benevolent) wel(=well)+willende(=wishing)

2.6.2 품사전환

현대영어 단어형성의 특징 가운데 하나는 품사전환(conversion)이라고 불리는 현상으로서, 형태상의 변화 없이 다른 품사의 단어로 사용되는 경우이다. 예를 들어 buy는 보통은 동사로 쓰이지만 That's a good *buy*(싸게 잘 샀다)라고 할 때에는 명사로 사용된 경우이다. 동사 특유의 어미(-an)가 있었던 고대영어에서는 기대하기 어려운 현상이다. 그러나 다음 예들에서 보듯 어미를 떼버리면 품사전환이라고 볼 수 있는 경우가 많이 있다. 다음은 동사와 명사가 대응하는 경우들이다.

bītan (=to bite)	—	bite (=bite)
ġēotan (=to pour)	—	gyte (=flood)
andswarian (=to answer)	—	andswaru (=answer)
blēdan (=to bleed)	—	blōd (=blood)
cemban (=to comb)	—	camb (=comb)
cuman (=to come)	—	cuma (=guest)
cuman (to come)	—	cyme (arrival)
dēman (=to judge)	—	dōm (=judgment)
endian (=to end)	—	ende (=end)
flēogan (=to fly)	—	flyge (=flight)
gyldan (=to gild)	—	gold (=gold)
hrēosan (=to fall)	—	hryre (=fall)
lǣran (=to teach)	—	lār (=learning)
lufian (=to love)	—	lufu (=love)
lēanian (=to reward)	—	lēan (=reward)
lēosan (=to lose)	—	lyre (=loss)
slītan (=to tear)	—	slite (tear)
sorgian (=to sorrow)	—	sorg (=sorg)
witan (=know)	—	wita (=wise man)
wuldrian (=to glorify)	—	wuldor (=glory)
wundrian (=to wonder at)	—	wundor (=wonder)
wyrcan (=to work)	—	weorc (=work)
ċēosan (=to choose)	—	cyre (=choice)

품사전환은 형용사와 동사 사이에서도 볼 수 있다.

beald (=bold)	—	byldan (=to embolden)
full (=full)	—	fyllan (=to fill)
fūs (=eager)	—	f̄ysan (=impel)
ġeorn (=eager)	—	gyrnan (=yearn for)
hāl (=whole)	—	h̄ælan (=to heal)
scearp (=sharp)	—	cyrpan (=to sharpen)
wōd (=mad)	—	wēdan (=to rage)
beorht (=bright)	—	beorhtian (=to shine)
ful (=corrupt)	—	fūlian (=to decay)
l̄ytel (=little)	—	l̄ytlian (=to diminish)
open (=open)	—	openian (=to open)
yfel (=evil)	—	yflian (=to inflict evil)

2.6.3 접두사

고대영어의 접두사는 전치사나 부사의 구실을 하는 경우와 첨가된 어간의 뜻을 바꾸는 두 가지 경우가 있다. 예를 들어 before의 뜻을 갖는 fore가 scēawian(=look at)과 결합하여 forescēawian이 되면 foresee라는 뜻이 되는데, 이 때 fore-는 단순한 부사의 구실을 하고 있을 따름이다.

그러나 다음에 열거한 접두사들은 그 자체 독립해서 사용될 수도 없는 단순한 접두사들이다.

an-/on-
(away) : āfaran (=to go awat),
(강조) : ācwellan (=to kill), āf̄ysan (=to drive away), āhēawan (=to cut away)
(별 뜻 없음) : āgalan (=to sing)

āġ-
(무한성) : āġhwelċ (=each). āġaer (=either)

be-/bī-

(about) : berīdan (=to ride round), besittan (=to surround)

(박탈) : bedǣlan (=to deprive), behēafdian (=to behead)

(자동사→타동사) : bestȳman (=to make wet), beaenċan (=to consider)

(강조) : becuman (=to come), belūcan (=to lock)

for-

(before) : forstandan (=to defend)

(상실, 파괴) : fordōn (=to destroy), forweorðan (=to perish)

(강조) : forbærnan (=burn up), fordīlġian (=destroy), forheard (=very hard)

ġe-

(together) : ġebrōðoru (=brothers), ġefēra (=fellow-traveller), ġesweostor
(=sisters)

(결과의 달성) : ġegān (=conquer), ġewinnan (=get by fighting)

(완수) : ġehīeran (=to succeed in hearing), ġesēon (=to succeed in seeing)

(별 뜻 없음) : ġebindan (=to bind), ġehātan (=to call)

(과거분사) :

(결과) : ġeweorc (=(military) work), ġewrit (=letter)

(내포) : ġehwā (=everyone), ġehwǣr (=everywhere)

on-/an-

(전치사 기능) :

(against, in return) : onġietan (=to perceive), onrǣs (=attack)

(해제) : onbindan (=to unbind), onlūcan (=to unlock)

or-

(박탈) : orsorg (=careless), ormǣte (=boundless)

tō-

(분리, 분할) : tōberstan (=to burst asunder), tōteran (=to tear to pieces),

(파괴) : tōfaran (=to go apart, disperse), tōweorpan (=to overthrow)

un-

(부정) : unmihtiġ (=weak), unġeliċ (=dissimilar), unġesǣliġ (=unhappy)

(비하) : unġiefe (=eveil gift), unlagu (=injustice), unweder (=bad weather), unwrītere (=bnad writer, careless scribe)

2.6.4 접미사

앞서 지적했던 것처럼 접미사는 첨가되는 어간의 문법범주를 바꾸게 되는데, 새로이 생성된 파생어의 문법범주는 접미사의 문법범주에 의해 결정된다. 현대영어에서 예를 든다면 -er이나 -ness가 첨가되는 파생어는 모두 명사이며, 한편 -ful이나 -y가 첨가되는 파생어는 형용사인 경우와 같다.

다음은 고대영어의 대표적인 파생명사 어미들이다.

-dōm	crīstendōm (=Christianity), hlāfordōm (=lordship), lǣċedōm (=medicine), martyrdōm (=martyrdom), arēowdōm (=slavery)
-end	ālīesend (=redeemer). būend (=dweller), ċīepend (=seller), hǣlend (=healer)
-ere	rīpere (=reaper), wrītere (=writer)
-hād	ċildhād (=childhood), woruldhād (=secular life)
-ing/-ung	weorðung (=honor), arōwung (=suffering)
-mǣl	fōtmǣl (=foot's length), ġēaremǣlum (=year by year)
-nes	beorhtnes (=splendor), hǣðennes (=heathendom), unrihtwīsnes (=inustice)

다음은 고대영어의 대표적인 파생형용사의 어미들이다. 고대영어의 대부분의 파생형용사는 명사에 접미사를 첨가해서 만들어진다.

-en	gylden (=golden), stǣnen (=of stone), hǣaen (=heathen)
-iġ	mihtiġ (=mighty), hāliġ (=holy),
-isc	Englisc (=English)
-full	ġelēafull (=pious), weorafull (=honorable)
-lēas	ārlēas (=dishonored, impious)
-liċ	folcliċ (=popular), heofonliċ (=heavenly), ċildliċ (=childlike)
-sum	hīersum (=obedient), ġedwolsum (=misleading), wynnsum (=delightful)
-weard	ufeweard (=upward), ēasteweard (=westward), hāmweard (=homeward)

파생부사는 현대영어와 마찬가지로 형용사에 접미사를 첨가해서 만들어진다. 다음이 그 예들이다.

-e	dēope (=deeply), fæste (=firmly), rihte (=rightly)
-līċe	blindlīċe (=blindly), sōalīċe (=truly), openlīċe (=openly), frēondlīċe (=amicably)
-inga/-unga	eallunga (=entirely), yrringa (=angrily)

3. 통사론

3.1 어순

3.1.1 형용사의 위치

굴절이 소실된 현대영어에서는 문법관계를 나타내는 중요한 단서가 어순이다. 예를 들어 현대영어에서 The lion kisses the man과 The man kisses the lion은 전혀 그 뜻이 다르다. 여기서 뜻의 차이를 가져오는 것은 어순뿐이다. 그러나 굴절이 발달했던 고대영어에서는 어순이 그리 중요하지 않다. 다음 세 문장은 모두 The lion kisses the man이란 동일한 뜻을 갖는다.

> Lēo cyssea guman.
> Gūman cyssea lēo.
> Guman lēo cyssea.

그러나 많은 부분에서 고대영어와 현대영어에는 공통점이 있다. 예를 들어 고대영어에서 형용사의 정해진 위치는 현대영어와 마찬가지로 수식하는 명사의 앞 자리이다. 다음이 그 예이다.

> *miċel* flōd (=a great flood)
> *hira* land (=their land)
> se *gōda* mann (=the good man)
> se *foresprecena* here (=the army before mentioned)

그러나 형용사가 수식하는 명사 뒤에 오는 경우도 적지 않다.

> fæder ūre (=*our* father)
> īğlanda *fela* (=many islands)
> eael *aysne* (=this country)

다음에서 보듯 직함이 고유명사와 함께 쓰일 때는 현대영어와 상이한 위치에 놓인다.

> Ælfred cyning (=King A.)
> Ælfmǣer abbod (=Abbot Æ.)
> sunu Bēanstānes (=B's son)
> cwēn Hrōðgāres (=H's queen)

두 개의 형용사가 하나의 명사를 수식할 때에는 다음에서 보듯 현대영어와 상이한 어순을 나타낸다.

> aū *yfla* aēow and *slāwa*! (=thou bad and slothful servant!)
> swīðe *micle* meras *fersce* (=very big fresh-water lakes)

3.1.2 목적어/보어의 위치

현대영어에서는 목적어와 보어가 있는 경우 SVO/C가 정해진 어순이며 고대영어에서도 많은 경우에 동일한 어순을 따른다.

> SVO　　hēo beswāc *hine* (=she betrayed him)
> SVC　　aæt Estland is swȳðe *myċel* (=Estonia is very large)

동시에 간접목적어와 직접목적어가 함께 사용되거나 목적어와 보어가 사용될 때에도 많은 경우에 고대영어와 현대영어는 동일한 어순을 갖는다.

> SVOC　　se cyning hēt hīe *feohtan* (=the king ordered them to fight)

SVO₁O   7ā sende se cyning *ðām earfum* ðone disc.
         (=Then the king sent the dish to the poor.)

그러나 강조나 리듬을 위해 정상적인 어순을 어기는 경우도 허다하다. 다음이 그 예들이다.

SOV   we *hie* ordredon (=we feared *them*)
         Ða reðan Iudei wedende *ðone halgan* stændon
            (=The cruel Jews in their rage stoned *the saint.*)
SVOO₁   ac hē forġēaf eorðlīċe ðing *mannum*
            (=but he gave earthly things to men)
OSV   *Micelne ġeleafan* hē hæfde (=Great faith he had.)
O₁SVO   *ðām acennedan Cyninge* wē bringað gold ···
            (=To the newborn King we bring gold ···)

비록 굴절이 풍부한 고대영어가 굴절이 소실된 현대영어보다 어순이 보다 자유로운 것은 사실이지만 고대영어에서도 이미 공통조어인 인구어(Indo-European)의 보다 풍부한 굴절에 비하면 이미 많은 부분이 소실된 상태였다. 예를 들어 많은 경우에 명사의 주격은 대격과 모양이 같은 경우가 허다하여 다음과 같은 예에서는 오로지 문맥만이 뜻을 말해준다.

     Enoch ġestrynde Irad and Irad ġestrynde Maruiahel···
       (=Enoch begat Irad and Irad begat Maruiahel)

위의 예에서 고유명사들은 주격과 대격의 모양이 같다. 따라서 이들의 문법 관계는 오로지 문장의 위치, 즉 문두에는 주로 주어가 온다는 사실에 의해 결정된다. 다시 말해 고대영어에서도 어순은 완전히 자유롭지는 못했다고 할 수 있다.
다음과 같은 예도 문맥만이 주어와 목적어를 구분해준다.

     Ðās seofon hīe ġecuron (=these seven they chose···=these seven chose them)

위의 예문의 뜻이 애매한 것은 hīe의 주격과 대격의 모양이 동일하여 they나 them

어느 쪽으로든 해석이 가능하기 때문이다.

3.1.3 도치

고대영어에서는 현대영어에서 보다 훨씬 더 많은 경우에 주어와 동사의 도치가
일어난다. 차례로 살펴보겠다. 첫째, 부사적 요소가 문두에 나올 때는 현대독일어에
서와 마찬가지로 거의 주어와 동사의 도치가 일어난다.

> Hēr *cōmon* tweġen aldormenn (=in this year two chiefs came)
> 7ā *cōm* þǣr reġen and miċel flōd, and þǣr *blēowon* windas,
>   (=Then there came rain and great flood, and there blew winds)
> Ġēa, būtan nettum *huntian* iċ mæġ (=Certainly I can hunt without nets.)
> 7ǣr *bið* swȳðe myċel ġewinn betwēonan him
>   (=There is much strife between them)
> ǣy ilcan ġēare *ġesette* Ælfred cyning Lundenburg
>   (=in the same year King Alfred occupied London)

드물기는 하지만 문두에 부사적 요소가 오는 경우에도 도치가 일어나지 않는 경
우가 있다.

> æfter þissum hē *fērde* tō Philistēa lande
>   (=after this he went to the land of the Philistines)

둘째, 강조를 위해 목적어나 보어가 문두에 오는 경우 도치가 일어난다.

> 목적어 : þā stōwe *habbaþ* ġiet his ierfenuman
>   (=that place his successors still have)
> 보　어 : mǣre *is* se God þe Daniēl on belīefþ
>   (=great is the God that Daniel believes in)

셋째, do 조동사가 없었던 고대영어에서 의문문을 만드는 가장 편한 방법은 도치
였다.

Ġehȳrt þū, sælida? (=Do you hear, sailor?)

Hwǣr *eart* þū nū, ġefera? (=Where are you now?)

Hwæt *sæġest* þū? (=What do you say?)

Hwilċe fixas *ġefēhst* ðū? (=What fishes do you catch?)

ne *sēowe* þū gōd sǣd on bīnum æcere? (=Did you not sow good seed in your field?

Ne *canst* þū huntian būton mid nettum? (Can you not hunt except with nets?)

넷째, 마찬가지 이유로 부정문에서도 도치가 사용된다.

Ne *eom* se here. (=The army did not come.)

ne *cwebe* iċ nū for þȳ ⋯ (=I do not say therefore ⋯)

다섯째, 명령문을 만드는 가장 흔한 방법 중의 하나가 도치이다.

Swiga ðū! (=Be silent!)

Forġif nū, Drihten, ūrum mōdum (=Grant now, oh Lord, to our hearts)

Lǣre mon siððan furður on Lædenġeðīode. (=Let one then instruct further in Latin.)

3.1.4 조동사와 본동사

현대영어에서 본동사는 조동사 바로 뒤에 놓이는 것이 상례이며 고대영어에서도 많은 경우에 그렇다.

se ādliga *wearð* ġehǣled on ðǣre ylcan nihte

(=the sick man was healed that very night)

그러나 현대독일어에서 그렇듯 조동사와 본동사가 떨어져 있는 경우도 많다.

Ēastengle *hæfdon* Ælfrede cyninge aaas ġeseald.

(=The East Angles had given King Alfred oaths)

he ne *meahte* onġemong oðrum monnum bion

(=he could not be among other men)

Hē *wolde* æfter ūhtsange oftost hine ġebiddan

(=After Matins, he would usually pray.)

þæs cyninges hǣs *wearþ* hrædlīċe ġefremed

(=the king's command was quickly carried out)

위의 예에서 hæfdon…ġeseald(=had…given)나 meahte…bion(=could…be) 등에서 조동사와 본동사는 현대영어에서와는 달리 떨어져있다. 다음 독일어의 경우를 참조하기 바란다.

Ich *habe* ein Brief *geschrieben*. (=I have written a letter.)

3.1.5 부사의 위치

현대영어에서도 그렇거니와 고대영어에서도 부사의 위치는 가장 유동적이라고 할 수 있다. 대개는 수식하는 동사나 형용사의 앞에 온다.

þǣr stōd (=stood there)

ne mihte (=could not)

hē *wel* cūþe Scyttisc (=he knew Gaelic well)

se bischop *þā* fērde (=the bishop then went)

and *munuclīċe* leofode (=and lived monastically)

swīðe ælmesġeorn (=very charitable)

ne는 늘 수식하는 말 앞에 온다. 그 결과 후속하는 말과 융합하여 하나의 단어가 되는 경우가 많다.

nis　　　(=ne+is)　　　(=isn't)

nǣron　(=ne+wǣron)　(weren't)

nabban (=ne+habban)　(haven't)

nolde　(=ne+wolde)　(wouldn't)

nǣniġ　(=ne+ǣniġ)　(=none)

nǣfre　(=ne+ǣfre)　(=never)

nā　　　(=ne+ā)　　　(=never, by no means)

3.1.6 전치사의 위치

고대영어에는 현대영어만큼 전치사가 흔하지 않았으나 더러 사용되기도 하였다. 대개는 현대영어와 마찬가지로 명사 앞에 놓였다.

> *on* huntoðe (=in hunting)
> *on* sumum stōwum (=in some places)
> *on* his āgnum lande (=in his own country)

그러나 다음에서 보듯 뒤에 오는 경우도 드물지 않다.

> 부사 뒤 : bǣr*tō*, bǣr*intō*, bǣr*æt*, hēr*inne*
> 대명사 뒤 : bus cweðende him *tō* (=saying thus to him)
>   him *biforan* (=before him)
>   him *betwēonan* (=between them)

심지어는 다음과 같은 경우도 있다.

> Ōswold him cōm *tō* (=O. came to him)
> him cōm miċel ēaca *tō* (=a great reinforcement came to him)
> be wē ġefyrn *ymbe* sprǣcon (=about which we spoke earlier)
> Ēadmunc cwæþ cynelīċe him *tō* (=Edmund said to him with kingly dignity)

3.2 격

3.2.1 주격

주격은 주어와 보어로 사용된다. 다음이 그 예들이다.

> 주어 : *þæt hūs* fēoll (=the house fell)
> 보어 : þū eart *fruma* (=thou art the beginning)
>   sē wæs betera ðonne *iċ* (=he was better than I)

주격은 호격(Vocative)으로도 쓰인다.

> 호격 : Đū iunga man (=You, young man)
> Ēalā *lēof hlāford* (=Oh, dear master)

3.2.2 속격

속격의 가장 중요한 기능은 소유와 근원을 나타내는 것이다.

> 소유 : *hiora* scipu (=their ships)
> 기원 : ides *Scyldinga* (=the lady of the Schyldings)

현대영어의 his murder에서 his가 murder의 주어(그가 행한 살인)가 되기도, 또는 목적어(그에 대한 살인)가 되기도 하는 것처럼 고대영어에서도 두 가지 용법이 존재한다. 다음이 그 예이다.

> 주　어 : *æs bisceopes* bodung (=the bishop's preaching)
> 목적어 : *folces* weard (=protector of the people)

고대영어의 속격은 때로 부사적으로 쓰이기도 한다.

> *dæges* ond *nihtes* (=by day and night)
> *ealles* (=altogether)
> *æs* (=therefore)

부사적 속격(Adverbial Genitive)이라고 불리는 이 용법은 다음과 같은 현대영어의 어말의 -s에서도 볼 수 있다.

> 시간 : always, evenings, nights, nowadays, sometimes, Sundays
> 공간 : afterwards, backwards, downwards, eastwards, homewards
> 양태 : crossways, sideways

동사에 따라서는 속격을 요구하는 것들이 있다. 다음이 그 예이다.

> hē hine *hlāfes* bitt (=he asks him for bread)
> sēo cwēn wundrode Salomones *wīsdōmes*
>   (=the queen wondered at Solomon's wisdom)

속격을 요구하는 중요한 동사 몇몇을 열거하면 다음과 같다.

> benǣman (=to deprive (of)), biddan (=to ask), brūcan (=to enjoy), helpan (=to help), onfōn (=to receive), wilnian (=to desire), wundrian (=to wonder (at)), āmyrran(=to hinder (from))

3.2.3 여격

여격의 가장 중요한 기능은 간접목적을 나타내는 것이다.

> ae *him* hringas ġeaf (=(he) who gave him rings)
> seġe *ānum lēodum* miccle lāare spell
>   (=report to your people a much more disagreeable message)

고대영어 시대에도 이미 간접목적을 tō라는 전치사를 사용하여 나태내기도 하였다.

> ġyfan (*tō*) *ǣniġum* (=give (to) anyone)

고대영어에는 절대여격(Dative Absolute)이라고 불리는 특수한 용법이 있는데, 이것은 라틴어의 절대탈격(Ablative Absolute)을 옮겨온 용법으로서 과거분사에 명사의 여격형을 더해 만든다. 현대영어의 독립분사구문과 비슷한 용법이다. 다음이 그 예이다.

> ūp sprungenre *sunnan*, hīe(=sumu sǣd) ādrūgodon
>   (=the sun rising up, they(=some of the seeds) dried up)

ġewunnenum *siġe* (=victory having been won)

ūtādrifenum *ǣm dēofle*, se dumba spræc

　　(=the devil (being) driven, out, the dumb spoke)

독립적인 형태를 잃어가고 있던 도구격(Instrumental Case)의 기능을 여격이 맡게되는데, 그 까닭에 고대영어의 여격의 용법이 속격 못지 않게 복잡하게 되었다. 도구격은 주로 도구나 행동의 양태를 나타낸다. 다음이 그 예이다.

　　도구 : *hondum* ġebrōden (=hand-woven)

　　양태 : hē ġeendode *yflum dēaae* (=he died (by) an evil death)

이와 같은 용법은 scēafmǣlum(=in sheaves)에서 보듯 본격적인 부사로 진전되었으며, 나아가 여격 어미 -e와 -um은 부사의 어미로 널리 쓰이게 되었다. 다음이 그 예이다.

　　-e (주로 형용사 뒤에서) : hlūde (=loudly), wīde (=widely)

　　-um (주로 명사 뒤에서) : miclum (=greatly), styċċemǣlum (=piecemeal)

3.2.4 대격

대격의 주된 기능은 직접목적어를 나타내는 것이다. 다음이 그 예이다.

　　hē ofslōg *aone aldormon* (=he killed th governor)

재귀대명사가 없던 고대영어에서는 대격이 재귀대명사의 역할을 했다.

　　þā behȳdde Adam *hine* (=then Adam hid himself)

　　swā swā *hine* selfne ġewiera (=as he himself pleases)

현대영어에서와 마찬가지로 고대영어에서도 대격은 시간이나 거리, 혹은 방향을 나타내는 부사적 용법을 갖는다.

시간 : hwȳ stande ġe hēr *ealne dæġ* īdle?

　　　(=Why do you stand here all day idle?)

거리 : iċ heonan nelle flēon fōtes *trym*

　　　(=I will not flee from here as much as a foot)

방향 : *hām* (=home(wards))

3.3 시제

3.3.1 현재형

고대영어에는 여타의 게르만어나 현대영어에서 그렇듯이 굴절 상으로는 현재와 과거의 두 시제 밖에 없었다. 미래시를 위해 라틴어처럼 별도의 정해진 굴절형은 없이 현재형이나 과거형으로 미래시를 나타냈다.

현대영어의 현재형이 그렇듯이 고대영어의 현재형은 현재시 뿐만 아니라 다음과 같은 여러 가지 기능을 가지고 있었다.

현재 :

　　bā bēowan *drincað* medo (=the slaves drink mead)

현재진행 :

　　ðēos woruld *nealæcð* bam ende (=this world is drawing near to its end)

미래 :

　　bas flotmenn *cumab* (=these seamen will come)

　　iċ *ārīse* and iċ *fare* tō mīnum fæder (=I will get up and go to my father)

　　Se mōna his leoht ne *selb* and steorran of heofone *feallab*.

　　　(=The moon will not give its light and stars will fall from heaven.)

　　gā ġē on mīnne wīnġeard, and iċ *selle* ēow bæt riht *bib*

　　　(=go into my vineyard, and I will give you what is right)

　　swā *bēob* bā fyrmestan ȳtemeste (=so the first shall be last)

　　ġif iċ *bēo* ġebunden mid seofon rāpum, sōna iċ *bēo* ġewield

　　　(=if I am bound with seven ropes, I shall at once be overcome.)

미래완료 :

　　sebe bæt *ġelæsteð*, bið him lēan ġearo

　　　(=a reward will be ready for him who does (shall have done) that)

3.3.2 과거형

과거형도 현재형 못지 않게 다양한 기능을 가지고 있다. 다음을 보자.

> 과거진행 :
>> 7ā bā menn *slēpon*, bā *cōm* his fēonda sum)
>>> (=while men were sleeping, one of his enemies came)
> 현재완료 :
>> iċ mid ealre heortan be *ġewilnode*
>>> (=I have wished for Thee with all my heart)
>> 7ās ‾ytemestan *worhton* āne tīd, and būu *dydest* hīe ġelīċe ūs, be *bǣron*
>> byrbenna on bisses dæġes hǣtan
>>> (=these last have worked one hour, and you have made them equal to us,
>>> who have borne burdens in the heat of this day)
> 과거완료 :
>> 7ā bā ġecōmon be ymbe bā endleoftan tīd *cōmon*
>>> (=when they came up who had come at the eleventh hour)

3.3.3 복합형

고대영어에도 비록 그 수는 많지 않으나 조동사+본동사의 복합시제가 더러 발견된다. 첫째는 willan(=will)/sculan(=shall)+동사원형의 결합이다. 많은 경우에 willan은 의지(volition)를, sculan은 필요(necessity)나 의무(obligation)를 나타낸다.

> forðǣm ġē *sculon* wēpan
>> (=because you will weep)
> iċ *wille* bissum ‾ytemestan sellan eall swā miċel swā bē
>> (=I mean to give to this last just as much as I give to you)

둘째는 habban(=have)/hæfde(=had)+과거분사의 결합형이다. 이 때 hæbbe+과거분사는 현재완료를, 그리고 hæfde+과거분사는 과거완료를 나타낸다.

nū iċ *hæbbe* ġestrīened ōbru twā (=now I have gained another two)

and hine *hæfde* ær Offa and Beortrīċ āflīemed

(=and Offa and Beorhtric had drfiven him into exile)

hæfde+목적어+과거분사의 형태가 단순한 과거를 나타내기도 하는데, 이 때 과거분사는 선행하는 목적어와 일치하는 변화를 한다. 가령 현대영어에서도 I have a letter written이라는 문장이 주어진다면 이것은 현재완료형이라기보다는 단순한 현재형으로 보아야 하는데, 이 때 written은 선행하는 목적어 letter를 수식하고 있는 경우와 같다.

hīe *hæfdon* hiera cyning āworpenne (=they had deposed their king)

이 예문에서 āworpenne(=deposed)는 선행하는 대격의 남성 단수형의 cyning에 일치하는 굴절형을 가지고 있다.

셋째는 wesan(=be)+과거분사의 모양으로 복합시제를 만든 경우이다.

bā hit *wæs* æfen ġeworden (=when it had become evening)

sibban hīe āfarene *wæron* (=after they had gone away)

여기서는 일종의 보어구실을 하고 있는 과거분사들이 주어의 성, 수, 격과 일치하고 있다.

넷째, wolde+본동사형은 현대영어에서와 마찬가지로 습관적인 동작을 나타낸다.

sēo *wolde* efsian ælċe ġēare bone sanct

(=she used to cut the saint's hair every year)

다섯째는 wesan(=be)+현재분사형으로서, 이것은 현대영어와는 달리 진행을 나타내지 않는다. 기능상 현재형과 거의 구별이 되지 않으나 표현을 생생하게 한다는 효과가 있다.

bā *wæs* se cyning openlīċe andettende bam biscope

(=Then the king openly confessed to the bishop)

이밖에 현대영어의 be+과거분사(타동사)에 해당하는 수동형이 있는데 여기에 대해서는 별도로 살펴보게 될 것이다.

3.4 형용사

우리는 앞서 형용사는 그 쓰임에 따라 두 가지 변화형을 갖는다는 사실을 알게되었다. 이른바 강변화(strong declension)과 약변화(weak declension)이다. 강변화는 형용사가 서술보어로 사용되거나, 혹은 수식하는 명사 앞에 형용사 밖에 없는 경우에 사용된다. 다음 예를 보자.

> 주격보어 :
> se mann is eald. (=The man is old.)
> ðā wurdon hī drēoriġe (=then they became sad)

> 명사와 단독으로 쓰일 때 :
> ealde menn (=old man)
> þær sint swīðe micle meras fersce
>   (=there are very large fresh-water lakes)

그 밖의 경우, 다시 말해 형용사 앞에 다른 한정어가 오는 경우에는 해당 명사의 성, 수, 격을 한정어가 나타내게 되어 형용사는 약변화형을 갖게 된다. 그 환경을 좀더 자세히 기술하면 다음과 같다. 첫째, 정관사 뒤에서는 약변화형이 사용된다.

> *se* ealda mann (=that old man)
> *se* æþela cyning (=the noble king)
> *þone* halgan līċhaman (=the holy body)
> *þæt* hāliġe hēafod (=the holy head)
> *þǣm* ġeswenctan folce (=to the harassed people)

둘째, 현대영어의 this의 뜻을 갖는 þes, þis, þēos 뒤에서는 약변화형이 사용된다.

> *þes* hālga cyning (=this holy king)

þ̄as earman landlēode (=these poor people)
þ̄eos nīwe lār (=this new doctrine)

셋째, 흔히 소유형용사 뒤에서 약변화형이 사용된다.

mīn ealda frēond (=my old friend)
þīne dīeglan goldhordas (=your hidden treasures)
mīne clǣnan handa (=my clean hands)
mid *his* micclan werode (=with his large force)

넷째, 형용사의 비교급에서 약변화형이 쓰인다.

se hālga is mǣrra (=the saint is more glorious)
þā wǣron ǣġðer ġe swiftran ġe unwealtran
(=they were both faster and steadier)

최상급에서는 형용사 앞에 대개 정관사가 오게 되므로 여기서도 약변화형이 사용된다.

þone mǣstan dǣl (=the largest part)

다섯째, 호격(vocative), 즉 상대방을 직접 부를 때 약변화형이 쓰인다.

Bēowulf lēofa (=dear Beowulf)
Dryhten, ælmihitiga, God! (=O Lord, almighty God!)
þū yfla þēow and slāwa! (=thou bad and slothful servant!)
ēalā þū lēofa cyning! (=Oh, beloved king!)

다시 정리하자면 강변화형은 형용사가 독립해서 사용될 때 쓰이며, 약변화형은 형용사 앞에 한정사나 소유대명사가 올 때 나타난다.

3.5 일치

3.5.1 주어와 동사의 일치

굴절이 발달한 모든 언어가 그렇듯이 고대영어에서도 많은 단어들이 그 쓰임에 따라 그 성과 수, 격, 인칭에 있어 일치해야 했다. 이것은 주어진 단어들이 동일한 하나의 문법적 기능을 수행한다는 것을 보여주는 한 방편이기도 하다.

우선 다루어야 할 것은 주어와 동사의 일치 현상인데, 다음에서 보듯 동사는 주어의 수와 인칭에 있어 일치했다.

> ðā *Deniscan* cōmon (=the Danes came)
> Eart bū se *Bēowulf*, sē þe wið Brecan wunne?
>   (=Are you the Beowulf that strove(2sg) against Breca?)

그러나 다음과 같은 경우에는 주어와 동사의 수가 일치하지 않는 경우가 생긴다. 첫째는 주어가 집합명사(collective noun)이거나 부정대명사(indefinite pronoun)일 때는 수의 불일치가 일어난다. 다음 예들을 보자.

> þonne rideð *ælċ*, and hit motan habban
>   (=then each man rides, and [they] can have it)
> þider urnon *swā hwelċ swā* þonne ġearo wearþ
>   (=whoever was(sg) then ready ran(pl) there)

위의 예문들에서 단수의 주어가 한번은 단수의 동사를, 그리고 뒤에서는 복수의 동사를 취하고 있다. 그밖에 다음과 같은 예도 있다.

주어와 동사의 불일치는 주어가 복합형일 때도 흔히 발견된다. 이때 동사는 대개 주어를 선행한다.

> þǣr sceal bēon *ġedrync and plega*
>   (=there must(sg) be drinking and merrymaking)
> ġefeaht *Æþered cyning ond Ælfred*
>   (=King Æthered and Ælfred fought(sg))
> þā ġegaderode *Æþered ond Æþelm ond þā cinges þeġnes*
>   (=then Æþered and Æþelm and the king's thanes assembled)

ætsomne cwōm *syxtiġ*

  (=sixty men came together)

3.5.2 대명사와 명사의 일치

원칙적으로 대명사는 그것이 지칭하는 명사와 성, 수, 격이 일치해야 한다. 다음
이 그 예들이다.

  anne flotan ··· se

    (=a pirate(m.) ··· he(=that))

  se hwæl ··· hē

    (=the whale(m.) ··· it)

  myċel sǣ ··· sēo is brādre

    (=great sea(f.) ··· it is broader)

  se hearpere ··· ðæs nama

    (=the harper, whose name)

  weall ··· hē is ġeworht of tiġelan

    (=wall(m.) ··· it is made of tile)

고대영어에서도 많은 경우에 문법성을 버리고 자연성을 따르는 경우가 발견된다.
다음이 그 예들이다.

  ðæt hearperes *wīf* ··· hire sawle

    (=the harper's wife(n.) ··· her soul)

  an swiðe ænliċ *wīf*, sio wæs haten Eurydice

    (=a most excellent wife(n.), who(f.) was called Eurydice)

  bæt mǣden ··· hēo wearð

    (=the maiden(n.) ··· she was)

위의 경우 모두에서 지칭하는 명사(wīf, mǣden)가 중성명사임에도 불구하고 이것
을 받고 있는 것은 자연성에 일치하는 여성 대명사이다. 많은 경우에 이처럼 문법
성이 쇠락하고 있는 것을 발견하게 된다.

3.5.3 분사

분사는 be나 become 따위의 계사(copula) 뒤에서는 주어와 일치한다. 이른바 주격보어이기 때문에 주어에 일치하는 것은 자연스럽다고 할 수 있다.

> wǣron hātene (=were called)
> ofslǽġene wǣrun (=were slain)

그러나 늘 그런 것은 아니다.

> rāpas bēoð of hwæles hȳde ġeworht (=the ropes are made(sg) of whales hide)

rāpas(=ropes)가 복수명사임에도 불구하고 단수 동사(bēoð)와 복수형의 분사(ġeworht)가 사용되고 있다.

habban이 과거분사와 함께 복합시제를 이루는 경우 과거분사는 많은 경우에 목적어와 일치한다.

> hīe hine ofslǽġenne hæfdon (=they had slain him)

한편 wesan(=be)이나 weoraan(=become)과 결합하여 복합시제를 이루는 경우에는 주로 주어에 일치한다.

> hīe wurdon ofslǽġene (=they were slain)
> be mid him ofslǽġene wæron (=who were killed with them)

위의 예들은 일반적인 경향을 보여줄 뿐이다. 위의 원칙을 따르지 않는 경우도 허다하다.

3.6 격지배

3.6.1 동사의 격지배

고대영어에서의 동사의 격지배는 현대영어와 많은 부분에서 일치한다. 예를 들어 현대영어에서 간접목적어가 사용될 위치에서 고대영어에서는 여격이 사용되며, 현대영어에서 동사의 목적어가 오는 위치에서는 고대영어에서도 대격이 사용된다. 우선 여격지배의 경우부터 알아보겠다.

> hē sealde ǣlcum ānne pening (=he gave each a penny)
> iċ ēow secge (=I say to you)
> hē aancode his Dryhtne (=he thanked his Lord)

이 밖에 여격을 지배하는 대표적인 자동사들을 아래에 열거해놓았다.

> andswarian (=to answer), bodian (=to announce), bēodan (=to offer), dēman (=to judge), fylgan (=to follow), losian (=to belost), onfōn (=to receive), wiðstandan (=to resist), ġelȳfan (=to believe)

현대영어에서와 마찬가지로 타동사 뒤에 쓰이는 대표적인 격은 대격이다. 다음이 그 예들이다.

> hē ofslōg aone aldormon (=he killed the governor)
> hē his hūs ofer stān ġetimbrode. (=he has built his house on a rock)
> And ne ġelǣd ðū ūs in costnunge, ac ālīes ūs of yfele.
>   (=And lead thou us not into temptation, but deliver us from evil)

다음은 여격과 대격이 동일 문장에 사용된 경우이다. 현대영어에서는 이런 경우의 여격을 간접목적어, 그리고 대격을 직접목적어라고 부르며, 이처럼 두 개의 목적어를 취하는 동사를 수여동사(dative verb)라고 부른다.

Ūrne ġedæġhwāmlican hlāf sele ūs tōdæġ.

 (=Give us our daily bread today.)

And forġief ūs ūre gyltas, swā swā wē forġiefað ūrum gyltendum.

 (=And forgive us our debts, as we forgive our debtors.)

고대영어에는 현대영어와는 달리 속격의 명사를 요구하는 경우가 있다. 주로 기쁨이나 감사, 욕망 등 감정을 나타내는 동사들이 속격을 요구한다. 다음이 그 예들이다.

 and hīe **ææs** *fæġnodon* (=and they rejoiced at that)

 ææs iċ *ġewilniġe* (=that I desire)

 ġif hē *rōhte* his fēores (=if he cared about his life)

속격을 요구하는 대표적인 동사들을 아래에 예시해놓았다.

 āmyrran (=to hinder (from)), belīðan (=to deprive (of)), āġēotan (=to drain (of)), berȳaan (=to despoil), bestrȳpan (=to strip), bīdan (=to wait for), blissian (=to rejoice (at)), brūcan (=to enjoy), fæġnian (=to rejoice), hēdan (=to look after), helpan (=to help). ġelīefan (=to believe), onmunan (=to care for), reccan (=to care), strīenan (=to beget), twēo(ga)n (=to doubt), aurfan (=to need), ayrstan (=to thirst (for)), wēnan (=to expect), wilnian (=to desire), wundrian (=to wonder at)

3.6.2 전치사의 격지배

굴절이 소실된 현대영어에서는 전치사 뒤에 오는 것이 여격인지 대격인지 알 수 없다. 예를 들어 towards me라고 할 때 me가 여격인지 대격인지 알 수 없다. 그러나 많은 경우 여격과 대격이 상이한 형태의 굴절형을 가졌었던 고대영어에서는 그 구분이 분명하다. 아래에 대격과 여격을 지배하는 대표적인 전치사들을 열거해놓았다.

 대격지배 :

 fore (=before), ġeond (=throughout), in (=into), ofer (=beyond), on (=into, against), ongēan (=towards), oa (=until), aurh (=through), wið (=against, towards, along), ymbe (=about)

여격지배 :
æfter (=after), ‾ær (=before), æt (=at), be (=about, by), betwēonan (=between), binnan (=within), būtan (=without, except), for (=for), fram (=from, by), mid (=with), of (=from) tō (=to)

다음 전치사들은 여격과 대격 모두를 지배한다.

ofer (=over), on (=on, in), under (=under)

현대독일어에서와 마찬가지로 동작을 나타낼 때에는 대격을, 그리고 정지된 장소를 나타낼 때에는 여격이 사용된다. 예를 들어 on이 대격형과 사용될 때에는 into의 뜻을, 여격형과 사용될 때에는 in의 뜻을 나타낸다. 다음 예를 보자.

여격 : *on* sele wunian (=to live in the hall)
        on ‾aæm landum eardodon Engle (=in the countries lived the Angles)

대격 : hīe furhton *on* a‾a burg (=they fought against the city)

그러나 그와 같은 구분은 늘 지켜지는 것도 아니며, 경우에 따라서는 아래에서 보듯 정반대의 경우도 발견된다. 첫 번째 예문에서는 동작을 나타내지 않는 경우임에도 불구하고 대격이 사용되었고, 반대로 두 번째 예문에서는 동작을 나타내고 있음에도 불구하고 여격이 사용되고 있다.

대격 : *on* ġehwæaere hand (=on both sides)
여격 : ymb twā ġēar aæs ae hē *on* Francum cōm
        (=about two years after he went to France)

흔하지는 않으나 전치사에 따라서는 속격을 지배하는 것도 있다. wia(=towards)나 tō가 대표적인 경우이다. 속격만을 취하는 전치사는 없다.

aā spearcan wundon *wiđ* **aæs** hrōfes (=the sparks flew towards the roof)

swilċe him *tō* gamenes (=as if for their sport)

tō **aæs** (=to such an extent, so)

3.6.3 형용사의 격지배

현대영어에서 형용사가 격을 지배하는 경우는 없다. 유일한 예외가 near이다. 굴절이 소실된 명사의 경우는 그 격을 알 수 없고, near 뒤에 대명사가 올 때는 near me, near him 등에서 보듯 굴절형이 사용된다. 여기서도 여격과 대격이 동일한 형태를 갖는 영어에서는 near 뒤의 격을 정확히 짚을 수 없다. 그러나 고대영어에서는 형용사가 지배하는 격의 모양을 정확히 알 수 있다.

첫째는 형용사가 속격을 지배하는 경우인데, 이것은 동사가 속격을 지배할 때처럼 형용사가 주로 기쁨이나 감사, 욕망 등 감정을 나타내는 경우에 속격이 사용되는 것을 볼 수 있다. 다음이 그 예들이다.

and hīe **aæs** *ġefæġene* wǣron (=and they were glad of that)

ġemyndiġ **ǣre** sōaan lāre (=mindful of the true doctrine)

wierđe sleġes (=deserving of death)

사용되고 있는 형용사가 '가까움'(nearness)과 '닮음'(likeliness)을 나타낼 때 대격이 사용된다.

Ēadmund clipode ānne biscop đe him *ġehendost* wæs

   (=Edmund summoned a bishop who was most intimate with him)

sē biđ *ġelīċ* **ǣm** dysigan menn

   (=he is like the foolish man)

3.7 가정법

3.7.1 주절에서의 가정법

현대영어에서는 고대영어만큼 가정법이 많이 쓰이지 않는다. 독일어나 프랑스어에는 아직도 많이 쓰인다. 현대영어에서는 다음 예들에서 볼 수 있듯이 주절에 소망, 요구, 충고 등의 동사나 형용사가 올 때 종속절에서 가정법이 쓰이는 경우가 있다. 대부분의 굴절이 사라진 현대영어에서도 아직도 -(e)s라는 어미를 간직하고 있는 3인칭 단수형에서만 그 쓰임을 확인할 수 있다.

> He *suggested* that she go to college.
> It is *desirable* that he do the work for himself.
> He *demanded* that it be postponed.

이런 경우 현대영어에서는 동사 앞에 should를 넣어 사용하기도 한다.

여기에 비하면 고대영어에서는 상당량의 가정법이 사용되고 있는데, 가정법이란 어떤 사항을 사실로서가 아니라 사고의 대상으로 주관적으로 파악하기 위한 표현 방법이다. 가정법이 독립한 문장에서 사용될 때에는 주로 소망이나 3인칭에 대한 명령을 나타낸다.

> aæs him sīe wuldor ā būtan ende
>   (=therefore glory be to Him ever without end)
> God aē sīe milde (=God be merciful to you.)
> Gōd ūre helpe (=may God help us)
> ne hē ealu ne drince oaae wīn (=nor shall he drink ale or wine)
> Tōbecume ðīn rīċe. (Thy kingdom come.)
> Ġeweorðe ðīn willa on eorðan swā swā on heofonum.
>   (=Thy will be done on earth, as in heavens.)
> ċild binnan ðrītegum nihta sīe ġefulwad
>   (=let a child be baptized within 30 nights)

3.7.2 종속절에서의 가정법

가정법은 명사절과 부사절 등의 종속절에서 사용되며, 특히 부사절에서 많이 사용된다. 우선 명사절에서의 가정법의 쓰임에 대해 알아보겠다. 가정법이란 위에서 언급했듯이 현실을 현실로서가 아니라 사고의 대상으로 다루고 있으므로 간접화법의 전달문이나 주절에 say, think, suggest 등의 동사가 올 때 많이 사용된다. 우선 간접화법에서의 가정법의 예부터 보자.

iċ him sæġde aæt hē forealdod wǣre (=I told him that he was very aged)

그러나 전달문의 내용이 사실일 때에는 다음에서 보듯 직설법이 사용된다.

hī hiere sæġde on hwǣm his strengau wæs
(=he told her what his strength consisted in)

다음은 주절에 소망과 필요, 충고나 명령의 뜻이 들어있는 경우이다.

aæs iċ ġewilniġe and ġewẏsce mid mōde, aæt iċ āna ne belīfe
(=this I desire and wish in my heart, that I may not remain alone)
hit nān wundor nys aæt se hālga cyning untrumnysse ġehǣle
(=it is no wonder that the holy king should heal sickness)
hēo hine lǣrde, aæt hē weoroldhād forlēte
(=she advised him that he should give up secular life)

가정법이 가장 많이 쓰이는 종속절은 부사절이다. 아래에 그 대표적인 용법과 예들을 제시해놓았다.

목적 :
hīe behȳddon aæt hēafod, aæt hit bebyrġed ne wurde
(=they hid the head, so that it should not be buried)
aæt heora ġelēaf wurde āwend eft tō Gode
(=in order that their faith might be turned again to God)

조건 :

    ġif mannes hēafod tōbrocen sīe (=if a man's head is broken)

    aās flotmenn aē cwicne ġebindaa, *būtan* aū mid flēame aīnum fēore ġebeorge

       (=these pirates will bind you alive, unless you save your life by flight)

    사실에 반대되는 불가능한 상황을 나타내기 위해 현대영어에서 if I were처럼 동사의 과거형을 쓰듯이 고대영어에서도 사실에 반대되는 상황을 나타내기 위해서는 동사의 과거형이 쓰였다. 다만 현대영어에서는 과거사실에 반대되는 상황을 위해서는 if I had been과 같은 과거완료형이 사용되지만 고대영어에서는 과거형이 현재와 과거 모두에 대한 불가능한 조건을 나타내는데 사용되었다.

    him wǣre bettere æt hē nǣfre ġeboren wǣre

    (=it would have been better for him if he had never been born)

양보 :

    God hielt Ēadmund hālne his līchman, aēah ae hē of moldan cōm

       (=God keeps Edmund's body whole, though he came from the earth)

    aēah man swā ne wēne (=although people do not think so)

    현대영어만큼 왕성하지는 않으나 고대영어에서도 이미 조동사를 사용한 가정법의 쓰임이 상당히 많이 발견된다. 소망, 요구, 명령을 나타내는 동사 뒤에서 흔히 scolde(=should)가 동사의 원형과 결합한 복합형이 발견된다.

    aū bǣde mē æt iċ scolde aē āwendan

    (=you asked me to translate the book for you)

    biddende aone Ælmihtigan æt hē him ārian scolde

    (=praying the Almighty to have mercy on him)

3.8 수동태

    수동태는 wesan/bēon(=be)이나 weoraan(=become)에 동사의 과거분사형을 더해 만든다는 점에서는 현대영어와 거의 비슷하다. wesan과 weoraan의 용법상의 차이는 분명치 않으나 대개 전자는 상태를, 그리고 후자는 동작을 나타낼 때 쓰인 것으로 보인다. 그러나 많은 경우 양자의 차이는 글을 쓰는 사람의 개인적 취향의 차이인 경우가 많다. 우선 수동태의 예를 보자.

nū is sēo bōc swīae nearolīċe ġesett
   (=now the book is composed in very summary fashion)
oa aæt hē eall wæs besett mid hiera scotungum
   (=until he was covered all over with their missiles)
hīe wurdon aā ġebrōhte tō āǣm biscope
   (=they were then brought to the bishop)
aæt hūs wearð ðā forburnen
   (=the house then was then burnt down)

고대영어에서는 be동사의 과거분사형이 없었으므로 과거수동태형이 이른바 대과거 수동태(pluperfect passive)의 구실을 대신했다. 다음이 그 예이다.

ae aæt hēliġe dūst on āhangen wæs
   (=on which the holy dust had been hung)

부정사의 수동태는 능동형으로 나타내었다.

aās aing sint tō dōnne (=these things are to be done)

여기에 대해서는 다음 부정사의 용법에서 다시 설명이 있을 것이다.

3.9 부정사

고대영어에서는 부정사가 두 가지 중 하나의 모양으로 나타난다. 첫째는 동사의 원형으로, 두 번째는 tō+부정사의 굴절형이다.

원형으로 사용되는 경우는 조동사로 사용된 cunnan(=know), (iċ) dearr(=dare), magan(=may), sculan(=shall), aurfan(=need), willan(=will) 뒤에 와서 복합시제를 이룰 때이다.

hwæt *sceal* iċ singan? (=what am I to sing?)

Ne *aurfe* wē ūs spillan (=We need not destroy each other)

아래의 예들에서는 부정사가 수동의 뜻으로 사용되고 있다.

aæt mǣste wæl ae wē secgan hīerdon

(=the greatest slaughter that we have heard tell of)

ġif sum dysiġ mann aās bōc rǣtt oaae rǣdan

(=if some foolish man reads this book or hears it read)

고대영어에서 흔히 쓰이는 것은 두 번째의 tō+부정사의 변화형이다. 명사구나 부사구로 사용된다. 아래 그 쓰임에 따라 예들을 분류해놓았다.

명사구 ('begin', 'teach', 'forbid' 따위 동사의 보어) :

Crīst and his apostolas ūs *tǣhton* ǣġaer tō healdenne

(=Christ and his apostles taught us to observe both)

hē *begann* aā tō winnenne wia aā Philistēos

(=he began then to fight against the Philistines)

cf. Peohtas *ongunnon* eardian aā noradǣlas aisses īeġlandes

(=the Picts began to inhabit the northern parts of this island)

형용사구 :

nū is *tīma* ūs of slǣpe tō ārīsenne

(=now it is time for us to arise from sleep)

mǣl is mē tō feran

(=it is time for me to go)

부사구 (목적) :

ūt *ēode* se sǣdere his sǣd tō sāwenne

(=the sower went out to sow his seed)

ān wulf *weara* āsend tō bewerienne aæt hēafod

(=a wolf had been sent to guard the head)

부사구 (형용사의 수식) :

 þæt weorc is swīþe *plēoliċ* mē tō underbeġinnenne

  (=that task is very hazardous for me to undertake)

 þā aūhte mē *hefiġtīeme* þē tō tīaienne þæs

  (=then it seemed to me burdensome to grant you that)

 iċ nū *forsceamiġe* tō secganne

  (=I am now very much ashamed to say)

부사구 (필요) :

 is *ēac* tō witenne (=it must also be known)

4. 작시법

  고대영어의 시를 읽을 때 가장 주목해야 할 것은 단어의 첫 부분의 운을 맞추는 두운법(alliteration)이다. 고대영어에는 현대영어와 같은 각운(rime)은 없다. 각운은 중세영어에 들어오면서 로망스 언어들에서 들여온 작시법이다. 강세가 항상 어두에 놓이던 고대영어에서는 두운이 자연스러운 작시법이다. 고대영어에 각운이 전혀 없는 것은 아니지만 3만행이 넘는 고대영어의 시 가운데서 각운만을 사용한 시는 하나도 없다.

  두운은 강세를 받는 단어의 어두 자음이나 모음을 맞추는 것을 말하는데, 시행을 전반과 후반으로 나눌 때, 전반의 강세를 받는 어두 자음과 후반의 첫 자음은 같게, 반대로 모음은 다르게 만드는 것을 뜻한다. 우선 아래에 열거한 *Beowulf*의 처음 5행을 살펴보자. 두운이 맞는 음들에 밑줄을 쳐놓았다.

1	Hwæt wē Gār-Dena	in ġeār-dagum
2	bēod-cyninga	brym gefrunon,
3	hū ða æbelingas	ellen fremedon.
4	Oft Scyld Scēfing	sceabena brēatum,
5	monegum mægbum	meodo-setla oftēah ;

  각 행을 전반과 후반으로 나누는 경계를 중간휴지(caesura[si : ǐú : rə])라고 한다. 위의 시행들의 두운에 대해 다음과 같은 사실들을 알게 된다. 첫째, 중간휴지를 중심으로 앞부분에서는 강세를 받는 음절의 어두 자음과 중간휴지 뒤의 첫 번째 단어의 어두 자음이 두운을 이룬다. 다시 말해 중간휴지 이후의 첫 번째 자음을 보면 두운을 이루는 자음을 알 수 있다. 둘째, 휴지의 전반부 시행에서 두운을 이루는 자음의 수는 일정치 않다. 4행과 5행에서는 전반부의 두 자음이 두운을 이루고 있다. 셋째,

모음이 두운을 이루는 경우에는 음의 종류는 개의치 않는다. 다른 모음이기만 하면 두운을 이루는 것으로 간주한다. 3행에서는 시행 전반부의 æ와 후반부의 e가 두운을 이룬다. 넷째, 1행은 이른바 교차두운(crossed alliteration)의 경우로서, 2차강세를 받는 음절의 어두음([d])들 간에서도 두운이 일어나고 있다. 다섯째, sp st, sc는 s가 아니라 동일한 sp, st sc와 두운을 이룬다. 여섯째, c는 ċ와, 그리고 g는 ġ와 비록 발음은 같지 않으나 두운이 맞는 것으로 간주한다. 이것은 구개음화가 널리 퍼지기 이전의 게르만어에서의 관습에 의한 것으로 보인다. 따라서 이들의 경우는 발음이 아니라 철자가 두운의 기준이 된다.

중간휴지 앞뒤의 시행에 나타나는 두운의 수와 위치에 따라 다음과 같은 세 가지 두운의 경우가 생긴다. 여기서 a는 두운이 맞는 음을 나타내며, ∥는 중간휴지를, | 은 운각 경계를 나타낸다.

(a)   a ∣ a ∥ a ∣ —   (4행과 5행)
(b)   a ∣ — ∥ a ∣ —   (2행)
(c)   — ∣ a ∥ a ∣ —   (3행)

(a)는 휴지 전반부에 두 운각 모두에 두운이 맞는 음이 있는 경우, 그리고 (b)는 전반부의 처음 운각에만 두운이 맞는 음이 있는 경우, 그리고 (c)는 전반부의 두 번째 운각에만 두운이 맞는 음이 있는 경우이다.

고대영어 시의 어휘의 한 특징은 이른바 Kennings라고 불리는 것으로서, 동일한 내용을 동의어나 비유로 나타내는 표현방법이다. 아래에 *Beowulf*에서 사용된 몇몇 예를 제시해놓았다.

sǣ (=sea) 단어 :   holm (=ocean), flōd (=flood), mere (=lake)
복합어 : hronrād (=whale-road), mereflōd (=mereflood)
구 :   ȳaa ġewealċ (=rolling of waters)

이밖에도 '검'을 hilde-lēoma (ray of battle)로, '육체'를 bān-hūs (bone's house)로, '태양'을 rodores candel (candle of the heaven)로 나타내는 등의 재미있는 표현도 있다.

Old English
고대영어

본문

산문

운문

Old English

ANGLO-SAXON PROSE (산문)

I. THE NEW TESTAMENT

THE LORD'S PRAYER (MATTHEW vi. 9-13)

1   Fæder ūre, ðū ðe eart on heofonum, sīe ðīn nama ġehālgod. Tōbecume ðīn rīċe. Ġeweorðe ðīn willa on eorðan swā swā on heofonum. Ūrne ġedæġhwāmlican hlāf sele ūs tōdæġ. And forġief ūs ūre gyltas, swā swā wē forġiefað ūrum gyltendum. And ne ġelǣd ðū ūs on costnunge,

5   ac ālīes ūs of yfele ⋯ Sōblīċe.

[fæder u ː re, Өu ː Өe ɛart on heovonum, si ː e Өi ː n nama yeha ː lgod. to ː beku ː me Өi ː n ri ː če. yeweorðe Өi ː n willa on eorðan swa ː swa ː on heovonum. u ː rne yedæyhwa ː mlikan hla ː f sele u ː s to ː dæy. and foryief u ː s u ː re gültas swa ː swa ː we ː foryievaӨ u ː rum gültendum. and ne yelɛ ː d Өu ː u ː s on kostnunge, ak a ː li ː es u ː s of üvele ⋯ so ː Өli ː če.]

1   fæder ūre=our father. OE에서는 형용사가 수식하는 명사 뒤에 오는 경우가 많았다. ðū ðe=thou that. 여기서 지시사 ðe(=that)는 관계대명사로 사용되었다. ðū의 [u ː]는 대모음추이 (the Great Vowel Shift)에 의해 [au]가 되므로 ðū는 현대영어의 thou에 해당한다. 한편 신 과 인간 사이의 대화에서는 thou가 대명사로 쓰인다. on heofonum=in heavens. on=in/ into. in의 뜻일 때에는 여격을, into의 뜻일 때에는 대격을 사용한다. 여기서 heofonum은 복수의 여격형이다. cf. on ēowrum heortum=in your heart. on costnunge=into temptation. ġehālgod=ġehālgian(=make holy)의 과거분사로서, 선행하는 sīe(=to be)와 더불어 수동태를 이룬다.

1-2   sīe, Tōbecume, Ġeweorðe는 각기 bēon(=to be), tōbecuman(=to arrive, come), ġeweorðan (=to become)의 가정법 단수 현재형으로서 '기원'을 나타낸다. ðīn의 [i ː]는 대모음추이에 의 해 [ay]가 되므로 ðīn은 현대영어의 thine에 해당한다. 그러나 의미상으로는 thine이 아니라 현대영어의 thy의 뜻으로 사용되었다. rīċe=kingdom. 독일어의 Reich와 동족어이다.

2   Ġeweorðe의 원형인 ġeweorðan은 독일어의 werden(=to become)과 동족어이다. swā swā=just as, as. 고대영어에는 이처럼 단음절의 단어를 겹쳐 사용하는 경우가 많았다. cf. bā bā=then when, when. Ūrne=our. wē(=we)의 단수 대격.

3   ġedæġhwāmlican=ġedæġhwāmliċ(=daily)의 단수 대격. hlāf=bread. 현대영어의 loaf의 옛날 형이다. OE의 brēad는 morsel, crumb의 뜻을 가지고 있었다. sele, forgief, ġelǣd, ālīes=각

기 sellan(=to give, sell), forġiefan(forgive), ġelǣædan(=to lead), ālīesan(=to release)의 단수 명령형이다. forġief ūs와 forġiefað ūrum gyltendum에서 ūs와 urum gyltendum은 모두 여격형이다. OE에서는 동사마다 일정한 격의 목적어를 지배하며 forġiefan은 여격지배 동사이다. sele=sellan(to give)의 단수 명령. 이처럼 본래 give라는 뜻으로 쓰였던 sellan은 점점 뜻이 좁아져 지금처럼 give for money(팔다)의 뜻이 되었다. gyltas[gültas]=gylt(=guilt, sin)의 복수 대격.

4 gyltendum=gyltend(=debtor)의 복수 여격. ne ġelǣd ðū ūs=you do not lead us. ne=no(t). OE에서는 아직 현대영어의 don't가 존재하지 않았으며, 부정의 명령은 여기서 보듯 단순히 동사 앞에 ne를 첨가하여 나타냈다. ðū는 현대영어에서와 마찬가지로 강조를 위해 삽입되었다. costnunge=temptation.

5 ac=but. ālīes=ālīesan(=to release)의 단수 명령. of yfele=from evil. sōblīċe=truly. 지금의 amen에 해당한다.

Our father, who art in heavens, thy name be hallowd. Thy kingdom come. Thy will be done on earth, as in heavens. Give us our daily bread today. And forgive us our debts, as we forgive our debtors. And lead thou us not into temptation, but deliver us from evil … Amen.

HOUSES BUILT ON A ROCK (MATTHEW vii. 24-7)

1 Ǽlc bāra be bās mīn word ġehīerþ, and bā wyrcþ, biþ ġelīc bǽm wīsan
were, sē his hūs ofer stān ġetimbrode. 7ā cōm bǣr reġen and miċel
flōd, and bǣr blēowon windas, and ahruron on bæt hūs, and hit nā ne
fēoll : sōblīce hit wæs ofer stān ġetimbrod.

5 And ǣlc bāra be ġehīerþ bās mīn word, and bā ne wyrcþ, sē biþ ġelīc
bǣm dysigan menn, be ġetimbrode his hūs ofer sandċeosol. 7ā rīnde
hit, and bǣr cōmon flōd, and blēowon windas, and āhruron on bæt hūs,
and bæt hūs fēoll ; and his hryre wæs miċel.

[ε : ǐc Θɑ : ra Θe Θɑ : s mi : n word yehi : erΘ, and Θɑ : würkΘ, biΘ yeǐ : ǐc Θe : m wi : zan
were, se : his hu : s over stɑ : n yetimbrode. Θɑ : ko : m Θe : r reyen and miċel flo : d,
and Θe : r ble : owon windas, and ɑ : hruron on Θæt hu : s, and hit nɑ : ne fe : oll :
so : Θli : ˇce hit wæs over stɑ : n yetimbrod.

and ε : ǐc Θɑ : ra Θe yehi : erΘ Θɑ : s mi : n word and Θɑ : ne würkΘ, se : biΘ yeǐ : č Θe : m
düzigan menn Θe yetimbrode his hu : s over sandčeozol. Θɑ : ri : nde hit, and Θe : r
ko : mon flo : d, and ble : owon windas, and ɑ : hruron on Θæt hu : s, and Θæt hu : s fe :
oll : and his hrüre wæs miċel.]

1 Ǽlc=each. Ǽlc bāra be에서 bāra는 se(=that)의 복수 속격. 따라서 ǽlc bāra는 each of
those의 뜻. be는 se의 남성 단수 주격형으로서 관계대명사로 쓰였다. 한편 이를 받는 대명
사로서는 his가 사용되고, 동사는 단수형의 biþ(=is)가 사용되는 것은 현대영어의 each 뒤
에는 단수형 동사가 오고 대명사는 he가 사용되는 관행과 일치한다. be bās mīn word
ġehīerþ=who these my words hears. 현대영어의 어순대로라면 be ġehīerþ bās mīn word
가 되었을 것이다. 한편 bās mīn word(=these my words)는 현대영어에서는 용납되지 않는
용법이다. 현대영어에서는 these words of mine으로 해야 옳다. ġehīerþ는 약변화 동사
hīeran(=to hear)의 3인칭 단수형. 여기서 단수형이 쓰인 것은 현대영어에서와 마찬가지로
선행사 ǽlc는 단수형의 동사로 받아야 하기 때문이다. mīn은 대모음추이를 거치면서 현대
영어의 mine이 되나 뜻은 my와 같다. bā wyrcþ는 여전히 관계대명사 be에 걸린다. 여기
서도 목적어가 동사 앞에 놓여 있다. 한편 wyrcþ는 약변화동사 wyrcan(=to work)의 3인칭
단수형. 주어가 3인칭 단수형을 요구하는 ǽlc이기 때문. bā는 지시사 sē(=the, that)의 복수
대격으로서 wyrcþ의 목적어.

1-2 bib ġelīc bǣm wīsan were의 bib는 bēon(=to be)의 3인칭 단수형. ġelīc는 현대영어의 like에 해당한다. 단 뒤에는 여격의 명사가 와야 한다. bǣm wīsan were(=the wise men)가 여격형이라는 것을 bǣm이 말해주고 있다. 현대영어에서는 near (him)나 like (me) 정도가 격을 지배하는 유일한 형용사이나 고대영어에서는 형용사가 격을 지배를 하는 것은 흔히 있던 일이다. were=men. 원형은 wer.

2 sē his hūs ofer stān ġetimbrode의 sē는 관계대명사. ġetimbrode는 timbrian(=to build)의 과거형. 당시 건물은 주로 나무(timber)로 된 것이었다. 7ā cōm bǣr reġen and miċel flōd=then came there rain and much flood. 현대독일어에서와 마찬가지로 문두에 부사적인 요소가 오면 주어와 동사는 도치된다. miċel=much.

3 flōd=flood. bǣr blēowon windas, and āhruron on bæt hūs의 blēowon과 āhruron은 각기 강변화동사 blāwan(=to blow)과 āhrēosan(=to fall)의 과거 복수형이다.

3-4 and hit nā ne fēoll에서의 hit는 중성의 3인칭 단수 주격형. nā ne fēoll의 nā ne는 2중부정형으로서, 현대영어처럼 긍정의 뜻을 갖는 것이 아니라 강한 부정을 나타낸다. 2중부정은 고대영어에서 흔히 볼 수 있던 용법이다. fēoll=fell. 원형은 feallan(=to fall).

4 hit wæs ofer stān ġetimbrod에서 우리는 고대영어에서도 수동형이 사용되었다는 것을 알 수 있다.

5-6 se bib ġelīc bǣm dysigan menn=that is like those foolish men. 여기서도 여격형을 요구하는 형용사 ġelīc 때문에 bǣm dysigan menn이라는 여격형이 사용되고 있다. bǣm은 se의 남성 복수 여격형. dysiġ=foolish.

6 sandċeosol=sand(=sand)+ceosol(=gravel). '모래 자갈밭'.

6-7 7ā rīnde hit에서도 부사 bā (=then)가 문두에 옴으로서 주어와 동사의 도치 현상이 일어나고 있다. 여기서 한 가지 주목할 것은 비인칭주어 hit(it)의 사용이다. It rains나 독일어의 Es regnet 등에서 볼 수 있듯이, 고대영어에서도 현대영어나 현대독일어와 마찬가지로 비인칭주어가 사용되었다.

8 his hryre에서 his는 hūs를 선행사로 하는 3인칭의 중성대명사 hit(=it)의 속격으로서 현대영어의 its에 해당한다. 한편 hryre는 동사 āhrēosan(=to fall)의 명사형으로서 fall, destruction, ruin 등을 뜻한다.

Each of those who hears these words of mine and works them, is like the wise man, who has built his house on a rock. Then there came rain and great flood, and there blew winds, and fell on that house, and it never fell : truly it was built on a rock.

And each of these who hears these words of mine, and does not work them, he is like the foolish man who has built his house on sand. Then it rained, and there came floods, and winds blew, and fell on that house, and the house fell ; and its fall was great.

THE PALSY CURED (MATTHEW ix. 1-7)

1　Đā āstāh hē on scip and oferseġlode, and cōm on his ċeastre. Đā
brōhton hīe him ǣnne laman, on bedde licgende. Đā ġeseah se Hǣlend
hiera ġelēafan, and cwæþ tō bǣm laman : 'Lā bearn, ġelīefe ðē ; bēoþ
ðīne synna forġiefene.' Đā cwǣdon sume ðā bōceras him betwēonan :
5　'Đes spricþ bismorsprǣċe.' Đā se Hǣlend ġeseah hiera ġebanc, ðā cwæð
hē : 'Tō hwȳ benċe ġe yfel on ēowrum heortum? Hwæt is ēaðeliċre tō
cweðenne, "Đē bēoþ forġiefene ðīne synna," oððe tō cweðenne, "Ārīs,
and gā"? Đæt ġē sōðlīċe witon, ðæt mannes sunu hæfþ anweald on
eorðan synna tō forġiefenne,' ðā cwæþ hē tō bǣm laman : 'Ārīs ;
10　nim ðīn bedd, and gang on ðīn hūs.' And hē ārās, and fērde tō his hūse.

[Θɑ꞉ ɑ꞉stɑ꞉x he꞉ on šip and overseylode, and ko꞉m on his čɛastre. Θɑ꞉
bro꞉xton hi꞉e him ɛ꞉nne laman, on bedde lidjende. Θɑ꞉ yezɛax se hɛ꞉lend hiera
yelɛ꞉əvan, and kwæΘ to꞉ Θɛ꞉m laman : 'lɑ꞉ beəm, yeli꞉eve Θe꞉ ; be꞉oΘ Θi꞉ne
sünna foryievene.' Θɑ꞉ kwɛ꞉don sume Θɑ꞉ bo꞉keras him betwe꞉onan : 'Θes spričΘ
bizmorsprɛ꞉če.' Θɑ꞉ se hɛ꞉lend jezɛax hiera yeΘaŋk, Θɑ꞉ kwæΘ he꞉ : 'to hwy꞉
Θenče ye꞉ üvel on e꞉owrum heortum? hwæt is e꞉əðeli꞉čre to꞉ kweden, "Θe꞉ be꞉oΘ
foryievene Θi꞉ne sünna," oΘΘe to꞉ kwedenne, "ɑ꞉ri꞉s, and gɑ꞉"? Θæt ye꞉ so꞉Θli꞉če
witon, Θæt mannes sunu hæfΘ anwɛald on eorðan sünna to꞉ foryievenne,' Θɑ꞉
kwæΘ he꞉ to꞉ Θɛ꞉m laman : 'ɑ꞉ri꞉s, nim Θi꞉n bedd and gang on Θi꞉n hu꞉s' and he꞉
ɑ꞉rɑ꞉s, and fe꞉rde to꞉ his hu꞉ze.]

1　Đā=at that time, then. āstāh on scip=went on board. 원형은 āstīgan(=to ascend).
oferseġlode=oferseġlian(=to cross by sailing)의 과거. ċeastre=원형은 ċeaster(=city). 현
재의 Chester, Winchester, Worcester, Lancaster 등의 지명에 남아있다. 이것은 본래 라틴
어의 castra(=camp)에서 온 말이다.

2　brōhton=brought. 원형은 bringan. ǣnne laman=ān(=one, a certain) lama(=lame)의 단수
대격. licġende=licġan(=to lie (low))의 현재분사. -ende는 현대영어의 -ing에 해당한다.
Đā(þā)=at that time, then. ġeseah=saw. 원형은 (ġe)sēon. Hǣlend=Saviour. cf. ġehǣlan
(=to heal).

3 hiera=their. hīe(=they)의 속격. ġelēafan은 ġelēafa(=belief, faith)의 대격. cwæb=quoth. 원형은 cweðan(=to say, speak). Lā=lo!, oh!. bearn=child, son. ġelīefe ðē의 ġelīefe는 ġelīefan (=believe)의 단수 명령형. ðē=thee. 강조를 위해 명령문에 주어가 사용된 경우이다. bēob= bēon(to be)의 3인칭 복수.

3-4 bēob…forġiefene=be forgiven. synna[sünna]=synn(=sin)의 복수 주격.

4 sume ðā bōceras=some of the scribes. him betwēonan=among them. 전치사 betwēonan 이 목적어(him=them)의 뒤에 놓인 것에 주목.

5 Ðes=this (man). bismorspræċe=bismorspræċ(=blasphemy)의 대격. ġebanc=mind, thought.

6 Tō hwȳ=why. benċe=(ġe)ðenċan(=to think)의 복수 2인칭 현재형. yfel=evil. ēowrum= your. ġe(=ye)의 속격. ēaðelicṙe=ēaðelic(=easy)의 비교급. ēaðelicṙe의 -re는 현대영어의 -er 에 해당한다. 한편 최상급을 위해서는 -ost/-est를 첨가했다. OE에는 현대영어의 more나 most에 해당하는 비교급은 없다.

6-7 tō cweðenne=to say. cweðenne는 cweðan(=to say)의 굴절부정사(inflected infinitive). Ðē= thee. þū(=thou)의 여격. forġiefan은 여격을 지배한다.

7 oððe=or.

7-8 Ārīs와 gā는 각기 ārīsan(=to arise)과 gān(=to go)의 단수 명령형.

8 Ðæt…ðæt에서 처음 Ðæt는 witon의 목적어이고, 뒤의 ðæt는 접속사이다. witon=(ġe) witan(=to know)의 복수 현재형. mannes sunu=man's son, 즉 인자(人子, 예수). cf. sunne=sun. hæfb=has. 원형은 habban (=to have). anweald=authority, rule.

9 synna=synn(=sin)의 복수. tō forġiefenne=to forgive. forġiefan의 굴절 부정사. tō cweðenne와 동일한 용법.

10 nim=(ġe)niman(=to take, seize)의 단수 명령형. 독일어의 nehmen과 동족어. gang= gangang (=go)의 단수 명령형. hūs는 대모음추이를 거치면 현대영어의 house가 된다. ārās=arose. 원형은 ārīsan. fērde=went. 원형은 fēran.

Then he went on board and sailed over, and came into his city. Then they brought to him a lame man, lying on a bed. Then the Saviour saw their faith and said to the lame man : 'Lo son, have thou trust ; thy sins are forgiven.' Then some of the scribes said among themselves : 'This (man) blasphemes.' When the Saviour saw their thought, then he said : 'Wherefore think ye evil in your hearts? Which is easier to say, "Thy sins are forgiven thee," or to say "Arise and go"? This ye know truly that the son of man hath power on earth to forgive sins,' then said he to the lame man : 'Arise ; take thy bed, and go to thy house.' And he arose, and went to his house.

THE PARABLE OF THE SOWER (MATTHEW xiii. 3-8)

1 Sōþlīċe ūt ēode se sāwere his sǣd tō sāwenne. And þā þā hē sēow,
sumu hīe fēollon wiþ weġ, and fuglas cōmon and ǣton þā. Sōþlīċe
sumu fēollon on stǣnihte, þǣr hit næfde miċle eorþan, and hrædlīċe ūp
sprungon, for þǣm þe hīe næfdon þǣre eorþan dīepan ; soblīċe, ūp

5 sprungenre sunnan, hīe ādrūgodon and forsċruncon, for þǣm þe hīe
næfdon wyrtruman. Sōþlīċe sumu fēollon on bornas, and þā bornas
wēoxon, and forbrysmdon þā. Sumu sōþlīċe fēollon on gōde eorþan, and
sealdon wæstm, sum hundfealdne, sum siextiġfealdne, sum brītiġfealdne.

[so ː θl̄iːče uːteːœde se saːwere his sɛːd toː saːwenne, and θɑ ː θɑ ː he ː se ː ow,
sumu hi ː e fe ː ollon wið wey, and fuglas ko ː mon and æ ː ton θɑ ː . so ː θliː če sumu
fe ː ollon on stɛ ː niçte, θɛ ː r hit nævde miče eorðan, and hrædli ː če u ː p sprungon,
for θɛ ː m θe hi ː e nævdon θɛ ː re eorðan di ː epan ː so ː θli ː če, u ː p sprungenre
sunnan, hi ː e ɑ ː dru ː godon and foršruŋkon, for θɛ ː m θe hi ː e nævdon würtruman.
so ː θli ː če sumu fe ː ollon on θornas, and θɑ ː θornas we ː okson, and forθrüzmdon
θɑ ː . sumu so ː θli ː če fe ː ollon on go ː de eorðan, and sɛəldon wæstm, sum hundfɛəldne,
sum siekstiyfɛəldne, sum θri ː tiyfɛəldne.]

1 ūt ēode에서 ūt는 대모음추이에 의해 현대영어의 out가 된다. ēode=went. 불규칙동사
gān(=to go)의 과거형이다. sāwere=sower. tō sāwenne=(in order) to sow. sāwenne의 원
형은 sāwan(=to sow). þā þā=when.

2 sumu hīe=some they. 현대영어의 some of them의 뜻이다. fēollon=fell. 원형은 feallan.
wiþ=along, against. cf. withstand. 현대영어의 with는 OE에서는 mid로 나타낸다. 이것은
독일어의 mit와 동족어이다. fugulas=fugol(bird)의 복수형. 독일어의 Vogel과 동족어이며
현대영어 fowl의 옛날 모습이다. ǣton=ate. 원형은 etan.

3 stǣnihte=stony ground. cf. stān=stone. þǣr=where. hit=sǣd. næfde=ne+hæfde=didn't
have. 한편 hæfde(=had)의 원형은 habban. miċle=miċel(=much)의 단수 대격. eorðan=
eorðe(=earth)의 단수 대격. hrædlīċe=quickly. 어미 -līċe는 현대영어의 -ly에 해당하며,
hræd는 early의 뜻.

4 sprungon=sprang. 원형은 springan. for þǣm þe=for that, namely, because. hīe(=they)=
sumu sǣd. þǣre=their. sē(=the, that)의 복수 속격.

4-5	ūp sprungenre sunnan=the sun (being) risen up. 라틴어의 절대탈격(Dative Absolute)을 모방한 절대여격(Dative Absolute)으로서, 현대영어의 분사구문에 해당한다.

4-5 ūp sprungenre sunnan=the sun (being) risen up. 라틴어의 절대탈격(Dative Absolute)을 모방한 절대여격(Dative Absolute)으로서, 현대영어의 분사구문에 해당한다.

5 ādrūgodon=dried up. 원형은 ādrūġian. cf. drȳġan(=to dry). forsċruncon=shrunk. 원형은 forsċrincan. cf. sċrincan(=to shrink). for bǣm be=because.

6 wyrtruman=wyrtruma(=root)의 단수 대격. bornas=born(=thorn)의 복수 대격.

7 wēoxon=grew. 원형은 weaxan. forbrysmdon=suffocated, choked. 원형은 forðrysm(i)an. cf. brysmian (=to strangle). þā=those. sē(=the, that)의 복수 대격. gōde는 대모음추이에 의해 현대영어의 good이 된다.

8 sealdon=gave. 원형은 sellan. wæstm=fruit. sum hundfealdne···=sum (sealde) hundfealdne (wæstm)··· -fealdne는 형대영어의 -fold에 해당한다. cf. twofold, threefold, manifold, ··· siextiġfealdne=sixtyfold. brītiġfealdne=thirtyfold.

Truly the sower went out to sow his seed. And while he was sowing, some of them fell along the way, and birds came and ate them. Truly some fell on stony ground, where it had not much earth, and quickly sprang up, because they had not the depth of earth ; truly, the sun rising up, they dried up and shrank up, because they had not roots. Truly some fell on thorns, and the thorns grew, and choked them. Some truly fell on good ground, and gave fruit, some hundredfold, some sixtyfold, some thirtyfold.

THE PARABLE OF THE WEEDS (MATTHEW xiii. 24-30)

1 　Heofona rīċe is ġeworden bǣm menn ġelīċ be sēow gōd sǣd on his
　æcere. Sōblīċe, þā þā menn slēpon, þā cōm his fēonda sum, and
　ofersēow hit mid coccele on middum bǣm hwǣte, and fērde banon.
　Sōblīċe, þā sēo wyrt wēox, and bone wæstm brōhte, þā ætīewde se
5 　coccel hine. 7ā ēodon bæs hlāfordes bēowas and cwǣdon : 'Hlāford, hū
　ne sēowe bū gōd sǣd on bīnum æcere? Hwanon hæfde hē coccel?' 7ā
　cwæb hē : '7æt dyde unhold mann.' 7ā cwǣdon bā bēowas, 'Wilt bū, wē
　gāb and gaderiab hīe?' 7ā cwæð hē : 'Nese : bylǣs ġē bone hwǣte
　āwyrtwalien, bonne ġe bone coccel gaderiab. Lǣtað ǣġber weaxan ob
10 　riptīman ; and on bǣm riptīman iċ secge bǣm rīperum : "Gadriab ǣrest
　bone coccel, and bindab sċēafmælum tō forbærnenne ; and gaderiab
　ðone hwǣte intō mīnum berne."'

1 　Heofona rīċe=heaven's kingdom. is ġeworden ġelīċ=is likened. ġelīċ의 접두사 ġe를 떼버
　리고 난 -līċ는 현대영어의 like에 해당한다. bǣm menn=se mann의 단수 여격. be=that. 관
　계대명사로 쓰였다. sēow=sowed. 원형은 sāwan. on his æcere의 æcere는 æcer(=field)의
　단수 여격.

2 　bā bā…bā=when…then. fēonda sum=some of his fiends.

3 　ofersēow=sowed over. 원형은 ofersāwan. hit=æcer. mid=with. coccele=tares, cockle(가라
　지). 잡초의 일종. fērde=went. 원형은 fēran. banon=thence.

4 　sēo wyrt=the herb. wēox=grew. 원형은 weaxan. wæstm=fruit. 주격과 대격의 모양이 같
　으며, 여기서는 대격으로 사용되었다. brōhte=brought. 원형은 bringan. ætīewde=showed.
　원형은 ætēowian. 뒤에 오는 hine와 함께 재귀동사로 사용되었다.

5 　hine=itself. 남성 단수 대격. ēodon=went. 원형은 gān. hlāfordes bēowas=master's slaves.
　cwǣdon=said. 원형은 cweðan. hū는 대모음추이를 거쳐 현대영어의 how가 된다.

6 　sēowe=sowed. 원형은 sāwan. bīnum=bīn의 남성 복수 여격. 여기서 복수형이 사용된 것은
　뒤에 오는 æcere가 복수이기 때문. Hwanon=whence. hē=æcer.

7 　dyde=did. 원형은 dōn. unhold=hostile. menn=men. Wilt=willan(=to will, wish)의 2인칭 단
　수 현재.

8 　gāb=gān(=to go)의 1인칭 복수 현재. 여기서는 미래시를 나타낸다. gaderiað=gaderian(=to
　gather)의 1인칭 복수 현재. 여기서도 미래시를 나타낸다. hīe=them. Nese=no. bylǣs=lest.
　ġe=you.

9 　āwyrtwalien=root up. cf. wyrt=plant. bonne=when. Lǣtað=lǣtan(=to let)의 복수 명령.

10 æġber=either. ob=up to, until.

10 riptīman=time of reaping, harvest. secge=secgan[sedĵan]의 1인칭 단수 현재형. 미래시를 나타낸다. Gaderiab=gaderian(=to gather)의 2인칭 복수 명령. ǣrest=first.

11 bindab=bindan (=to bind)의 복수 명령. sċēafmǣlum=sheaf by sheaf. sċēaf=sheaf. sċēafm ǣlum은 sċēafmǣl의 복수 여격으로서 여기서는 도구의 여격(instrumental dative) 기능을 갖는다. 도구의 여격은 행위의 양태를 나타낸다. cf. hē ġeendode yflum dēaae(=he died (by) an evil death). sċēafmǣl의 -mǣl은 독일어의 einmal(=once) 등에 그 잔재가 남아있다. tō forbærnenne=to burn up. forbærnenne는 forbærnan(=to burn utterly)의 굴절부정사. tō 와 함께 목적을 나타낸다.

12 mīnum=mīn(=my)의 복수 여격. berne=bern(=barn)의 여격.

    The kingdom of heaven may be compared to someone who sowed good seed in his field ; but while everybody was asleep, an enemy came and sowed weeds among the wheat, and then went away, so when the plants came up and bore grain, then the weeds appeared as well. And the slaves of the householder came and said to him, 'Master, did you not sow good seed in your field? Where, then, did these weeds come from?' He answered, 'An enemy has done this.' The slaves said to him, 'Then do you want us to go and gather them?' But he replied, 'No ; for in gathering the weeds you would uproot the wheat along with them. Let both of them grow together until the harvest ; and at harvest time I will tell the reapers, "Collect the weeds first and bind them in bundles to be burned, but gather the wheat into my barn."'

1   Sōðlīċe sum monn hæfde twēġen suna. 7ā cwæð sē ġingra tō his
    fæder, 'Fæder, sele mē mīnne dǣl mīnre ǣhte be mē tō ġebyreb.' 7ā
    dǣlde hē him his ǣhta. Ðā æfter fēawum dagum eall his þing ġegaderode
    sē ġingra sunu ond fērde wrǣclīċe on feorlen rīċe ond forspilde þǣr his
5   ǣhta, libbende on his gǣlsan.

    Ðā hē hīe hæfde eall āmierrede, þā wearð miċel hungor on þām rīċe
    and hē wearð wǣdla. 7ā fērde hē and folgode ānum burhsittendum
    menn þæs rīċes ; ðā sende hē hine tō his tūne þæt hē hēolde his swīn.
    Ðā ġewilnode hē his wambe ġefyllan of þām bēancoddum be ðā swīn
10 ǣton, and him mon ne sealde.

    7ā bebōhte hē hine ond cwæð, 'Ēalā, hū fela hȳrlinga on mīnes fæder
    hūse hlāf ġenōhne habbað, ond iċ hēr on hungre forweorðe! Iċ ārīse
    ond iċ fare tō mīnum fæder and iċ secge him, "Ēalā, fæder, iċ syngode
    on heofonas and beforan þē ; nū iċ ne eom wierðe þæt iċ bēo þīn sunu
15 nemned ; dō mē swā ānne of þīnum hȳrlingum."'

1   twēġen=two. suna=sunu(=son)의 복수 대격. ġingra=ġeong(=young)의 비교급. fæder=father.
2   sele=sellan(=to give)의 단수 명령. mē=iċ의 단수 여격. 대모음추이에 의해 현대영어의
    me[mi :]가 된다. mīnne dǣl=my share (내 몫). ǣhte=possessions, property. cf. āgen=to
    own. mē tō=to me. ġebyreb=belongs. 원형은 ġebyrian(=to belong).
3   dǣlde=dǣlan(=to divide, give out)의 과거. ġegaderode=gathered. 원형은 ġegaderian.
4   ond=and. n 앞에서는 a와 o가 자유롭게 교체하였다. cf. lond=land.fērde=fēran(=to go,
    journey)의 과거. wrǣclīċe=abroad. feorlen=distant. rīċe=kingdom. forspilde=wasted. 원
    형은 forspillan. þǣr=there.
5   libbende=libban(=to live)의 현재분사. cf. on bedde licgende=lying on a bed. gǣlsan=gǣlsa
    (=wantonness, luxury)의 단수 여격.
6   Ða…þā=when…then. āmierrede=wasted, squandered, destroyed. 원형은 āmierran. wearð=
    weorðan(=happen, become)의 과거. miċel hungor=대 기근.
7   wǣdla=poor man. folgode=followed. 원형은 folgian. 뒤에는 여격(ānum burhsittendum
    menn)이 온다. 독일어에서도 마찬가지이다. cf. Folgen Sie mir! burhsittendum=city-
    dwelling. burh=city. 동사에 어미 -end(=-ing)가 첨가된 현재분사형으로 여기서는 뒤에 오
    는 menn을 수식하는 형용사로 사용되었다.

8 menn=mann의 단수 여격. tūne=field. þæt hē hēolde his swīn의 hēolde는 healdan(=to hold, guard)의 가정법. 전체의 뜻은 that he may guard his swine의 뜻. swīn은 대모음추이에 의해 현대영어의 swine이 된다. 여기서 þæt는 so that의 뜻.

9 ġewilnode=desired. 원형은 ġewilnian. wambe=belly, stomach. ġefyllan=to fill. 돼지는 유태인들에게 가장 더러운 것 중의 하나이다. 따라서 이 젊은이가 돼지 먹이도 마음껏 먹지 못했다는 것은 더 이상 내려갈 수 없는 밑바닥까지 내려갔다는 것을 의미한다. bēancoddum=bean-pod(콩깍지).

9-10 be þā swīn æton의 be는 관계 대명사로서 æton(=ate)의 목적어.

10 sealde=sellan(=to give)의 과거.

11 bebōhte=bethought. 원형은 bebenċan(=bethink, consider). bebenċan은 재귀동사로서 뒤의 hine(=him)가 himself의 구실을 하고 있다. Ēalā=lo! alas! fela=much, many. hȳrlinga=hireling, hired servant, farm labourer.

12 ġenōhne=enough. cf. G. genug. habbað=have. 원형은 habban. forweorðe=forweorðan(=to perish)의 1인칭 단수 현재.

12-13 ārīse, fare, secge는 각기 ārīsan(=to arise), faran(=to go), secgan(=to say)의 현재형으로서 미래시를 나타낸다. faran은 현대영어의 farewell(party)에 그 잔재가 남아있다.

13 syngode=(have) sinned. 원형은 syngian.

14 þē=thee. þū(=thou)의 단수 여격. ne eom=am not. wierðe=worthy. bēo=bēon(=to be)의 가정법 현재.

15 nemned=named. 원형은 nemnan. dō=dōn(=to do)의 단수 명령. dō mē=make me.

There was a man who had two sons. The younger of them said to his father, 'Father, give me the share of the property that will belong to me.' So he divided his property between them. A few days later the younger son gathered all he had and traveled to a distant country, and there he squandered his property in dissolute living.

When he had spent everything, a severe famine took place throughout that country, and he began to be in need. So he went and hired himself out to one of the citizens of that country, who sent him to his fields to feed the pigs. He would gladly have filled himself with the pods that the pigs were eating ; and no one gave him anything.

But when he came to himself he said, 'How many of my father's hired hands have bread enough and to spare, but here I am dying of hunger! I will get up and go to my father, and I will say to him, "Father, I have sinned against heaven and before you ; I am no longer worthy to be called your son ; treat me like one of your hired hands."'

THE PARABLE OF LOST SON (2) (LUKE xv. 20-32)

1　Ond hē ārās bā ond cōm tō his fæder. And bā ġiet bā hē wæs feorr his
fæder, hē hine ġeseah ond wearð mid mildheortnesse āstyred and
onġēan hine arn ond hine beclypte ond cyste hine. Ðā cwæð his sunu,
'Fæder, iċ syngode on heofon ond beforan ðē ; nū iċ ne eom wierbe
5　bæt iċ bīn sunu bēo ġenemned.' Ðā cwæb sē fæder tō his beowum,
'Bringað hræðe bone sēlēstan ġeġierelan and scrȳdað hine, ond sellað
him hring on his hand and ġescȳ tō his fōtum ; ond bringað ān fǣtt
stierċ and ofslēað, ond uton etan and ġewistfullian ; for bām bēs mīn
sunu wæs dēad, ond hē ġeedcwicode ; hē forwearð, ond hē is ġemētt.'
10　Ðā ongunnon hīe ġewistlǣcan.

Sōðlīċe his ieldra sunu wæs on æcere ; ond hē cōm, and bā hē bām
hūse ġenēalǣhte, he ġehīerde bone swēġ ond bæt werod. 7ā clipode hē
ānne bēow ond āscode hine hwæt bæt wǣre. Ðā cwæð hē, '7īn brōðor
cōm ; and bīn fæder ofslōh ān fǣtt ċealf, for bām be hē hine hālne
15　onfēng.'

Ðā bealg hē hine ond nolde in gān. 7ā ēode his fæder ūt ond ongann
hine biddan. Ðā cwæb hē his fæder andswariende, 'Efne swā fela ġēara
iċ bē bēowode, ond iċ nǣfre bīn bebod ne forġīemde ; and ne sealdest
bū mē nǣfre ān ticċen bæt iċ mid mīnum frēondum ġewistfullode ; ac
20　siððan bēs bīn sunu cōm be his spēde mid miltestrum āmierde, bū
ofslōge him fǣtt ċealf.' Ðā cwæb hē, 'Sunu, bū eart mid mē, ond ealle
mīne bing sint bīne ; bē ġebyrede ġewistfullian ond ġeblissian, for bām
bēs bīn broðor wæs dēad, ond hē ġeedcwicode ; hē forwearð, and hē is
ġemētt.'

1　ārās=arose. 원형은 ārīsan. fæder=fæder의 단수 여격. bā…bā=when. feorr=(a)far.
2　his fæder, hē에서 hē는 앞의 주어(his fæder)를 반복하고 있다. ġeseah=saw. 원형은
ġesēon. wearð=became. 원형은 weorðan. mildheortnesse=loving-kindness, mercy. wearð
…āstyred=was moved. āstyred=āstirian(=stir, agitate)의 과거분사.

3 onġēan=towards, against. arn=ran. 원형은 irnan. beclypte[beklüpte]=embraced. 원형은 beclyppan. cyste[küste]=kissed. 원형은 cyssan.

4 nū는 대모음추이에 의해 현대영어의 now가 된다.

6 Bringað=bringan(=to bring)의 복수 명령. hræðe=quickly. sēlēstan=best. ġeġierelan= garment. sċrȳdað=sċrȳdan(=to clothe)의 복수 명령. sellað=sellan(=to give)의 복수 명령.

7 hring[hriŋ]=ring. ġesċy[yešü：]=shoes. fōtum은 대모음추이에 의해 현대영어의 foot가 된다.

7-8 bringað ān fæt stierċ and ofslēað=bringað and ofslēað ān fæt stierċ. fætt stierċ=fat calf. ofslēað=ofslēan(=to kill)의 복수 명령.

8 uton etan=let us eat. for þām=because. þes mīn sunu=this son of mine.

9 ġeedwicode=revived. 원형은 ġeedwician(=to revive, bring to life again). forwearð= perished. 원형은 forweorðan. ġemētt=ġemētan(=to find)의 과거분사.

10 ongunnon=began. 원형은 onginnan. ġewistlǣċan=to feast.

11 ieldra=eald(=old)의 비교급.

12 ġenēalǣhte=approached. 원형은 ġenēalǣċan. ġehīerde=heard. 원형은 ġehīeran. sweġ= noise. werod=troop, multitude. clipode=called. 원형은 clipian(=to call, cry out).

13 ānne þēow=a servant. āscode[a：skode]=asked. 원형은 āscian[a：skian]. wǣre=wesan(=to be)의 가정법 과거.

14 ċealf=calf. for þām þe=because. hālne=healthy, sound, whole.

15 onfēng=received. 원형은 onfōn.

16 bealg=became angry. 원형은 belgan. hine=재귀대명사. nolde=ne+wolde. ongann=began. 원형은 onginnan.

17 biddan=to ask, entreat. andswariende=andswarian(=to answer)의 현재분사. cwæþ… andswariende=대답하여 가로되. Efne=behold, lo. swā fela ġēara=so many years.

18 þēowde=served. 원형은 þēowan. nǣfre=never. bebod=command. forġiemde=forġieman (=to neglect)의 과거. sealdest=gave. 원형은 sellan.

19 tiċċen[titčen]=kid. ġewistfullode=ġewistfullian(=to feast)의 가정법 과거. 앞의 þæt와 함께 '잔치를 베풀 수 있도록'의 뜻. ac=but.

20 siððan=afterwards, after since. spēde=wealth. miltestrum=miltestre(=prostitute)의 복수 여격.

21 ofslōge=killed. 원형은 ofslēan.

22 sint=are. þīne는 대모음추이에 의해 현대영어의 thine이 된다. þē(=to thee)는 여격. 여격의 동사가 사용된 것은 ġebyrian(=be fitting, behove)이 여격을 요구하기 때문. ġebyrede= ġebyrian(=be fitting, behove)의 과거. þē ġebyrede=…하는 것이 너에게 어울린다. ġeblissian=rejoice. for þām=because.

So he set off and went to his father. But while he was still far off, his father saw him and was filled with compassion ; he ran and put his arms around him and kissed him. Then the son said to him, 'Father, I have sinned against heaven and before you ; I am no longer worthy to be called your son.' But the father said to his slaves, 'Quickly, bring out a robe—the best one—and put it on him ; put a ring on his finger and sandals on his feet. And get the fatted calf and kill it, and let us eat and celebrate ; for this son of mine was dead and is alive again ; he was lost and is found!' And they began to celebrate.

Now his elder son was in the field ; and when he came and approached the house, he heard music and dancing. He called one of the slaves and asked what was going on. He replied, 'Your brother has come, and your father has killed the fatted calf, because he has got him back safe and sound.'

Then he became angry and refused to go in. His father came out and began to plead with him. But he answered his father, 'Listen! For all these years I have been working like a slave for you, and I have never disobeyed your command ; yet you have never given me even a young goat so that I might celebrate with my friends. But when this son of yours came back, who has devoured your property with prostitutes, you killed the fatted calf for him!' Then the father said to him, 'Son, you are always with me, and all that is mine is yours. But we had to celebrate and rejoice, because this brother of yours was dead and has come to life ; he was lost and has been found.'

THE PARABLE OF THE LOST SHEEP (MATTHEW xviii. 12-14)

1   Ġif hwelċ mann hæfb hund sċēapa, and him losab ān of bǣm, hū, ne
    forlǣt hē bā nigon and hundnigontiġ on bǣm muntum, and gǣb, and
    sēċb bæt ān be forwearb? And ġif hit ġelimpb bæt hē hit fint, sōblīċe iċ
    ēow seċġe bæt hē swībor ġeblissab for bǣm ānum bonne ofer bā
5   nigon and hundnigontiġ be nā ne losodon.

1   Ġif=if. hwelċ=which, any(one), some(one). hund sċēapa에서 hund(=hundred)나 būsend
    (=thousand)는 굴절하지 않는 경우가 많으며 항상 속격을 취한다. sċēapa는 sċēap(=sheep)
    의 속격이다. cf. eahta hund mīla=eight hundred miles. fēower būsend wera=four thousand
    men. him losab=he loses. 원형은 losian(=to be lost). ān of bǣm=one of them.
2   forlǣt=leaves. 원형은 forlǣtan(=to leave, abandon). nigon and hundnigontiġ=nine and
    ninety=ninety-nine. hundnigontiġ=ninety. cf. hundseofontiġ=seventy, hundeahtatiġ=eighty.
    muntum=munt(=mountain)의 복수 여격. gǣb=goes. 원형은 gān.
3   sēċb=seeks. 원형은 sēċan(=to seek). be forwearb=the lost (sheep). forwearban=to be lost.
    ġelimpb, fint는 각기 ġelimpan(=to happen)과 findan(=to find)의 직설법의 변화형인데, 이
    들이 ġif(=if)절에 속해 있으면서도 가정법이 아니고 직설법의 모양으로 사용된 것은 현대
    영어의 if it rains 등에서 보듯 주어진 사건을 사실의 반대가 아닌 현실로 받아들이기 때문
    이다.
4   swībor=swībe(=exceedingly)의 비교급. ġeblissab=rejoices. 원형은 ġeblissan. bonne=than.
5   be=that. 관계대명사. losodon=losian(=to lose)의 과거.

If a shepherd has a hundred sheep, and one of them has gone astray, does
he not leave the ninety-nine on the mountains and go in search of the one
that went astray? And if he finds it, truly I tell you, he rejoices over it more
than over the ninety-nine that never went astray.

THE PARABLE OF THE TEN YOUNG WOMEN (MATTHEW xxv. 1-13)

1　　7onne bib heofona rīċe ġelīċ b̄æm tīen f̄æmnum, be bā lēohfatu nāmon,
and fērdon onġēan bone br̄ydguman. Hiera fīf w̄æron dysiġe, and fīf
glēawe. Ac bā fīf dysigan nāmon lēohfatu, and ne nāmon nānne ele mid
him ; bā glēawan nāmon ele on hiera fatum mid b̄æm lēohfatum.

5　　Ða sē br̄ydguma ielde, bā hnappodon hīe ealle, and slēpon. Witodlīċe
tō middre nihte man hrīemde, and cwæb : 'Nū sē br̄ydguma cymb ;
farab him tōġēanes.' 7ā ārison ealle bā f̄æmnan, and glenġdon hiera
lēohfatu.

　　Ða cw̄ædon bā dysigan tō b̄æm wīsum : 'Sellab ūs of ēowrum ele, for
bām ūre lēohfatu sind ācwenċtu.' 7ā andswarodon bā glēawan, and
10　cw̄ædon : 'Nese, b̄y l̄æs be wē and ġē næbben ġenōg. Gāb tō b̄æm
ċīependum, and bycgab ēow ele.'

　　Witodlīċe, bā hīe fērdon, and woldon bycgan, bā cōm se br̄ydguma ;
and bā be ġearwe w̄æron ēodon inn mid him tō b̄æm ġieftum ; and sēo
duru wæs belocen.

15　　7ā æt nīehstan cōmon bā ōbre f̄æmnan, and cw̄ædon : 'Dryhten,
dryhten, l̄æt ūs inn.' 7ā andswarode hē him, and cwæð : 'Sōb iċ ēow
secge, ne cann iċ ēow.' Witodlīċe, waciab, for b̄æm be ġē nyton ne
bone dæġ ne bā tīd.

1　　7onne=then. tīen=ten. f̄æmnum=f̄æmne(=maiden)의 복수 여격. 형용사 ġelīċ(=like)는 여격
형을 요구한다. lēohfatu=lēohtfæt(=lamp)의 복수 대격. cf. lēoht(=light), fæt=vessel, cup.
nāmon=took. 원형은 niman.

2　　onġean bone br̄ydguman=towards the bridegroom. Hiera=their. hira fīf=five of them.
dysiġe=foolish.

3　　glēawe=wise. nānne=no, none ele=oil.

4　　him=them. hīe(=they)의 복수 여격. fatum=fæt(=vat, vessel)의 복수.

5　　ielde=delayed. 원형은 ieldan. hnappodon=hnappian(=to nap)의 과거. Witodlīċe=truly.

6　　tō middre nihte=at midnight. 한편 nihte의 발음은 [niçte]. hrīemde=cried out. 원형은
hrīeman. Nū=now. cymb[kümθ]=comes. 원형은 cuman. farab=faran(=to go, proceed,
march)의 복수 명령.

7　him tōġēanes=towards them. glenġdon=glengan(=to trim)의 과거.

8　bā dysigan=the foolish ones. tō bǣm wīsum=to the wise ones. Sellaþ=sellan(=to give)의 복수 명령. of ēowrum ele=of your oil. ēowerum은 þū(=thou)의 복수 속격. 한편 of는 프랑스어의 부분관사와 같은 구실을 하고 있다. 즉 "당신들 기름 가운데 일부를"의 뜻.

9　ūre=our. ācwenċte=ācwenċan(=to quench)의 과거.

10　Nese=no. þȳ lǣs þe=lest⋯should. næbben=ne+habban(=to have)의 2인칭 복수 가정법 현재. Gāþ=gān(=to go)의 복수 명령.

11　ċīependum=ċīepend(=merchant)의 복수 여격. bycgaþ=bycgan(=to buy)의 복수 명령.

12　woldon=willan(=to wish)의 과거.

13　ġearwe=ġearu(=ready)의 복수 주격. þe ġearwe wǣron=those who were ready. ēodon=gān(=to go)의 과거. ġieftum=ġiefta(=marriage)의 복수 여격.

14　belocen=locked. 원형은 belūcan(=to lock, shut up).

15　æt nīehstan=in the next place, thereupon. ōþre(ōþer)=other. Dryhten=lord, the Lord.

16　lǣt=lǣtan(=to let)의 단수 명령.

17　cann=cunnan(=to know)의 1인칭 단수 현재. waciaþ=wacian(=to be awake)의 2인칭 복수 명령. nyton=ne+witon=do not know.

Then the kingdom of heaven will be like this. Ten bridesmaids took their lamps and went to meet the bridegroom. Five of them were foolish, and five were wise. When the foolish took their lamps, they took no oil with them ; but the wise took flasks of oil with their lamps.

As the bridegroom was delayed, all of them became drowsy and slept. But at midnight there was a shout, 'Look! Here is the bridegroom! Come out to meet him.' Then all those bridesmaids got up and trimmed their lamps.

The foolish said to the wise, 'Give us some of your oil, for our lamps are going out.' But the wise replied, 'No! there will not be enough for you and for us ; you had better go to the dealers and buy some for yourselves.'

And while they went to buy it, the bridegroom came, and those who were ready went with him into the wedding banquet ; and the door was shut.

Later the other bridesmaids came also, saying, 'Lord, lord, open to us.' but he replied, 'Truly I tell you, I do not know you.' Keep awake therefore, for you know neither the day nor the hour.

THE PARABLE OF THE GOOD SAMARITAN (LUKE x. 30-35)

1   Sum mann fērde fram Hierusalem tō Hiericho ond becōm on þā
scaðan, þā hine berēafodon and tintregodon hine ond forlēton hine
sāmcwicne. 7ā ġebyrede hit þæt sum sācerd fērde on þām ilcan weġe ;
and þā hē þæt ġeseah, hē hine forbēag. Ond eall swā sē dīacon, þā hē
5 wæs wið þā stōwe ond þæt ġeseah, hē hine ēac forbēag. Đā fērde sum
Samaritanisc monn wið hine ; þā hē hine ġeseah, þā wearð hē mid
mildheortnesse ofer hine āstyred. 7ā ġenēalǣhte hē ond wrāð his
wunda ond on āġēat ele and wīn ond hine on his nīeten sette and ġelǣdde
on his lǣċehūs and hine lācnode ; ond brōhte ōðrum dæġe twēġen
10 peningas and sealde þām lǣċe ond bus cwæð, 'Beġīem his ; ond swā
hwæt swā þū māre tō ġedēst, bonne iċ cume, iċ hit forġielde bē.'

---

1   becōm=becuman(=to meet with, fall among, happen)의 과거.

2   scaðan=thieves, robbers.. þā=they. hine=him. berēafodon=deprived, stripped. 원형은 berēofan. cf. ModE, to bereave. tintregodon=tortured. 원형은 tintregian. cf. tintreg= torture. forlēton=forlǣtan(=to abandon)의 과거.

3   sāmcwicne=half-dead, half-alive. ġebyrede=happened. 원형은 ġebyrian. ġebyrede hit=it so happened. sācerd=priest. ilcan=ilca(=same)의 단수 여격. weġe=weġ(=way)의 단수 여격.

4   forbēag=turned away, 원형은 forbūgan. eall swā=just as, likewise. eall=all. swā=as. dīacon=deacon(副祭).

5   wið=opposite. stōwe=place. ēac=also.

7   mildheortnesse=loving-kindness, mercy. āstyred=aroused. 원형은 āstyrian(=to arouse, stir). wearð…āstyred=was moved. ġenēalǣhte=approached. 원형은 ġenēalǣċan. cf. ModE, near. wrāð=wrapped. 원형은 wrīðan.

8   wunda=wound. on āġēat=poured on. 원형은 āġēotan. ele=oil. nīeten=animal. sette=settan(=to set)의 과거 단수. ġelǣdde=led. 원형은 ġelǣdan(=to lead).

9   lāċehūs=hospital. lācnode=healed, treated with medicine. 원형은 lācnian. brōhte=brought. 원형은 bringan. ōðrum dæġe=the next day. twēġen=two.

10   peningas=pening(=penny, 현재 미국의 10센트 동전 크기)의 복수 대격. sealde=sellan(=to give)의 과거. lǣċe=physician. Beġīem=beġīeman(=take care of)의 단수 명령형. beġīeman 은 속격을 요구한다.

10-11 swā hwæt swā=whatever. cf. swā hwā swā=whoever.

māre=more. ġedēst=ġedōn(=do)의 2인칭 단수. bonne=when. forġielde=forġieldan(=to repay)의 현재형으로서 선행하는 cume(=come)과 함께 미래시를 나타낸다.

A man was going down from Jerusalem to Jericho, and fell into the hands of robbers, who stripped him, beat him, and went away, leaving him half dead. Now by chance a priest was going down that road ; and when he saw him, he passed by on the other side. So likewise a Levite, when he came to the place and saw him, passed by on the other side. But a Samaritan while traveling came near him ; and when he saw him, he was moved with pity. He went to him and bandaged his wounds, having poured oil and wine on them. Then he put him on his own animal, brought him to a inn, and took care of him. The next day he took out two denarii, gave them to the innkeeper, and said, 'Take care of him ; and when I come back, I will repay you whatever more you spend.'

THE RICH MAN AND LAZARUS (LUKE xvi. 19-31)

1   Sum weliġ man wæs, ond hē wæs ġescrȳdd mid purpuran ond mid twīne and dæġhwāmlīċe rīċelīċe ġewistfullode. Ond sum wǣdla wæs, on naman Lazarus, sē læġ on his dura, swīðe forwundod, and wilnode þæt hē hine of his crumum ġefylde þē of his bēode fēollon ; ond him nān

5   monn ne sealde, ac hundas cōmon and his wunda liccodon.

    Ðā wæs ġeworden þæt sē wǣdla forðfērde, ond hine englas bǣron on Abrahames grēadan ; þā wearð sē weliga dēad and wæs on helle bebyrġed. Ðā āhōf hē his ēagan ūp, þā hē on þām tintregum wæs, ond ġeseah feorran Abraham, ond Lazarum on his grēadan. Ðā hrīemde hē

10   and cwæð, 'Ēalā fæder Abraham, ġemiltsa mē, ond send Lazarum þæt hē dyppe his fingres lib on wætere ond mīne tungan ġecēle ; for þām þe iċ eom on þissum līeġe cwielmed.'

    Ðā cwæð Abraham, 'Ēalā sunu, ġebenċ þæt þū gōd onfēnge on þīnum līfe, ond ġelīċe Lazarus onfēng yfel ; nū is þēs ġefrēfred, ond þū eart

15   cwielmed. And on eallum þissum, betweox ūs ond ēow is miċel dwolma ġetrymed ; þā ðe willað heonon tō ēow faran ne magon, nē banon faran hider.'

    Ðā cwæð hē, 'Fæder, iċ bidde þē þæt ðū sende hine tō mīnes fæder hūse ; iċ hæbbe fīf ġebrōðru ; þæt hē cȳðe him þæt hīe ne cumen on

20   þissa tintrega stōwe.' 7ā sæġde Abraham him, 'Hīe habbað Moysen and wītegan ; hīe hlysten him.' Ðā cwæð hē, 'Nese, fæder Abraham, ac hīe dōð dǣdbōte ġif hwelċ of deaðe tō him færð.' Ðā cwæð hē, 'Ġif hīe ne ġehīerab Moysen ond þā wītegan, nē hīe ne ġelīefað þēah hwelċ of dēaðe ārīse.'

---

1   weliġ=wealthy, rich. Sum weliġ man wæs=There was a rich man. ġescrȳdd=ġescrȳ dan(=to clothe)의 과거분사. purpuran=purple robe.

2   twīne=linen. dæġhwāmlīċe=daily. rīċelīċe=sumptuously. cf. rīċe=kingdom. līċe=like. ġewistfullode=feasted. 원형은 ġewistfullian. wǣdla=poor man, beggar.

2-3 on naman Lazarus=with the name Lazarus.

3 læġ=lay. 원형은 licgan[lidjan]. duru=duru (=door)의 단수 여격. swīðe=strongly, very. forwundod=wounded seriously. 원형은 forwundian. wilnode=wished. 원형은 wilnian.

4 cruman=crumb. ġefylde=ġefyllan(=to fill)의 가정법. bē of his bēode fēollon=that fell from his table.

4-5 ond him nān monn ne sealde=no one gave him. nān…ne은 부정의 강조를 나타낸다. sealde의 원형은 sellan.

5 hundas=dogs. 현대영어 hound의 옛날 모습이다. cf. G. Hund. wunda=wound. liccodon=liccian(=to lick)의 과거.

6 wæs ġeworden=happened. cf. ġeweorðan(=to become). forðfērde=died. 원형은 forðfēran. engelas=angels. bǣron=carried. 원형은 beran.

7 grēadan=bosom. be weliga=the rich one. helle=hell.

8 bebyrġed=buried. 원형은 bebyrġan. āhōf=raised. 원형은 āhebban(=to raise, lift up). ēagan=eyes. tintregum=torment. 원형은 tintreġ.

9 feorran=afar. hrīemde=cried out. 원형은 hrīeman.

10 Ēalā=lo, behold. ġemiltsa=ġemiltsian(=to pity, show mercy)의 단수 명령. send=sendan (=to send)의 단수 명령.

11 dyppe=dyppan(=to dip)의 가정법. '…할 수 있도록'의 뜻. lib=joint, limb. tungan=tongue. ġecēle=ġecēlan(=to cool)의 가정법. for bām be=because.

12 eom=am. līeġe=flame. cwielmed=tormented. 원형은 cwielman.

13 ġebenċ=ġebenċan(=to think)의 단수 명령. onfēnge=onfōn(=to take)의 과거.

14 ġefrēfred=comforted. 원형은 ġefrēfran(=to console, comfort).

15 on eallum bissum=on eall bis(=on all of this)의 복수 여격. "여기에 더하여, 이것 말고도". betweox=between. ēow=ġe(=bū(=thou))의 복수)의 여격/대격. miċel=much. 여기서는 big 의 뜻. dwolma=empty space.

16 ġetrymed=prepared. 원형은 ġetrymman. bā be willað=those who wish. heonon=hence. magon=magan(=to be able, can)의 3인칭 복수 현재. banon=thence.

17 hider=hither.

18 bidde=ask, entreat, pray. 원형은 biddan. sende=sendan의 가정법. fæder=fæder의 속격.

19 hæbbe=habban(=to have)의 1인칭 단수 현재. ġebrōðru=ġebrōðor (=brother)의 복수 대격. cȳðe=cȳðan(=to make known, inform)의 가정법. cumen=cuman (=to come)의 가정법.

20 tintrega stōwe=place of torment. sæġde=said. 원형은 secgan. Moysen=Moses.

21 wītegan=prophet, wise man. hlysten=hlystan(=to listen to)의 가정법.

22 dōð=dōn(=to do)의 3인칭 복수 현재. dǣdbōte=penance, reparation. '속죄'. cf. dǣd=deed, bōt=remedy, cure. hwelċ of deaðe=some of the dead. færð=goes. 원형은 faran.

23 ġelīefað=believe. 원형은 ġelīefan. bēah[θe : əx]=in spite of, though.

24 ārīse=ārīsan(=to arise)의 가정법 3인칭 단수 현재로서 미래시를 나타낸다.

There was a rich man who was dressed in purple and fine linen and who feasted sumptuously every day. And at his gate lay a poor man named Lazarus, covered with sores, who longed to satisfy his hunger with what fell from the rich man's table ; even the dogs would come and lick his sores.

The poor man died and was carried away by the angels to be with Abraham. The rich man also died and was buried. In Hades, where he was being tormented, he looked up and saw Abraham far away with Lazarus by his side. He called out, 'Father Abraham, have mercy on me, and send Lazarus to dip the tip of his finger in water and cool my tongue ; for I am in agony in these flames.'

But Abraham said, 'Child, remember that during your lifetime you received your good things, and Lazarus in like manner evil things ; but now he is comforted here, and you are in agony. Besides all this, between you and us a great chasm has been fixed, so that those who might want to pass from here to you cannot do so, and no one can cross from there to us.'

He said, 'Then, father, I beg you to send him to my father's house—for I have five brothers—that he may warn them, so that they will not also come into this place of torment.' Abraham replied, 'They have Moses and the prophets ; they should listen to them.' He said, 'No, father Abraham ; but if someone goes to them from the dead, they will repent.' He said to him, 'If they do not listen to Moses and the prophets, neither will they be convinced even if someone rises from the dead.'

THE PARABLE OF THE UNFORGIVING SERVANT (MATTHEW xviii. 23-35)

1   For þām is heofona rīċe anlīċ þām cyninge þe his bēowas ġerādegode.
Ond þā hē þæt ġerād sette, him wæs ān brōht sē him sceolde tīen
būsend punda. And þā hē næfde hwanon hē hit āgulde, hine hēt his
hlāford ġesellan, ond his wīf ond his ċild ond eall þæt hē āhte. 7ā

5 āstreahte sē bēow hine and cwæð, 'Hlāford, ġehafa ġebyld on mē, and
iċ hit þē eall āġielde.' 7ā ġemiltsode sē hlāford him ond forġeaf him
þone gylt.

    7ā sē bēowa ūt ēode, hē ġemētte his efenbeowan sē him sceolde ān
hund peninga ; ond hē nam hine þā and forbrysmode hine ond cwæð,

10 'Āġief þæt þū mē scealt.' And þā āstreahte his efenbēowa hine ond bæd
hine ond bus cwæð, 'Ġebyldiga, ond iċ hit be eall āġiefe.' Hē ðā nolde ;
ac fērde ond wearp hine on cweartern, oð ðæt hē him eall āġeafe.

    Ðā ġesāwon his efenbēowas þæt, ðā wurdon hīe swīðe ġeunrōtsode
ond cōmon and sæġdon hira hlāford ealle þā dǣde. Ðā clipode his

15 hlāford hine and cwæb tō him, 'Ēalā þū lȳbra bēowa, ealne þīnne gylt
iċ ðē forġeaf, for þām þe ðū mē bǣde ; hū ne ġebyrede þē ġemiltsian
þīnum efenðēowan, swā swā iċ þē ġemiltsode?' Ðā wæs sē hlāford
ierre, ond scealde hine þām wītnerum, oð þæt hē eall āgulde.

    Swā dēb mīn sē heofonlīca Fæder ġif ġē of ēowerum heortum ēowerum

20 brōðrum ne forġiefab.

---

1   anlīċ=like. cyninge=king. bēowas=servants, slaves. ġerādegode=ġerādegian(=to call to
an account)의 과거.

2   ġerād=account. ān=one (man). brōht=brought. 원형은 bringan. sē는 관계대명사.
sceolde=sculan(=to owe)의 과거.

3   būsend=thousand. punda=pound. næfde=ne(=not)+hæfde(=had). hwanon=whence. hit=
tīen būsend punda. āgulde=āġieldan(=to pay)의 과거. hēt=commanded. 원형은 hātan.

4   ġesellan=to sell. ċild=child. āhte=possessed. 원형은 āgan.

5   āstreahte=āstreċċan(=to stretch, prostrate oneself)의 과거. hine=himself. ġehafa=ġehabban
(=to have)의 단수 명령. ġebyld=patience.

6 āġielde=āġieldan(=to pay)의 단수 현재로서 미래시를 나타낸다. þē=to thee. ġemiltsode= ġemiltsian(=to show mercy)의 과거. forġeaf=forgave. 원형은 forġiefan.

7 gylt=debt, guilt.

8 ġemētte=encountered. 원형은 ġemētan. efenþēowan=fellow-servants.

9 peninga=pennies. 미국의 10센트 동전 크기의 은전. nam=seized. 원형은 niman. forþrysmode= forþrysmian(=to strangle, choke)의 과거.

10 Āġief=āġiefan(=to pay)의 단수 명령. scealt=sculan(=to owe)의 2인칭 단수 현재. bæd= entreated. 원형은 biddan.

11 Ġebyldiga=ġebyldigian(=to be patient)의 단수 명령. nolde=ne+wolde(=willan의 과거).

12 wearp=threw. 원형은 weorpan. cwearten=prison. oð=till.

13 ġesāwon=saw. 원형은 ġesēon. swīðe=greatly. ġeunrōtsode=was sad. 원형은 ġeunrōtsian (=to be sad).

14 dǣde=deed, act. clipode=cried out. 원형은 clipian.

15 [yþra=wicked.

16 hū=how. ġebyrede=ġebyrian(to happen)의 과거.

18 ierre=angry. sealde=sellan(=to send)의 과거. wītnerum=wītnere(torturer)의 복수 여격.

19 dēþ=dōn(=to do)의 3인칭 단수 현재로서 미래시를 나타낸다. ēowerum=your. heortum= heorte(=heart)의 복수 여격.

For this reason the kingdom of heaven may be compared to a king who wished to settle accounts with his slaves. When he began the reckoning, one who owed him ten thousand talents, was brought to him ; and, as he could not pay his lord ordered him to be sold, together with his wife and children and all his possession, and payment to be made. So the slave fell on his knees before him, saying, 'Have patience with me, and I will pay you everything.' And out of pity for him, the lord of that slave released him and forgave him the debt.

But that same slave, as he went out, came upon one of his fellow slaves who owed him a hundred denarii ; and seizing him by the throat, he said, 'Pay what you owe.' Then his fellow slave fell down and pleaded with him, 'Have patience with me, and I will pay you.' But he refused ; then he went and threw him into prison until he would pay the debt.

When his fellow slaves saw what had happened, they were greatly distressed, and they went and reported to their lord all that had taken place. Then his lord summoned him and said to him, 'You wicked slave! I forgave you all that debt because you pleaded with me. Should you not have had mercy on your fellow slave, as I had mercy on you? And in anger his lord handed him over to be tortured until he would pay his entire debt.

So my heavenly Father will also do to every one of you, if you do not forgive your brother or sister from your heart.

THE PARABLE OF THE TENANTS IN THE VINEYARD (MARK xii. 1-9)

1   Sum monn him plantode wīnġeard and betȳnde hine ond dealf ānne
    sēað ond ġetimbrode ānne stīepel ond ġesette hine mid eorðtilium and
    fērde on elbēodiġnesse.

    7ā sende hē tō þām tilium his bēow on tīde þæt hē þæs wīnġeardes
5   wæstm onfēnge. Ðā swungon hīe bone ond forlēton hine īdelhendne.
    And eft hē him sende ōðerne bēow, and hīe bone on hēafde
    ġewundodon ond mid tēonum ġeswenċton. Ond eft hē him sumne
    sende, ond hīe bone ofslōgon.

    7ā hæfde hē þā ġīet ānne lēofostne sunu ; þā sende hē æt nīehstan
10 him bone ond cwæð, 'Witodlīċe mīnne sunu hīe forwandiað.' Ðā cwǣdon
    þā tilian him betwēonum, 'Hēr is sē ierfenuma ; uton ofslēan hine,
    bonne bið ūru sēo ierfeweardness.' Hīe þā ofslōgon hine and wurpon
    wiðūstan bone wīnġeard.'

    Hwæt dēð þæs wīnġeardes hlāford? Hē cymð ond fordēð þā tilian
15 and seleð ōðrum bone wīnġeard.

---

1   monn(=mann)=man. plantode=planted. 원형은 plantian. wīnġeard=vineyard. betȳnde=
    enclosed. 원형은 betȳnan. hine=wīnġeard. dealf=dug. 원형은 delfan. ānne=one.

2   sēað=pit, cistern. ġetimbrode=built. 원형은 ġetimbrian. stīepel=tower. ġesette=ġesettan
    (=to set, place, appoint)의 과거. eorðtilium=farmers. cf. eorð=earth, tilian=to till.

3   fērde=went. 원형은 fēran(=to go, journey). elbēodiġnesse=residence in a foreign country.
    cf, elbeodiġ=foreign.

4   sende=sent. 원형은 sendan. tilium=farmer. bēow=slave, servant. tīde=time.

5   wæstm=crop. onfēnge=onfōn(=to receive)의 가정법. swungon=beat. 원형은 swingan(=to
    beat, strike). forlēton=forlǣtan(=to leave, abandon, release)의 과거. īdelhendne=empty-
    handed.

6   eft=again. ōðerne=second, another, other. hēafde=head. 원형은 hēafod.

7   ġewundodon=wounded. 원형은 ġewundian. tēonum=tēona (=injury)의 복수 여격.
    ġeswenċton=ġeswenċan(=to afflict)의 과거. sumne=someone.

8   ofslōgon=ofslēan(=to strike down, kill)의 과거.

9   ġīet=yet, still. lēofostne=lēof(=)의 최상급 lēofost의 단수 대격.

9-10 æt nīehstan=in the next place, thereupon. nīehst=nēah(=near)의 최상급.

10 him=to them. Witodlīċe=certainly. forwandiað=respect. 원형은 forwandian.

11 tilian=farmers. him betwēonan=among themselves. 현대영어의 감각으로는 betwēonan him 으로 해야 옳다. him은 hē(=he)의 복수 대격. Hēr=here. ierfunuma=heir. uton ofslēan=let us kill.

12 þonne=then. bið=is. ūru=ours. ierfeweardness=the inheritance. ofslōgon=killed. 원형은 ofslēan. wurpon=threw. 원형은 weorpan.

13 wiðūstan=outside.

14 dēð=dōn(=to do)의 3인칭 단수 현재. hlāford=master. cymð=comes. 원형은 cuman. fordēð=fordōn(=to ruin, destroy)의 3인칭 단수 현재로서 미래시를 나타낸다.

15 seleð=sellan(=to give)의 3인칭 단수 현재로서 미래시를 나타낸다. ōðrum=ōþer(=other)의 복수 여격.

A man planted a vineyard, put a fence around it, dug a pit for the wine press, and built a watchtower ; then he leased it to tenants and went to another country.

When the season came, he sent a slave to the tenants to collect from them his share of the produce of the vineyard. But they seized him, and beat him, and sent him away empty-handed. And again he sent another slave to the m ; this one they beat over the head and insulted. Then he sent another, and that one they killed. and so it was with many others ; some they beat, and others they killed.

He had still one other, a beloved son. Finally he sent him to them, saying, 'They will respect my son.' But those tenants said to one another, 'This is the heir ; come, let us kill him, and the inheritance will be ours.' So they seized him, killed him, and threw him out of the vineyard.

What then will the owner of the vineyard do? He will come and destroy the tenants and give the vineyard to others.

THE PARABLE OF THE WORKERS IN THE VINEYARD (MATTHEW xx. 1-16)

1　　Heofona rīċe is ġelīċ b̄æm hīredes ealdre be on ǣrnemerġen ūt ēode
āh̄yrian wyrhtan on his wīnġeard. Ġewordenre ġecwidrǣdenne b̄æm
wyrhtum, hē sealde ǣlcum ānne pening wiþ his dæġes weorce, and
āsende hīe on his wīnġeard. And þā hē ūt ēode ymbe underntīd, he
5　　ġeseah ōþre on strǣte īdle standan. 7ā cwæþ hē : 'Gā ġē on mīnne
wīnġeard, and iċ selle ēow bæt riht biþ.' And hīe þā fērdon. Eft hē ūt
ēode ymbe þā siextan and nigoþan tīd, and dyde b̄æm swā ġelīċe. 7ā
ymbe þā endleoftan tīd hē ūt ēode, and funde ōþre standende, and þā
sæġde hē : 'Hw̄y stande ġē hēr ealne dæġ īdle?' 7ā cwǣdon hīe : 'For
10　 b̄æm þe ūs nān mann ne h̄yrode.' 7ā cwæþ hē : 'And gā ge on mīnne
wīnġeard.'

　　　Sōblīċe þā hit wæs ǣfen ġeworden, þā sæġde se wīnġeardes hlāford
his ġerēfan : 'Clipa þā wyrhtan, and āġief him hiera mēde ; onġinn fram b̄æm
ȳtemestan oþ þone fyrmestan.' Eornostlīċe þā þā ġecōmon þe ymbe þā
15　 endleoftan tīd cōmon, þā onfēngon hīe ǣlċ his pening. And þā þe b̄ær
ǣrest cōmon wēndon þæt hīe scolden māre onfōn ; þā onfēngon hīe
syndriġe peningas. 7ā ongunnon hīe murcnian onġeah þone hīeredes
ealdor, and þus cwǣdon : '7ās ȳtemstan worhton āne tīd, and þū dydest
hīe ġelīċe ūs, þe b̄æron byrþenna on þisses dæġes hǣtan.' 7ā cwæþ hē
20　 andswariende hiera ānum : 'Ēalā þū frēond, ne dō iċ þē nānne tēonan ;
hū ne cōme þū tō mē tō wyrċenne wiþ ānum peninge? Nim þæt þīn is,
and gā ; iċ wille þissum ȳtemestan sellan eall swā miċel swā þē. Obþe
ne mōt iċ dōn þæt iċ wille? Hwæþer þe þin ēage mānfull is for b̄æm þe
iċ gōd eom? Swā bēoþ þā fyrmestan ȳtemeste, and þā ȳtemestan
25　 fyrmeste ; sōblīċe maniġe sind ġeclipode, and fēawe ġecorene.

1　hīredes=hīred(=family, household)의 단수 속격. ealdre=ealdor(=chief, master)의 단수 여
　격. b̄æm hīredes ealdre=to the master of [a] household. ǣrnemerġen=early morning. ūt
　ēode=went out. 여기서 보듯 부사가 동사 앞에 오는 것은 고대영어에서 흔히 볼 수 있는

현상이다. ēode(=went)의 원형은 gān. ūt ēode=went out. ēode=gān(=to go)의 과거.

2   āhȳrian=to hire. wyrhtan=wyrhta(=worker, laborer)의 복수 대격.

2-3   Ġewordenre ġecwidrǣdenne bǣm wyrhtum=An agreement having been made with the workers. 절대여격(dative absolute)의 예. 고대 영어 성격의 원본인 라틴어의 절대탈격을 그대로 모방한 용법임. 이 분사구문의 주어는 ġecwidrǣden(=agreement)인데, 현대영어에 서라면 주격이 사용될 것이 여기서는 여격형이 사용되고 있다. Ġewordenre=ġeweorþan (=to happen, come out)의 과거분사.

3   wyrhtum=wyrhta(=worker, laborer)의 복수 여격. sealde=sellan(=to give). ǣlcum=ǣlċ (=each)의 여격. wiþ=against, in return for. weorce[weorke]=work.

4   āsende=sent. 원형은 āsendan. hīe=them. wīnġeard=vineyard. ymbe=about. underntīd=the third hour of the day, 9 a.m.

5   strǣte=street. īdle standan=stand idle. Gā ġe=go ye! Gā는 소망을 나타내는 가정법이다.

6   selle=I [will] give. þæt=that which, what. 관계대명사. þæt riht biþ=what is right. þæt는 선행사를 내포하는 관계대명사. Eft=again, afterwards, then.

7   siextan and nigoþam tīd=the sixth and ninth hour of the day=at noon and at three o'clock. dyde þǣm swā ġelīċe=did to that so like=did like to that. swā는 불필요하게 들어가 있다.

8   endleoftan tīd=the eleventh hour of the day=at five o'clock. funde=findan(=to find)의 과거. standende=standan(=to stand)의 현재분사로서 standing workers의 뜻.

9   ealne dæġ=all day. adverbial accusative의 경우이다. Hwȳ stande ġē hēr ealne dæġ īdle=why do you stand here all day idle? stande ġē=stand ye.

9-10   For þǣm þe=because.

10   hȳrode=hired. 원형은 hȳrian.

12   þā…þā=when. ǣfen=evening.

13   ġerēfan=officer, bailiff. Clipa=clipian(=to call, summon)의 단수 명령. āġief=āġiefan(=to give, deliver)의 단수 명령. mēde=pay, reward. onġinn=onginnan(=to begin)의 단수 명령.

13-14   þǣm ȳtemestan=the last. ūterra(=outer, exterior)의 최상급으로서 뒤의 fyrmestan (=first) 와 마찬가지로 명사로 사용되었다.

14   fyremestan=first. Eornostlīċe=in truth, indeed. þā þā ġecōmon þe=when those came who. ġecōmon=came.

15   onfēngon=began. 원형은 onfēon. ǣlċ=each. þā þe=whose who.

16   wēndon=thought, expected. 원형은 wēnan. scoldon=sculan(=ought to, have to)의 과거. māre=miċel(=much)의 비교급. more. onfōn=receive.

16-17   þā onfēngon hīe syndriġe peningas=then received they separate pennies(or 'separately, pennies').

17   syndriġe=separate. onfēngon=onfōn(=to receive)의 복수 과거. murcnian=to grumble, complain. onġeah=towards. hīerede=guardian, keeper.

18   ealdor=elder, leader. āne tīd=one hour.

19   þē=관계대명사. bǣron=beran(=to carry, bear)의 과거. byrþenna=byrþen(=burden)의 복수

대격. hǣtan=heat. byrþenna on þisses dæġes hǣtan=the burdens in this dayġs heat.
20 andswariende=andswarian(=to answer)의 현재분사. hiera ānum=one of them. Ēalā þū
frēond=O thou friend. nānne=no, none. tēonan=injury, insult.
21 hū ne cōme þū···=Didn't you come···? tō wyrċenne=to work. 원형은 ġewyrċan.
Nim=niman(=to take)의 단수 명령.
22 eall swā miċel swā þē=exactly as much as to thee. Obbe=or. mōt=may.
23 Hwæþer be=whether. 여기서 be는 별 뜻이 없다. Hwæþer be 뒤에는 직접 의문이 온다.
ēage=eye. mānfull=wicked, evil.
23-24 for þǣm þe iċ gōd eom=because I am good.
24 maniġe=many. ġeclipode=summoned. 원형은 ġeclipian. fēawe=few. ġecorene=chosen. 원
형은 cēosan.

For the kingdom of heaven is like a landowner who went out early in the
morning to hire laborers for his vineyard. After agreeing with the laborers
for the usual daily wage, he sent them into his vineyard. When he went out
about nine o'clock, he saw others standing idle in the marketplace ; and he
said to them, 'You also go into the vineyard, and I will pay you whatever is
right.' So they went. When he went out again about noon and about three
o'clock, he did the same. And about five o'clock he went out and found
others standing around. went out and found others standing around ; and he
said to them, 'Why are you standing here idle all day?' They said to him,
'Because no one has hired us.' He said to them, 'You also go into the
vineyard.'

When evening came, the owner of the vineyard said to his manager, 'Call
the laborers and give them their pay, beginning with the last and then going
to the first.' When those hired about five o'clock came, each of them received
the usual daily wage.' Now when the first came, they thought they would
receive more ; but each of them also received the usual daily wage. And
when they received it, they grumbled against the landowner, saying 'These
last worked only one hour, and you have made them equal to us who have
borne the burden of the day and the scorching heat.' But he replied to one of
them, 'Friend, I am doing you no wrong ; did you not agree with me for the
usual daily wage? Take what belongs to you and go ; I choose to give to

this last the same as I give to you. Am I not allowed to do what I choose with what belongs to me? Or are you envious because I am generous? So the last will be first, and the first will be last ; for many are called, but few chosen.

THE PARABLE OF THE THREE SERVANTS (MATTHEW xxv. 14-30)

1   Sum mann fērde on el-bēodiġnesse, and clipode his bēowas, and betǣhte
him his ǣhta. And ānum hē sealde fīf pund, sumum twā, sumum ān :
ǣġhwelcum be his āgnum mæġne ; and fērde sōna.

7ā fērde sē be bā fīf pund underfēng, and ġestrīende ōbru fīfe. And
5   eall-swā sē be bā twā underfēng, ġestīende ōbru twā. Witodlīċe sē be
bæt ān underfēng fērde, and bedealf hit on eorban, and behȳdde his
hlāfordes feoh.

Witodlīċe æfter miclum fierste cōm bāra hlāford, and dihte him ġerād.
7ā cōm sē be bā fīf pund underfēng, and brōhte ōbru fīfe, and cwæb :
10   'Hlāford, fīf pund bū sealdest mē ; nū iċ ġestrīende ōbru fīfe.' 7ā cwæb
his hlāford tō him : 'Bēo blībe, bū gōda bēow and ġetrēowa : for bǣm
be bū wǣre ġetrēowe ofer lȳtlu bing, iċ ġesette bē ofer miclu. Gā intō
bīnes hlāfordes blisse.' 7ā cōm sē be bā twā pund underfēng, and cwæb :
'Hlāford, twā pund bū mē sealdest ; nū iċ hæbbe ġestrīened ōbru twā.'
15   7ā cwæb his hlāford tō him : 'Ġeblissa, bū gōda bēow and ġetrēowa :
for bæm be bū wǣre ġetrēowe ofer fēa, ofer fela iċ bē ġesette. Gā on
bīnes hlāfordes ġefēan.'

7ā cōm sē be bæt ān pund underfēng, and cwæb : 'Hlāford, iċ wāt bæt
bū eart heard mann : bū rīpst bǣr bū ne sēowe, and gadrast bǣr bū ne
20   sprenġdest. And iċ fērde ofdrǣdd, and behȳdde bīn pund on eorban. Hēr
bū hæfst bæt bīn is.' 7ā andswarode his hlāford him, and cwæb : '7ū yfla
bēow and slāwa, bū wistest bæt iċ rīpe bǣr iċ ne sāwe, and iċ gadriġe bǣr
iċ ne strēdde : hit ġebyrede bæt bū befæste mīn feoh myneterum, and iċ
nāme, bonne iċ cōme, bæt mīn is, mid bǣm gafole. Ānimab bæt pund
25   æt him, and sellab bǣm be mē bā tīen pund brōhte. Witodlīċe ǣlcum
bāra be hæfb man selb, and hē hæfb ġenōg ; bǣm be næfb, bæt him byncb
bæt hē hæbbe, bæt him bib ætbrogden. And weorpab bone unnyttan
bēowan on bā ūterran bēostru ; bǣr bib wōp and tōba grist-bitung.'

1   el-bēodiġesse=living abroad. cf. el-bēodiġ=foreign. fērde on el-bēodiġesse=went on a travel.

2   betǣhte=committed, entrusted. 원형은 betǣċan. ǣhta=property. anum, sumum은 각기 ān (=one)과 sum(=a certain one)의 여격.

3   ǣġhwelcum=ǣġhwelċ(=each)의 여격. be=according to. āgnum=agen(=own)의 여격. mæġne=mæġen(=capacity)의 여격. sōna=at once ; then.

4   sē be=the one who. underfēng=received. 원형은 underfōn. ġestrīende=gaiend. 원형은 strīenan. ōbru=other. 원형은 ōber.

5   eall-swā=in the same way.

6   bedealf=bedelfan(=to bury, hide by digging)의 과거. behȳdde=hid. 원형은 behȳdan.

7   feoh=money ; property.

8   miclum=much. miċel(=much)의 복수 여격. fierste=period, time. bāra=their. dihte=dihtan (=to arrange, command, dictate)의 과거. ġerād=reckoning, account.

11   Bēo=Well done. bēon(=to be)의 가정법 단수 현재. blībe=glad, merry. gōda=good. god (=god)와 구별할 것. ġetrēowa=true, faithful.

12   lytlu=little. 원형은 lytel. bing=thing. ġesette=ġesettan(=to set, place, appoint)의 현재형으로서 미래시를 나타낸다. miclu=many things. 원형은 miċel.

13   blisse=joy, gladness.

15   Ġeblissa=ġeblissian(=to rejoice)의 단수 명령.

16   fēa=few.

17   ġefēan=joy.

18   wāt=knew. 원형은 witan.

19   heard=hard, severe. gadrast=ġegadrian(=to gather)의 2인칭 단수 현재.

20   sprenġdest=sprenġan(=to sow)의 2인칭 단수 현재. ofdrǣdd=afraid. ofdrǣdan(=to dread) 의 과거분사.

21   yfla=evil, bad. 원형은 yfel.

22   slāwa=slothful, slow. wistest=witan(=to know)의 2인칭 단수.

23   strēdde=strew. 원형은 strēdan(=to strew, scatter). ġebyrede=ġebyrian(=to befit)의 과거. hit ġebyrede bæt=it was befitted that. befæste=befdstan(=to commit, entrust)의 가정법. myneterum=money changer. cf. Lt. moneta.

24   nāme=take. 원형은 niman. gafole=interest. Ānimab=āniman(=to take away).

25   æt=from. brōhte=brought. 원형은 bringan. ǣlcum=ǣlċ(=each, every)의 여격.

26   hæfb=habban(=to have)의 3인칭 단수 현재. selb=sellan(=to give, send)의 3인칭 단수로서 미래시를 나타낸다. hæfb=habban(=to have)의 3인칭 단수 현재로서 미래시를 나타낸다. næfb=ne+habban. bynccb=byncan(=to seem)의 3인칭 단수 현재.

27-28   bæt him bynb bæt hē hæbbe=그가 가지고 있다고 생각되는 것.

27   ætbrogden=ætbreġdan(=to take away)의 과거분사. weorpab=weorpan(=to throw)의 단수 명령. unnyttan=useless, unprofitable.

28   ūterran=outer. bēostru=darkness. bǣr bib=there is(=will be). wōp=weeping. cf. wēpan

(=to weep). tōba=tōb(=tooth)의 속격. grist-bitung=gnashing of teeth.

For it is as if a man, going on a journey, summoned his slaves and entrusted his property to them ; to one he gave five talents, to another two, to another one, to each according to his ability. Then he went away.

The one who had received the five talents went off at once and traded with them, and made five more talents. In the same way, the one who had the two talents made two more talents. But the one who had received the one talent went off and dug a hole in the ground and hid his master's money.

After a long time the master of those slaves came and settled accounts with them. Then the one who had received the five talents came forward, bringing five more talents, saying 'Master, you handed over to me five talents ; see, I have made five more talents.' His master said to him, 'Well done, good and trustworthy slave ; you have been trustworthy in a few things. I will put you in charge of many things ; enter into the joy of your master.' And the one with the two talents also came forward, saying, 'Master, you handed over to me two talents ; see, I have made two more talents.' His master said to him, 'Well done, good and trustworthy slave ; you have been trustworthy in a few things. I will put you in charge of many things ; enter into the joy of your master.'

Then the one who had received the one talent also came forward, saying, 'Master, I knew that you were a harsh man, reaping where you did not sow, and gathering where you did not scatter seed ; so I was afraid, and I went and hid your talent in the ground. Here you have what is yours.' But his master replied, 'You wicked and lazy slave! You knew, did you, that I reap where I did not sow, and gather where I did not scatter? Then you ought to have invested my money with the bankers, and on my return I would have received what was my own with interest. So take the talent from him, and give it to the one with the ten talents. For to all those who have, more will be given, and they will have an abundance ; but from those who have nothing, even what they have will be taken away. As for this worthless slave, throw him into the outer darkness, where there will be weeping and gnashing of teeth.'

THE SERMON ON THE MOUNT (MATTHEW v. 1-10)

1   Sōðlīċe þā sē Hǣlend ġeseh þā menigu, hē āstah on þone munt ; and
þā hē sæt, þā genēalǣhton his leorningenihtas tō him. And hē ontȳnde
his mūð and lǣrde hī, and cwæð, 'Ēadige synt þā gāstlīcan bearfan, for
þām hyra ys heofena rīċe. Ēadige synt þā līðan, for þām þe hī eorðan
5   āgun. Ēadige synt þā ðe nū wēapað, for þām þe hī bēoð ġefrēfrede.
Ēadige synt þā ðe rihtwīsnesse hingriað and byrstað, for þām þe hī
bēoð ġefyllede. Ēadige synt þā mildheortan, for þām þe hī
mildheortnysse begytað. Ēadige synt þā clǣnheortan, for þām þe hī
God ġesēoð. Ēadige synt þā ġesybsuman, for þām ðe hī beoð Godes
10   bearn ġenemnede. Ēadige synt þā þe ēhtnysse boliað for rihtwīsnysse,
for þām þe hyra ys heofonan rīċe.'

1   Hǣlend=Savior (healer). cf. hǣlan=to heal, cure. ġeseh=ġeseah=saw. menigu=multitude.
āstāh=went up. 원형은 āstīgan. munt=mountain, hill.

2   genēalǣhton=approached. 원형은 genēalǣċan. cf. nēah=near. leorningcnihtas=disciples.
leorning(=learning)+cnihtas(=knights). ontȳnde=opened. 원형은 ontȳnan.

3   mūð=mouth. lǣrde=taught. 원형은 lǣran. hī(e)=them. Ēadige=blessed, happy, rich. cf.
ēad=happiness, bliss. synt=sind=are. gāstlīcan=spiritually. bearfan=needy.

4   hyra=hiera=their(s). ys=is. heofona=heofon(=heaven)의 복수 속격. līðan=līðe(=gentle,
kind, gracious)의 복수. hī(e)=they.

5   āgun=āgnian(=to own, possess)의 3인칭 복수 현재. nū=now. wēapað=wēopan (=to weep)
의 복수 현재. bēoð=are. ġefrēfrede=comforted. 원형은 frēfran.

6   rihtwīsnesse=righteousness. hingriað=hunger for. byrstað=byrstan(=to thirst for)의 복수
현재.

7   ġefyllede=filled up. 원형은 fyllan. mildheortan=gentle, merciful. mildheortnysse=mercy.

8   begytað=get, obtain. 원형은 beġietan. clǣnheortan=pure-hearted. cf. clǣne=clean.

9   ġesēoð=see. 원형은 ġesēon. ġesybsuman=peaceful.

10   ġenemnede=named. ēhtnysse=persecution. cf. ehtan=to persecute. boliað=bolian(=to endure,
suffer)의 복수 현재.

When Jesus saw the crowds, he went up the mountain ; and after he sat
down, his disciples came to him. Then he began to speak, and taught them,

saying : 'Blessed are the poor in spirit, for theirs is the kingdom of heaven. Blessed are those who mourns, for they will be comforted. Blessed are the meek, for they will inherit the earth. Blessed are those who hunger and thirst for righteousness, for they will be filled. Blessed are the merciful, for they will receive mercy. Blessed are the pure in heart, for they will see God. Blessed are the peacemakers, for they will be called children of God. Blessed are those who are persecuted for righteousness' sake, for theirs is the kingdom of heaven.

II. THE OLD TESTAMENT

THE CREATION (1) (GENESIS i. 1-13)

1   On anġinne ġesceōp God heofenan and eorðan. Sēo eorðe sōðlīċe wæs
ȳdel and ǣmtiġ, and bēostra wǣron ofer þǣre niwelnisse brādnisse,
and Godes gāst wǣs ġeferod ofer wæteru. God cwæð þā : 'Ġeweorðe
lēoht.' And lēoht wearð ġeworht. God ġeseah þā þæt hit gōd wæs ;
5   and hē ġedǣlde þæt lēoht fram þām bēostrum, and hēt þæt lēoht dæġ
and þā bēostra niht. 7ā wæs ġeworden ǣfen and morgen ān dæġ. God
cwæð þā eft : 'Ġewurðe nū fæstnis tōmiddes þām wæterum, and tōtwǣme
þā wæteru fram þām wæterum.' And God ġeworhte þā fæstnisse, and
tōtwǣmde þā wæteru þe wǣron under þǣre fæstnisse fram þām þe
10   wǣron bufan þǣre fæstnisse. Hit wæs þā swā ġedōn. And God hēt þā
fæstnisse heofonan. And wæs þā ġeworden ǣfen and morgen ōðer dæġ.
   God sōðlīċe cwæð, 'Bēon ġegaderode þā wæteru þe sind under þǣre
heofenan, and ætēowiġe drīġnis.' Hit wæs swā ġedōn. And God ġeċīġde
þā drīġnisse eorðan, and þǣra wætera ġegaderunga hē hēt sǣs. God
15   ġeseah þā þæt hit gōd wæs, and cwæð, 'Spritte sēo eorðe grōwende
gærs and sǣd wirċende, and æppelbǣre trēow wæstm wirċende æfter
his cinne, þæs sǣd siġ on him silfum ofer eorðan.' Hit wæs þā swā
ġedōn. And sēo eorðe forð ātēah grōwende wyrte and sǣd berende be
hire cinne, and trēow westm wirċende and ġehwilċ sǣd hæbbende æfter
20   his hīwe. God ġeseah þā þæt hit gōd wæs. And wæs ġeworden ǣfen
and mergen sē bridda dæġ.

(고대영어 성경의 번역은 주로 Ælfric에 의해 이루어졌는데, 흠정판(King James' Authorized
Version)의 번역가들이 희랍어와 히브리어의 원문에서 번역한 것과는 달리 그는 라틴어의
Vulgate 판에서 번역하였다. 그 결과 특히 구약의 경우 그 내용이 현재의 번역본들과 일치
하지 않는 곳이 더러 있다.)

1 　on anġienne=in the beginning. anġinn=beginning. ġesceōp=created. 원형은 ġescieppan. Sēo=the. sē(=the)의 중성 주격.

2 　ȳdel(=īdel)=empty. ǣmtiġ=empty, void. bēostra=darkness. bǣre niwelnisse brādnisse= the abyss's surface. niwelnisse=chasm, abyss. brādnisse=broadness, surface.

3 　gāst=breath, soul, spirit. ġeferod=ġeferian(=to carry, bring)의 과거분사. wæteru=water. Ġeweorðe=ġeweorðn(=to become)의 가정법으로서 '기원'을 나타낸다.

4 　lēoht=light. wearð=became. 원형은 weorðan. ġeworht=ġewyrċan(=to work, make, build)의 과거분사.

5 　ġedǣlde=ġedǣlan(=to separate, divide)의 과거. hēt=hātan(=to call, command, name)의 과거.

6 　niht[niçt]=night. ǣfen=evening.

7 　eft=again. fæstnis=firmness. tōmiddes=amidst, among. tōwǣme=tōwǣman(=to divide)의 가정법으로서 '기원'을 나타낸다.

9 　be=관계대명사.

10 　bufan=over, above. ġedōn=done. 원형은 ġedōn.

12 　Bēon=bēon(=to be)의 가정법으로서 '기원'을 나타낸다. ġegaderode=ġegaderian(=to gather)의 과거.

13 　ætēowiġe=ætēowian(=to show, appea)의 가정법. drīġnis(=drȳġnes)=dryness. ġeċīġde= ġeċīeġan(=to name)의 과거.

15 　Spritte=spryttan(=to sprout, yield fruit)의 단수 명령. grōwende=growing. 원형은 grōwan.

16 　gærs=grass, herb. gærs가 현대영어의 grass가 되는 현상을 환치(metathesis)라고 부른다. sǣd=seed, fruit. wirċende=wyrċan(=to work, do)의 현재분사. æppelbǣre=fruit-bearing. trēow=tree. wæstm=fruit, growth.

17 　cinne(=cynn)=kind, kin. siġ(=sīe)=is. bēon(=to be)의 가정법. silfum(=selfum)=self.

18 　forð=forth. ātēah=produced. 원형은 ātēon(=to produce, draw out). forð ātēah=ātēah forð. wyrte=herb, root. sǣd berende=seed-bearing. be=according to.

19 　westm(=wæstm)=fruit. ġehwilċ(=ġehwelċ)=each.

20 　hīwe=appearance, form, species, kind, color. mergen(=morgen)=morning.

21 　bridda=third. brīe(=three)의 서수.

　　In the beginning when God created the heavens and the earth, the earth was a formless void and darkness covered the face of the deep, while a wind from God swept over the face of the waters. The God said, 'Let there be light' ; and there was light. And god saw that the light was good ; and God separated the light from the darkness. God called the light Day, and the darkness he called Night. And there was evening and there was morning, the first day. And God said, 'Let there be a dome in the midst of the waters, and let it separate the waters from the waters.' So God made the dome and separated the waters that were under the dome from the waters that were above the dome. And it was so. God called the dome Sky. And there was evening and there was morning, the second day.

And God said, 'Let the waters under the sky be gathered together into one place, and let the dry land appear.' And it was so. God called the dry land Earth, and the waters that were gathered together he called Seas. And God saw that it was good. Then God said, 'Let the earth put forth vegetation : plants yielding seed, and fruit trees of every kind on earth that bear fruit with the seed in it.' And it was so. The earth brought forth vegetation : plants yielding seed of every kind, and trees of every kind bearing fruit with the seed in it. And god saw that it was good. And there was evening and there was morning, the third day.

THE CREATION (2) (GENESIS i, 14-23)

1　　God cwæð þā sōðlīċē : 'Bēo nū lēoht on b̄ære heofenan fæstnysse, and
tōdǣlen dæġ and nihte, and bēon tō tācnum and tō tīdum, and tō
dagum and tō ġēarum. And hī scīnen on b̄ære heofenan fæstnysse, and
ālīhten þā eorðan.' Hit wæs þā swā ġeworden. And God ġeworhte twā
5　 miċele lēoht, þæt māre lēoht tō þæs dæġes līhtinge, and þæt l̄æsse lēoht
tō b̄ære nihte līhtinge ; and steorran hē ġeworhte, and ġesette hiġ on b̄ære
heofenan, þæt hiġ scinen ofer eorðan, and ġīmden þæs dæġes and b̄ære
nihte, and tōdǣlden lēoht and bēostra. God ġeseah þā þæt hit gōd wæs.
And wæs ġeworden ̄æfen and mergen sē fēorða dæġ.

10　　God cwæð ēac swilċe : 'Tēon nū þā wæteru forð swimmende cynn
cucu on līfe, and flēogende cinn ofer eorðan under b̄ære heofenan
fæstnisse.' And God ġesceōp þā þā miċelan hwalas, and eall libbende
fisc-cinn and stiriġendlīċ, þe þā wæteru tugon forð on heora hīwum,
and eall flēogende cinn æfter heora cinne. God ġeseah þā þæt hit gōd
15　wæs, and blētsode hiġ, þus cweðende : 'Weaxað and bēoð ġemeniġfilde,
and ġefillað b̄ære s̄æ wæteru ; and þā fugelas bēon ġemeniġfilde ofer
eorðan.' And þā wæs ġeworden ̄æfen and mergen sē fīfta dæġ.

1　Bēo=bēon(=to be)의 가정법 단수 현재. fæstnysse=firmament, firmness.
2　tōdǣlen=separate, divide. bēo=bēon(=to be)의 가정법 복수 현재. tācnum=tācen(=sign, token)의 복수 여격. tīdum=tīd(=time, season)의 복수 여격.
3　hī(=hīe)=they. scinen[šinen]=shine.
4　ālīhten=light, illuminate.
6　līhtinge=light, illumination. l̄æsse=less. steorran=stars.
7　hiġ(=hīe)=they/them. þæt hiġ scien=that they may shine. ġīmden=rule over. 원형은 ġīeman. 속격을 지배한다.
8　bēostra=darkness.
9　fēorða=fourth. fēower(=fourth)의 서수.
10　ēac=also. swilċe=likewise. Tēon=tēon(=to draw, pull)의 복수 명령. swimmende=swimman(=to swim)의 현재분사. cynn=kind, kin.
11　cucu(=cwic)=living, alive. flēogende=flēogan(=to fly)의 현재분사.

12 ġescēop=creatred. 원형은 ġescieppan(=to create, shape). hwalas=whales. libbende=libban (=to live)의 현재분사.

13 fisc-cinn[fiš-kin]=race of fishes. striġendliċ=moving. tugon=create. 원형은 tēon. heora=their. hīwum=appearance, species.

15 blētsode=blētsian(=to bless)의 과거. Weaxað, bēoð는 각기 weaxan(=to grow, increase)과 bēon(=to be)의 복수 명령. ġemenīġfilde=ġemenīġfyldan(=to multiply, increase)의 과거분사.

16 ġefillað=ġefyllan(=to fill)의 복수 명령. sǣ=sea. fugelas=birds. 원형은 fugol.

17 fīfta=fifth. fīf(=five)의 서수.

And God said, 'Let there be lights in the dome of the sky to separate the day from the night ; and let them be for signs and for seasons and for days and years, and let them be lights in the dome of the sky to give light upon the earth.' And it was so. God made the two great lights —the greater light to rule the day and the lesser light to rule the night—and the stars. God set them in the dome of the sky to give light upon the earth, to rule over the day and over the night, and to separate the light from the darkness. And god saw that it was good. And there was evening and there was morning, the fourth day.

And god said, 'Let the waters bring forth swarms of living creatures, and let birds fly above the earth across the dome of the sky.' So God created the great sea monsters and every living creature that moves, of every kind, with which the waters swarm, and every winged bird of every kind. And God saw that it was good. God blessed them, saying, 'Be fruitful and multiply and fill the waters in the seas, and let birds multiply on the earth.' And there was evening and there was morning, the fifth day.

1   God cwæð ēac and swilċe : 'Lǣde sēo eorðe forð cuce nītenu on heora
cinne, and crēopende cinn and dēor æfter heora hīwum.' Hit wæs þā
swā ġeworden. And God ġeworhte þǣre eorðan dēor æfter hira hīwum,
and þā nītenu and eall crēopende cynn on heora cynne. God ġeseah þā

5   þæt hit gōd wæs, and cwæð : 'Uton wirċean man tō andlīcnisse and tō
ūre ġelīcnisse, and hē siġ ofer þā fixas and ofer þā fugelas, and ofer þā
dēor and ofer ealle ġesceafta, and ofer ealle þā crēopende be stiriað on
eorðan.' God ġescēop þā man tō his andlīcnisse, tō Godes andlīcnisse
hē ġescēop hine. Werhādes and wīfhādes hē ġescēop hiġ. And God hiġ

10   blētsode, and cwæð : 'Wexað and bēoð ġemeniġfilde, and ġefillað þā
eorðan ; and ġewildað hiġ, and habbað on ēowrum ġewealde þǣre sǣ
fixas, and þǣre lyfte fugelas, and ealle nȳtenu be stiriað ofer eorðan.'
God cwæð þā : 'Efne, iċ forġeaf ēow eall gærs and wyrta sǣd berende
ofer eorðan, and ealle trēowu þā be habbað sǣd on him silfon heora

15   āgenes cynnes, þæt hiġ bēon ēow tō mete. And eallum nȳtenum, and
eallum fugelcynne, and eallum þām be stiriað on eorðan, on þām þē ys
libbende līf, þæt hiġ habben him tō ġereordienne.' Hit wæs þā swā
ġedōn. And God ġeseah ealle þā bing be hē ġeworhte, and hiġ wǣron
swīðe gōde. Wæs þā ġeworden ǣfen and mergen sē sixta dæġ.

---

1   Lǣde=lǣdan(=to lead, derive)의 단수 명령. cuce=living, alive. nītetu=animal.
2   crēopende=crēopan(=to creep)의 현재분사. dēor=animal, beast. 현재영어 deer의 옛날 모
      습이다. cf. 독일어 Tier(=animal).
5   Uton=let us. wirċean(=wyrċan)=work, make. andlīcnisse=likeness, resemblance.
6   ġelīcnisse=image, likeness. siġ(=sīe)=bēon(=to be)의 가정법으로서 기원을 나타낸다.
      fixas=fisc[fiš](=fish)의 복수.
7   stiriað=stirs, moves. 원형은 styrian.
8   ġescēop=ġescieppan(=to create)의 과거.
9   Werhādes=male sex. wīfhādes=female sex. hiġ(=hīe)=them.
10   blētsode=blessed. 원형은 blētsian. Wexað, bēoð, ġefillað는 각기 weaxan(=to grow,
      increase), bēon(=to be), ġefyllan(=to fill)의 복수 명령. ġemeniġfilde=ġemeniġfyldan(=to

multiply)의 과거분사.

11 ġewildaŏ=ġewieldan(=to have power over)의 복수 명령. habbaŏ=habban(=to have)의 복수 명령. ēowrum=bū(=thou)의 복수 속격. ġewealde=power, dominion.

12 lyfte=air, sky. cf. 독일어의 Luft(=air). nȳtenu=animals. Efne=behold, lo.

13 forġeaf=gave utterly. 원형은 forġiefan. gærs=grass. wyrta=herb, plant, root. berende=beran(=to bear)의 현재분사.

14 trēowu=trees. silfon=self.

15 āgenes=own. mete=food, feast.

16 fugelcynne=race of birds. ys=is.

17 libbende līf=living life. tō ġereordienne=to feed.

19 swīŏe=exceedingly, very.

　　And God said, 'Let the earth bring forth living creatures of every kind : cattle and creeping things and wild animals of the earth of every kind.' And it was so. God made the wild animals of the earth of every kind, and the cattle of every kind, and everything that creeps upon the ground of every kind. And god saw that it was good. So God created humankind in his image, in the image of god he created them ; male and female he created them. God blessed them, and God said to them, 'Be fruitful and multiply, and fill the earth and subdue it ; and have dominion over the fish of the sea and over the birds of the air and over every living thing that moves upon the earth.' God said, 'See, I have given you every plant yielding seed that is upon the face of all the earth, and every tree with seed in its fruit ; you shall have them for food. And to every beast of the earth, and to every bird of the air, and to everything that creeps on the earth, everything that has the breath of life, I have given every green plant for food.' And it was so. God saw everything that he had made and indeed, it was very good. And there was evening and there was morning, the sixth day.

1   Ēac swelċe sēo nǣdre wæs ġēapre bonne ealle bā ōðre nīetenu be God
    ġeworhte ofer eorðan ; and sēo nǣdre cwæð tō bām wīfe : 'Hwȳ
    forbēad God ēow bæt ġe ne ǣten of ælcum trēowe binnan Paradīsum?'
    7æt wīf andwyrde : 'Of bāra trēowa wæstme be sind on Paradīsum wē etað :
5   and of bæs trēowes wæstme, be is onmiddan neorxenawange, God
    bebēad ūs bæt wē ne ǣten, ne wē bæt trēow ne hrepoden bȳ lǣs be wē
    swulten.' 7ā cwæð sēo nǣdre eft tō bām wīfe : 'Ne bēo ġe nāteshwōn
    dēade, bēah be ġe of bām trēowe eten. Ac God wāt sōðlīċe bæt ēowre
    ēagan bēoð ġeopenode on swā hwelċum dæġe swā ġe etað of bām
10 trēowe ; and ġē bēoð bonne englum ġelīċe, witende ǣġðer ġe gōd ġe
    yfel.' 7ā ġeseah bæt wīf bæt bæt trēow wæs gōd tō etanne, be bām be
    hire būhte, and wlitiġ on ēagum and lustbǣre on ġesihðe ; and ġenam
    bā of bæs trēowes wæstme and ġeæt, and sealde hire were : hē æt bā.
    And hira bēġra ēagan wurdon ġeopenode : hīe oncnēowon bā bæt hīe
15 nacode wǣron, and sīwodon him fīclēaf and worhton him wǣdbrēċ.

1   Ēac=also, and. swelċe=such. nǣdre=snake, serpent. ġeappre=ġeap(=deceitful, astute)의 비
    교급. bonne=than. nīetenu=nīeten(=beast, animal, cattle)의 복수. be=that. 관계대명사.
2   ġeworhte=made. 원형은 ġewyrċan. ofer eorðan=on the earth. cwæð=said. cweðan(=to
    say)의 3인칭 단수 현재로서 초기 현대영어의 quoth가 그 잔재이다. Hwȳ=why. forbēad=
    forbade. 원형은 forbēadan.
3   ēow=ġe(=you)의 여격. ǣten=etan(=to eat)의 2인칭 복수. forbēad God ēow bæt ġe ne ǣ
    ten=commanded…that you should not eat. ne는 forbēad(=forbade)의 뜻을 부정하는 것이 아
    니라 강조한다. ælcum=ælċ(=each)의 단수 여격. trēow=tree. binnan=within. Paradīsum=
    Paradīsus(=Paradise)의 단수 여격. 선행하는 전치사 binnan이 여격을 요구한다.
4   andwyrde=answered. 원형은 andwyrdan. bāra=se(=the, that)의 복수 속격. wæstme=
    wæstm(=fruit)의 단수 여격. be=that. 관계대명사. wē etað=we eat. 그러나 여기서는 we do
    eat로 번역해야.
5   onmiddan=in the middle of. 여격을 지배한다. neorxenawange=Paradise.
6   bebēad=commanded, ordered. 원형은 bebēodan. ne wē bæt trēow ne hrepoden bȳ lǣs
    be=nor might we touch that tree lest…. 여기서도 이중부정은 강조를 나타낸다. hrepoden=
    hrepian(=to touch)의 가정법. bȳ lǣs (be)=lest.

132 고대영어

7   swulten=sweltan(=to die)의 가정법. 7ā=then. Ne bēo ġē=You will not be. nāteshwōn= not at all.

8   dēade=dead. bēah be=although. wāt=knows. 원형은 witan. ēowre=ġe(=you)의 속격.

9   ēagan=ēage(=eye)의 복수 대격. bēoð=bēon(=to be)의 과거 복수형으로서 미래시를 나타낸다. ġeopenode=opened. 원형은 ġeopenian. swā hwelċum…swā=whatsoever. etað=eat. 원형은 etan.

10 englum=engel(=angel)의 복수 여격. 후속하는 형용사 ġeliċe(=like)가 여격을 지배한다. witende=witan(=to know)의 현재분사. ǣġðer…ġe=both…and.

11 ġeseah=sēon(=to see)의 과거. gōd tō etanne=good to eat. be bām be=as, according as.

12 hire būhte=it seemed to her. būhte는 비인칭 동사로서 원형은 bynċan. wlitiġ=beautiful. lustbǣre=desirable. ġesihðe=sight. ġenam=took. 원형은 ġeniman.

13 ġeǣt=ate. sealde=gave. 원형은 sellan. were=wer(=husband)의 단수 여격. hē ǣt bā=he ate them.

14 hira=their. beġra=bēġen(=both)의 복수 속격. wurdon ġeopenode=were opened. wurdon= weorðan(=to become, happen)의 과거. oncnēowon=recognized. 원형은 oncnāwan.

15 nacode=naked. sīwodon=stitched together. 원형은 sīwian. him…him=모두 themselves의 뜻. ficlēaf=figleaf. worhton=made. 원형은 wyrċan. wǣdbrēċ=breeches.

   Now the serpent was more crafty than any other wild animal that the Lord God had made. He said to the woman, 'Did God say, "You shall not eat from any tree in the garden"? 'The woman said to the serpent, 'We may eat of the fruit of the trees in the garden ; but God said, "You shall not eat of the fruit of the tree that is in the middle of the garden, not shall you touch it, or you shall die." 'But the serpent said to the woman, 'You will not die ; for God knows that when you eat of it your eyes will be opened, and you will be like God, knowing good and evil.' So when the woman saw that the tree was good for food, and that it was a delight to the eyes, and that the tree was to be desired to make one wise, she took of its fruit and ate ; and she also gave some to her husband, who was with her, and he ate. Then the eyes of both were opened, and they knew that they were naked ; and they sewed fig leaves together and made loincloths for themselves.

THE FALL OF MAN (2) (GENESIS iii, 8-19)

1   Eft þā þā God cōm and hīe ġehīerdon his stefne, þǣr hē ēode on
neorxenawange ofer middæġ, þā behȳdde Adam hine, and his wīf ēac
swā dyde, fram Godes ġesihðe onmiddan þām trēowe neorxenawanges.
God clipode þā Adam, and cwæð : 'Adam, hwǣr eart þū?' Hē cwæð :
5   7īne stefne iċ ġehīerde, lēof, on neorxenawange, and iċ ondrēd mē, for
þām þe iċ eom nacod, and iċ behȳdde mē.' God cwæð : 'Hwā sæġde þē
þæt þū nacod wǣre, ġif þū ne ǣte of þām trēowe þe iċ þē bebēad þæt
þū of ne ǣte?' Adam cwæð : '7æt wīf þæt þū mē forġēafe tō ġefēran,
sealde mē of þām trēowe, and iċ ǣt.' God cwæð tō þām wīfe : 'Hwȳ
10 dydest þū þæt?' Hēo cwæð : 'Sēo nǣdre bepǣhte mē and iċ ǣt.'

    God cwæð tō þǣre nǣdran : 'For þām þe þū þis dydest, þū bist
āwierġed betweox eallum nīetenum and wilddēorum. 7ū gǣst on þīnum
brēoste and etst þā eorðan eallum dagum þīnes līfes. Iċ sette fēondrǣdene
betweox þē and þām wīfe and þīnum ofspringe and hire ofspringe ; hēo
15 tōbrȳt þīn hēafod and þū sierwst onġēan hire hō.'

    Tō þām wīfe cwæð God ēac swelċe : 'Iċ ġemaniġfealde þīne iermða
and þīne ġeēacnunga ; on sārnesse þū ācenst ċild and þū bist under
weres onwealde and hē ġewielt þē.' Tō Adame hē cwæð : 'For þām þe
þū ġehīerdest þīnes wīfes stefne and þū ǣte of þǣm trēowe, þe iċ þē
20 bebēad þæt þū ne ǣte, is sēo eorðe āwierġed on þīnum weorce ; on
ġeswincum þū etst of þǣre eorðan eallum dagum þīnes līfes. 7ornas
and brēmēlas hēo āspryt þē, and þū etst þǣre eorðan wyrta. On swāte
þīnes andwlitan þū brȳcst þīnes hlāfes, oð þæt þū ġewende tō eorðan,
of þǣre þe þū ġenumen wǣre, for þām þe þū eart dūst and tō dūste
25 wierbst.'

---

1   þā þā…þā=when…then. ġehīerdon=heard. 원형은 ġehīeran. stefne=stefn(=voice)의 단수
대격. ēode=went. 원형은 gān.
2   ofer middæġ=after midday. behȳdde=hid. 원형은 behȳdan. hine=himself. 고대영어에서는

인칭대명사가 재귀대명사의 구실도 했다.

3 dyde=did. 원형은 dōn. ġesihðe=sight, vision, presence.

4 clipode=called. 원형은 clipian.

5 lēof=beloved, dear. iċ ondrēd mē=I was afraid. 여기서 mē는 재귀대명사로서 번역할 필요
가 없다. 초기 현대영어의 Fear thee not과 같은 표현에 해당된다.

5-6 for þām þe=because. sæġde=secgan(=to say)의 과거.

7 þe=that. 관계대명사. bebēad=commanded. 원형은 bebēodan.

8 forġeafe=gave. 원형은 forġīefan. ġefēran(=companion, comrade)의 단수 대격.

9 sealde=gave. 원형은 sellan.

10 bepæhte=deceived. 원형은 bepæċan.

11 For þām þe=as, since. bist=are. bēon(=to be)의 2인칭 단수 현재.

12 āwierġed=cursed. āwierġan(=to curse)의 과거분사. betweox=between, among, wilddēorum=
wild beast cf. dēor=wild animal. 현대영어의 deer가 그 현대형이다. gǣst=gān(=to go)의 2
인칭 단수 현재형으로서 미래시를 나타낸다. þīnum=þīn(=thy)의 복수 여격.

13 brēoste=breast. etst=etan(=to eat)의 2인칭 단수 현재로서 여기서도 미래시를 나타낸다.
eorðan=earth(흙). eallum dagum=all the days. þīnes līfes=of thy life. sette=settan(=to
put, set)의 현재로서 미래시를 나타낸다. fēondrǣdene=enmity.

14 ofspringe=offspring.

15 tōbrȳt=tōbrȳtan(=to crush)의 3인칭 단수 현재. sierwst=sierwan(=to contrive, plot)의 현
재로서 미래시를 나타낸다. onġēan=against. hō=hōh(=heel)의 단수 여격.

16 ġemaniġfealde=multiply, increase. iermða=misery.

17 ġeēacnunga=child-bearing, conception. sārnesse=pain. ācenst=ācennan(=to bring forth,
give birth to)의 현재로서 미래시를 나타낸다.

18 weres=man's, husband's. onwealde=authority, power, ġewielt=rule, control. 원형은
ġewealdan.

19 be iċ bē의 be는 관계대명사.

20 is sēo eorðe āwierġed=the earth is cursed. weorce=work, task, deed.

21 ġeswincum=ġeswincan(=hardship, toil)의 복수 여격. 원형은 ġeswinc. 초기현대영어의
swink가 그 잔재. þornas=thorns.

22 brēmēlas=brambles, briers. hēo=she. 선행하는 sēo eorðe가 여성명사이므로 hēo가 사용되
었다. āspryt=āspryttan(=to sprout, bring forth)의 현재. wyrta=herb, plant. swāte=sweat.

23 andwlitan=face. brȳcst=enjoy, use, benefit from. 원형은 brūcan. hlāfes=bread. þīnes
hlāfes는 속격으로서 선행하는 동사 brȳcst가 속격을 요구하기 때문이다. oð þæt=until.
ġewende=ġewendan(=to return)의 현재.

24 of þǣre þe=from which. ġenumen=taken. 원형은 niman. dūst=dust.

25 wierbst=will return. 원형은 weorðan.

They heard the sound of the Lord God walking in the garden at the time
of the evening breeze, and the man and his wife hid themselves from the

presence of the Lord God among the trees of the garden. But the Lord God called to the man, and said to him. 'Where are you?' He said, 'I heard the sound of you in the garden, and I was afraid, because I was naked ; and I hid myself.' He said, 'Who told you that you were naked? Have you eaten from the tree of which I commanded you not to eat?' The man said, 'The woman whom you gave to be with me, she gave me fruit from the tree, and I ate.' Then the Lord God said to the woman, 'What is this that you have done?' The woman said, 'The serpent tricked me, and I ate.'

The Lord God said to the serpent, 'Because you have done this, cursed are you among all animals and among all wild creatures ; upon your belly you shall go, and dust you shall eat all the days of your life. I will put enmity between you and the woman, and between your offspring and hers ; he will strike your head, and you will strike his heel.'

To the woman he said, 'I will greatly increase your pangs in childbearing ; in pain you shall bring forth children, yet your desire shall be for your husband, and he shall rule over you.' And to the man he said, 'Because you have listened to the voice of your wife, and have eaten of the tree about which I commanded you, "You shall not eat of it," cursed is the ground because of you ; in toil you shall eat of it all the days of your life ; thorns and thistles it shall bring forth for you ; and you shall eat the plants of the field. By the sweat of your face you shall eat bread until you return to the ground, for out of it you were taken ; you are dust, and to dust you shall return.'

THE FLOOD (1) (GENESIS vi, 11-vii, 9)

1 7ā wæs eall sēo eorðe ġewemmed ætforan Gode, and āfylled mid
unrihtwīsnysse. 7ā ġeseah God bæt sēo eorðe wæs ġewemmed, for bam
be ǣlċ flǣsc ġewemde his weġ ofer eorðan.

And God cwæð bā tō Noe : 'Ġeendung ealles flǣsces cōm ætforan
5 mē. Sēo eorðe ys āfylled mid unrihtwīsnysse fram heora ansīne, and iċ
fordō hiġ mid bǣre eorðan samod. Wirċ bē nū ǣnne arc of āhēawenum
bordum. And bū wircst wununge binnan bām arce, and clǣmst
wiðinnan and wiðūtan mid tyrwan.'

*   *   *

Noe sōðlīċe dide ealle bā bing be him God behēad.
10 And God cwæð tō him : 'Gang in tō bām arce, and eall bīn hīwrǣden.
7ē iċ ġeseah sōðlīċe rihtwīsne ætforan mē on bissere mǣġðe. Nim in tō
bē of eallum clǣnum nītenum seofen and seofen ǣġðres ġecyndes, and
of bām unclǣnum twām and twām ; and of fugelcinne seofen and seofen
ǣġðres ġecyndes, bæt sǣd sī ġehealden ofer ealre eorðan brādnisse. Iċ
15 sōðlīċe sende rēn nū ymb seofon niht ofer eorðan fēowertiġ daga and
fēowertiġ nihta tōgædere, and iċ ādīleġie ealle bā edwiste be iċ
ġeworhte ofer eorðan brādnisse.' Noe bā dide ealle bā bing be him God
bebēad. And hē wæs bā six hund ġeara on ylde, bā bā bæs flōdes
wæteru ȳðedon ofer eorðan.

20 Hwæt! 7ā Noe ēode in tō bām arce and his brī suna and his wīf and
his suna wīf for bæs flōdes wæterum. Ēac swilċe bā nītenu of eallum
cinne and of eallum fugelcynne cōmon tō Noe in tō bām arce, swā swā
God bebēad.

---

1 ġewemmed=defiled. 원형은 ġewemman(=to defile, destroy). ætforan=before, in the sight
of. āfylled=filled. 원형은 āfyllan.
2 unrihtwīsnysse=unrighteousness.
2-3 for bam be=because.

3   flǣsc=flesh.

4   Ġeendung=end. cōm=came. 원형은 cuman.

5   ānsīne=face, view, sight.

6   fordō=fordōn(=to destroy)의 현재로서 미래시를 나타낸다. hiġ(=hīe)=them. s a m o d = together. Wirċ=wyrċan(=to make, work)의 단수 명령. arc=ark. āhēawenum=āhēawenan (=to cut away, hew)의 과거분사.

7   bordum=board. wircst=make. wununge=dwelling. binnan=within, inside. clǣmst=clǣ man(=to caulk, smear)의 단수 명령.

8   wiðinnan=within. wiðūtan=outside. tyrwan=pitch, tar.

9   behēad=commanded. 원형은 behātan.

10   Gang=gangan(=to go, walk)의 단수 명령. arce=ark. hīwrǣden=family, household.

11   rihtwīsne=righteous. bissere=bes(=this)의 속격. mǣġðe=country, people, tribe.　N i m = niman(=to take)의 단수 명령.

12   clǣnum nīetum=clean animals. clean/unclean animals의 구별에 대해서는 Leviticus(레위기) 11장을 참조할 것). seofen=seven. ǣġðres=each, either. ġecyndes=species, kind.

13   unclǣn=unclean. twām=two. fugelcinne=race of birds. seofon=seven.

14   sǣd=seed. sī=is. bēon(=to be)의 가정법. þæt…sī=that…may. ġehealden=ġehealden(=to hold)의 과거분사. brādnisse=surface, broadness.

15   rēn=rain. nū=now. ymb=about, around. fēowertiġ=forty. daga=days.

16   nihta=nights. tōgædere=together. ādīleġie=ādīleġian(=to destroy)의 현재로서 미래시를 나타낸다. edwiste=being.

18   six hund ġeara=six hundred years. ylde(=ieldo)=age.

19   yðedon=yðiġan(=to flow, flood)의 과거.

20   Hwæt=lo, behold. ēode=went. 원형은 gān. brī=three.

21   for þæs=because of. Ēac=also. swilċe=likewise.

22   swā swā=just as.

Now the earth was corrupt in God's sight, and the earth was filled with violence. And god saw that the earth was corrupt ; for all flesh had corrupted its ways upon the earth.

And God said to Noah, 'I have determined to make an end of all flesh, for the earth is filled with violence because of them ; now I am going to destroy them along with the earth. Make yourself an ark of cypress wood ; make rooms in the ark, and cover it inside and out with pitch.

*   *   *

Noah did this ; he did all that God commanded him.

Then the Lord said to Noah, 'Go into the ark, you and all your household, for I have seen that you alone are righteous before me in this generation. Take with you seven pairs of all clean animals, the male and its mate ; and a pair of the animals that are not clean, the male and its mate ; and seven pairs of the birds of the air also, male and female, to keep their kind alive on the face of all the earth. For in seven days I will send rain on the earth for forty days and forty nights ; and every living things that I have made I will blot out from the face of the ground.' And Noah did all that the Lord had commanded him. Noah was six hundred years old when the flood of waters came on the earth.

And Noah with his sons and his wife and his sons' wives went into the ark to escape the waters of the flood. Of clean animals, and of animals that are not clean, and of birds, and of everything that creeps on the ground, two and two, male and female, went into the ark with Noah, as god had commanded Noah.

THE FLOOD (2) (GENESIS vii, 10-24)

1   7ā on bām eahtoðan dæġe, þā þā hiġ inne wǣron, and God hiġ belocen
hæfde wiðūtan, þā ȳðode þæt flōd ofer eorðan. On bām ōðrum mōnðe,
on bām seofentēoðan dæġ þæs mōnðes, þā āsprungon ealle wyllspringas
þǣre miċelan niwelnisse, and þǣre heofonan wæterbēotan wǣron
5   ġeopenode. And hit rīnde þā ofer eorðan fēowertiġ daga and fēowertiġ
nihta on ān. Wæs þā ġeworden miċel flōd, and þā wæteru wǣron
ġemeniġfilde, and āhefdon ūpp þone arc, and ȳðedon swīðe, and
ġefyldon þǣre eorðan brādnisse ; witodlīċe sē arc wæs ġeferud ofer þā
wæteru.

10 And þæt wæter swīðrode swīðe ofer þā eorðan ; wurdon þā behelede
ealle þā hēhstan dūna under ealre heofenan. And þæt wæter wæs fīftȳne
fæðma dēop ofer þā hēhstan dūna. Wearð þā fornumen eall flǣsc be
ofer eorðan styrode, manna and fugela, nȳtena and crēopendra. And
ǣlċ þing þe līf hæfde wearð ādȳd on þām dēopan flōde, būton þām
15 ānum þe binnan þām arce wǣron. 7æt flōd stōd þā swā ān hund daga
and fīftiġ daga.

---

1   eahtoðan=eighth. belocen=belūcan(=to lock, shut up)의 과거분사.
2   wiðūtan=outside.
3   seofentēoðan=seventeenth. mōnðes=of the month. āsprungon=āsrþingan(=to spring
forth)의 과거. wyllspringas=spring (of water).
4   niwelnisse=chasm, abyss. þǣre=there. wæterbēotan=torrent.
5   ġeoepenode=ġeopenian(=to open)의 과거분사. fēowertiġ=forty.
6   on ān=continuously. cf. ān=one.
7   ġemenīġfilde=ġemenīġfyllan(=to increase)의 과거분사. āhefdon=āhebban(=to raise, lift up,
heave)의 과거분사. ūpp=up. ȳðedon=surged. cf. ȳð=wave. swīðe=exceedingly, very.
8   ġefyldon=destroyed. 원형은 ġefyllan. brādnisse=bredth, surface. witōdlīċe=truly.
ġeferud=ġeferian(=to carry, bring)의 과거분사.
10 swīðrode=became strong. 원형은 swīðrian. wurdon=weorðan(=to become)의 과거.
behelede=behelian(to cover)의 과거분사.
11 hēhstan=hēah(=high)의 최상급. dūna=hill. cf. down. fīftȳne=fifteen.

12 fæðma=fathom. dēop=deep. fornumen=destroyed. 원형은 forniman.
13 styrode=stirred, moved. 원형은 styrian. manna=mann(=man)의 복수 속격으로서 선행하는 flǽsc(=flesh)에 걸린다. crēopendra=creeping things. 원형은 crēopan(=to creep). '기어다니는 것들의'.
14 ādȳd=ādȳdan(=to kill)의 과거분사. būton=except. 여격을 지배한다.
15 ānum=ān(=one)의 복수 여격. binnan=within. stōd=stood. 원형은 standan.

And after seven days (they were in and God locked them outside,) the waters of the flood came on the earth. On the seventeenth day of the month, on that day all the fountains of the great deep burst forth, and the windows of the heavens were opened. The rain fell on the earth forty days and forty nights on end. The waters increased, and bore up the ark. The waters swelled and increased greatly on the earth ; and the ark floated on the face of the waters.

The waters swelled so mightily on the earth that all the high mountains under the whole heaven were covered ; the waters swelled above the mountains, covering them fifteen cubits deep. And all the flesh died that moved on the earth, birds, domestic animals, wild animals, all swarming creatures that swarm on the earth, and all human beings. Every living thing on the face of the earth was wiped out except those who were in the ark. And the waters covered the earth for one hundred and fifty days.

ABRAHAM AND ISAAC (1) (GENESIS xxii, 1-8)

1   God wolde þā fandian Abrahāmes ġehīersumnesse, and clipode his naman, and cwæþ him þus tō : 'Nim þīnne āncennedan sunu Isaāc, þe þū lufast, and far tō þām lande Visionis hraþe, and ġeoffra hine þǣr uppan ānre dūne.'

5   Abrahām þā ārās on þǣre ilcan nihte, and fērde mid twǣm cnapum tō þǣm fierlenan lande, and Isaāc samod, on assum rīdende. 7ā on þone þriddan dæġ, þā hīe þā dūne ġesāwon, þǣr þǣr hīe tō scoldon tō ofslēanne Issāc, þā cwæþ Abrahām tō þǣm twǣm cnapum þus : 'Andbīdiaþ ēow hēr mid þǣm assum sume hwīle! Iċ and þæt ċild gāþ

10   unc tō ġebiddenne, and wit siþþan cumaþ sōna eft tō ēow.'

     Abrahām þā hēt Isaāc beran þone wudu tō þǣre stōwe, and hē self bær his sweord and fȳr. Isaāc þā āscode Abrahām his fæder : 'Fæder mīn, iċ āsciġe hwǣr sēo offrung sīe ; hēr is wudu and fȳr.' Him andwyrde se fæder : 'God foresċēawaþ, mīn sunu, him self þā offrunge.'

15   Hīe cōmon þā tō þǣre stōwe þe him ġesweotolode God ; and hē þǣr wēofod ārǣrde on þā ealdan wīsan, and þone wudu ġelōgode swā swā hē hit wolde habban tō his suna bærnette, siþþan hē ofslæġen wurde. Hē ġeband þā his sunu, and his sweord ātēah, þæt hē hine ġeoffrode on þā ealdan wīsan.

---

1   wolde=wished. 원형은 willan. fandian=to test. ġehȳrsumnesse=obedience. clipode=clipian (=to call, summon)의 과거.

2   cwæþ him þus tō=spoke to him thus. OE에서는 여기서 보듯 종종 전치사가 목적어 뒤에 오는 경우가 있다. Nim=take. niman(=to take)의 단수 명령. āncenned=(adj.)only begotten.

3   lufast=lufian(=to love)의 2인칭 단수 현재. far=go. faran(=to go)의 단수 명령. cf. ModE, to fare, farewell. þām lande Visionis=the land of Moriah. 히브리어의 Moriah는 vision의 뜻. hraþe=quickly. ġeoffra=ġeoffrian(=to offer, sacrifice)의 단수 명령. uppan=upon, on.

4   ānre dūne=one of the mountains. dūne=hill. cf. ModE, down.

5   ārās=arose. 원형은 ārīsan. ilcan=same. fērde=went. twǣm=two. cnapum=boys. cf. G. Knabe(=boy).

6   fierlenan=distant. samod=together. assum=assa(=ass)의 복수 여격. rīdende=riding. rīdan

(=to ride)의 현재분사.

7 ġesāwon=saw. 원형은 ġesēon.

7-8 þā dūne ġesāwon, þær þær hīe tō scoldon tō ofslēaane=the mountain where they must (go) to slay. tō scoldon=had to. þær þær=where. 관계부사.

8 ofslēanne=kill, slay. 원형은 ofslēan.

9 Andbīdiaþ=andbīdian(=to await)의 단수 명령. eow=ġē(=you)의 재귀대명사. 동사 andbīdian (=to await)는 현대영어의 wait와는 달리 재귀대명사를 요구한다. hēr=here. sume=some, a certain. sume hwīle=for some time. hwīle=while, time. gāð=gān(=to go)의 1인칭 복수 현재로서 미래시를 나타낸다.

10 unc=wit(1인칭 양수)의 대격. 후속하는 ġebiddenne의 재귀대명사. 여기서는 번역할 필요가 없다. tō ġebiddenne=to pray. 원형은 ġebiddan. 흔히 재귀대명사와 함께 쓰인다. unc tō ġebiddenne=to pray. wit=1인칭 양수. '우리 둘'. sibban=afterwards, then. cumaþ=cuman (=to come)의 복수 현재로서 미래시를 나타낸다. sōna=soon, immediately.

11 hēt=ordered. 원형은 hātan. beran=bear. wudu=wood. stōwe=place.

12 bær=beran(=to bear, carry)의 과거. sweord=sword. fȳr=fire. āscode=ascian[askian]의 과거.

13 hwær=where. iċ āsciġe hwær sēo offrung sīe=I ask where the offering is. sīe=bēon(=to be)의 가정법 현재로서 지금 당장 제물이 없으므로 가정법이 사용되었다. offrunge= offering, sacrifice.

14 andwyrde=answered. forscēawaþ=forescēawian(=to provide)의 현재형으로서 미래시를 나타낸다. cf. fore(=pre)+scēawian(=see). God forescēawaþ him self þā offrunge=God himself will provide the offering (for himself). him self=현대영어 himself의 모습이 보인다.

15 ġesweotolode=ġesweotolian(=to show)의 과거.

16 wēofod=altar. ārærde=raised up. 원형은 āræran. on þā ealdan wīsan=in the ancient manner. wīsan=fashion, way. ġelōgode=arranged. 원형은 ġelōgian. cf. lodge. suna= suna(=son)의 속격.

17 bærnette=burning. ofslæġen wurde=would be killed. wurde는 weorþan(=to become, happen)의 가정법 과거로서 과거중 미래(future-in-the-past)를 나타낸다.

18 ġeband=ġebindan(=to tie)의 과거, ātēah=ātēon(=to draw)의 과거. ġeoffrode=might offer. ġeoffrian(=to offer)의 가정법 과거. 선행하는 þæt와 함께 that…may의 뜻을 갖는다.

19 ealdan=old.

After these things God tested Abraham. He said to him, 'Abraham!' And he said, 'Here I am.' He said, 'Take your son, your only son Isaac, whom you love, and go to the land of Moriah, and offer him there as a burnt offering on one of the mountains that I shall show you.

So Abraham rose early in the morning, saddled his donkey, and took two of his young men with him, and his son Isaac ; he cut the wood for the burnt offering, and set out and went to the place in the distance that God had shown him. On the third day Abraham looked up and saw the place far away. Then Abraham said to his young men, 'Stay here with the donkey ; the boy and I will go over there ; we will worship, and then we will come back to you.'

Abraham took the wood of the burnt offering and laid it on his son Isaac, and he himself carried the fire and the knife. so the two of them walked on together. Isaac said to his father Abraham, 'Father!' And he said, 'Here I am, my son.' He said, 'The fire and the wood are here, but where is the lamb for a burnt offering?' Abraham said, 'God himself will provide the lamb for a burnt offering, my son.' So the two of them walked on together.

When they came to the place that God had shown him, Abraham built an altar there and laid the wood in order. He bound his son Isaac, and laid him on the altar, on top of the wood. Then Abraham reached out his hand and took the knife to kill his son.

ABRAHAM AND ISAAC (2) (GENESIS xxii, 11-19)

1   Mid þǣm þē hē wolde þæt weorc beġinnan, þā clipode Godes engel
arodlīċe of heofonum : 'Abrahām! Hē andwyrde sōna. Se engel him
cwæþ tō : 'Ne ācwele þū þæt ċild, ne þīne hand ne āstreċe ofer his
swēoran! Nū iċ oncnēow sōþlīċe þæt þū swīþe ondrǣtst God, nū þū
5   þīnne āncennedan sunu ofslēan woldest for him.'

    7ā beseah Abrahām sōna under bæc, and ġeseah þǣr ānne ramm
betwix þǣm brēmlum be þǣm hornum ġehæft ; and hē āhefde bone
ramm tō þǣre offrunge, and hine þǣr ofsnāþ Gode tō lāce for his sunu
Isaāc. Hē hēt þā þā stōwe *Dominus uidet*, þæt is 'God ġesiehþ', and
10 ġiet is ġesæġd swā, *In monte Dominus uidebit*, þæt is, 'God ġesiehþ on
dūne.'

    Eft clipode se engel Abrahām, and cwæþ : Iċ sweriġe þurh mē selfne,
sæġde se Ælmihtiga, nū þū noldest ārian þīnum āncennedan suna, ac þē
wæs mīn eġe māre þonne his līf, iċ þē nū blētsiġe, and þīnne ofspring
15 ġemaniġfielde swā swā steorrran on heofonum, and swā swā
sandċeosol on sǣ ; þīn ofsrping sceal āgan hiera fēonda gatu. And on
þīnum sǣde bēoþ ealle bēoda ġeblētsode, for þǣm þe þū
ġehīersumodest mīnre hǣse þus.

    Abrhām þā ġeċierde sōna tō his cnapum, and fērde him hām swā
20 mid heofonlicre blētsunge.

1   Mid þǣm be=when, while. weorc=work. engel=angel.
2   arodlīċe=quickly.
2-3 him cwæþ tō=cwæþ tō him.
3   ācwele=ācwellan(=to kill)의 단수 명령. Ne ācwele=do not kill. ne…ne는 강조를 나타낸
다. āstreċe=āstreċċan(=to stretch out)의 단수 명령.
4   swēoran=neck. oncnēow=knew, perceived, understood. 원형은 oncnāwan. Nū Iċ
oncnēow…, nū þū=Now I perceive…now that thou. Nū…nū는 상관접속사(correlative
conjunction). swīþe=greatly. ondrǣtst=dread, fear. 원형은 ondrǣdan. 두 번째 nū=since,
now that.
6   beseah=saw. 원형은 besēon. under=under. bæc=back. under bæc=behind. ramm=ram.
7   betwix=between. brēmlum=brambles. 단수형은 brēmel. be=by. hornum=horns.

8   ġehæft=ġehæftan(=to hold fast)의 과거분사. āhefde=āhebban(=to raise, lift up)의 과거.

8   ofsnab=slaughtered. 원형은 ofsnīban. Gode tō lāce=as a sacrifice to God. lāce=offering, gift.

9   hēt=called. 원형은 hātan. bā bā에서 첫 번째 bā=then, 두 번째 bā=sēo(=she(=stōwe))의 단수 대격. Domunus uidet(=videt)=The Lord sees. ġesiehþ=sees. 원형은 sēon.

10   ġiet=yet. ġesǣd=called. 원형은 secgan. In monte Dominus uidebit=on the mountain the Lord will see.

12   sweriġe=swear. 원형은 swerian.

13   Ælmihtiga=almighty, Lord. nū=now that. noldest=did not desire. ārian=spare.

14   eġe=fear. māre=more. bonne=than. blētsiġe=bless. 원형은 blētsian. ofspring=offspring.

15   ġemaniġfielde=will increase. 원형은 ġemaniġfieldan.

16   sandċeosol=gravel. sǣ=sea. sceal=ought to. āgan=possess. fēonda=fēond(=enemy)의 속격. gatu=gates. 원형은 ġeat.

17   sǣde=seed. ðēoda=peoples. for bǣm be=because.

18   ġehiersumodest=obeyed. 원형은 ġehīersumian. hǣse=command.

19   ġeċierde=returned. 원형은 ġeċierran. hām=home.

20   heofonlicre=heavenly. 원형은 heofonliċ. blētsunge=blessing.

But the angel of the Lord called to him from heaven, and said, 'Abraham, Abraham!' And he said, 'Here I am.' He said, 'Do not lay your hand on the boy or do anything to him ; for now I know that you fear God, since you have not withheld your son, your only son, from me.'

And Abraham looked up and saw a ram, caught in a thicket by its horns. Abraham went and took the ram and offered it up as a burnt offering instead of his son. So Abraham called that place 'The Lord will provide' ; as it is said to this day, 'On the mount of the Lord it shall be provided.'

The angel of the Lord called to Abraham a second time from heaven, and said, 'By myself I have sworn, says the Lord : Because you have done this, and have not withheld your son, your only son, I will indeed bless you, and I will make your offspring as numerous as the stars of heaven and as the sand that is on the seashore. And your offspring shall possess the gate of their enemies, and by your offspring shall all the nations of the earth gain blessing for themselves, because you have obeyed my voice.'

So Abraham returned to his young men, and they arose and went together to Beersheba ; and Abraham lived at Beersheba.

SAMSON (JUDGES xiii-xv)

1   Ān mann wæs eardiende on Israhēla aēode, Manuē ġehāten, of āǣre
mǣġae Dan. His wīf wæs untīemende, and hīe wunodon būtan ċilde.
Him cōm aā gangende tō Godes engel, and cwæa aæt hīe scolden
habban sunu him ġemǣnne : 'Sē bia Gode hāliġ fram his ċildhāde ;

5   and man ne mōt hine efsian oaae bescieran, ne hē ealu ne drince nǣfre
oaae wīn, ne nāht fūles ne aicge ; for āǣm ae hī onġina tō ālīesenne
his folc, Israhēla aēode, of Philistēs aēowte.'

   Hēo ācēnde aā sunu, swā swā hiere sæġde se engel, and hēt hine
Samson ; and hē swīae wēox, and God hine blētsode, and Godes

10 gāst wæs on him. Hē weara aā mihtiġ on miċelre strengae, swā aæt hē
ġelǣhte āne lēon be weġe, ae hine ābītan wolde, and tōbræġd hīe tō
styċċum, swelċe hē tōtǣre sum ēaaeliċ tiċċen.

   Hē begann aā tō winnenne wia aā Philistēos, and hiera fela ofslōg
and tō scame tūcode, aēah ae hīe anweald hæfden ofer his lēode. 7ā

15 fērdon aā Philistēi fora æfter Samsone, and hēton his lēode aæt hīe hine
āġēafen tō hiera answealde, aæt hīe wrecan mihten hiera tēonrǣdenne
mid tintregum on him. Hīe aā hine ġebundon mid twǣm bæstenum
rāpum and hine ġelǣddon tō āǣm folce. And aā Philistēiscan aæs
fæġnodon swīae ; urnon him tōġēanes ealle hlȳdende, woldon hine

20 tintreġian for hiera tēonrǣdenne. 7ā tōbræġd Samson bēġen his ermas,
aæt aā rāpas tōburston ae hē mid ġebunden wæs. And hē ġelǣhte aā
sōna sumes assan ċinnbān ae hē āǣr funde, and ġefeaht wia hīe, and
ofslōg ān aūsend mid aæs assan ċinnbāne, and cwæa tō him selfum :
'Iċ oflōg witodlīċe ān aūsend wera mid aæs assan ċinnbāne.' Hē weara

25 aā swīae ofayrst for āǣm wundorlican sleġe, and bæd aone heofonlican
God aæt hē him āsende drincan, for āǣm ae on āǣre nēawiste næs nān
wæterscipe. 7ā arn of āǣm ċinnbāne, of ānum tēa, wæter ; and Samson
aā dranc, and his Dryhtne aancode.

(여기 인용한 글은 성경을 직접 번역한 것이 아니고 Ælfric이 해당 부분을 풀어 쓴 것이다.)

1   eardiende=eardian(=to live)의 현재분사. aēode=people, nation. Manuē ġehāten=called Manoah.

2   mǣġae=tribe. untīemende=barren. cf. tīerman=bring forth. wunodon=lived. 원형은 wunian. būtan ċilde=without child.

3   Him cōm aā gangende tō Godes engel=aā Godes engel cōm gangende tō him=God's angel came approaching to them. gangende=gān(=advance, proceed)의 현재분사.

4   ġemǣnne=shared, in common. ċildhāde=childhood.

5   efsian=cut the hair. bescieran=cut off the hair of, shear. ealu=ale.

6   nāht=nothing. fūles=foul, impure. aicge=take, eat, drink. 원형은 ġebicgan. onġina tō ālīesenne=will liberate. onġina=begin. 원형은 onġinnan. tō ālīesenne=to liberate. ālīesenne= ālīesan의 굴절 부정사.

7   aēowte=servitude. 원형은 aēowot.

8   ācēnde=gave birth to. 원형은 ācennan. hēt=called, named. 원형은 hātan.

9   swīae=greatly. wēox=grew. 원형은 weaxan. blētsode=blessed. 원형은 bletsian.

9-10 Godes gāst=God's spirit.

10 mihtiġ=mighty, strong. miċelre=more. miċel의 비교급. strengae=strength. swā aæt=so that.

11 ġelǣhte=caught. 원형은 ġelǣdan. lēon=lion. be weġe=on the way. ae=lēo(=the lion)를 선행사로 하는 관계대명사. hine=Samson. ābītan=devour. tōbræġd=tore to pieces. 원형은 tōbreġdan.

12 styċċum=pieces. swelċe=as if. tōtǣre=tear to pieces. 원형은 tōteran. ēaaeliċ=weak. tiċċen=kid.

13 aā=then. tō winnenne=to fight. 원형은 winnan. wia=against. hiera fela=many of them. ofslōg=slaughtered. 원형은 ofslēan.

14 tō scame=with ignominy. tūcode=harassed. 원형은 tūcian. aēah=although. anweald=rule, authority, power.

14-15 7ā fērdon aā Philistēi=Then went the Philistines. 처음 7ā는 부사(=then)이고 두 번째 aā(=those)는 지시대명사이다. fērdon=went. 원형은 fēran.

15 hēton=ordered. 원형은 hātan.

16 āġēafen=deliver. 원형은 āġiefan. aæt hīe wrecan mihten=so that might avenge. wrecan=avenge. mihten=might. 원형은 magan. tēonrǣdenne=humiliation.

17 tintregum=torment. 원형은 tintreġ. ġebundon=bound. 원형은 ġebindan.

17-18 bæstenum rāpum=two ropes of basts(=the inner bark of line, 인피(靭皮)).

18 ġelǣddon=led, brought.

19 fæġnodon=rejoiced. 원형은 fæġnian. swīae=greatly. urnon=ran. 원형은 irnan. tōġēanes= towards. hlȳdende=hlȳdan(=to shout)의 현재분사.

20 tōbræġd=pulled apart. bēġen his earmas=both of his arms.

21 tōburston=broke asunder. 원형은 tōberstan. ae hē mid ġebunden wæs=which he was

22 sōna=at once. assan ċinnbān=jawbone of an ass. ae hē ǣr funde=which he there found. fundan의 원형은 findan. ġefeaht=fought. 원형은 feohtan.

23 cwæa tō him selfum=said to himself.

24 witodlīċe=indeed. wera=men.

25 ofayrst=thirsty. for ǣm wundorlican sleġe=because of the wondrous slaughter. bæd=asked. 원형은 biddan.

26 āsende=āsendan(=to send)의 가정법. drincan=drink(n). for ǣm ae=because, for. nēawiste=nearest. nēah(=near)의 최상급. næs=ne+wæs. nān=none, no. nys nān=부정의 강조를 나타낸다.

27 wæterscipe=piece of water, water. arn=ran. 원형은 irnan. of ǣm ċinnbāne=from the jawbone. of ānum tēa=teeth. 원형은 tōa.

28 his Dryhtne=to God. aancode=thanked. 원형은 aancian.

A man was living among the people of Israel called Manoah from the clan of the Danites. His wife was sterile, and they lived without children. Then the angel of God came appearing to them and said that they should have a son between them ; 'He will be the holy God from his childhood ; and no one of you must cut his hair, nor drink wine or eat anything unclean ; because he will liberate his folk, the Israelites from the hands of the Philistines.'

She gave birth to a son, just as they heard from the angel, and named him Samson ; and he grew fast, and God blessed him, and the Spirit of the Lord was on him. He then became strong in his later mature years, so that he caught a lion on the way, which wanted to devour him, and tore him to pieces, as if he were to bite a weak kid.

He then began to fight again against the Philistines, and slaughtered many of them and with ignominy harassed them although they had power over his people. Then the Philistines went forth after Samson, and called his people that they should take him according to their rule, so that they might revenge on him with torture for the humiliation. They then bound him with two ropes made of basts and brought him from the people. And the Philistines were very rejoiced on account of that ; all Philistines ran to meet him shouting, wanted to torture him for their humiliation. Then Samson thrust both of his arms apart, so that the ropes which he was bound with were shattered. And he then brought at once a jawbone of an ass which he found around, and fought against them, and struck down a thousand men with the jawbone of an ass, and said to himself : 'I have killed indeed a thousand men with a donkey's jawbone.' He then became very thirsty for the terrible slaughter, and asked the heavenly God that he should give him something to drink, for there was not a water-place near him. Then water came out from one of the teeth of the jawbone ; and Samson drank it, and thanked God.

III. ÆLFRIC

COLLOQUY (1)

The Monk

1   *Discipuli* : Wē ċildru biddaþ þē, ēalā lārēow, þæt þū tǣċe ūs sprecan on Lēden ġereorde rihte, for þām unġelǣrede wē syndon, and ġewemmodlīċe wē sprecaþ.

    Magister : Hwæt wille ġē sprecan?

5   *D* : Hwæt rēċe wē hwæt wē sprecan, būton hit riht sprǣċ sȳ and behēfe, næs īdel oþþe fracoð?

    M : Wille ġē bēon beswungen on leornunge?

    D : Lēofre is ūs bēon beswungen for lāre þænne hit ne cunnan ; ac wē witon þē bilewitne wesan, and nellan onbelǣdan swingla ūs būton þū 10 bēo tō ġenȳdd fram ūs.

    M : Iċ āxie þē, hwæt spricst þū? Hwæt hæfst þū weorces?

    Discipulus : Iċ eom ġeanwyrde munuc, and iċ singe ǣlċe dæġ seofon tīda mid ġebrōþrum, and iċ eom bysgod on rǣdinga and on sange ; ac bēah hwæþere iċ wolde betwēnan leornian sprecan on Lēden ġereorde.

15   *M* : Hwæt cunnon þās, þīne ġefēran?

    D : Sume synt yrþlingas, sume scēaphyrdas, sume oxanhyrdas, sume ēac swylċe huntan, sume fisceras, sume fugeleras, sume ċēapmenn, sume sceōwyrhtan, sealteras, bæceras.

The Ploughman

    M : Hwæt sæġest þū, yrþling? Hū begǣst þū þīn weorc?

20   *Arator* : Ēalā, lēof hlāford, þearle iċ deorfe ; iċ gā ūt on dæġrǣd, þȳwende oxan tō felda, and ġeocie hiġ tō sȳl. Nis hit swā stearc winter þæt iċ durre lūtian æt hām, for eġe mīnes hlafordes ; ac ġeġeocodan oxan and ġefæstnodum sceare and cultre mid þǣre sȳl, ǣlċe dæġ iċ

sceal erian fulne æcer obþe māre.

25   *M* : Hæfst bū æniġne ġefēran?

A : Iċ hæbbe sumne cnapan b̄ywendne oxan mid gād-īsene, þe ēac swilċe nū hās is for ċylde and hrēame.

M : Hwæt māre dēst bū on dæġ?

A : Ġewislīċe bænne, māre iċ dō. Iċ sceal fyllan binnan oxena mid
30   hīeġ, and wæterian hiġ, and heora scearn beran ūt.

M : Hiġ, hiġ, miċel ġedeorf is hit.

A : Ġē, lēof, miċel ġedeorf hit is, forþām iċ neom frēoh.

(Ælfric은 라틴어 문법책을 쓰고 거기에 대한 일종의 부교재로 Colloquy를 역시 라틴어로 썼다. 사람들이 그것을 고대영어로 번역한 것이 여기 실린 글이다.

이 글은 라틴어를 배우려는 학생들과 교사와의 대화 형식을 취하고 있다. 눈여겨볼 것은 학생들의 직업이 다양하여 당시 Anglo-Saxon 시대의 생활상을 엿볼 수 있다는 점이고, 또 한가지는 교사가 학생들을 가르침에 있어 Socrates의 잘 알려진 산파법을 사용하고 있다는 점이다. Socrates는 학생들은 임산부가 뱃속에 아기를 품고 있듯이 이미 답을 가지고 있다는 전제하에, 교사가 할 일은 산파가 몸 속의 아기를 밖으로 꺼내듯이 이미 학생들이 가지고 있는 답을 끄집어내는 일 뿐이라고 생각한다. Colloquy의 교사는 직업엔 귀천이 없다는 사실을 스스로는 일언반구 하지 않으면서 명쾌히 가르치고 있다.)

1   Discipuli=Lt. discipulus(=pupil, scholar, disciple)의 복수형. ċildru=children. 단수형은 ċild. biddaþ=ask. 원형은 biddan. ēalā=oh. lārēow=teacher, master, preacher. cf. lār=wisdom, learning, teaching. t̄æċe=t̄æċan(=to teach)의 가정법 현재. sprecan=to speak.

2   Lēden=Latin. ġereorde=language. rihte=rightly, correctly. for þām=because. unġel̄æ rede=ignorant. syndon=are. ġewemmodlīċe=corruptly(=ungrammatically).

4   wille ġe=want you=do you want.

5   Hwæt rēċe wē···?=what care we···?=what do we care···?=we don't care. 수사의문문이다. rēċe=care. 원형은 rēċan. būton=if. s̄y(=sīe)=bēon(=to be)의 가정법.

6   behēfē=suitable, befitting, useful. 앞에 있는 spr̄æċ를 수식한다. næs=not. īdel=worthless, vain, empty. fracoð=base, impious. cf. ModE, fraked.

7   beswungen=beswingan(=to flog, beat)의 과거분사. on leornunge=during learning.

8   Lēofre=lēof(=dear, beloved)의 비교급. Lēofre is ūs bēon···=It is dearer to us to be···=We would rather be··· lāre=learning. hit=lāre. lāre는 여성명사이므로 본래는 hēo(=whe)로 받아야 하나 여기서 보듯 고대영어에서는 종종 문법성(grammatical gender) 대신 자연성(natural gender)를 쓰는 경우가 있었다. cunnan=know.

9 witon=know. 원형은 witan. bilewitne=kind, gentle, merciful. nellan=ne+willan=be unwilling. onbelǣdan=inflict upon. swingla=whip, blow. 원형은 swingell.

10 ġenȳdd=compelled. 원형은 ġenȳdan. fram ūs=by us.

11 āxie=ask. 원형은 āscian. Hwæt hæfst þū weorces?=Hwæt weorces hæfst þū? weorces= works.

12 ġeanwyrde=known, professed(선서하고 수도회에 들어간). ǣlċe=each,

12-13 seofon tīda=seven times.

13 mid=with. ġebrōþrum=brethren(=fellow monks). 원형은 ġebrōðor. bysgod=occupied, busy. rǣdinga=reading. sange=song.

14 bēah hwæbere=however, nevertheless. wolde=would like. betwēonan=in the meantime.

15 þās=뒤에 오는 þīne ġefēran과 동격. '이 사람들' 정도의 뜻. ġefēran=companion, comrade.

16 synt=are. yrblingas=farmer, ploughman. sċēaphyrdas=shepherds. oxanhyrdas=oxherds.

17 ēac swylċe=also likewise. huntan=hunters. 원형은 hunta. fisceras=fishermen.   원형은 fiscere. fugeleras=fowlers. 원형은 fugelere. ċēapmenn=merchants, traders.

18 sċeōwyrht=shoemakers, leatherworkers. 단수는 sċeōwyrhts. sealteras=salters. 당시 고기를 소금에 절이는 일은 식품 생산의 중요한 과정 중의 하나였다. bæceras=bakers. 원형은 bæcere.

19 begǣst=perform, practice. 원형은 begān.

20 Arator=Lt. ploughman. lēof hlāford=dear lord. 여기서는 선생님(lārēow)이 주인(hlāford) 역을 담당하고 있다. 그렇다면 여기 등장하는 각종 직업인들도 실은 학생들이 대역을 하고 있는 것이라고 볼 수 있다. bearle=very. deorfe=labour. 원형은 deorfan. dæġrǣd=dawn. cf. ModE, dayred.

21 bȳwende=bȳwan(=to urge, drive)의 현재분사. felda=field. ġeocie=yoke. 원형은 ġeocian. sȳl=sūl(=plough)의 단수 여격. cf. ModE, sullow. Nis=ne+is. stearc=sever. cf. ModE, stark.

21-22 Nis hit swā stearc winter bæt=It isn't so stark a winter that…=There is no winter so severe that…

22 durre=dare. 원형은 durran. lūtian=lie hidden. hām=home. for eġe mīnes hladordes=for fear of my lord. eġe=fear, terror. ġeġeocodan=yoked. 원형은 ġeġeocian(=to yoke).

23 ġefæstnodum=fastened. 원형은 ġefæstnian. sceare=ploughshare(쟁깃 날). cultre=colter(보 습 끝의 날카로운 날). 원형은 culter. sȳl=sulh(=plough)의 단수 여격.

24 sceal=shall. 원형은 sculan. erian=plough. fulne=full. 원형은 full.

26 sumne=a certain. cnapan=boy, youth, child. bȳwendne=drive. 원형은 bȳwendan. gād-īsen= goad-iron, cattle-prod. be=who. 관계대명사. ēac=also.

27 hās=hoarse. ċylde=cold. hrēame=shouting. cf. ModE, ream.

28 dēst=dost=dōn(=to do)의 2인칭 단수. on=during.

29 Ġewislīċe=certainly. bænne(bonne)=than. bænne māre=still more. fyllan=fill. binnan oxan=oxen's bins. binnan=bin. 원형은 binn. hī(e)ġ=hay.

30 wæterian=water. heora=their. scearn=dung, muck. beran=bear, carry.

31 Hiġ=oh. ġedeorf=toil, labour.

neom=ne eom=am not. frēoh=free. 당시의 농부는 농노(serf) 신분인 경우가 많았다.

The Monk

Pupils : Oh master, we children beg that you will teach us to speak Latin correctly, because we are unlearned and speak badly.

Master : What do you want to talk about?

Pupils : We don't care what we talk about, as long as it is accurate and useful conversation, and not frivolous or filthy.

Master : Are you prepared to be beaten while learning?

Pupils : We would rather be beaten for the sake of learning than be ignorant. But we know that you are kind and unwilling to inflict blows on us unless we compel you to.

Master : I ask you (indicating a particular pupil), what do you say to me? What is your work?

Monk : I am a professed monk, and every day I sing seven times with the brethren, and I am busy with reading and singing, but nevertheless, between-times I want to learn to speak the Latin language.

Master : What do your friends do?

Monk : Some are ploughmen, some shepherds, some oxherds ; some again, huntsmen, some fishermen, some fowlers, some merchants, some shoe-makers, salters, bakers.

The Ploughman

Master : What do you say, ploughman? How do you carry out your work?

Ploughman : Oh, I work very hard, dear lord. I go out at daybreak driving the oxen to the field, and yoke them to the plough ; for fear of my lord, there is no winter so severe that I dare hide at home ; but the oxen, having been yoked and the share and coulter fastened to the plough, I must plough a full acre or more every day.

Master : Have you any companion?

Ploughman : I have a lad driving the oxen with a goad, who is now also hoarse because of the cold and shouting.

Master : What else do you do in the day?

Ploughman : I do more than that, certainly. I have to fill the oxen's bins with hay, and water them, and carry their muck outside.

Master : Oh, Oh! It's hard work.

Ploughman : It's hard work, sir, because I am not free.

COLLOQUY (2)

The Shepherd

1 *M* : Hwæt seġst bū, scēaphyrde? Hæfst bū ǣniġ ġedeorf?

Opillio : Ġēa, lēof, iċ hæbbe. On forewerdne morgen iċ drīfe mīne scēap tō heora lǣse, and stande ofer hiġ on hǣte and on ċyle mid hundum, þē lǣs wulfas forswelġen hiġ ; and iċ āġenlǣde hiġ tō heora 5 locan, and melce hiġ tweowa on dæġ, and heora locan iċ hebbe on bǣrtō, and ċȳse and buteran iċ dō, and iċ eom ġetrȳwe mīnum hlāforde.

The Oxherd

M : Ēalā, oxanhyrde, hwæt wyrcst bū?

Bubulcus : Ēalā, mīn hlāford, miċel iċ ġedeorfe. 7ænne sē yrbling unscenþ þā oxan, iċ lǣde hiġ tō lǣse, and ealle niht iċ stande ofer hiġ, 10 waciende for bēofan, and eft on ǣrne mergen iċ betǣċe hiġ þām yrblinge wel ġefylde and ġewæterode.

The Hunter

M : Is þēs of þīnum ġefērum?

Disipulus : Ġēa, hē is.

M : Canst bū ǣniġ þing?

15 *Venator* : Ǣnne cræft iċ cann.

M : Hwylcne is?

V : Hunta iċ eom.

M : Hwæs?

V : Cinges.

20 *M* : Hū begǣst bū þīnne cræft?

V : Iċ breġde mē max, and sette hiġ on stōwe ġehæppre, and ġetyhte mīne hundas þæt wilddēor hiġ ēhton, oþ þæt hiġ þē cumen tō þām nettum unforscēawodlīċe, and þæt hiġ swā bēon begrȳnode ; and iċ ofslēa hiġ on bām maxum.

25   *M* : Ne canst þū huntian būton mid nettum?

    V : Ġēa, būton nettum huntian iċ mæġ.

    M : Hū?

    V : Mid swiftum hundum iċ betǣċe wilddēor.

    M : Hwilċe wilddēor swīþost ġefēhst þū?

30   *V* : Iċ ġefēo heortas, and bāras, and rānn, and rǣgan, and hwīlum

haran.

    M : Wǣre þū tō dæġ on huntnoðe?

    V : Iċ næs, forþām sunnandæġ is, ac ġystrandæġ iċ wæs on

huntunge.

35   *M* : Hwæt ġelǣhtest þū?

    V : Twēġen heortas and ǣnne bār.

    M : Hū ġefēng þū hiġ?

    V : Heortas iċ ġefēng on nettum, and bār iċ ofslōh.

    M : Hū wǣre þū dyrstiġ ofstician bār?

40   *V* : Hundas bedrifon hine tō mē, and iċ þǣr tōġēanes standende

fǣrlīċe ofsticode hine.

    M : Swīþe brīste þū wǣre þā.

    V : Ne sceal hunta forhtfull wesan, forþām mislīċe wilddēor

wuniað on wudum.

45   *M* : Hwæt dēst þū be þīnre huntunge?

    V : Iċ sylle cynge swā hwæt swā iċ ġefō, forþām iċ eom hunta his.

    M : Hwæt sylþ hē þē?

    V : Hē scrȳt mē wel, and fētt, and hwīlon sylþ mē hors obbe bēah

þæt þē lustlīcor mīnne cræft iċ begange.

---

1   ġedeorf=toil, labor

2   forewerdne=early. drīfe=drive.

3   lǣse=pasture. hǣte=heat. ċyle(ċiele)=cold, chill.

4   hundum=dogs. þē lǣs=the less=lest…should. wulfas=wolves. forswelġen=devour. 원형은
    forswelgan. āġenlǣde=lead back. 원형은 āġenlǣdan.

5   locan=enclosure, sheepfold. melce=milk. 원형은 melcan. tweowa on dæẏ=twice a day. hebbe=raise, lift, move. 원형은 hebban.

5-6   on bǣrtō=in addition. bǣrtō=thereto.

6   ċȳse=cheese. buteran=butter. ġetrȳwe=faithful, loyal.

8   Bubulcus=Lt. oxherd. ġedeorfe=ġedeorfan(=do laboriously)의 1인칭 단수 현재. 7ænne=bonne=then.

9   unscenb=unharness. 원형은 unscennan.

10   waciende=wæċċan(=to watch)의 현재분사. bēofan=thief. eft=again. ǣrne=early. betǣċe=entrust. 원형은 betǣċan.

11   ġefyled=fed. 원형은 ġefyllan. ġewæterode=watered. 원형은 ġewæterian.

13   Ġēa=yes.

15   Venator=Lt. hunter. cræft=skill.

19   Cinges=king's.

20   begǣst=perform, practice. 원형은 begān.

21   breġde=weave. 원형은 breġdan. max=net. Iċ breġde mē max=I weave net for myself. cf. ModE. I bought me a hat. stōwe=place. ġehæppre=ġehæp(=convenient, suitable)의 비교급. ġetyhte=train. 원형은 ġetyhtan.

22   wilddēor=wild animal. ēhton=attack, pursue, chase. ob bær…bē=until.

23   nettum=net. unforscēawodlīċe=unexpectedly, unawares, suddenly. begrȳnode=begrīnian (=to ensnare)의 과거분사.

24   ofslēa=kill. 원형은 ofslēan.

28   betǣċe=pursue, hunt. 원형은 betǣċan.

29   swībost=mostly. ġefēhst=catch. 원형은 ġefōn.

30   heortas=harts, stags. bāras=boars. rānn=roebuck. rā(=roebuck)의 복수 속격. rǣgan=roe deers. hwīlum=sometimes. haran=hares.

32   tō dǣġ=today.

33   forbām=because. sunnandæġ=Sunday. ġystrandæġ=yesterday. cf. G. gestern.

35   ġēlǣhtest=capture. 원형은 ġelæċċan.

39   dyrstiġ=daring, venturesome. ofstician=pierce, stab.

40   bedrifon=drive, chase. 원형은 bedrīfan. tōġeanes=toward.

41   fǣrliċe=suddenly.

42   Swībe=very, strongly. brīste=daring, bold.

43   Ne sceal=shouldn't be. sceal의 원형은 sculan. forhtfull=fearful, timid. wesan=be. 원형은 bēon. mistlīċe=various, diverse. manifold, miscellaneous.

44   wuniað=dwell. wudum=wood.

45   huntunge=game.

46   swā hwæt swā=whatever.

48   scrȳt=clothes. 원형은 scrȳdan. fētt=feed. 원형은 fēdan. hwīlon=sometimes. bēah=bēag=ring, bracelet.

þæt bē=so that. lustlīcor=lustlīċe(=gladly, willingly)의 비교급. begange=perform. 원형은 begangan.

The Shepherd

Master : What do you say shepherd? Do you have any work?

Shepherd : I have indeed, sir. In the early morning I drive my sheep to their pasture, and in the heat and in cold, stand over them with dogs, lest wolves devour them ; and I lead them back to their folds and milk them twice a day, and move their folds ; and in addition I make cheese and butter ; and I am loyal to my lord.

The Oxherd

Master : Oh, oxherd, what do you work at?

Oxherd : Oh, I work hard, my lord. When the ploughman unyokes the oxen, I lead them to pasture, and I stand over them all night watching for thieves ; and then in the early morning I had them over to the ploughman well fed and watered.

The Hunter

Master : Is this one of your companions?

Oxherd : Indeed, he is.

Master : Do you know how to do anything?

Huntsman : I know one trade.

Master : Which?

Huntsman : I am a huntsman.

Master : Whose?

Huntsman : The king's.

Master : How do you carry out your trade?

Huntsman : I weave myself nets and set them in suitable place, and urge on my dogs so that they chase the wild animals until they come into the nets unawares and are thus ensnared ; and I kill them in the nets.

Master : Don't you know how to hunt without nets?

Huntsman : I can hunt without nets, certainly.

Master : How?

Huntsman : I hunt for wild animals with fast dogs.

Master : Which animals do you mostly catch?

Huntsman : I catch stags and wild boars and roe-buck and does, and sometimes hares.

Master : Were you out hunting today?

Huntsman : I wasn't, because it's Sunday ; but I was out hunting yesterday.

Master : What did you catch?

Huntsman : Two stags and a boar.

Master : How did you take them?

Huntsman : I took the stags in nets, and the boar I killed.

Master : How did you dare stick a boar?

Huntsman : The dogs drove it towards me, and I stuck it quickly, standing there in its path.

Master : You were very brave then.

Huntsman : A huntsman mustn't be afraid, because all sorts of wild animals live in the woods.

Master : What do you do with your game?

Huntsman : Whatever I take I give to the king, since I am his huntsman.

Master : What does he give you?

Huntsman : He clothes and feeds me well, and sometimes gives me a horse or ring so that I follow my trade the more willingly.

COLLOQUY (3)

The Fisherman

1   *M* : Hwylcne cræft canst þū?

Piscator : Iċ eom fiscere.

M : Hwæt beġytst þū of þīnum cræfte?

P : Biġleofan and scrūd and feoh.

5   *M* : Hū ġefēhst þū fixas?

P : Iċ āstīġe mīn scip, and weorpe mīne max on eā, and angil oððe ǣs iċ weorpe, and spyrtan, and swā hwæt swā hiġ ġehæftað iċ ġenime.

M : Hwæt ġif hit unclǣne fixas bēoþ?

10   *P* : Iċ ūtweorpe þā unclǣnan ūt, and ġenime mē clǣne tō mete.

M : Hwǣr ċȳpst þū þīne fixas?

P : On ċeastre.

M : Hwā byġþ hī?

P : Ċeasterware. Iċ ne mæġ swā fela ġefōn, swā fela swā iċ mæġ

15   ġesyllan.

M : Hwilċe fixas ġefēhst þū?

P : Ǣlas, and hacodas, ǣlepūtan, sceotan and lampredan, and swā hwylċe swā on wætere swymmaþ.

M : For hwī ne fixast þū on sǣ?

20   *P* : Hwīlum iċ dō, ac seldan, forþām miċel rēwet mē is tō sǣ.

M : Hwæt fēhst þū on sǣ?

P : Hǣringas and leaxas, mereswȳn and ostran and crabban, muslan, winewinclan, sǣcoccas, facge and flōc and loppestran, and fela swylċes.

25   *M* : Wilt þū fōn sumne hwæl?

P : Niċ,

M : For hwī?

P : Forhwan plyhtlīċ bing hit is ġefōn hwæl. Ġebeortlīcre is mē faran tō ēa mid mīnum scipe, bænne faran mid manegum scipum on

30 hutunge hranes.

M : For hwī swā?

P : Forbām lēofre is mē ġefōn fisc bæne iċ mæġ ofslēan, be nā bæt ān mē, ac ēac swylċe mīne ġefēran mid ānum sleġe hē mæġ besenċan obbe ġecwylman.

35 *M* : And beah mæniġe ġefōb hwælas, and ætberstab frēcnysse, and miċelne sceat banon beġytab.

P : Sōb bū seġst, ac iċ ne ġebrīstige, for mīnes mōdes nytenysse.

2	Piscator=Lt. fisherman. fiscere=fisherman.
3	beġystst=get, acquire. 원형은 beġietan. of=from
4	Biġleofan=food. scrūd=clothing. feoh=money.
5	ġefēhst=catch. 원형은 ġefōn. fixas=fix(=fish)의 복수.
6	āstīġe=ascend. 원형은 āstīgan. weorpe=throw, cast. ēa=water, river. angil(=angel)=fishhook.
7	oððe=or. ǣs=bait. spyrtan=basket. swā hwǣt swā=whatever. ġehæftas=catch. 원형은 ġehæftan. ġenime=take. 원형은 ġeniman.
9	unclǣne fiscas=unclean fish. cf. Deuteronomy(신명기) 14 : 10. 'And whatever (fish) does not have fins and scales you shall not eat ; it is unclean for you.'
10	ūtweorpe=throw out. mete=food. mē⋯tō mete=for my food.
11	c̄ypst=c̄ypan(=to sell, buy)의 2인칭 단수.
12	ċeastre=city. cf. Lt. castra=camp. cf. Lancaster, Manchester.
13	byġb=buys. 원형은 bycgan.
14	Ċeasterware=citizens. swā⋯swā=as⋯so.
15	ġesyllan(=ġesellan)=sell.
17	Ǣlas=eels. hacodas=pike(창꼬치). ǣlepūtan=burbot(모오캐. 대구과의 민물 고기). sceotan=trout(송어). lampredan=lamprey(칠성장어).
17-18	swā hwylċe swā=whatever.
18	swymmab=swim.
19	fixast=(fiscian, fixian)의 2인칭 단수.
20	Hwīlum=sometimes. seldan(=seldon)=seldom. rēwet=rowing.
22	Hǣringas=herring(청어). leaxas=salmon(연어). mereswȳn=porpoise(돌고래). ostran=oyster. crabban=crab.
23	muslan=shellfish(조개). winewinclan=periwinkle(총알고둥). sǣcoccas=cockle(새조개). facge=

plaice(가자미). floōc=flounder(가자미류). loppestran=lobster.

24 swylċes=likewise.

25 hwæl=whale.

26 Niċ=ne+iċ=not me.

28 Forhwan=because. plyhtlīċ=dangerous. Ġebeortlīcre=ġebeorhtlīċ(=safe)의 비교급.

29 manegum=maniġ(=many)의 복수 여격.

30 hranes=whale.

32 lēofre=lēof(=dear)의 비교급. lēofre is mē=(it) is more agreeable to me=I prefer.
bæne(=bone)=sē(=that)의 단수 대격으로서 여기서는 목적격의 관계대명사로 쓰였다.

32-33 nā bæt ān=no only.

33 ac ēac=but also. swilċe=likewise. sleġe=blow, stroke. besenċan=sink, drown.

35 beah=however. ætberstab=escape. frēcnysse=danager.

36 miċelne=much. sceat=money. banon=thence. beġytab=acquire. 원형은 beġietan.

37 Sōþ=true. seġst=say. 원형은 secgan. ġebrīstige=dare. 원형은 ġebrīstian. mōdes=mind,
heart, courage. nytenysse=ignorance, sloth.

The Fisherman

Master, indicating another : What trade do you follow?

Fisherman : I am a fisherman.

Master : What do you gain from your trade?

Fisherman : Food and clothing and money.

Master : How do you catch the fish?

Fisherman : I board my boat and cast my net into the river ; and throw in a hook and bait and baskets ; and whatever they catch I take.

Master : What if the fishes are unclean?

Fisherman : I throw the unclean ones away, and take the clean ones for food.

Master : Where do you sell your fish?

Fisherman : In the city.

Master : Who buys them?

Fisherman : The citizens. I can't catch as many as I can sell.

Master : Which fish do you catch?

Fisherman : Eels and pike, minnows and burbot, trout and lampreys and whatever swims in the water.

Master : Why don't you fish in the sea?

Fisherman : Sometimes I do, but rarely, because it is a lot of rowing for me to the sea.

Master : What do you catch in the sea?

Fisherman : Herrings and salmon, porpoises and sturgeon, oysters and crabs, mussels, winkles, cockles, plaice and flounders and lobsters, and many similar things.

Master : Would you like to catch a whale?

Fisherman : Not me!

Master : Why?

Fisherman : Because it is a risky business catching a whale. It's safer for me to go on the river with my boat, than to go hunting whales with many boats.

Master : Why so?

Fisherman : Because I prefer to catch a fish that I can kill, rather than a fish that can sink or kill not only me but also my companions with a single blow.

Master : Nevertheless, many catch whales and escape danger, and make a great profit by it.

Fisherman : You are right, but I dare not because of my timid spirit!

COLLOQUY (4)

The Fowler

1 *M* : Hwæt sæġst bū, fugelere? Hū beswīcst bū fugelas?

Auceps : On feala wīsan iċ beswīce fugelas. Hwīlum mid nettum, mid grīnum, mid līme, mid hwistlunge, mid hafoc, mid treppan.

M : Hæfst bū hafoc?

5 *A* : Iċ hæbbe.

M : Canst bū temian hiġ?

A : Ġēa, iċ cann. Hwæt sceoldon hiġ mē, būton iċ cūbe temian hiġ?

Venator : Syle mē ǣnne hafoc.

A : Iċ sylle lustlīċe ġyf bū sylst mē ǣnne swyftne hund. Hwylcne

10 hafoc wilt bū habban, bone māran hwæber be bæne lǣssan?

V : Syle mē bæne māran.

M : Hū āfēdst bū bīne hafocas?

A : Hiġ fēdab hiġ sylfe and mē on wintra, and on lengten iċ lǣte hiġ ætwindan tō wuda ; and iċ ġenime mē briddas on hærfæste, and

15 temiġe hiġ.

M : And for hwī forlǣtst bū bā ġetemedon ætwindan fram bē?

A : Forbām iċ nelle fēdan hiġ on sumera, forbām be hiġ bearle etab.

M : And maniġ fēdab bā ġetemedan ofer sumor bæt eft hiġ

20 habban ġearuwe.

A : Ġēa, swā hiġ dōb, ac iċ nelle deorfan ofer hiġ, forbām iċ cann ōbre nā bæt ǣnne, ac ēac swilċe maniġe ġefōn.

The Merchant

M : Hwæt sæġst bū, mangere?

Mercator : Iċ secge bæt behēfe iċ eom, ġe cinge and ealdormannum

25 and weligum and eallum folce.

M : And hū?

Mer : Iċ āstiġe mīn scip mid mīnum hlæstum, and rōwe ofer sǣlīċe dǣlas, and ċȳpe mīne þing, and bycge þing dȳrwyrðe þā on þisum lande ne bēoþ ācennede, and iċ hit tō ġelǣde ēow hider mid micclan
30 plihte ofer sǣ, and hwīlum forlidenesse iċ þolie mid lyre ealra mīnra þinga, unēaþe cwic ætberstende.

M : Hwylċe þing ġelǣdst þū ūs?

Mer : Pællas and sīdan, dēorwyrþe ġymmas and gold, selcūþe rēaf and wyrtġemang, wīn and ele, ylpesbān and mæstling, ǣr and tin,
35 swefel and glæs, and bylċes fela.

M : Wilt þū syllan þīne þing hēr eal swā þū hī ġebohtest þǣr?

Mer : Iċ nelle. Hwæt þænne mē fremode mīn ġedeorf? Ac iċ wille hīe ċȳpan hēr luflīcor þonne iċ ġebycge þǣr, þæt sum ġestrēon mē iċ beġyte. 7anon ic mē āfēde and mīn wīf and mīnne sunu.

---

1 beswīcst=deceive, trap. 원형은 beswīcan. fugelas=fugol(=bird)의 복수 대격. cf. G. Vogel (=bird).

2 Auceps=Lt. bird-catcher, fowler. feala=many, much. wīsan=manner, way. nettum=net.

3 grīnum=snare. līme=bird-lime(새 잡는 끈끈이). hwistlunge=whistling. hafoc=hawk. treppan=trap.

6 temian=tame, train.

7 sceoldon=be good, be of use. 원형은 sculan. būton=except. cūþe=know. 원형은 cunnan.

8 Syle=sellan(=to give)의 단수 명령.

9 sylle=send. 뒤에 fafoc가 생략되었다. lustlīċe=gladly, willingly. sylst=give. swyftne= swift.

10 māran=māra(=more, larger)의 단수 대격. lǣssan=lǣs(=less, smaller)의 단수 대격.

12 āfēdst=feed. 원형은 āfēdan.

13 hiġ sylfe=themselves. lengten=springtime. lǣte=let. 원형은 lǣtan.

14 ætwindan=escape. ġenime=take. 원형은 ġeniman. mē=for myself. briddas=birds. bridd>bird는 대표적인 환치(metathesis)의 예이다. hærfæste=autumn.

16 for hwī=why. forlǣtst=release. 원형은 forlǣtan. þā ġetemedon=those tamed.

17 nelle=ne wille=do not wish. sumera=summer. 원형은 sumor. þearle=vigorously, exceedingly.

18 etaþ=eat.

20 ġearuwe=ready. 원형은 ġearu.

21 deorfan=labor, work.

22 nā···ac ēac=not···but also. ēac=also.

23 mangere=merchant.

24 Mercator=Lt. merchant. behēbe=necessary. ġe...and=ġe···ġe=both···and.
ealdormannum=ealdormann(=nobleman)의 복수 여격.

25 weligum=wealthy, prosperous.

27 hlæstum=load, freight. sǣlīċe=of the sea.

28 dǣlas=region, part. ċype=sell. bycge=buy. 원형은 bycgan. dȳrwyrðe=precious.

29 ācennede=produced. 원형은 ācennan. hit=what I have bought. ġelǣde=lead, bring.
hider=hither.

30 plihte=peril, danger. hwīlum=sometimes. forlidenesse=shipwreck. bolie=suffer. lyre=loss.
mīnra=my. 원형은 mīn.

31 unēabe=with difficulty. ætberstende=escape.

33 Pællas=silk robe. sīdan=silk. dēorwyrbe=valuable, precious. ġymmas=gem, jewel.
selcūbe=strange, novel. rēaf=dress.

34 wyrtġemang=spices, perfume. ele=oil. ylpesbān=ivory. mæstling=bronze. ǣr=copper.

35 swefel=sulphur. glæs=glass. bylċes=such, of that sort.

36 eal swā=just as. ġebohtest=bought. 원형은 ġebycgan.

37 bænne(=bonne)=then. fremode=fremian(=to profit, benefit)의 과거. ġedeorf=toil, labor.

38 luflīcor=luflīċ(=dearly)의 비교급. bæt=so that. ġestrēon=gain.

39 beġyte=acquire. 원형은 beġietan. 7anon=thence.

The Fowler

Master : What do you say, fowler? How do you trap birds?

Fowler : I trap birds in many ways : sometimes with nets, sometimes
with snares, sometimes with lime, by whistling, with a hawk or with a trap.

Master : Have you got a hawk?

Fowler : I have.

Master : Do you know how to tame them?

Fowler : Yes, I know how. What good would they be to me unless I
knew how to tame them?

Huntsman : Give me a hawk.

Fowler : I will give you one willingly, if you will give me a fast dog.
Which hawk will you have, the bigger one or the smaller?

Huntsman : Give me the bigger one.

Master : How do you feed your hawks?

Fowler : They feed themselves, and me, in winter ; and in the spring I let them fly away to the woods ; and in the autumn I take young birds and tame them.

Master : Any why do you let those you have tamed fly away from you?

Fowler : Because I don't want to feed them in the summer, since they eat too much.

Master : Yet many feed the tamed ones throughout the summer, in order to have them already again.

Fowler : Yes, so they do. But I don't want to go to so much trouble over them, because I know how to catch others—not just one, but many more.

The Merchant

Master : What do you say, merchant?

Merchant : I say that I am useful both to king and ealdormen, and to the wealthy and to all people.

Master : And how?

Merchant : I board my ship with my cargo and sail to lands overseas, and sell my goods, and buy precious things which aren't produced in this country. And in great danger on the sea I bring them back to you here ; and sometimes I suffer shipwreck with the loss of all my goods, scarcely escaping alive.

Master : What things do you bring us?

Merchant : Purple cloth and silks, precious jewels and gold, unusual clothes and spices, wine and oil, ivory and bronze, copper and tin, sulphur and glass and many similar things.

Master : Do you want to sell your goods here for just what you paid for them there?

Merchant : I don't want to. What would my labour benefit me then? I want to sell dearer here than I buy there so that I gain some profit, with which I may feed myself and my wife and my sons.

COLLOQUY (5)

The Shoemaker

1   *M* : 7ū sceōwyrhta, hwæt wyrcst bū ūs nytwyrbnesse?

   Sutor : Witodlīċe mīn cræft is behēfe bearle ēow, and nēodbearf.

   M : Hū?

   S : Iċ bycge h̄yda and fell, and ġearcie hiġ mid mīnum cræfte and

5   wyrċe of him ġescȳ mistlīċes cynnes, swyftlēras and sceōs, leberhosa
and butericas, brīdelbwangas and ġer̄ædu, flaxan oððe pinnan and
h̄ydiġe fatu, spurleberu and hælftra, pusan and f̄ætelsas, and nān ēower
nele oferwintran būton mīnum cræfte.

The Salter

   M : Sealtere, hwæt ūs fremab bīn cræft?

10   *Salinator* : 7earle fremab mīn cræft ēow eallum. Nān ēower blisse
brȳcð on ġererdinge oððe mete, būton mīn cræft ġistlībe him bēo.

   M : Hū?

   S : Hwylċ manna werodum burhbrȳcb metum būton swæċċe
sealtes? Hwā ġefylb his cleofan oððe hēddernu, būton mīnum cræfte.

15   Efne ̄ælċ buterġebwēor and c̄ȳsġerunn losab ēow, būton iċ hyrde
ætwese ēow, be ne furbum wyrtum ēowrum būton mē brūcab.

The Baker

   M : Hwæt seġst bū, bæcere? Hwām fremab bīn cræft, oððe
hwæðer wē būton bē magon līf ādrēogan?

   Pistor : Ġē magon burh sum fæc būton mīnum craæfte līf ādrēogan,

20   ac nā lange nē tō wel. Sōblīċe, būton mīnum cræfte ælċ bēod ̄æmtiġ bib
ġesewen ; and, būton hlāfe, ̄ælċ mete tō wl̄ættan byb ġehwyrfed. Iċ
ġestrangie mannes heortan ; iċ eom mæġen wera, and furbum lītlingas
nellab forbīġean mē.

The Cook

M : Hwæt secgab wē be cōce, hwæber wē beburfon hine on
25　ǣnigum cræfte?

Cocus : Ġif ġē mē ūt ādrīfab fram ēowrum ġefērscype, ġē etab
grēne ēowre wyrta and ēowre fǣscmettas hrēawe, and furbum fǣtt
brob ġē magon būton mīnum cræfte ne habban.

M : Wē ne reċċab be bīnum cræfte, nē hē ūs nēodbearf is, forbām
30　wē sylfe magon sēoban bā bing be tō sēobenne synd, and brǣdan bā
bing be tō brǣdene synd.

C : Ġif ġē forbȳ mē fram ādrīfab, bæt ġē bus dōn, bonne bēo ġē
ealle brǣlas, and nān ēower ne bib hlāford ; and bēah hwæbere būton
mīnum cræfte ġē ne etab.

1　nytwyrbnesse=utility, use.

2　Witodlīċe=truly. behēfe=necessary. bearle=exceedingly. nēodbearf=necessity, need.

4　hȳda=hide, skin. fell=hide, skin. ġearcie=prepare. 원형은 ġearcian.

5　wyrċe=make. 원형은 wyrċan. ġescȳ=shoes. mistlīċe=various. cynnes=kin. swyftlēras=
slippers. sceōs=scōh(=shoe)의 복수. leberhosa=leather gaiters.

6　butericas=leather bottles. brīdelbwangas=reins. ġerǣdu=trappings (마구들). flaxan=flasks,
bottles. pinnan=leather flasks. 단수는 pinne.

7　hȳdiġe=made of leather. fatu=fæt(=vat, vessel, cup)의 복수. spurleberu=spur-strap(박차
끈). hælftra=hælfter(=halter)의 복수 대격. pusan=bags. fǣtelsas=fǣtels(=pouch, sack)의
복수 대격. nān ēower=none of you.

8　nele=ne wille. oferwintran=live through the winter.

9　fremab=fremian(=profit, avail, benefit)의 2인칭 단수.

10　Salinator=Lt. salter. blisse=bliss.

11　brȳcð=enjoys. 원형은 brūcan(=enjoy (the use of), use). ġererdinge=meal. mete=food.
ġistlībe=hospitable.

13　werodum=sweet. burhbrȳcb=enjoys fully. 원형은 burhbrūcan. swæċċe=flavor, taste.

14　cleofan=cellar. hēddernu=storehouse.

15　Efne=lo. buterġebwēor=butter-curd. ċysġerunn=rennet. hyrde=guard, keeper.

16　ætwese=be present. furbum=even. wyrtum=herb, root. brūcab=use, enjoy.

18　ādrēogan=carry on, endure.

19　Pistor=Lt. baker. fæc=period of time.

20　nā⋯nē=neither⋯nor. bēod=table. ǣmtiġ=empty.

21 ġesewen=ġesēon(=seem)의 과거분사. hlāfe=loaf, bread. wlǣttan=disgust, loathing. byb=is. ġehwyrfed=ġehwierfan(=to turn, convert, transform)의 과거분사.

22 ġestrangie=strengthen. mæġen=strength, power, might. wera=man. furþum=even. lītlingas=infant, child.

23 nellab=ne willab. forbīġean=turn away.

24 be=concerning. cōcem=cook. beburfon=beburfan(to need)의 현재 복수.

26 Cocus=Lt. cook. ādrīfaþ=drive away. ġefērscype=companionship. etaþ=eat.

27 grēne=green, uncooked. wyrta=herb, vegetable. flǣscmettas=flesh, meat. hrēawe=raw. furþum=even. fǣtt=fat.

28 broþ=broth, soup.

29 reċċaþ=care for. 원형은 reċċan. hē=bīnum cræfte. nēodþearf=necessity, need.

30 wē sylfe=we ourselves. sēoðan=boil. tō sēoþenne synd=to be boiled. synd=sind=are.

31 tō brǣdan synd=to be roasted. tō brǣdene=to roast.

32 forþȳ=therefore. þonne=then.

33 brǣlas=slave, serf. hweæþere=however, yet.

The Shoemaker

Master : You shoemaker, what do you work at for our use?

Shoemaker : My trade is certainly very useful and necessary to you.

Master : How so?

Shoemaker : I buy hides and skins, and by my craft prepare them and make them into various kinds of footwear, slippers and shoes, leggings and leather bottles, reins and trappings, flasks and leather vessels, spur-straps and halters, bags and purses. And not one of you would want to pass the winter without my craft.

The Salter

Master : Salter, what good is your craft to us?

Salter : My craft is very useful to all of you. Not one of you enjoys satisfaction in a meal or food, unless he entertain my craft.

Master : How so?

Salter : What man enjoys pleasant foods to the full without the flavor of salt? Who fills his pantry or storeroom without my craft? Indeed you will lose all butter and cheese-curd unless I am present with you as a preservative ; you couldn't even use your herbs without me.

The Baker

Master : What do you say, baker? What is the use of your trade ; or can we survive without you?

Baker : You might live without my trade for a while, but neither for long nor very well. Truly, without my craft every table would seem empty ; and without bread all food would turn distasteful. I make people's hearts strong ; I am the stamina of men, and even the little ones are unwilling to pass me by.

The Cook

Master : What shall we say of the cook? Do we need his craft in any way?

The Cook says : If you expel me from your society, you'll eat your vegetables raw and your meat uncooked ; and you can't even have a good broth without my art.

Master : We don't care about your art ; it isn't necessary to us, because we can boil things that need boiling, and roast the things that need roasting, for ourselves.

The Cook says : However, if you drive me out so as to do that, then you'll all be servants, and none of you will be lord. And without my craft you still won't be able to eat.

COLLOQUY (6)

Critique of the Occupations

1   *M* : Ēalā, munuc, þe mē tō spricst, efne iċ hæbbe āfandod þē
habban gōde ġefēran, and þearle nēodbearfe ; and iċ āhsie þē, hwā sind
hiġ?

   D : Iċ hæbbe smiþas, īsenesmiþas, goldsmiþ, seolforsmiþ, ārsmiþ,
5   trēowwyrhtan, and manegra ōþra mistlīcra cræfta biġgengeras.

   M : Hæfst þū ǣniġne wīsne ġebeahtan?

   D : Ġewislīċe iċ hæbbe. Hū mæġ ūre ġegaderung būton ġebeahtende
bēon wissod?

   M : Hwæt seġst þū, wīsa? Hwilċ cræft þē is ġebūht betwux þās
10   furþra wesan?

   Consilarius : Iċ secge þē, mē is ġebūht Godes bēowdom betweoh
þās cræftas ealdorscipe healdan, swā swā hit is ġerǣd on godspelle,
'Fyrmest sēċeað Godes rīċe and his rihtwīsnesse, and þās þing ealle
bēoþ tōġeīehte ēow.'

15   *M* : And hwilċ þē is ġebūht betwux woruld-cræftas healdan
ealdordōm?

   D : Eorþtilþ, forþām sē yrþling ūs ealle fētt.

   Sē smiþ seġð : Hwanon bēo þām yrþlinge sȳlanscear oððe culter,
þe nā gāde hæfþ būton of mīnum cræfte. Hwanon bēo fiscere angel,
20   oððe sceōwyrhtan æl, oððe sēamere nǣdl? Nis hit of mīnum ġeweorce?

   Se ġebeahtend andswerað : Sōþ witodlīċe sæġst þū, ac eallum ūs
lēofre is, wīcian mid þē yrþlinge þonne mid þē. Forþām sē yrþling sylð
ūs hlāf and drenċ. Hwæt sylst þū ūs on þīnre smibban, būton īsenne
fȳrspearcan, and swēġinga bēatendra slecgea, and blāwendra byliga?

25   *Sē trēowwyrhta seġð* : Hwilċ ēower ne notaþ mīnum craæfte,
þonne hūs and mistlīċe fatu and scipu ēow eallum iċ wyrċe?

   Se smiþ andwyrt : Ēalā trēowwyrhta, forhwī swā spricst þū, bonne ne furbum ān byrl būton mīnum cræfte bū ne miht dōn?

    Se ġebeahtend sæġþ: Ēalā ġefēran and gōde wyrhtan, uton

30   tōwurpon hwætlīcor þās ġeflitu, and sȳ sibb and ġebwǣrnyss betweoh
ūs, and framige ūrum ġehwylcum ōþrum on his cræfte, and ġedwǣrian
symble mid þām yrþlinge. And þis ġebeaht iċ sylle eallum wyrhtum,
þæt ānra ġehwylċ his cræft ġeornlīċe begange ; forþām sē þe his cræft
forĺæt, hē biþ forĺæten fram þām cræfte. Swā hwæðer þū sȳ swā

35   mæsseprēst, swā munuc, swā ċeorl, swā cempa, begā oððe behwyrf þē
sylfne on þisum ; and bēo þæt þū eart, forþām miċel hȳnð and sceamu
hit is menn, nelle wesan þæt þæt hē is and þæt hē wesan sceal.

1   munuc=monk. āfandod=āfandian(=to find out)의 과거.

2   nēodbearfe=necessary. āhsie=ask. 원형은 ācsian.

4   smiþas=smiths. īsenesmiþas=iron-smiths. goldsmiþ=goldsmith. seolforsmiþ=silversmith.
ārsmiþ=coppersmith.

5   trēowwyrhtan=carpenters. cf. trēo(w)=tree, wood. manegra=traders, merchants. 원형은
manegere. ōþra=other. mistlīcra=various. biġgengeras=bigengere(=worker)의 복수.

6   ǣniġne=any. wīsne=wise. ġebeahtan=counsellor, adviser.

7   Ġewislīċe=certainly. ġegaderung=gathering, company. ġebeahtende=counsellor.

8   wissod=directed. 원형은 wissian.

9   wīsa=wise man. ġebuht=thought. 원형은 ġebenċcan. betwux(=betweoh, betweox)=
between, among.

10 furþra=superior. wesan=be.

11 Consilarius=Lt. counsellor. mē ist ġebuht=it seems to me. Gōdes bēowdom=service of
God.

12 ealdorscipe=supremacy. healdan=hold. ġerǣd=ġerǣdan(=to read)의 과거분사.
godspelle=gospel.

13 Fyrmest=first of all. cf. Luke 12 : 31. 'Instead, strive for his kingdom, and these things
will be given to you as well.' sēċeað=sēċan(=to seek)의 단수 명령. rīċe=kingdom.
rightwīsnesse=righteousness.

14 tōġeīehte=added to. 원형은 tōġeīeċan.

15 woruld-cræftas=worldly occupation. healdan=held.

16 ealdordōm=superiority.

17 Eorþtilþ=agriculture. yrþling=farmer, ploughman. fētt=feed. 원형은 fēdan.

18 sȳlanscear=plowshare. culter=coulter(보습 바로 앞에 달린 풀 베는 날).

19 gāde=goad(몰이 막대기). fiscere=fisher. angel=fishhook.

20   ǽl=awl(송곳). sēamere=tailor. nǽdl=needle. Nis=ne is. ġeweorce=work.

21   andwerab=answers. 원형은 andwyrdan.

22   lēofre=lēof(=dear)의 비교급. wīcian=dwell. sylð=gives. 원형은 sellan.

23   drenċ=drink. sylst=give. 원형은 sellan. smibban=smithy(대장간).

23-24   īsenne fȳrspearcan=iron sparks.

24   swēġinga=sound. bēatendra=beating. 원형은 bēatan. slecgea=slecg(=sledge-hammer)의 복수 속격. blāwendra=blowing. 원형은 blāwan. byliga=bylg(=bellows)의 복수 속격.

25   notab=use. 원형은 notian.

26   fatu=fæt(=vessel, vat)의 복수 속격. wyrċe=work. 원형은 wyrċan.

27   forhwī=why.

28   furbum=even. byrl=hole. miht=may. 원형은 magan.

29   wyrhtan=workers. uton=let us.

30   tōwurpon(=tōwearpan)=put on end to. hwætlīcor=hwætlīċe(=quickly)의 비교급. ġeflitu=dispute. sȳ=sīe=let there be. bēon(=to be)의 가정법. sibb=peace. ġebwǣrnyss=concord.

31   framige=benefit. 원형은 framian. ġehwylcum=every one, 원형은 ġehwelċ, ġehwylċ.. ōbrum=others. ġedwǣrian=agree.

32   symble(=simble, simle)=always. ġebeaht=counsel, advice. sylle=give. wyrhtum=worker.

33   ānra ġehwylċ=each one. ġeornlīċe=eagerly, zealously. begange=begangan(=perform)의 가정법.

34   forlǽt=abandon. Swā hwæðer···swā=whichsoever···may be.

35   mæsseprēst=priest. ċeorl=peasant. cempa=soldier. begā=begān(=to practice)의 단수 명령. behwyrf=behwyrfan(=to prepare)의 단수 명령.

35-36   bē sylfne=yourselves.

36   bēo=bēon의 단수 명령. bēo þæt þū eart=be what you are. eart=are. hȳnð=humiliation, disgrace. sceamu(=scamu)=shame.

37   menn=men. nelle=ne wille. wesan=be. þæt þæt=that which.

Critique of the Occupations

Master : Oh monk, you who are speaking to me. Now, I have found that you have good and very necessary companions ; and who are these I ask you?

Monk : I have craftsmen : blacksmiths, a goldsmith, silversmith, coppersmith, carpenters and workers in many other different crafts.

Master : Have you got any wise counsellor?

Monk : Certainly I have. How can our community be directed without a counsellor?

Master : What do you say, wise man? Which trade among these seems to you to be superior?

Counsellor : I tell you, to me the service of God seems to hold the first place among these crafts, just as it reads in the gospel : Seek first the kingdom of god and his righteousness, and all these things shall be added unto you.

Master : And which among the secular arts seems to you to hold the first place?

Counsellor : Agriculture, because the ploughman feed us all.

The Smith says : Where does the ploughman get his plough-share or coulter or goad, except by my craft? Where the fisherman his hook, or the shoemaker his awl, or the tailor his needle? Isnt it from my work?

The Counsellor answers : What you say is in fact true. But we would all prefer to live with you, ploughman, than with you, because the ploughman gives us bread and drink. You, what do you give us in your smithy but iron sparks, and the noise of hammers beating and bellow blowing?

The Carpenter says : Which of you doesn't make use of my craft, when I make houses and various vessels and boats for you all?

The Blacksmith answers : Oh, carpenter, why do you talk like that when you couldn't pierce even one hole without my craft?

The Counsellor says : Oh, friends and good workmen, let us bring these arguments to an end quickly, and let there be peace and concord between us, and let each one of us help the others by his craft. And let us always agree with the ploughman, where we find food for ourselves and fodder for our horses. And I give this advice to all workmen, that each one pursue his trade diligently ; for he who abandons his craft will be abandoned by his craft. Whoever you are, whether priest or monk or peasant or soldier, exercise yourself in this, and be what you are ; because it is a great disgrace and shame for a man not to want to be what he is, and what he has to be.

(tr. Swanton)

KING EDMUND (1)

1 Sum swībe ġelǣred munuc cōm sūban ofer sǣ fram sancte Benedictes
stōwe, on Æbelredes cyninges dæġe, tō Dūnstāne ærċebiscope, brim
ġēarum ǣr hē forbfērde, and se munuc hātte Abbo. 7ā wurdon hīe æt
sprǣċe, ob þæt Dūnstān reahte be sancte Ēadmunde, swā swā Ēadmundes
5 sweordbora hit reahte Æbelstāne cyninge, þā þā Dūnstān ġeong mann
wæs, and se sweordbora wæs forealdod mann. 7ā ġesette se munuc
ealle þā ġereċednesse on ānre bēċ, and eft, þā þā sēo bōc cōm tō ūs,
binnan fēam ġēarum, þā āwendon wē hit on Englisc, swā swā hit
hēræfter stent. Se munuc þā Abbo binnan twǣm ġēarum ġewende hām
10 tō his mynstre, and wearb sōna tō abbode ġesett on bǣm ilcan
mynstre.

Ēadmund se ēadiga, Ēastengla cyning, wæs snotor and weorbfull, and
weorbode simle mid æbelum bēawum bone ælmihtigan God. Hē wæs
ēabmōd and ġebungen, and swā ānrǣd burhwunode bæt hē nolde
15 ābūgan tō bismerfullum leahtrum, ne on nāwbre healfe hē ne āhielde
his bēawas, ac wæs simle ġemyndiġ bǣre sōþan lāre : 'Ġif bū eart tō
heafodmenn ġesett, ne āhefe bū bē, ac bēo betwix mannum swā swā ān
mann of him.' Hē wæs cystiġ wǣdlum and widewum swā swā fæder,
and mid welwillendnesse ġewissode his folc simle tō rihtwīsnesse, and
20 bǣm rēbum stīerde, and ġesǣliġlīċe leofode on sōbum ġelēafan.

Hit ġelamp bā æt nīehstan bæt bā Deniscan lēode fērdon mid
sciphere, herġiende and slēande wīde ġēond land, swā swā hiera
ġewuna is. On bǣm flotan wǣron 3ā fyrmestan hēafodmenn Hinguar and
Hubba, ġeānlǣhte burh dēofol, and hīe on Norbhymbralande ġelendon
25 mid æscum, and āwēston bæt land, and bā lēode ofslōgon. 7ā ġewende
Hinguar ēast mid his scipum, and Hubba belāf on Norbhymbralande,
ġewunnenum siġe mid wælhrēownesse. Hinguar bā becōm tō
Ēastenglum rōwende on bǣm ġēare be Ælfred æbeling ān and twentiġ

ġēara wæs, sē be Westseaxna cyning sibban wearb mǣre. And se
foresæġda Hinguar fǣrlīċe, swā swā wulf, on land bestealcode, and bā
lēode slōg, weras and wīf and bā unwittigan ċild, and tō bismere
tūcode bā bilewitan crīstenan.

(여기 실린 글은 Ælfric의 성인전(*Lives of the Saints*)에서 가져온 것이다. Edmund는 855년
에 14세의 나이로 East Anglia의 왕이 되었다가 869년에 바이킹 군에 의해 살해당한다. 그
뒤 그는 성인으로 추앙 받는다. 여기 실린 글은 10세기말에 쓰여진 것으로 짐작된다. 여기
서 한가지 주목할 것은 운문만큼 엄격하지는 않지만 산문에서도 두운이 지켜지고 있다는
사실이다. 다음을 참고하기 바란다. 해당 철자에 밑줄을 쳐놓았다.

    Ēadmund se ēadiga,   Ēastengla cyning,
    wæs snotor and weorbfull,   and weorbode simle
    mid æbelum bēawum   bone ælmihtigan God.)

30

1   swībe=very, greatly. ġelǣred=learned. cf. lǣran=to teach, educate. cf. lār=teaching.
sūban=from the south. cf. sūb=south. sancte=saint. cf. Lt. sancti(=sacred).

1-2   sancte Benetictes stōwe=프랑스의 Fleury에 있는 수도원. 지금은 St. Fleury-sur-Loire라
고 부르며, 여기에 Benedict의 유골이 모셔져 있다고 알려져 있다. stōwe=place.

2   Dūnstāne=그는 뒤에(959) Canterbury 대주교가 된 사람으로서, 몇몇 앵글로색슨 왕들의
자문에 응했으며, 그 스스로는 Fleury 수도원에 자문을 구했다. ærċebiscope=archbishop.

3   forbfērde=died. 원형은 forbfēran. brim ġēarum ǣr hē forbfērde=three years before he
died. brim ġēarum은 brīe ġēar(=three years)의 복수 여격. 여기서 보듯 고대영어에서는 여
격으로 시간을 나타내는 경우가 있었다. cf. hwilum=at times. hātte=hātan(=to call, name,
command)의 과거분사로서 was called의 뜻. wurdon=happened. 원형은 weorban.

3-4   wurdon hīe æt sprǣċe=they came into conversation. sprǣċe=speech, conversation.

4   ob=until, up to. reahte=reċċan(=to tell, narrate)의 과거. be=about, concerning. Ēadmunde=
Edmund가 죽은 것은 869년.

5   sweordbora=sword bearer. bā bā=when. ġeong=young.

6   forealdod=aged. forealdian(=to grow old)의 과거분사. ġesette=set.

7   ġereċednesse=narrative. cf. reċċan(=to narrate). bēċ=bōc(=book)의 여격. 이 책의 이름은
Passio Sancti Eadmund. eft=afterwards, again.

8   binnan=within. āwendon=translated, changed.

9   hēræfter=hereafter, after this. stent=stand. 원형은 standan. ġewende=returned. hām=home.

10   mynstre=monastery. sōna=at once, then. abbode=abbot. ilcan=same.

12   Ēadmund=855년에 14세의 나이로 왕이 되었다. ēadiga=blessed. snotor=wise, prudent.
weorbfull=worthy, honorable.

13   weorbode=honored. 원형은 weorbian. simle=always, ever. æbelum=noble. 원형은 æbele.

bēawum=custom, habit. 복수형은 virtues, morality의 뜻. ælmihtigan=almighty.

14 ēabmōd=humble. ġebungen=virtuous, excellent. ānrǣd=constant, resolute. burhwunode= continued, remained. 원형은 burhwunian. nolde=ne wolde.

15 ābūgan=bend, swerve, submit. bismerfullum=shameful. leahtrum=leahtor(=vice, sin, crime)의 복수 여격.

15-16 nāwbre…ne…ne=neither…nor. ne on nāwbre healfe hē ne āhielde his bēawas=nor did he turn away on either side from his good practices=neither did he turn away from his good practices. 부정사를 반복하는 것은 부정을 강조하기 위해서이다. healfe=half. āhielde=āhieldan(=to incline, bend)의 과거.

16 ġemyndiġ=mindful. ġemyndiġ는 속격을 지배한다. cf. ModE. mindful of. sōþan=true. lāre=teaching, doctrine.

17 heafodmenn=ruler. āhefe…bē=raise yourself. 원형은 āhebban. āhefe와 뒤에 나오는 bēo는 모두 소망이나 명령을 나타내는 가정법의 형태이다.

17-18 swā swā ān mann of him=as one of them.

18 cystiġ=charitable. wǣdlum=wǣdla(=poor man)의 복수 여격. widewum=widew(=widow) 의 복수 여격.

19 welwillendnesse=benevolence. ġewissode=ġewissian(=to guide)의 과거. rihtwisnesse= righteousness.

20 rēbum=the cruel. cf. rēbe=cruel. 형용사가 명사로 쓰인 경우임. stīerde=stīeran(=to restrain)의 과거. ġesǣliġlīce=happily, blessedly. leofode=lived. 원형은 libban. ġelēafan= belief, faith.

21 ġelamp=happened. 원형은 ġelimpan. nīehstan=nēah(=near)의 최상급. æt nīehstan=at last. lēode=people. fērdon=went. 원형은 fēran(=to go, travel).

22 sciphere=fleet. herġiende=ġeherġian(=to ravage, plunder)의 현재분사. slēande=slēan(=to kill)의 현재분사. ġēond=through(out).

22-23 swā swā hiera ġewuna is=as their custom is. ġewuna=habit, custom.

23 flotan=fleet. fyrmestan=first. hēafodmenn=(=head-man)=ruler, captain.

24 ġeānlǣhte=ġeānlǣċan(=to unite)의 과거분사. 선행하는 Hinguar and Hubba를 수식한다. dēofol=devil. Norþhymbralande=Northumbria. ġelendon=landed. 원형은 ġelendan.

25 æscum=(ash-tree)=warship. āwēston=āwēstan(to lay waste, ravage)의 과거.

26 ēast=eastwards. belāf=remained. 원형은 belīfan.

27 ġewunnenum=ġewinnan(=to win)의 과거분사의 복수 대격. siġe=victory. gewunnenum siġe=victory having been won. wælhrēownesse=cruelty.

28 rōwende=rōwan(=to row)의 현재분사. æþeling=prince.

28-29 ān and twentiġ ġeara=one and twenty=twenty-one. Alfred 대왕은 871년에 21세의 나이 로 West-Saxon의 왕이 되었다.

29 sē þe=Ælfred æþeling을 선행사로 하는 관계대명사. wearþ=weorþan(=to become)의 과거. mǣre=famous, glorious, great.

29-30 se foresæġda=the aforesaid. 원형은 foresecgan.

færlīċe=suddenly. wulf=wolf. bestealcode=went stealthily. 원형은 bestealcian(move stealthily).

31 weras=men. unwittigan=innocent, simple. bismere=insult, shame, ignominy. tō bismere= with ignominy.

32 tūcode=harassed, afflicted. 원형은 tūcian. bilewitan=innocent. crīstenan=Christians. 단수 는 crīsten.

In the time of King Æthelred a certain very learned monk came from the south over the sea from St. Benoit sur Loire to Archbishop Dunstan, three years before he died ; and the monk was called Abbo. Then they talked together until Dunstan told the story of St Edmund, just as Edmund's sword-bearer had told the story of St Edmund, when Dunstan was a young man and the sword-bearer was a very old man. Then the monk set down all the information in a book ; and afterwards, when the book came to us a few years later, then we translated it into English, just as it stands hereafter. Then within two years the monk Abbo returned home to his monastery and was straightway appointed abbot in that very monastery.

The blessed Edmund, King of East Anglia, was wise and honourable, and by his noble conduct ever glorified Almighty God. He was humble and virtuous, and continued resolutely thus so that he would not submit to shameful sins ; nor did he alter his conduct in any way, but was always mindful of that true teaching : 'You are appointed ruler?' do not exalt yourself, but be amongst men as one of them.' He was as generous as a father to the poor and to widows, and with benevolence always guided his people towards righteousness, and restrained the violent, and lived happily in the true faith.

Then eventually it happened that the Danish people came with a pirate force, harrying and slaying widely throughout the land, as their custom is. In that fleet, united by the devil, were the very important leaders Ivar and Ubbi ; and they landed with warships in Northumbria, and wasted the land and slew the people. Then Ivar turned eastward with his ships and Ubbi remained behind in Northumbria, having won victory with savagery. Then Ivar came sailing to East Anglia in the year in which prince Alfred (he who afterwards became the famous King of Wessex) was twenty-one years old ; and the aforesaid Ivar abruptly stalked over the land like a wolf, and slew the people : men and women and the innocent children, and humiliated the honest Christians.

KING EDMUND (2)

1   Hē sende þā sōna siþþan tō þǣm cyninge bēotliċ ǣrende, þæt hē
ābūgan scolde tō his mannrǣdenne, ġif hē rōhte his fēores. Se
ǣrendraca cōm þā tō Ēadmunde cyninge, and Hinguares ǣrende him
arodlīċe ābēad : "Hinguar ūre cyning, cēne and siġefæst on sǣ and on
5 lande, hæfþ fela lēoda ġeweald, and cōm nū mid fierde fǣrlīċe hēr tō
lande, þæt hē hēr wintersetl mid his werode hæbbe. Nū hǣtt hē þē
dǣlan þīne dīeglan goldhordas and þīnra ieldrena ġestrēon arodlīċe wiþ
hine, and þū bēo his undercyning, ġif þū cwic bēon wilt, for þǣm þe þū
næfst þā miht þæt þū mæġe him wiþstandan.

10   Hwæt þā Ēadmund cyning clipode ānne biscop þe him þā ġehendost
wæs, and wiþ hine smēade hū hē þǣm rēþan Hinguare andwyrdan
scolde. 7ā forhtode se biscop for þǣm fǣrlican ġelimpe, and for þæs
cyninges līfe, and cwæþ þæt him rǣd þūhte þæt hē tō þǣm ġebuge þe
him bēad Hinguar. 7ā swigode se cyning, and beseah tō þǣre eorþan,
15 and cwæþ þā æt nīehstan cynelīċe him tō : 'Ēalā þū biscop, tō bismere
sind ġetāwode þās earman landlēode, and mē nū lēofre wǣre þæt iċ on
ġefeohte fēolle, wiþ þǣm þe mīn folc mōste hiera eardes brūcan.' And
se biscop cwæþ : 'Ēalā þū lēofra cyning, þīn folc līþ ofslæġen, and þū
næfst þone fultum þæt þū feohtan mæġe, and þās flotmenn cumaþ,
20 and þē cwicne ġebindaþ, būtan þū mid flēame þīnum fēore ġebeorge,
oþþe þū þē swā ġebeorge þæt þū būge tō him.' 7ā cwæþ Ēadmund
cyning, swā swā hē full cēne wæs : '7æs iċ ġewilniġe and ġewȳsce mid
mōde, þæt iċ āna ne belīfe æfter mīnum lēofum beġnum, þe on hiera
bedde wurdon mid bearnum and and wīfum fǣrlīċe ofslæġene fram
25 þissum flotmannum. Næs mē nǣfre ġewuneliċ þæt iċ worhte flēames,
ac iċ wolde swīþor sweltan, ġif iċ þorfte, for mīnum āgnum earde, and
se ælmihtiga God wāt þæt iċ nylle ābūgan fram his bīgengum ǣfre, ne
fram his sōþan lufe, swelte iċ, libbe iċ.'

Æfter þissum wordum hē ġewende tō þǣm ǣrendracan þe Hinguar
30 him tō sende, and sæġde him unforht : "Witodlīċe þū wǣre wierþe
sleġes nū, ac iċ nylle āfȳlan on þīnum fūlum blōde mīne clǣnan handa,
for þǣm þe iċ Crīste folgiġe, be ūs swā ġebȳsnode ; and iċ blīþelīċe
wille bēon ofslæġen þurh ēow, ġif hit swā God foresċēawaþ. Far nū
swīþe hraþe, and sæġe þīnum rēþan hlāforde : "Ne āþȳhþ nǣfre Ēadmund
35 Hinguare on līfe, hǣþnum heretogan, būtan hē tō Hǣlende Crīste ǣrest
mid ġelēafan on þissum lande ġebūge."

---

1 bēotliċ=arrogant, threatening. ǣrende=errand, message.

2 ābūgan scolde=should submit. mannrǣdenne=allegiance. abūgan scolde tō his mannrǣdenne
=submit to his service=submit to being a underking to the pagan Hinguar. rōhte=cared.
원형은 reċċan. rōhte는 직설법과 모양은 같으나 여기서는 가정법으로 쓰였다. fēores=life.
원형은 feorh.

3 ǣrendraca=messenger. Ēadmunde cyninge=cyninge Ēadmunde=king Edmund.

4 arodlīċe=quickly. ābēad=announced. 원형은 ābēodan. cēne=brave, bold. siġefæst=victorious.

5 fela=many. ġeweald=ġewealdan(=rule, control, have power over)의 과거분사. fierde=
army.

6 þæt…habbe=that…may have. habbe는 habban의 가정법 현재형이다. wintersetl=winter-
quarters. werode=troop.

6-7 hǣtt hē þē dǣlan=he orders you to divide. hǣtt=orders. 원형은 hātan.

7 dǣlan=to divide, to part. dīeglan=secret. 원형은 dīegol. goldhordas=treasures. þīnra=
your.
ieldrena=ancestors'. 원형은 ieldran. ġestrēon=possession. arōdlīċe=quickly.

8 bū bēo=명령을 나타내는 가정법이다. undercyning=under-king, tributary king. cwic=
alive. for þǣm þe=because.

9 næfst=ne hæfst. miht=might, power. wiþstandan=withstand, resist.

10 Hwæt=well, lo! clipode=summoned, called. 원형은 clipian. biscop=bishop. ġehendost=
ġehende(=near, at hand, intimate)의 최상급.

11 smēade=considered. 원형은 smēaġan.

11-12 andwyrdan scolde=should answer.

12 forhtode=feared. 원형은 forhtian. fǣrlican=sudden. ġelimpe=event, emergency.

13 rǣd=advice, counsel. þūhte=seemed. 원형은 þynċan. him rǣd þūhte=it seemed advisable
to him.

13-14 þæt hē tō þǣm ġebuge þe him bēad Hinguar=that he should submit to that which
Hinguar demanded of him. ġebuge=ġebūgam(=to bend, submit)의 가정법 현재. bēad=
offered, commanded. 원형은 bēodan.

14   swigode=swigian(=to be silent)의 과거. beseah=looked. 원형은 besēon.

15   cynelīċe=like a king, royally.

15-16 tō bismere sind ġetāwode=are profaned. tō bismere=with ignomity.

16   ġetāwode=afflicted. 원형은 ġetāwian. earman=poor, wretched. landlēode=people of a country. mē lēofre wǣre=I would rather. lēof=dear, pleasant. ġefeohte=fight(ing).

17   fēolle=fēallan(=to fall)의 가정법 현재. wiþ þǣm þe mīn folc mōste hiera eardes brūcan=두 가지 해석이 가능하다. 첫째는 wiþ þǣm þe가 on condition that의 뜻이 있으므로 against him who would possess my people's land로 해석할 수 있으며, 다른 한 가지 해석은 wiþ 가 against의 뜻을 가지고 있으므로 against him who might possess my people's land로 해석하는 것이다. folc=people. mōste=mōt(=may)의 과거. 과거형 현재 동사(preterite-present verb). eardes=country, land. brūcan=possess, make use of.

18   līþ=lie. 원형은 licgan.

19   næfst=ne+hæfst. fultum=forces, troops. mæġe=can. flotmenn=pirate, sailor. cumaþ= cuman(=to come)의 복수형으로서 여기서는 미래시를 나타낸다.

20   cwicne ġebindaþ=bind alive. 여기서도 현재형으로 미래시를 나타낸다. flēame=flight. cf. flōn=to flee. fēore=life. 원형은 feorh.

21   þū bē swā ġebeorge þæt þū būge tō him=save yourself in that you submit=save yourself by submitting. ġebeorge=save. 원형은 beorgan. swā…þæt의 swā는 thus의 뜻.

22   swā swā=as. cēne=brave. ġewilniġe=desire. 원형은 ġewilnian. ġewȳsce=wish. 원형은 ġewȳscan.

23   mōde=heart, mind, spirit. mid mōde=with my heart, in my mind. āna=one. belīfe=remain. lēofum=dear, beloved. beġnum=thane (왕의 근위병), retainer (신하).

24   bearnum=beran(=child)의 복수 여격. fǣrlīċe=suddenly, quickly. ofslæġene=ofslēan(=to slay)의 과거분사로서 앞의 wurdon(=became)과 함께 수동태를 이룬다.

25   Næs=ne wæs. nǣfre=never. cf. ne+æfre(=ever). ġewuneliċ=customary, habitual. worhte=worked. 원형은 wyrċan. flēames=flēme(=flight)의 속격. 이처럼 wyrċcan은 속격을 지배하는 경우가 많았다.

26   wolde=I would rather. swīþor=rather. þorfte=þearf(=need)의 과거형 현재 동사.

27   wāt=knows. 원형은 witan(과거형 현재 동사). nylle=ne wille. bīgengum=worship. ǣfre=ever.

28   sōþan=true. lufe=love. swelte iċ, libbe iċ=whether I die or live. whether I die or live. swelte=sweltan(=to die)의 가정법 현재형. libbe= libban(=to live)의 가정법 현재형.

29   ġewende=turned.

30   unforht=dauntless, unafraid.

30-31 wǣre wierþe sleġes=were worthy of death=you deserve to be killed. wierþe=deserving. cf. werþ=worth.

31   sleġes=killing, slaughter. cf. slēan=to slay.
     nylle=ne+wil(l)e. āfȳlan=to defile. fūlum=foul, impure. blōde=blood. clǣnan=clean, pure. handa=hand.

32   folgiġe=follow. 원형은 folgian. ġebȳsnode=ġebȳsnian (=to set an example, to instruct by example)의 과거. cf. bȳsen=example, model. be ūs swā ġebȳsnode=who thus set an example for us. blībelīċe=gladly.

33   ofslæġen=slain. foresċēawab=pre-ordains. 원형은 foresċēawian. Far=go! 원형은 faran.

34   hrabe=quickly. rēban=fierce, cruel. hlāforde=lord, master. ābȳhb=submit. 원형은 ābūgan. næfre=never.

35   on līfe=while living. hǣbnum=heathen. heretogan=army leader, general. cf. here=army.

36   ġelēafan=belief, faith. ġebūge=bend, submit.

Then immediately afterwards he sent an arrogant message to the king that if he cared for his life, he should submit to do him homage. The messenger came to King Edmund and quickly announced Ivar's message to him : 'Ivar our King, brave and victorious by sea and by land, has subdued many nations and now suddenly landed here with an army, so that he might take winter quarters here with his host. Now he orders you to divide your secret treasures and the wealth of your forbears with him quickly, and if you want to live, you will be his under-king, because you haven't the power to be able to resist him.'

Well, then King Edmund summoned a certain bishop who was very near at hand, and discussed with him how he should answer the savage Ivar. Then the bishop was afraid because of the unexpected disaster, and for the king's life, and said that he thought it advisable that he should submit to what Ivar commanded. Then the king was silent and looked at the ground, and then eventually said to him, regally : 'Oh bishop! this wretched nation is humiliated, and I would rather fall in battle against him who might possess my people's land.' And the bishop said : 'Alas, dear king, your people lie slain, and you have not the forces to be able to fight ; and these pirates will come and bind you alive, unless you save your life by flight, or save yourself by submitting to him thus.' Then said King Edmund, very brave as he was : 'This I desire and wish with my heart, that I alone should not be left, after my beloved thegns, who with wives and children were suddenly slain in their beds by these pirates. It was never my custom to take flight, but I would rather die for my own country if I must ; and Almighty God knows that I would never turn away from his worship, nor from his true love, whether I die or live.'

After these words he turned to the messenger that Ivar had sent to him and said to him, unafraid : 'You would certainly deserve death now, but I would not dirty my clean hands in your filthy blood, for I follow Christ, who set us an example thus ; and I will cheerfully be slain by you if God so ordains it. Go very quickly now and say to your savage lord : "Edmund will never while living submit to the heathen war-leader, Ivar, unless he first submit in this land to Christ the Saviour in faith."'

KING EDMUND (3)

1   7ā ġewende se ǣrendraca arodlīċe onweġ, and ġemētte be weġe bone wælhrēowan Hinguar mid ealre his fierde fūse tō Ēadmunde, and sæġde b̄ǣm ārlēasan hū him ġeandwyrd wæs. Hinguar bā bebēad mid bieldu b̄ǣm sciphere bæt hīe bæs cyninges ānes ealle cēpan scolden, be his
5 h̄ǣse forseah, and hine sōna bindan.

    Hwæt bā Ēamund cyning, mid b̄ǣm be Hinguar cōm, stōd innan h̄is healle, bæs H̄ǣlendes ġemyndiġ, and āwearp his wǣpnu ; wolde ġeefenl̄æċan Crīstes ġeb̄ysnungum, be forbēad Petre mid wǣpnum tō winnenne wib bā wælhrēowan Iūdēiscan. Hwæt bā ārlēasan bā Ēadmund
10 ġebundon, and ġebismrodon huxlīċe, and bēoton mid sāglum, and swā sibban l̄æddon bone ġelēaffullan cyning tō ānum eorbfæstum trēowe, and tīeġdon hine b̄ærtō mid heardum bendum, and hine eft swungon langlīċe mid swipum ; and hē simle clipode betwix b̄ǣm swinglum mid sōbum ġelēafan tō H̄ǣlende Crīste ; and bā h̄ǣbnan bā for his ġelēafan
15 wurdon wōdlīċe ierre, for b̄ǣm be hē clipode Crīst him tō fultume. Hīe scuton bā mid gafelucum, swelċe him tō gamenes, tō, ob bæt hē eall wæs besett mid hiera scotungum, swelċe īles byrsta, swā swā Sebastiānus wæs. 7ā ġeseah Hinguar, se ārlēasa flotmann, bæt se æbela cyning nolde Crīste wibsacan, ac mid ānr̄ædum ġelēafan hine ǣfre
20 clipode. Hēt hine bā behēafdian, and bā h̄ǣbnan swā dydon. Betwix b̄ǣm be hē clipode tō Crīste bā ġiet, bā tugon bā h̄ǣbnan bone hālgan tō sleġe, and mid ānum swenġe slōgon him of bæt hēafod, and his sāwol sībode ġes̄ǣliġ tō Crīste. 7ær wæs sum mann ġehende, ġehealden burh God beh̄ydd b̄ǣm h̄ǣbnum, be bis ġehīerde eall, and hit eft sæġde, swā
25 swā wē hit secgab h̄ēr.

    Hwæt bā se flothere fērde tō scipe, and beh̄yddon bæt hēafod bæs hālgan Ēadmundes on b̄ǣm biccum brēmlum, bæt hit bebyrġed ne wurde. 7ā æfter fierste, sibban hīe āfarene wǣron, cōm bæt landfolc tō,

be bær tō lāfe wæs bā, bǣr hiera hlāfordes līċ læġ būtan hēafde, and
30 wurdon swībe sārġe for his sleġe on mōde, and hūru bæt hīe næfdon
bæt hēafod tō bǣm bodiġe. 7ā sæġde se scēawere, be hit ǣr ġeseah, bæt
bā flotmenn hæfdon bæt hēafod mid him ; and wæs him ġebūht, swā
swā hit wæs full sōb, bæt hīe behȳdden bæt hēafod on bǣm holte
forhwega.

1 ǣreadraca=messenger. arodlīċe=quickly. onweġ=away. ġemētte=met. 원형은 ġemētan.
   be weġe=on the way.
2 wælhrēowan=cruel. fierde=army. fūse=hastening.
3 bǣm ārlēasan=to the wicked. 여기서는 형용사가 명사로 사용되었다. hū him ġeandwyrd=
   how he was answered. bebēad=commanded. 원형은 bebēodan. bieldu=arrogance.
4 sciphere=fleet. bæs cyninges ānes=only the king. 여기서 속격이 사용된 것은 후속하는
   cēpan이 속격을 요구하기 때문. cēpan=look out for.
5 hǣse=command. forseah=forsēon(=to despise, scorn)의 과거.
6 Hwæt=well, lo! mid bǣm be=when. stōd=stood. 원형은 standan. healle=hall. ġemyndiġ=
   mindful. āwearp=threw. 원형은 āweorpan. wǣpnu=weapon. 원형은 wǣpen.
8 ġeefenlǣċan=imitate. ġebȳsnungum=example. forbēad=forbade. 원형은 forbēodan.
8-9 be forbēad Petre mid wǣpnum tō winnenne wib bā wælhrēowan Iūdēiscan=John : 18
   : 10-11을 참조할 것. tō winnenne=to fight. 원형은 winnan.
9 wælhrēowan=cruel. Iūdēiscan=Jews. 원형은 Iūdēas/Iūdēi. Hwæt=well, lo! ārlēasan=
   wicked, impious. bā ārlēasan=those wicked men.
10 ġebundon=bound. 원형은 ġebindan. ġebismrodon=ġebismrian(=to teat with ignominy)의
   과거. huxlīċe=ignominiously, with insult. bēoton=beat. 원형은 bēatan. sāglum=rod, staff.
   원형은 sāgol.
11 sibban=afterwards. lǣddon=led. 원형은 ġelǣdan(=to lead). ġelēaffullan=believing, pious,
   devout. eorbfæstum=firm in the earth. trēowe=tree.
12 tīeġdon=tied. 원형은 tīeġan. bǣrtō=thereto, to it. heardum=hard, strong. bendum=bond.
   eft=again, afterwards. swungon=swingan(=to beat)의 과거.
13 langlīċe=for a long time. swipum=whip. 원형은 swipu. simle=continually. swinglum=
   flogging, stroke. 원형은 swingel.
13-14 mid sōbum ġelēafan=with true faith.
14 bā hǣbnan=the heathen.
15 wurdon=became. 원형은 weorban. wōdlīċe=madly. ierre=angry. tō fultume=to help. 원형
   은 fultumian.
16 scuton…tō=shot at. 원형은 scēotan. gafelucum=spear, javelin. swelċe=as if, as it were.
   swelċe him tō gamenes=as if to amuse themselves. gamenes=sport.

17 besett=occupied, composed. 원형은 settan. scotungum=shooting, missile. īles=hedgehog. byrsta=bristle.

18 Sebastiānus=로마 시대의 순교자. 무수한 화살을 맞는 형벌을 받았다. æbela=noble.

19 wibsacan=deny. ānrǣdum=constant, resolute. ǣfre=every, always.

20 Hēt=hātan(=to order)의 과거. behēafdian=behead. hǣbnan=behead. dydon=did. 원형은 dōn.

20-21 Betwix bǣm be=while. tugon=dragged. 원형은 tēon.

21-22 tō sleġe=to kill. cf. slēan=slay.

22 swenġe=stroke, blow. cf, swingan=beat. slōgon=slaughtered. 원형은 slēan(=to slaughter, kill). slōgon him of bæt hēafod=struck the head from him=beheaded him. hēafod=head. sāwol=soul.

23 sībode=went, journeyed. 원형은 sīban. ġesǣliġ=happy, blessed. ġehende=near, at hand. ġehealden=kept. 원형은 ġehealdan. burh=through, by.

23-24 ġehealden burh God behȳdd bǣm hǣbnum=kept hidden from the heathens by God.

24 behȳdd=hidden. 원형은 behȳdan. ġehierde=heard.

25 secgab=say. 원형은 secgan.

26 flothere=army from a fleet, army of pirates. fērde=went. behȳddon=behȳdan(=to hide)의 과거.

27 biccum=thick, dense. 원형은 bicce. brēmlum=bramble. 원형은 brēmel.

27-28 bæt hit bebyrġed ne wurde=so that it would not be buried. bebyrġed=bebyrġan(=to bury)의 과거분사.

28 fierste=period, time. āfarene=gone. 원형은 āfaran. landfolc=people of a country.

29 lāfe=remnant, remains. tō lāfe bēon=to remain, be left. līċ=body, corpse.

30 sārġe=sorrowful, sad, sorry. 원형은 sāriġ. mōde=heart, mind, spirit. on mōde=앞의 sārġe 를 수식한다. hūru=especially, indeed. næfdon=ne+hæfdon.

31 bodiġe=body. scēawere=witness.

32 wæs him ġebūht=it seemed to him. ġebūht의 원형은 ġebenċan.

33 holte=wood. forhwega=somewhere.

Then the messenger went away quickly and met the savage Ivar on the way hastening to Edmund with his entire army, and told the wicked man how he was answered. Then Ivar resolutely commanded the men of the war-ships that they should all seize only the king, who had scorned his behest, and immediately bind him.

Well, then when Ivar came, King Edmund stood within his hall, mindful of the Saviour, and threw aside his weapons ; he would imitate the example of Christ, who forbade Peter to fight against the savage Jews with weapons.

So, then those wicked men bound Edmund and insulted him shamefully, and beat him with cudgels, and afterwards led the faithful king thus to a tree rooted in the ground, and tied him to it with tight bonds, and afterwards flogged him with whips for a long time ; and amidst the floggings he unceasingly called on Christ the Saviour with true faith ; and then, because of his faith, the heathen became insanely angry because he called on Christ to help him. Then, as if for sport, they shot at him with darts, until he was entirely covered with their missiles, like the bristles of a hedgehog, just as Sebastian was. When the wicked pirate Ivar saw that the noble king would not renounce Christ, but ever called on him with steadfast faith, he ordered him to be beheaded ; and the heathens did so. While he still called on Christ the heathens dragged the saint away to slaughter and with one blow struck off his head, and his blessed soul went to Christ. There was at hand a certain man, hidden from the heathen by god, who heard all this and afterward told it just as we tell it here.

Well, then the pirate force returned to ship, and hid the head of the holy Edmund in the dense brambles, so that it would not be buried. Then after a time, when they had gone away, the inhabitants who were left there came to where their lord's headless body lay, and were very sorrowful at heart because of his slaughter, and in particular because they did not have the head to the body. Then the observer who previously saw it, said that the pirates had taken the head with them, and he thought, as was perfectly true, that they had hidden the head somewhere in the wood.

KING EDMUND (4)

Hīe ēodon þā ealle endemes tō þǣm wuda, sēċende ġehwǣr, ġeond
bȳflas and brēmlas, ġif hīe āhwǣr mihten ġemētan þæt hēafod. Wæs
ēac miċel wundor þæt ān wulf wearþ āsend, þurh Godes wissunge, tō
bewerienne þæt hēafod wiþ þā ōþru dēor ofer dæġ and niht. Hīe ēodon
þā sēċende and simle clipiende, swā swā hit ġewuneliċ is þǣm þe on
wuda gāþ oft : 'Hwǣr eart þū nū, ġefēra?' And him andwyrde þæt
hēafod : 'Hēr, hēr, hēr ; and swā ġelōme clipode andswariende him
eallum, swā oft swā hiera ǣniġ clipode, oþ þæt hīe ealle becōmon þurh
þā clipunge him tō. Þā læġ se grǣga wulf þe bewiste þæt hēafod, and
mid his twǣm fōtum hæfde þæt hēafod beclypped, grǣdiġ and hungriġ,
and for Gode ne dorste þæs hēafdes onbierġan, ac hēold hit wiþ dēor.
Þā wurdon hīe ofwundrode þæs wulfes hierdrǣdenne, and þæt hālġe
hēafod hām feredon mid him, banciende þǣm Ælmihtigan ealra his
wundra. Ac se wulf folgode forþ mid þǣm hēafde, oþ þæt hīe tō tūne
cōmon, swelċe hē tam wǣre, and ġewende eft sibban tō wuda onġēan.
Þā landlēode þā sibban lēġdon þæt hēafod tō þǣm hālgan bodiġe, and
bebyriġdon hine swā hīe sēlest mihton on swelcre hrǣdinge, and
ċiriċan ārǣrdon sōna him onuppan. Eft þā on fierste, æfter fela ġēarum,
þā sēo hergung ġeswāc, and sibb wearþ forġiefen þǣm ġeswenċtan
folce, þā fēngon hīe tōgædre and worhton āne ċiriċan weorþlīċe þǣm
hālgan, for þǣm þe ġelōme wundru wurdon æt his byrġenne, æt þǣm
ġebedhūse þǣr hē bebyrġed wæs. Hīe woldon þā ferian mid folclicum
weorþmynde þone hālgan līchaman, and lecgan innan þǣre ċiriċan. Þā
wæs miċel wundor þæt hē wæs eall swā ġehāl swelċe hē cwic wǣre,
mid clǣnum līchaman, and his swēora wæs ġehālod, þe ǣr wæs forslæġen,
and wæs swelċe ān seolcen brǣd ymbe his swēoran rēad, mannum tō
sweotolunge hū hē ofslæġen wæs. Ēac swelċe þā wunda, þe þā
wælhrēowan hæbnan mid ġelōmum scotungum on his līċe macodon,

wǣron ġehǣlde burh bone heofonlican God ; and he līb swā ansund ob

30 bisne andweardan dæġ, andbīdiende ǣristes and bæs ēċan wuldres. His
līchama ūs cȳbb, be līb unformolsnod, bæt hē būtan forliġre hēr on
worulde leofode, and mid clǣnum līfe tō Crīste sībode.

1　endemes=together. sēċende=seeking. 원형은 sēċan. ġehwǣr=everywhere. ġeond=through (out).

2　bȳflas=bushes. 원형은 bȳfel. āhwǣr=anywhere. mihten=might, ġemētan=meet, find.

3　wundor=wonder, miracle. wulf=wolf. āsend=sent. wissunge=guidance, direction.

3-4　tō bewerienne=to defend.

4　dēor=wild beasts, animal. cf. G. Tier(=animal). cf, ModE, deer.

5　clipiende=calling. ġewuneliċ=customary, habitual.

6　wuda=wood. gāb=goes. 원형은 gān. oft=often. ġefēra=companion.

7　ġelōme=frequent.

8　hiera ǣniġ=any of them. becōmon=came, arrived. 원형은 becuman.

9　clipunge=calling. læġ=lay. grǣga=grey. 원형은 grǣġ. bewiste=watched over. 원형은 bewitan.

10　fōtum=feet. beclypped=embraced. grǣdiġ=greedy. hungriġ=hungry.

11　for Gode=because of God. dorste=dared. 원형은 dearr. onbierġan=eat, taste. hēold=held. 원형은 healdan. wib dēor=against beasts.

12　ofwundrode=astonished. hierdrǣdenne=guardianship.

13　feredon=went. 원형은 ferian. banciende=thanking. 원형은 bancian.

14　folgode=followed. 원형은 folgian. forb=forth. tūne=village.

15　swelċe hē tam wǣre=as if he were tame. onġēan=towards.

16　landlēode=people of a country. lēġdon=lecgan(=to lay)의 과거

17　sēlest=wel(=well)의 최상급. swā hīe sēlest mihton=as best they could, as well as they could. hrǣdinge=haste, hurry.

18　ċiriċan=church ārǣrdon=built. 원형은 ārǣran. onuppan=upon, above.

19　hergung=raving, pillage. ġeswāc=ceased. 원형은 ġeswīcan. sibb=peace. forġiefen=given. ġeswenċtan=afflicted. 원형은 swenċan.

20　fēngon=seized. 원형은 fōn. fēngon tōgædre=joined together. tōgædre=together. worhton=wyrċan(=to work, make, build)의 과거. weorblīċe=honourably.

21　byrġenne=tomb. cf. byrġan=to bury.

22　ġebedhūse=oratory, chapel. cf. ġebed=prayer. cf. biddan=to pray. bebyrġed=buried. 원형은 bebyrġan. woldon=wished. 원형은 willan. ferian=carry. cf. faran=to go. folclicum=popular, public, common. 원형은 folcliċ.

23　weorbmynde=honour. līchaman=body. lecgan=lay. innan=within, inside. 원형은 inne.

24　ġehāl=whole, uninjured. cwic=alive.

25 sweora=neck. ġehālod=healed. 원형은 hālian. forslæġen=forslēan(=to cut through)의 과거
분사.

26 swelċe=as it were. seolcen=silken. brǣd=thread. rēad=red. mannum=mann(=man)의 복수 여
격.

27 sweotolunge=sign, manifestation. wunda=wound.

28 wælhrēowan=cruel. macodon=made. 원형은 macian.

29 ġehǣlde=healed. 원형은 hǣlan. heofonlican=heavenly. 원형은 heofonliċ. ansund=sound,
whole, uncorrupted.

30 andweardan=present. andbīdende=awaiting. 원형은 andbīdian. cf. bīdan=to wait.
ǣristes=resurrection. cf. ārīsan=to arise. ēċan=eternal. wuldres=glory. 원형은 wuldor.

32 cȳbb=make known, tell. 원형은 cȳban. cf. cūb=known. unformolsnod=undecayed.
forliġre=fornication. 원형은 forliġer.

32 worulde=world. leofode=lived. 원형은 libban. sībode=journeyed. 원형은 sībian.

Then they all went in a body to the wood, searching everywhere through bushes and brambles, to see if they could find the head anywhere. There was moreover a great miracle, in that a wolf was sent by God's guidance to protect the head against the other beasts by day and night. Then they went searching, and continually calling out, as is usual among those who frequent the woods, 'Where are you now, comrade?' And the head answered them : 'Here, here, here!', and called out frequently thus, answering them all, as often as any of them called out, until they all came to it by means of the calling. There lay the grey wolf who watched over the head, and had embraced the head with his two feet, ravenous and hungry, and because of God dare not eat the head, but kept it safe from the beasts. Then they were amazed at the wolf's care, and thanking the almighty for all his miracles, carried the holy head home with them ; but as if he were tame, the wolf followed the head along until they came to the town, and afterwards turned back to the wood again.

Then afterwards the inhabitants laid the head with the holy body, and buried it as best they could in such haste, and erected a chapel over it forthwith. Then in time, when after many years the raids stopped and peace was restored to the afflicted people, they joined together and built a church worthy of the saint, because miracles were frequently performed at his grave in the oratory where he was buried. They wished then to carry the holy body with universal veneration and lay it within the church. Then there was a great miracle, in that he was just as whole as if he were alive, with unblemished body ; and his neck, which was previously cut through, was healed, and there was, as it were, a silken thread red about his neck as an indication to men of how he was slain. Likewise the wounds which the savage heathens had made in his body with repeated missiles, were healed by the heavenly God. And he lies uncorrupt thus to this present day, awaiting resurrection and the eternal glory. His body, which lies here undecayed, proclaims to us that he lived here in the world without fornication, and journeyed to Christ with a pure life.

KING EDMUND (5)

1   Sum widewe wunode, Ōswyn ġehāten, æt þæs hālgan byrġenne, on
ġebedum and fæstennum manigu ġēar sibban. Sēo wolde efsian ǣlċe
ġēare þone sanct, and his næġlas ċeorfan sȳferlīċe mid lufe, and on
scrīne healdan tō hāliġdōme on wēofode. Þā weorbode þæt landfolc
5 mid ġelēafan þone sanct, and Þēodred biscop bearle mid ġiefum on
golde and on seofre, þǣm sancte tō weorbmynde.

    Þā cōmon on sumne sǣl unġesǣlġe þēofas eahta on ānre nihte tō þǣm
ārweorban hālgan : woldon stelan þā māþmas þe menn þider brōhton,
and cunnodon mid cræfte hū hīe inn cuman mihten. Sum slōg mid
10 slecge swībe þā hæpsan, sum hiera mid fēolan fēolde ymbūtan, sum ēac
underdealf þā duru mid spade, sum hiera mid hlǣdre wolde onlūcan þæt
ēagbȳrel ; ac hīe swuncon on īdel, and earmlīċe fērdon, swā þæt se
hālga wer hīe wundorlīċe ġeband, ǣlcne swā hē stōd strūtiende mid
tōle, þæt hiera nān ne mihte þæt morb ġefremman ne hīe banon āstyrian ;
15 ac stōdon swā ob merġen. Menn þā þæs wundrodon, hū þā weargas
hangodon, sum on hlǣdre, sum lēat tō ġedelfe, and ǣlċ on his weorce
wæs fæste ġebunden. Hīe wurdon þā ġebrōhte tō þǣm biscope ealle,
and hē hēt hīe hōn on hēam ġealgum ealle ; ac hē næs nā ġemyndiġ hū
se mildheorta God clipode burh his wītegan þās word be hēr standab :
20 *Eos qui ducuntur ad mortem eruere ne cesses*, 'Þā þe man lǣtt tō
dēabe ālīes hīe ūt simle.' And ēac þā hālgan canōnas ġehādodum
forbēodab, ġe biscopum ġe brēostum, tō bēonne ymbe þēofas, for þǣm
be hit ne ġebyreb þǣm be bēob ġecorene Gode tō beġnienne þæt hīe
ġebwǣrlǣċan scylen on ǣnġes mannes dēabe, ġif hīe bēob Dryhtnes
25 beġnas. Eft þā Þēodred biscop sċēawode his bēċ, hē sibban behrēowsode
mid ġeōmrunge þæt hē swā rēbne dōm sette þǣm unġesǣlgum
bēofum, and hit besārgode ǣfre ob his līfes ende, and þā lēode bæd
ġeorne þæt hīe him mid fæsten fullīċe brīe dagas, biddende þone

Ælmihtigan bæt hē him ārian scolde.

1 widewe=widow. wunode=lived. 원형은 wunian. Ōswyn ġehāten=called Ōswyn. byrġenne
=tomb.

2 fæstennum=fast. manigu=many. 원형은 maniġ. manigu ġēar=for many years. efsian=cut
the hair of.

3 sanct=saint. næġlas=nail. 원형은 næġel. ċeorfan=cut. sȳferlīċe=with purity, chastely.
lufe=love. 원형은 lufu.

4 scrīne=shrine. healdan=kept. hāliġdōme=relic. wēofode=altar. weorbode=weorbian(=to
worship)의 과거.

5 bearle=very, greatly, thoroughly. ġiefum=gift.

6 weorbmynde=esteem.

7 sǣl=time, occasion. unġesǣlġe=unhappy, accursed, wretched. bēofas=thieves.

8 ārweorban=venerable. cf. weorb=worth, value. woldon=wished. 원형은 willan. stelan=
steal. mābmas=treasure. 원형은 mābum. bider=thither, there.

9 cunnodon=tried. 원형은 cunnian. cuman mihten=could come. slōg=slēan(=to strike)의 과
거.

10 slecge=hammer. hæpsan=hasp, fastening. fēolan=file. fēolde=filed. 원형은 fēolian. ymbūtan
=round, around.

11 underdealf=dug under. 원형은 underdelfan. duru=door. spade=spade. 원형은 spadu.
hlǣdre=ladder. 원형은 hlǣder. onlūcan=unlock.

12 ēagbȳrel=(=eye-hole) window. swuncon=labored, toiled. 원형은 swincan. īdel=idle. on īdel
=in vain. earmlīċe=miserably, wretchedly. fērdon=fared. 원형은 fēran. swā bæt=in that.

13 wundorlīċe=wonderfully, in a miraculous way. ġeband=bindan(=to bind)의 과거. ǣlcne=
each, every, all. 원형은 ǣlċ. stōd strūtiende=stood rigid, stiff.

14 tōle=tool. nān=none. morb=crime. ġefremman=perform, commit. hīe=themselves. banon=
thence, from there. āstyrian=stir, move.

15 merġen=morning. bæs=뒤에 오는 hū절을 받고 있다. wundrodon=wondered, marvelled. 원
형은 wundrian. weargas=felon, criminal.

16 hangodon=hung. 원형은 hangian. ēat=bent. 원형은 lūtan(=to bend). ġedelfe=digging.
weorce=work.

18 hōn=hang. hēam=high. 원형은 hēah. ġealgum=gallows. 원형은 ġealga. ġemyndiġ=
mindful.

19 mildheorta=(=mind-hearted) merciful. wītegan=prophet.

20 *Eos qui ducuntur ad mortem enere ne cesses*=Do not fail to release those who are led to
death. lǣtt=let. 원형은 lǣtan.

21 dēabe=death. ālīes=redeem, liberate. 원형은 ālīesan. canōnas=canons. ġehādodum=ordained,
clerical. cf. hādian=ordain.

22 forbēodaþ=forbid. 원형은 forbēodan. ġe…ġe=both…and. prēostum=priests. tō bēonne
ymbe=to concern themselves with. bēonne=be.

23 ġebyreþ=befit, 원형은 ġebyrian. ġecorene=chosen 원형은 ċēosan. beġnienne=serve.

24 ġebwærlæċan=agree. scylen=ought to, must. 원형은 sceal. ænġes=anyone's. 원형은 æniġ.

25 beġnas=servants. 원형은 beġen. scēawode=examined. 원형은 scēawian. bēċ=books.
behrēowsode=repented. 원형은 behrēowsian. cf. hrēowan=repent.

26 ġeōmrunge=grief, lamentation. rēbne=cruel. 원형은 rēbe. dōm=judgement, sentence. sette
=set, appointed.

27 besārgode=lamented. 원형은 besārġian. cf. sāriġ=sorry. æfre=ever, always. lēode=people.
bæd=prayed. 원형은 biddan.

28 ġeorne=eagerly, earnestly. fæsten=fast. fullīċe=fully. biddende=praying. biddan의 현재분
사.

29 ārian=have mercy on. scolde=should.

A certain widow called Oswyn lived in prayer and fasting at the saint's
tomb for many years afterwards ; each year she would cut the hair of the
saint and cut his nails, circumspectly, with love, and keep them as relics in
a shrine on the altar. Then the inhabitants venerated the saint with faith, and
Bishop Theodred richly endowed the monastery with gifts of gold and silver
in honour of the saint.

Then at one time there came wretched thieves, eight in a single night, to
the venerable saint ; they wanted to steal the treasures which men had
brought there, and tried how they could get in by force. One struck at the
bolt violently with a hammer ; one of them filed around it with a file ; one
also dug under the door with a spade ; one of them with a ladder wanted to
unlock the window. But they laboured in vain and fared miserably, inasmuch
as the holy man miraculously bound them, each as he stood rigid with his
tool, so that none of them could commit that sinful deed nor move away
from there, but they stood thus till morning. Then men marvelled at how the
villains hung there, one up a ladder, one bent in digging, and each was
bound fast in his labour. Then they were all brought to the bishop, and he
ordered them all to be hung on a high gallows. But he was not mindful of
how the merciful God spoke through his prophet the following words : *Eos*

qui ducuntur ad mortem eruere ne cesses, 'Always redeem those whom they lead to death' ; and also the holy canons forbid those in orders, both bishops and priests, to be concerned with thieves, for it is not proper that those who are chosen to serve God should be a party to any man's death, if they are the Lord's servants. Then after Bishop Theodred had examined his books, he repented, with lamentation, that he had appointed so cruel a judgement to those wretched thieves, and regretted it to the end of his life, and earnestly prayed the people to fast with him a whole three days, praying to the Almighty that he would have mercy on him.

KING EDMUND (6)

1   On þæm lande wæs sum mann, Lēofstān ġehāten, rīċe for worulde
and unwittiġ for Gode. Sē rād tō þæm hālgan mid rīċetere swīþe, and
hēt him ætēowian orgellīċe swīþe þone hālgan sanct, hwæþer hē ġesund
wǣre ; ac swā hraþe swā hē ġeseah þæs sanctes līchaman, þā āwēdde
5   hē sōna, and wælhrēowlīċe grymetode, and earmlīċe ġeendode yflum
dēaþe. 7is is þæm ġelīċ þe ġelēaffulla pāpa Gregōrius sæġde on his
ġesetnesse be þæm hālgan Laurentie, þē līþ on Rōmebyriġ, þæt menn
woldon sċēawian simle hū hē lǣġe, ġe gōde ġe yfle ; ac God hīe ġestilde
swā þæt þǣr swulton on þǣre sċēawunge āne seofon menn ætgædre. 7ā
10   ġeswicon þā ōþre tō sċēawienne þone martyr mid m e n n i s c u m
ġedwylde.

Fela wundra wē ġehīerdon on folclicre sprǣċe be þæm hālgan
Ēadmunde, þe wē hēr nyllaþ on ġewrite settan, ac hīe wāt ġehwā. On
þissum hālgan is sweotol, and on swelcum ōþrum, þæt God ælmihtiġ
15   mæġ þone mann ārǣran eft on dōmes dæġ ansundne of eorþan, sē þe
hielt Ēadmunde hālne his līchaman oþ þone miclan dæġ, þēah þe hē of
moldan cōme. Wierþe is sēo stōw for þæm weorþfullan hālgan þæt hīe
man weorþiġe and wel ġelōġiġe mid clǣnum Godes þēowum tō Crīstes
þēowdōme ; for þæm þe se hālga is mǣrra þonne menn magon
20   āsmēaġan.

Nis Angelcynn bedǣled Dryhtnes hālgena, þonne on Englalande
licgaþ swelċe hālgan swelċe þes hālga cyning, and Cūþberht se ēadiga,
and sancte Æþelþrÿþ on Ēliġ, and ēac hiere sweostor, ansunde on
līchaman, ġelēafan tō trymminge. Sind ēac fela ōþre on Angelcynne
25   hālgan, þe fela wundra wyrċaþ, swā swā hit wīde is cūþ, þæm
Ælmihtigan tō lofe, þe hīe on ġelīefdon. Crīst ġesweotolaþ mannum
þruh his mǣran hālgan þæt hē is ælmihtiġ God þe macaþ swelċ
wundru, þēah þe þā earman Iūdēi hine eallunga wiþsōcen, for þæm þe

hīe sind āwierġde, swā swā hīe wȳscton him selfum. Ne beob nān
30 wundru ġeworht æt hiera byrġennum, for bǣm be hīe ne ġelīefab on
bone lifiendan Crīst ; ac Crīst ġesweotolab mannum hwǣr se sōba
ġelēafa is, bonne hē swelċ wundru wyrcb burh his hālgan wīde ġeond
bās eorban. 7æs him sīe wuldor ā mid his heofonlican Fæder and bǣm
Hālgan Gāste, ā būtan ende. Amen.

1   worulde=world.
2   unwittiġ=foolish, innocent, simple. rād=rode. 원형은 rīdan. rīċetere=arrogance.
3   him=them. ætēowian=show. orgellīċe=proudly, insolently. ġesund=sound, healthy,
    uncorrupted.
4   swā hrabe swā=as soon as. āwēdde=went mad. 원형은 āwēdan.
5   wælhrēowlīċe=savagely, cruelly. grymetode=roared, raged. 원형은 grymetian. earmlīċe=
    miserably, wretchedly. ġeendode=ended. 원형은 ġeendian. yflum=evil. 원형은 yfel.
6   ġelīċ=like. ġelēaffulla=believing, pious, devout. pāpa=pope.
7   ġesetnesse=decree, law, narrative. Laurentie=St. Lawrence는 258년에 순교했다. Rōmebyriġ=
    city of Rome. cf. burg=fortified place, city.
8   scēawian=look at, examine, observe. ġe gōde ġe yfle=both good and evil. ġestilde=
    stopped. 원형은 ġestillan.
9   swā bæt=inasmuch as. swulton=sweltan(=to die)의 과거. scēawunge=seeing, examination.
    āne=at one time, at once. āne seofon menn ætgædere=a band of seven men together.
    ætgædre=together.
10 ġeswicon=ceased. 원형은 ġeswīcan. tō scēawienne=to examine. martyr=martyr. menniscum=
    human.
11 ġedwylde=error.
12 Fela=many. folclicre=popular, public, common. 원형은 folcliċ. sprǣċe=speech. be=about,
    concerning.
13 nyllab=ne+willab. ġewrite=writing. hīe=them. 앞에 나오는 wundra(=wonders)를 가리킨
    다. wāt=witan(=to know)의 3인칭 단수. ġehwā=everyone. ac hīe wāt ġehwā=but everyone
    knows of them.
14 sweotol=clear, evident, manifest. swelcum=such. 원형은 swelċ.
15 mæġ=can. ārǣran=raise. dōmes dæġ=Judgement day. ansundne=sound, whole.
16 hielt=hold. 원형은 healdan. hālne=whole, uninjured. sē be hielt Ēadmunde hālne=that
    who keeps Edumund's body whole. miclan dæġ=great day. beah=though.
17 moldan=earth. Wierbe=worthy, deserving. cf. weorb=worth, value. weorbfullan=worthy,
    honourable.
18 weorbiġe=honor, worship. ġelōgiġe=place, furnish.

19   bēowdōme=service. mǣrra=glorious, great. 원형은 mǣre.
20   āsmēġan=conceive, consider, think of. 원형은 āsmēaġan.
21   Nis=ne+is. Angelcynn=the English nation, England. bedǣled=bedǣlan(=to deprive)의 과
      거. bonne=now. Dryhtnes=Lord's. 원형은 Dryhten. bonne=since.
22   licgab=lie. 원형은 licgan. Cūbberht se ēadiga=the blessed Cuthbert.
23   Æbelbrȳb on Ēliġ=St. Æthelthryth(680년 사망)는 Ely의 대 수녀원장(abbess)이었으며, 그
      녀의 여동생 이름은 Seaxburg였다. sweostor=sister.
24   ġelēafan tō trymminge=as a confirmation of the faith. trymminge=confirmation,
      strengthening. Sind=are.
24-25 Angelcynne hālgan=English saints.
25   wyrċab=worked. 원형은 wyrċan. cub=known. 원형은 cunnan.
26   lofe=praise, glory. ġesweotolab=shows. 원형은 ġesweotolian.
27   macab=makes. 원형은 macian.
28   bēah=though. earman=poor, wretched, despicable. Iūdēi=Jews. eallunga=entirely. wibsōcen=
      denied, renounced. 원형은 wibsacan.
28-29 for bǣm be hīe sind āwierġde=wherefore they are accused. cf. Matthew 27 : 25. 'Then
      the people as a whole answered, "His blood be on us and on our children!"'
29   āwierġde=cursed, accursed. 원형은 āwierġan. wȳscton=wished. 원형은 wȳscan.
      him selfum=themselves.
30   ġeworht=ġewyrċan(=to work)의 과거분사. byrġennum=tombs. 원형은 byrġen. cf. byrian=
      to bury.
31   lifiendan=libban(=to live)의 현재분사.
32   ġelēafa=belief, faith. bonne=now, since. ġeond=through(out), as far as.
33   wuldor=glory. ā=ever. mid=with. heofonlican=heavenly.
34   Gāste=spirit. se Hālga Gāst=The Holy Ghost(Spirit). būtan ende=without end.

    There was in that land a certain man called Leofstan, powerful before the
world and foolish before God, who rode to the saint with great arrogance,
and insolently ordered them to show him whether the holy saint was
uncorrupted ; but as soon as he saw the saint's body, he immediately went
insane and roared savagely and ended miserably by an evil death. This is
like what the faithful Pope Gregory said in his treatise about the holy
Lawrence who lies in Rome, that men, both good and evil, were forever
wanting to see how he lay ; but God stopped them, inasmuch as there once
died seven men together in the looking ; then the others left off looking at
the martyr with human foolishness.

We have heard in common talk of many miracles concerning the holy Edmund, which we will not set down here in writing ; but everyone knows of them. By this saint, and by others such, it is clear that Almighty God is able to raise man again at Judgement day, incorruptible from the earth, he who keeps Edmund whole in his body until the great day, although he came from the earth. The place was worthy of the venerable saint, in that men honoured it and supplied it well for Christ's service with pure servants of God, because the saint is more glorious than men might conceive. The English nation is not deprived of the Lord's saints, since in England lie such saints as this saintly king, and the blessed Cuthbert, and in Ely Æthelthryth, and her sister also, incorrupt in body, for the confirmation of the faith. There are also many other saints among the English who work many miracles—as is widely known—to the praise of the Almighty, in whom they believed. Through his glorious saints Christ makes clear to men that he who performs such miracles is Almighty God, even though the wretched Jews completely rejected him ; wherefore they are damned, just as they wished for themselves. There are no miracles performed at their graves, for they do not believed in the living Christ ; but Christ makes clear to men where the true faith is, inasmuch as he performs such miracles through his saints widely throughout this earth. Wherefore to him, with his heavenly Father and the Holy Spirit, be glory for ever. Amen.

(tr. Swanton)

HOMILIES

ST. CUTHBERT

1 7es forsǣda hālga wer wæs ġewunod bæt hē wolde gān on niht tō sǣ, and standan on ðām sealtan brymme oð his swȳran, syngende his ġebedu. 7ā on sumere nihte hlosnode sum ōðer munuc his færeldes, and mid sleaccre stalcunge his fōtswabum filiġde, oð bæt hī bēġen tō sǣ

5 becōmon. Ðā dyde Cūðberhtus swā his ġewuna wæs, sang his ġebedu, on sǣliċere ȳðe standende oð bone swȳran, and syððan his cnēowa on ðām ċeosle ġebīġde, āstrehtum handbredum tō heofenlicum rodere. Efne ðā cōmon twēġen sēolas of sǣlicum grunde, and hī mid heora flȳse his fēt drȳġdon and mid heora blǣde his leoma beðedon, and siððan mid

10 ġebēacne his blētsunge bǣdon, licgende æt his fōton on fealwum ċeosle. 7ā Cūðberhtus ðā sǣlican nȳtenu on sund āsende mid sōðre blētsunge, and on meriġenliċere tīde mynster ġesōhte. Wearð bā se munuc miċċlum āfyrht, and ādliġ on ǣrne-meriġen hine ġeēadmētte tō ðæs hālgan cnēowum, biddende bæt hē his ādl eallunge āflīġde and his

15 fyrwitnysse fæderlīċe miltsode. Se hālga ðā sōna andwyrde : 'Iċ ðīnum ġedwylde dearnunge miltsiġe, ġif ðū ðā ġesihðe mid swīgan bediġlast, oð bæt mīn sāwul heonon sīðiġe, of andwerdum līfe ġelaðod tō heofonan.' Cūðberhtus ðā mid ġebede his scēaweres sēocnysse ġehǣlde and his fyrwites ganges gylt forġeaf.

(여기 인용한 St. Cuthbert와 다음의 St. Gregory는 *Sermones Catholicae*(*Catholic Homilies*)라는 이름의 Ælfric 설교집에서 가져온 것이다. 설교집에는 통상적인 설교 외에 몇몇 성인들의 생애도 소개하고 있다. 여기 실린 글이 그 경우이다.)

1   Cuthbert=Lindisfarne의 주교(bishop)(685-7)였다. forsǣda=aforesaid. wer=man. bes fores ǣda hālga wer=this aforesaid holy man=Cuthbert. ġewunod=accustomed. 원형은 ġewunian. wolde gān=would go. wolde의 원형은 willan.

2   sealtan=salt. brymme=brim(=sea, ocean)의 단수 여격. swȳran=swēora(=neck)의 단수 대

격. syngende=singing.

3 ġebedu=ġebed(=prayer)의 복수 대격. on sumere nihte=one night. hlosnode=heard, listened. 원형은 hlosnian. munuc=monk. færeldes=journey, expedition.

4 sleaccre=sleac(=stealthy)의 단수 여격. stalcunge=stalking. fōtswabum=fōtswæð(=footprint, footstep)의 복수 여격. filiġde=followed. 원형은 filiġan. oð=up to. bēġen=both.

5 ġewuna=custom, wont.

6 sǣliċere=sǣliċ(=of the sea)의 단수 여격. ȳðe=yð(=wave)의 단수 여격. syððan(=siððan)= since, afterwards. cnēowa=cnēo(w)(=knee)의 복수 대격.

7 ċeosle=ċeosol(=gravel)의 단수 여격. ġebīġde=bent, bowed. 원형은 gebīgan. āstrehtum= stretched out. 원형은 āstreċċan. handbredum=palm of a hand. āstrehtum handbredum= (his) palms (being) stretched out. 라틴어의 절대탈격(Dative Absolute)을 모방한 절대여격 (Dative Absolute)으로서, 현대영어의 분사구문에 해당한다. rodere=rodor(=sky, heaven)의 단수 여격.

7-8 Efne ðā=just then. Efne=just.

8 sēolas=seolh(=seal)의 복수. 원형은 seolh. grunde=ground, bottom, depth. heora=their. flȳse=fur, sealskin.

9 fēt=fōt(=foot)의 복수. drȳġdon=dried. 원형은 drȳġan. blǣde=breath. leoma=lim(=limb)의 복수 대격. beðedon=bathed. 원형은 beðian(=to bathe).

10 ġebēacne=ġebēacn(=sign)의 단수 여격. blētsunge=blessing. bǣdon=biddan(=to beg)의 과거. licgende=lying. licgan(=to lie)의 현재분사. fōton=fōtum. 후기 West Saxon의 모습이다. fealwum=fealu(=fallow, dusky, brown)의 단수 여격.

11 nȳtenu=animal. sund=sea, water. 여기서는 대격으로 사용되었다. āsende=sent forth. sōðre=true, just.

12 meriġenliċere=meriġenliċ(=morning)의 단수 여격. tīde=time. mynster=monastery, convent. ġesōhte=ġesēċan(=to seek, visit)의 과거.

13 miċċlum=greatly, much. āfyrt=frightened. 원형은 āfyrhtan. ādliġ=ill. ǣrne-meriġen= early morning. ġeēadmete=humiliated. 원형은 ġeēdmēdan(=to humble, humiliate).

14 cnēowum=cnēo(w)(=knee)의 여격. adl=illness. eallunge=altogether, entirely. āflīġde= āflīġan(=to drive away)의 가정법 과거.

15 fyrwitnysse=curiosity. fæderlīċe=paternally. miltsode=miltsian(=to pity, have compassion on)의 가정법 과거. andwyrde=answered. 원형은 andwyrdan.

16 ġedwylde=ġedwyld(=error)의 단수 여격. dearnunge=secretly. ġesihðe=sight. swīgan= swīġe(=silence)의 여격. bediġlast=conceal. 원형은 bediġlian.

17 sāwul=soul. heonon=hence. sīðiġe=depart. 원형은 sīðian. andwerdum=andweard(=present) 의 단수 여격. ġelðod=invited 원형은 ġeladian.

18 scēaweres=scēawere(=spectator, spy)의 단수 속격. sēocnysse=sēocnes(=sickness)의 단수 대격. ġehǣlde=ġehǣlan(=to heal)의 과거.

19 fyrwites=fyrwit(=curiosity)의 단수 속격. ganges=gang(=journey, going, walk)의 단수 속격. forġeaf=forġiefan(=to forgive)의 과거.

This aforesaid saint was wont that he would go at night to the sea and stand in the salt sea up to his neck, singing his prayers. Then (on) one night another monk listened for his journey and with stealthy stalking followed his footsteps, till they both came to the sea. Then Cuthbert did as was his wont, sang his prayers, standing in the waves of the sea up to the neck, and afterwards bent his knees in the gravel, with (his) palms stretched out to the heavenly sky. Just then came two seals from the ground of the sea, and they dried his feet with their fur and warmed his limbs with their breath, and afterwards with sign(s) begged his blessing, lying at his feet on the brown gravel. Then Cuthbert sent the sea-animals to the water with just blessing, and on the morning-tide visited the monastery. Then the monk was much frightened, and ill in the early morning humbled himself at the saint's knees, entreating that he drove away his illness altogether, and paternally had mercy on his curiosity. The saint then soon answered : 'I shall secretly have mercy on thy error, if thou concealest the sight with silence till my soul depart hence from the present life, invited to heavens.' Cuthbert then healed his observer's sickness with prayer and forgave his guilt of the journey of curiosity.

ST. GREGORY

1   7ā underġeat se pāpa be on bām tīman bæt apostoliċe setl ġesæt, hū
se ēadiga Grēgōrius on hālgum mæġnum bēonde wæs, and hē bā hine
of b̄ære munuclican drohtnunge ġenam, and him tō ġefylstan ġesette,
on diaconhāde ġeendebyrdne. 7ā ġelamp hit æt sumum s̄æle, swā swā
5   ḡyt for oft dēð, bæt Englisce ċypmenn brōhton heora ware tō Rōmāna
byriġ, and Grēgōrius ēode be ð̄ære str̄æt tō ðām Engliscum mannum,
heora ðing sceawiġende. 7ā ġeseah hē betwux ðām warum ċypecnihtas
ġesette, bā w̄æron hwītes līċhaman and fæġeres andwlitan menn, and
æðelīċe ġefexode. Grēgōrius ðā behēold b̄æra cnapena wlite, and befrān
10   of hwilċere bēode hī ġebrōhte w̄æron. 7ā s̄æde him man bæt hī of
Englalande w̄æron, and bæt ð̄ære ðēode mennisc swā wlitiġ w̄ære. Eft
ðā Grēgōrius befrān, hwæðer bæs landes folc Crīsten w̄ære ðe h̄æðen.
Him man s̄æde bæt hī h̄æðene w̄æron. Grēgōrius ðā of inweardre
heortan langsume sicċetunge tēah, and cwæð : 'Wālāwā, bæt swā
15   fæġeres hīwes menn sindon ðām sweartan dēofle underðēodde!' Eft hē
āxode hū ð̄ære ðēode nama w̄ære, be hī of cōmon. Him wæs ġeandwyrd
bæt hī Angle ġenemnode w̄æron. 7ā cwæð hē : 'Rihtlīċe hī sind Angle
ġehātene, for ðan ðe hī engla wlite habbað, and swilcum ġedafenað bæt
hī on heofonum engla ġefēran bēon.' Ḡyt ðā Grēgōrius befrān, hū ð̄ære
20   scīre nama w̄ære be ðā cnapan of āl̄ædde w̄æron. Him man s̄æde bæt ðā
scīrmen w̄æron Dēre ġehātene. Grēgōrius andwyrde : 'Wel hī sind Dēre
ġehātene, for ðan ðe hī sind fram graman ġenerode and tō Crīstes
mildheortnysse ġeċȳġede.' Ḡyt ðā hē befrān : 'Hū is ð̄ære lēode cyning
ġehāten?' Him wæs ġeandswarod bæt se cyning Ælle ġehāten w̄ære.
25   Hwæt, ðā Grēgōrius gamenode mid his wordum tō ðām naman, and
cwæð : 'Hit ġedafenað bæt Alleluia sȳ ġesungen on ðām lande, tō lofe
bæs ælmihtigan Scyppendes.' Grēgōrius ðā sōna ēode tō ðām pāpan bæs
apostlican setles, and hine bæd bæt hē Angelcynne sume lārēowas

āsende, ðe hī tō Crīste ġebiġdon and cwæð bæt hē sylf ġeard wǣre bæt

30 weorc tō ġefremmenne mid Godes fultume, ġif hit ðām pāpan swā
ġelīcode.

1   underġeat=perceived. 원형은 underġietan. se pāpa=the pope. 당시의 법왕은 Pelagius
    II(578-590)였다. apostolīċe=apostolic. '사도의', '로마교황의'. setl=seat, throne. ġesæt=
    ġesittan(=to occupy)의 과거.

2   ēadiga=blessed. hālgum=hāliġ(=holy)의 복수 여격. mæġnum=mæġen(=host, troop)의 복수
    여격. bēonde=thriving, prosperous.

3   munuclican=monastic 원형은 munucliġ. drohtnunge=condition, state. ġenam=took. 원형
    은 ġeniman(=to take). him tō ġefylstan ġesette=appointed him as helper. ġefylstan=
    ġtfylsta(=helper)의 단수 여격. ġesette=placed. 원형은 ġesettan.

4   diaconhāde=deaconship. ġeendebyrdne=ordained. 원형은 ġeendebyrdan. ġelamp=happened.
    원형은 ġelimpan. sǣle=time, season.

4-5 swā swā ġȳt for oft dēð=as it still very often does.

5   ġȳt=ġiet=yet. for=very. oft=often. ċȳpmenn=merchants. ware=waru(ware, article of
    merchandise)의 복수.

6   byriġ=burg(=town, fortified palace)의 여격. be=along. strǣt=street.

7   heora=their. sceawiġende=scēawian(=to observe, espy)의 현재분사. ġeseah=saw. 원형은
    ġesēon. betwux=between, among. ċȳpecnihtas=slave.

8   hwītes=white. liċhaman=body. fæġeres=fair, beautiful. andwlitan=face, countenance.

9   æðelīċe=excellently. ġefexode=haired. behēold=behealdan(=to behold, observe)의 과거.
    wlite=beauty, appearance. befrān=asked. 원형은 befrīnan.

10 hwilċere=which. bēode=nation, people. sǣde=said. 원형은 secgan.

11 mennisc[menniš]=people, nation. wlitiġ=beautiful. Eft=again.

12 hwæðer…ðe=whether…or. Crīsten=Christian. hǣðen=heathen.

13-14 of inweadre heortan=from depths of his heart.

14 langsume=long, prolonged. siċċetunge=sigh. tēah=drew. 원형은 tēon. Wālāwā=alas!

15 fæġeres=beautiful. hīwes=appearance, form. cf. ModE hue. sweartan=black, dark, evil.
    dēofle=dēofol(=devil)의 단수 여격. underðēodde=underðēodan(=to subject)의 과거.

16 āxode=asked. 원형은 āscian[a : skian]. be hī of cōmon=from which they came.
    ġeandwyrd=ġeandwyrdan(=answer)의 과거분사.

17 Rihtlēċe=rightly.

18 ġehātene=ġehātan(=to call)의 과거분사. for ðan ðe=for ðǣm ðe=because. engla wlite=
    angels' appearance. swilcum=such. ġedafenæð=ġedafenian(=to be fitting)의 3인칭 단수
    현재.

19 ġefēran=companions.

20 scīre=shire, district. ālǣdde=ālǣdan(=to lead away)의 과거분사.

21 scīrmen=shiremen. Dēre=Deira(Northumbria의 왕국으로서 지금의 Yorkshire에 해당한다) 의 주민. Deira가 라틴어의 de īrā(=from anger)와 발음이 비슷한 것을 빗대어 fram gramman이라는 말을 재미있게 쓰고 있다.

22 graman=rage, anger. ġenerode=saved, delivered. 원형은 ġenerian.

23 mildheortnysse=mercy. ġecȳġede=ġecȳġan (=to invoke, summon)의 과거분사. Ġyt=still. lēode=people, tribe people.

24 Ælle=Deira의 초대 왕(559–588).

25 gamenode=gamenian(=to joke, jest)의 과거.

26 sȳ=bēon(=to be)의 가정법 단수 현재. ġesungen=sung. 원형은 ġesingan. lofe=praise.

27 ælmitigan=almighty. 원형은 ælmitiġ. Scyppendes=Creator's. sōna=at once, immediately, soon.

28 bæd=biddan(=to beg, ask)의 과거. Angelcynne=English race. lārēowas=teacher, preacher.

29 āsende=āsendan(=to send)의 가정법 과거. ġebīġdon=ġebīġan(=to convert (heathen))의 가 정법. he sylf=he himself. ġeard=ready.

30 weorc=work. tō ġefremmenne=to perform. fultume=help.

31 ġelīcode=ġelīcian(=to please)가정법 과거.

Then perceived the pope who at that time sat on the apostolic seat, how the blessed Gregory was thriving in the holy troops, and he then picked him up from the monastic condition, and made him his helper, being ordained to deaconhood. Then it happened at one time (=one day), as it yet very often does, that English merchants brought their wares to the city of Rome, and Gregory went along the street to the English men, seeing their things. Then he saw, among the wares, slaves set, who were men of white body and fair face, and excellently haired. Gregory then beheld the appearance of those boys, and asked from which country they were brought. Then he was told that they were from England, and that people of that country were so beautiful. Then again Gregory asked whether the folk of the land was Christian or heathen. They told him that they were heathen. Gregory then drew a long sigh from the depth of his heart, and said, 'Alas! that men of so fair appearance are subject to the black devil.' Again he asked how the name of the nation was, where they came from. He was answered that they were named Angles. Then said he, 'Rightly they are called Angles, because they have angels' appearance, and it befits such people that they should be angels' companions in heavens! Still Gregory asked how the name of the shire was, from which they were led away. They told him that the shiremen were called Deirians. Gregory answered, 'They are well called Deirians, because they are delivered from ire, and invoked to Christ's mercy.' Still he asked 'How is the king of the people called?' He was answered that the king was called Ælle. What! then Gregory joked with his words to the name, and said, 'It is fitting that Halleluiah be sung in the land, in praise of the almighty Creator,' Then Gregory at once went to the pope of the apostolic seat, and entreated him that he should send some preachers to the English, whom they converted to Christ, and said that he himself was ready to perform the work with god's help, if it so pleased the pope.

IV. BEDE'S *ECCLESIASTICAL HISTORY OF THE ENGLISH PEOPLE*

DESCRIPTION OF BRITAIN

1   Britannia bæt īġland hit is norbēastlang ; and hit is eahta hund mīla
lang, and twā hund mīla brād. 7onne is be sūðan him on ōðre healfe
bæs sǣs earmes Gallia Belgica ; and on westhealfe on ōðre healfe ðæs
sǣs earmes is Ibernia bæt īġland. Ibernia, bæt wē Scotland hātab, hit
5   is on ǣlċe healfe ymbfangen mid gārsecge ; and for bon be sēo sunne
bǣr gǣb nēar on setl bonne on ōðrum landum, bǣr sindon līðran wederu
bonne on Britannia. 7onne be westannorðan Iberia is bæt ȳtemeste land
bæt man hǣt Thīla, and hit is fēawum mannum cūb for bǣre oferfyrre.
Hēr sindon on Brytene bām īġlande fīf ġebēodu, Englisc. Brytwylsc,
10   Scyttisc, Pihtisc and Bōc-læden. Ǣrest wǣron būend bisses landes
Bryttas ; bā cōmon of Armenia, and ġesǣton sūðanwearde Brytene
ǣrest. 7ā ġelamp hit bæt Pihtas cōmon sūðan of Scithia mid langum
scipum nā manigum, and bā cōmon ǣrest on Norb-Ibernian ūp, and bǣr
bǣdon Scottas bæt hī bǣr mōsten wunian ; ac hī noldon him lȳfan, for
15   bon be hī cwǣdon bæt hī ne mihton ealle ætgædere ġewunian bǣr. And
bā cwǣdon Scottas : 'Wē magon ēow hwǣðere rǣd ġelǣran. Wē witon
ōðer īġland hēr be ēastan bǣr ġē magon eardian, ġif ġē willab. And ġif
hwā ēow wibstent, wē ēow fultumiab, bæt ġē hit magon ġegangan.' 7ā
fērdon bā Pihtas, and ġefērdon bis land norðanweard. Sūðanweard hit
20   hæfdon Bryttas, swā swā wē ǣr cwǣdon ; and bā Pihtas him ābǣdon
wīf æt Scottum, on bā ġerād bæt hī ġecuron heora cynecynn ā on bā
wīfhealfe ; bæt hī hēoldon swā lange sibban. And bā ġelamp ymbe
ġēara ryne bæt Scotta sum dǣl ġewāt of Ibernian on Brytene, and
bæs landes sumne dǣl ġeēodon, and wæs heora heretoga Rēoda ġehāten ;

25 from bām hī sind ġenemnede Dālrēodi.

(Bede(c.672-735)는 Northumbria에서 일생을 보낸 성직자로서 그는 다방면에 걸친 글을 남겼다. 그의 대표작인 *Historia ecclesiastica gentis Anglorum*(*Ecclesiastical History of the English People*)은 Julias Caesar가 영국 땅을 침략했던 BD 60년부터 시작하여 그가 글쓰기를 그만둔 AD 731년까지의 일을 기록하고 있다. 그는 라틴어로 글을 썼으며 *Historia*도 라틴어로 쓰여졌던 것을 Alfred왕(871-99)이 고대영어로 번역토록 한 것이다.)

1 īġland=island. nōrbeastlang=extending to the north-east. eahta hund mīla=eight hundred (of) miles. mīla는 mīl(=mile)의 속격으로서, 이처럼 수사 뒤의 명사가 속격을 취하는 경우가 많다.

2 twā hund mīla brād=two hundred mile broad. 7onne=then. be=by. be sūðan에서처럼 방향을 나타내기 위해 be를 사용하는 관행은 현대영어의 *be*yond에서도 볼 수 있다.

2-3 on ōðre healfe…on ōðre healfe=on one side…on the other side.

3 bæs sæs earmes=of the sea's arm. westhealfe=western side. cf. healf=half.

4 Iberia bæt īġland=Hiberia the island=Iberian which is island. Scotland의 sc는 [š]가 아니라 [sk]로 읽힌다. 한편 지금의 Scotland에 살고 있는 Gaelic족은 본래 Ireland에 살다가 Scotland로 건너 왔기 때문에 옛날에 Scotland라면 지금의 Ireland를 가리킨다. hātab=call. 원형은 hātan.

5 ælċe=each. ymbfangen=ymbfōn(=surround, encompass)의 과거분사. mid gārsecge=with ocean. for bon be=for bǣm be=because.

6 gǣb=goes. 원형은 gān(=to go). nēar=nēah(=near)의 비교급. setl=setting (of the sun). bonne=than. sindon=sind(=are). līðran=līðe(=mild, gentle)의 비교급. wederu=weder (=weather)의 복수.

7 7onne=then. westannorðan=north-western. ȳtemeste=outermost. ūtera(=outer)의 최상급.

8 man=one. hǣt=calls. 원형은 hātan. fēawum mannum cūb=known to few. fēawum= fēa(we)(=few)의 복수 여격. cūb=known. cf. cunnan=to know. oferfyrre=oferfierro(=too great distance)의 단수 여격.

9 ġebēodu=ġebēode(=language)의 복수. Brytwylsc=[brütwülš]=British(=Welsh).

10 Scyttisc=[skütiš]=Scotch(=Irish). Pihtisc=[piçtiš]=Pictish. Bōc-læden=Book Latin=Latin language. Vulgar Latin에 대한 문어체 라틴어를 가리킨다. Ǣrest=ǣr(=previously, before)의 최상급. būend=inhabitant.

11 Bryttas=the Britons. Armenia는 Armonica의 잘못. (Sweet). ġesǣton=ġesittan(=to occupy)의 과거. sūðewearde=southern (part of a place).

12 ġelamp hit=it happened. ġelimp의 원형은 ġelimpan. of=from.

12-13 langum scipum=warship. cf. Lt. navis longa(=long ship).

13 nā manigum=not many. ūp는 윗줄의 cōmon에 연결된다.

14 bǣdon=begged, asked. 원형은 biddan. mōsten=mōtan (=may)의 가정법 과거 복수.

wunian=dwell. noldon=ne+woldon. cf. woldon=willan(=to desire)의 복수 과거. him=hīe (=they)의 여격. ſyfan=līefan(=to allow).

15   mihton=might. 원형은 magan(=may). ealle ætgædere=all together.

16   magon=may. 원형은 magan(=may). hwæðere=however. rǣd=advice, counsel. cf. G. Rat= advice). ġefǣran=teach. witon=know. 원형은 witan.

17   hēr be ēastan=here to the east=to the east of this. eardian= settle, occupy.

18   hwā=any one. wibstent=resists. 원형은 wibstandan. fultumiab=help. 원형은 fultumian. ġegangan=overrun.

19   fērdon=went. 원형은 fēran. ġefērdon=ġefēran(=to gain victory)의 복수 과거. norðanweard=northward.

20   hæfdon=had. swā swā=just as, as. ǣr=previously. cf. ModE, ere. ābǣdon=ābiddan(=to obtain by asking)의 복수 과거.

21   wīf=wife. æt Scottum=from the Irish. on bā ġerād bæt=on the condition that. ġecuron=ġeċēosan(=choose)의 복수 과거. cynecynn=royal line. ā=always.

22   wīfhealfe=female side in inheritance or descent. hēoldon=held. 원형은 healdan. lange sibban=long afterwards.

23   ryne=running course. ymbe ġēara ryne=in the course of years. ryne=course. sum dǣl= some part. ġewāt=departed. 원형은 ġewītan. of=from.

24   ġeēodon=overran. 원형은 ġegān. heretoga=general. ġehāten=called. ġenemnede=ġenemnan (=to name, call)의 과거.

Britain the island it is extending to the north-east ; and it is eight hundred miles long, and two hundred miles broad. Then is to the south to it on one side of the arm of the sea Belgic Gaul ; and on the west side on the other side of the arm of the sea is Hibernia(=Ireland) the island. Hibernia, which we call Scotland, it is on every side surrounded with ocean ; and because the sun there sets nearer to it than in other lands, there are milder weathers than in Britain. Then to the northwest of Ireland is that outermost land which they call Thule, and it is known to few men on account of excessive distance.

Here are in Britain the island five languages, English, British(=Welsh), Scottish(=Irish), Pictish, and Latin. First the inhabitants of this island were Britons ; they came from Armorica, and occupied southern Britain first. Then it happened that Picts came from the south from Scythia with warships not many, and they first came up into North Ireland, and there begged the Irish that they might remain there ; but they would not permit them, because they said that they could not dwell there all together. And then said the Irish : 'We can however teach you advice. We know another island to the east of this where you can dwell, if you will. And if anybody resists you, we help you, that you may conquer it.' Then went the Picts, and overran this land northward. Southward Britons had it, just as we said before ; and the Picts obtained for themselves women from the Irish, on the conditions that they should choose their royal family always on the woman's-side ; that they kept so long afterwards. And then it happened in the course of years that some part of the Irish departed from Ireland to Britain, and overran a part of the land, and their leader was called Rēoda ; from him they are named Dālrēodi.

THE SETTLEMENT OF THE ANGLES, SAXONS AND JUTES

1 Đā was ymb fēower hund wintra and nigon ond fēowertiġ fram ūres
Drihtnes menniscnysse æt Martiānus cāsere rīċe onfēng and VII ġēar
hæfde. Sē wæs syxta ēac fēowertigum fram Agustō aām cāsere. Đā
Angelaēod and Seaxna wæs ġelaðod fram aām foresprecenan cyninge,
5 and on Breotone cōm on arim myclum scypum, and on ēastdǣle ayses
ēalondes eardungstōwe onfēng aurh ðæs ylcan cyninges bebod, ae hī
hider ġelaðode, æt hī sceoldan for heora ēðle compian and feohtan.
And hī sōna compedon wið heora ġewinnan, ae hī oft ǣr norðan
onherġedon ; and Seaxan aā siġe ġeslōgan. 7ā sendan hī hām ǣrenddracan
10 and hēton secgan aysses landes wæstmbǣrnysse and Brytta yrgao.
And hī aā sōna hider sendon māran sciphere strengran wiġhena ; and
wæs unoferswīðendliċ weorud, aā hī tōgædere ġeaēodde wǣron. And
him Bryttas sealdan and ġeafan eardungstōwe betwih him, æt hī for
sibbe and hǣlo heora ēðles campodon and wunnon wið heora fēondum,
15 and hī him andlyfne and āre forġēafen for heora ġewinne.

Cōmon hī of arim folcum ðām strangestan Germānie, æt of Seaxum
and of Angle and of Gēatum. Of Gēata fruman syndon Cantware and
Wihtsǣtan, æt is sēo ðēod ae Wiht æt ēalond oneardað. Of Seaxum,
æt is, of ðām lande ae mon hāteð Ealdseaxan, cōman Ēastseaxan and
20 Sūðseaxan and Westseaxan. And of Engle cōman Ēastengle and
Middelengle and Myrċe and eall Norðhembra cynn ; is æt land ðe
Angulus is nemned, betwyh Gēatum and Seaxum ; is sǣd of aǣre tīde
ae hī ðanon ġewiton oð tō dæġe æt hit wēste wuniġe. Wǣron ðā ǣrest
heora lāttēowas and heretogan tweġen ġebrōðra. Hengest and Horsa.
25 Hī wǣron Wihtgylses suna, aæs fæder wæs Witta hāten, aæs fæder
wæs Wihta hāten, aæs fæder wæs Wōden nemned, of ðæs strynde
moniġra mǣġða cyningcynn fruman lǣdde. Ne wæs ðā ylding tō aon
æt hī hēapmǣlum cōman māran weorod of aām aēodum ae wē ǣr

ġemynegodon. And aæt folc ðe hider cōm ongan weaxan and myclian
30 tō ðan swīðe aæt hī wǣron on myclum eġe aām sylfan landbīgengan ðe
hī ǣr hider laðedon and cȳġdon.

Æfter aissum hī aā ġeweredon tō sumre tīde wið Pehtum, aā hī ǣr
aurh ġefeoht feor ādrifan. And aā wǣron Seaxan sēċende intingan and
tōwyrde heora ġedāles wið Bryttas. Cȳðdon him openlīċe and sǣdon,
35 būton hī him māran andlyfne sealdon, aæt hī woldan him sylfe niman
and herġian aǣr hī hit findan mihton. And sōna ðā bēotunge dǣdum
ġefyldon ; bærndon and herġedon and slōgan fram ēastsǣ oð westsǣ,
and him nǣniġ wiðstōd. Ne wæs unġelīċ wræcc aām ðe iū Chaldēas
bærndon Hierusaleme weallas and ðā cynelican ġetimbro mid fȳre
40 fornāman for ðæs Godes folces synnum. Swā aonne hēr fram aǣre
ārlēasan ðēode, hwæðere rihte Godes dōme, nēh ċeastra ġehwylċe and
land forhereġeode wǣron. Hruran and fēollan cynelico ġetimbro and
ānlīpie, and ġehwǣr sācerdas and mæsseprēostas betwih wībedum
wǣron slæġene and cwylmde ; biscopas mid folcum būton ǣniġre āre
45 scēawunge ætgædere mid īserne and līġe fornumene wǣron. And ne
wæs ǣniġ sē ðe bebyrignysse sealde aām ðe swā hrēowlīċe ācwealde
wǣron. And moniġe ðǣre earman lāfe on wēstenum fanggene wǣron
and hēapmǣlum sticode. Sume for hungre heora fēondum on hand ēodon
and ēcne aēowdōm ġehēton, wiððon ae him mon andlifne forġefe ;
50 sume ofer sǣ sāriġende ġewiton ; sume forhitiende in ēðle ġebīdan and
aearfendum līfe on wuda and on wēstenue and on hēan clifum
sorġiende mōde symle wunodon.

---

1 ymb=around. fēower hund=four hundreds. wintra=winters. nigon ond fēowertiġ=nine
   and forty=forty-nine.
2 Drihtnes=Lord's. menniscnysse=incarnation. Martiānus=Marcian. AD 450-7 사이의 로마
   황제. cāsere=emperor. rīċe=power. onfēng=took. 원형은 onfōn.
2-3 VII ġēar hæfde=held for seven years.
3 Sē=He. syxta ēac fēowertigum=the sixth-plus-fortieth=the forty-sixth (emperor). ēac=
   moreover. Agusto=Augustus (27 BC-AD 14). 로마의 초대 황제.

4 Angelaēod ond Seaxna=the Angle nation and (the nation) of Saxons=the Anglo-Saxon people. wæs ġelaðod=was invited. ġelaðod=ġelaðian(=to invite)의 과거분사. fram=by. foresprecenan cyninge=aforementioned king(=Vortigern).

5 arim=arīe(=three)의 복수 여격. myclum scypum=Bede의 라틴어 원문에서는 'long ships' 로 표현되어 있다. ēastdǣle=eastern part.

6 ēalondes=of the island. eardungstōwe=place of settlement. onfēng=received. 원형은 onfōn. ylcan=same. cyninges bebod=decree. ae=who. hī=them.

7 aæt=(on condition) that. for heora ēðle=for their native land=Britain. heora(=their)는 침략 자들이 아니라 British를 가리킨다. 그러나 다음 문장의 heora는 침략자들을 가리킨다. compian=campain(=fight). feohtan=fight.

8 compedon=campian(=to fight)의 과거. ġewinnan=adversaries. hī=them(=the British). ǣr= previously. norðan=from the north.

9 onherġedon=(that) harassed. 원형은 onherġian. siġe=victory. ġeslōgan=won, strike. 원형 은 ġeslēan. hām=home. ǣrenddracan=messengers.

10 hēton=commanded (them). 원형은 hātan. secgan=to tell about. wæstmbǣrnysse=fertility. Brytta=of the Britons. yrgao=cowardice.

11 māran=more. sciphere=ship-army, fleet. strengran=stronger. 원형은 strang. wiġhena= wiġa(=warrior)의 복수 속격.

12 unoferswīðendliċ=invincible. weorud=company, band, host. ġeaēodde=joined, united. 원형 은 ġeaēodan.

13 sealdan=gave. 원형은 sellan. ġeafan=granted. 원형은 ġiefan. betwih=among. him=them. aæt=so…that.

14 sibbe=peace. hǣlo=security. campodon=fought. 원형은 campian. wunnon=struggled. 원형 은 winnan. fēondum=fēond (=enemy)의 복수여격.

15 andlyfne=andlēan(=reward)의 단수 대격. āre=ār(=benefit)의 단수 대격. forġēafen=gave. 원형은 forġiefan. ġewinne=labor, war.

16 of=from. folcum=tribes. strangestan=most powerful. strang(=strong)의 최상급. Germānie= of the Germans. Seaxum=the Saxons.

17 Angle=the Angles. Ġēatum=the Jutes. Of Ġēata fruman syndon=From the origin of the Jutes are…=Descended from the Jutes are…. fruman=origin. Cantware=inhabitants of Kent.

18 Wihtsǣtan=inhabitants of Wight people. ðēod=people. Wiht=Isle of Wight. ēalond=island. oneardað=oneardian(=to inhabit)의 현재 단수.

19 mon hāteð=man called. Ealdseaxan=Old Saxony.

21 Myrċe=Mercians. Norðhembra=of the Northumbrians. cynn=race. Is aæt land ðe=that is the land that….

22 Angulus=Angles의 라틴어. betwyh(betwux)=among, between.

22-23 is sǣd of āǣre tīde ae hī ðanon ġewiton oð tō dæġe aæt=hit is sǣd aæt, of āǣre tīde ae…=it is said that from the time they left until the present…. tīde=time.

23 ðanon=from there. ġewiton=departed. 원형은 ġewitan. wēste=desolate. wuniġe=remains. 원형은 wunian. ǣrest=at first.

24 lāttēowas=leaders. heretogan=commanders. tweġen ġebrōðra=two brothers.

25 wæs Witta hāten=was called Wihta. aæs=whose.

26 strynde=stock, race.

27 monigra=maniġ(=many)의 복수 속격. mǣġða=tribes. cyningcynn=royal line. fruman ǣdde=took origin=derived their origin. ylding=delay. tō aon=after that.

28 hēapmǣlum=in troops, in droves. aæt hī cōman māran weorod=that more troops came.

29 ġemynegodon=mentioned. 원형은 ġemynegian. ongan=began. 원형은 onġinnan. weaxan= grow. myclian=increase.

30 tō aan swīðe aæt=to such an extent that. on myclum eġe=as a great terror=a cause of great terror. eġe=fear, dread, terror. landbīgengan=native inhabitants.

31 laðedon=invited. 원형은 laðian. ċȳġdon=summoned. 원형은 ċīeġan.

32 ġeweredon=made an (defensive) alliance. 원형은 ġewerian. tō=at. sumre=a certain. wið= with. Pehtum=the Picts. aā=whom.

33 aurh ġefeoht=through battle. feor=far. ādrifan=had driven away. sēċende=seeking. 원형 은 sēċan. intingan=occasion, cause.

34 tōwyrde=opportunity. heora ġedāles wið Bryttas=for their breaking from the Britons. ġedāl=separation. Ċȳðdon=proclaiemd. 원형은 ċȳaan. openlīċe=openly.

35 būton=unless. andlyfne=andleofen(=food, money)의 단수 대격. aæt hī woldan him sylfe=they would ⋯ for themselves. niman=seize.

36 herġian=plunder. hī hit findan mihton=they might find it. 여기서 hit는 andleofen을 가리 킨다. 주목할 것은 선행사인 andleofen이 여성명사임에도 불구하고 여기서는 중성의 대명 사 hit가 사용되었다는 사실이다. 자연성(natural gender)의 예이다. bēotunge=threats. dǣdum=with deeds. 원형은 dǣd.

37 ġefyldon=ġefyllan(=to fulfill)의 과거. bærndon=bærnan(=to burn)의 과거. herġedon= plundered. 원형은 herġian. slōgan=slēan (=to slay)의 과거. ēastsǣ=eastern sea. westsǣ= western sea.

38 nǣniġ=none. wiðstōd=resisted. 원형은 wiðstand. unġelīċ=unlike. wræcc=vengeance. 원형 은 wracu. iū=formerly. Chaldēas=Chaldeans.

39 weallas=walls. cynelican=royal, public. ġetimbro=buildings. fȳre=fire.

40 fornāman=destroyed. 원형은 forniman. synnum=sin. Swā aonne hēr=Thus, therefore(aonne), at this time(hēr). fram=on account of.

41 ārlēasan=impious. ðēode=people. hwæðere rihte Godes dōme=and indeed by God's just decree. hwæðere=nevertheless, yet. rihte=right. dōm=decree. nēh ċeastra=neighboring towns. ġehwylċe=each. 속격과 함께 쓰인다.

42 forhereġeode=forherġian(=to ravage)의 과거분사. Hruran=Crumbled. 원형은 hrēosan. fēollan=fell. 원형은 feallan.

42-43 cynelico ġetimbro ond ānlīpie=royal private buildings.

43   ānlīpie(ānlēpe)=private. ġehwǣr=everywhere. sācerdas=priests. mæsseprēostas=mass-priests(=secular priests). 일반 신도들의 지도를 담당한다. betwih= among. wībedum=altars.

44   slæġene=slēan(=to slay)의 과거분사. cwylmde=murdered. 원형은 cwylmian. būton= without. æniġre=any. āre=of respect.

45   scēawunge=regard, show. ætgædere=bishops and people together. mid īserne=with iron (sword). līġe=fire. fornumene=forniman(=to destroy)의 과거분사.

45-46   ne wæs æniġ sē ðe=there was none, he who⋯=there was no one who⋯.

46   bebyrignysse=burial. sealde=might give. aām=to those. hrēowlīċe=cruelly. ācwealde= ācwellan(=to kill)의 과거분사.

47   moniġe=many. ðǣre=se(=that)의 단수 속격. earman=wretched. lāfe=remnant. wēstenum= wēsten(=wasteland)의 복수 여격. fanggene=fōn(=to capture)의 과거분사.

48   hēapmǣlum=in troops. sticode=stician(=to stab, butcher)의 과거분사. butchered. fēondum= fēond(=enemy)의 복수 여격. on hand ēodon=went into the hand=yielded to=surrendered to. ēodon=went. 원형은 gān.

49   ēcne=perpetual. aēowdōm=servitude. ġehēton=promised. 원형은 ġehātan. wiðaon ae= provided that. mon=someone, people. andlifne=andleofen(=food)의 대격. forġefe=gave. 가정법.

50   sāriġende=grieving. 원형은 sārian. ġewiton=went. 원형은 ġewītan. forhitiende=in fear. ēðle=native land. ġebīdon=remained. 원형은 ġebīdan.

51   aearfende=needy. wuda=wudu(=forest)의 단수 여격. hēan=hēah(=high)의 단수 대격. clifum=crags.

52   sorġiende=sorgian(=to grieve)의 현재분사. mōde=heart, mind. symle=continuously. wunodon=lived. 원형은 wunian.

It was about four hundred and forty-nine years after our Lord's incarnation that the Emperor Martian acceded to the throne and he held it for seven years. He was also the forty-sixth after the emperor Augustus. Then the people of the Angles and Saxons were invited by the aforesaid king [Vortigern] and came to Britain in three large ships, and they received a place to live in the east part of the island through the instruction of that same king who invited them here, so that they might battle and fight on behalf of the homeland. And immediately, they fought against their enemies who had often previously attacked them from the north ; and the Saxons won the victory. Then they sent a messenger home and instructed him to speak about the fertility of this land and the cowardice of the Britons. And straightaway they sent here more naval forces with stronger warriors ; and this was to be an invincible army when they were united together. And the Britons offered and gave them a place to live among themselves, so that for peace and for prosperity they would fight and battle for their homeland against their enemies, and they gave them provisions and property because of their battles.

They came from among the three most powerful Germanic tribes, those of the Saxons, the Angles and the Jutes. Of Jutish origins are the people in Kent and people of the Isle of Wight : that is the people who inhabit the Isle of Wight. From the Saxons, that is from that land which is called Saxony, come those in Essex, Sussex and Wessex. And from the Angles come the East Anglians and Middle Anglians and Mercians and all the people of Northumbria. That land which is called Angeln is between Jutland and Saxony ; it is said that from the time they left there until the present day that it remains deserted. The first of their leaders and commanders were two brother, Hengest and Horsa. They were the sons of Wihtgyls, whose father was called Wihta, this Wihta's father was named Woden, from whose lineage many tribes of royal races claimed their origin. It was not long before many troops came in crowds from those people that we mentioned before. And the people who came here began to expand and grow to the extent that they were a great terror to those same inhabitants who had previously invited and summoned them here.

After this, they were united by agreement with the Picts, whom they had previously driven far away through battle. And then the Saxons were seeking a cause and opportunity for their separation from the Britons. They informed them openly and said to them that unless they gave them more provisions they would take it and plunder it themselves wherever they might find it. And immediately the threat was carried out ; they burned and ravaged and murdered from the east coast to the west, and no one withstood them. This was not unlike the former vengeance of the Chaldeans when they burned the walls of Jerusalem and destroyed the royal buildings with fire because of the sins of the people of god. Thus here because of the graceless people, yet with the righteous judgement of God, nearly every city and land was ravaged. Royal private buildings were razed to the ground, and everywhere priests and mass-priests were murdered and killed among their altars ; bishops with the people, without being shown any mercy, were destroyed with sword and fire together. And nor was there any burial given to those who were so cruelly killed. And many of the wretched survivors were captured in the wastelands and stabbed in groups. Because of hunger, some went into the hands of the enemy and promised perpetual slavery with the provision that they be given sustenance ; some went sorrowing over the sea ; some remaiend, always fearful, in their native land, and lived in deprivation in the deserted woods or dwelled on high cliffs, always with a mournful mind.

(tr. Treharne)

V. ANGLO-SAXON CHRONICLE

THE VIKING INVASION

1   855 Hēr hǣane menn ǣrest on Scēapīeġe ofer winter sǣton. And āy
ilcan ġēare ġebōcode Ǣaelwulf cyning tēoaan dǣl his landes ofer eall
his rīċe Gode tō lofe, and him selfum tō ēċre hǣlu ; and āy ilcan ġēare
fērde tō Rōme mid miċelre weoranesse, and āǣr wæs twelf mōnaa

5   wuniende, and aā him hāmweard fōr. And him aā Carl Francna cyning
his dohtor ġeaf him tō cwēne ; and æfter āǣm tō his lēodum cōm, and
hīe aæs ġefæġene wǣron. And ymb twā ġēar aæs ae hē on Francum
cōm, hē ġefōr ; and his līċ līa æt Wintanċeastre. And hē rīcsode
nigontēoae healf ġēar.

10   865 Hēr sæt hǣaen here on Tenet, and ġenāmon fria wia Cantwarum,
and Cantware him feoh ġehēton wia aām friae ; and under āǣm friae
and āǣm feohġehāte se here hine on niht ūp bestæl, and oferhergode
ealle Cent ēastewearde.

866 Hēr fēng Ǣaelred Ǣaelbryhtes brōaor tō Westseaxna rīċe. And āy

15   ilcan ġēare cōm miċel here on Angelcynnes land, and wintersetl nāmon
on Ēastenglum, and āǣr ġehorsode wurdon ; and hīe him wia fria
nāmon.

867 Hēr fōr se here of Ēastenglum ofer Humbre-mūaan tō Eoforwīcċeastre on Norahymbre. And āǣr wæs miċel unġeawǣrnes āǣre

20   aēode betwix him selfum, and hīe hæfdon hiera cyning āworpenne
Ōsbryht, and unġecyndne cyning underfēngon Ǣllan. And hīe late on
ġēare tō āǣm ġeċierdon aæt hīe wia aone here winnende wǣron ; and hīe
aēah micle fierd ġegadrodon, and aone here sōhton æt Eoforwīcċeastre ;

and on aā ċeastre brǣcon, and hīe sume inne wurdon. And aǣr wæs

25 unġemetliċ wæl ġeslægen Noraanhymbra, sume binnan, sume būtan, and aā cyningas beġen ofslæġene ; and sēo lāf wia aone here fria nam.

868 Hēr fōr se ilca here innan Mierċe tō Snotingahām, and aǣr wintersetl nāmon ; and Burgred Mierċna cyning and his witan bǣdon Æaelred Westseaxna cyning and Ælfred his brōaor aæt hīe him ġefultumoden

30 aæt hīe wia aone here ġefuhten. And aā fērdon hīe mid Westseaxna fierde innan Mierċe oa Snotingahām, and aone here aǣr mētton on aǣm ġeweorce ; and aǣr nān hefeliċ ġefeoht ne weara, and Mierċe fria nāmon wia aone here.

869 Hēr fōr se here eft tō Eoforwīċċeastre and aǣr sæt i ġear.

35 870 Hēr rād se here ofer Mierċe innan Ēastengle and wintersetl nāmon æt 7eodforda. And aȳ wintra Ēadmund cyning him wia feaht and aa Deniscan siġe nāmon and aone cyning ofslōgon and aæt land all ġeēodon.

(Alfred왕에 의해 시작된 *Anglo-Saxon Chronicle*은 한국의 삼국사기에 해당하는 문헌이다. 891년에 시작되었으며, AD 43년의 Julius Caesar의 영국 침략에서 시작하여 Alfred 시대까지의 역사적 사건들을 연대순으로 기록하고 있다. 작업이 시작된 891년에서 AD 43년까지의 850년간의 기사는 Bede의 *Historia Ecclesiastica*에 의존하고 있다. 작업은 Norman Conquest 이후에도 계속되다가 Stephen왕이 서거하는 1154년에 끝난다.)

1 Hēr=here=at this point in the series=at this date=in this year. 매해 기사 첫 머리에 상투적으로 쓰이는 표현이다. hǣane men=heathen men. ǣrest=first. sǣton=remained. 원형은 sittan.

1-2 aȳ ilcan ġēare=in the same year. ilcan=same. ġebōcode=ġebōcian(=to grant by charter)의 과거. tēoaan dǣl=tenth part. tēoaan=tenth. dǣl=part, share.

3 Gode tō lōfe=to the glory of God. lōf=glory, fame. him selfum tō ēċre hǣlu=for his own perpetual security. ēċe=eternal. hǣlo=security, safety.

4 miċelre=much. weoranesse=splendor.

5 wuniende=wunian(=to stay)의 현재분사. hāmweard=homewards. fōr=traveled. 원형은

faran.

6   his dohtor ġeaf him tō cwēne=gave him his daughter for a queen. tō his lēodum=to his people.

7   ġefæġene=happy, glad. ymb=about. on=from.

8   ġefōr=ġefēran(=to go, journey, depart)의 과거. 여기서는 '서거했다'의 뜻. liċ=body. līa= licgan(=to lie)의 3인칭 단수. Wintanċeastre=Winchester. rīcsode=ruled. 원형은 rīcsian.

9   nigontēoae=nineteen. nigontēoae healf=nineteen and a half.

10   sæt=remained. 원형은 sittan. hǣaen=heathen. here=army. Tenet=Thanet. ġenāmon=took. 원형은 ġeniman. fria=peace. Cantwarum=inhabitants of Kent.

11   him=to them. feoh=money. ġehēton=promised. 원형은 ġehātan.

12   feohġehāte=promise of money. hiene=뒤에 오는 bestelan의 재귀대명사. ūp=up. bestæl= bestelan(=to steal away)의 과거. 재귀대명사(hiene)와 함께 쓰인다. oferhergode= oferherġean(=to overrun, ravage)의 과거.

13   ealle Cennt ēastewearde=all the east of Kent. ēastwearde=eastwards.

14   fēng=took. 원형은 fōn. fēng tō rīce=succeeded to the throne.

15   ilcan=same. ġeare=year. wintersetl=winter quarters. nāmon=took. 원형은 niman.

16   ġehorsode=ġehorsian(=to provide with horses)의 과거분사. wurdon=became. 원형은 weoraan.

16-17   hīe him wia fria nāmon=they made peace with them.

18   fōr=travelled. 원형은 faran. of=from. Humbre=Humber 강. mūaan=mouth.

18-19   Eoforwiċċeastre=York. Norahymbre=Northumbria. unġeawǣrnes=discord, conflict.

20   aēode=people. betwix=between. him selfum=themselves. hæfdon=had. 원형은 habban. āworpenne=āweorpan(=to throw away)의 과거분사.

21   unġecyndne=alien. underfēngon=accepted. 원형은 underfōn. late on ġeare=late in that year.

22   aǣm=후속하는 aæt절의 선행사. tō aǣm ġeċierdon aǣt=they turned to (that, namely) fighting against the Danish army. ġeċierdon=ġeċierran(=to turn, come)의 과거. aæt=so that. winnende=winnan(=to struggle)의 현재분사. wǣron=were. aēah=though, however.

23   micle fierd=national army, Anglo-Saxon army ġegadrodon= gathered. 원형은 ġegadrian. sōhton=sought. 원형은 sēċan(=to seek). Eoforwīċċeastre= York.

24   ċeastre=town, fort. brǣcon=broke. 원형은 brecan. hīe sume=some (of) them. inne wurdon=got in. wurdon=became. 원형은 weoraan.

25   unġemetliċ=immense. wæl=slaughter. ġeslæġen=slēan(=to slay)의 과거분사. binnan= within. būtan=outside.

26   beġen=both. sēo=bēon(=to be)의 가정법 현재. lāf=leaving, remnant, survivor

27   fōr=travelled. 원형은 faran. Mierċe=Mercia. Snotingahām=Nottingham.

28   witan=adviser. bǣdon=biddan(=to ask)의 과거.

29   ġefultumadon=fultumian(=to help)의 가정법 과거.

30   ġefuhton=fought. 원형은 ġefeohtan. fērdon=fēran(=to go, journey)의 과거.

31 innan=within, into. mētton=met. 원형은 mētan.

32 ġeweorce=work, fortification. nān=no. hefeliċ=heavy, serious. weara=happened. 원형은 weoraan.

34 eft=again. sæt=dwelled. 원형은 sittan. i ġear=one year.

35 rād=rode. 원형은 rīdan.

36 āy wintra=that winter. Ēadmund cyning him wia feaht=King Edmund fought with them. feaht=fēon(=to fight)의 과거.

37 Deniscan=the Danes=Vikings. siġe=victory. ofslōgon=slayed. 원형은 ofslēan.

38 ġeēodon=ġegān(=to overrun, conquer)의 과거.

855 In this year, for the first time, the heathen men settled in Sheppey during the winter. And in the same year King Æthelwulf granted a tenth part of his land by charter over all his kingdom, to the glory of God and for his own perpetual salvation. And in the same year he went to Rome with great splendour, and he stayed there for twelve months, and then journyed homewards. And then Charles, king of the Franks, gave him his daughter for a queen, and after that he came back to his people and they were happy at that. And about two years after he came back from Francia, he died, and his body lies at Winchester, and he ruled for eighteen and a half years.

865 In this year the heathen Viking army remained in Thanet, and made a peace with the people of Kent ; and the people of Kent promised them money in order to have that peace. And under the peace and the promise of money, the Viking army moved away stealthily by night and ravaged all of eastern Kent.

866 In this year Æaelred, Æaelberth's brother, succeeded to the kindgon of the West Saxons ; and in the same year a great Viking army arrived in the land of the English and took winter quarters in East Anglia, and there they were given horses, and they made peace with them.

867 In this year the Viking army travelled from East Anglia over the mouth

of the River Humber to the city of York in Northumbria ; and there was great conflict of that people among themselves ; and they had deposed Osberht their king and accepted an alien king, Ælla. And it was late in that year when they turned their attention to fighting against the Viking army, and even so, they gathered a great army and went after the Viking army at York and stormed the city, and some of them got inside ; and there was violent slaughter of the Northumbrians there, some inside, some outside, and the kings were both killed, and those who survived made peace with the Viking army. And in the same year, Bishop Ealhstan died, and he held that see for fifty years at Sherborne, and his body lies there in the town.

868 In this year that same Viking army travelled into Mercia to Nottingham, and took winter quarters there. And Burhred, king of the Mercians, and his witan asked Æaelred, king of Wessex, and Ælfred, his brother, that they help them fight against the Viking army. And then they travelled with the West Saxon army into Mercia up to Nottingham, and there they met the Viking army in that fortified place, and no serious battle happened there, and the Mercians made a peace with the Viking army.

869 In this year the Viking army went to York again, and remained there for one year.

870 In this year the Viking army rode through Mercia into East Anglia, and took winter quarters at Thetford. And that winter King Edmund fought against them, and the Danes gained the victory, and murdered the king, and occupied the entire region.

(tr. Treharne)

ALFRED'S WAR WITH THE DANES

1 897   7ȳ ilcan ġēare drehton bā herġas on Ēastenglum ond on
Norðhymbrum Westseaxna lond swīðe be bǣm sūðstæðe mid
stælherġum, ealra swībust mid bǣm æscum be hīe fela ġēara ǣr
timbredon. 7ā hēt Ælfred cyng timbran lang scipu onġēn ðā æscas ;
5 bā wǣron ful nēah tū swā lange swā bā ōðru ; sume hæfdon LX āra,
sume mā ; bā wǣron ǣġðer ġe swiftran, ġe unwealtran, ġe ēac hīerran
bonne bā ōðru ; nǣron nāwðer ne on Frēsisc ġescæpene ne on Denisc,
būton swā him selfum ðūhte bæt hīe nyttwyrðoste bēon meahten. 7ā
sumum ċirre bæs ilcan ġēares cōmon bǣr sex scipu tō Wiht, ond bǣr
10 myċel yfel ġedydon, ǣġðer ġe on Defenum ġe wel hwǣr be ðǣm
sǣriman. 7ā hēt se cyng faran mid nigonum tō bāra nīwena scipa ; ond
forfōron him bone mūðan foran on ūtermere. 7ā fōron hīe mid brim
scipum ūt onġēn hīe, ond brēo stōdon æt ufeweardum bǣm mūðan on
drȳġum ; wǣron bā menn uppe on londe of āgāne. 7ā ġefēngon hīe
15 bāra brēora scipa tū æt ðǣm mūðan ūteweardum, ond bā menn
ofslōgon, ond bæt ān oðwand ; on bǣm wǣron ēac bā menn ofslæġene
būton fīfum ; bā cōmon for bȳ on weġ be bāra ōberra scipu āsǣton. 7ā
wurdon ēac swīðe unēðelīċe āseten : brēo āsǣton on ðā healfe bæs
dēopes ðe ðā Deniscan scipu āseten wǣron, ond bā ōðru eall on ōbre
20 healfe, bæt hira ne mehte nān tō ōðrum. Ac bā bæt wæter wæs āhebbad
fela furlanga from bǣm scipum, bā ēodon ðā Deniscan from bǣm brim
scipum tō bǣm ōðrum brim be on hira healfe beebbade wǣron, ond hīe
bā bǣr ġefuhton. 7ǣr wearð ofslæġen Lucumon cynges ġerēfa, ond
Wulfheard Frīesa, ond Æbbe Frīesa, ond Æðelhere Frīesa, ond Æðelferð
25 cynges ġenēat, ond ealra monna, Frēsiscra ond Engliscra LXII, ond bāra
Deniscena CXX. 7ā cōm bǣm Deniscum scipum bēh ǣr flōd tō, ǣr bā
Crīstnan mehten hira ūt āscūfan, ond hīe for ðȳ ūt oðrēowon. 7ā wǣron
hīe tō bǣm ġesārgode bæt hīe ne mehton Sūðseaxna lond ūtan

berōwan, ac hira bǣr tū sǣ on lond wearp ; ond bā menn mon lǣdde tō
30 Winteċeastre tō bǣm cynge, ond hē hīe ðǣr āhōn hēt ; ond bā menn
cōmon on Ēastengle be on bǣm ānum scipe wǣron swīðe forwundode.

1 7̄y=þæt의 조격(instrumental case). ilcan=same. drehton=harassed, afflicted. 원형은
dreċċan. herġas=here(=army, predatory troop)의 복수. here는 현대영어의 harry(=침략하
다)와 동일 어원의 단어로서 Danish army의 뜻으로 사용되었다. Ēastenglum=
Eastengle(=East-Anglia)의 여격.

2 Norðhymbrum=Norðhymbre(=Northumbria)의 여격. Westseaxna=Westseaxe(=West Saxons)
의 속격. swīðe=greatly. be=along. sūðstæðe=sūðstæð(=south coast)의 여격. stælherġum=

3 stælhere=stælhere(=predatory army)의 복수 여격. earla=eall(=all)의 속격. swībust
(=swībost)=swībe(=greatly)의 최상급. æscum=æsc(=ash-tree(물푸레나무)). 여기서는 물푸
레나무로 만든 덴마크의 배를 가리킨다. fela ġeara ǣr=few years before.

4 timbredon=built. hēt=bade. 원형은 hātan(=to bid). onġēan=against.

5 ful nēah=full nearly. tū swā lange swā=twice as long as. LX=(L(50)+X(10))=60.
āra=ār(=oar)의 복수 속격.

6 mā=more. ǣġðer ġe···ġe=both···and. swiftran=swift(=swift)의 비교급. unwealtran=
unwealt(=steady)의 복수 비교급. ēac=also. hīerran=higher. hēah(=high)의 비교급.

7 bā ōðru=the others. nǣron=were not. ne(=not)+wǣron(=were). nāwðer=neither. nāwðer···
ne(···ne)=neither···nor(···nor).
on Frēsisc=on the Frisian (Danish) model. ġescæpene=ġescieppan(=to shape, make)의 과
거분사. 선행하는 nǣron과 함께 수동태를 이룬다. on Denisc =in a Danish manner.

8 būton=but. ðūhte=seemed. 원형은 ðynċan. nyttwyrðoste=nyttwyrðe(=useful)의 최상급.
meahten=magan(=may)의 가정법 과거 복수.

9 ċirre=ċierr(=time, occasion)의 단수 여격.

10 ġedydon=did. 원형은 ġedōn. Defenum=Eevon. ǣġðer ġe···ġe=both···and. wel hwǣr=
nearly everywhere.

11 sǣriman=coast. cyng=king. nigon=nine. nīwena=nīew(=new)의 복수 속격.

12 forfōron=obstructed, blockaded. 원형은 forfaran. 주어는 앞의 nigonum···nīwena scipa.
mūðan=mūða(=mouth of river)의 단수 대격. foran=in front. utermere=outsersea, open
sea.

12-13 fōron···ūt=went out. fōron은 faran(=march)의 복수 과거. mid brim schipum=with three
ships.

13 stōdon=stood. 여기서는 좌초했다는 뜻. 원형은 standan. ufeweardum=upper, further up.

14 drȳġum=dry. uppe=up, above. uppe on=above on, upon. āgāne=went away. 원형은 āgān.
ġefangon=ġefōn(=to catch, seize)의 복수 과거.

15 bāra brēora scipa tū=two of those three ships. brēora=brīe(=three)의 속격. tū=two. 원형
은 twēgen. ūteweardum=outward, extreme. æt bǣm mūðan ūteweardum=outseide the

mouth of the river.

16   ofslōgon=killed. 원형은 ofslēan. oðwand=escaped. 원형은 oðwindan. wǣron···ofslæġene=
were killed.

17   būton fīfum=except five. for bȳ=뒤의 be와 함께 한 덩어리가 되어 because의 뜻. on
weġ=away. oberra=ober(=other)의 복수 속격. āsǣton=āsittan(=to run aground)의 복수 과
거.

18   wurdon=weorðan(=to become, come about)의 복수 과거로서 후속하는 āseten과 더불어 수
동태를 이룬다. swīðe unēðelīċe=very inconveniently. āseten=āsittan(=to run aground)의
과거분사. healfe=side.

19   dēopes=depth. ðe ðā Deniscan=where those Danish.

20   mehte=might. 원형은 magan. āhebbad=ebbed away. 원형은 āhebbian.

21   fela=many. furlanga=furlong. 220 yards, ⅛ mile. ēodon=went. 원형은 gān.

22   beebbade=stranded. 원형은 beebbian.

23   ġefuhton=fought. 원형은 ġefeohtan. ġerēfa=reeve, officer, prefect. 지방 행정관.

24   Wulfheard Frīesa=Wulfheard the Frisian.

25   ġenēat=comrade, vassal. LXII=62.

26   CXX=120. bēh(=beah)=yet, however. 통상적으로 문장 한 가운데 놓인다. ǣr···ǣr=before.

27   āscūfan(=āscēofan)=pushed away. 원형은 āscūfan. for ðy=therefore. oðrēowon=oðrōwan
(=to row away)의 복수 과거.

28   tō bǣm···bæt=to that (degree)···that, so···that. ġesārgode=wounded. 원형은 ġesārgian.

29   berōwan=row round. bǣr=there. sǣ=sea. wearp=weorpan(=to throw, cast)의 단수 과거.
mon(=man) lǣdde=one led, i.e. were led.

30   āhōn=to hang. āhōn hēt=ordered to hang.

31   forwundode=badly wounded. 원형은 forwundian.

The same year the (Danish) armies in East Anglia and in Northumbria much
harassed the West Saxons' land along the south coast with plundering
armies, especially with the ships of war that they had built many years
before. Then King Alfred bade build long ships to oppose the (Danish) ships ;
they were full nearly twice as long as the others ; some had sixty oars, some
more ; they were both swifter and steadier and also higher than the others :
(they) were made neither on the Frisian (model), nor yet on the Danish, but
(only) so as it seemed to (the King) himself that they might be most useful.
Now at a certain season of the same year there came six ships to Wight,
and there much harm they did, both in Devon and nearly everywhere by the
sea-coast. Then the King gave orders to go (against them) with nine of the

new ships, and they blockaded from them the mouth (of the river) on the outer sea. Then they (i.e. the Danes) went out with three ships against them, and three stood aground at the upper part of the mouth ; the men had gone away into the land ; then they (i.e. English) took two of the three (Danish) ships on the outside of the mouth and killed the men, and the one (ship) escaped : in that too were the men slain but five. They got away because the others' (i.e. Englishmen's) ships had run aground. They too ran aground in a most inconvenient way,—three ran aground on that side of the water where the Danish ships were grounded, and the others all on the other side, so that none of them might (get) to the others. But when the water had ebbed many furlongs from the ships, the Danes went from the three ships to the other three (English ships) that were stranded on their side, and there they fought them. There Lucumon the king's reeve was slain, and (so was) Wulfheard the Frisian, and Ebba the Frisian, and Etherhere the Frisian, and Ethelfrith the king's companion, and in all, of Frisians and Englishmen, two and sixty ; and of Danes, a hundred and twenty. But, however, the tide reached the Danish ships before the Christians were able to shove theirs off, and they (i.e. Danes) therefore rowed away. And they were so wounded that they could not row round the south Saxons's land ; but two of the ships the sea cast ashore there, and the men were taken to Winchester to the King, and he gave orders (to his men) to hang them (forthwith) ; and the men that were in the one (i.e. the third) ship came to East Anglia, sore wounded.

VI. APOLLONIUS OF TYRE

APOLLONIUS OF TYRE (1)

1   Ðā Apollonius þæt ġehīerde, hē þām ġehīerdsumode and ēode forð mid
þām menn, oð þæt hē becōm tō ðæs cyninges healle. Ðā ēode sē mann
in beforan tō ðām cyninge and cwæð, "Sē forlidena monn is cumen, be
ðū æfter sendest, ac hē ne mæġ for scame in gān būton scrūde." Ðā
5   hēt sē cyning hine sōna ġescrȳdan mid weoðfullum scrūde ond hēt hine
in gān tō ðǣm ġereorde.

Ðā ēode Apollonius in and ġesæt bǣr him ġetāht wæs onġean ðone
cyning. Ðǣr wearð ðā sēo beġnung in ġeboren ond æfter bǣm cynelīċ
ġebeorscipe ; ond Apollonius nān ðing ne ǣt, ðēah ðe ealle ōðre menn
10   ǣton and blīðe wǣron. Ac hē behēold þæt gold ond þæt seolfor ond ðā
dēorwierðan rēaf ond þā bēodas and ðā cynelīcan beġnunga.

Ðā ðā hē þis eall mid sārnesse behēold, ðā sæt sum eald ond sum
æfestiġ ealdormann be þām cyninge. Mid þȳ be hē ġeseah þæt
Apollonius swā sārlīċe sæt ond eall þing behēold ond nān ðing ne ǣt,
15   ðā cwæð hē tō ðām cyninge, "Ðū gōda cyning, efne þēs monn, be þū
swā wel wið ġedēst, hē is swīðe æfestful for ðīnum gōde." Ðā cwæð sē
cyning, "7ē misþyncð ; sōðlīċe þēs ġeonga mann ne æfestað on nānum
ðingum ðe hē hēr ġesiehð, ac hē cȳðð þæt hē hæfð fela forloren.

Ðā beseah Arcestrates sē cyning blīðe andwlitan tō Apollonio ond
20   cwæð, "Ðū ġeonga monn, bēo blīðe mid ūs and ġehyht on God þæt þū
mōte self tō ðām sēlrum becuman." Mid þȳ ðe cyning þās word
ġecwæð, ðā fǣringa bǣr ēode in ðæs cyninges ġeong dohtor ond cyste
hire fæder ond ðā ymbsittendan. 7ā hēo becōm tō Apollonio, þā ġewende
hēo onġean tō hire fæder and cwæð, "Ðū gōda cyning ond mīn sē
25   lēofosta fæder, hwæt is þēs ġeonga mann þe onġean ðē on swā
weorðlīcum setle sitt mid sārlīcum ondwlitan? Nāt iċ hwæt hē

besorgað." Ðā cwæð sē cyning, "Lēofe dohtor, bēs ġeonga monn is forliden, ond hē ġecwēmde mē manna betst on ðǣm plegan ; for ðām iċ hine ġelaðode tō ðisum ūrum ġebēorscipe. Nāt iċ hwæt hē is nē hwanon hē is ; ac ġif ðū wille witan hwæt hē sīe, āsca hine, for ðām bē ġedafenað þæt þū wite.

Ðā ēode þæt mæġden tō Apollonio ond mid forwandiendre sprǣċe cwæð, "Ðēah ðū stille sīe and unrōt, þēah iċ þīne æðelborennesse on ðē ġesēo. Nū bonne, ġif ðē tō hefiġ ne bynċe, seġe mē þīnne noman, ond þīn ġelimp āreċe mē." Ðā cwæð Apollonius, "Ġif ðū for nēode āscast æfter mīnum naman, iċ secge þē, iċ hine forlēas on sǣ ; ġif ðū wilt mīne æðelborennesse witan, wite ðū þæt iċ hīe forlēt on Tharsum." Þæt mæġden cwæð, "Seġe mē ġewislīcor, þæt iċ hit mæġe understandan."

(*Apollonius of Tyre*는 원래 기원전 2, 3세기 경 희랍에서 생겨난 이야기로서 중세에 구라파 각국에 널리 퍼져있던 이야기 중의 하나이다. 여러 차례 라틴어로 번역되었을 뿐만 아니라 거의 모든 구라파 언어로 번역되었으며, 고대영어 번역은 그 중 이른 번역 중의 하나이다. 고대영어판은 라틴어 번역본을 대본으로 삼고 있다. Shakespeare도 *Pericles, Prince of Tyre*라는 제목으로 이 이야기를 극화하고 있다. *Apollonius*는 고대영어에서 유례를 찾기 힘든 산문체 소설이기도 하다.

이야기는 당대 중세 소설들(romance)의 전형적인 모습을 가지고 있다. 우연한 기회에 Antioch왕의 딸과의 불륜을 발견하게 된 Apollonius는 신변의 위험을 느껴 도망가다가 Cyrenaica(지금의 Libya 지방)에서 파선을 당하게 된다. 일행 중 혼자 살아남은 그는 그곳 Cyrenaican의 Arecestrates왕의 공놀이에 참가했다가 왕에게 깊은 인상을 주게 되어 왕의 만찬에 초대받게 된다. 여기 인용한 글은 바로 이 장면부터 시작된다.

본문에서 우리는 만찬에 참석했던 왕의 공주가 Apollonius에 첫눈에 반하게 되는 것을 알게 된다. 이 대목은 고대영어 문학에서 여성의 심리를 그린 몇 안 되는 경우에 해당한다.

그 두 사람은 결혼하게 되어 Apollonius의 고향으로 가던 중 다시 풍랑을 만나게 되면서 공주는 아기를 조산하다 죽게 되어 상자에 담아 바다에 버리게 된다. 그러나 실은 공주가 죽지 않고 살아나게 되며, 한편 Apollonius는 딸과 헤어지게 된다. 그 뒤 Apollonius는 파란만장 속에 극적으로 죽은 줄 알았던 아내와 딸을 다시 만나게 되고 고향에 돌아가 왕이 되어 행복하게 산다는 것이 이야기의 줄거리이다.)

1 Ðā=when. ġehīerd=heard. ġehīerdsumode=obeyed. 원형은 (ġe)hīersumian. ēode forð= went forth. ēode=went. 원형은 gān.

2   oð=up to. becōm=came. 원형은 becuman. healle=heall(=hall)의 단수 여격. Đā ēode sē mann in=then the man went in.

3   beforan=in front of, in the presence of. forlidena=shipwrecked.

3-4 be ðu æfter sendest=whom you sent for.

4   ne mæġ…in gān=can not come in. mæġ의 원형은 magan. scame([šame])=shame. būton= except. scrūde=clothed. 원형은 scrȳdan([šrü : dan]).

5   hēt=commanded. 원형은 hātan. sōna=immediately, soon. ġescrȳdan=clothed. weorðfullum=worthy, honorable (dress), glorious. cf. weorð=worth. scrūde=clothing.

6   ġereorde=meal, banquet.

7   ġesæt=sat. 원형은 ġesittan. bǣr him ġetāht=where he was directed. ġetāht의 원형은 ġet ǣċan(=teach, show, direct). onġēan=against, opposite.

8   wearð=became, happened. 원형은 weorðan. beġnung=service. ġeboren=carried. 원형은 ġeberan.

8-9 cyneliċ ġebeorscipe=royal feast.

9   ǣt=ate. 원형은 etan. ðēah=although, in spite of.

10   blīðe=joyful. behēold=gazed, looked. 원형은 behealdan. seolfor=silver.

11   dēorwierðan=valuable, precious, costly. rēaf=dress. bēodas=tables. beġnunga=여기서는 식기류.

12   Đā ða…ðā=When…then. sārnesse=pain, grief. eald=old.

13   æfestiġ=envious. ealdorman=nobleman. be=beside, by. Mid bȳ be…ðā=when…then.

14   sārlīċe=painfully, with grief.

15   efne=behold.

16   wið=against, towards. ġedēst=did. 원형은 dōn. swīðe=very. æfestful=envious. gōde= possessions.

17   7ē misbyncð=misbynċan(=to appear incorrectly)의 3인칭 단수 현재. cf. bynċan=to seem. æfestað=is envious. 원형은 æfestian.

17-18 on nānum ðingum=on nothing. on이 여격과 함께 쓰인 거의 유일한 예.

18   hēr=here. ġesiehð=sees. 원형은 ġesēon. cȳðð=cȳðan(=to make known, inform)의 3인칭 단 수 현재. fela=much, many. forloren=forlēosan(=to lose)의 과거분사.

19   beseah=looked. 원형은 besēon. blīðe=happy. andwlitan=face.

20   bēo=bēon(=to be)의 단수 명령. bēo blīðe=be happy. mid ūs=with us. ġehyht=ġehyhtan (=to hope, trust)의 단수 명령.

21   mōte=be permitted. 원형은 magan(=to be able). self=yourself. sēlrum=better. becuman= become.

21-22 Mid bȳ ðe…ðā=when…then.

22   ðā=then. fǣringa=by chance, suddenly. ġeong=young. cyste=kissed. 원형은 cyssan.

23   ðā ymbesittendan=those sitting around, neighbor. cf. ymbe(=around)+sittan(=to sit)+ end(=ing). 7ā…bā=When…then. ġewende=turned. 원형은 wendan.

26   weorðlīcum=honorable. 원형은 weorðlīċ. setle=seat. sārlēcum=painful, grievous. 원형은

sārliċ. ondwlitan(andwlitan)=face. Nāt=ne wāt=don't know. 원형은 wītan.

27 besorgaðð=besorgian(=to be sorry for, be trouble about)의 3인칭 단수 현재.

28 ġecwēmde=pleased. 원형은 ġecwēman. manna=of men. mann의 복수 속격. betst=best. plegan=game, play. manna betst on ðǣm plegan=the best of the men in the (ball) game. for ðām=therefore.

29 ġelaðode=ġeladian(=to invite)의 과거. ġebēorshipe=feast. Nāt…ne=neither…nor. hwanon= whence.

30 ġif ðū wille witan=if you wish to know. wille는 willan(=to wish)의 가정법 2인칭 단수 현재. witan=to know. wille=willan(=to wish)의 가정법. sīe=bēon(=to be)의 가정법 3인칭 단수 현재. āsca=āscian(=to ask)의 단수 명령. for ðām=because.

30-31 bē ġedafenað bæt…=it is proper for you that.

31 ġedafenian= to be fitting, suit. wite=witan(=to know)의 가정법 2인칭 단수 현재.

32 forwandiendre=forwandian(=to hesitate)의 현재분사. forwandiendre sprǣċe=respectful speech.

33 Ðēah…bēah=Though…nevertheless. bēah=though, in spite of. stille=still, quiet. sīe=bēon 의 가정법 2인칭 단수 현재. unrōt=sad. cf. rōt=cheerful. bēah(ðēah)=though. æðelborennesse= nobility of birth.

34 ġesēo=see. 원형은 ġesēon. Nū bonne=now then. ġif ðē tō hefiġ ne bynċe=if it does not seem too oppressive to you. ðē는 여격. hefiġ=heavy. bynċe=bynċcan(=to appear, seem)의 가정법. seġe=secgan(=to say)의 단수 명령. noman(naman)=name.

35 ġelimp=happening, event. āreċe=āreċċan(=to tell, relate)의 단수 명령. for nēode=needs must. nēode=need, necessity. āscast=ask. 원형은 āscian[a : skiən].

36 forlēas=lost. 원형은 forlēosan. sæ=sea.

37 wilt=willan(=to wish)의 가정법 2인칭 단수 현재. wite bū=witan(=to know)의 단수 명령. bū는 강조를 위한 것. forlēt=left. 원형은 forlǣtan. Tharsum=Tarsus(도시 이름).

38 mæġden=maiden, girl. ġewislīcor=more precisely. ġewislīċe (=certain)의 비교급. bæt=so that. mæġe=magon(=can)의 가정법. understan=understandan (=to understand)의 가정법.

When Apollonius heard that, he obeyed and went along with the man until he came to the king's hall. Then the man went in first to the king and said : 'The shipwrecked man for whom you sent has come, but he cannot, for shame, enter without clothing.' Then the king ordered him to be immediately clothed with honorable garment and go in to the feast.

Then Apollonius went in and sat where he was directed, opposite the king. Then the service was carried in there, and after that a royal feast. And Apollonius ate nothing although all other men ate and were happy ; but he gazed at the gold and the silver and the costly apparel and the tables and the royal plate.

While he gazed at all this in sadness, a certain old and envious nobleman was sitting by the king. When he saw that Apollonius sat so sorrowfully and gazed at all things and ate nothing, then he said to the king : 'Good king, behold, this man whom you have so much favoured is very envious of your wealth.' Then said the king : 'You are mistaken. In fact this young man envies nothing that he sees there. But he reveals that he has suffered great loss.'

Then with a cheerful face Arcestrates the king turned to Apollonius and said : 'Young man, be happy with us and trust to God that you may yourself come to better things.' While the king was saying these words, by chance the king's young daughter came in and kissed her father and those sitting around. Then when she came to Apollonius, she turned back to her father and said : 'Good king, and my dearest father, who is this young man who sits opposite you in so honourable a seat with a sorrowful face? I do not know what he is troubled about.' Then said the king : 'Dear daughter, this young man is shipwrecked : and he pleased me best of all men in the game, so I invited him to this feast of ours. I do not know who he is nor where he comes from. But if you want to know who he is, ask him, because it is proper that you should know.'

Then the girl went to Apollonius and with respectful words said : 'Although you are silent and unhappy, I still see in you your noble birth. Now therefore, if it does not seem too grievous, tell me your name and relate to me what has happened to you.' Then Apollonius said : 'If you needs must ask for my name, I tell you that I lost it at sea. If you want to know my nobility, know that I left it in Tarsus.' The girl said : 'Tell me more exactly, so that I can understand.'

APOLLONIUS OF TYRE (2)

1 Apollonius þā sōðlīċe hire āreahte eall his ġelimp ond æt þǣre sprǣċe
ende him fēollon tēaras of ðǣm ēagum. Mid þȳ þe sē cyning þæt
ġeseah, hē bewende hine ðā tō ðǣre dehter ond cwæð, "Lēofe dohtor,
þū ġesyngodest ; mid þȳ þe þū woldest witan his naman and his
5 ġelimp, þū hafast nū ġeednīwod his ealde sār. Ac iċ bidde þē þæt þū
ġiefe him swā hwæt swā ðū wille."

   Ðā ðā ðæt mæġden ġehīerde þæt hire wæs ālīefed from hire fæder þæt
hēo ǣr hire self ġedōn wolde, ðā cwæð hēo tō Apollonio, "Apolloni,
sōðlīċe þū eart ūre. Forlǣt þīne murcnunge, ond nū iċ mīnes fæder
10 lēafe hæbbe, iċ ġedō ðē weliġne." Apollonius hire þæs bancode, and sē
cyning blissode on his dohtor welwillendnesse ond hire tō cwæð,
"Lēofe dohtor, hāt feċċan þīne hearpan, and ġeċīeġ ðē tō þīne frīend,
ond āfeorsa fram þām ġeongan his sārnesse."

   Ðā ēode hēo ūt ond hēt feċċan hire hearpan, and sōna swā hēo
15 hearpian ongann, hēo mid wynsumum songe ġemengde þǣre hearpan
sweġ. Ðā ongunnon ealle þā menn hīe herian on hire swēġcræfte, ond
Apollonius āna swīgode. Ðā cwæð sē cyning, "Apolloni, nū ðū dēst
yfele, for ðǣm þe ealle menn heriað mīne dohtor on hire swēġcræfte,
and þū āna hīe swīġiende tǣlst." Apollonius cwæð, "Ēalā ðū gōda
20 cyning, ġif ðū mē ġelīefst, iċ secge þæt iċ onġiete þæt sōðlīċe þīn
dohtor ġefēoll on swēġcræft, ac hēo næfð hine nā wel ġeleornod. Ac hāt
mē nū sellan þā hearpan ; þonne wāst þū þæt þū ġīet nāst." Arcestrates
sē cyning cwæð, "Apolloni, iċ oncnāwe sōðlīċe þæt þū eart on eallum
þingum wel ġelǣred."

25 Ðā hēt sē cyning sellan Apollonie þā hearpan. Apollonius þā ūt ēode
and hine scrȳdde ond sette ānne cynehelm uppan his hēafod ond nam
þā hearpan on his hond and in ēode and swā stōd þæt sē cyning and
ealle þā ymbsittendan wēndon þæt hē nǣre Apollonius ac þæt hē wǣre

Apollines, ðāra hǣðenra god. Đā wearð stilness ond swīġe ġeworden
30 innan ðǣre healle, and Apollonius his hearpenæġel ġenam, ond hē bā
hearpestrengas mid cræfte āstyrian ongonn ond bǣre hearpan swēġ
mid wynsumum songe ġemengde. Ond sē cyning self ond ealle bē bǣr
andwearde wǣron miċelre stefne clipodon and hine heredon. Æfter
bissum forlēt Apollonius bā hearpan ond plegode ond fela fæġerra
35 binga bǣr forðtēah be bām folce unġecnāwen wæs ond unġewuneliċ,
and heom eallum bearle līcode ǣlċ bāra binga ðe hē forðtēah.

1   āreahte=told. 원형은 āreċċan. ġelimp=happening, event.

1-2 æt bǣre sprǣċe ende=at the end of the speech.

2   fēollon=fell. 원형은 feallan. tēaras=tears. of=from. ēagum=eyes. 단수형은 ēage. him
fēollon tēaras of ðǣm ēagum=from him fell tears from the eyes=tears fell from his eyes.
Mid bȳ be=when.

3   bewende hine=turned himself. ðā=then. dehter=dohtor(=daughter)의 단수 여격.

4   ġesyngodest=ġesyngian(=to wrong)의 과거. bū ġesyngodest=you have done wrong.

5   hafast=habban(=to have)의 2인칭 단수 현재. ġeednīwod=renewed. 원형은 ġeednīwian.
sār=pain, wound, grief. bidde=ask.

6   ġiefe=ġiefan(=to give)의 가정법. swā hwæt swā=whatever.

7   Đā ðā=when. hire wæs ālīefed=to her it was allowed=she was allowed. ālīefed=allowed.
원형은 ālīefan.

7-8 bæt hēo ǣr hire self ġedōn wolde=what she already herself wanted to do.

8   ǣr=before. hire self=herself. ġedōn wolde=wished to do.

9   bū eart ūre=you are ours=you are one of us. Forlǣt=forlǣtan(=to leave, abandon)의 단수
명령. murcnunge=grief, complaint. fæder=fæder's. fæder(=father), mōdor(=mother), brōðor
(=brother), sweostor(=sister), dohtor(=daughter) 등 -or로 끝나는 가족 관계를 나타내는 단
어들은 단수형에서는 모든 격이 동일한 형태를 갖는다.

10 lēafe=permission. ġedō=ġedōn(=to do)의 1인칭 단수형으로서 미래시를 나타낸다. weliġne=
wealthy, prosperous. bancode=thanked. 원형은 bancian. blissode=rejoiced. 원형은 blissian.

11 dohtor=daughter's. welwillendnesse=benevolence.

12 hāt feċċan bīne hearpan=command thy harp to be brought. hāt=hātan(=to command)의
단수 명령. feċċan=fetch. ðē tō=to you. ġeċieġ=ġeċieġan(=to call)의 단수 명령. frīend=
frēond(=friend)의 복수 대격.

13 āfeorsa=āfeorsian(=to remove)의 단수 명령.

14 ēode…ūt=went out. sōna swā=as soon as.

15 ongann=began. 원형은 onginnan. mid wynsmum=pleasing, delightful. 원형은 wynsum.
songe=song. ġemengde=ġemengan=(to mix, combine, mingle)의 과거.

16 sweġ=sound, melody, music. ongunnon=began. 원형은 onġinnan. hīe=her. hērian=to praise. on=for. swæġcræfte=musical skill.

17 āna=alone. swīgode=was silent. 원형은 swigian. dēst=dōn(=to do)의 2인칭 단수 현재.

17-18 dēst yfele=do wrong.

19 swīġiende=(swīġian)의 현재분사=being silent. hīe swīġiende tǣlst=insult her by being silent. tǣlst=blame, censure. 원형은 tǣlan.

20 ġelīefest=permit, believe. onġiete=perceive.

21 ġefēoll on swēġcræft=has fallen into musical craft=she has made a start in the craft. næfð=ne hæfð=has not. hæfð=habban(=to have)의 3인칭 단수 현재. hine=it=swēġcræft. ġeleornod=learned. 원형은 ġeleornian.

21-22 hāt mē nū sellan bā hearpan=now command a harp to be brought to me.

22 sellan=give. bonne=then. wāst=know. ġiet=yet. nāst=ne wāst=do not know. bonne wāst þū þæt þū ġief nāst=then you will understand what you do not now as yet understand.

23 oncnāwe=recognize. 원형은 oncnāwan.

24 ġelǣred=learned.

26 hine scrȳdde=dressed himself. 원형은 scrȳdan. sette=set. ānne=a. cynehelm=garland, royal crown. hēafod=head. nam=took. 원형은 niman.

28 wēndon=imagined, believed, thought. 원형은 wēnan. nǣre=ne wǣre=was not. wǣre는 가정법. Apollines=Apollo.

29 ðāra=se(=the)의 복수 속격. hǣðenra=heathena(=heathen)의 복수 속격. swīġe ġeworden=became silent.

30 innan=in. hearpenæġel=harp nail=plectrum. ġenam=tool.

31 hearpestrengas=harp-strings. āstyrian=stir.

33 andwearde=present. miċelre stefne=with great voice. stefne(=voice)의 원형은 stefen. clipodon=cried out. 원형은 clipian. heredon=praised. 원형은 herian.

34 plegode=played. 원형은 pleġian. fæġerra=beautiful, pleasant.

35 forðtēah=brought out. 원형은 forðtēon. þe=that. 관계 대명사. folce=people. unġecnāwen=unknown. unġewunelīċ=unusual.

36 heom eallum þearle līcode=to them all it pleased=it pleased them all. þearle=greatly. līcode=pleased. 원형은 līcian. ǣlċ þāra þinga=each of those things. ðe=that. 목적격의 관계 대명사.

Then Apollonius told her truly all his circumstances, and at the end of the speech tears fell from his eyes. When the king saw that, he turned himself towards his daughter and said : 'Dear daughter, you have done wrong. In wanting to know his name and what has happened to him, you have now renewed his old sorrow. But I bid you give him whatever you will.'

Then when the girl heard that her father permitted what she herself already wished to do, then said she to Apollonius : 'Apollonius, you are truly one of us! Leave your grief ; and now I have my father's leave, I will make you wealthy.' Apollonius thanked her for this. And the king rejoiced at his daughter's kindness, and said to her : 'Dear daughter, order your harp to be fetched, entertain your friends and take away the young man's sadness.'

Then she went out and ordered her harp to be fetched : and as soon as she began to play, she accompanied the sound of the harp with beautiful song. Then all the men began to praise her for her musical skill, and Apollonius alone kept silent. Then said the king : 'Apollonius, now you are doing wrong, because all men praise my daughter for her musical skill and you alone censure her by remaining silent.' Apollonius said : 'Oh you good king, if you will forgive me, I say that I perceive that your daughter has fallen into the way of musical skill, but she has not learned it well. But order the harp to be given to me now ; then you will understand what you do not yet understand.' Arcestrates the king said : 'Apollonius, I know truly that you are well taught in all things.'

Then the king ordered Apollonius to be given the harp. Then Apollonius went out and dressed himself and set a garland on his head and took the harp in his hand and went in and stood thus, so that the king and all those sitting around imagined that he was not Apollonius but that he was Apollo, the god of the heathens. Then there was stillness and silence within the hall. And Apollonius took his plectrum and began to strike the harp-strings with skill, and accompanied the sound of the harp with beautiful song. And the king himself and all who were present there called out with a loud voice and praised him. After this Apollonius left the harp and played and performed there many pleasing things, which were unknown and unfamiliar in that country, and each of the things he performed pleased them all greatly.

APOLLONIUS OF TYRE (3)

1 Sōðlīċe mid þȳ þe þæs cyninges dohtor ġeseah þæt Apollonius on
eallum gōdum cræftum swā wel wæs ġetogen, þā ġefēoll hire mōd on
his lufe. Ðā æfter þæs bēorscipes ġeendunge cwæð þæt mæġden tō ðām
cyninge, "Lēofa fæder, þū līefdest mē lȳtle ǣr þæt iċ mōste ġiefan
5 Apollonio swā hwæt swā iċ wolde of þīnum goldhorde." Arcestrates sē
cyning cwæð tō hire, "Ġief him swā hwæt swā ðū wille."

Hēo ðā swīðe blīðe ūt ēode and cwæð, "Lārēow Apolloni, iċ ġiefe þē
be mīnes fæder lēafe twā hund punda goldes ond fēower hund punda
ġewihte seolfres ond þone mǣstan dǣl dēorweorðes rēafes ond twēntiġ
10 ðēowra monna." And hēo þā þus cwæð ðǣm bēowum mannum, "Berað
þās þing mid ēow þe iċ behēt Apollonio, mīnum lārēowe, ond lecgað
innan būre beforan mīnum frēondum." Þis wearð þā þus ġedōn æfter þǣre
cwēne hǣse, ond ealle þā menn hire ġiefa heredon ðe hīe ġesāwon.

Ðā sōðlīċe ġeendode sē ġebēorscipe, ond þā menn ealle ārison and
15 grētton þone cyning ond ðā cwēne ond bǣdon hīe ġesunde bēon and
hām ġewendon. Ēac swelċe Apollonius cwæð, "Ðū gōda cyning ond
earmra ġemiltsiend ond þū cwēn lāre lufiend, bēon ġē ġesunde." Hē
beseah ēac tō ðām bēowum monnum þe þæt mæġden him forġiefen
hæfde ond him cwæð tō, "Nimað þās þing mid ēow þe mē sēo cwēn
20 forġeaf, and gān wē sēċan ūre ġiesthūs þæt wē magon ūs ġerestan."
Ðā ondrēd þæt mæġden þæt hēo nǣfre eft Apollonium ne ġesāwe swā
hræðe swā hēo wolde ond ēode þā tō hire fæder and cwæð, "Ðū gōda
cyning, līcað ðē wel þæt Apollonius, þe burh ūs tōdæġ ġegōdod is, þus
heonon fare, ond cumen yfele menn ond berēafien hine?" Sē cyning
25 cwæð, "Wel þū cwæde. Hāt him findan hwǣr hē hine mæġe weorðlīcost
ġerestan.

Ðā dyde þæt mæġden swā hire beboden wæs, ond Apollonius onfēng
þǣre wununge ðe him ġetǣht wæs ond ðǣr in ēode Gode þanciende ðe

him ne forwiernde cynelīċes weorðscipes and frōfres. Ac bæt mæġden
hæfde unstille niht mid bǣre lufe onǣled bāra worda and sanga be hēo
ġehīerde æt Apollonie, ond nā leng hēo ġebād ðonne hit dæġ wæs, ac
ēode sōna swā hit lēoht wæs and ġesæt beforan hire fæder bedde. Ða
cwæð sē cyning, "Lēofe dohtor, for hwȳ eart ðū bus ǣrwacol?
Ðæt mæġden cwæð, "Mē āweahton bā ġecneordnessa be iċ ġiestrandæġ
ġehierde. Nū bidde iċ ðē for ðām bæt bū befæste mē ūrum cuman
Apollonie tō lāre."

   Ðā wearð sē cyning bearle ġeblissod ond hēt feċċan Apollonium ond
him tō cwæð, "Mīn dohtor ġiernð bæt hēo mōte leornian æt ðē ðā
ġesǣligan lāre ðe bū canst, and ġif ðū wilt bisum bingum ġehīersum
bēon, iċ swerie ðē burh mīnes rīċes mæġenu bæt swā hwæt swā ðū on
sǣ forlure iċ ðē bæt on lande ġestaðelie." Ðā ðā Apollonius bæt
ġehīerde, hē onfēng bām mæġdene tō lāre ond hire tāhte swā wel swā
hē self ġeleornode.

1-2   mid bȳ be···bā=when···then.
2   ġetogen=instructed 원형은 ġetēon. mōd=mind, heart.
2-3   ġefēoll hire mōd on his lufe=her heart fell into his love. mōd=heart, mind. lufe=love.
3   bēorscipe=feast. ġeendung=end.
4   līefdest=granted. 원형은 līefan. ſytel ǣr=a little before. mōste=mōtan(=to be permitted,
      be able)의 과거.
5   swā hwæt swā=whatever. of=from. goldhorde=tresury.
7   swīðe=very. blīðe=happy. Lārēow=teacher, master. ġiefe=give. 원형은 ġiefan.
8   be=by, according to. fæder=father's. fæder는 단수형이 모두 같다. lēafe=permission. hund=
      hundred. punda=pounds. fēower=four.
9   ġewihte=weight. seolfres=silver. 원형은 seolfor. mǣstan=most, greatest. bone mǣstan
      dǣl=the greatest portion=a great quantity of. dǣl=share, portion. dēorweorðes=costly,
      valuable, precious. rēafes=clothing.
10   ðēowra monna=serving men. Berað=beran(=to carry)의 복수 명령.
11   mid ēow=with you. be iċ behēt=that I promised. be=목적격의 관계대명사. behēt=behātan
      (=to promise)의 과거. lecgað=lecgan(=to lay)의 복수 명령.
12   būre=chamber. wearð=was. ġedōn=done. æfter=according to.
13   cwēne=queen. hǣse=command. ġiefa=gifts. 원형은 ġiefu. heredon=praised. 원형은 herian.
      hīe=them. ġesāwon=seen. 원형은 ġesēon.

14 ġeendode=ended. 원형은 ġeendian. ārison=arose. 원형은 ārīsan.

15 grētton=greeted. 원형은 grētan. bǣdon=bade. 원형은 biddan. ġesunde=healthy, wound, uninjured, whole. bēon=to be. bǣdon hīe ġesunde bēon=bade them be healthy=said farewell to them.

16 hām=home. ġewendon=turned. 원형은 ġewendan. Ēac=also. swelċe=likewise.

17 earmra=poor, wretched, miserable. ġemiltsiend=pitying. 원형은 ġemiltsian. earmra ġemiltsiend=pitier of the poor. lāre=of learning. lufiend=loving. lāre lufiend=lover of learning. bēon ġē ġesunde=be healthy. bēon=bēon(=to be)의 가정법 복수형으로서 기원을 나타낸다.

18 beseah=looked. be bæt=that which.

18-19 forġiefen hæfde=had given.

19 Nimað=niman(=to take)의 복수 명령.

20 forġeaf=gave. 원형은 forġiefan. gān=go. seċan=to seek. gān we seċan=let us go to seek. ġiesthūs=guesthouse, lodging, inn. bæt we magon…=that we can…. ūs=ourselves. ġerestan=to rest.

21 ondrēd=was afraid. 원형은 ondrǣdan. eft=again. ġesāwe=would see. ġesēon(=to see)의 가정법 과거. swā=as.

22 hræðe=quickly. swā hræðe swā hēo wolde=as quickly as she wished.

23 līcað=(does it) please 원형은 līcian. ġegōdod=enriched. 원형은 ġegōdian.

24 heonon=from here. fare=should go. 원형은 faran. berēafien=should rob. berēafian(=to rob)의 가정법.

25 Wel þū cwǣde=well thou (have) said=you are right. Hāt him findan hwǣr hē hine mæġe…=Command them to find for him (a place) where…. mæġe=magan(=can)의 가정법. weorðlīcost=weorðlīċe(=honourably)의 최상급.

27 beboden=command. onfēng=accepted. 원형은 onfōn.

28 wununge=dwelling. ġetāht=assigned. 원형은 ġetǣċan. anciende=thanking. cf. bancian(=to thank)+ende(=ing).

29 forwiernde=denied. 원형은 forwiernan. cynelīċes=regal. weorðscipe=dignity. frōfres= comfort. 원형은 frōfor.

30 unstille=restless. onǣled=enflamed. 원형은 onǣlan. worda=words. sanga=songs.

31 æt=from. nā leng=no longer. ġebād=waited. 원형은 ġebīdan. ðonne=when.

32 lēoht=light. sōna swā hit lēoht wæs=as soon it was light. ġesæt=sat. 원형은 ġesittan.

33 for hwȳ=why. ǣrwacol=early awake. cf. ǣr(=early)+wacol(=awake).

34 āweahton=awakened. 원형은 āweċċan. ġecneordnessa=accomplishments. ġiestrandæġ= yesterday.

35 bidde=ask, entreat. 원형은 biddan. for ðām=therefore. befæste=entrust. 원형은 befæstan. ūrum=our. 뒤에 오는 cuman, Apollonie와 함께 모두 단수 여격형이다. cuman=guest.

36 tō=for.

37 bearle=very, strongly, exceedingly. ġeblissod=pleased. 원형은 ġeblissian. hēt feċċan…

=commanded (them) to bring….

38 ġiernð=desires. 원형은 ġiernan. mōte=can. leornian=to learn. æt ðē=from you.

39 ġesǣliġan=beneficial. canst=know. cnāwan의 2인칭 단수 현재. ġehīersum=obedient, amenable.

40 swerie=swear. 원형은 swerian. burh mīnes rīċes mæġenu=by the powers of my kingdom. mæġen=power. swā hwæt swā=whatever.

41 forlure=lost. 원형은 forlēosan. ġestaðelie=restore. 원형은 ġestaðelian. Ðā ðā=When.

42 tāhte=taught. 원형은 tǣċan. swā wel swā=as well as.

43 ġeleornode=learned.

Truly, when the king's daughter saw that Apollonius was so well educated in all accomplishments, then her heart fell in love with him. Then at the end of the entertainment, the girl said to the king : 'Dear father, a little earlier you gave me permission to give Apollonius whatever I wanted from your treasury.' Arcestrates the king said to her : 'Give him whatever you want.'

She then went out very happy and said : 'Master Apollonius, with my father's permission, I give you two hundred pounds in gold and four hundred pounds weight of silver, and a great quantity of costly clothing, and twenty serving men.' And she then said to the serving men thus : 'Carry with you these things which I have promised my master Apollonius, and lay them within the chamber in front of my friend.' Then this was done thus according to the princess' command, and all those men who saw her gifts praised them.

Then in fact the entertainment ended, and everybody got up and addressed the king and the queen, and bade them farewell, and went home. Similarly Apollonius said : 'Farewell good king and pitier of the poor, and you princess, lover of learning.' Then he turned to the serving men that the girl had given him, and said to them : 'Take these things with you that the princess has given me, and let us go and seek our lodgings so that we may rest.' Then the girl was afraid that she might not see Apollonius again as soon as she would wish, and went then to her father and said : 'Good king, are you content that Apollonius, who has been enriched by us today, should go hence and that evil men should come and rob him?' The king said : 'You are right.

Bid them find him a place where he may rest most honourably.'

Then the girl did as she was commanded, and Apollonius accepted the dwelling that was assigned to him, and entered, thanking God who had not denied him regal dignity and comfort. But the girl had a restless night, inflamed with love of the words and songs that she had heard from Apollonius. And when it was day she could wait no longer, but as soon as it was light went and stood beside her father's bed. Then said the king : 'Dear daughter, why are you awake so early?' The girl said : 'The accomplishments which I heard yesterday kept me awake. Now I entreat you, therefore, that you entrust me to our guest Apollonius for instruction.'

Then the king was very pleased, and ordered Apollonius to be fetched and said to him : 'My daughter longs to be instructed by you in the delightful arts you possess ; and if you will agree to this, I swear to you by the power of my kingdom, that whatever you lost at sea I will restore to you on land.' Then when Apollonius heard that, he accepted the girl for instruction, and taught her as well as he himself had learned.

1   Hit ġelamp ðā æfter aissum binnan fēawum tīdum aæt Arcestrates sē
cyning hēold Apollonius hond on honda and ēodon swā ūt on ðǣre
ċeastre strǣte. 7ā æt nīehstan cōmon ðǣr gān onġean hīe arīe ġelǣrede
weras ond æaelborene aā longe ǣr ġierndon aæs cyninges dohtor. Hīe
5   ðā ealle arīe tōgædere ānre stefne grētton ðone cyning. Ðā smearcode
sē cyning and him tō beseah and aus cwæð, 'Hwæt is aæt, aæt ġē mē
ānre stefne grētton?' Ðā andswarode heora ān and cwæð, 'Wē bǣdon
ġefyrn aīnre dohtor, ond aū ūs oftrǣdlīċe mid elcunge ġeswenċtest. For
ðām wē cōmon hider tōdæġ aus tōgædere. Wē sindon aīne ċeasterġewaran
10   of æðelum ġebyrdum ġeborene ; nū bidde wē aē aæt aū ġeċēose aē ānne
of ūs arim, hwelcne aū wille aē tō āðume habban.' Ða cwæð sē cyning,
'Næbbe ġe nā gōdne tīman āredodne ; mīn dohtor is nū swīðe bisiġ
ymbe hire leornunge. Ac, aē lǣs ae iċ ēow ā leng slacie, āwrītað
ēowere noman on ġewrite ond hire morgenġiefe. 7onne āsende iċ aā
15   ġewritu mīnre dehter aæt hēo self ġeċēose hwelcne ēower hēo wille.'
Ðā dydon ðā cnihtas swā, ond sē cyning nam ðā ġewritu and
ġeinseġlode hīe mid his hringe and sealde Apollonio aus cweðende,
'Nim nū, lārēow Apolloni, swā hit aē ne mislīcie, ond bring aīnum
lǣringmæġdene.
20   Ðā nam Apollonius aā ġewritu and ēode tō ðǣre cynelīcan healle. Mid
aām ae aæt mæġden ġeseah Apollonium, aā cwæð hēo, "Lārēow, hwȳ
gǣst ðū āna?' Apollonius cwæð, 'Hlǣfdiġe, ⋯ nim ðās ġewritu ðe aīn
fæder aē sende ond rǣd.' Ðæt maġden nam ond rǣdde aāra arēora
cnihta naman, ac hēo ne funde nā aone noman aǣron ae hēo wolde.
25   Ðā hēo aā ġewritu oferrǣdd hæfde, ðā beseah hēo tō Apollonio and
cwæð, 'Lārēow, ne ofaynċð hit ðē ġif iċ aus wer ġeċēose?' Apollonius
cwæð, 'Nā, ac iċ blissie swīðor ðæt aū meaht ðurh ðā lāre ae aū æt mē
underfēnge aē self on ġewrite ġecȳðan hwelcne heora aū wille. Mīn

willa is aæt aū ðē wer ġeċēose ǣr ðū self wille.' 7æt mæġden cwæð, 'Ēalā lārēow, ġif ðū mē lufodest, aū hit besorgodest.' Æfter aissum wordum hēo mid mōdes ānrǣdnesse āwrāt ōðer ġewrit ond aæt ġeinseġlode and sealde Apollonio. Apollonius hit aā ūt bær on ðā strǣte ond sealde aām cyning. Ðæt ġewrit wæs aus ġewriten : '7ū gōda cyning and mīn sē lēofosta fæder, nū aīn mildheortnes mē lēafe sealde aæt iċ self mōste ċēosan hwelcne wer iċ wolde, iċ secge ðē tō sōðe, aone forlidenan monn iċ wille. And ġif ðū wundrie aæt swā scamfæst fǣmne swā unforwandiendlīċe ðās word āwrāt, aonne wite aū aæt iċ hæbbe purh weax āboden, ðe nāne scame ne conn, aæt iċ self ðē for scame secgan ne mihte.'

1 Hit ġelamp=it happend. 원형은 ġelimpan. binnan=within. fēawum tīdum=few hours.

2 hēold=held. 원형은 healdan. hond on honda=hand in hand. ēodon=went. 원형은 gān. swā=in this fashion(손을 잡은 채로). ūt=out.

3 ċeastre strǣte=city street. æt nīehstan=thereupon. cōmon ðǣr gān onġean hīe=there came walking. arīe ġelǣrede weras ond æaelborene=arīe ġelǣrede ond æaelborene weras=three learned and nobly-born men. arīe=three. ġelǣrede=learned.

4 weras=men. æaelborene=of noble birth. aā=관계대명사. longe(=lange)=for a long time. ǣr=previously, formerly. ġierndon=desired. 원형은 ġiernan.

5 ānre stefne=with one voice. 원형은 stefn. grētton=greeted. 원형은 grētan. smearcode= smiled. 원형은 smearcian.

6 beseah=looked. 원형은 besēon. ġē=ye. 2인칭 복수 주격.

7 heora ān=one of them. bǣdon=asked. 원형은 biddan.

8 ġefyrn=long ago. oftrǣdlīċe=frequently. elcunge=delay. ġeswenċtest=harassed. 원형은ġeswenċan.

9 ċeasterġewaran=citizens.

10 of æðelum ġebyrdum ġeborene=born of noble family. æðelum=noble. 원형은 æðele. ġebyrdum=birth. ġeborene=born. 원형은 ġeberan. bidde wē aē=we ask you. ġeċēose= ġeċēoan(=to choose)의 가정법.

10-11 ānne of ūs arim=one of us three.

11 hwelcne=hwilċ(=which)의 단수 대격. āðume=son-in-law.

12 Næbbe=ne hæbbe=don't have. āredodne=found. 원형은 āredian. swīðe bisiġ=very busy.

13 ymbe=with. leornunge=learning. aē lǣs ae=lest…should. leng slacie=slacian(=to delay)의 가정법. āwrītað=āwrītan(=to write down)의 복수 명령.

14 noman(=naman)=names. ġewrite=letter. morgenġiefe=gift from husband to wife on

morning after wedding. 7onne=then. āsende=send.

15 dehter=dohtor(=daughter)의 단수 여격. aæt=so that. ġeċēose=ġeċēosan(=to choose)의 가
정법. hwelcne ēower=which of you.

16 cnihtas=young men. nam=took. 원형은 niman.

17 ġeinseġlode=sealed. 원형은 ġeinseġlian. hringe=ring. sealde=gave. 원형은 sellan.

18 lārēow=teacher, master. mislīcie=displeases. 원형은 mislīcian.

19 l͞æringmæġdene=(girl) pupil.

20 cynelīcan healle=royal hall.

20-21 Mid aām ae=when.

22 g͞æst=come. 원형은 gān. āna=alone. H͞læfdiġe=lady.

22-23 ðe aīn fæder aē sende=which your father sends you.

23 r͞æd=r͞ædan(=to read)의 단수 명령.

23-24 arēora cnihta naman=the names of the three (young men).

24 wolde=wished. 원형은 willan.

25 oferr͞ædd=read through. 원형은 oferr͞ædan.

26 ofaynċð=displeases. 원형은 ofaynċan.

27 Nā=no. blissie=rejoice. meaht=might. 원형은 magan. lāre=teaching. ae=관계대명사.

28 underfēnge=received. 원형은 underfōn. aē self=yourself. ġeċy͞ðan=announce.

29 willa=wish. wille=wish.

30 Ēalā=oh! besorgodest=(you are) sorry. 원형은 besorgian.

31 mōdes=mind, heart. ānr͞ædnesse=resolution. āwrāt=wrote down. 원형은 āwrītan.

32 sealde=gave. 원형은 sellan. bær=carried. 원형은 beran.

34 mildheortnes=kindness. lēafe=permission. mōste=be allowed to. 원형은 mōtan.

36 forlidenan=shipwrecked. wundrie=wonder. 원형은 wundrian. scamfæst=modest. fæmne=
maid.

37 unforwandiendlīċe=without bashfulness. wite=witan(=to know)의 단수 명령.

38 weax=wax. āboden=announced. 원형은 ābēodan. ðe nāne scame ne conn=which does
not know shame. conn=knows. 원형은 cunnan. ðē=to you.

39 secgan ne mihte=could not say.

Then it happened a few hours after this, that Arcestrates the king held
Apollonius hand in hand and thus went out into the city street. Then at
length there came walking towards them three learned and nobly-born men,
who for a long time had desired the king's daughter. Then they all three
together greeted the king with one voice. Then the king smiled and turned to
them and said thus : 'What is it, that you greet me with once voice?' Then
one of them answered and said : 'We asked for your daughter long ago and

you have continually tormented us by delay. Therefore we have come here today together thus. We are your citizens, born of noble family. Now we entreat you to choose which of us three you want to have as son-in-law.' Then said the king : 'You have not hit upon a good time. My daughter is now very busy with her studies. But lest I should delay you longer, write down your names and her marriage-gift in a letter ; then I will send the letters to my daughter so that she herself may choose which of you she wants.' Then the young men did so, and the king took the letters and sealed them with his ring and gave them to Apollonius, saying thus : 'Now Master Apollonius, if you do not object, take and carry them to your pupil.'

Then Apollonius took the letters and went to the royal hall. Then when the girl saw Apollonius she said : 'Master, why do you come alone like this?' Apollonius said : 'Lady, ⋯ take and read these letters which your father sends you.' The girl took them and read the names of the three young men, but she did not find there the name she wanted. When she had read over the letters, then she turned to Apollonius and said : 'Mater, will it not grieve you if I should choose a husband thus?' Apollonius said : 'No. But I should rejoice much more if you could, through the instruction which you have received from me, yourself declare in writing which one of them you want. My wish is that you should choose a husband whom you yourself wish.' The girl said : 'Oh mster, if you loved me, you would be sorry about it.' After these words she, with a resolute mind, wrote another letter and sealed it and gave it to Apollonius. Apollonius then carried it out into the street and gave it to the king. The letter was written thus : 'Good king, and my dearest father, now that your kindness has given me permission to choose for myself what husband I wanted, I say to you truly, I want the shipwrecked man ; and if you should wonder that so modest a woman wrote those words so shamelessly, then know that I have declared by means of wax, which knows no shame, what I could not for shame say to you myself.'

APOLLONIUS OF TYRE (5)

1   Ðā ðā sē cyning hæfde aæt ġewrit oferrǣdd, aā niste hē hwelcne
forlidenne hēo nemde, beseah ðā tō ðǣm arim cnihtum ond cwæð,
'Hwelċ ēower is forliden?' Ðā cwæð heora ān, sē hātte Ardalius, 'Iċ
eom forliden.' Sē ōðer him andwyrde and cwæð, 'Swīga ðū! Ādl aē
5   fornime, aæt aū ne bēo hāl nē ġesund! Mid mē aū bōccræft leornodest,
ond ðū nǣfre būton aǣre ċeastre ġeate from mē ne cōme. Hwǣr ġefōre
ðū forlidennesse?' Mid ðy ae sē cyning ne meahte findan hwelċ heora
forliden wǣre, hē beseah tō Apollonio and cwæð, 'Nim ðū, Apolloni, ais
ġewrit ond rǣd hit. Ēaðe mæġ ġeweorðan aæt aū wite aæt iċ nāt, ðū ðe
10   aǣr ondweard wǣre.' Ðā nam Apollonius aæt ġewrit and rǣdde, and
sōna swā hē onġeat aæt hē ġelufod wæs from ðām mæġdene his
ondwlita eall ārēodode. Ðā sē cyning aæt ġeseah, aā nam hē Apollonies
hand ond hine hwōn fram aām cnihtum ġewende and cwæð , 'Wāst aū
aone forlidenan monn?' Apollonius cwæð, 'Ðū gōda cyning, ġif aīn
15   willa bið, iċ hine wāt.' Ðā ġeseah sē cyning aæt Apollonius mid rosan
rude wæs eall oferbrǣded, aā onġeat hē aone cwide and aus cwæð tō
him, 'Blissa, blissa, Apolloni, for ðǣm ae mīn dohtor ġewilnað aæs ðe
mīn willa is. Ne mæġ soðlīċe on ayllīcum aingum nān aing ġeweorðan
būton Godes willan.' Arcestrates beseah tō ðām arim cnihtum and cwæð,
20   'Sōð is aæt iċ ēow ǣr sæġde, aæt ġē ne cōmon on ġedafenlīcre tīde
mīnre dohtor tō biddenne ; ac aonne hēo mæġ hī fram hire lāre
ġeǣmettigian, aonne sende iċ ēow word.' Ðā ġewendon hīe hām mid
aisse ondsware.

And Arcestrates sē cyning hēold forð on Apollonius hond hine lǣdde
25   hām mid him, nā swelċe hē cuma wǣre ac swelċe hē his āðum wǣre.
Ðā æt nīehstan forlēt sē cyning Apollonius hand ond ēode āna intō
ðǣm būre aǣr his dohtor inne wæs, and aus cwæð, 'Lēofe dohtor,
hwone hafast aū ðē ġecoren tō ġemæċċan?' Ðæt mæġden aā fēoll tō

hire fæder fōtum ond cwæð, 'Ðū ārfæsta fæder, ġehīer aīnre dohtor
30 willan. Iċ lufie aone forlidenan mann ðe wæs aurh unġelimp beswicen.
Ac āȳ [æs ae aē twēonie aǣre sprǣċe, Apollonium iċ wille, mīnne
lārēow, ond ġif aū mē him ne selest, aū for[ǣtst ðīne dohtor.' Sē
cyning ðā sōðlīċe ne meahte āræfnan his dohtor tēaras, ac ārǣrde hīe
ūp and hire tō cwæð, 'Lēofe dohtor, ne ondrǣd aū ðē ǣniġes ainges. 7ū
35 hafast ġecoren aone wer ae mē wel līcað.' Hē ēode ðā ūt and beseah tō
Apollonio ond cwæð, 'Lārēow Apolloni, iċ smēade mīnre dohtor mōdes
willan ; ðā āreahte hēo mē mid wōpe betweox ōðre sprǣċe aās aing aus
cweðende, "7ū ġeswōre Apollonio, ġif hē wolde ġehīersumian mīnum
willan on lāre, aæt aū woldest him ġeinnian swā hwæt swā sēo sǣ him
40 ætbrǣġd. Nū for ðām ae hē ġehīersum wæs aīnre hǣse and mīnum
willan, iċ fōr æfter him."

1   Ðā ðā=when. niste=ne+wiste=did not know. 원형은 witan.
3   heora ān=one of them. hātte=called. 원형은 hātan.
4   Swīga=swīgan(=to keep quiet)의 단수 명령. Ādl=disease.
5   fornime=forniman(=to seize)의 가정법. aæt aū ne bēo hāl nē ġesund!=so that you be
    neither whole nor sound! bōccræft=book-learning. leornodest=learned. 원형은 leornian.
6   ċeastre ġeate=city gates. ġefōre=traveled. 원형은 ġefaran.
7   Mid ðy ae=when. meahte=could. 원형은 magan.
9   Ēaðe=easily. mæġ=may. 원형은 magan. mæġ ġeweorðan aæt=it may happen. wite=know.
    원형은 witan. ðū ðe=thou who. ðe=관계대명사.
10 ondweard=present.
11 sōna swā=as soon as. onġeat=perceived. 원형은 onġietan. ġelufod=ġelufian(=to love)의
    과거분사.
12 ondwlita(andwlita)=face. ārēodode=reddened, blushed. 원형은 ārēodian.
13 hwōn=hwā(=who)의 도구격. aām cnihtum ġewende=turned away. 원형은 ġewendan.
    Wāst=know. 원형은 witan.
14-15 ġif aīn willa bið=if you please.
15 wāt=know. 원형은 witan. rosan=rose.
16 rude=redness. oferbrǣded=covered. 원형은 oferbrǣdan. onġeat=understood. 원형은 onġietan.
    cwide=remark.
17 Blissa=blissian(=to rejoice)의 단수 명령. ġewilnað=desired. 원형은 ġewilnian. aæs ðe=
    that which.
18 ayllīcum=such. aingum=thing.

19 būton Godes willan=without God's will.

20 ġedafenlīcre tīde=suitable time.

21 tō biddenne=to ask. 원형은 biddan. lāre=learning, study.

22 ġeǣmettiġian=ġeǣmettiġan(=to free, empty)의 과거분사.

23 ondsware=answer.

24 hēold=held. 원형은 healdan. lǣdde=led. 원형은 lǣdan.

25 nā swelċe=not as. cuma=guest. āðum=son-in-law.

26 æt nīehstan=thereupon. forlēt=forlǣtan(=to let go)의 과거. āna=alone.

27 būre=chamber.

28 hwone=whom. hwā(=who)의 대격. ġemæċċan=husband. fēoll=fell. 원형은 feollan.

29 ārfæsta=kind. ġehīer=ġehīeran(=listen)의 단수 명령.

29-30 dohtor willan=daughter's will. fæder(=father), mōdor(=mother), brōdor(=brother), sweostor (=sister), dohtor(=daughter) 등 가족 관계를 나타내는 말들은 단수에서 주격으로 속격을 나타낸다.

30 aurh=through, by. unġelimp=misfortune. beswicen=betrayed.

31 āy lǣs ae=lest···should. twēonie=doubt. 원형은 twēonian.

32 selest=give. 원형은 sellan. forlǣtst=forsake. 원형은 forlǣtan.

33 meahte=could. 원형은 magan. ārǣfnan=endure. tēaras=tears. ārǣrde=reared.

34 ondrǣd=ondrǣdan(=to be afraid of)의 단수 명령. æniġes ainges=anything.

35 wer=man. līcað=pleases. 원형은 līcian.

36 smēade=examined. 원형은 smēaġan.

37 āreahte=told. 원형은 āreċċan. wōpe=weeping.

38 cweðende=cweaan(=to say)의 현재분사. ġeswōre=swore. 원형은 ġeswerian. ġehīersumian=obey.

39 ġeinnian=supply. 원형은 ġeinnian. swā hwæt swā=whatever.

40 ætbræġd=took away. 원형은 ætbreġdan. for ðām ae=because. ġehīersum=obedient. hǣse= command.

Then when the king had read over the letter, he did not know which shipwrecked man she meant. Then he turned to the three young men and said ：'Which of you has been shipwrecked?' Then one of them who was called Arcadius said ：'I have been shipwrecked.' Another answered him and said ：'You keep quiet! Plague take you, so that you be neither whole nor sound! You studies book-learning with me, and you have never been outside the city gates without me. Where did you suffer shipwreck?' When the king could not find which of them had been shipwrecked, he turned to Apollonius and said ：'Apollonius, you take this letter and read it. It may well be that you who were present there may know what I do not know.' Then Apollonius took and read the letter, and as soon as he realized that he was loved by the girl his face completely reddened. When the king saw that, then he took Apollonius' hand and went with him a little apart from the young men, and said : 'Do you know the shipwrecked man?' Apollonius said : 'Good king, if you please, I know him.' When the king saw that Apollonius was all suffused with blushes, then he understood the remark and said to him thus : 'Rejoice, rejoice, Apollonius, for my daughter desires that which is my will! Nor truly, may anything happen in such matters except by the will of God.' Arcestrates turned to the young men and said : 'What I said to you earlier — that you did not come at a suitable time to ask for my daughter — is true ; but when she can be freed from her studies, then I will send you word.' Then they went home with this answer.

And Arcestrates the king therefore held Apollonius' hand, and led him home with him, not as if he were a visitor, but as if he were his son-in-law. Then eventually he let go of Apollonius' hand and went alone into the chamber where his daughter was and spoke thus : 'Dear daughter, whom have you chosen as a husband?' The girl then fell at her father's feet and said : 'Kind father, listen to your daughter's desire. I love the shipwrecked man who was betrayed by misfortune. But lest you are unclear as to those words, I want Apollonius, my teacher, and if you will not give him to me you forsake your daughter.' Then truly the king could not bear his daughter's tears, but raised her up and said to her : 'Dear daughter, do not be afraid for anything. You have chosen the man that pleases me well.' Then he went out and turned to Apollonius and said : 'Master Apollonius, I have enquired into the desire of my daughter's heart. Weeping, she then told me these things, saying thus among other words : "You swore to Apollonius that if he would assent to my wish and teach me, you would restore to him whatever the sea took away from him. Now, because he was obedient to your command and my wish, I went after him."

(tr. Swanton)

VII. ALFRED

ALFRED'S PREFACE TO *PASTORAL CARE* (1)

1   Ælfred kyning hāteð grētan Wǣrferð biscep his wordum luflīċe ond
frēondlīċe ; ond ðē cȳðan hāte ðæt mē cōm swīðe oft on ġemynd,
hwelċe wiotan iū wǣron ġiond Angelcynn, ǣġðer ġe godcundra hāda ġe
woruldcundra ; ond hū ðā ġesǣliġlica tīda ðā wǣron ġiond Angelcynn ;
5   ond hū ðā kyningas ðe ðone onwald hæfdon ðæs folces on ðām dagum
Gode ond his ǣrendwrecum hērsumedon ; ond hū hīe ǣġðer ġe hiora
sibbe ġe hiora siodo ġe hiora onweald innanbordes ġehīoldon, ond ēac
ūt hiora ēðel ġerȳmdon ; ond hū him ðā spēow ǣġðer ġe mid wīġe ġe
mid wīsdōme ; ond ēac ðā godcundan hādas hū ġiorne hīe wǣron ǣġðer
10   ġe ymb lāre ġe ymb liornunga, ġe ymb ealle ðā ðīowotdōmas ðe hīe
Gode dōn scoldon ; ond hū man ūtanbordes wīsdōm ond lāre hieder on
lond sōhte, ond hū wē hīe nū sceoldon ūte beġietan, ġif wē hīe habban
sceoldon.
      Swǣ clǣne hīo wæs oðfeallenu on Angelcynne ðæt swīðe fēawa
15   wǣron behionan Humbre ðe hiora ðēninga cūðen understondan on
Englisc oððe furðum ān ǣrendġewrit of Lǣdene on Englisc āreċċean ;
ond iċ wēne ðætte nōht moniġe beġiondan Humbre nǣren. Swǣ fēawa
hiora wǣron ðæt iċ furðum ānne ānlēpne ne mæġ ġeðenċean be sūðan
Temes ðā ðā iċ tō rīċe fēng. Gode ælmihtegum sīe ðonc ðætte wē nū
20   ǣniġne onstal habbað lārēowa. Ond for ðon iċ ðē bebīode ðæt ðū dō swǣ
iċ ġelīefe ðæt ðū wille, ðæt ðū ðē ðissa woruldðinga tō ðǣm ġeǣmetiġe,
swā ðū oftost mæġe, ðæt ðū ðone wīsdōm ðe ðē God sealde ðǣr ðǣr ðū
hiene befǣstan mæġe, befǣste. Ġeðenċ hwelċ wītu ūs ðā becōmon for
ðisse worulde, ðā ðā wē hit nōhwæðer ne selfe ne lufodon, ne ēac
25   ōðrum monnum ne lēfdon ; ðone naman ānne wē lufodon ðætte wē
Crīstne wǣren, ond swīðe fēawa ðā ðēawas.

Đā iċ ðā ðis eall ġemunde, ðā ġemunde iċ ēac hū iċ ġeseah, ǣr ðǣm
ðe hit eall forhergod wǣre ond forbærned, hū ðā ċiriċean ġiond eall
Angelcynn stōdon māðma ond bōca ġefylda, ond ēac miċel meniġeo

30 Godes ðīowa ; ond ðā swīðe l̄ytle fiorme ðāra bōca wiston, for ðǣm ðe
hīe hiora nānwuht onġietan ne meahton, for ðǣm ðe hīe nǣron on hiora
āgen ġeðīode āwritene. Swelċe hīe cwǣden : 'Ūre ieldran, ðā ðe ðās
stōwa ǣr hīodon, hīe lufodon wīsdōm, ond ðurh ðone hīe beġēaton welan
ond ūs l̄æfdon. Hēr mon mæg ġīet ġesīon hiora swæð, ac wē him ne

35 cunnon æfter spyriġean, ond for ðǣm wē habbað nū ǣġðer forl̄æten ġe
ðone welan ġe ðone wīsdōm, for ðǣm ðe wē noldon tō ðǣm spore mid
ūre mōde onlūtan.'

(이 글은 Alfred대왕(871-899)이 Gregory법왕의 대표작 가운데 하나인 *Cura Pastoris*
(*Pastoral Care*)를 스스로 번역하여 각 교구로 보내면서 딸려보낸 편지의 양식을 띠고 있
다. 890년경에 쓰여진 글이다. 당시는 스칸디나비아인들의 침략에 의해 영국이 말할 수 없
는 곤경에 처해있던 시기이다. Alfred대왕은 문화적 창달 없이는 군사적 승리도 기대하기
어렵다는 신념 하에 여러 가지 어려움에도 불구하고 중요한 문헌들의 보존과 번역에 남다
른 관심을 기울이고 있으며, 여기서 보듯 스스로도 번역에 참가하고 있다. Alfred대왕은 한
국의 세종대왕에 버금가는 훌륭한 임금이다.)

1 Ælfred kyning=King Alfred. kyning(cyning)=king. 고대영어에서 k는 거의 쓰이지 않았다.
hāteð=hātan(=commands)의 3인칭 단수 현재. 여기서는 자기(Ælfred kyning)를 3인칭으로
취급하고 있다. grētan=to greet. Wǣrferð biscep=Bishop Wærferth(873-915). hāteð
grētan Wǣrferð biscep=commands Bishop Wærferth to be greeted. 명령을 나타내는
hāteð 따위 동사 뒤의 원형동사는 수동태로 번역된다. 따라서 hāteð grētan Wǣrfers biscep
his wordum=commands bishop Wærferth to be greeted with his(Ælfred's) words=sends
greetings to bishop Wærferth. wordum=word(=word)의 복수 여격. 여기서는 부사적으로
사용되고 있다. luflīċe=affectionately.

2 frēondlīċe=lovingly, in friendly fashion. ðē=to thee. cȳðan=make known. hāte=hātan(=to
command)의 1인칭 단수 현재. 여기서는 자기를 본래의 1인칭으로 취급하고 있다. 이와 같
은 인칭의 변경은 Alfred의 글에서 종종 보인다. ðē cȳðan hāte=command you to be
informed. cȳðan=inform, make known. cōm=(it) has come. mē…on ġemynd=into my
mind. ġemynd=mind, remembrance. hwelċe=what.

3 wiotan=wita(=wise man)의 복수. iū(ġeō)=formerly, of old. wǣron=were. ġiond(ġeond)=
through(out). Angelcynn=England, the English people. ǣġðer ġe…ġe=both…and.

godcundra=godcund(=divine, religious)의 복수 속격. hāda=office, order. godcundra hāda는 앞의 wiotan을 수식하고 있다.

4 woruldcundra=woruldcund(=secular)의 복수 속격. 뒤에 hāda가 생략되었다. hū=how. ġes æliġlica=ġesǣliġliċ=blessed, happy. 원형은 ġesǣliġliċ. tīda=time. ðā=then.

5 onwald=authority, power.

6 ǣrendwrecum=ǣrendraca(=messenger, minister)의 복수 대격. hērsumedon=obeyed. 원형은 hīersumian(=to obey, be obedient). hiora=hī(=he)의 복수 속격.

7 sibbe=peace. siodo=morality. innanbordes=at home, within the nation. ġehīoldon=held. 원형은 ġehealdan.

8 eðel=territory. ġerȳmdon=extended. 원형은 ġerȳman. him ðā spēow=it prospered for them then=they prospered then. spēow=succeeded. 원형은 spōwan. wīġe=war, battle.

9 wīsdōme=wisdom. ġiorne=eager. 원형은 ġeorn.

10 liornunga=learning. ðīowotdōmas=service. ðe=that. 목적격의 관계대명사.

11 Gode=God의 단수 여격. ūtanbordes=from abroad. Bede 시대에 Northumbria는 기독교 학문의 중심지로서 대륙의 수요에 맞추기 위해 많은 책이 필사되었다. hieder(hider)=hither. sōhte=sēċan(=to seek)의 과거.

12 hīe=lār의 단수 대격. nū=now. sceoldon=should. ūte=outside, abroad. beġietan=to gain, acquire.

14 Swǣ…ðæt=so…that. hīo=hīe. clǣne=clean, complete. oðfeallenu=oðfeallan(=to fall away, decline)의 여성 주격 단수형 과거분사로서 선행하는 hīo(=lār)에 일치하고 있다. 한편 oðfeallenu는 선행하는 wæs와 함께 과거완료를 나타낸다. swīðe fēawa=very few.

15 behionan=on this side of. ðeninga=divine service. cūðen=well known.

16 furðum=further. ǣrendġewrit=letter. of=from. Lǣdene=Lǣden(=Latin)의 단수 여격. on= onto. āreċċean=translate.

17 wēne=think. 원형은 wēnan. ðætte=ðæt ðe=that. nōht(nānwuht)=nothing. beġiondan (beġeondan)=beyond. beġiondan Humbre=beyond the Humber=Northumbria. nǣren=ne wǣren=were not.

17-8 Swǣ fēawa hiora wǣron ðæt=so few of them were that. furðum=even.

18 ānne ānlēpne ne=not a single one. ānlēpne=ānlēpe(=single)의 단수 대격. ġeðenċean= think. be sūðan Temes=to the south of the Thames.

19 ðā ðā iċ tō rīce fēng=when I succeeded to the kingdom=when I came to the throne. fēng=caught, seized. 원형은 fōn. ælmihtegum=almighty. 원형은 ælmihtiġ. sīe=bēon(=to be)의 가정법. ðonc=thanks (for).

20 ǣniġne=any. onstal=supply. lārēowa=teacher. ǣniġne onstal habbað lārēowa=have some supply of teachersə for ðon=therefore, and so. bebīode=bebēodan(=to command)의 1인칭 단수 현재.

20-21 ðæt ðū dō swǣ iċ ġelīefe ðæt ðū wille=that you do as I believe you desire.

21 ġelīefe=believe. ðissa woruldðinga=of these world-affairs=of the affairs of this world. ġe ǣmetiġe=ġeǣmetiġan(=to disengage, free)의 가정법. swǣ ðū oftost mæġe=as you

oftenest can=as often as you can. ðe ðē=that which. 관계대명사.

21-22 ðæt ðū ðē ðissa woruldðinga tō ðæm ġeæmetiġe=that you disengage yourself from worldly affairs for that.

22 ðær ðær=there where=wherever. 관계부사.

23 hiene(hine)=hē(=wīsdōm)의 단수 대격. befæstan=apply. Ġeðenc=ġeðenċan(=to think)의 단수 명령. wītu=wite(=punishment)의 복수. 여기서는 Scandinavian invasion을 가리키고 있다. for=on account of, because of.

24 ðā ðā=when. hit=선행사는 wīsdōm. 남성인 wīsdōm을 hē 대신 자연성의 hit가 대신하고 있다. selfe=ourselves. nōhwæder…ne ēac=neither…nor. selfe=ourselves. lufodon=loved. 원형은 lufian.

25 monnum=mann(=nan)의 복수 여격. lēfdon=læfan(=to leave)의 과거 .

25-26 ðone naman ānne wē lufodon ðætte wē Crīstne wǣren=we loved only the name that we were Christians=we loved only to be called Christians. ānne=only. ðone naman을 수식한다.

26 swīðe fēawa ðā ðēawas=(we loved) very few (of the) practices=very few (of us) (loved) the practices. ðēawas=ðāaw(=practice)의 복수 대격. fēawa 뒤에 lufodon이 생략되었다.

27 Ðā…ðā=when…then. ġemunde=remembered. 원형은 ġemunan.

27-28 ær ðæm ðē=before.

28 forhergod=ravaged. 원형은 forherġian. forbærned=burned (up). 원형은 forbærnan. ċiriċean= churches. 원형은 ċiriċe.

29 stōdon=stood. 원형은 standan. māðma=māðm(=treasure)의 복수 속격. bōca=bōc(=book)의 복수 속격. ġefylda=ġefyllan(=to fill, replenish)의 과거분사. stōdon māðma ond bōca ġefylda=were full of books and of treasures. māðum=treasure. ġefylda=ġefyllan(=to fill) 의 과거분사. ond ēac=and also. meniġeo=multitude.

30 ðīowa(ðīow)=servant, slave. ðā swīðe lytle fiorme ðāra bōca wiston=they knew very little use of the books=they had very little benefit from the books. fiorme=benefits. wiston=knew. 원형은 witan. for ðǣm ðe=because.

31 hiora nānwuht=none of them. nānwuht=nothing, not at all. onġiotan=understand. 원형은 onġietan. meahton=magan(=can)의 복수 과거. nǣron=ne+wǣren=were not.

32 āgen=own. ġeðīode(ġeðēode)=language. āwritene=āwrītan (=to write)의 과거분사. Swelċe hīe cwǣden=(It is) as if they had said. ieldran=elders, ancestors. ðā ðe=those who.

33 stōwa=places. hīodon=held, kept. 원형은 healdan. beġēaton=acquired. 원형은 beġietan(=to acquire, get). welan=prosperity, riches.

34 lǣfdon=left. 원형은 lǣfan. Hēr=ðās stōwa. mon(man(n))=man. ġīet=yet, still. ġesīon (ġesēon)=see. swæð=track.

34-35 ac wē him ne cunnon æfter spyriġean=ac wē ne cunnon æfter him spyriġean=we cannot follow after him. 고대영어에서는 이처럼 전치사가 (대)명사 뒤에 오는 경우도 있다.

35   cunnon=cannot. spyriġean=follow.

35   for ðæm=therefore.

35-36   ǣġðer…ġe…ġe…=both…and. forlǣten=forlǣtan(=to abandon, forsake)의 과거분사.

36   noldon=ne+woldon=did not wish. spore=track, trail.

37   mōde=mind. onlūtan=bow, incline, bend down.

    King Alfred sends greetings to Bishop Wærferth with his loving and friendly words, and would declare to you that it has very often come to my mind what wise men there were formerly throughout the English people, both in sacred and in secular orders ; and how there were happy times then throughout England ; and how the kings who had rule over the people in those days were obedient to God and his messengers, and both maintained their peace and their morality and their authority at home, and also enlarged their territory abroad ; and how they prospered both in warfare and in wisdom ; and also how zealous the sacred orders were both about teaching and about learning and all the services which they had to perform for God ; and how men from abroad came here to this land in search of knowledge and instruction, and how we should now have to get them from abroad, if we were to have them.

    So complete was its decay among the English people that there were very few this side of the Humber who could comprehend their services in English, or even translate a letter from Latin into English ; and I imagine that there were not many beyond the Humber. There were so few of them that I cannot even remember a single one south of the Thames when I succeeded to the kingdom. Thanks be to Almighty God that now we have any supply of teachers. And therefore I command you to do, as I believe you wish, that you disengage yourself as often as you can from the affairs of this world, so that you can apply the wisdom which god has given you wherever you are able to apply it. Think what punishments then came upon us on account of this world when we neither loved it [wisdom] ourselves nor allowed it to other men—we loved only to be called Christians, and very few loved the virtues.

When I remembered all this, then I also remembered how, before it was all ravaged and burnt, I have seen how the churches throughout all England stood filled with treasures and books, and there was also a great multitude of god's servants—they had very little benefit from those books, because they could not understand anything of them, since they were not written in their own language. As if they had said : 'Our forefathers who formerly held these places loved knowledge, and through it they acquired wealth and left it to us. One can see their footprints here still, but we cannot follow after them and therefore we have now lost both the wealth and the knowledge because we would not bend our mind to that course.'

ALFRED'S PREFACE TO *PASTORAL CARE* (2)

1　Ðā iċ ðā ðis eall ġemunde, ðā wundrade iċ swīðe swīðe ðāra gōdena
wiotona ðe ġiū wǣron ġiond Angelcynn, ond ðā bēċ ealla be fullan
ġeliornod hæfdon, ðæt hīe hiora ðā nǣnne dǣl noldon on hiora āgen
ġeðīode wendan. Ac iċ ðā sōna eft mē selfum andwyrde, ond cwæð :
5　'Hīe ne wēndon aætte ǣfre menn sceolden swǣ reċċelēase weorðan,
ond sīo lār swǣ oðfeallan ; for ðǣre wilnunga hīe hit forlēton, ond
woldon ðæt hēr ðȳ māra wīsdōm on londe wǣre ðȳ wē mā ġeðēoda
cūðon.'

Ðā ġemunde iċ hū sīo ǣ wæs ǣrest on Ebrēisc ġeðīode funden, ond
10　eft, ðā hīe Crēacas ġeliornodon, ðā wendon hīe hīe on hiora āgen
ġeðīode ealle, ond ēac ealle ōðre bēċ. Ond eft Lǣdenware swǣ same,
siððan hīe hīe ġeliornodon, hīe hīe wendon ealla ðurh wīse wealhstodas
on hiora āgen ġeðīode. Ond ēac ealla ōðra Crīstena ðīoda sumne dǣl
hiora on hiora āgen ġeðīode wendon. For ðȳ mē ðyncð betre, ġif īow
15　swǣ ðyncð, ðæt wē ēac suma bēċ, ðā ðe nīedbeðearfosta sīen eallum
monnum tō wiotonne, ðæt wē ðā on ðæt ġeðīode wenden ðe ealle
ġecnāwan mæġen, ond ġedōn, swǣ wē swīðe ēaðe magon mid Godes
fultume, ġif wē ðā stilnesse habbað, ðætte eall sīo ġioguð ðe nū is on
Angelcynne frīora monna, ðāra ðe ðā spēda hæbben ðæt hīe ðǣm
20　befēolan mæġen, sīen tō liornunga oðfæste, ðā hwīle ðe hīe tō nānre
ōðerre note ne mæġen, oð ðone first ðe hīe wel cunnen Englisc ġewrit
ārǣdan. Lǣre mon siððan furður on Lǣdenġeðīode ðā ðe mon furðor
lǣran wille, ond tō hīerran hāde dōn wille.

Ðā iċ ðā ġemunde hū sīo lār Lǣdenġeðīodes ǣr ðissum āfeallen wæs
25　ġiond Angelcynn, ond ðēah moniġe cūðon Englisc ġewrit ārǣdan, ðā
ongan iċ, onġemang ōðrum mislīcum ond maniġfealdum bisgum ðisses
kynerīċes ðā bōc wendan on Englisc ðe is genemned on Lǣden
Pastoralis, ond on Englisc *Hierdebōc*, hwīlum word be worde, hwīlum

andġit of andġiete, swǣ swǣ iċ hīe ġeliornode æt Pleġmunde mīnum
ærcebiscepe, ond æt Assere mīnum biscepe, ont æt Grimbolde mīnum
mæsseprīoste, ond æt Iōhanne mīnum mæsseprēoste. Siððan iċ hīe ðā
ġeliornod hæfde, swǣ swǣ iċ hīe forstōd, ond swǣ iċ hīe andġitfullīcost
āreċċean meahte, iċ hīe on Englisc āwende ; ond tō ǣlcum biscepstōle
on mīnum rīce wille āne onsendan ; ond on ǣlcre bið ān æstel, sē bið
on fīftegum mancessa. Ond iċ bebīode on Godes naman ðæt nān mon
ðone æstel from ðǣre bēċ ne dō, ne ðā bōc from ðǣm mynstre—uncūð
hū longe ðǣr swǣ ġelǣrede biscepas sīen, swǣ swǣ nū, Gode ðonc,
wel hwǣr siendon. For ðy iċ wolde ðætte hīe ealneġ æt ðǣre stōwe
wǣren, būton sē biscep hīe mid him habban wille, oððe hīo hwǣr tō
lǣne sīe, oððe hwā ōðre bī wrīte.

1   wundrade=wundrian(=to wonder)의 과거. 후속하는 ðāra gōdena wiotona와 ðæt hīe…가
목적어이다. swīðe swīðe=very much.

1-2   ðāra gōdena witona ðe…=about those good wise men who….

2   ġiū(ġeō)=formerly, of old. ealla=ðā bēċ(=those books)와 동격. be fullan=completely. cf.
full=full.

3   ġeliornod=learned. 원형은 ġeleornian. nǣnne=nān(=none)의 단수 대격. hiora ðā nǣnne
dǣl=not any part of them. dǣl=portion. ðā=at that time. noldon=ne+weldon=did not wish.
cf. weldon=wished. 원형은 willan. 뒤에 오는 wendan에 걸린다. wēndan=imagined,
expected. 원형은 wēnan.

5   ǣfre=ever. reċċelēase=negligent, careless.

6   sīo=bēon(=to be)의 가정법. lār=teaching. oðfeallan=decay, fall away, decline. for ðǣre
wilnunga=on purpose, deliberately. forlēton=forlǣtan(=to abandon, neglect, forsake)의 과
거. hit forlēton의 hit는 번역하는 일.

7   hēr…on londe=here…in this land. ðy…ðy=이들은 ðæt의 도구격(instrumental case)으로서
현대영어의 the more…, the more…의 전신이다. 직역하면 by that much…by that much
(그만큼 많으면 그만큼 더). māra=more. mā=more. ġeðēoda=languages.

8   cūðon=know. 원형은 cunnan.

9   sīo ǣ=the Law. Pentateuch(모세 5경)(구약성서의 처음 다섯 편). Ebrēisc ġeðīode=the
Hebrew language.

10   ðā…ðā=when…then. hīe=10행에 나타나는 세 개의 hīe 가운데서 첫 번째 것과 마지막 것
은 여성 단수 대격으로서 선행하는 ǣ에 일치하고 있으며, 가운데 hīe는 주격 복수형으로서
Crēacas에 일치한다. Crēacas=the Greeks. 본래 히브리어로 쓰여졌던 구약성경은 뒤에 북

아프리카에 사는 유대인들을 위해 희랍어로 번역되었고, 다시 로마 제국에 있는 기독교신 자들을 위해 라틴어로 번역되었다. Alfred는 이와 같은 성경 번역의 역사를 개관함으로써 성경을 자국어로 번역하는 정당성을 강조하고 있다.

11 ealle=두 개의 ealle 중 처음 것은 단수 여성 대격으로서 선행하는 hīe(=ǣ)에 일치하며, 두 번째 ealle는 후속하는 bēċ를 가리킨다. ealle ōðre bēċ는 구약성경의 나머지 부분을 가리 킨다. Lǣdenware=the Romans. swǣ same=likewise, in the same way. same=similarly.

12 siððan hīe hīe ġeliornodon, hīe hīe wendon ealla=after they(Lǣdenware) had learned them(bēċ), they translated them all. 여기서도 주어를 반복하고 있다. 두 번 나타나는 hīe hīe에서 각기 처음 hīe(=they)는 주어로, 두 번째 hīe(=them)는 목적어로 사용되고 있다. ġeliornodon의 원형은 ġeleornian(=to learn). wealhstodas=translators.

13 ðīoda=peoples, nations. sumne dǣl hiora=some part of them(=the biblical books). For ðy =therefore.

14 ðyncð=seems. 원형은 ðynċan(=to appear). betre=better.

14-15 ġif īow swǣ ðyncð=if it seems so to you. 여기서 īow(=ēow)라는 복수형을 쓴 것은 Alfred가 지금부터는 Wærferth주교뿐만 아니라 책을 받게 될 전국의 주교들에게 이야기하 고 있기 때문.

15 suma=some. ðā ðe=those which. nīedbeðearfosta=nīedbeðearf(=necessary)의 최상급.

15-16 eallum monnum=for all the people. ðā=suma bēċ를 선생사로 하는 them의 뜻일 수도 있 고, 아니면 then의 뜻을 갖는 단순한 부사일 수도 있다. tō wiotonne=to know. 원형은 witan. witonne는 witan의 굴절형 부정형.

17 ġecnāwan mæġe=may understand. ġedōn=done. 원형은 ġedōn. swǣ wē swīðe ēaðe magon=as we can (do) very easily. ēaðe=easily.

18 fultume=help, support. stilnesse=peace. ġioguð=young people, youth.

19 frīora=frīo(=free)의 복수 속격. frīora monna=Angelcynne를 수식한다. ðāra ðe=those of who. ðæt=with which. spēda=opportunity.

20 befēolan=apply oneself. liornunga=learning. oðfæste=oðfæstan(=to set)의 과거분사. ðā hwīle ðe=while, as long as.

20-21 tō nānre ōðerre note ne mæġen=cannot be set to any other employment.

21 oð ðone first ðe=until. cunnen=cunnan(=to know)의 가정법. ġewrit=writing.

22 ārǣdan=read. Lǣre=teach. 원형은 lǣran. ðā ðe=those who.

23 hīerran=hēah(=high)의 비교급. hāde=office, order. dōn=do. tō hīerran hāde dōn=advance to a higher position=promote.

24 āfeallen=fallen off. 원형은 āfeallan. āfeallan wæs는 과거완료.

25 ond ðēah=and yet. cūðon=can. 원형은 cunnan. ārǣdan=read.

26 ongan=began. 원형은 onginnan. onġemang=among. ōðrum=ōðer(=other)의 복수 여격. mislicum=misliċ(=various)의 복수 여격. maniġfealdum=maniġfeald(=manifold)의 복수 여 격. bisgum=bisgu(=concern, occupation, care)의 복수 여격.

26-27 ðisses kyneriċes=of this kingdom. ġenemned=nemnan(=to call, name)의 과거분사.

28 Hierdebōc=Shepherd's book. hwīlum=sometimes. word be worde=word for word.

29	andġit of andġiete=sense from sense=according to the (general) sense. andġit=meaning, sense. of=from. swǣ swǣ=just as. hīe=여성 단수 대격으로서 선행사는 Hierdebōc.
29-31	Plegmunde(Mercian)···Assere(Welsh)···Grimbolde(Flanders)···Iōhanne(대륙의 Saxon)=Alfred왕이 밖에서 모셔온 학자들이다.
30	ærċebiscepe=ærċebiscop(=archbishop)의 단수 여격. biscepe=biscop(=bishop)의 단수 여격.
31	mæsseprīoste=mass-priest. mæsseprēoste의 철자가 달라진 것에 주목할 것. 당시 철자가 고정되지 않았던 사정을 여실히 보여준다.
32	swǣ swǣ···절과 swǣ절은 그가 *Cura Pastoralis*를 잘못 이해했거나 오역했을 가능성을 겸손하게 인정하고 있다. forstōd=understood. 원형은 forstandan. andġitfullicost= andġitfullīċe(=clearly, intelligibly)의 최상급.
33	āreċċean=translate. meahte=could. 원형은 magan. āwende=translate. ǣlcum=ælċ(=each)의 중성 단수 여격. biscepstōle=episcopal. āne=āne bōc.
34	onsendan=send. ǣlcre=ælċ(=each)의 여성 단수 여격. bið=is. æstel=book-marker. 라틴어의 indicatorium.
34-35	sē bið on fiftegum mancessa=it will be worth fifty mancuses.
35	mancessa=mancus(=a gold coin worth 30 silver pence)의 복수 속격. bebīode=command. 원형은 bebēodan.
36	dō=take. 원형은 dōn. uncūð=(it is) unknown.
36-37	uncūð hū longe=(it being) uncertain how long.
37	ġelǣrede=learned. ġelǣran(=to teach, advise)의 과거분사.
37-38	swǣ swǣ nū, Gode ðonc, well hwǣr siendon=as now, thanks to God, there are nearly everywhere. sīen=가정법 복수 현재. Gode ðonc=thanks be to God.
38	wel hwǣr=well-nigh everywhere. For ðy=therefore. wolde=desire. hīe=the book and æstel. ealneġ=always. ðǣre stōwe=that place=the church.
39	būton=except.
39-40	hīo hwǣr tō lǣne sīe=it is to be lent out anywhere. hwǣr=where, somewhere. lǣne=loan.
40	hwā=someone. bī wrīte=copy. cf. bī(be)=about. wrīte=write.

When I remembered all this, then I wondered greatly at those good wise men who formerly existed throughout the English people and had fully studied all those books, that they did not wish to translate any part of them into their own language. But then I immediately answered myself and said : 'They did not imagine that men should ever become so careless and learning so decayed ; they refrained from it by intention and hoped that there would be the greater knowledge in this land the more languages we knew.'

Then I remembered how the law was first found in the Hebrew language, and afterwards, when the Greeks learned it, they translated it all into their own language, and all the other books as well. And afterwards in the same way the Romans, when they had learned them, they translated them all into their own language through learned interpreters. and all other Christian nations also translated some part of them into their own language. Therefore it seems better to me, if it seems so to you, that we also should translate certain books which are most necessary for all men to know, into the language that we can all understand, and also arrange it, as with God's help we very easily can if we have peace, so that all the youth of free men now among the English people, who have the means to be able to devote themselves to it, may be set to study for as long as they are of no other use, until the time they are able to read English writing well ; afterwards one may teach further in the Latin language those whom one wishes to teach further and wishes to promote to holy orders.

Then when I remembered how the knowledge of Latin had previously decayed throughout the English people, and yet many could read English writing, I began amidst other various and manifold cares of this kingdom to translate into English the book which is called *Pastoralis* in Latin and 'Shepherd's Book' in English, sometimes word for word, sometimes in a paraphrase, as I learned it from my archbishop Plegmund, and my bishop Asser, and my priest Grimbold and my priest John. When I had learned it, I translated it into English as I understood it and as I could interpret it most intelligibly ; and I will send one to every bishopric in my kingdom ; and in each there will be a book-marker worth fifty mancuses. And in the name of god I command that no one remove the book-marker from the book, nor the book from the minster ; it is uncertain how long there may be such learned bishops, as now, thanks be to God, there are almost everywhere ; therefore I desire that they should always lie at that place, unless the bishop want to have it with him, or it be anywhere on loan, or anyone be copying it.

(tr. Swanton)

VIII. WULFSTAN

ON FALSE GODS (1)
De Falsis Deis

1 Ēalā, ġefyrn is aæt ðurh dēofol fela ainga misfōr and aæt mancynn tō
swȳðe Gode mishȳrde and aæt hǣðenscype ealles tō wīde swȳðe
ġederede and ġyt dereð wīde. Ne rǣde wē aēah āhwār on bōcum aæt
man ārǣrde ǣniġ hǣðenġyld āhwār on worulde on eallum aām
5 fyrste ae wæs ǣr Nōes flōde. Ac syððan aæt ġewearð aæt Nembroð and
ðā entas worhton aone wundorlican stȳpel æfter Nōes flōde, and him ðā
swā fela ġereorda ġelamp, aæs ae bēċ secgað, swā ðæra wyrhtena wæs.
7ā syððan tōfērdon hȳ wīde landes and mancyn aā sōna swȳðe wēox.
And ðā æt hȳhstan wurdon hī bepæhte aurh ðone ealdan dēofol ae
10 Ādam iū ǣr beswāc, swā aæt hī worhton wōlīċe and ġedwollīċe him
hǣaene godas and ðone sōðan God and heora āgenne scyppend forsāwon
ae hȳ tō mannum ġescōp and ġeworhte.

Hī nāmon ēac him ðā aæt tō wisdōme, aurh dēofles lāre, aæt hȳ
wurðedon him for godas aā sunnan and ðone mōnan for heora
15 scīnendan beorhtnesse and him lāc aā æt nȳhstan aurh dēofles lāre
offrodon and forlēton heora Drihten ae hȳ ġescōp and ġeworhte. Sume
men ēac sǣdan be ðām scīnendum steorrum aæt hī godas wǣron and
āgunnan hȳ weorðian ġeorne and sume hȳ ġelȳfdon ēac on fȳr for
his fǣrlicum bryne, sume ēac on wæter, and sume hȳ on ðā eorðan,
20 forðan ae hēo ealle aing fēdeð. Ac hȳ mihton ġeorne tōcnāwan, ġif hī
cūðon aæt ġescead, aæt sē is sōð God ae ealle aās ðing ġescōp ūs
mannum tō brīce and tō note for his miclan gōdnesse ae hē mancynne
ġeūðe. Ðās ġesceafta ēac ealle dōð swā swā him ġedihte heora āgen
scyppend and ne magon nān aing dōn būtan ūres Drihtnes aafunge,

25 forðām ae nān ōðer scyppend nis būton se āna sōða God ae wē on
ġelȳfað and wē hine ǣnne ofer ealle ōðre aing lufiad and wurðiaa mid
ġewissum ġelēafan, cweaende mid mūðe and mid mōdes incundnesse
aæt sē ān is sōð God ae ealle ðing ġescōp and ġeworhte.

(이 글의 필자인 Wulfstan은 Worcester와 York에서 각기 주교와 대주교의 일을 맡았던 사람이다. 이 글은 Ælfric의 설교를 기초로 쓰여진 것으로서 당시 게르만족들 사이에 만연했던 이교 신에 대한 숭배를 경계하기 위해 쓰여졌다. 초기 중세 게르만족들이 기독교적 신과 이교도적 신을 혼동했던 사실의 한 예가 게르만어와 로망스어의 요일 이름이다. 예를 들어 게르만인들은 수요일(Mercury)에 대해 이교도의 Woden을 사용하고 있다. 그 결과 '수요일'은 프랑스어로는 mercredi인데 비해 영어에서는 Wednesday가 되었다. 설교자인 동시에 대중 연설자였던 Wulfstan의 글은 격정적인 동시에 직설적이다. 조용하고 명상적이었던 학자풍의 Ælfric의 글과 대조를 이룬다.)

1   Ēalā=Alas. ġefyrn=long ago. ðurh=because of. dēofol=devil. fela=many. 단수 취급을 받는다. misfōr=went wrong. 원형은 misfaran. mancynn=mankind. tō=too.

2   swȳðe=greatly. mishȳrde=disobeyed. 여격과 함께 쓰인다. 원형은 mishȳran. hǣðenscype= paganism. ealles tō wīde=altogether too widely.

3   ġederede=did harm. 원형은 (ġe)derian. ġyt=still. dereð=injured. 원형은 derian. rǣde= rǣdaa라고 해야 옳다. aēah=however. āhwǣr=anywhere.

4   ārǣrde=established. 원형은 ārǣran. hǣðenġyld=idolatry.

5   fyrste=time. ǣr=before. Nōes flōde=Noah's flood. cf. Gen 7-8. syððan=later. ġewearð= happened. 원형은 weorðan.

5-6   Nembroð and ðā entas=Nimrod and the giants. Gen 10.8-10에 의하면 Noah의 후손인 Nimrod는 힘이 세고 건장한 사냥꾼이긴 하였으나 여기서 암시하고 있듯이 Gen 6.4의 거인과는 관계가 없으며, Gen.11.1-9의 Babel 탑과도 관계가 없다. 중세에 퍼졌던 이와 같은 생각은 Augustine 등이 퍼트린 이야기의 탓이다.

6   entas=giants. worhton=built. 원형은 wyrċan. wundorlican=wonderful. stȳpel=tower.

6-7   him ðā swā fela ġereorda ġelamp=then as many languages came about (were created) for them. 여기서 swā는 다음에 나오는 swā와 짝으로 쓰인 것이다.

7   ġereorda=languages. ġelamp=happened, turned out. 원형은 ġelimpan. aæs ae bēċ secgað= according to what books say. wā ðæra wyrhtena wæs=as there were workmen.

8   tōfērdon=dispersed. 원형은 tōfēran. hȳ=they. landes=by land, across the land. wēox= increased. 원형은 weaxan.

9   æt hȳhstan=at last=in the end. bepǣhte=deceived. 원형은 bepǣċan. dēofol=devil. iū=long ago.

10   beswāc=betrayed. 원형은 beswīcan. worhton=made. 원형은 wyrċan. wōlīċe=perversely.

ġedwollīċe=heretically. him=for themselves.

11 sōðan=true. āgenne=own. scyppend=creator. forsāwon=scorned. 원형은 forsēon.

12 tō=as. ġescōp=created. 원형은 (ġe)scieppan. ġeworhte=made. 원형은 (ġe)wyrċan.y.

13 nāmon=took. 원형은 (ġe)niman. ēac=also. æt=it. tō=as. wisdōme=wisdom. lāre=teaching. hȳ=hī=they.

14 wurðedon=worshipped. 원형은 weorðian. him=for themselves. wurðedon과 함께 사용된 관계대명사이며 여기서는 번역하지 않아도 무방하다.

15 scīnendan=shining. 원형은 scīnan. beorhtnesse=brightness. him=(to) them. lāc=sacrifices. æt nȳhstan=at length, in the end, finally.

16 offrodon=offered. 원형은 offrian. forlēton=abandoned. 원형은 forlǣtan. Drihten=Lord, God.

17 sǣdan=said. 원형은 secgan. be=about. scīnendum steorrum=shining stars.

18 āgunnan=began. 원형은 āginnan. weorðian=whorship. ġeorne=earnestly. ġelȳfdon= believed. 원형은 ġelīefan. fȳr=fire.

19 fǣrlicum=sudden. 원형은 fǣrliċ. bryne=heat.

20 forðan ae=because. fēdeð=nourishes. 원형은 fēdan. mihton=could. 원형은 magan. ġeorne= readily. tōcnāwan=understand.

21 cūðon æt ġescead=knew reason=had the power of reason. ġescead=reason, distinction.

22 brīce=enjoyment. note=use. 원형은 notu. for=because of. miclan gōdnesse=great goodness.

23 ġeūðe=granted. 원형은 (ġe)unnan. Ðās=These. ġesceafta=created things. dōð=does. 원형 은 dōn. ġedihte=directed. 원형은 (ġe)dihtan. āgen=own.

24 būtan=without. aafunge=consent.

25 nis=is not. āna=only. on=in.

26 ġelȳfað=believe. 원형은 (ġe)lȳfan. ǣnne=alone. wurðiaa=worship. 원형은 weoraian.

27 ġewissum=sure. ġelēafan=faith. mōdes=of heart. incundnesse=conviction.

28 ān=alone.

Now, it was long ago that, because of the Devil, many things went wrong and that mankind disobeyed God too much, and that paganism all too widely inflicted damage—and widely inflicts damage still. We do not read anywhere in books, though, that they set up any idolatory anywhere in the world during all the time which was before Noah's flood. But then it happened that after Noah's flood, Nimrod and the giants wrought the marvellous tower ; and as the book tells, it came to pass that there were as many languages as there were workmen. Then afterwards they dispersed into distant lands, and then mankind soon greatly increased. And then at last they were deceived by the old Devil who had long before betrayed Adam, so that they perversely and heretically made pagan gods for themselves and scorned the true God and their own Creator who created and fashioned them as men.

Moreover, through the teaching of the Devil, they took it for wisdom to worship the sun and the moon as gods on account of their shining brightness ; and then at last, through the teaching of the Devil, offered them sacrifices and forsook their Lord who had created and fashioned them. Some men also said that the shining stars were gods, and began to worship them earnestly ; and some believed in fire on account of its sudden heat, some also in water, and some believed in the earth because it nourished all things. But they might have readily discerned, if they had the power of reason, that he is the true God who created all things for the enjoyment and use of us men, which he granted mankind because of his great goodness. Moreover, these created thins act entirely as their own Creator ordained for them, and can do nothing except by our Lords's consent, for there is no other Creator but the one true God in whom we believe. And with sure faith we love and worship him alone over all other things, saying with our mouths and with conviction of heart, that he alone is the true God, who has created and fashioned all things.

On False Gods (2)

1 Ġyt ðā hǣaenan noldon bēon ġehealdene on swā fēawum godum swā
hȳ hæfdan ac fēngon tō wurðienne æt nȳhstan mistliċe entas and
streċe woruldmen ae mihtiġe wurdan on woruldafelum and eġesfulle
wǣran aā hwȳle ae hȳ leofedon, and heora āgenum lustum fūllīċe
5 fullēodan. Ān man wæs on ġeardagum eardiende on aām īġlande ae
Crēta hātte se wæs Saturnus ġehāten, and sē wæs swā wælhrēow aæt
hē fordyde his āgene bearn, ealle būtan ānum, and unfæderelīċe macode
heora līf tō lyre sōna on ġeogoðe. Hē lǣfde swāaēah unēaðe ǣnne tō
līfe, aēah ðe hē fordyde aā brōðra elles, and sē wæs Iōuis ġehāten
10 and sē wearð hetol fēond. Hē āflȳmde his āgene fæder eft of ðām ylcan
foresǣdan īġlande ae Crēta hātte and wolde hine forfaran ġeorne ġif hē
mihte. And se Iōuis wearð swā swȳðe gāl aæt hē on his āgenre
swyster ġewīfode ; sēo wæs ġenamod Iūno and hēo wearð swȳðe hēaliċ
gyden æfter hǣðenscype ġeteald.
15 Heora twā dohtra wǣron Minerua and Uēnus. 7ās mānfullan men ae
wē ymbe specað wǣron ġetealde for ðā mǣrostan godas aā on ðām
dagum and aā hǣðenan wurðodon hȳ swȳðe aurh dēofles lāre. Ac se
sunu wæs swāaēah swȳðor on hǣðenscype ġewurðod aonne se fæder
wǣre and hē is ġeteald ēac ārwurðost ealra aǣra goda ae aā hǣðenan
20 on ðām dagum for godas hæfdon on heara ġedwylde. And hē hātte 7or
ōðrum naman betwux sumum aēodum, ðone Denisca lēoda lufiað swȳ
ðost and on heora ġedwylde weorðiaa ġeornost. His sunu hātte Mars,
se macode ǣfre ġewinn and wrōhte, and saca and wraca hē styrede
ġelōme. Ðysne yrming ðfter his forðsīðe wurðodon aā hǣðenan ēac
25 for hēaliċne god and swā oft swā hȳ fyrdedon oððe tō ġefeohte woldon,
aonne offrodon hȳ heora lāc on ǣr tō weorðunge aissum ġedwolgode.
And hȳ ġelȳfdon aæt hē miclum mihte heom fultumian on ġefeohte,
forðan ae hē ġefeoht and ġewinn lufude on līfe.

1 Ġȳt=yet. noldon=would not. ġehealdene=restricted. on=to. fēawum=few.

2 fēngon tō wurðienne=took to worshipping. wurðienne는 weorðian(=to worship)의 굴절 부정형. æt nȳhstan=in the end. mistlīċe=various. entas=giants.

3 streċe woruldmen=violent men of the earth=human being. migtiġe=mightyŋ strong. wurdan=became. woruldafelum=worldly powers. eġesfulle=awe-inspiring.

4 aā hwȳle ae=as long as. leofedon=lived. 원형은 libban. lustum=joy. fūllīċe=foully.

5 fullēodan=followed. 원형은 fullġan. ġeardagum=former days. eardiende=living.

6 hātte=hātan(=to call, name)의 과거분사. se=관계대명사의 who, 혹은 인칭대명사의 he 어느 쪽으로도 해석이 가능하다. wælhrēow=savage.

7 fordyde=did away with. āgene=own. bearn=child. unfæderelīċe=unlike a father. macode heora līf tō lyre=made their lives to destruction=destroyed their lives. macode=made. 원형은 macian. lyre=destruction.

8 sōna=early. ġeogoðe=youth. 원형은 ġeogua. ſæfde=left. 원형은 ſæfan. ſæfde…tō līfe=left …alive. swāaēah=nevertheless. unēaðe=reluctantly.

9 fordyde=did away with, destroyed. 원형은 fordōn. elles=otherwise. Iōuis=Jove.

10 wearð=became. hetol=savage. āfľȳmde=expelled. 원형은 āfľȳman(āflīeman). ylcan=same.

11 foresædan=aforesaid. forfaran=destroy.

12 swȳðe=greatly, strongly. gāl=wanton.

12-13 on his āgenre swyster ġewīfode=took his own sister as a wife.

13 ġewīfode=took to wife. 원형은 ġewīfian. Iūno=Juno. hēaliċ=extaled.

14 gyden=goddess. æfter=according to. ġeteald=reckoned.

15 Minerua=Minerva. Uēnus=Venus. mānfullan=wicked.

16 ymbe=about. mærostan=greatest.

17 wurðodon=honored, worshipped. 원형은 weorðian. lāre=teaching.

17-18 se sunu=Jove.

18 swāaēah=aēah=though. swȳðor=more greatly. aonne=than.

19 ārwurðost=most honorably. ealra=all. 원형은 eall.

20 ġedwylde=error.

21 ōðrum naman=by another name. Thor는 Jove(=Jupiter)와 동일시되는데, 이것은 아마도 그가 게르만족의 신들 가운데서 위계가 가장 높기 때문일 것이다. 기독교로 개종하기 이전에 그는 영국에서 Thunor(=thunder)로 알려지고 숭상되었다. betwux=among. aēodum= nations. ðone=whom. lēoda=people.

23 ġewinn=strife. wrōhte=contention. saca=conflict. wraca=enmity. 원형은 wracu. styrede= stirred up. 원형은 styrian.

24 ġelōme=often. yrming=wretch. forðsīðe=journey forth=death.

25 swā oft swā=as often as, whenever. fyrdedon=went to war. 원형은 fyrdian. oððe=or. tō ġefeohte woldon=wanted (to go) into battle. ġefeohte=battle, fight.

26 lāc=offering. on ǣr=beforehand, in advance. weorðunge=honor(to+d). edwolgode=false god.

27   ġelȳfdon=believed. 원형은 ġelīefan. miclum=greatly. fultumian=assist.
28   on līfe=when alive.

Yet the heathen would not be satisfied with as few gods as they had previously, but in the end took to worshipping various giants and violent men of the earth who became strong in worldly power and were awe-inspiring while they lived, and foully followed their own lusts. In former days there was a certain man living in the island called Crete who was called Saturn, and who was so savage that he destroyed his own sons—all but one—and unlike a father destroyed them early in childhood. Reluctantly he left one alive however, although he had destroyed all the brothers otherwise ; and he was called Jove, and he became a malignant enemy. He afterwards drove his own father out of that same aforesaid island called Crete and would readily have killed him if he could. And this Jove was so very lecherous that he took to wife his own sister, who was named Juno ; and she became a very important goddess according to pagan reckoning. Their two daughters were Minerva and Venus. These wicked men about whom we speak were reckoned the greatest gods in those days, and through the teaching of the Devil the heathen greatly honoured them. But the son, though, was more worshipped in paganism than the father was, and he is also reckoned the most honourable of all those whom the heathen in their error, took for gods in those days. And he whom the Danish people love most and, in their error most earnestly worship, was called by the other name Thor among certain nations. His son was called Mars, who always brought about strife and contention ; and he frequently stirred up conflict and enmity. After his death the heathen also honoured this wretch as an important god. And as often as they went to war or intended to do battle, then they offered their sacrifices beforehand in honour of this false god ; and they believed that he could assist them in battle because he loved battle and conflict when alive.

ON FALSE GODS (3)

1   Sum man ēac wæs ġehāten Mercurius on līfe, se wæs swȳðe facenfull
and, ðeah full snotorwyrde, swicol on dǣdum and on lēasbreġdum.
Ðone macedon aā hǣðenan be heora ġetæle ēac heom tō mǣran gode
and æt wega ġelǣtum him lāc offrodon oft and ġelōme aurh dēofles
5 lāre and tō hēagum beorgum him brōhton oft mistliċe loflāc. Ðes
ġedwolgod wæs ārwurðe ēac betwux eallum hǣðenum on aām dagum
and hē is Ōðon ġehāten ōðrum naman on Denisce wīsan. Nū secgað
sume aā Denisce men on heora ġedwylde aæt se Iōuis wǣre, ae hȳ 7or
hātað, Mercuries sunu, ae hī Ōðon namiað, ac hī nabbað nā riht,
10 forðan ae wē rǣdað on bōcum, ġe on hǣðenum ġe on Crīstenum, aæt se
hetula Iōus tō sōðan is Saturnes sunu. And sum wīf hātte Uēnus ; sēo
wæs Iōues dohtor and sēo wæs swā fūl and swā fracod on gālnysse
aæt hyre āgen brōðor wið hȳ ġehǣmde, aæs ae man sǣde, aurh dēofles
lāre, and ðā yfelan wurðiað aā hǣðenan ēac for hēaliċe fǣmnan.
15   Maneġe ēac ōðre hǣaene godas wǣron mistlīċe fundene and ēac
swylċe hǣaene gyldena on swȳðlicum wyrðmente ġeond middaneard,
mancynne tō forwyrde, ac aās synd aā fyrmestan ðēh aurh hǣðenscipe
ġetelde, aēah ðe hȳ fūlīċe leofodon on worulde. And se syrwienda
dēofol ae ā swīcað embe mancyn ġebrōhte aā hǣðenan men on ðām
20 hēalicon ġedwylde, aæt hī swā fūle him tō godum ġecuran ae heora
fūlan lust heom tō lage sylfum ġesettan and on unclǣnnesse heora līf
eal lyfedan aā hwīle ðe hī wǣran. Ac sē bið ġesǣliġ ae eal swylċ
oferhogað and ðone sōðan Godd lufað and weorðað ae ealle aing ġescōp
and ġeworhte. Ān is ælmihtiġ God on arȳm hādum, aæt is fæder and
25 suna and hāliġ gāst. Ealle aā ðrȳ naman befēhð ān godcund miht and
is ān ēċe God, waldend and wyrhta ealra ġescheafta. Him symle sȳ lof
and weorðmynt in ealra worulda woruld ā būtan ende. Āmen.

1   facenfull=crafty.

2   snotorwyrde=plausible in speech. swicol=deceitful. dǣdum=dǣd(=deed)의 복수 여격. lēasbreġdum=trickeries.

3   Ðone=Him. ġetæle=reckoning. heom=for themselves. mǣran=renowned, great.

4   æt wega ġelǣtum=at the junctions of ways=at crossroads. 액을 피하기 위해 여행자의 신인 Mercury의 형상을 교차로에 세우는 오래된 관습은 게르만족에게서 가져온 것으로 보인다. ġelǣte=junction.

5   tō hēagum beorgum=on the high hills. hēagum=high. 원형은 hēah. beorgum=hill. 원형은 beorg. loflāc=praise-offerings=offerings in honor of the god.

6   ġedwolgod=false god. ārwurðe=honorable.

7   wīsan=manner.

8   sume aā Denisce men=some of the Danish men. ġedwylde=error.

9   ae hī Ōðon namiað=앞의 sunu가 아니라 그 앞의 Mercuries를 수식한다. on=among. nabbað=do not have=nā(=not)+habbað(=have).

10   ġe…ġe=both…and. hetula=savage. 원형은 hetol.

11   tō sōðan=in truth. fūl=foul. fracod=wicked. gālnysse=lust.

13   ġehǣmde=copulated.

14   ðā yfelan=that evil (woman). for=as. fǣmnan=woman.

15   mistlīċe=in various ways. fundene=devised. 원형은 findan.

16   swylċe=likewise. on swȳðlicum wyrðmente=were held in great honor. swȳðlicum=great. wyrðmente=esteem. ġeond middaneard=throughout the world.

17   forwyrde=ruin. fyrmestan=foremost. ðēh(ðēah)=however. aurh=in.

18   syrwienda=scheming. ā=ever.

19   swīcað=is treacherous. embe=towards.

20   hēalicon=profound. æt=so that. fūle=vile (people). ġecuran=chose. 원형은 ġecēosan.

20-21   ae heora fūlan lust heom tō lage sylfum ġesettan=who (had) made their vile lust as a law for themselves. lage=law. 원형은 lagu. unclǣnnesse=uncleanness, impurity.

22   wǣran=existed. aā hwīle ðe hī wǣran=as long as they lied. ġesǣliġ=blessed. swylċ=such.

23   oferhogað=scorns, despises. 원형은 oferhogian.

24   Ān is ælmihtiġ God on arȳm hādum=one in three persons.

25   befēhð=encompass. 원형은 befōn. godcund=divine. is=(he) is.

26   ēċe=eternal. waldend=ruler. wyrhta=maker. symle=ever. sȳ=be. 가정법. lof=praise.

27   weorðmynt=esteem. in ealra worulda woruld ā būtan ende=for ever and ever, world without end.

    There was also a certain man called Mercury in life, who was very crafty and, although very clever in speech, deceitful in his actions and in trickeries.

Him also the heathen made for themselves a great god according to their reckoning, and over and again, through the teaching of the devil, offered him sacrifices at crossroads and often brought him various sacrifices of praise on the high hills. This false god also was venerated among all the heathen in those days, and in the Danish manner he is called by the other name Odin. Now some of those Danish men say in their error that Jove, whom they call Thor, was the son of Mercury, whom they name Odin ; but they are not right because we read in books, both pagan and Christian, that the malignant Jove is in fact Saturn's son. And a certain woman called Venus was the daughter of Jove, and she was so foul and so abandoned in lechery that through the teaching of the Devil, her own brother copulated with her so they said. And the heathen also worship that evil creature as an exalted woman.

Many other heathen gods also were devised in various ways, and heathen goddesses likewise held in great honour throughout the world to the ruin of mankind ; but these, though, are reckoned the most important in paganism, although they lived foully in the world. And the scheming Devil, who always deceives mankind, brought those heathen men into profound error so that they chose as gods for themselves and for as long as they lived spent all their lives in uncleanness. But blessed is he who completely scorns such affairs and loves and honours the true God who created and fashioned all thing. Almighty God is one in three persons, that is Father and son and Holy Spirit. All three names encompass once divine power and one eternal God, ruler and maker of all creation. To him for ever be praise and honour in all worlds, world without end. Amen.

(tr. Swanton)

WULFSTAN'S ADDRESS TO THE ENGLISH (1)

Sermo Lupi ad Anglos quando Dani maxime persecuti sunt eos, quod fuit anno millesimo XIIII ab incarnatione domini nostri Iesu Cristi.

1 Lēofan men, ġecnāwað þæt sōð is : ðēos woruld is on ofste, and hit nēalǣcð þām ende ; and ðȳ hit is on worulde ā swā leng swā wyrse, and swā hit sceal nȳde for folces synnan fram dæge tō dæge ǣr Antecrīstes tōcyme yfelian swȳðe ; and hūru hit wyrð þænne eġesliċ

5 and grimliċ wīde on worulde.

Understandað ēac ġeorne þæt dēofol þās þēode nū fela ġēara dwelode tō swȳðe, and þæt lȳtle ġetrȳwða wǣron mid mannum, þēah hī wel sprǣcan ; and unrihta tō fela rīcsode on lande, and næs ā fela manna be smēade ymbe þā bōte swā ġeorne swā man scolde ; ac dæġhwāmlīċe

10 man īhte yfel æfter ōðrum, and unriht rǣrde and unlaga maneġe ealles tō wīde ġynd ealle þās ðēode. And wē ēac for ðām habbað fela byrsta and bismra ġebiden ; and ġyf wē ǣniġe bōte gebīdan sculan, þonne mōte wē þæs tō Gode earnian bet þonne wē ǣr ðison dydon. For ðām mid miclan earnungan wē ġeearnodon þā yrmða þe ūs on sittað, and

15 mid swȳðe miclan earnungan wē þā bōte mōtan æt Gode ġerǣċan ġyf hit sceal heonanforð gōdiende wurðan⋯

Ac sōð is þæt iċ secge, þearf is þǣre bōte, for þām Godes ġerihta wanedan tō lange innan þysan earde on ǣġhwylcum ende, and folclaga wyrsedan ealles tō swȳðe, and hāliġnessa syndon tō griðlēase wīde,

20 and Godes hūs syndon tō clǣne berȳpte ealdra ġerihta and innan bestrȳpte ǣlcra ġerisena ; and wydewan syndon wīde fornȳdde on unriht tō ċeorle, and tō mæniġe foryrmde and ġehȳnede swȳðe, and earme men sindon sāre beswicene and hrēowlīċe besyrwde and ūt of ðisan earde wīde ġesealde swȳðe unforworhte fremdum tō ġewealde, and cradolċild

25 ġebēowode þurh wælhrēowe unlaga for lȳtelre þȳfðe wīde ġynd þās þēode ; and frēoriht fornumene, and ðrælriht ġenerwde, and ælmesriht

ġewanode. And, hraðost is tō cwebenne, Godes laga lāðe and lāra
forsewene ; and ðæs wē habbað ealle burh Godes yrre bysmor ġelōme,
ġecnāwe sē ðe cunne, and se byrst wyrð ġemǣne, bēah man swā ne
30　wēne, ealre bisse bēode, būtan God ġebeorge.

(Wulfstan은 늘 라틴어의 Lupus(=wolf)라는 필명으로 글을 썼다. 이 글이 쓰여진 1014년
은 Æthelred왕(978-1016) 치세의 마지막 부분에 해당한다. 덴마크 인들의 침략에 왕은
백성들을 덴마크 왕 Svein의 지배하에 남겨놓고 스스로는 Normandy로 도망을 간 때이
다. 나라는 말할 수 없는 곤경에 빠지게 되고 도덕은 땅에 떨어진 때이기도 하다.
Wulfstan은 묵시록적인 이미지를 원용하여 신의 가리킴에 등을 돌린 이 백성들이 당하
게 될 징벌을 강조하고 있다.)

Sermo Lupi ad Anglos quando Dani maxime persecuit sunt eos, quod fuit anno
millesimo XIIII ab incarnatione domini nostri Iesu Cristi=The Sermon of the Wolf to
the English, when the Danes were most severly persecuting them, which was in the
thousand and fourteenth year from the incarnation of our Lord Jesus Christ.
1　Lēofan=beloved. ġecnāwað=ġecnāwan(=to know)의 복수 명령. bæt sōð is=what(that
which) is true 또는 what the truth is. sōð는 형용사일 수도, 혹은 명사일 수도 있다. ðēos
woruld=this world. on=in. ofste=haste.
2　nēalǣcð=is nearing. 원형은 nēalēċan. bȳ=therefore. hit is on worulde ā swā leng swā
wyrse=it is ever so longer so worse=the longer it goes on, the worse it will get. ā=
always, continuously, for ever. wyrse=worse.
3　sceal=must. nȳde=necessarily. for=on account of. synnan=sin. fram dæġe tō tæġe=from
day to day.
3-4　ǣr Antecrīstes tōcyme=before the arrival of antichrist.
4　tōcyme=coming, arrival. yfelian=grow worse. swȳðe=exceedingly. hūru=indeed. wyrð=
will become. eġeslić=dreadful, awful.
5　grimlić=terrible, cruel. wīde=widely.
6　Understandað=understandan(=to understand)의 복수 명령. ēac=also. ġeorne=clearly,
carefully, earnestly. dēofol=the Devil. bēode=bēod(=people)의 단수 대격. fela ġeara=for
many years. dwelode=led astray. 원형은 dwelian.
7　tō swȳðe=greatly. lȳtle=few. ġetrȳwða=loyalties. cf. trēow=true. mid mannum=among
men. bēah=though. wel=fair.
8　sprǣcan=spoke. 원형은 sprecan. unrihta=wrongs. rīcsode=rīcsian (=to prevail)의 단수 과
거. fela rīcsode에서처럼 fela는 종종 단수형의 동사와 사용되었다. næs=was not. cf.
ne(=not)+wæs(=was). 이것도 fela가 단수 동사와 사용된 경우이다. ā=ever.
9　smēade=smēaġan(=to ponder, think)의 단수 과거. 주어는 앞의 fela이다. ymbe=about.

bōte=remedy. swā ġeorne swā man scolde=as eagerly as we should. dæġhwāmlīċe=
daily.

10 īhte=increased. 원형은 ‾ycan. unriht=injustice, wrong. rǣrde=committed. 원형은 rǣran.
unlaga=unlawful acts. cf. lagu=law. maneġe=many. ealles=altogether.

11 ġynd(ġeond)=throughout. for ðām=therefore. byrsta=injuries. 단수형은 byrst.

12 bismara=insults. 단수형은 bismer. ġebiden=endured. 원형은 ġebīdan. ġyf…bonne=if…
then. ǣniġe=any. ġebīdan=expect. 원형은 bīdan.

13 mōte wē=we must. mōte의 원형은 mōtan. tō=from. earnian=earn. bet=better. ǣr ðison=
formerly, hitherto. ðison=ðes(=this)의 여격.

14 earnungan=deservings, merit. ġeearnodon=earned. 원형은 ġeearnican. yrmða=miseries.
be ūs on sittað=that oppress us.

15 æt=from. ġerǣċan=obtain. heonanforð=henceforth, from here.

16 gōdiende=improved. 원형은 gōdian.

17 sōð=true. þearf=need. ġerihta=what is right, privilege, .

18 wanedan=dwindled away. 원형은 wanian. tō lange=too long. innan=within. earde=
country, region. þēode=nation. ǣġhwylċum=every, each. 원형은 ǣġhwylċ. ende=end,
region, limit, part. folclaga=public law.

19 wyrsedan=grew worse, deteriorated. 원형은 wyrsian. tō swȳðe=greatly. hāliġnessa=
sanctuaries. tō griðlēase=too much unprotected, violated. wīde=widely.

20 clǣne=utterly, completely. berȳpte=plundered. 원형은 berȳpan. ealdra=old. eald(=old)의
비교급.

21 bestrȳpte=stripped. 원형은 bestrȳpan. ǣlcra=ælċ(=each)의 복수 속격. ġerisena=what is
seemly, decent. ǣlcra ġerisena=of everything that is decent. wydewan=widuwe(=widow)
의 복수 주격. syndon=bēon(=to be)의 3인칭 복수 현재. wīde=widely, far and wide.
fornȳdde=compelled, forced. 원형은 fornȳdan. on unriht=wrongly.

22 ċeorle=man. fornȳdde on unriht tō ċeorle=compelled to a husband=force to marry. 당시
미망인은 교회의 허가 하에 1년 후에 재혼할 수 있었으나 가능하면 재혼하지 않는 것이 미
덕으로 여겨졌다. tō mæniġe=too many. foryrmde=reduced to poverty. 원형은 foryrman.
ġehȳnede=humiliated. 원형은 ġehȳnan. earme=poor.

23 sāre=grievously, sorely. beswicene=deceived. 원형은 beswīcan. rēowlīċe=cruelly.
besyrwde=ensnared. 원형은 besyrwan.

24 ġesealde=sold. 원형은 ġesellan. swȳðe=completely. unforworhte=uncondemned, innocent.
fremdum=to foreigners. ġewealde=control, power. fremdum tō ġewealde=to strangers
into power=into the power of strangers. 10세기 후반 Viking 족의 침공 시 시장에서 앵글
로 색슨인들을 사고 파는 것은 흔한 일이었다. cradolċild=child in the cradle, infant.
bloodthirsty.

25 ġebēowode=enslaved. 원형은 ġebēowian. wælhrēowe=cruel, savage. unlaga=violation of
law. ‾lytelre=petty. ‾byfþe=theft. ġynd(ġeond)=throughout.

26 þēode=nation, people. frēoriht=rights of free persons. fornumene=taken away. 원형은

forniman. ðrǣlfriht=rights of slaves. 앵글로 색슨 시대에도 노예 제도가 존속했다. ġenerwde=restricted. 원형은 nierwan. ælmesriht=right to alms.

27 ġewanode=dwindled. 원형은 ġewanian. hraðost tō cwebenne=quickest is to tell=to be brief. hrabe=quickly. lāðe=hated. lāra=teachings.

28 forsewene=despised. 원형은 forsēon. bæs=(because) of that. habbað=experience. 원형은 habban. yrre=anger. bysmor=shame, disgrace, insult. ġelōme=frequently.

29 ġecnāwe=ġecnāwan(=know)의 가정법으로서 기원을 나타낸다. cunne=cunnan(=to able to) 의 가정법 현재 3인칭 단수. byrst=injury. ġemǣne=common. bēah=though. ġecnāwe sē ðe cunne=let (him) understand, he who can. ġemǣne=common.

30 wēne=believe. 원형은 wēnan. ealre bisse bēode=for all this nation. būtan=except. ġebeorge=protect, defend. 원형은 ġebeorgan.

Beloved men, recognize what the truth is : this world is in haste and it is drawing near the end, and therefore the longer it is the worse it will get in the world. And it needs must thus become very much worse as a result of the people's sins prior to the advent of Antichrist ; and then, indeed, it will be terrible and cruel throughout the world.

Understand properly also that for many years now the Devil has led this nation too far astray, and that there has been little loyalty among men although they spoke fair, and too many wrongs have prevailed in the land. And there were never many men who sought a remedy as diligently as they should ; but daily they added one evil to another, and embarked on many wrongs and unlawful acts, all too commonly throughout this whole nation. And on that account, we have also suffered many injuries and insults. And if we are to expect any remedy then we must deserve better of God than we have done hitherto. Because we have earned the miseries which oppress us by great demerit, we must obtain the cure from God, if it is to improve henceforth by very great merit.…

But it is true what I say ; there is need of a remedy, because God's dues have for too long dwindled away in every region within this nation, and the laws of the people have deteriorated all too much, and sanctuaries are commonly violated, and the houses of God are completely despoiled of ancient rights, and stripped of everything decent inside. And widows are wrongfully forced to take a husband. And too many are harassed and greatly humiliated, and poor men are painfully deceived and cruelly enslaved and, completely innocent, commonly sold out of this country into the power of foreigners, and through cruel injustice children in the cradle are enslaved for petty theft commonly throughout this nation, and the rights of freemen are taken away and the rights of slaves restricted, and the right to alms diminished ; and, to be brief, God's laws are hated and his teachings scorned. And therefore, through God's anger, we are all frequently put to shame ; let him realize it who can. And although one might not imagine so, the harm will become common to this entire nation, unless God defend us.

WULFSTAN'S ADDRESS TO THE ENGLISH (2)

1   For ðām hit is on ūs eallum swutol and ġesȳne þæt wē ǣr bisan oftor
brǣcon þonne wē bēttan, and ðȳ is þisse þēode fela onsǣġe. Ne dohte
hit nū lange inne ne ūte, ac wæs here and hunger, bryne and blōdġyte
on ġewelhwylċon ende oft and ġelōme ; and ūs stalu and cwalu, strīc

5   and steorfa, orfcwealm and uncoðu, hōl and hete and rȳpera rēaflāc
derede swȳðe bearle, and ūs ungylda swȳðe ġedrehton, and ūs
unwedera foroft wēoldan unwæstma.

    For þām on bisan earde wæs, swā hit þinċan mæġ, nū fela ġēara
unrihta and tealte ġetrȳwða ǣġhwǣr mid mannum. Ne bearh nū foroft

10   ġesib ġesibbum bē mā be fremdan, ne fæder his bearne, ne hwīlum
bearn his āġenum fæder, ne brōðor ōðrum. Ne ūre nǣniġ his līf ne
fadode swā swā hē scolde, ne ġehādode regollīċe ne lǣwede lahlīċe ; ac
worhtan lust ūs tō lage ealles tō ġelōme, and nāðor ne hēoldon ne lāre
ne lage Godes ne manna swā swā wē scoldan. Ne ǣnig wið ōberne

15   ġetrēowlīce bōhte swā rihte swā hē scolde, ac mǣst ǣlċ swicode and
ōðrum derede wordes and dǣde ; and hūru unrihtlīċe mǣst ǣlċ ōberne
æftan hēaweð mid scandlican onscytan and mid wrōhtlācan : dō māre
ġyf hē mæġe.

    And scandliċ is tō specenne þæt geworden is tō wīde and eġesliċ is tō

20   witanne þæt oft dōð tō maneġe, þe drēogað þā yrmbe þæt scēotað
tōgædere and āne cwenan ġemǣnum ċēape bicgað ġemǣne and wið þā
āne fȳlbe ādrēogað, ān after ānum and ǣlċ æfter ōðrum, hundum
ġeliċċast þe for fȳlbe ne scrīfað, and syððan wið weorðe syllað of lande
fēondum tō ġewealde Godes ġesceafte and his āġenne ċēap þe hē dēore

25   ġebohte.

    Ēac wē witan ful ġeorne hwǣr sēo yrmð ġeweard þæt fæder ġesealde
his bearn wið weorðe, and bearn his mōdor, and brōðor sealde ōberne
fremdum tō ġewealde ūt of ðisse þēode ; and eal þæt syndon micle and

egeslice dǣda, understande sē ðe wille. And gȳt hit is mǣre and ēac
mǣniġfealdre bæt dereð bisse bēode. Mǣniġe syndan forsworene and
swȳðe forlogene, and wed synd tōbrocene oft and ġelōme ; and bæt is
ġesȳne on bisse bēode bæt ūs Godes yrre hetelīċe on sit, ġecnāwe sē ðe
cunne.

1   swutol=clear, evident. ġesȳne=visible, evident. swutol and ġesȳne나 4행에 나오는 oft and
     ġelōme처럼 동의어를 병렬하는 표현 방법은 Wulfstan이 즐겨 쓰던 수사법 중의 하나이다.
     ǣr bisan=before. oftor=more often. oft(=often)의 비교급.

2   brǣcon=broke. 원형은 brecan(=to break, transgress). bonne=than. bēttan=atoned. 원형은
     bētan. ðy=therefore. is bisse bēode fela onsǣġe=much is assailing this nation. onsǣġe
     (adj)=attacking, assailing. 여격을 요구한다.

2-3 Ne dohte hit=It has not availed=Things have not thrived(prospered). dohte=dugan(=to be
     of no use, avail, thrive)의 3인칭 단수 과거.

3   inne ne ūte=neither in nor out=everywhere. here=devastation. bryne=burning, fire, flame.
     blōdġyte=bloodshed.

4   ġewelhwylcon=nearly every. 원형은 ġewelhwilċ. ende=region. oft and ġelōme=often and
     frequently=over and over again. ġelōme=frequently, often, constantly. stalu=theft.
     cwalu=murder. strīc=plague. 이 단어는 Wulfstan의 글에서만 발견된다.

5   steorfa=pestilence. orfcwealm=cattle-plague, murrain. uncobu=disease. hōl=slander, malice.
     hete=hatred. rȳpera=rȳpere(=robber)의 복수 속격. rēaflāc=robbery, plundering.

6   derede=injured, harmed. 원형은 derian. bearle=hard, harshly, violently. ungylda=excessive
     taxes. ġedrehtan=oppressed. 원형은 ġedreċċan.

7   unwedera=bad weather, storm. foroft=very often. wēoldan=wealdan(=to cause, wield,
     control, manage)의 과거. unwæstma=crop failures. cf, wæstm=fruit.

8   swā hit binċan mæġ=so it might be thought. binċan(bynċan)=to seem, appear, think.
     tealte=unstable, wavering.

9   ġetrȳwða(ġetreowb)=loyalties. ǣghwǣr=everywhere. mid mannum=among men.
     bearh=protects. 원형은 beorgan. 여격을 지배한다.

10 ġesib=kinsman. 주격. ġesibban=kinsman. 여격이 사용된 것은 앞에 나온 동사 bearh
     (beorgan)가 여격을 지배하기 때문. bē mā be=any more than. fremdan=strangers. bearne=
     child. 역시 여격이다. ne fæder his bearne=ne bearh fæder his bearne=nor a father
     protects his child. hwīlum=sometimes.

11 āġenum=own(=father). ōðrum=ōðrum brōðor. Ne=nor. ūre=of us. nǣniġ=none.

12 fadode=regulated, arranged. 원형은 fadian. ne ġehādode regollīċe ne=neither those in
     holy orders(those consecrated) according to the rule. ġehādian=consecrate, ordain.
     regollīċe=according to rule. lāwede=unlearned, lay. lahlīċe=lawfully.

13 worhtan=(we) have made. 원형은 wyrċan. lust=joy, pleasure. lage=lagu(=law)의 여격. ūs=for us. tō ġelōme=too often. nāðor=neither. hēoldon=held. 원형은 healdan.

14 wið=towards.

15 ġetrēowlīċe=loyally. bōhte=has intended. 원형은 benċan(=to think). mǣst=almost. ǣlċ=everyone. swicode=has betrayed. 원형은 swician.

16 wordes and dǣde=in word and deed. hūru=certainly, truly.

17 æftan=in the back, from behind. hēaweð=stabs. 원형은 hēawan. scandlican=shameful. onscytan=attacks. wrōhtlācan=wrongful accusation, calumny.

17-18 dō māre gyf hē mæġe=let him do more if he can. dū=dūn(=to do)의 단수 명령.

19 scandliċ=shameful. tō sprecenne=to speak. bæt=what. ġeworden=ġeweorban(=to become, happen)의 과거분사. tō wīde=widely. eġesliċ=dreadful, fearful.

19-20 tō witanne=to know.

20 bæt=what. dōð=did. 원형은 dōn. maneġe(=maniġ)=many. drēogað=commit, undergo. 원형은 drēogan. yrmþe=atrocity, crime. sċēotað=(they) put in (club). 원형은 sċēotan.

21 tōgædere=together. āne cwenan ġemǣnum ċēape bicgað ġemǣne=buy a woman in common(ġemǣne) as a joint(ġemǣnum) purchase. cwenan=cwene(=woman)의 단수 대격. ġemǣnum=ġemǣne(=joint, in common)의 단수 여격. ċēap=purchase. bicgað=bicgan(=to buy)의 3인칭 단수.

22 āne=one. fylbe=foul sin. ādrēogað=commit, practice. 원형은 ādrēogan. hundum=dogs.

23 ġeliċċast=most like. 여격을 지배한다. 원형은 ġeliċ. hundum ġeliċċast=just like dogs. scrīfað=care about. 원형은 scrīfan. syððan=later, wið weorðe=for a price. syllað=give up. 원형은 sellan.

24 fēondum=enemy. ġewealde=power, control. Godes ġesceafte=God's creature=the woman. āġenne=own. ċēap=purchase. dēore=dearly.

25 ġebohte=bought. 원형은 ġebicgan.

26 ġeorne=well, clearly. hwǣr=where. ġesealde=sold. 원형은 ġesellan.

28 micle=much. 원형은 miċel.

29 dǣda=deed. understande=understandan(=to understand)의 가정법 3인칭 단수 현재. 기원을 나타낸다. ġyt=yet. māre=greater.

30 mæniġfealdre=mæniġfeald(=manyfold, numerous, diverse)의 비교급. dereð=injures. 원형은 derian. forsworene=forsworn. 원형은 forswerian.

31 forlogene=perjured. 원형은 forlēogan. wed=pledges. tōbrocene=tōbrecan(=to break to pieces, destroy, violate)의 과거분사.

32 ġesȳne=visible, evident. yrre=anger. heteliċe=violently, terribly.

For it is clear and evident in us all that we have hitherto more often transgressed than we have atoned, and therefore many things fall upon this nation. For long now, nothing has prospered here or elsewhere, but in every region there has been devastation and famine, burning and bloodshed over and again. And stealing and slaughter, plague and pestilence, murrain and disease, slander and hatred, and the plundering of robbers have damaged us very severly ; and excessive taxes have greatly oppressed us, and bad weather has very often caused us crop-failures.

Wherefore for many years now, so it seems, there have been in this country many injustices and unsteady loyalties among men everywhere. Now very often kinsman will not protect a kinsman any more than a stranger, nor a father his son, nor sometimes a son his own father, nor one brother another. Nor has any of us regulated his life just as he ought, neither clerics according to rule, nor laymen according to the law. But all too frequently, we have made lust a law to us, and have kept neither the teachings nor the laws of God or man just as we ought ; nor has anyone intended loyalty towards another as justly as he ought, but almost all men have betrayed and injured others by word and deed ; and in any case, almost all men wrongfully stab others in the back with shameful attack ; let him do more if he can.

And it is shameful to speak of what has too commonly happened, and it is dreadful to know what many too often do, who practice that wretchedness that they club together and buy one woman in common as a joint purchase, and with the one commit filth one after another and each after the other just like dogs who do not care about filth ; and then sell for a price out of the land into the power of enemies the creature of God and his own purchase that he dearly bought.

Also we know well where the wretchedness has occurred that father has sold son for a price, and son his mother, and one brother has sold another into the power of foreigners ; and all these are grave and dreadful deeds, let him understand who will. And yet what is injuring this nation is greater and also more multifarious. Many are forsworn and greatly perjured, and pledges are broken over and again ; and it is evident in this nation that the wrath of God violently oppresses us, let him realize it who can.

WULFSTAN'S ADDRESS TO THE ENGLISH (3)

1   Nis ēac nān wundor bēah ūs mislimpe, for ðām wē witan ful ġeorne
bæt nū fela ġeara men nā ne rōhton foroft hwæt hȳ worhtan wordes
oððe dǣde ; ac wearð bes bēodscype, swā hit binċan mæġ, swȳðe
forsyngod burh mæniġfealde synna and burh fela misdǣda, burh morðæda
5   and ðurh māndǣda, burh ġītsunga and ðurh ġīfernessa, burh stala and
burh strūdunga, burh mansylena and ðurh hǣðene unsida, burh
swicdōmas and ðurh searocræftas, burh lahbrycas and ðurh ǣswicas,
burh mǣġrǣsas and ðurh manslihtas, burh hādbrycas and ðurh
ǣwbrycas, burh sibbleġeru and ðurh mistliċe forligru. And ēac syndan
10   wīde, swā wē ǣr cwǣdan, burh āðbrycas and ðurh wedbrycas and ðurh
mistliċe lēasunga forloren and forlogen mā bonne scolde, and
frēolsbricas and fæstenbricas wīde ġeworhte oft and ġelōme.
    And bȳ is nū ġeworden wīde and sīde tō ful yfelan ġewunan bæt
menn swȳðor scamað nū for gōddǣdan bonne for misdǣdan ; for ðām
15   tō oft man mid hōcere gōddǣda hyrweð and godfyrhte lehtreð ealles tō
swȳðe, and swȳðost man tǣleð and mid olle ġegrēteð ealles tō ġelōme
bā ðe riht lufiað and Godes eġe habbað be ǣnigum dǣle.
    Ān bēodwita wæs on Brytta tīdum, Gildas hātte, sē āwrāt be heora
misdǣdum, hū hī mid heora synnan swā oferlīċe swȳðe God ġegrǣmedon
20   bæt hē lēt æt nȳhstan Engla here heora eard ġewinnan and Brytta
duguðe fordōn mid ealle.
    Ac utan dōn swā ūs bearf is, warnian ūs be swilcan ; and sōð is bæt
iċ secge, wyrsan dǣda wē witan mid Englum sume ġewordene aonne
wē mid Bryttan āhwār gehȳrdan ; and ðȳ ūs is bearf miċel bæt wē ūs
25   bebenċan, and wið God sylfne bingian ġeorne. And utan dōn swā ūs
bearf is, ġebūgan tō rihte, and be suman dǣle unriht forlǣtan, and
bētan swȳðe ġeorne bæt wē ǣr brǣcan. And utan God lufian and Godes
lagum fyliġean, and ġelǣstan swȳðe ġeorne bæt bæt wē behētan bā wē

fulluht underfēngan oððon bā be æt fulluhte ūre forespecan wǣron.

30 And utan word and weorc rihtlīċe fadian, and ūre inġeðanc clǣnsian
ġeorne, and āð and wedd wǣrlīċe healdan, and sume ġetrȳwða habban
ūs betwēonan būtan uncræftan, and utan gelōme understandan bone
miclan dōm be wē ealle tō sculan, and beorgan ūs ġeorne wið bone
weallendan bryne helle wītes, and ġeearnian ūs bā mǣrða and ðā

35 myrhða be God hæfð ġeġearwod bām ðe his willan on worulde
ġewyrcað. God ūre helpe. Amen.

1 Nis=ne is. bēah=even if. ūs mislimpe=(it) goes wrong for us. 원형은 mislimpan. ġeorne=
clearly.

2 fela ġeara=for many years. rōhton=cared about. 원형은 reċċan. foroft=very often. hȳ
(hīe)=they. worhtan=did. 원형은 wyrċan.

3 bēodscype=nation. swā hit binċan mæġ=so it seems. binċan(bynċan)=seem, appear.

4 mæniġfealde=manifold, numerous. misdǣda=misdeed. morðdǣda=deadly deeds.

5 māndǣda=evil deeds. gītsunga=avarice. ġīfernessa=greed.

6 strūdunga=robberies. mansylena=sale of men. hǣðene unsida=heathen abuses. 당시 이
교도들의 제물 바치기, 점치기, 우상숭배 등에 대해서는 이를 다스리는 엄격한 법이 있었
다. unsida(abuses)의 원형은 unsidu.

7 swicdōmas=deceptions. searocræftas=frauds. lahbrycas=law-breaches. 원형은 lahbryċe.
ǣswicas=transgressions.

8 mǣġrǣsas=attacks on kinsmen. manslihtas=manslaughters. hādbrycas=injuries to those
in holy orders. 원형은 hādbryċe. 이와 같은 범죄에 대해서도 엄격한 처벌이 가해졌다.

9 ǣwbrycas=adulteries. 원형은 ǣwbryċe. sibbleġeru=acts of incest. mistliċe=various,
diverse. forligru=fornications. syndan(=are)=뒤에 나오는 forloren과 forlogen이 여기에 걸
린다.

10 āðbrycas=oath-breakings. 원형은 āðbryċe. wedbrycas=pledge-breakings. 원형은 wedbryċe.

11 lēasunga=falsehoods. forloren=destroyed, lost. 원형은 forlēosan. forlogen=perjured. 원형
은 forlēogan. mā bonne scolde=more (people) than should have been).

12 frēolsbricas=failures to observe festivals. 원형은 frēolsbriċe. fæstenbricas=fast-breakings.

13 bȳ=by that. is nū ġeworden wīde and sīde tō ful yfelan ġewunan=it has become a
very evil custom. sīde=widely. wīde and sīde=far and wide. ġewunna=custom.

14 menn swȳðor scamað=it shames people more greatly=people are more greatly ashamed.
swīðor=swīðe(=very, exceedingly)의 비교급. goddǣdan=good deeds.

15 tō oft=very often. hōcere=insult. hyrweð=derides. hyrwan. godfyrhte=God-fearing (people)
lehtreð=reviles. 원형은 lehtrian.

15-16 ealles tō swȳðe=all too much.

16 swȳðost=most of all, especially. tǣleð=slanders. 원형은 tǣlian. olle=contempt. ġegrēteð=
    attacks. 원형은 grētan. ealles tō ġelōme=all too often.

17 þā=those. ðe=관계대명사. riht=justice. eġe=fear. be=to. dǣle=extent.

18 bēodwita=learned man. Brytta=of the Britons. Gildas=5, 6세기경의 문필가. 그는 *De
    excidio Britanniae*('On the ruin of Britain')라는 글에서 Briton인들은 그들이 지은 죄값으
    로 천사의 군대(Angle족)에 의해 멸망했다고 개탄하고 있다. hātte=called. āwrāt=wrote.
    원형은 āwrītan. be=about.

19 oferlīċe=excessively. ġegrǣmedon=provoked. 원형은 ġegremian.

20 æt nȳhstan=at length, last. nȳhst는 nēah (=near)의 최상급. eard=country. ġewinnan=
    conquer.

21 duguðe=nobility. fordōn=destroy.

22 utan=let us. þearf=need. warnian=warn. be swilcan=an about such (things). soð=true.

23 wyrsan=worse. mid=among.

24 āhwǣr=anywhere. ġehȳrdan=heard.

25 bebenċan=bring to mind, reflect on. God sylfne=God himself. þingian=intercede.

26 ġebūgan=bow. dǣle=part, share, extent. forlǣtan=forsake.

27 bētan=atone for, amend, compensate. þæt=what. bræcan=broke. 원형은 brecan.

28 fyliġean=follow. 원형은 fylġan. ġelǣstan=fulfil. behētan=promised. 원형은 behātan.

29 fulluht=baptism. underfēngan=received. 원형은 underfōn. oððon=or. orespecan=sponsors.

30 fadian(v)=order. inġeðanc=inner thought=conscience. clǣnsian=cleanse, purify.

31 āð=oath. wedd=pledge. wærlīċe=carefully. healdan=hold, keep. sume ġetrȳwða=some
    loyalties.

32 būtan=without. uncræftan=deceits.

33 dōm=decree, judgement. sculan=must (come). beorgan=protect, defend. wið=against.

34 weallendan=surging. weallan (=well up)의 현재분사. bryne=burning, fire. helle wītes=of
    hell torment. ġeearnian=earn. mǣrða=glories. 원형은 mǣrþu.

35 myrhða=joys. ġeġearwod=prepared. 원형은 ġeġearwian.

36 God ūre helpe=May God help us. helpe는 helpan(=to help)의 가정법으로서 기원을 나타낸
    다. ūre가 사용된 것은 동사 helpan이 속격을 요구하기 때문.

    And is it no wonder things go badly for us though. For we know full well
that for many years now men have too often not cared what they did by
word or deed ; but this nation, so it seems, has become totally sinful through
manifold sins and through many misdeeds : through deadly sins and through
evil deeds, through avarice and through greed, through theft and through
pillaging, through the selling of men and through heathen vices, through
betrayals and through plots, through breaches of the law and through legal

offences, through attacks on kinsmen and through manslaughters, through injury done to those in holy orders and through adulteries, through incest and through various fornications. And commonly also, as we said before, more than should be are ruined and perjured through the breaking of oaths and through the breaking of pledges and through various lies. And failure to observe festivals and the breaking of fasts occurs commonly over and again.

And therefore it has now reached such an evil state of affairs far and wide, that men are now more ashamed of good deeds than of misdeeds ; because too often they dismiss good deeds with derision, and godfearing people are abused all too much, and especially reviled and treated with contempt are those who love justice and fear God in any action.

There was a historian in the time of the Britons called Gildas. He wrote about their misdeeds, how by their sins they angered God so very excessively that finally he allowed the host of the English to conquer their land and to destroy the nobility of the Britons altogether.

But let us do as is necessary for us—warn ourselves by such things. And it is true what I say ; we know of worse deeds among the English than we have anywhere heard of among the Britons. And therefore it is very necessary that we reflect about ourselves and earnestly plead with God himself. And let us do as is necessary for us—bow to justice and in some part to leave off injustice, and to compensate very carefully for what we previously broke. And let us love God and follow God's laws, and very diligently practise what we promised when we received baptism—or those who were our sponsors at baptism. And let us order words and works aright, and earnestly cleanse our conscience, and carefully keep oath and pledge, and have some loyalty between us without deceit. And let us frequently consider the great Judgement to which we must all come, and carefully defend ourselves against the suffering flame of hell-torment, and earn for ourselves those glories and those joys which God has prepared for them that work his will in the world. May God help us. Amen.

(tr. Swanton)

Old English

ANGLO-SAXON VERSE (운문)

IX. RELIGIOUS POEMS

CAEDMON'S HYMN

1 Nū wē sculon herian   heofonrīċces Weard,
  Meotodes meahte   and his mōdġeaanc,
  weorc Wuldor-Fæder,   swā hē wundra ġehwæs,
  ēċe Dryhten,   ōr onsteade.

5 Hē ǣrest sċēop   eorðan bearnum
  heofon tō hrōfe,   hāliġ Scieppend ;
  7ā middanġeard   mann-cynnes Weard,
  ēċe Dryhten,   æfter tēode,
  fīrum foldan,   Frēa eallmihtiġ.

(기독교를 주제로 한 최초의 고대영어 문헌이다. 전통적인 게르만족의 작시법을 사용하고 있다. 각행은 중간휴지(casura)에 의해 전후반으로 나누어지며, 두운(alliteration)을 지키고 있다. Caedmon's Hymn은 원래 Bede의 *Ecclesiastical History of the English People* (*Historia Ecclesiastica Gentis Anglorum*)에 들어있던 것이다. Caedmon은 이 밖에도 성경을 주제로 한 많은 작품을 쓴 것으로 알려져 있으나 현재 남아있는 것은 이 기도문뿐이다. 배우지 못한 한낱 목동이었던 그가 어떻게 시를 쓸 수 있었는지는 수수께끼이다.)

1 herian=praise, glorify. Weard=gurdian.
2 Meotodes=creator's. meahte=miht(=might)의 단수 대격. mōdġebanc=conception, purpose of mind.
3 weorc wuldorfæder=action of the glory-father. weorc=work. Wuldor-Fæder=Father of Glory, God. swā=how. wundra ġehwæs=each of the marvels. wundra=wundor(=wonder, miracle)의 복수 속격. ġehwæs=hwā(=who)의 속격=whose.
4 ēċe=eternal. Dryhten=lord. ōr=beginning. onstealde=establish. 원형은 onstellan.
5 ǣrest=first. sċēop=created. 원형은 scieppan. eorðan bearnum=for the children of the earth=for humankind of the earth. bearnum=bearn(=child)의 복수 여격.
6 tō=as. hrōfe=roof. hāliġ=holy. Scieppend=creator. cf. scieppan=to create.
7 7ā=then. middanġeard=middle earth=the world. manncynnes=mankind.
8 tēode=tēon(=to make, prepare, adorn)의 과거.

9   fīrum foldan=made/adorned the earth for men *or* made/adorned it(=middle-earth) for the men of the earth. fīrum=fīras(=people)의 복수 여격. foldan=earth. 원형은 folde. Frēa=the Lord. eallmihtiġ=almighty.

Now we must praise the Guardian of Heaven,
the might of the Lord and His purpose of mind,
the work of the Glorious Father ; for He,
God Eternal, established each wonder,
He, Holy Creator, first fashioned
heaven as a roof for the sons of men.
Then the Guardian of Mankind adorned
this middle-earth below, the world for men,
Everlasting Lord, Almighty King.

                                        (tr. Crossley-Holland)

The Dream of the Rood (1)

1   Hwæt, iċ swefna cyst   secgan wylle

hwæt mē ġemǣtte   tō midre nihte

syðban reordberend   reste wunedon.

    7ūhte mē bæt iċ ġesāwe   syllicre trēow

5   on lyft lǣdan,   lēohte bewunden,

bēama beorhtost.   Eall bæt bēacen wæs

begoten mid golde.   Ġimmas stōdon

fæġere æt foldan scēatum ᛬   swylċe bǣr fīfe wǣron

uppe on bām eaxleġespanne.   Behēoldon bǣr engel Dryhtnes ealle

10   fæġere burh forðġesceaft.   Ne wæs ðǣr hūru fracodes ġealga

ac hine bǣr behēoldon   hāliġe gāstas,

men ofer moldan   ond eall bēos mǣre ġesceaft.

    Sylliċ wæs se siġebēam   ond iċ synnum fāh,

forwunded mid wommum.   Ġeseah iċ wuldres trēow,

15   wǣdum ġeweorðode,   wynnum scīnan,

ġeġyred mid golde.   Ġimmas hæfdon

bewriġene weorðlīċe   wealdendes trēow.

Hwæðre iċ burh bæt gold   onġytan meahte

earmra ǣrġewin   bæt hit ǣrest ongan

20   swǣtan on bā swīðran healfe.   Eall iċ wæs mid sorgum ġedrēfed,

forht iċ wæs for bǣre fæġran gesyhðe.   Ġeseah iċ bæt fūse bēacen

wendan wǣdum ond blēom ;   hwīlum hit wæs mid wǣtan bestēmed,

beswyled mid swātes gange,   hwīlum mid since ġeġyrwed.

Hwæðre iċ bær licgende   lange hwīle

25   behēold hrēowċeariġ   hǣlendes trēow,

oððæt iċ ġehȳrde   bæt hit hlēoðrode,

ongan bā word sprecan   wudu sēlēsta ᛬

    '7æt wæs ġēara iū, iċ bæt ġȳta ġeman,

þæt iċ wæs āhēawen   holtes on end,

30   āstyred of stefne mīnum.   Ġenāman mē ðǣr strange fēondas,

ġeworhton him bǣr tō wǣfersȳne,   hēton mē heora wergas hebban.

Bǣron mē ðǣr beornas on eaxlum   oððæt hīe mē on beorg āsetton,

ġefæstnodon mē bǣr fēondas ġenōge.   Ġeseah iċ þā frēan mancynnes

efstan elne mycle   þæt hē mē wolde on ġestīgan.

35   Þǣr iċ þā ne dorste   ofer Dryhtnes word

būgan oððe berstan,   þā iċ bifian ġeseah

eorðan sċēatas.   Ealle iċ mihte

fēondas ġefyllan, hwæðre iċ fæste stōd.

(이 시는 예수가 못 박힌 십자가를 의인화하여 1인칭의 증언 형식을 빌어 예수의 죽음을 그리고 있다. 의인화(prosopopeia)는 당시 흔히 사용되던 표현 양식이다. 초기 게르만족의 기독교 작품들이 그렇듯이 이 시의 예수는 악마와 대항해 싸우는 용감한 투사의 이미지를 지니고 있다. 대개의 고대영어 시들이 그렇듯이 본래는 제목이 없던 것을 현대 학자들이 지금처럼 작명한 것이다. 때로는 *A Vision of the Cross*라고도 불린다. 스코트랜드의 Dumfriesshire의 Ruthwell에 세워져있는 십자가 석조물의 한 면에 이 시의 일부가 새겨져 있다.)

1   Hwæt=What. 시의 첫 머리에서는 Listen!이나 Lo!의 뜻으로 사용된다. iċ swefna cyst= the choicest(best) dream. swefna=swefn(=dream)의 복수 속격. cyst=ċēosan(=to choose)에 서 나온 명사. swefna cyst와 hwæt절은 모두 secgan의 목적어이다. secgan=tell. wylle= will.

2   mē ġemǣtte=it dreamed to me=I dreamed. 원형은 ġemǣtan으로서 비인칭 동사이며, 여격 의 (대)명사를 의미상의 주어로 사용한다. tō=at. midre=mid.

3   syðban=when. syðban reordberend reste wunedon=when (the) voice-bearers remained at rest. reordberend=reord(=voice)+berend(=bearing)=voice-bearers=human beings. 이런 표현 방식을 완곡 대칭법(kenning)이라고 한다. 그밖에 고대영어에서 흔히 쓰이는 용법으 로 바다(sea)를 뜻하는 hwælweġ(=whale's way) 등이 있다. cf. berend=beran(=to bear) +end(=-ing). wunedon=remained. 원형은 wunian.

4   Þūhte=(It) seemed. 원형은 þynċan. mē=to me. ġesāwe=saw. 원형은 ġesēon. syllicre= syllic(=wonderful)의 비교급으로서 most wondrous의 뜻. 이른바 절대비교급이다.

5   on lyft lǣdan=lifted into the air. ġesāwe 뒤에 오는 원형 동사는 수동의 뜻을 갖는다. lyft=air. cf. G. Luft. lǣdan=lead. lēohte=lēoht(=light)의 여격으로서 도구를 나타낸다. with light. bewunden=wrapped round. 원형은 bewindan.

6 bēama=of beams. beorhtost=beorht(=bright)의 최상급.

6-7 Eall þæt bēacen wæs begoten=all drenched. 원형은 beġēeotan. bēacen=beacon. '등화'와 '표지(sign)'의 두 가지 뜻을 갖는다.

7 Ġimmas=Gems. stōdon=appeared, existed.

8 fæġere=beautiful(ly), æt foldan sċēatum=at the surface of the earth=at the foot of the cross. foldan=earth. sċēatum=sċēat(=surface)의 복수 여격. swylċe=likewise. bǣr fīfe wǣron=there were five (gems).

9 uppe=above. eaxleġespanne=shoulder-link=the cross-beam. 다섯 개의 보석은 사각형 주변에 하나, 그리고 중앙에 하나 박혀 있었을 것이다. (quincunx).

9-10 Behēoldon þǣr engel Dryhtness ealle fæġere burh forðġesceaft=All (those) fair by eternal decree beheld there the angel of the Lord. 이 문장의 주어는 ealle이며, engel Dryhtness는 예수나 십자가를 나타낸다. Behēoldon=beheld. 원형은 behealdan. Dryhtnes= drihten(drihten)(=the Lord)의 단수 속격. forðġesceft=preordination, eternal decree. ealle fæġere burh forðġesceaft(=all those fair by eternal decree)는 11행의 hāliġe gāstas를 나타낸다.

10 hūru=truly. fracodes=a criminal's. ġealga=gallows.

11 hine=it. 선행사는 앞줄의 ġealga. behēoldon=beheld. hāliġe=holy. gāstas=spirits, ghost.

12 moldan=(the) earth. bēos=this. mǣre=glorious. ġesceaft=creation.

13 Syllič=wonderful. siġebēam=victory-tree. synnum=by sins. fāh=stained, decorated.

14 forwunded=forwundian(=wound badly)의 과거분사. wommum=faults. Ġeseah=saw. 원형은 ġesēon. wuldres=of glory.

15 wǣdum ġeweorðode=adorned with garments. wǣdum=wǣd(=clothing)의 복수 여격=with garments. ġeweorðode=ġeweorbian(=to adorn)의 과거분사. wynnum=winn(=joy)의 복수 여격. sċīnan=shine, shining.

16 ġegyred=adorned. 원형은 ġyrwan. Ġimmas=Gems. hæfdon=habban(to have)의 과거.

17 bewriġene=covered. 원형은 bewrēon. weorðlīċe=splendidly. wealdendes=of the ruler.

18 Hwæðre=Yet. burh=beyond. onġytan(onġietan)=perceive. meahte=could. 원형은 magan.

19 earmra ǣrġewin=the former struggle of wretched ones=those who crucified Christ. the former struggle of wretched ones. 예수와 십자가가 겪은 고통을 지칭하는 듯. earmra= wretched, poor. ǣrġewin=former struggle. þæt=in that. ǣrest=first. ongan=began. 원형은 onġinnan.

20 swǣtan=to bleed. on þā swīðran healfe=on the right side. cf. John, 19 : 34. 'But one of the soldiers with a spear opened his side, and immediately there came out blood and water.' swīðra=right. sorgum=sorrows. gedrēfed=afflicted. 원형은 ġedrēfan.

21 forht=frightened. for=before. fæġran=fæġer(=beautiful)의 단수 여격. ġesyhðe=sight. fūse= eager. bēacen=beacon, sign.

22 wendan=change. wǣdum ond blēom=in respect of garments and colors. blēom=color. hwīlum=at times. wǣtan=wetness, water. bestēmed=bestēman(=to drench)의 과거분사.

23 beswyled=beswillan(=to soak)의 과거분사. swātes=of blood. gange=motion, flow. since=

treasure. ġeġyrwed=adorned. 원형은 ġyrwan.

24 Hwæðre=Nevertheless. licgende=lying. 원형은 licgan. lange hwīle=for a long time.

25 hrēowċeariġ=distressed, cruelly wretched. hǣlendes=Saviour's.

26 oððæt=until. ġehȳrde=heard. 원형은 ġehīeran. hlēoðrode=spoke. 원형은 hlēobrian.

27 ongan=began. 원형은 onginnan. þā=these. sprecan=to speak. wudu=tree. sēlēsta=best.

28 7æt wæs gēara=long ago. iū=once. ġȳta=still. ġeman=remember. 원형은 ġemunan.

29 āhēawen=hewn. 원형은 āhēawan. holtes on end=from the end of the forest.

30 āstyred=removed. of=from. stefne=root. Genāman=Seized. 원형은 ġeniman. strange= strong. fēondas=enemies.

31 ġeworhton him þǣr tō wæfersȳne=they made me into a spectacle for themselves there. ġeworhton=made. 원형은 ġewyrċan. him=for themselves. wæfersȳne=spectacle, show. hēton=commanded. 원형은 hātan. wergas=criminals. hebban=to raise.

32 Bǣron=Carried. 원형은 beran. beornas=men. eaxlum=shoulders. beorg=hill. āsetton=set up. 원형은 āsettan.

33 ġefæstnodon mē þǣr fēondas ġenōge=enemies enough (i.e. many enemies) secured me there. ġefæstnodon=ġefæstnian(=to establish, fasten)의 과거. ġenōge=enough. frēan=lord. mancynnes=of mankind.

34 efstan=hurry. elne mycle=with great fortitude. elne=ellen(=strength, courage, fortitude)의 단수 여격. mycle=miċel(=much)의 단수 여격. þæt hē mē wolde on ġestīgan=(in) that he wanted to ascent onto me=in his wish to ascend onto me. þæt=because. ġestīgan=ascend.

35 dorste=dared. 원형은 durran. ofer=against. Dryhtnes word=the Lord's word.

36 būgan=bend. berstan=break. þā=when. bifian=shake. þā bifan ġeseah=when I saw⋯. cf. Matthew 27 : 51. 'At that moment the curtain of the temple was torn in two, from top to bottom. The earth shook, and the rocks were split.'

37 eorðan=earth's. scēatas=surface. Ealle=다음 줄의 frēondas를 수식한다. mihte=I could have. 원형은 magan.

38 ġefyllan=knock down. hwæðre=nevertheless.

   Listen! I will describe the best of dreams

   which I dreamed in the middle of the night

   when, far and wide, all men slept.

      It seemed that I saw a wondrous tree

   soaring into the air, surrounded by light,

   the brightest of crosses ; that emblem was entirely

   cased in gold ; beautiful jewels

   were strewn around its foot, just as five

   studded the cross-beam. All the angels of God,

fair creations, guarded it. That was no cross
of a criminal, but holy spirits and men on earth
watched over it there—the whole glorious universe.

   Wondrous was the tree of victory, and I was stained
by sin, stricken by guilt. I saw this glorious tree
joyfully gleaming, adorned with garments,
decked in gold ; the tree of the Ruler
was rightly adorned with rich stones ;
yet through that gold I could see the agony
once suffered by wretches, for it had bled
down the right hand side. Then I was afflicted,
frightened at this sight ; I saw that sign often change
its clothing and hue, at times dewy with moisture,
stained by flowing blood, at times adorned with treasure.
yet I lay there for a long while
and gazed sadly at the Saviour's cross
until I heard it utter words ;
the finest of trees began to speak :
   'I remember the morning a long time ago
that I was felled at the edge of the forest
and severed from my roots. Strong enemies seized me,
bade me hold up their felons on high,
made me a spectacle. Men shifted me
on their shoulders and set me on a hill.
Many enemies fastened me there. I saw the Lord of Mankind
hasten with such courage to climb upon me.
I dared not bow or break there
against my Lord's wish, when I saw the surface
of the earth tremble. I could have felled
all my foes, yet I stood firm.

Onġyrede hine þā ġeong hæleð, þæt wæs God ælmihtiġ,

40 strang ond stīðmōd. Ġestāh hē on ġealgan hēanne,

mōdiġ on maniġra ġesyhðe, þā hē wolde mancyn lȳsan.

Bifode iċ þā mē se beorn ymbclypte. Ne dorste iċ hwæðre būgan tō eorðan,

feallan tō foldan scēatum, ac iċ sceolde fæste standan.

Rōd wæs iċ ārǣred, āhōf iċ rīċne cyning,

45 heofona hlāford ; hyldan mē ne dorste.

7urhdrifan hī mē mid deorcan næġlum ; on mē syndon þā dolg ġesīene,

opene inwidhlemmas ; ne dorste iċ hira nǣnigum sceððan.

Bysmeredon hīe unc būtū ætgædere. Eall iċ wæs mid blōde bestēmed

begoten of þæs guman sīdan siððan hē hæfde his gāst onsended.

50 Feala iċ on þām beorge ġebiden hæbbe

wrāðra wyrda. Ġeseah iċ weruda God

bearle benian. 7ystro hæfdon

bewriġen mid wolcnum wealdendes hrǣw,

scīrne scīman ; sceadu forð ēode,

55 wann under wolcnum. Wēop eal ġesceaft,

cwīðdon cyninges fyll. Crīst wæs on rōde.

Hwæðere þǣr fūse feorran cwōman

tō þām æðelinge. Iċ þæt eall behēold.

Sāre iċ wæs mid sorgum ġedrēfed, hnāg iċ hwæðre þām secgum tō handa

60 ēaðmōd elne mycle. Ġenāmon hīe þǣr ælmihtiġne God,

āhōfon hine of ðām hefian wīte. Forlēton me þā hilderincas

standan stēame bedrifenne ; eall iċ wæs mid strǣlum forwundod.

Ālēdon hīe ðǣr limwēriġne, ġestōdon him æt his līċes hēafdum ;

behēoldon hīe ðǣr heofenes Dryhten ond hē hine ðǣr hwīle reste,

65 mēðe æfter ðām miclan ġewinne. Ongunnon him þā moldern wyrċan

beornas on banan ġesyhðe ;   curfon hīe ðæt of beorhtan stānē,

ġesetton hīe ðǣron sigora wealdend.   Ongunnon him þā sorhlēoð galan

earme on þā ǣfentīde   þā hīe woldon eft sīðian

mēðe fram þām mǣran bēodne.   Reste hē ðǣr mǣte weorode.

70   Hwæðere wē ðǣr grēotende   gōde hwīle

stōdon on staðole,   stefn ūp ġewāt

hilderinca.   Hrǣw cōlode,

fæġer feorgbold.   7ā ūs man fyllan ongan

ealle tō eorðan ;   þæt wæs eġesliċ wyrd!

75   Bedealf ūs man on dēopan sēabe.   Hwæðre mē þǣr Dryhtnes beġnas

frēondas ġefrūnon, ···

ġyredon mē   golde ond seolfre.

---

39   Ongyrede hine þā geong hæleð=Then the young hero stripped himself. 그러나 성경에
보면 로마 군병들이 예수의 옷을 벗긴 것으로 되어 있다. cf. Matthew 27 : 28. 'They
stripped him and put a scarlet robe on him, ···' Onġyrede=stripped, unclothed. 원형은
onġyrwan. ġeong=young. hæleð=man, hero, warrior.

40   stīðmōd=resolute. Ġestāh=Climbed. 원형은 ġestīgan. ġealgan=gallows. hēanne=high.

41   mōdig=brave. on maniġra=of many. mancyn=mankind. ſȳsan=redeem.

42   Bifode=tremble. 원형은 bifian. þā=when. beorn=warrior, hero. ymbclypte=embraced. 원
형은 ymbclyppan. būgan=bend.

43   sceolde=had to. 원형은 sculan.

44   Rōd=cross. ārǣred=raised. 원형은 ārǣran. āhōf=lifted, raised. 원형은 āhebban. rīċne=
mighty.

45   heofona=of the heavens. hlāford=lord. hyldan=bend. mē=myself.

46   7urhdrīfan=Pierced. 원형은 burhdrīfan. deorcan=dark. næġlum=nails. syndon=are. dolg=
scars. ġesīene=visible.

47   inwidhlemmas=malicious wound. hira=of them. nǣnigum=none. sceððan=injure.

48   Bysmeredon=Mocked. 원형은 bysmerian. unc=us (dual). būtū=both. ætgædere=together.
blōde=blood. bestēmed=drenched. 원형은 bestēman.

49   begoten of þæs guman sīdan=(drenched and) soaked (with blood) from that man's side.
begoten=beġēotan(=to pour over)의 과거분사. 앞줄의 iċ를 수식한다. siððan=when.
gāst=spirit. onsended=sent forth. 원형은 onsendan.

50-1   Feala···wrāðra wyrda=many cruel events. wrāðra=wrāð(=cruel)의 복수 속격. wyrda=
happening, event. iċ on þām beorge ġebiden=suffered, endured. ġebiden의 원형은

ġebīdan. beorge=hill. hæbbe=have.

51 weruda=of hosts. 원형은 werod.

52 bearle=harshly. benian=stretch out. 7ystro=Darkness. hæfdon=had.

53 bewriġen=bewrēon(=cover, hide)의 과거분사. hidden. wolcnum=clouds. wealdendes= ruler's. hrǣw=corpse.

54 scīrne scīman=shining splendor (of light). 앞줄의 wealdendes hrǣw와 동격. sceadu forð ēode=a shadow went forth. cf. Matthew 27 : 45. 'Now from the sixth hour there was darkness over the whole earth.' forð=forth. ēode=went. 원형은 gān.

55 wann=dark. Wēop=Wept. 원형은 wēpan. ġesceaft=creature, created things.

56 cwīðdon=lamented. 원형은 cwīban. fyll=death.

57 Hwæðere=yet. fūse feorran cwōman=eager (people) came from afar. feorran=from afar. cwōman=came. 원형은 cuman. 요한복음에 비추어 볼 때 Arimathea의 Joseph와 Nicodemus 를 가리킨다. cf. John 19 : 38-9. 'After these things, Joseph of Arimathea, who was a disciple of Jesus, though a secret one because of his fear of the Jews, asked Pilate to let him take away the body of Jesus. Pilate gave him permission ; so he came and removed his body. Nicodemus, who had at first come to Jesus by night, also came, bringing a mixture of myrrh and aloes, weighing about a hundred pounds.'

58 æðeliðnge=prince. behēold=beheld. 원형은 behealdan.

59 Sāre=Grievously. sorgum=sorg(=sorrow)의 복수 여격=with sorrows. ġedrēfed=afflicted. 원형은 drēfan. hnāg=bent. 원형은 hnīgan. hwæðre=however. bām secgum tō handa=to the men to hand=to the hands of the men. secg=man, retainer, warrior.

60 ēaðmōd=humble. elne=ellen(=zeal)의 단수 여격. mycle=much. 원형은 miċel. Genāmon= Seized.

61 āhōfon=raised. 원형은 āhebban. hefian=heavy, dire. wīte=torment. Forlēton=Left. bā= then 또는 the의 해석이 모두 가능하다. hilderincas=warriors.

62 stēame=with moisture. bedrifenne=spattered. 원형은 bedrīfan. strǣlum=arrows. 46행에 나왔던 næġlum(=nails)을 화살에 비유하고 있다. forwundod=wounded badly. 원형은 foreunfisn.

63 Ālēdon=Laid down. 원형은 ālecgan. limwēriġne=limb-weary (one). gestōdon him æt his līces hēafdum=they placed themselves at his body's head. ġestōdon=stood. 원형은 ġestandan. him=themselves. līċes=body's. hēafdum=head.

64 hine=himself. reste=restan(=to rest)의 과거.

65 mēðe=worn out. miclan=great. ġewinne=struggle. moldern=tomb. wyrcan=make.

66 beornas=men. on banan ġesyhðe=in the sight of the slayer. 십자가가 스스로를 예수의 살해자라고 부르고 있다. banan=bana(=slayer)의 단수 속격. ġesyhðe=presence. curfon= crved. 원형은 ċeorfan. beorhtan=bright. stānē=rock.

67 ġesetton=placed. ðǣron=therein. sigora=of victories. wealdend=ruler, the Lord. sorhlēoð= song of sorrow. galan=sing.

68 earme=wretched. 떠나려고 하는 사람들을 수식하고 있다. æfentīde=eveningtime. eft=

back. sīðian=travel, go.

69 mēðe=worn out. mǣran=famous. bēodne=prince. mǣte weorode=with a small company. 예수는 무덤 안에 혼자 있었으므로 small company는 일종의 곡언(litotes)적 표현으로서 alone의 뜻이다. 아니면 세 명의 Mary였거나, 무덤의 경비를 맡았던 로마 군병일 수도 있다. cf. Matthew 27 : 61, 65-6. mǣte=small. weorode=company.

70 Hwæðere=but. wē=예수가 못 박힌 십자가와 그 옆의 두 동료 십자가를 지칭한다. grēotende=grēotan(=to lament)의 현재분사. gōde hwīle=for a good while.

71 staðole=fixed position. ūp ġewāt=went upward=passed away. 원형은 ġewītan.

72 hilderinca=warriors'. Hrǣw=corpse. cōlode=grew cold. 원형은 cōlian.

73 fæġerfair=fair, beautiful. feorgbold=soul's dwelling (body). fyllan=strike down. ongan= began. 원형은 onġinnan.

74 eġeslīċ=dreadful. wyrd=fate.

75 Bedealf=Buried. 원형은 bedelfan. sēabe=pit.

75-6 mē⋯ġefrūnon=heard about me. begnas와 frēondas가 주어이다. beġnas=thegns, noblemen, retainers.

76 ġefrūnon=heard of. 원형은 ġefriġnan. 76행의 후반은 사라졌으나 그 내용을 짐작하기에 어렵지 않다. 다음 줄과 함께 '땅에 묻혔던 십자가를 오랜 세월 끝에 St. Helena가 찾아내어 귀한 유물로 장식했다'는 내용이었을 것이다.

77 ġyredon=adorned. 여격과 함께 쓰인다. 원형은 ġyrwan. seolfre=silver.

Then the young warrior, God Almighty,

stripped Himself, firm and unflinching. He climbed

upon the cross, brave before many, to redeem mankind.

I quivered when the hero clasped me,

yet I dared not bow to the ground,

fall to the earth. I had to stand firm.

A rood was I raised up ; I bore aloft the mighty King,

the Lord of Heaven. I dared not stoop.

They drove dark nails into me ; dire wounds are there to see,

the gaping gashes of malice ; I dared not injure them.

They insulted us both together ; I was drenched in the blood

that streamed from the Man's side after He set His spirit free.

On that hill I endured many grievous trials ;

I saw the God of Hosts stretched

on the rack ; darkness covered the corpse

of the Ruler with clouds, His shining radiance.

    Shadows swept across the land, dark shapes
under the clouds. all creation wept,
wailed for the death of the King ; Christ was on the cross.

    Yet men hurried eagerly to the Prince
from afar ; I witnessed all that too.
I was oppressed with sorrow, yet humbly bowed to the hands of men,
and willingly. There they lifted Him from His heavy torment,
they took Almighty God away. The warriors left me standing there,
stained with blood ; sorely was I wounded by the sharpness of
        spear-shafts.
They laid Him down, limb-weary ; they stood at the corpse's head,
they beheld there the Lord of Heaven ; and there He rested for a while,
worn-out after battle. And then they began to build a sepulchre ;
        under his slayers' eyes, they carved it from the gleaming stone,
and laid therein the Lord of Victories. Then, sorrowful at dusk,
they sang a dirge before they went, weary,
from their glorious Prince ; He rested in the grave alone.

    But we still stood there, weeping blood,
long after the song of the warriors
had soared to heaven ; the corpse grew cold,
the fair human house of the soul. Then our enemies
began to fell us ; that was a terrible fate.
They buried us in a deep pit ; but friends
and followers of the Lord found me there
and girded me with gold and shimmering silver.

THE DREAM OF THE ROOD (3)

    Nū ðū miht ġehȳran,   hæleð mīn se lēofa,

þæt iċ bealuwara weorc   ġebiden hæbbe,

80 sāra sorga.   Is nū sǣl cumen

þæt mē weorðiað   wīde ond sīde

menn ofer moldan   ond eall bēos mǣre ġesceaft

ġebiddaþ him tō þyssum bēacne.   On mī bearn Godes

brōwode hwīle ;   forþon iċ þrymfæst nū

85 hlīfiġe under heofenum   ond iċ hǣlan mæġ

ǣġhwylċne ānra   þāra þe him bið eġesa tō mē.

Iū iċ wæs ġeworden   wīta heardost

lēodum lāðost   ǣr þan iċ him līfes weġ

rihtne ġerȳmde,   reordberendum.

90 Hwæt, mē þā ġeweorðode   wuldres ealdor

ofer holmwudu,   heofonrīċes weard.

swylċe swā hē his mōdor ēac.   Mārian sylfe,

ælmihtiġ God   for ealle menn

ġeweorðode   ofer eall wīfa cynn.

95   Nū iċ þē hāte,   hæleð mīn se lēofa,

þæt ðū þās ġesyhðe   secge mannum,

onwrēoh wordum   þæt hit is wuldres bēam,

sē ðe ælmihtiġ God   on brōwode

for mancynnes   manegum synnum

100 ond Ādomes   ealdġewyrhtum.

Dēad hē þǣr byriġde,   hwæðere eft Dryhten ārās

mid his miclan mihte   mannum tō helpe.

Hē ðā on heofenas āstāg.   Hider eft fundaþ

on þysne middanġeard   mancynn sēċan

105 on dōmdæġe   Dryhten sylfa

ælmihtiġ God   on his englas mid

þæt hē þonne wile dēman,   se āh dōmes ġeweald.

ānra ġehwylcum   swā hē him ǣrur hēr

on þyssum lǣnum   līfe ġeearnaþ.

110 Ne mæġ þǣr ǣniġ   unforht wesan

for þām worde   þe se wealdend cwyð.

Frīneð hē for þǣre mæniġe   hwǣr se man sīe,

sē ðe for Dryhtnes naman   dēaðes wolde

biteres onbyriġan,   swā hē ǣr on ðām bēame dyde.

115 Ac hīe þonne forhtiað   ond fēa bencaþ

hwæt hīe tō Crīste   cweðan onġinnen.

Ne þearf ðǣr þonne ǣniġ   anforht wesan,

þe him ǣr in brēostum bereð   bēacna sēlēst

ac ðurh ðā rōde sceal   rīċe ġesēċan

120 of eorðweġe   ǣġhwylċ sāwl.

sēo þe mid wealdende   wunian benċeð.

78 ðū miht geh̄yran=you can hear. hæleð=man. lēofa=beloved.

79 bealuwara=dwellers in iniquity, evil men. weorc=work, deed. ġebiden=endured. 원형은 ġebīdan. hæbbe=have.

80 sāra=sore, painful. sorga=sorrow. s̄æl=time. cumen=come.

81 weorðiað=(shall) worship. wīde=far. sīde=wide.

82 menn=people. moldan=earth. mǣre=splendid, famous. ġesceaft=creation.

83 ġebiddaþ=(shall) pray. 원형은 ġebiddan. him=바로 앞의 동사 ġebiddan은 여격의 재귀대명사를 취한다. bēacne=beacon, sign. bearn=son.

84 brōwode=suffered. 원형은 brōwian. forþon=therefore. þrymfæst=glorious.

85 hlīfiġe=rise up, tower. 원형은 hlifian. h̄ælan=heal, save. mæġ=can. 원형은 magan.

86 ǣġhwylċne ānra=each of ones=each one. ǣġhwylċne=each. ānra=ān(=one)의 복수 속격. þāra þe him bið egesa tō me=of those who in whom is fear of me=of those who have fear for me. eġesa=awe.

87 Iū=long ago. wæs geworden=was (had) become=became. 원형은 weorþan. wīta=of punishments. heardost=heard(=cruel)의 최상급.

88 lēodum=to people. lāðost=lāð(=hateful)의 최상급. ǣr þan=before that=before.

88-9 him līfes weġ rihtne=the right way of life for them.

89 ġerȳmde=opened up. 원형은 ġerȳman. reordberendum=for the speech-bearers, for humans.

90 Hwæt=Lo! ġeweorðode=honored. 원형은 ġeweorbian. wuldres=wuldor(=glory)의 단수 속격. ealdor=prince.

91 ofer holmwudu=above the trees of the forest. heofonrīċes=kingdom of heaven. 단수 속격. weard=guardian.

92 swylċe swā hē=just as he. 93행의 ælmihtiġ God을 지칭한다. ēac=likewise. Mārian=Mary. sylfe=(her)self.

93 for=before.

94 geweorðode ofer eall wīfa cynn=above all womankind (lit. the race of women). wīfa=wīfa(=woman)의 복수 속격. cynn=kin, kind.

95 hāte=command. 원형은 hātan.

96 þās=this. ġesyhðe(ġesihðe)=sight. secge=tell. mannum=to people.

97 onwrēoh=reveal. 원형은 onwrēon. wordum=in words. wuldres=wuldor(=glory)의 단수 속격. bēam=tree, cross.

98 sē ðe ælmihtiġ God on brōwode=that on which almighty God suffered.

99 mancynnes manegum synnum=many sins of mankind.

100 Ādomes=Adam's. ealdġewyrhtum=deeds of old. 하나님에 대한 Adam과 Eve의 불복종을 가리킨다.

101 Dēad=Death. byrigde=tasted. 원형은 byriġan. hwæðere=however. eft=afterwards. ārās=arose. 원형은 ārīsan.

102 mihte=power. tō=as. helpe=a benefit.

103 on=to. āstāg=ascended. āstīgan. Hider=Here. eft=again. fundab=(will) come. 원형은 fundian.

194 middanġeard=world. sēċan=to seek.

105 dōmdæge=judgement day.

106 englas=angels. mid=as well.

107 bæt=in as much as, because. wile=will. 원형은 willan. dēman=judge. 여격과 함께 쓰인다. se=who. āh=possesses. 원형은 āgan. dōmes ġeweald=(the) power of judgement.

108 ānra gehwylcum=each one. ǣrur=earlier.

109 lǣnum=transitory. ġeearnab=deserves. 원형은 ġeearnian.

110 Ne mæġ bǣr ǣniġ unforht=No one can be unafraid. wesan=be.

111 for=because of. wealdend=ruler, the Lord. cwyð=(will) say.

112 Frīneð=(Will) ask. 원형은 friġnan. for=before. mæniġe=multitude. hwǣr=where. sīe=bēon (=to be)의 가정법 단수 현재.

113 sē=he. wolde=willan(=to wish)의 과거 복수.

114 biteres=bitter. 앞줄의 dēaðes를 수식한다. onbyriġan=taste. 속격과 함께 쓰인다. ǣr=formerly.

115 Ac hīe bonne forhtiað=will be afraid. 원형은 forhtian. fēa=scarcely. benċab=imagine,

think. 원형은 benċan.

116 onġinnen=may begin.

117 Ne bearf=No need. bonne=however. ǣnig=any. anforht=terrified. wesan=to be.

118 brēostum=in his breast. bereð=bears. bēacna=sign. sēlēst=the best (of).

119 rōde=cross. sceal=shall. rīċe=kingdom. ġesēċan=seek out.

120 of=away from. eorðweġe=the earthly path. ǣġhwylċ=each. sāwl=soul.

121 sēo=she who. 선행사는 sāwl. wunian=to dwell. benċeð=desires. 원형은 benċan.

Now, my loved men, you have heard

how I endured bitter anguish

at the hands of evil men. Now the time is come

when men far and wide in this world,

and all this bright creation, bow before me ;

they pray to this sign. On me the Son of God

suffered for a time ; wherefore I now stand on high,

glorious under heaven ; and I can heal

all those who stand in awe of me.

Long ago I became the worst of tortures,

hated by men, until I opened

to them the true way of life.

Lo! The Lord of Heaven, the Prince of Glory,

honoured me over any other tree

just as He, Almighty God, for the sake of mankind

honoured Mary, His own mother,

before all other women in the world.

Now I command you, my loved man,

to describe your vision to all men ;

tell them with words this is the tree of glory

on which the Son of God suffered once

for the many sins committed by mankind,

and for Adam's wickedness long ago.

He sipped the drink of death. Yet the Lord rose

with His great strength to deliver man.
Then He ascended into heaven. The Lord Himself,
Almighty God, with His host of angels,
will come to the middle-world again
on Domesday to reckon with each man.
Then He who has the power of judgement
will judge each man just as he deserves
for the way in which he lived this fleeting life.
No-one then will be unafraid
as to what words the Lord will utter.
Before the assembly, He will ask where that man is
who, in God's name, would undergo the pangs of death,
just as He did formerly upon the cross.
The men will be fearful and give
scant thought to what they say to Christ.
But no-one need be numbed by fear
who has carried the best of all signs in his breast ;
each soul that has longings to live with the Lord
must search for a kingdom far beyond the frontiers of this world.

Ġebæd iċ mē bā tō bam bēame   blīðe mōde,

elne mycle,   bǣr iċ āna wæs

mǣte werede.   Wæs mōdsefa

125   āfȳsed on forðweġe,   feala ealra ġebād

langunghwīla.   Is mē nū līfes hyht

bæt iċ bone siġebēam   sēċan mōte

āna oftor   bonne ealle men,

well weorbian.   Mē is willa tō ðām

130   myċel on mōde   ond mīn mundbyrd is

ġeriht tō bǣre rōde.   Nāh iċ rīcra feala

frēonda on foldan   ac hīe forð heonon

ġewiton of worulde drēamum,   sōhton him wuldres cyning,

lifiab nū on heofenum   mid hēhfædere,

135   wuniab on wuldre,   on iċ wēne mē

daga ġehwylċe   hwænne mē Dryhtnes rōd,

be iċ hēr on eorðan   ǣr scēawode,

on bysson lǣnan   līfe ġefetiġe

ond mē bonne ġebringe   bǣr is blis myċel,

140   drēam on heofonum,   bær is Dryhtnes folc

ġeeseted tō symle   bǣr is singal blis,

ond mē bonne āsette   bǣr iċ sybban mōt

wunian on wuldre,   well mid bām hālgum

drēames brūcan.   Sī mē Dryhten frēond,

145   sē ðe hēr on eorban   ǣr brōwode

on bām ġealgtrēowe   for guman synnum.

Hē ūs onlȳsde   ond ūs līf forġeaf,

heofonlicne hām.   Hiht wæs ġenīwad

mid blēdum ond mid blisse   bām be bǣr bryne bolodan.

150 Se sunu wæs sigorfæst   on bām sīðfate

mihtiġ ond spēdiġ   þā hē mid maniġeo cōm,

gāsta weorode,   on Godes rīċe,

anwealda ælmihtiġ,   englum tō blisse

ond eallum þām hālgum   þām þe on heofonum ǣr

155 wunedon on wuldre,   þā heora wealdend cwōm,

ælmihtiġ God, þ̄ær ēðel wæs.

122	Ġebæd=Pryaed. blīðe mōde=with glad heart.
123	elne=ellen(=zeal)의 단수 여격. āna=alone.
124	mǣte=small. werede=werod(=company)의 단수 여격. mōdsefa=(my) spirit.
125	āfȳsed=urged. 원형은 āfȳsan. forðweġe=the journey ahead.
125-6	feala ealra ġebād langunghwīla=experienced many of all periods longing=very many periods of longing. 주어는 mōdsefa. feala(fela)=many. ealra=eall(=all)의 복수 속격. ġebād= endured. 원형은 ġebīdan.
126	langunhwīla=period of longing. hyht=hope.
127	siġebēam=tree of victory. sēċan=seek. mōte=may. 원형은 mōtan.
128	āna=alone. oftor=more often. þonne=than.
129	well=properly. weorþian=to worship.
129-30	Mē is willa tō ðām mycel on mōde=for me the desire for that is great in my heart.
130	mundbyrd=hope of protection.
131	ġeriht=directed. Nāh iċ=I do not have. 원형은 āgan. rīcra=powerful. feala=many.
132	foldan=earth. heonon=from here. sōhton him=sought out for themselves.
133	ġewiton=departed. 원형은 ġewitan. drēamum=joy. wuldres=wuldor(=glory)의 단수 속격.
134	hēhfædere=the high father=God the father.
135	wuniaþ=dwell. 원형은 wunian. iċ wēne mē=I hope for/look forward to. wēne=hope. 원형은 wēnan. 재귀대명사는 번역하지 않아도 무방하다.
136	ġehwylċe=each. 복수 속격과 사용된다. hwænne=when.
137	scēawode=beheld. 원형은 scēawian.
138	on=from. lǣnan=transitory. ġefetiġe=may fetch. ġefetian(=to fetch)의 가정법 단수 현재.
139	ġebringe=ġebringan(=to bring)의 가정법 단수 현재. þ̄ær=where. blis=happiness.
141	ġeseted=placed. 원형은 ġesettan. tō=at. symle=the feast. 원형은 sym(b)el. singal= continuous.
142	āsette=set down. 원형은 āsettan. sybban=then. mōt=can, may. 원형은 mōtan.
143	well=fittingly. hālgum=saints.
144	brūcan=enjoy. 속격과 함께 사용된다. Sī mē Dryhten frēond=May the Lord be a friend to me. Sī=Be.

145 brōwode=suffered.

146 ġealgtrēowe=gallows-tree. for guman synnum=for men's sins. guman=of man. *nether*

147 onlȳsde=set free. 원형은 onlȳsan. forġeaf=gave. 원형은 forġiefan.

148 heofonlicne hām=heavenly home. Hiht=Hope. ġenīwad=renewed. 원형은 ġenīwian.

149 blēdum=splendor. bām be=for them who…. 십자가에 못 박히고 나서 승천하는 사이 예수가 지옥을 정복(Harrowing of Hell)하여 유황불로부터 구해낸 착한 사람들을 가리킨다. bryne=burning. bolodan=suffered. 원형은 bolian.

150 sigorfæst=victorious. sīðfate=expedition.

151 spēdig=successful. bā=when. maniġeo=the multitude.

152 gāsta=spirit. weorode(werod)=(with a) host.

153 anwealda=ruler. englum tō blisse=to the delight of the angels.

154 hālgum=to the saints. 뒤에 tō blisse가 생략되었다. ǣr=before.

155 wunedon=lived. 원형은 wunian.

156 ēðel=homeland.

Then I prayed to the cross, eager
and light-hearted, although I was alone
with my own poor company. My soul
longed for a journey, great yearnings
always tugged at me. Now my hope in this life
is that I can turn to that tree of victory
alone and more often than any other man
and honour it fully. These longings master
my heart and mind, and my help comes
from holy cross itself. I have not many friends
of influence on earth ; they have journeyed on
from the joys of this world to find the King of Glory,
they live in heaven with the High Father,
dwell in splendour. Now I look day by day
for that time when the cross of the Lord,
which once I saw in a dream here on earth,
will fetch me away from this fleeting life
and lift me to the home of joy and happiness
where the people of God are seated at the feast

in eternal bliss, and set me down
where I may live in glory unending and share
the joy of the saints. May the Lord be a friend to me,
He who suffered once for the sins of men
here on earth on the gallows-tree.
He has redeemed us ; He has given life to us,
and a home in heaven.
                              Hope was renewed,
blessed and blissful ; , for those who before suffered burning.
On that journey the Son was victorious,
strong and successful. When He, Almighty Ruler,
returned with a thronging host of spirits
to God's kingdom, to joy amongst the angels
and all the saints who lived already
in heaven in glory, then their King,
Almighty God, entered His own country.

                                        (tr. Crossley-Holland)

X. HISTORIC POEMS

THE BATTLE OF MALDON (1)

··· brocen wurde.

Hēt bā hyssa hwæne   hors forlǣtan

feor āfysan   and forð gangan,

hicgan tō handum   and tō hige gōdum.

5   7ā bæt Offan mǣg   ǣrest onfunde

bæt se eorl nolde   yrhðo gebolian,

hē lēt him bā of handon   lēofne flēogan

hafoc wið bæs holtes   and tō āǣre hilde stōp.

Be bām man mihte oncnāwan   bæt se cniht nolde

10   wācian æt bām wīge   bā hē tō wǣpnum fēng.

Ēac him wolde Ēacdrīc   his ealdre gelǣstan,

frēan tō gefeohte ;   ongan bā forð beran

gār tō gūae.   Hē hæfde gōd gebanc

bā hwīle be hē mid handum   healdan mihte

15   bord and brād swurd ;   bēot hē gelǣste

bā hē ætforan his frēan   feohtan sceolde.

     Ðā bǣr Byrhtnōð ongan   beornas trymian,

rād and rǣdde,   rincum tǣhte

hū hī sceoldon standan   and bone stede healdan

20   and bæd bæt hyra randas   rihte hēoldon

fæste mid folman   and ne forhtedon nā.

7ā hē hæfde bæt folc   fægere getrymmed,

hē līhte bā mid lēodon   bǣr him lēofost wæs,

bǣr hē his heorðwerod   holdost wiste.

25   7ā stōd on stæðe   stīðlīce clypode

wīcinga ār,   wordum mǣlde ;

sē on bēot ābēad   brimlīðendra

ǣrǣnde tō þām eorle   bǣr hē on ōfre stōd :

'Mē sendon tō þē   sǣmen snelle,

30   hēton ðē secgan   þæt þū mōst sendan raðe

bēagas wið gebeorge   and ēow betere is

þæt gē bisne gārrǣs   mid gafole forgyldon

þon wē swā hearde   hilde dǣlon.

Ne þurfe wē ūs spillan   gif gē spēdaþ tō þām.

35   Wē willað wið þām golde   grið fæstnian.

Gyf þū þat gerǣdest   þe hēr rīcost eart,

þæt þū þīne lēoda   lȳsan wille,

syllan sǣmannum   on hyra sylfra dōm

fēoh wið frēode   and niman frið æt ūs,

40   wē willaþ mid þām sceattum   ūs tō scype gangan,

on flot fēran   and ēow friþes healdan.'

(*Anglo-Saxon Chronicle*은 991년에 Essex의 Maldon에서 Viking침략자들과 싸우던 그 지방의 태수(ealdorman) Byrhtnoth가 전사한 사실을 적고 있다. 이 시는 그 전투를 묘사한 것이다. 당시 영국은 Æthelred(the Unready)의 치세 하에서 군과 국민의 사기가 땅에 떨어져 있던 때이다. 자신에 차있던 Byrhtnoth가 '자존심 때문에'(for his ofermōde(=because of his pride)) 강을 건너오지 못하던 적군에게 도강을 허가한 잘못으로 스스로는 전사하고 Odda 의 겁 많은 세 아들이 도망가는 것을 계기로 전세는 일시에 기울게 된다. 그러나 전사들은 일치 단결하여 나라를 지키고 태수의 죽음을 안갚음하기 위해 처절히 싸우나 모두 죽고 만다. 물론 이 전투는 두 나라 군대 사이에 있었던 수많은 전투 중의 하나이며 실제보다는 더 시적으로 미화되었을 것이라는 것도 짐작할 수 있다. 여기 인용한 글은 David Casley라는 사람이 필사해두었던 것이 1731년의 화재에서 일부 소실된 나머지 부분이다. 처음 50행과 끝의 100행 가량이 소실되었으나 시 전체의 이해에는 큰 지장이 없다. 본문의 이해를 위해 다음 지도를 참조하기 바란다.)

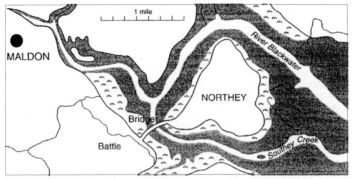

(B. Mitchel, 2001⁶. *A Guide to Old English.* Blackwell, 240)

1 ⋯brocen wurde=시의 첫 부분은 소실되었다. brocen=broken. 원형은 breecan. 짐작컨대 Viking들의 침략에 맞서 Byrhtnoth가 군병들을 모집하여 Pante강가에 포진하게 된 내력이 적혀 있었을 것이다.

2 Hēt bā hyssa hwæne hors forlǣtan=He (i.e. Byrhtnoth) commanded ⋯to release. 후속하는 afysan, gangan, hicgan도 모두 forlǣtan(=to release)에 걸린다. bā=then. hyssa=of warriors. 원형은 hyse. hwæne=each. 원형은 hwā. hors=(his) horse.

3 feor=far. afysan=drive off. gangan=go.

4 hicgan tō handum=to think about (their) hands 또는 set (their) mind on (their) hands= concentrate on the work that their hands must now do, wielding sword and spear in combat. hicgan(hycgan)=think. hiġe(hyġe)=courage. gōdum=noble.

5 7ā=When. bæt=it. onfunde의 목적어이나 번역에서는 무시하는 것이 좋다. Offan=Offa's. mǣ ġ=kinsman. ǣrest=first. onfunde=realized. 원형은 onfindan.

6 eorl=nobleman. nolde=ne+wilde=wouldn't. yrhðo=cowardice. ġebolian=tolerate.

7 lēt=let. of handon=from his hands. 본래는 handum으로 해야 옳다. 이처럼 –um 대신 사용되는 –on의 예는 23행에서도 볼 수 있다(lēodon).

7-8 hē lēt him bā of handon lēofne flēogan hafoc=hē lēt bā (then) of handon lēofne hafoc flēogan=he then let his beloved falcon fly from his hands. lēofne=beloved. flēogan=fly.

8 hafoc=falcon, hawk. wið=towards. 소유격과 함께 쓰인다. holtes=wood. hilde=battle. stōp=advanced. 원형은 steppan.

9 Be=By. bām=that. man mihte oncnāwan=one could understand. oncnāwan=to recognize. cniht=young man.

10 wācian=weaken. wīġe=battle. bā=now. tō wǣpnum fēng=grasped at weapons=grabbed (his) weapons. wǣpnum의 원형은 wǣpen. fēng의 원형은 fōn.

11 Ēac=In addition to. ealdre=leader. ġelǣstan=to support. 여격과 함께 쓰인다.

12 frēan=lord. 11행의 ealdre와 함께 wolde⋯ġrlǣstan의 여격 목적어이다. tō=in. ġefeohte= fight. ongan=began. beran=to carry.

13 gār=spear. gūbe=battle. gōd=firm. ġebanc=purpose.

14 bā hwīle be=in the period that=while, as long as. mid=with.

15 bord=shield. brād=broad. swurd=sword. bēot=vow. ġelǣste=fulfilled. 원형은 ġelǣstan.

16 ætforan=in front of. frēan=lord. feohtan=battle. sceolde=had to. 가정법.

17 Đā bǣr Byrhtnōð=Then there…. 그가 부하들에게 이처럼 자세한 지시를 내리는 것은 거기 모인 병졸들이 전투 경험이 없는 신참병들이라는 것을 나타내는 것과 동시에 Byrhtnoth가 경험이 많은 지휘관이라는 사실도 알려준다. beornas=warriors. trymian=to arrange.

18 rād=rode (about). 원형은 rīdan. rǣdde=instructed. 원형은 rǣdan. rincum=men. tǣhte=showed. 원형은 tǣċan.

19 stede=position. healdan=keep.

20 bǣd=ordered. 원형은 biddan. randas=shields. rihte=properly. hēoldon=hēaldan(=keep)의 가정법이므로 hēalden으로 해야 옳다. hēaldon은 과거형이다. 그러나 이처럼 과거형 어미와 가정법 어미를 혼용하는 것은 후기 고대영어의 한 특징이기도 하다.

21 fæste=firmly. folman=hands. forhtedon=be afraid. 원형은 forhtian. nā=not at all.

22 hæfde=had. folc=troop. fæġere=carefully.

23 līhte=dismounted. 원형은 līhtan. mid lēodon=among the people. lēodon은 복수 여격이 요구되는 현재의 위치에서 lēodum 대신 사용되었다.

24 heorðwerod=hearth-troop. holdost=loyalest. wiste=knew (to be). 원형은 witan.

25 stæðe=shore. stīðlīċe=fiercely. clypode=shouted. 원형은 clypian. 시인은 같은 내용을 stīðlīce clypode, wordum mǣlde, ābēad brimlīðendra라는 세 가지 다른 표현으로 반복하고 있다.

26 wīcinga=the Vikings'. ār=messenger. wordum mǣlde=spoke out with (his) words. mǣlde=spoke. 원형은 mǣlan.

27 sē=여기서는 hē(=he)와 sē(=who)의 두 가지 해석이 모두 가능하다. on bēot=in boast, in threat=threateningly. ābēad=declared. 원형은 ābēodan. brimlīðendra=seafarers'.

28 ǣrende=message. ōfre=bank. 원형은 ōfer

29 sendon=have sent. bē=bū(=you)의 단수 여격. sǣmen=sailors. snelle=bold.

30 hēton ðē secgan=(they) commanded (me) to say to you. mōst=must. raðe=quickly.

31 bēagas=treasures. wið=in exchange for. ġebeorge=protection. ēow=for you. betere=better.

32 ġē=you. gārrǣs=spear-storm. gafole=tribute. forġyldon(forġieldan)=buy off. 원형은 forġieldan(forġyldan).

33 bon=than. 보다 흔하게는 bonne가 사용된다. hearde=형용사(fierce, cruel)로 사용되어 hilde(=battle)를 수식하는 것으로, 혹은 부사(fiercely, cruelly)로 사용되어 dǣlon(=share)을 수식하는 것으로 볼 수도 있다. hilde=battle. dǣlon=share. 원형은 dǣlan.

34 burfe wē=정확한 모습은 burfab이나 뒤에 대명사가 올 때에는 여기서 보듯 어미가 -e로 줄기도 한다. burfe=need, must. 원형은 burfian. ūs=each other. spillan=destroy, kill. gif gē spēdab tō bām=if you are prosperous (enough) for that=if you have money enough to buy us off.

35 grið=truce. fæstnian=fix.

36 þat=it. ġerǣdest=decide. 원형은 ġerǣdan. be hēr rīcost eart=if you, who are the most powerful here. 산문에서라면 앞의 þū 바로 뒤에 놓였을 것이다. rīcost=rīċe(=rich, powerful)의 최상급.

37 lēoda=people. ꞁysan=redeem, release, ransom.

38 syllan=give. 원형은 sellan. on hyra sylfra dōm=at the judgement of them themselves=at their own judgement (choice). 평화를 위해 지불해야 할 대가의 정도는 Vikings들이 정한다. hyra(hira)=their. sylfra=themselves. dōm=judgement, choice.

39 fēoh=money. frēode=goodwill. niman=accept. fri∂=peace. æt=from.

40 sceattum=money. ūs tō scype gangan=take ourselves off to our ships. 동작을 나타내는 동사와 함께 사용되는 재귀대명사는 번역하지 않아도 무방하다.

41 on flot fēran=go to sea. flōt=sea. fēran=go. ēow=with you. friþes=of peace. healdan=keep. 속격과 함께 사용된다.

⋯ may have become broken.

Then he commanded each one of the warriors to let his horse go,

to drive it far away and to advance on foot,

to turn thoughts to hands and to be of good courage.

Then when Offa's kinsman first found

that the earl would nor endure cowardice

he let fly from his hands his beloved

hawk into th wood, and stepped into battle ;

by that a man might perceive that the warrior would not

weaken at that battle when he took up his weapons.

In addition to him, Eadric wanted to serve his leader,

his lord in the fight, so he began then to carry forward

his spear into battle. He had a firm mind

as long as he could hold with his hands

his shield and broad sword ; he fulfilled his boast

when he was obliged to fight in front of his lord.

Then Byrhtnoth began to encourage the warriors there,

he rode about and gave them advice, taught the warriors

how they should stand and maintain the position,

and urged them to hold their shields properly,

securely with their hands, and not to be afraid at all.
When he had suitably arrayed that host,
he dismounted among the men where it was most pleasing to him to be,
where he knew his retainers to be most loyal.
Then there stood on the bank, and fiercely called out
a messenger of the Vikings, he spoke with words,
he announced in a boast a message of the seafarers
to the earl where he stood on the bank of the river.
'Bold seamen have sent me to you,
they command me to tell you that you must quickly send
rings in return for protection, and it will be better for you
that you buy off this storm of spears with a tribute
than that we should take part in such a hard battle.
We will not need to destroy one another if you are sufficiently wealthy ;
we will establish a truce in exchange for that gold.
If you, the one who is most powerful here, decide upon this,
that you want to ransom your people,
give the seamen — what they judge for themselves —
money for peace, and accept protection from us,
and we will go to our ships with that tribute,
set sail and maintain that peace with you.'

THE BATTLE OF MALDON (2)

Byrhtnōð mabelode,   bord hafenode,
wand wācne æsc,   wordum mǣlde,
yrre and ānrǣd   āgeaf him andsware :
45   'Gehȳrst bū, sǣlida.   hwæt bis folc segeð?
Hī willað ēow tō gafole   gāras syllan,
ǣttrynne ord   and ealde swurd,
bā heregeatu   be ēow æt hilde ne dēah.
Brimmanna boda, ābēod eft ongean,
50   sege bīnum lēodum   miccle lābre spell,
bæt her stynt unforcūð   eorl mid his werode
be wile gealgean   ēbel bysne,
Æbelrēdes eard, ealdres mīnes,
folc and foldan.   Feallan sceolon
55   hǣbene æt hilde.   Tō hēanlic mē binceð
bæt gē mid ūrum sceattum   tō scype gangon
unbefohtene   nū gē bus feor hider
on ūrne eard   in becōmon.
Ne sceole gē swā sōfte   sinc gegangan ;
60   ūs sceal ord and ecg   ǣr gesēman,
grim gūðplega,   ǣr wē gofol syllon.'
Hēt bā bord beran,   beornas gangan
bæt hī on bām ēasteðe   ealle stōdon.
Ne mihte bǣr for wætere   werod tō bām ōðrum.
65   7ǣr cōm flōwende   flōd æfter ebban,
lucon lagustrēamas.   Tō lang hit him būhte,
hwænne hī tōgædere   gāras bēron.
Hī bǣr Pantan strēam   mid prasse bestōdon,
Ēastseaxena ord   and se æschere.

70 Ne mihte hyra ǣnig   ōþrum derian,

būton hwā burh flānes flyht   fyl genāme.

    Se flōd ūt gewāt ;   þā flotan stōdon gearowe,

wīcinga fela,   wīges georne.

Hēt þā hæleða hlēo   healdan þā bricge

75 wigan wīgheardne,   se wæs hāten Wulfstān,

cāfne mid his cynne :   þæt wæs Cēolan sunu

be ðone forman man   mid his francan ofscēat

be bǣr baldlīcost   on þā bricge stōp.

Þǣr stōdon mid Wulstāne   wigan unforhte,

80 Ælfere and Maccus,   mōdige twēgen ;

þā noldon æt bām forda   flēam gewyrcan

ac hī fæstlīce   wið ðā fȳnd weredon

þā hwīle þe hī wǣpna   wealdan mōston.

---

42 Byrhtnōð maþelode, bord hafenode=maþelode와 hafenode가 운(rhyming)을 맞추고 있다
는 사실에 주목하기 바란다. 고대영어에서는 매우 드문 일이긴 하나 가끔 압운이 발견된
다. maþelode=spoke. 원형은 maþelian. hafenode=lifted. 원형은 hafenian.

43 wand=brandished. 원형은 windan. wācne=slender. æsc=ash-spear. wordum mǣlde=
spoke with words. 원형은 mǣlan.

44 yrre=angry. ānrǣd=single-minded. āġeaf=gave back. 원형은 āġiefan. andsware=andswaru
(=answer)의 단수 대격.

45 Gehȳrst=Hear. 원형은 ġehȳran. sǣlida=seaman. seġeð=says. 원형은 secgan.

46 tō=as. gafole=tribute. gāras=spears. syllan=sellan(=give).

47 ǣttrynne=poisonous. 원형은 ǣtterne. 실제로 독을 발랐다기보다 deadly나 fatal과 같은 뜻
의 은유적 표현이다. ord=(spear-)point. ealde=ancient. swurd=sword.

48 hereġeatu=war-gear. ēow=to you. æt=in. hilde=battle. dēah=be of use.

49 Brimmanna=seamen's. cf. brim(=sea)+man(=man). boda=messenger. ābēod=ābēodan(=to
report)의 명령형. eft=again. onġean=back.

50 lēodum=to the people. miccle lāþre spell=a much more unpleasant tale (than they
expect). miccle=much. lāþre=lāþ(=hostile)의 비교급. spell=tale, message.

51 stynt=stands. 원형은 standan. unforcūð=undisgraced, honorable. eorl=nobleman, warrior.
werode=troop.

52 wile=will. ġealgean=defend. 원형은 ġeealgian. ēþel=homeland.

53 eard=country. ealdres mīnes=my lord's=Æþelrēdes를 수식한다. 지금까지 Byrhtnoth는 스

스로를 3인칭으로 지칭해 왔다.

54 foldan=land. Feallan sceolon=are destined to fall.

55 hǣþene=heathens. Tō=too. hēanliċ=humiliating, shameful. mē binceð=(it) seems.

56 ūrum=our. sceattum=money, property. gangon=should go. gongan(=to go)의 가정법 현재 복수.

57 unbefohtene=unfought. feor=far. hider=hither.

58 on=into. becōmon=have come. 원형은 becuman.

59 sōfte=easily. sinc=treasure. ġegangan=gain. 원형은 ġegongan.

60 ord=point, spear. ecg=(sword-)edge. ġesēman=reconcile, bring to an agreement.

60-1 ǣr⋯ǣr=first⋯before.

61 grim=fierce. gūðplega=battle-game. syllon=sellan(=to give)의 가정법 현재 단수.

62 bord=shield. beran=bear, carry. beornas=warrior. gangan=go, advance. 원형은 gongan.

63 bæt=so that. ēasteðe=river-bank.

64 Ne mihte þǣr for wætere werod=뒤에 reach나 come에 해당하는 동사가 생략되었다. 전체의 뜻은 Neither troop can get to the other because of the flood tide. 밀물이 섬과 육지를 연결하는 길(causeway)을 덮어버렸기 때문이다.

65 cōm=came. flōwende=flowing. 원형은 flōwan. flōd=flood(-tide). ebban=ebb(-tide).

66 lucon lagustrēamas=the sea-currents locked=the rising tide submerged the causeway, completely encircling the island. lucon=locked. 원형은 lūcan. lagustrēamas=river. him=to them. būhte=(it) seemed. 원형은 bynċan.

67 hwænne hī tōgædere gāras bēron=when (until) they could bring spears together (bring spears against each other).

68 Pantan=Pante. 단수 속격. strēam=river. mid prasse=in battle array. bestōdon=stood around, stood alongside.

69 Ēastseaxena=East Saxons'. ord=vanguard. æschere=ship=army=the Vikings. 물푸레나무 (ash-wood)는 창 자루나 배를 만드는 데 사용되었다.

70 hyra=of them. ōðrum=to the other. derian=do harm.

71 būton=unless. hwā=someone. flānes=arrow's. flyht=flight. fyl=death. ġenāme=ġeniman (=to take)의 가정법 과거.

72 ġewāt=went. 원형은 ġewītan. flotan=seafarers. ġearowe=ready.

73 wīcinga=Viking. fela=many. 복수 속격과 함께 쓰인다. wīges=wīġ(=war)의 단수 속격. georne=eager for. 속격과 함께 쓰인다.

74 Hēt=다음 줄의 wigan(=a warrior)이 목적어이다. hæleða hlēo=the protector of the heroes= Byrhtnoth에 대한 별명(epithet)이다. healdan=keep. bricge=causeway(둑길).

75 wigan=a warrior. wīġheardne=war-hardened. se=who.

76 cāfne mid his cynne=he was as bold as all his kin were known to be. cāfne=bold. mid= along with, like. cynne=kin. Cēolan sunu=Ceola's son=Wulfstan.

77 forman=first. francan=spear. ofscēat=pierced. 원형은 ofscēotan.

78 baldlīcost=most boldly. baldlīċe(=bold)의 최상급. on=onto. stōp=advanced. 원형은 steppan.

79 unforhte=unafraid.

80 mōdige=heroic. twēġen=pair.

81 bā=they. æt=from. forda=ford. flēam gewyrcan=flee, yield. flēam=flight. ġewyrċan=take.

82 ac=but. fæstlīċe=resolutely. wið=against. fӯnd=enemies. weredon=defended. 원형은 werian.

83 bā hwīle be=as long as. wæpna=weapon. 원형은 wæpen. wealdan=to wield. 속격과 함께
    사용된다. mōston=were able. mōtan의 가정법 복수 과거.

  Byrhtnoth made a speech ; he lifte his shield,

shook his slender ash spear, spoke forth with words

angry and resolute, and gave him an answer :

'Do you hear, seafarer, what this army says?

They will give you spears as tribute,

the poisoned spear-tip and ancient swords,

that war-gear that will not be of use to you in battle.

Messenger of the seamen, report back again,

tell your people a much more hateful message :

that here stands, with his troop, an earl of untainted reputation,

who will defend this native land,

the country of Æthelred, my lord's

people and ground. The heathens

will fall in battle. It seems too shameful to me

that you should go to your ships with our tribute

without a fight now that you have come this far

here into our land.

You shall not get treasure so easily :

weapon-tip and edge shall arbitrate between us first,

the fierce game of battle, before we give you tribute.'

  Then he commanded the warriors to advance bearing shields,

so that they all stood on the bank of the river.

One army could not get at the other because of the water there ;

where the tide came flowing after the ebb

streams of water enclosed the land. It seemed too long to them until they could brandish spears togher.

They stood there alonside the River Pante in military formation,

the East Saxon vanguard and the Viking army ;

not one of them was able to injure any other

unless someone received death from the flight of a missile.

The tide went out ; the seamen stood ready,

many Vikings, eager for battle.

Then the protector of the heroes commanded the causeway to be defended

by a warrior fierce in war called Wulfstan,

as brave as all his family (he was Ceola's son),

who with his spear shot the first man

who stepped most boldly onto that causeway.

There stood with Wulfstan fearless warriors,

Ælfere and Maccus, two brave men,

who would not take flight from that ford,

but they firmly resisted the enemy

as long as they were able to brandish their weapons.

THE BATTLE OF MALDON (3)

7ā hī bæt ongēaton   and georne gesāwon
85 bæt hī bǣr bricgweardas   bitere fundon,
ongunnon lytegian bā   lāðe gystas,
bǣdon bæt hī ūpgangan   āgan mōston,
ofer bone ford faran,   fēban lǣdan.

Ðā se eorl ongan   for his ofermōde
90 ālȳfan landes tō fela   lābere ðēode.
Ongan ceallian bā   ofer cald wæter
Byrhtelmes bearn ;   beornas gehlyston :
'Nū ēow is gerȳmed,   gāð ricene tō ūs,
guman tō gūbe ;   God āna wāt
95 hwā bǣre wælstōwe   wealdan mōte.'

Wōdon bā wælwulfas   (for wætere ne murnon)
wīcinga werod,   west ofer Pantan :
ofer scīr wæter   scyldas wēgon,
lidmen tō lande   linde bǣron.

100 7ǣr ongēan gramum   gearowe stōdon
Byrhtnōð mid beornum ;   hē mid bordum hēt
wyrcan bone wīhagan   and bæt werod healdan
fæste wið fēondum.   7ā wæs feohte nēh,
tīr æt getohte.   Wæs sēo tīd cumen
105 bæt bǣr fǣge men   feallan sceoldon.
7ǣr wearð hrēam āhafen,   hremmas wundon,
earn ǣses georn ;   wæs on eorban cyrm.
Hī lēton bā of folman   fēolhearde speru,
grimme gegrundene   gāras flēogan ;
110 bogan wǣron bysige,   bord ord onfēng.
Biter wæs se beadurǣs,   beornas feollon

on gehwæðere hand,   hyssas lāgon.

Wund weard Wulfmǣr,   wælrǣste geċēas,

Byrhtnōðes mǣg :   hē mid billum wearð,

115   his swustersunu,   swīðe forhēawen.

7ær wærd wīcingum   wiberlēan āgyfen.

Gehȳrde iċ þæt Ēadweard   ānne slōge

swīðe mid his swurde,   swenges ne wyrnde,

þæt him æt fōtum   fēoll fǣge cempa ;

120   þæs him his ðēoden   þanc gesǣde

bām būrþēne,   þā hē byre hæfde.

---

84 hī=they. 86행에 나오는 þā lāðe gystas(=those hateful strangers)를 받고 있다. ongēaton= realized. 원형은 onġietan. ġeorne=clearly. ġesāwon=saw. 원형은 ġesēon.

85 briċgweardas=causeway-guardians. bitere=fierce. fundon=had met. 원형은 findan.

86 ongunnon=began. 원형은 onġinnan. lytegian=guile, deceive. 다른 곳에서는 발견되지 않 는 단어이다. lāðe=hateful. gystas=strangers.

87 bǣdon=implored. 원형은 biddan. ūpgangan=passage, access. āgan=have.

88 faran=go. fēþan=soldiers. lǣdan=lead.

89 for=because of. ofermōde=대개는 over-pride나 too much pride로 해석된다. 그러나 상대방 으로 하여금 둑길을 넘어오게 한 것은 작전상의 실수일 수는 있어도 교만으로 보기는 어렵 다는 관점에서 over-exuberance나 excess of courage로 번역하자는 제안도 있다(Marsden, 258).

90 ālyfan=yield to. 뒤에는 여격이 온다. landes tō fela=too much land. 나라의 태반을 빼앗긴 상황에서 '너무 많은 땅'이라는 표현은 자조적인 느낌마저 준다. lāþere=more hateful. ðēode=people. 단수 여격.

91 ċeallian=call out, shout. ofer=across. cald=cold.

92 Byrhtelmes bearn=the son of Byrhtelm=Byrhtnoth. beornas=men, warriors. ġehlyston= listened. 원형은 ġehlystan.

93 Nū ēow is ġerȳmed=(a space) has been cleared for you. 동사의 원형은 ġerȳman. gāð= come. 원형은 gān. ricene(recene)=quickly.

94 guman=men. gūþe=battle, combat. āna=alone. wāt=knows.

95 hwā=who. wælstōwe=place of battle. wealdan=control. mōte=may.

96 Wōdon=Advanced. 원형은 wadan. wælwulfas=slaughter-wolves. murnon=paid heed. 원형 은 murnan.

97 werod=company, band.

98 scīr=clear, bright, gleaming. wēgon=carried. 원형은 wegan.

99 lidmen=seamen. linde=(linden-)shield.

100 ongēan=facing. gramum=foes. ġearowe=ready. 원형은 ġearo.

101 mid bordum=의미상으로는 다음 줄의 wīhagan 뒤에 와야 한다. hēt=commanded. 목적어는 다음 줄의 bæt werod(=the army)이며, 명령의 내용은 첫째, wyrcan bone wīhagan mid bordum할 것과, 둘째 healdan fæste wið fēondum할 것의 두 가지이다.

102 wīhagan=battle-hedge. 병사들이 방패를 촘촘히 붙여서 만드는 방패 벽.

103 fæste=firmly. feohte=fighting. nēh=near.

104 tīr=glory. ġetohte=battle. tīd=time. cumen=come.

105 fǣġe=fated, doomed to die.

106 wearð=was. 원형은 weorðan. hrēam=shouting. āhafen=raised. hremmas=ravens. wundon=circled. 원형은 windan.

107 earn=eagle. ǣses=carrion. ġeorn=eager. ċyrm=shout, uproar.

108 lēton=let. 원형은 lǣtan. folman=hand. fēolhearde=file-hard 또는 hardened by files. speru=spears. 원형은 spere.

109 grimme=cruelly. ġegrundene=ground. gāras=spears. flēogan=fly.

110 bogan=bows. bysiġe=busy. bord=shield. ord=point, spear. onfēng=received. 원형은 onfōn.

111 beadurǣs=onslaught. 원형은 beadu.

112 ġehwæðere=either. hand=side. hyssas=warriors. 원형은 hyse. lāgon=lay (dead). 원형은 licgan.

113 Wund=Wounded. 원형은 wundian. weard=wearð=became, was. 이처럼 ð와 d를 혼동하는 것은 후기의 원고들에서는 흔히 있던 일이다. 116행의 wærd(=wearð)도 마찬가지 경우이다. wælrǣste=slaughter-bed=a resting place among the slain. ġeċēas=chose. 원형은 ġeċēosan.

114 mǣġ=kinsman. billum=swords.

115 his swustersunu=his (Byrhtnoth's) sister's son=Wulfmær. 게르만족에게 있어 여자 형제 쪽의 조카에 대한 애정은 남다른 것이 있었다. swīðe=violently. forhēawen=forhēawan(=to cut down)의 과거분사.

116 wærd=was. wiberlēan=requital. āġyfen=āġiefan(=to give back)의 과거분사.

117 Gehȳrde iċ=여기서 1인칭이 사용된 것은 극적인 효과를 높이기 위해 시인 자신이 목격자인 양 기술하기 위한 것. Gehȳrde=Heard. 원형은 ġehieran. ānne=one man. slōge=struck. 원형은 slēan.

118 swenges=blows. 단수 속격. wyrnde=withheld. 속격과 함께 쓰인다. 원형은 wyrnan.

119 him æt fōtum=at his feet. cempa=champion, fighter.

120-1 bæs him his ðēoden banc ġesǣde bām būrbēne=for that his lord said to him, to the chamberlain, thanks. ðēoden=lord. banc=thnks.

121 būrbēnd=bower-thane=Edward. byre=opportunity.

When the Vikings perceived this and saw plainly
that they had found there fierce causeway-defenders,

they began to use cunning, the hateful strangers :
they requested that they should be allowed a passage to land,
to travel over the ford, to lead the foot-soldiers.
Then the earl, because of his pride, began
to allow too much land to a more hateful nation.
He began to call out then over the cold water,
this son of Byrhtelm — the warriors listened :
'Now a passage is granted to you, come quickly to us
as men to battle ; God alone knows
who will be allowed to control the place of slaughter.'
    The wolves of slaughter advanced ; they did not care about the water,
that host of Vikings. West over the Pante,
over the shining water, they bore their shields ;
the sailors carried their lime-wood shields to land.
There against the hostile ones stood ready
Byrhtnoth with his men. He commanded the army
to make a battle-wall with shields and to hold fast
against the enemies. The battle was near then,
glory in the fray ; the time had come
that fared men should fall there.
An outcry was raised there ; ravens circled in the air,
the eagle eager for carrion ; there was uproar on earth.
Then from their hands they let fly spears as hard as files,
sharpened missiles ;
bows were busy, the shield received the sword-point.
Bitter was the rush of battle ; warriors fell
on either side, soldiers lay dead.
Wulfmær was wounded, he chose death in battle,
the kinsman of Byrhtnoth, son of his sister :
he was cruelly cut down with swords.
Requital was given to the Vikings there.

I heard that Eadweard killed one

fiercely with his sword — he did not withhold the blow —

so that at his feet a doomed warrior fell,

for which his lord gave thanks

to his chamberlain when he had the chance.

(tr. Treharne)

THE BATTLE OF BRUNANBURH (1)

1   Hēr Æbelstān cyning   eorla dryhten,
      beorna bēahgifa   ond his brōbor ēac,
      Ēadmund æbeling,   ealdorlangne tīr
      geslōgon æt sæcce   sweorda ecgum

5   ymbe Brūnanburh.   Bordweal clufan,
      hēowan heabolinde   hamora lāfan,
      afaran Ēadweardes,   swā him geæbele wæs
      from cnēomǣgum   bæt hī æt campe oft
      wib lābra gehwæne   land ealgodon,

10   hord ond hāmas.   Hettend crungun,
      Sceotta lēoda   ond scipflotan
      fæge fēollan,   feld dænede
      secge swāte   siðban sunne ūp
      on morgentīd,   mǣre tungol,

15   glād ofer grundas,   Godes condel beorht,
      ēces Drihtnes,   oð sīo æbele gesceaft
      sāh tō setle.   7ær læg secg mænig
      gārum āgēted,   guma norberna
      ofer scild scoten,   swilce Scittisc ēac,

20   wērig, wīges sæd.   Wesseaxe forð
      ondlongne dæg   ēorodcistum
      on lāst legdun   lābum bēodum,
      hēowan hereflēman   hindan bearle
      mēcum mylenscearpan.   Myrce ne wyrndon

25   heardes hondplegan   hæleba nānum
      bǣra be mid Anlāfe   ofer ǣra gebland
      on lides bōsme   land gesōhtun,
      fæge tō gefeohte.   Fīfe lægun

on bām campstede cyningas giunge,

30 sweordum āswefede, swilce seofene ēac

eorlas Anlāfes, unrīm heriges

flotan ond Sceotta. 7ǣr geflēmed wearð

Norðmanna bregu, nēde gebēded,

tō lides stefne lītle weorode ;

35 crēad cnear on flot, cyning ūt gewāt

on fealene flōd, feorh generede.

(*Anglo-Saxon Chronicle*의 937년 항목에는 Wessex의 왕 Æðelstan과 그의 동생 Edmund (이들은 Alfred대왕의 손자들이다)가 하나님의 도움에 의해 Brunanburh에서 Olaf의 군대를 격퇴했다는 기사가 실려있다. 이 시는 그 전투 장면을 묘사한 것이다. Olaf의 군대는 그가 Dublin에서 이끌고 온 Norse인, Constantine 3세가 이끄는 Scot인, 그리고 Strathclyde에서 온 Briton인의 연합군이었다. *The Battle of Maldon*과는 달리 Brunanburh는 승리의 기록이 다. Brunanburh가 영국의 서북방의 어느 고장이었을 것이라는 것 이상 정확한 위치는 알려져 있지 않다.)

1 Hēr=Here=In this year. *Chronicle*을 시작하는 상투적인 표현이다. Æbelstān=전투가 벌어 졌을 때의 나이는 16세이다. 재위 기간은 924-39. 그 뒤를 이어 동생 Edmund(939-46)가 왕 위에 오른다. 이들의 부왕은 Edward(899-924)이다. eorla=of men. dryhten=lord.

2 beorna=warriors'. bēahġifa=ring=giver=lord. ēac=also.

3 æbeling=prince. ealdorlangne=life-long. tīr=glory.

4 ġeslōgon=won. 원형은 ġeslēan. sæċċe=battle. sweorda ecgum=by the edges of swords.

5 ymbe=at, near. Bordweal=Shield-wall. clufan=split. 원형은 clēofan.

6 hēowan=hacked. 원형은 hēawan. heabolinde=linden-shields. hamora lāfan=with the legacies of hammers=swords forged by the blacksmith's hammer. hamora lāf=swords. hamora=hammer. lāf=what is left, legacy.

7 afaran=sons. swā=as. him=in them. ġeæbele=inborn.

8 cnēomǣġum=ancestors. 그들의 가장 빛나는 선조는 Alfred(871-99) 대왕이다. campe= combat.

9 wib=against. lābra=of foes. ġehwǣne=each. 속격과 함께 쓰인다. ealgodon=defended. 원 형은 ealgian.

10 hord=treasure-board. hāmas=homes. Hettend=Enemies. crungun=fell. 원형은 crincgan.

11 Sceotta lēoda ond scipflotan=People of the Scots and seamen (i.e. Vikings). 이들이 침략 군의 중요한 두 세력이었다.

12 fæġe=fated. feld=field. dænede=flowed(?). 원형은 dennian. 이 단어의 정확한 뜻은 알려져

있지 않다.

13 secge swāte=with the blood of men. secge=man, warrior. swāte=blood.

14 morgentīd=morning. mǣre=glorious. tungol=star.

15 glād=glided. 원형은 glīdan. grundas=ground. condel=candle. beorht=bright.

16 ēċes=eternal. Drihtnes=앞줄의 Godes와 함께 condel에 걸린다. oð=until. sīo=bēon(=to be) 의 가정법 현재 단수. æbele=noble. ġesceaft=creation.

17 sāh=sank. 원형은 sīgan. setle=rest. læġ=lay. 원형은 licgan. secg=(a) man.

18 gārum=by spears. āġēted=destroyed. 원형은 āġēotan. guma norberna=many a north man (Norseman). 앞줄의 mæniġ의 수식을 받는다.

19 ofer=above. scild=shield. scoten=hit, shot. 원형은 scēotan. swilċe=likewise. Scittisc= Scots(man).

20 wēriġ=weary. wīġes=battle. sæd=sated with, weary of. 속격과 함께 쓰인다. Wesseaxe= Westseaxe=The West Saxons. forð=onwards.

21 ondlongne dæġ=for the entire day. ēorodċistum=troops.

22 on lāst legdun lāþum þēodum=followed in the track (pursued the trail) of the hostile peoples. lāst=track. legdun=laid. 원형은 lecgan. lāþum=hostile. þēodum=people.

23 hēowan=cut down, hewed. 원형은 hēawan. hereflēman=fugitives. hindan=from behind. þearle=violently.

24 mēcum mylenscearpan=with swords mill-sharp=sharpened by the grindstone. mēcum= mēċe(=sword)의 복수 여격. Myrċe=Mercians. wyrndon=withheld. 원형은 wyrnan. 속격 과 함께 사용된다.

24-6 ne wyrndon heardes hondplegan hæleþa nānum þǣra þe=did not withhold hard hand-to-hand combat from any of the warriors who….

25 heardes=fierce, hard. hondplegan=hand-to-hand combat. hæleþa=man, warrior. nānum= none.

26 þǣra þe=those who. þǣra=se(=that)의 복수 속격. Anlāfe=Olaf. Dublin에서 쳐들어온 Vikings의 지휘관이었다. ǣra=of waves. ġebland=turmoil.

27 lides=ship's. bōsme=bosom. ġesōhtun=invaded. 원형은 ġesēċan.

28 fæġe=fated (men). ġefeohte=battle. lǣgun=lay (dead). 원형은 licgan.

29 campstede=battlefield. ġiunge=young.

30 āswefede=put to sleep. 원형은 āswebban.

31 unrīm=(and) a countless number. heriġes=the army. 단수 속격. 원형은 here.

32 flotan=(the army) of sailors (Vikings). ġeflēmed=put to flight. 원형은 ġeflȳman. wearð= was.

33 bregu=chief. 원형은 brego. nēde=by necessity. ġebēded=forced. 원형은 ġebēdan.

34 stefne=prow. lītle weorode=with little company.

35 crēad=hastened. 원형은 crūdan. cnear=boat, small ship. flot=sea. ġewāt=went. 원형은 ġewītan.

36 fealene=grey. 원형은 fealu. flōd=tide. feorh=life. ġenerede=saved. 원형은 ġenerian.

Æthelstan, the King, ruler of earls
and ring-giver to men, and Prince Eadmund
his brother, earned this year fame everlasting
with the blades of their swords in battle
at Brunanburh ; with their well-wrought weapons
both Eadweard's sons cleaved the linden shields,
cut through the shield-wall ; as was only fitting
for men of their lineage, they often carried arms
against some foe in defence of their land,
their treasure, their homes. The enemy perished,
fated Scots and seafarers
fell in the fight ; from the hour when that great
constellation the sun, the burning candle
of God eternal, first glides above the earth
until at last that lordly creation
sinks into its bower, the battlefield flowed
with dark blood. Many a warrior lay there,
spreadeagled by spears, many a Norse seafarer
stabbed above his shield and many a weary Scot,
surfeited by war. All day,
in troops together, the West Saxons
pursued those hateful people,
hewed down the fugitives fiercely from behind
with their sharpened swords. The Mercians did not stint
hard handplay to any of the heroes
who, fated to fight, sought this land
with Anlaf, sailed in the ship's hold
over the surging sea. Five young kings
sprawled on that field of battle,
put to sleep by swords ; likewise seven
of Anlaf's earls and countless in the host,

seafarers and Scots. There, the Norse king
was forced to flee, driven to the ship's prow
with a small bodyguard ; the little ship
scurried out to sea, the king sped
over the dark waves and so saved his life.

THE BATTLE OF BRUNANBURH (2)

Swilce þær ēac se frōda   mid flēame cōm
on his cȳbbe norð,   Costontīnus ;
hār hilderinc   hrēman ne borfte
40   mæcan gemānan.   Hē wæs his mǣga sceard,
frēonda gefylled   on folcstede
beslagen æt sæcce   ond his sunu forlēt
on wælstōwe   wundun forgrunden,
giungne æt gūðe.   Gelpan ne borfte
45   beorn blandenfeax   bilgeslehtes,
eald inwidda,   ne Anlāf bȳ mā.
Mid heora herelāfum   hlehhan ne borftun
bæt hēo beaduweorca   beteran wurdun
on campstede   cumbolgehnāstes,
50   gārmittinge,   gumena gemōtes,
wǣpengewrixles,   bæs hī on wælfelda
wib Ēadweardes   afaran plegodan.
Gewitan him bā Norbmen   nægledcnearrum,
drēorig daraða lāf,   on Dinges-Mere
55   ofer dēop wæter   Difelin sēcan
eft Īreland,   æwiscmōde.
Swilce bā gebrōber   bēgen ætsamne,
cyning ond æbeling,   cȳbbe sōhton,
Wesseaxena land,   wīges hrēmige.
60   Lētan him behindan   hrǣ bryttian
saluwigpādan,   bone sweartan hræfn,
hyrnednebban,   ond bane hasewanpādan
earn æftan hwīt,   ǣses brūcan,
grǣdigne gūðhafoc   ond bæt grǣge dēor,

65 wulf on wealde.   Ne wearð wæl māre

   on bis ēiglande   ̄æfre gīeta

   folces gefylled   beforan bissum

   sweordes ecgum,   bæs be ūs secgað bēc,

   ealde ūðwitan,   sibban ēastan hider

70 Engle ond Seaxe   ūp becōman

   ofer brād brimu   Brytene sōhtan,

   wlance wīgsmibas   Wēalas ofercōman,

   eorlas ārhwate   eard begēatan.

37 Swilċe=Likewise. frōda=wise (man). mid=in. flēame=flight. cōm=went

38 ċybbe=native land. 원형은 ċybbu. norð=(went) north. Costontīnus=Constantine Ⅲ 당시 Pict족과 Scot족의 통합 왕이었다.

39 hār=hoary. hilderinc=warrior. hrēman=to exult. borfte=had cause. 원형은 burfan.

40 mæcan ġemānan=(about) the shared swords=about the battle. mæcan=mēċe(=sword)의 복수 여격. ġemunan=think about. m̄æga=kinsmen. 복수 속격이다. sceard=bereft of.

41 frēonda ġefylled=(bereft of kinsmen,) of friends felled⋯. ġefylled의 원형은 ġefyllan. folcstede=battlefield.

42 beslaġen=struck down. 원형은 beslēan. sæċċe=strife, battle. sunu=sons. forlēt=left. 원형은 forl̄ætan.

43 wælstōwe=place of slaughter. wundun=wound. forgrunden=forgrindan(=to grind to pieces, destroy)의 과거분사로서 행위자는 여격으로 나타낸다.

44 ġiungne=young (men). gūðe=battle. Gelpan=to boast (of+g).

45 beorn=warrior. blandenfeax=gray-haired. bilġeslehtes=sword-clash. 단수 속격.

46 inwidda=malicious foe. ne Anlāf b̄y mā=nor Olaf the more=and no more did Olaf.

47 Mid=Among. heora=their. herelāfum=army-remnants. hlehhan=to rejoice.

48 hēo=they. beaduweorca beteran wurdun=were (had been) superior in battle-deeds. beaduweorca=warlike deed. wurdun=was. 원형은 weorban.

49 campstede=battle-field. cumbolġehnāstes=clash of standards.

50 gārmittinge=meeing of spears. gumena=men's. ġemōtes=encounter.

51 w̄æpenġewrixles=exchange of weapons. bæs=afterwards, because. wælfelda=field of slaughter.

52 afaran(eafera)=sons, offsprings, descendants. plegodan=contended. 원형은 plegian.

53 Ġewitan=Departed. 원형은 ġewītan. him=themselves. 움직임을 나타내는 동사와 사용된 재귀대명사는 번역하지 않는 것이 보통이다. næġledcnearrum=in (their) nailed ships.

54 drēoriġ=sad. daraða lāf=the remnants of spears=those left untouched by the spears.

daraða의 원형은 daroð. lāf=remnant. Dinges-Mere=분명치는 않으나 Ireland 맞은 편에 있는 영국 서해안의 어느 강어귀로서 아마도 지금의 River Dee일 가능성이 높다.

55 Difelin=Dublin. sēċan=to make for.
56 eft=again. æwiscmōde=ashamed, humiliated.
57 ġebrōþer=brothers. bēġen=both. ætsamne=together.
58 c̄ybbe=home.
59 wīġes=of battle. hrēmige=exulting. 속격과 함께 쓰인다.
60 Lētan=(They) left. 원형은 l̄ætan. hr̄æ=corpses. 원형은 hr̄æw. bryttian=to divide out.
61 saluwiġpādan=dark-plumaged. sweartan=black. hræfn=raven. 앞뒤에 세 형용사 saluwiġpādan, sweartan, hyrnednebban의 수식을 받는다.
62 hyrnednebban=horny-beaked. hasewanpādan=dark-coated.
63 earn æftan hwīt=the eagle white from behind=with white tail. earn=eagle. æftan=from behind. hwīt=white. ̄æses=carrion. brūcan=to enjoy. 속격과 함께 사용된다. 60행의 bryttian 과 함께 Lētan에 걸린다.
64 gr̄ædiġne=greedy. gūðhafoc=war-hawk. gr̄æġe=grey. dēor=beast.
65 wulf=wolf. on=from. wealde=forest.
65-67 Ne wearð wæl māre on þis ēiglande ̄æfre ġīeta folces ġefylled=Never yet···had there been a greater slaughter of people killed ···. wæl=slaughter. ̄æfre=ever.
66 ēiġlande(īġland)=island. ġīeta=yet.
67 folces=65행의 māre에 걸린다. ġefylled=fulfilled. 원형은 ġefyllan.
68 þæs þe=according to what. bēc=books.
69 ūðwitan=authorities. siþþan=since.
70 ūp=ashore. becōman=came.
71 brād=broad. brimu=ocean. sōhtan=sought out. 원형은 sēċċan.
72 wlance=proud. wīġsmiþas=war-smiths, warrior. Wēalas=Welshmen. ofercōman=overcame. 원형은 ofercuman.
73 eorlas=noblemen. ārhwate=eager for glory. eard=country. beġēatan=acquired. 원형은 beġietan.

Constantine, too, (a man of discretion)
fled north to the comforts of his own country ;
deprived of kinsmen and comrades cut down
in the strife, that old warrior
had no reason whatsoever to relish
the swordplay ; he left his son
savaged by weapons on that field of slaughter,
a mere boy in battle. That wily, grizzled warrior

had no grounds at all to boast about the fight,

and neither did Anlaf ; with their leavings

of an army, they could scarcely exult

that things went their own way

in the thick of battle - at the crash of standards

and the clash of spears, at the conflict of weapons

and struggle of men - when they grappled

on that slaughter-field with Eadweard's sons.

Then the Norsemen made off in their nailed boats,

and survivors shamed in battle,

they crossed the deep water from Dingesmere

to the shelter of Dublin, Ireland once more.

Likewise both brothers together,

king and prince, returned to Wessex,

their own country, exulting in war.

They left behind them to devour the corpses,

relish the carrion, the horny-beaked raven

garbed in black, and the grey-coated

eagle (a greedy war-hawk)

with its white tail, and that grey beast,

the wolf in the wood. Never, before this,

were more men in this island slain

by the sword's edge-as books and aged sages

confirm-since Angles and Saxons sailed here

from the east, sought the Britons over the wide seas,

since those warsmiths hammered the Welsh,

and earls, eager for glory, overran the land.

(tr. Crossley-Holland)

XI. ELEGIES AND LYRICS

Deor

1   Welund him be wurman   wræces cunnade,
      ānhȳdig eorl   earfoba drēag,
      hæfde him tō gesībbe   sorge ond longab,
      wintercealde wræce.   Wēan oft onfond
5   sibban hine Nīðhād on   nēde legde,
      swoncre seonnobende   on sȳllan monn.
      7æs oferēode, bisse swā mæg.

      Beadohilde ne wæs   hyre brōbra dēab
      on sefan swā sār   swā hyre sylfre bing,
10 bæt hēo gearolīce   ongieten hæfde
      bæt hēo ēacen wæs.   Ǣfre ne meahte
      brīste gebencan   hū ymb bæt sceolde.
      7æs oferēode, bisses swā mæg.

      Wē bæt Mǣðhilde   monge gefrugnon
15 wurdon grundlēase   Gēates frīge,
      bæt hī sēo sorglufu   slǣp ealle binōm.
      7æs oferēode,   bisses swā mæg.

      Ðēodrīc āhte   brītig wintra
      Mǣringa burg ; bæt wæs monegum cūb.
20   7æs oferēode, bisses swā mæg.

      Wē geāscodan   Eormanrīces
      wylfenne gebōht.   Āhte wīde folc

Gotena rīces. 7æt wæs grim cyning.
Sæt secg monig   sorgum gebunden,
25 wēan on wēnan,   wȳscte geneahhe
bæt bæs cynerīces   ofercumen wǣre.
7æs oferēode, bisses swā mæg.

Siteð sorgcearig   sǣlum bidǣled,
on sefan sweorceð,   sylfum binceð
30 bæt sȳ endelēas   earfoda dǣl.
Mæg bonne gebencan   bæt geond bās woruld
wītig Dryhten   wendeb geneahhe :
eorle monegum   āre gescēawað,
wīslicne blǣd,   sumum wēana dǣl.

35 7æt ic bī mē sylfum   secgan wille,
bæt ic hwīle wæs   Heodeninga scop,
dryhtne dȳre.   Mē wæs Dēor noma.
Āhte ic fela wintra   folgað tilne,
holdne hlāford,   obbæt Heorrenda nū,
40 lēoðcræftig monn,   londryht gebāh
bæt mē eorla hlēo   ǣr gesealde.
7æt oferēode,   bisses swā mæg.

(이 시는 신화나 전설에 나오는 비극적 삽화들을 소개함으로써 주인의 사랑을 잃은 자신의
슬픔을 극복해보려는 의도에서 쓰여진 것이다. 각 연(stanza)은 그것대로 각기 독립한 이야
기를 다루고 있으며 그 끝은 '그 큰 슬픔들이 지나갔듯이 나의 이 슬픔도 지나갈지어다'라
는 후렴으로 끝나고 있다. 이처럼 후렴이 있고 또 시가 연(stanza)으로 구분돼 있다는 점에
서도 고대영어의 다른 시들에 비해 매우 독특하다.)

1   Welund=게르만족들 사이에 잘 알려진 대장장이로서 그를 놓치기 싫어한 Nithhad 왕이 도
망가지 못하게 그의 발뒤꿈치를 끊어 놓는다. 여기에 분노한 Welund는 왕의 두 아들을 죽

이고 딸 Beadohild를 겁탈하여 11행에서 보듯 애를 임신하게 만든다. 그리고는 쇠로 날개를 만들어 도망을 간다. him=for him. be=through, by means of. wurman(wyrmum)=wyrm(=serpent)의 복수 여격=among the serpents. 여기서 '뱀'은 뱀을 그린 칼이나 Welund에 가해지고 있는 속박에 대한 은유로 보아야 할 듯. wræces=wræc(=exile, persecution, misery)의 단수 속격. cunnade=experienced. 속격과 함께 사용된다. 원형은 cunnian.

2   ānh̄ydiġ=strong-minded, resolute. eorl=man. earfoþa=miseries. drēag=suffered. 원형은 drēogan.

3   tō=as. ġesīþþe=companion. sorge=sorrow. longaþ=langoþ(=longing)의 단수 대격.

4   winterċealde=wintry-cold. wræce=wracu(=suffering)의 단수대격. Wēan=Misfortunes. onfond=experienced. 원형은 onfindan.

5   siþþan=after. hine…on=on him. nēde=constraints, fetters. leġde=laid. 원형은 licgan.

6   swoncre=supple. seonobende=sinew-bonds. seono(=sinew)+bend(=bond). 이 자체로서는 fetters made from sinew의 뜻이지만, fetters of rope applied to the sinews 그 어느 쪽으로도 번역이 가능하다. 왕이 Welund의 발뒤꿈치를 잘라 놓았다는 전설을 따르는 경우에는 후자의 해석이 타당하겠으나 swoncre seonobende(=supple sinew-bonds)를 Welund가 당하고 있는 고초(nēde)에 대한 비유로 본다면 전자의 해석도 가능하다. (Marsden, 319). s̄y llan=good. monn=man.

7   7æs oferēode, þisse swā mæġ=That passed away, this also may. oferēode=passed away. 원형은 ofergān.

8   Beadohilde=to Beadohild. Nithhad의 딸로서 Welund에 겁탈당하고 애를 갖게 된다. hyre(hire)=her.

9   sefan=(her) heart. swā=as. sār=grievous. hyre sylfre=of her herself=her own. þing=situation.

10   þæt=in that (or when). ġearolīċe=clearly. onġieten=realized. 원형은 onġietan.

11   ēacen=pregnant. Æfre ne meahte=Never could (she)…. Æfre=ever. meahte=magan(=can)의 과거.

12   brīste=confidently. ġeþenċan=think. hū ymb þæt sceolde=how in respect of that it must (be)=what must needs become of that.

14   Mǣðhilde=of Mæthhild. monge=그 뜻을 알 수 없으나 뒤에 오는 gefrugnon(=heard)의 목적어라는 점을 감안해서 affair라는 해석이 제안되었다. 그밖에도 monge를 mōne(=moan)로 고쳐 읽으려는 시도도 있다. ġefrugnon=heard. 원형은 ġefriġnan.

15   wurdon=became. grundlēase=boundless. Gēates friġe=the affections of Geat.

16   þæt hī sēo sorglufu slǣp ealle binōm=in that that unhappy love deprived her of sleep completely. hī(hīe)=(목적격의) her(=Mæthhild). sorglufu=sad love. slǣp=sleep. ealle=completely, altogether. binōm=deprived. 원형은 beniman.

18   Ðēodrīc=동 고트족의 왕 Theodoric(493-526). 게르만족들 사이에서는 폭군으로 알려져 있었다. āhte=ruled. 원형은 āgan. brītiġ wintra=thirty winters=thirty years.

19   Mǣringa burg=stronghold of Mærings. monegum=maniġ(=many)의 단수 여격=too many. cūþ=known.

21 ġeāscodan=learned, discovered. 원형은 ġeascian [yea : skian]. Eormanrīces=고딕 왕 Eormanric (-375). 역시 폭군이었다.

22 wylfenne=savage. ġebōht=mind. wīde=widely.

23 Gotena=of the Goths. grim=cruel.

24 secg=(a) man. ġebunden=fettered (by). 여격에 의해 행위자를 나타낸다.

25 wēan on wēnan=in expectation of sorrow. wēan=woe, misfortune. wēnan=think, imagine, expect. wȳscte=wished. 원형은 wȳscan [wi : šan]. ġeneahhe=often.

26 bæs cynerīċes ofercumen wǣre=as regards the kingdom, it might be defeated.

28 sorgceariġ=sorrowing (man). sǣlum=from joys. bidǣled=cut off. 원형은 bidǣlan.

29 sefan=spirit. sweorceð=grows dark. 원형은 sweorcan. sylfum=to himself. binceð=(it) seems. 원형은 bynċcan.

30 sȳ=is. 가정법 단수 현재. earfoda=hardship. 원형은 earfoba. dǣl=(his) share (of).

31 Mæġ=(I) can. ġeond=throughout.

32 wītiġ=wise. wendeb=changes (things), causes change. 원형은 wendan. ġeneahhe=in abundance.

33-4 eorle monegum ⋯ sumum=to many a man ⋯to some ⋯. eorle=nobleman. monegum= many. āre=mercy. ġescēawað=shows. 원형은 ġescēawian.

34 wīsliċne=certain. blǣd=success.

35 bī(be)=about.

36 hwīle=for a time. Heodeninga=of the Heodenings. Heoden 왕(노르만족의 Heðinn)의 일가. scop=poet, singer.

37 dȳre(dēore)=dear. Mē wæs Dēor noma=Deor was my name. Dēor=bold, brave, dear, animal 등의 뜻을 갖는다.

38 Āhte=Possessed. 원형은 āgan. folgað=position. tilne=good. 원형은 til.

39 holdne=loyal. 원형은 hold. obbæt=ob=until. Heorrenda=중세 고지대독일어의 서사시 Kudrun 에 나오는 유명한 가수 Hôrant를 가리킬 수도 있다. 노르웨이 문학에서 Hjarrandi는 Heðinn(36행)의 아버지이다. nū=now.

40 lēoðcræftiġ=song-skilled. londryht=land-entitlement. ġebāh=received. 원형은 ġebicgan.

41 hlēo=protector. ǣr=previously. ġesealde=granted. 원형은 sellan.

Weland well knew about exile ;

that strong man suffered much ;

sorrow and longing and wintry exile

stood him company ; often he suffered grief

after Nithhad fettered him, put supple bonds

of sinew upon the better man.

    That passed away, this also may.

To Beadohild, her brothers' death
was less cause for sorrow than her own state
when she discovered she was
with child ; she could never think
anything but ill would come of it.
> That passed away, this also may.

Many of us have learned that Geat's love
for Mæthild grew too great for human frame,
his sad passion stopped him from sleeping.
> That passed away, this also may.

For thirty years Theodric ruled
the Mæring stronghold ; that was known to many.
> That passed away, this also may.

We have heard of the wolfish mind
of Ermanaric ; he held wide sway
in the realm of the Goths. He was a cruel king.
Many a warrior sat, full of sorrow,
waiting for trouble, often wishing
that his kingdom might be overcome.
> That passed away, this also may.

If a man sits in despair, deprived of all pleasure,
his mind moves upon sorrow ; it seems to him
that there is no end to his share of hardship.
Then he should remember that the wise Lord
brings many changes ;
to many a man he grants glory,
certain fame, to others a sad lot.

I will say this about myself,

that once I was a scop of the Heodeningas,

dear to my lord. Deor was my name.

For many years I had a fine office

and loyal lord, until now Heorrenda,

a man skilled in song, has received the land

that the guardian of men first gave to me.

   That passed away, this also may.

(tr. Crossley-Holland)

THE WIFE'S LAMENT (1)

1   Ic bis giedd wrece   bī mē ful geōmorre,
mīnre selfre sīb.   Ic ðæt secgan mæg
hwæt ic yrmba gebād,   sibban ic ūp wēox,
nīwes obbe ealdes,   nā mā bonne nū.

5   Ā ic wīte wonn   mīnra wræcsība.

        Ǣrest mīn hlāford gewāt   heonan of lēodum
ofer ȳba gelāc ;   hæfde ic ūhtceare
hwǣr mīn lēodfruma   londes wǣre.
Ðā ic mē fēran gewāt   folgab sēcan,

10   winelēas wrecca,   for mīnre wēabearfe.

        Ongunnon bæt bæs monnes   māgas hycgan
burh dyrne gebōht,   bæt hȳ todǣlden unc,
bæt wit gewīdost   in woruldrīce
lifdon lāðlīcost ;   ond mec longade.

15   Hēt mec hlāford mīn   hēr heard niman ;
āhte ic lēofra lȳt   on bissum londstede,
holdra frēonda.   Forbon is mīn hyge geōmor.
Ðā ic mē ful gemæcne   monnan funde,
heardsǣligne,   hygegeōmorne,

20   mōd mibendne,   morbor hycgendne.
Blīðe gebǣro,   ful oft wit bēotedan
bæt unc ne gedǣlde   nemne dēað āna,
ōwiht elles ;   Eft is bæt onhworfen ;
is nū fornumen   swā hit nā wǣre,

25   frēondscipe uncer.   Sceal ic feor ge nēah
mīnes felalēofan   fǣhðu drēogan.

(이 시는 시집 식구들에게 쫓겨나 남편과 헤어지게 된 어느 아내의 비통함을 그린 작품이
다. 그러나 헤어지게 된 사정은 자세하지 않다. 짐작컨대 이 부인은 타관에서 온 사람이며

남편은 어떤 모반에 가담했다가 유배당한 듯 하다. 여기에 대해 어떤 이는 이 작품을 기독교적인 우화로 읽을 것을 제안한다. 이 경우 아내는 Jerusalem(즉 히브리 사람들)과 교회를 가리키고, 그녀가 겪은 고통과 슬픔은 구약에 나오는 신의 백성들, 나아가 현세의 기독교 신자들이 겪은 고통을 가리킨다고 생각할 수 있다.)

1　ġiedd=tale. wrece=tell. 원형은 wrecean. bī me ful ġeōmorre=about me very melancholy=about my very melancholy self. bī(be)=about. ġeōmorre=sorrowful, sad, gloomy.

2　mīnre selfre sib=the experience of my self=my own experience. sib=experience.

3　yrmþa=troubles. ġebēd=experienced, endured. 원형은 ġebīdan. siþþan=after. ūp=up. wēox=grew. 원형은 weaxan.

4　nīewes oþþe ealdes=of new or of old=recently or of old. nō=never. mā=more.

5　Ā=Always. wīte=torment. wonn=suffered. 원형은 winnan. mīnra wræcsīþa=(the torment) of my miserable journeys. wræcsīða=misery.

6　Ǣrest=First, hlāford=lord, master. ġewāt=went. 원형은 ġewītan. heonan=hence. lēodum=(his) people.

7　ȳþa ġelāc=the play(or rolling) of the waves. ȳþa=waves. ġelāc=rolling, tumult. ūhtceare=anxiety before dawn. cf. ūhta=period just before dawn. cearo=care. 원형은 cearu.

8　hwǣr mīn lēodfruma londes wǣre=(as to) where in the land my leader of men might be. lēodfruma=leader of a people, lord.

9　iċ mē fēran ġewāt folgaþ sēċan=I went traveling. mē=myself. 동작을 나타내는 동사와 별 뜻 없이 사용되는 경우가 있다. 백성들의 지도자(lēodfruma)인 그의 남편은 신하들(folgaþ)을 데리고 여행중이며 아내가 찾고 나선 것이 바로 이들이다. fēran=set out, go. folgaþ=retinues, retainers. cf. folgian=follow. sēċan=seek.

10　winelēas=friendless. cf. wine=friend, lord. wreċċa=wanderer, fugitive, exile, outcast. wēabearfe=grievous need, woeful need.

11　Ongunnon=began. þæt=뒤에 오는 hycgan의 목적어. monnes=man's. māgas=kinsmen. 원형은 mǣġ. hycgan=to plot.

12　dyrne=secret. ġebōht=design. hȳ(hīe)=they. todǣlden=todǣlan(=to separate)의 가정법. unc=us two.

13　wit=we two. ġewīdost=most widely. 원형은 ġewīde. woruldrīċe=world-kingdom=this world.

14　lifdon=(have) lived. 원형은 libban. lāðlīcost=most wretchedly. mec longode=I pine. 원형은 longian. meċ=me.

15　Hēt=Commanded. hēr heard niman=원본에서는 hērheard niman으로 되어 있다. 이 경우 몇 가지 상이한 해석이 가능하다. 하나는 hērh(hearh, hearg)(=grove, sanctuary) eard (=abode) niman(=take)으로 나누어 전체의 뜻을 'My lord commanded me to take up this residence in a grove(sanctuary)'로 해석하는 것이다. 또 다른 해석은 hērheard를 hēr(=here)와 heard(cruel(ly))로 나누어 전체의 뜻을 'My cruel lord commanded me to be seized here'로 해석하는 것이다. 세 번째는 heard를 hearde(=cruelly)로 읽어 'cruelly commanded me'로

해석하는 것. 그리고 마지막 해석은 heard에서 어두의 h가 무의미하게 들어간 것으로 보고 전체를 hēr(=here) eard(=abode) niman(=take)로 나누어 전체의 뜻을 'to take up residence here'로 해석하는 것이다. 그러나 27행에 견주어 볼 때는 첫 번째 해석이 가장 타당할 듯 하다.

16　āhte=possessed. 원형은 āgan. lēofra=leof(=beloved, dear)의 복수 속격. 여기서는 loved ones의 뜻. fyt=few. londstede=region, country.

17　holdra=loyal, friendly. Forþon=Therefore. hyġe(hiġe)=spirit. ġeōmor=sad.

18　ful ġemæcne monnan=very suitable man=자기 남편. ġemæcne=ġemæc(=suitable)의 단수 대격. funde=found. 원형은 findan.

19　heardsǣliġne=ill-fortuned, unhappy. cf. heard(=bitter)+sæliġ(=happy). hyġeġeōmorne= sad-spirited. cf. hyġe(=spirit)+ġeōmor(=sad).

20　mōd=heart. mīþendne=concealing. 원형은 mīþan. morþor=murder. hycgendne=plotting. 원형은 hycgan(hicgan).

21　Blīðe=friendly, cheerful. ġebǣro=demeanour. Blīðe ġebǣro(=with a happy demeanour)는 앞줄 끝을 콤마로 끝내는 경우에는 남편이 모의를 꾸미는 모습을, 여기서처럼 마침표로 끝 내는 경우에는 뒤의 wit(=we two)를 수식하게 된다. wit=we two. bēotedan=vowed. 원형 은 bēotian.

22　unc ne ġedǣlde⋯ōwiht elles=nothing else would separate us except⋯. ġedǣlde= separate. 원형은 ġedǣlan. nemne=except. dēað=death. āna=only.

22-23　unc ne ġedǣlde⋯ōwiht elles=nothing else would separate us (except⋯.)

23　Eft=Now. onhworfen=reversed, changed. 원형은 onhworfan(onhwerfan).

24　fornumen=taken away. 원형은 forniman. 이 단어는 원본에는 없던 것을 앞 뒤 문맥에 맞 춰 추측해서 삽입한 것이다. swā=as if. swā hit nā wǣre=as if it had not never been.

25　frēondscipe=friendship. 여기서는 love의 뜻. uncer=wit(=we two)의 단수 속격=our. Sceal= must. feor=far. ġe=and. nēah=near.

26　felalēofan=dearly loved. fǣhðu=fǣhðo(=feud)의 대격. drēogan=suffer.

I draw these words from my deep sadness,

my sorrowful lot. I can say that,

since I grew up, I have not suffered

such hardships as now, old or new.

I am tortured by the anguish of exile.

First my lord forsook his family

for the tossing waves ; I fretted at dawn

as to where in the world my lord might be.

In my sorrow I set out then,
a friendless wanderer, to search for my man.
But that man's kinsmen laid secret plans
to part us, so that we should live
most wretchedly, far from each other
in this wide world ; I was seized with longings.

My lord asked me to live with him here ;
had few loved ones, loyal friends
in this country ; that is reason for grief.
Then I found my own husband was ill-starred,
sad at heart, pretending, plotting
murder behind a smiling face. How often
we swore that nothing but death should ever
divide us ; that is all changed now ;
our friendship is as if it had never been.
Early and late, I must undergo hardship
because of the feud of my own dearest loved one.

THE WIFE'S LAMENT (2)

Heht mec mon wunian   on wuda bearwe,

under āctrēo   on bām eorðscræfe.

Eald is þes eorðsele,   eal ic eom oflongad ;

30   sindon dena dimme,   dūna ūphēa,

bitre burgtūnas   brērum beweaxne,

wīc wynna lēas.   Ful oft mec hēr wrāþe begeat

fromsīþ frēan.   Frȳnd sind on eorþan,

lēofe lifgende,   leger weardiað,

35   þonne ic on ūhtan   āna gonge

under āctrēo   geond þās eorðscrafu.

Þær ic sittan mōt   sumorlangne dæg,

þær ic wēpan mæg   mīne wræcsīþas,

earfoþa fela.   Forþon ic æfre ne mæg

40   þære mōdceare   mīnre gerestan,

nē ealles þæs longaþes   þe mec on þissum līfe begeat.

Ā scyle geong monn   wesan geōmormōd,

heard heortan gebōht ;   swelce habban sceal

blíþe gebǣro,   ēac þon brēostceare,

45   sinsorgna gedreag.   Sȳ æt him sylfum gelong

eal his worulde wyn,   sȳ ful wīde fāh

feorres folclondes,   þæt mīn frēond siteþ

under stānhliþe   storme behrīmed,

wine wērigmōd,   wætre beflōwen

50   on drēorsele.   Drēogeþ se mīn wine

micle mōdceare ;   hē gemon tō oft

wynlicran wīc.   Wā bið þǣm þe sceal

of langoðe   lēofes ābīdan.

27 Heht=Commanded. 원형은 hātan. Heht meċ mon=I was commanded (by my husband).
mon=the woman's husband. wunian=to dwell. on wuda=of trees. bearwe=bearu(=grove)
의 단수 여격.

28 āctrēo=oaktree. eorðscræfe=earth-cave. cf. eorð(=earth)+scræf(=cave).

29 Eald=old. eorðsele=earth-dwelling. cf. eorð(=earth)+sele(=house). eal=all. eom=bēon(=to
be)의 1인칭 단수=am. eom oflongad=seized with longing. 원형은 oflongian(=to seize with
longing).

30 dena=dales. 원형은 dena. dimme=dark. dūna=hills. uphēa=high.

31 bitre=bitter, grim. 원형은 biter. burgtūnas=fortified enclosures. brērum=with briars. 원형
은 brēr. beweaxne=overgrown. 원형은 beweaxan.

32 wīċ=abode, habitation. wynna=pleasure, benefit. lēas=without. 속격을 요구한다. Ful oft
meċ hēr wrāðe beġeat=took hold of cruelly here=caused me pain. beġeat=beġietan(=to
lay hold of, assail)의 3인칭 단수 과거. 주어는 다음 줄의 fromsīb frēan.

33 fromsīb=departure. frēan=(of my) lord. 원형은 frēa. Frȳnd=friends.

34 lēofe=beloved. lifġende=living. 원형은 libban. leġer=beds. 모양은 원형과 같으나 여기서는
복수 대격. 현대영어의 lair가 그 잔재이다. weardiað=occupy. 원형은 weardiġan. leġer
weardiað=occupy their beds=are in bed together.

35 ūhtan=dawn. āna=alone. gonge=walk. 원형은 gongan.

36 ġeond=around.

37 mōt=must. 원형은 mōtan. sumorlangne dæġ=the summer-long day.

38 wēpan=weep, bewail. wræcsības=miseries.

39 earfoba=hardships. fela=many. Forbon=because. æfre ne=never.

40 mōdceare=heart-sorrow. ġerestan=find rest from. 속격을 요구하는 동사이다.

41 longabes=longing. be=that. 관계대명사.

42 Ā=always. scyle=sculan(=must)의 가정법 3인칭 단수. 가정법이므로 뜻이 약간 약해져
may have to 정도의 뜻. ġeong=young. wesan=be. ġēomormōd=sad-hearted, serious.

43 heard=hard. heortan=heart. ġebōht=ġebenċan. sceal=must. sculan의 3인칭 단수. sceal은
앞의 scyle과는 달리 직설법이므로 강한 must의 뜻. blibe=cheerful. ġebæro=behavior. ēac
bon=in addition to that, besides, moreover. brēostceare=heart-care. cf. brēost(=breast)+
cearu(=care).

45 sinsorgna=sinsorg(=constant sorrow)의 복수 속격. ġedreag=host. ġelong=belonging to.

45-6 Sȳ…sȳ=두 가지 해석이 가능하다. 하나는 이들 가정법 동사를 기원을 나타내는 것으로 간
주하여 Let all his joy in the world be dependent(ġelong) on himself, let him be…로 해석
하거나 아니면 이들 가정법 동사를 단순한 가정을 나타내는 것으로 간주하여 Whether all
his joy in the world be…(or) whether he be…의 두 가지 해석이 가능하다. Sȳ
(sīe)=bēon(=to be)의 가정법 단수 현재. ġelong=dependent on.

46 worulde=woruld(=world)의 단수 속격. wyn=pleasure, benefit. fāh=guilty.

47 feorres folclondes=in a far country. 이처럼 고대영어에서는 속격으로 장소를 나타내는
경우가 있다.

48 stānhliþe=stone slope. storme=by the storm. behrīmed=frost-coated. 원형은 behrīman.

49 wine=friend. wērigmōd=sad-spirited. wætre=wæter(=water)의 단수 여격=by water. beflōwen= beflōwan(=to surround by water, flow around)의 과거분사.

50 drēorsele=sad abode. Drēogeþ=(will) endure. 원형은 drēogan. se mīn wine=that friend of mine.

51 micle=great. ġemon=(will) remember, think about. 원형은 ġemunan.

52 wynlicran=more pleasant. 원형은 wynliċ. wīċ=abode. Wā=woe. sceal=shall. 원형은 scullan.

53 of langoðe=in longing. abīdan=await.

Men forced me to live in a forest grove,

under an oak tree in the earth-cave.

This cavern is age-old ; I am choked with longings.

Gloomy are the valleys, too high the hills,

harsh strongholds overgrown with briars :

a joyless abode. The departure of my lord so often

cruelly seizes me. There are lovers on earth,

lovers alive who lie in bed,

when I pass through this earth-cave alone

and out under the oak tree at dawn ;

there I must sit through the long summer's day

and there I mourn my miseries,

my many hardships ; for I am never able

to quiet the cares of my sorrowful mind,

all the longings that are my life's lot.

Young men must always be serious in mind

and stout-hearted ; they must hide

their heartaches, that host of constant sorrows,

behind a smiling face.

Whether he is master

of his own fate or is exiled in a far-off land —

sitting under rocky storm-cliffs, chilled
with hoar-frost, weary in mind,
surrounded by the sea in some sad place —
my husband is caught in the clutches of anguish ;
over and again he recalls a happier home.
Grief goes side by side with those
who suffer longing for a loved one.

(tr. Crossley-Holland)

THE WANDERER (1)

1   Oft him ānhaga   āre gebīdeð,
       metudes miltse,   bēah be hē mōdcearig
       geond lagulāde   longe sceolde
       hrēran mid hondum   hrīmcealde s̄æ,
5   wadan wræclāstas.   Wyrd bið ful ār̄æd.

       Swā cwæb eardstapa,   earfeba gemyndig,
       wrābra wælsleahta,   winem̄æga hryre.
       Oft ic sceolde āna   ūhtna gehwylce
       mīne ceare cwīðan.   Nis nū cwicra nān
10   be ic him mōdsefan   mīnne durre
       sweotule āsecgan.   Ic tō sōbe wāt
       bæt bib in eorle   indryhten bēaw
       bæt hē his ferðlocan   fæste binde,
       healde his hordcofan,   hycge swā hē wille.
15   Ne mæg wērig mōd   wyrde wiðstondan,
       ne se hrēo hyge   helpe gefremman.
       Forðon dōmgeorne   drēorigne oft
       in hyra brēostcofan   bindað fæste.
       Swā ic mōdsefan   mīnne sceolde
20   of earmcearig   ēðle bid̄æled
       frēom̄ægum feor,   feterum s̄ælan,
       sibban gēara iū   goldwine mīne
       hrūsan heolstre biwrāh   ond ic hēan bonan
       wōd wintercearig   ofer wabema gebind,
25   sōhte seledrēorig   sinces bryttan
       hw̄ær ic feor obbe nēah   findan meahte
       bone be in meoduhealle   mīne wisse
       obbe mec frēondlēasne   frēfran wolde,

weman mid wynnum.　　Wāt sē be cunnað

30　hū slīben bið　　sorg tō gefēran

bām be him lȳt hafað　　lēofra geholena.

Warað hine wræclāst,　　nales wunden gold,

ferðloca frēorig,　　nalæs foldan blǣd.

Gemon hē selesecgas　　ond sincþege.

35　hū hine on geoguðe　　his goldwine

wende tō wiste.　　Wyn eal gedrēas.

(한 때 영주(lord) 아래서 영화를 누리던 신하가 영주가 죽은 뒤에 방랑자가 된 자기의 슬픔을 노래한 시이다.)

1　Oft=often. 시에서는 많은 경우에 always의 뜻으로 쓰인다. him=for himself. ānhaga=solitary one. āre=ār(=grace, favor, pity)의 단수 대격. ġebīdeð=ġebīdan(=to wait for, endure, experience, obtain)의 과거.

2　metudes=metod(=creator, ordainer, God)의 단수 속격. miltse=mercy, favor. þēah þe=though. mōdceariġ=sad at heart, anxious of mind.

3　ġeond=across. lagulāde=sea-way. longe=far. sceolde=must.

4　hrēran mid hondum=stir with hands. hrēran=move, stir. hrīmċealde=ice-cold. hrīm (=frost)+ċeald(=cold). sǣ=sea.

5　wadan=travel. wræclāstas=paths of exile. cf. wræc(=misery, persecution)+lāst(=track, step). Wyrd=fate. ful=fully. ārǣd=determined. 원형은 ārǣdan.

6　Swā cwæþ=so spoke. eardstapa=wanderer. earfeþa=earfoþe(=hardship, suffering, misery)의 복수 속격. ġemyndiġ=recalling, mindful of. 속격형과 함께 쓰인다.

7　wrāþra=of enemies. wælsleahta=slaughters. winemǣga=dear kinsmen. hryre=fall, death.

8　seeolde=have had to. āna=alone. ūhtna ġehwylċe=at each dawn. ūhte=period before dawn, early morning. ġehwylċ=each.

9　ceare=sorrow. cwīðan=lament. Nis=nue=is=(there) is not. cwicra nān=none of living-ones=not one living. cwicra=cwic(=living)의 복수 속격.

10　be iċ him=who…to him=to whom. mōdsefan=heart. durre=dare. 원형은 durran.

11　sweotule=openly, clearly, plainly. āsecgan=express. tō sōþe=as a truth, in truth, truly. tō=as. sōþe=truth. wāt=know. 원형은 wītan.

12　biþ=(it) is. eorle=nobleman. indryhten=excellent. þēaw=custom, practice, virtue.

13　ferðlocan=heart. fæste=fast, firmly. binde=bindan(=to bind)의 가정법 현재 단수.

14　healde=healdan(=to hold, keep)의 가정법 현재 단수. hordcofan=trasure-chamber=treasury of his thoughts. cf. hord(=hoard, treasure)+cofa(=closet, chamber). hycge swā hē

15 wēriġ=weary. mōd=heart. wyrde=fate. wiðstondan=resist. 여격과 함께 쓰인다.

15-16 Ne…ne=neither…nor.

16 hrēo=troubled. hyġe=mind, spirit. helpe=help. ġefremman=provide.

17 Forðon=therefore. dōmġeorne=복수 명사로 쓰인 형용사=those eager for glory. drēoriġne= 명사로 쓰인 형용사=a sorrowful thing, sorrowful mind.

18 brēostcofan=breast-chamber=heart.

19 mōdsefan mīnne=my heart. sceolde…sǣlan(=must bind)의 목적어. sceolde=(have) had to.

20 earmceariġ=care-worn, wretchedly anxious. ēðle=ēðel(=homeland)의 단수 여격. bidǣ led=deprived of. 여격과 함께 쓰인다. 원형은 bidǣlan.

21 frēomǣġum=frēomǣġ(=noble kinsman)의 복수 여격=from noble kinsmen. feor=far. feterum=with fetters. sǣlan=bind.

22 sibban gēara iū=since years ago. sibban=since. gēara=once. iū=long ago. goldwine= gold-friend=lord.

23 hrūsan heolstre biwrāh=(since) covered…with the darkness of the earth. hrūsan=earth. heolstre=heolstor(=darkness)의 단수 여격. biwrāh=hid, covered. 원형은 bewrēon. hēan= dejected, despised. bonan=from there.

24 wōd=went. 원형은 wadan. winterċeariġ=winer-sad. wabema=of waves. 원형은 wabum. ġebind=mingling.

25 sōhte=sought. 원형은 sēċan. seledrēoriġ=hall-sad=sad for the lack of a hall. sinces=of treasure. bryttan=giver.

26 obbe=or. meahte=might.

27 bone=him. meoduhealle=mead-hall. mīne wisse=might know of my own (i.e., my origins or people). wisse=knew. 원형은 witan.

28 meċ=me. frēondlēasne=friendless. frēfran=comfort. wolde=willan(=to wish)의 과거.

29 wēman=entice (me). wynnum=wynn(=pleasure, joy, delight)의 목수 여격. Wāt=Know. sē=he. be cunnað=experiences (it).

30 slīben=cruel. sorg=grief. tō=as. ġefēran=companion.

31 bām=for him. him=himself. lyt=little. lēofra=dear. ġeholena=comrades.

32 Warað hine wræclāst=the path of an exile claims him. Warað=Preoccupies. 원형은 warian. nales=not. wunden=twisted, coiled.

33 ferðloca=breast, heart. frēoriġ=frozen. nalæs=not, in no way. foldan=folda(=earth)의 단수 속격. blǣd=splendor, blessings, riches.

34 Ġemon=remembers. 원형은 ġemunan. selesecgas=hall-men. sincbeġe=treasure-receiving.

35 hine=다음 줄 wenede의 목적어. ġeoguðe=(his) youth. gold-wine=lord.

36 wende=entertained. 원형은 wenian. wiste=feast. Wyn=delight, joy. ġedrēas=perished. 원형은 ġedrēosan.

Often the wanderer pleads for pity
and mercy from the Lord ; but for a long time,
sad in mind, he must dip his oars
into icy waters, the lanes of the sea ;
he must follow the paths of exile : fate is inflexible.
　　Mindful of hardships, grievous slaughter,
the ruin of kinsmen, the wanderer said :
　　'Time and again at the day's dawning
I must mourn all my afflictions alone.
There is no one still living to whom I dare open
the doors of my heart. I have no doubt
that it is a noble habit for a man
to bind fast all his heart's feelings,
guard his thoughts, whatever he is thinking.
The weary in spirit cannot withstand fate,
and nothing comes of venting spleen :
wherefore those eager for glory often
hold some ache imprisoned in their hearts.
Thus I had to bind my feelings in fetters,
often sad at heart, cut off from my country,
far from my kinsmen, after, long ago,
dark clods of earth covered my gold-friend ;
I felt that place in wretchedness,
ploughed the icy waves with winter in my heart ;
in sadness I sought far and wide
for a treasure-giver, for a man
who would welcome me into his mead-hall,
give me good cheer (for I boasted no friends),
entertain me with delights. He who has experienced it
knows how cruel a comrade sorrow can be
to any man who has few loyal friends :

for him are the ways of exile, in no wise twisted gold ;
for him is a frozen body, in no wise the fruits of the earth.
He remembers hall-retainers and treasure
and how, in his youth, his gold-friend
entertained him. Those joys have all vanished.

THE WANDERER (2)

Forþon wāt sē þe sceal his winedryhtnes
lēofes lārcwidum longe forþolian,
ðonne sorg ond slǣp somod ætgædre
earmne ānhogan oft gebindað.

40

7inceð him on mōde þæt hē his mondryhten
clyppe ond cysse ond on cnēo lecge
honda ond hēafod, swā hē hwīlum ǣr
in gēardagum giefstōlas brēac.

45

Ðonne onwæcneð eft winelēas guma,
gesihð him biforan fealwe wēgas,
baþian brimfuglas, brǣdan febra,
hrēosan hrīm ond snāw, hagle gemenged.
7onne bēoð þy hefigran heortan benne,

50

sāre æfter swǣsne. Sorg bið genīwad.
7onne māga gemynd mōd geondhweorfeð.
Grēteð glīwstafum georne geondscēawað
secga geseldan. Swimmað oft on weg.
Flēotendra ferð nō þǣr fela bringeð

55

cūðra cwidegiedda. Cearo bið genīwad
þām þe sendan sceal swīþe geneahhe
ofer waþema gebind wērigne sefan.
Forþon ic geþencan ne mæg geond þās woruld
for hwan mōdsefa mīn ne gesweorce

60

þonne ic eorla līf eal geondþence,
hū hī fǣrlīce flet ofgēafon,
mōdge maguþegnas. Swā þes middangeard
earla dōgra gehwām drēoseð ond fealleþ.
Forþon ne mæg wearþan wīs wer ǣr hē āge

65   wintra d̅æl in woruldrīce.   Wita sceal gebyldig,

      ne sceal nō tō hātheort   ne tō hrædwyrde,

      ne tō wāc wiga   ne tō wanh̅ydig,

      ne tō forht ne tō fægen   ne tō feohgīfre

      ne n̅æfre gielpes tō georn   ̅ær hē geare cunne.

70   Beorn sceal gebīdan,   bonne hē bēot spriceð,

      obbæt collenferð   cunne gearwe

      hwider hrebra gehygd   hweorfan wille.

---

37   Forbon wāt…brēac까지의 긴 문장은 전체가 wāt(=knows)의 목적어로서, He who must
      long forgo his beloved lord's counsels knows (that) when sorrow and sleep both together
      constrain the wretched solitary, it seems to him…의 뜻이 된다. wāt=knows, understands.
      원형은 witan. 뒤에 'these things'라는 의미상의 목적어는 생략되었다. sceal=must. sē
      be=he who. winedryhtnes=friendly lord's.

38   lēofes=dear. lārcwidum=counsel, precepts. longe(lange)=for a long time. forbolian=do
      without. 여격과 함께 쓰인다.

39   ðonne=when. sorg=sorrow. sl̅æp=sleep. somod=at the same time. ætgædre=together.

40   earmne=wretched. ānhogan=ānhoga(=solitary one)의 단수 대격. ġebindað=hold fast. 원형
      은 ġebindan.

41   7inceð=it seems. 원형은 bynċan. mondryhten=lord, master.

42   clyppe=embraces. 원형은 clyppan. cysse=kisses. 원형은 cyssan. cnēo=(his) knees. lecge=
      lays. 원형은 lecgan. 여기 나온 일련의 동작들은 군신간의 유대를 확인하기 위한 의식을
      나타낸다.

43   honda ond hēafod=hand and head.

43-4 swā hē hwīlum ̅ær in ġēardagum ġiefstōlas brēac=just as from time to time he used
      to make use of the throne in days of old. swā=just as. hwīlum=at times. ̅ær=before.

44   ġēardagum=days of old. giefstōlas=ġiefstōl(=gift-throne)의 단수 속격. brēac=brūcan(=to
      make use of, enjoy benefit from)의 과거.

45   Ðonne=then. onwæcneð=awakes. 원형은 onwæcnan. eft=again. winelēas=friendless.
      guma=man.

46   ġesihð=sees. 원형은 ġesēon. biforan=before. 여격과 함께 쓰인다. fealwe=fealu(=gray)의
      복수 대격. 현대영어의 fallow. wēgas=waves.

47   babian brimfuglas=(sees) seabirds bathing. babian=bathe. brimfuglas=seabirds. br̅ædan=
      spread(ing). febra=wings. feber(=feather)의 단수 대격.

48   hrēosan=fall(ing). hrīm=frost. haġle=hæġl(=hail)의 단수 여격. ġemenged=mingled. 원형은
      ġemengan.

49   7onne=then. bēoð=are. b̅y=the. sē(=that)의 조격. hefiġran=hefiġ(=heavy, grievous)의 비

교급. heortan=heart's. benne=wounds.

50 sāre æfter swǣsne=painful (i.e., the wounds) in pursuit of (in longing for) the beloved (one). sāre=painful, sore. swǣsne=swǣs(=beloved, dear)의 단수 대격. ġenīwad=renewed. 원형은 ġenīwian.

51 māga=mǣġ(=kinsman)의 복수 속격. ġemynd=memory. ġeondhweorfeð=goes through. 원형은 ġeondhweorfan. cf. ġeond(=through)+hweorfan(=to move, come).

52 Grēteð=greets. glīwstafum=joyfully. georne=eagerly. ġeondscēawað=ġeondscēawian(= to regard, survey)의 3인칭 단수 현재형.

53 secga=of men. ġeseldan=companions. Swimmað oft on weġ=Often (Always) they drift away.

54-5 Flēotendra ferð nō bǣr fela bringeð cūðra cwidegiedda=The spirit of the floating ones does not bring there many familiar utterances. Flēotendra=of the floating ones=of the swimmers=of the speechless birds. flēotendra는 flēotan(=to float)의 복수 속격의 현재분사형으로서 여기서는 명사 구실을 한다. ferð=heart, spirit. fela=many.

55 cūðra=cūð(=familiar)의 복수 속격. cwideġiedda=spoken utterance, speech. Cearo=care.

56 bām=in him. swīþe=very. ġeneahhe=often.

57 wabema=wabum(=wave)의 복수 속격. ġebind=binding, mingling. wēriġne=wēriġ(=weary)의 단수 대격. sefan=spirit.

58 Forþon=therefore. ġebenċan=think. ne mæġ=cannot. 원형은 magan. ġeond=in. woruld= world.

59 for hwan=for what=why. mōdsefa=mind, spirit. ġesweorce=grow dark. 원형은 ġesweorcan.

60 eorla=warrior. līf=life. ġeondbenċe=contemplate.

61 hī=they. fǣrlīċe=quickly, suddenly. flet ofġēafon=give up the floor (of the mead-hall)= died. flet=floor. ofġeafon의 원형은 ofġiefan(=abandon).

62 mōdġe=mōdiġ(=brave)의 복수. magubeġnas=young retainers. middanġeard=world.

63 earla dōgra ġehwām=on each of all days=each and every day. dōgra=dōgor(=day)의 복수 속격. ġehwām=each, every. drēoseð=declines. 원형은 drēosan. fealleþ=falls. 원형은 feallan.

64 wearþan=become. wīs=wise. wer=a man. āge=has. 원형은 āgan.

65 wintra dǣl in woruldrīce=a deal of winters in the kingdom of the world=in this world. Wita=a wise man. sceal=should (be). ġebyldiġ=patient.

66 nō tō=not too⋯. hātheort=fiery. ne=nor. hrædwyrde=hasty of speech.

67 wāc=weak. wiġa=warrior. wanhȳdiġ=reckless, foolhardy, rash.

68 forht=fearful. fæġen=joyful, glad. feohġīfre=wealth-greedy. cf. feoh(=money)+ġīfre(=greedy).

69 nǣfre=never. ġielpes(ġylpes)=boasting. ġeorn=eager for. 속격과 함께 쓰인다. ǣr hē ġeare cunne=before he clearly knows=before he is fully aware of what his boast may entail. ġeare(ġearwe)=really, well.

70 Beorn=warrior. ġebīdan=wait. bēot=boast. spriceð=utters. 원형은 sprecan.

71 obbæt=until. collenferð=stout-hearted, bold-spirited. ġearwe=fully.

72 hwider=where. hrebra=hreber(=breast, heart)의 복수 속격. ġehyġd=thought, intention. hweorfan=to turn. wille=will.

A man who lacks advice for a long while
from his loved lord understands this,
that when sorrow and sleep together
hold the wretched wanderer in their grip,
it seems that he clasps and kisses
his lord, and lays hands and head
upon his lord's knee as he had sometimes done
when he enjoyed the gift-throne in earlier days.
Then the friendless man wakes again
and sees the dark waves surging around him,
the sea-birds bathing, spreading their feathers,
frost and snow falling mingled with hail.

Then his wounds lie more heavy in his heart,
aching for his lord. His sorrow is renewed ;
the memory of kinsmen sweeps through his mind ;
joyfully he welcomes them, eagerly scans
his comrade warriors. Then they swim away again.
Their drifting spirits do not bring many old songs
to his lips. Sorrow upon sorrow attend
the man who must send time and again
his weary heart over the frozen waves.

And thus I cannot think why in the world
my mind does not darken when I brood on the fate
of brave warriors, how they have suddenly
had to leave the mead-hall, the bold followers.
So this world dwindles day by day,
and passes away ; for a man will not be wise
before he has weathered his share of winters

in the world. A wise man must be patient,
neither too passionate nor too hasty of speech,
neither too irresolute nor too rash in battle ;
not too anxious, too content, nor too grasping,
and never too eager to boast before he knows himself.
When he boasts a man must bide his time
until he has no doubt in his brave heart
that he has fully made up his mind.

THE WANDERER (3)

Ongietan sceal glēaw hæle   hū gǣstlic bið
bonne ealre bisse worulde wela   wēste stondeð,
swā nū missenlīce   geond bisne middangeard
winde biwāune   weallas stondab
hrīme bihrorene.   Hrȳðge bā ederas,
wōriað bā wīnsalo,   waldend licgað
drēame bidrorene.   Dugub eal gecrong
wlonc bī wealle ;   sume wīg fornōm.
ferede in forðwege,   sumne fugel obbǣr
ofer hēanne holm,   sumne se hāra wulf
dēaðe gedǣlde,   sumne drēorighlēor
in eorðscræfe   eorl gehȳdde.
Ȳbde swā bisne eardgeard   ælda scyppend
obbæt burgwara   breahtma lēase
eald enta geweorc   īdlu stōdon.
    Sē bonne bisne wealsteal   wīse gebōhte
ond bis deorce līf   dēope geondbenceð,
frōd in ferðe,   feor oft gemon
wælsleahta worn   ond bās word ācwið :
'Hwǣr cwōm mearg? Hwǣr cwōm mago? Hwǣr cwōm mābbumgyfa?
Hwǣr cwōm symbla gesetu?   Hwǣr sindon seledrēamas?
Ēalā beorht būne!   Ēalā byrnwiga!
Ēalā bēodnes brym!   Hū sēo brāg gewāt,
genāp under nihthelm   swā hēo nō wǣre.
Stondeð nū on lāste   lēofre dugube
weal wundrum hēah,   wyrmlicum fāh.
Eorlas fornōman   asca brȳbe,
wǣpen wælgīfru,   wyrd sēo mǣre,

ond þās stānhleoþu   stormas cnyssað,

hrīð hrēosende   hrūsan bindeð,

wintres wōma.   7onne won cymeð,

nīpeð nihtscūa,   norþan onsendeð

105   hrēo hæglfare   hæleþum on andan.

Eall is earforðlic   eorþan rīce ;

onwendeð wyrda gesceaft   weoruld under heofonum.

Hēr bið feoh l͞æne,   hēr bið frēond l͞æne,

hēr bið mon l͞æne,   hēr bið m͞æg l͞æne,

110   eal þis eorþan gesteal   īdel weorþeð!

Swā cwæð snottor on mōde,   gesæt him sundor æt rūne.

Til biþ sē þe his trēowe geheldeþ :   ne sceal n͞æfre his torn tō

    rycene

beorn of his brēostum ācy͞þan   nemþe hē ͞ær bā bōte cunne,

eorl mid elne gefremman.   Wel bið þām þe him āre sēceð,

115   frōfre tō fæder on heofonum   þ͞ær ūs eal sēo fæstnung stondeð.

---

73   Onġietan=Realize. glēaw=prudent. hæle=man. g͞æstliċ=awful, ghostly. bið=it will be.

74   wela=riches. wēste=desolate.

75   missenlīċe=in various places. ġeond=throughout. middanġeard=middle-earth=earth.

76   winde biwāune=blown by wind. winde는 wind(=wind)의 여격으로서 수동태 문장의 행위자를 나타낸다. biwāune=biwāwan(=to blow upon)의 과거분사. weallas=wall. 76행은 산문에서라면 weallas stondaþ winde biwāune(=the wall stand wind-blown)가 될 것이다.

77   hrīme bihrorene=covered by frost. hrīm=frost. bihrorene=covered. bihrēosan(=to cover)의 과거분사. Hrȳðġe=Storm-beaten. 원형은 hrȳþiġ. ederas=buildings. 원형은 edor.

78   wōriað=crumble. 원형은 wōrian. wīnsalo=wine-halls. 원형은 wīnsæl. waldend=rulers. licgað=lie (dead).

79   drēame=joy. bidrorene=deprived. 여격과 함께 쓰인다. 원형은 bidrēosan. Duguþ=Noble company. ġecrong=fell. 원형은 ġecringan.

80   wlonc=proud. bī=near. wealle=wall. sume=some. wīġ=war. fornōm=destroyed, took away. 원형은 forniman.

81   ferede=carried. 원형은 ferian. in forðweġe=on the onward path=to death and whatever follows. fugel=bird. obþær=bore away. 원형은 obþeran.

82   hēanne=hēah(=high)의 단수 대격. holm=ocean. hāra=grey. wulf=wolf.

83   dēaðe ged͞ælde=received a share of in death. drēoriġhlēor=sad-faced. 다음 줄의 eorl을

수식한다.

84 eorðscræfe=earth-grave. ġehȳdde=buried. 원형은 ġehȳdan.

85 Ȳbde=Laid waste. 원형은 ȳban. eardġeard=habitation, world. ælda=men's. scyppend= creator. scyppan(scieppan)=to shape.

86 obbæt=till. burgwara=of citizens. breahtma=of the revelries. lēase=deprived.

87 eald=old, ancient. enta=giants 복수 속격. ġeweorc=constructions. enta ġeweorc=the works of giants. 당시 큰 건물을 흔히 거인의 작품이라고 불렀다. īdlu=empty. 원형은 īdel.

88 Sē=He who. wealsteal=wall-place. ġebohte=(has) considered. 원형은 ġebenċan.

89 deorce=gloomy, dark. dēope=deeply. wīse=wisely. ġeondbenċeð=contemplates. 원형은 ġeondbenċean.

90 frōd=wise. ferðe=heart. feor=far back. ġemon=recalls. 원형은 ġemunan.

91 wælsleahta=wælsleaht(=slaughter)의 복수 속격. worn=a multitude. 복수 속격과 함께 쓰인다. ācwið=utters. 원형은 ācweðan.

92 Hwǣr cwōm mearg=Where did the horse go? cwōm=went. 원형은 cuman. mearg= mearh(=horse)의 단수 주격. mago=kinsman. māðbumġyfa=treasure-giver. cf. māðm= treasure.

93 cwōm=cuman(=to come, go)의 3인칭 단수 과거로서 주어는 ġesetu(=places). 이처럼 단수형의 동사가 복수형의 주어를 받는 것은 고대영어에서는 드물지 않은 현상이다. symbla= of banquets. ġesetu=places. seledrēamas=hall-pleasures.

94 Ēalā beorht būne=Alas, the bright goblet! beorht=bright. būne=goblet. byrnwiġa=mailed warrior.

95 bēodnes=prince's. brym=majesty. brāg=time period. ġewāt=went, set out. 원형은 ġewītan.

96 ġenāp=grew dark. 원형은 ġenīpan. nihthelm=cover of night. swā hēo nō wǣre=as though it had never been. 대과거 시제(pluperfect tense)가 없던 고대영어에서는 이런 경우를 대과거로 번역하는 것이 좋다.

97 on lāste lēofre dugube=in the track of the dear company=after their departure(=death). lāste=track. dugube=noble band (of warriors).

98 weal=wall. wundrum=wondrously. wyrmlicum=with snake patterns. fāh=decorated.

99 Eorlas=The men. fornōman=took off. 원형은 forniman. asca=of ash(-spears). brȳbe=hosts.

100 wǣpen=weapons. wælgīfru=slaughter-greedy. wyrd=fate, destiny. mǣre=splendid.

101 stānhleobu=rocky slopes. 원형은 stānhlib. cnyssað=batter, press.

102 hrīð=snowstorm. hrēosende=falling. 원형은 hrēosan. hrūsan=earth.

103 wintres wōma=howling of winter. 7onne=Then. 그러나 앞의 마침표를 콤마로 바꾸면 접속사 when으로 해석할 수도 있다. won(wann)=dark. 다음 줄의 nihtscūa를 수식. 그렇다면 nihtscūma는 cymeð와 nīþeð의 주어가 되는데, 이런 어색함 때문에 편집자에 따라서는 won을 주어로 보아 won cymeð(=darkness comes)와 nihtscūa nīþeð(=night deepens)의 두 문장으로 나눌 것을 제안하고 있다. cymeð=comes. 원형은 cuman.

104 nīþeð=darkens. nihtscūa=night=shadow. norþan=from north. onsendeð=sends. 주어는 nihtscūa.

105 hrēo=fierce. hæġlfare=hailstorm. 원형은 hæġlfaru. hælebum=to men. on=as. andan=terror.

106 Eall is earfoðlic eorþan rīce=Eall(=All)이 주어인 경우 eorþan rīce(the kingdom of earth) 는 부사구가 되어 전체의 뜻은 All in the kingdom of earth…가 될 것이나 만약에 eorþan rīce(the kingdom of earth)가 주어인 경우에는 Eall(=entirely)이 부사가 되어 전체의 뜻은 The whole kingdom…이 될 것이다. earfoðliċ=full of hardship.

107 onwendeð=changes. wyrda ġesceaft=the disposition of the fates=the ordained course of events. wyrda=wyrd(=happening, event)의 복수 속격. ġesceaft=creation, created thing.

108 feoh=wealth. lǣne=temporary. cf. lǣnan=to lend.

109 mǣġ=kinsman.

110 ġesteal=foundation. īdel=empty. weorþeð=will become. 원형은 weorþan.

111 snottor=wise man. ġesæt=sat. 원형은 ġesittan. him=himself. 번역하지 않아도 무방하다. sundor=apart. æt rūne=rūne는 consultation이나 (secret) counsel의 뜻인데, 여기서는 스스로에게 자문을 구하고 있으므로 in contemplation나 in thought 정도로 번역하는 것이 좋다.

112 Til=Worthy. trēowe=faith. ġeheldeþ=keeps. 원형은 ġehealdan. ne sceal=주어는 다음 줄의 beorn. torn=anger. rycene(recene)=hastily.

112-3 ne sceal nǣfre his torn tō rycene beorn of his brēostum ācȳþan=a man must never too hastily (rycene) reveal his anger from his breast.

113 beorn=man. brēostum=breast. ācȳþan=make know, reveal. nembe=unless. ǣr=beforehand. bōte=the remedy.

114 eorl=nobleman. elne=courage. ġefremman=to effect. Wel bið þām þe him=It will be well for the one (þām) who for himself…. āre=mercy. sēċeð=seeks. 원형은 sēċan.

115 frōfre=comfort. 원형은 frōfor. ūs=for us. fæstnung=permanence.

A wise man must fathom how eerie it will be

when all the riches of the world stand waste,

as now in diverse places in this middle-earth

walls stand, tugged at by winds

and hung with hoar-frost, buildings in decay.

The wine-halls crumble, lords lie dead,

deprived of joy, all the proud followers

have fallen by the wall : battle carried off some,

led them on journeys ; the bird carried one

over the welling waters ; one the grey wolf

devoured ; a warrior with downcast face

hid one in an earth-cave.

Thus the Maker of Men laid this world waste

until the ancient works of the giants stood idle,

hushed without the hubbub of inhabitants.

    Then he who has brooded over these noble ruins,

and who deeply ponders this dark life,

wise in his mind, often remembers

the many slaughters of the past and speaks these words :

Where has the horse gone? Where the man? Where the giver of gold?

Where is the feasting-place? And where the pleasures of the hall?

I mourn the gleaming cup, the warrior in his corselet,

the glory of the prince. How that time has passed away,

darkened under the shadow of night as if it had never been.

Where the loved warriors were, there now stands a wall

of wondrous height, carved with serpent forms.

The savage ash-spears, avid for slaughter,

have claimed all the warriors—a glorious fate!

Storms crash against these rocky slopes,

sleet and snow fall and fetter the world,

winter howls, then darkness draws on,

the night-shadow casts gloom and brings

fierce hailstorms from the north to frighten men.

Nothing is ever easy in the kingdom of earth,

the world beneath the heavens is in the hands of fate.

Here possessions are fleeting, here friends are fleeting,

here man is fleeting, here kinsman is fleeting,

the whole world becomes a wilderness.'

So spoke the wise man in his heart as he sat apart in thought.

Brave is the man who holds to his beliefs ; nor shall he ever

show the sorrow in his heart before he knows how he

can hope to heal it. It is best for a man to seek

mercy and comfort from the father in heaven where security stands
for us all.

(tr. Crossley-Holland)

XII. EPIC : BEOWULF

MS. COTT VITELLIUS A. XV
Fol. 160ᵃ (reduced). (ll. 1352-77.)

MS. COTT VITELLIUS A. XV
Fol. 160ᵃ (reduced). (ll. 2428-50.)

(F. Klaeber, 1950. *Beowulf and The fight at Finnsburg*, Heath & Co.)

(The Geography of *Beowulf*)
(M. Alexander, ed. 1995. *Beowulf*, Penguin Classics, p. ix.)

GENEALOGIES

DANISH ROYAL FAMILY

Scyld Scefing
|
Beowulf (the Dane)
|
Healfdene

Heorogar   Hrothgar   Halga   daughter
           (m. Wealtheow)   (m. Onela,
                                            the Swede)

Heoroweard   Hrethric   Hrothmund   Freawaru   Hrothulf
                                          (m. Ingeld)
                                     the Heathobard

GEAT ROYAL FAMILY

Hrethel

Herebeald   Hæthcyn   Hygelac   daughter
                           (m. Hygd)   (m. Ecgtheow,
                                       the Wægmunding)

daughter   Heardred   Beowulf
(m. Eofor)

SWEDISH ROYAL FAMILY (SCYLFINGS)

Ongentheow

Ohthere   Onela
             (m. Healfdene's daughter)

Eanmund   Eadgils

m.=married to.

(M. Alexander, ed. 1995. *Beowulf*, Penguin Classics, 230.)

SCYLD SCEFING AND HIS LINEARITY (1)

1   Hwæt wē Gār-Dena   in geārdagum,
         bēodcyninga   brym gefrūnon,
         hū ða æbelingas   ellen fremedon!
         Oft Scyld Scēfing   sceabena brēatum,

5   monegum mǣgbum   meodosetla oftēah ;
         egsode eorlas,   syððan ǣrest wearð
         fēasceaft funden ;   hē bæs frōfre gebād :
         wēox under wolcnum,   weorðmyndum bāh,
         oð bæt him ǣghwylc   ymbsittendra

10   ofer hronrāde   hȳran scolde,
         gomban gyldan :   bæt wæs gōd cyning!
         Ðǣm eafera wæs   æfter cenned
         geong in geardum,   bone God sende
         folce tō frōfre ;   fyrenðearfe ongeat,

15   bæt hīe ǣr drugon   aldorlēase
         lange hwīle ;   him bæs Līffrēa,
         wuldres Wealdend,   woroldāre forgeaf ;
         Bēowulf wæs brēme   — blǣd wīde sprang —
         Scyldes eafera,   Scedelandum in.

20   Swā sceal geong guma   gōde gewyrcean,
         fromum feohgiftum   on fæder bearme,
         bæt hine on ylde   eft gewunigen
         wilgesības,   bonne wīg cume,
         lēode gelǣsten ;   lofdǣdum sceal

25   in mǣgba gehwǣre   man gebēon.

(*Beowulf*는 고대영어로 된 최초의 서사시(epic)이며, 고대영어의 가장 대표적인 작품이다. 그러나 이야기의 배경은 덴마크와 남부 스웨덴(Geats)이며, 등장인물도 영국인이 아닌 스칸디나비아 인들이다. 이야기는 4, 5세기에 시작된 게르만 민족의 대이동 이전에 이미 널

리 펴져 있던 것이므로 영국인들도 영국 땅에 이주해오기 이전에 이미 그 내용을 알고 있었을 것이다. 여러 가지 정황으로 보아 시는 8세기 중엽에 쓰여졌을 것으로 짐작되며, 현존하는 원고는 1,000~1,010년 사이에 쓰여진 것으로 알려져 있다. 1731년의 런던 화재 때 원고의 일부가 그슬렸다. 원고는 분명히 두 사람의 필생(scribe)에 의해 필사되었는데, 첫 부분(1~1939행)을 베낀 사람이 뒷부분을 베낀 사람보다 훨씬 당시의 철자에 충실하고 있다.

이야기의 내용은 Hrothgar 왕 치하의 덴마크의 백성들을 잡아먹는 괴물 Grendel과 그의 어머니를 퇴치하기 위해 Geats에서 달려온 Beowulf가 이들 괴물을 퇴치하는 이야기이다. 뒤에 Beowulf는 자기 고향으로 돌아가 왕이 된다. 비록 이교도들의 이야기를 다루고 있으나 작자는 분명히 기독교를 알고 있으며, 어떤 이는 Beowulf를 예수로 빗댄 우화로 읽을 것을 제안하고 있으나 이것은 지나친 시도로 여겨진다.)

1 Hwæt=본래의 뜻은 what이지만 여기서처럼 시행의 첫머리에서 청중의 주의를 끌기 위해 사용되기도 한다. Listen! 정도의 뜻이다. Gār-Dena=Spear-Danes. cf. gār=spear. ġēardagum=days of yore. 원형은 ġēardagas.

1-2 wē…ġefrūnon=we have heard. 원형은 ġefriġnan.

2 bēodcyninga=king of a people. þrym=power.

3 hū ða æbelingas ellen fremedon=how those princes accomplished glorious deeds. hū=how. æbelingas=prince, hero. ellen=(deeds of) valor. fremedon=accomplished. 원형은 fremian.

4 Oft=Often. Scyld Scēfing=덴마크의 Scylding 왕조의 창시자이다. sceabena=enemy. 원형은 sceaba. brēatum=troop.

5 monegum=many. 원형은 monig. mæġbum=mæġb(=nation)의 복수 여격. meodosetla oftēah=(he) deprived them of mead-benches. meodosetla=mead-bench. oftēah=took away. 원형은 oftēon.

6 eġsode=terrified. 원형은 eġesian. eorlas=warriors. syððan=after. ǣrest=first.

6-7 wearð funden=was found. wearð=became. 원형은 weorban. funden=found. 원형은 findan.

7 fēasceaft=destitute. þæs=for that(=his destitute condition). frōfre=consolation. gebād=experience. 원형은 ġebīdan.

8 wēox=grew up. 여기서는 prospered 정도의 뜻으로서 같은 줄에 나오는 bāh와 동의어. 원형은 weaxan. wolcnum=wolcen(=cloud)의 복수 여격. weorðmyndum=honour. bāh=prospered. 원형은 bēon.

9 oð þæt=until. ǣġhwylċ=each. ymbsittendra=surrounding people.

10 hronrāde=whale-road. hron(=whale)+rāde(=ride). ocean에 대한 전형적인 대칭법(kenning)이다. hȳran=obey. scolde=had to. 원형은 sculan.

11 gomban=tribute. gyldan=pay. gōd=good. cyning=king. gōd cyning=Scyld는 '좋은 임금' 정도가 아니었다. 시에서 흔히 나타나는 완곡표현(litotes)의 한 예이다.

12 Ðǣm=To him. eafera=child. æfter=afterward. cenned=brought forth, begot. 원형은 cennan.

13 ġeong=young. ġeardum=ġeard(=court)의 복수 여격. þone=whom. sende=send. 원형은 sendan.

14 folce=people. tō=for. frōfre=comfort. 원형은 frōfor. fyrenðearfe=dire distress. onġeat=perceived. 원형은 onġietan.

15 ǣr=formerly. drugon=endure. 원형은 drēogan. aldorlēase=without a lord.

16 hwīle=time. him=to him. Līf-frēa=Lord of Life.

17 wuldres=glory. 원형은 wuldor. Wealdend=Ruler. woroldāre=worldly honor. forġeaf=give. 원형은 forġiefan.

18 Bēowulf=Scyld의 아들이며 Healfdene의 아버지. wæs brēme=renowned. blǣd=fame. wīde=far. sprang=spread. 원형은 springan.

19 eafera=offspring. Scedelandum=southern Scandinavian.

20 Swā=Thus, in such a way. ġeong=young. guma=man. gōde=good deed. ġewyrċean=accomplish, bring about. 원형은 ġewyrċan.

21 fromum=splendid. feoh-ġiftum=rich gift. fæder=father. bearme=protection.

22 ylde=old age. 원형은 yldo. eft=afterwards. ġewunigen=remanied. 원형은 ġewunian.

23 wilġesīþas=dear companion. þonne=when. wīġ=war. cume=cuman(=to come)의 가정법 단수 현재.

24 lēode=people. ġelǣsten=serve. lofdǣdum=praiseworthy deed. sceal=will, is sure to. 원형은 sculan.

25 mǣġþa=nation. ġehwǣre=each. 원형은 ġehwā. ġebēon=prosper.

Listen!

The fame of Danish kings
in days gone by, the daring feats
worked by those heroes are well known to us.
　　Scyld Scefing often deprived his enemies,
many tribes of men, of thier mead-benches.
He terrified his foes ; yet he, as a boy,
had been found a waif ; fate made amends for that.
He prospered under heaven, won praise and honour,
until the men of every neighbouring tribe,
across the whale's way, were obliged to obey him
and pay him tribute. He was a noble king!
Then a son was born to him, a child

in the court, sent by God to comfort
the Danes ; for He had seen their dire distress,
that once they suffered hardship for a long while,
lacking a lord ; and the Lord of Life,
King of Heaven, granted this boy glory ;
Beow was renouned — the name of Scyld's son
became known throughout the Norse lands.
By his own mettle, likewise by generous gifts
while he still enjoys his father's protection,
a young man must ensure that in later years
his companions will supoort him, serve
their prince in battle ; a man who wins renown
will always prosper among any people.

Him ðā Scyld gewāt   tō gescæphwīle,
fēlahrōr, fēran   on Frēan wǣre.
Hī hyne bā ætbǣron   tō brimes faroðe,
swǣse gesības,   swā hē selfa bæd,

30   benden wordum wēold   wine Scyldinga,
lēof landfruma   lange āhte.
7ǣr æt hȳðe stōd   hringedstefna,
īsig ond ūtfūs,   æbelinges fær ;
ālēdon bā   lēofne bēoden,

35   bēaga bryttan   on bearm scipes,
mǣrne be mæste ;   bǣr wæs mādma fela
of feorwegum,   frætwa, gelǣded.
Ne hȳrde ic cȳmlīcor   cēol gegyrwan
hildewǣpnum   on heaðowǣdum,

40   billum ond byrnum ;   him on bearme læg
mādma mænigo,   bā him mid scoldon
on flōdes ǣht   feor gewītan.
Nalæs hī hine lǣssan   lācum tēodan,
bēodgestrēonum,   bon bā dydon,

45   be hine æt frumsceafte   forð onsendon
ǣnne ofer ȳðe   umborwesende.
7ā gȳt hīe him āsetton   segen gyldenne
hēah ofer hēafod,   lēton holm beran,
gēafon on gārsecg ;   him wæs gēomor sefa,

50   murnende mōd.   Men ne cunnon
secgan tō sōðe,   selerǣdende,
hæleð under heofenum,   hwā bǣm hlæste onfēng.

26   Him···gewāt=He departed. ġewāt=went. 원형은 ġewītan. tō=at. ġescæphwīle=appointed

time.

27 fēlahrōr=very strong. fēran=go, journey. Frēan=Lord. wǣre=protection.

28 Hī=They. hyne=him. bā=then. ætbǣron=carried. 원형은 ætberan. brimes=sea. faroðe= current, sea.

29 swǣse=dear. ġesības=retainer. selfa=self. bæd=asked. 원형은 biddan.

30 benden=while. wēold=ruled. 원형은 wealdan. wine Scyldinga=the friend of the Danes= the lord of the Danes. wine=friend. Scyldinga=Danes.

31 lēof=dear. landfruma=king. lange=for long. āhte=possessed. 원형은 āgan.

32 7ǣr=there. hȳðe=harbour. stōd=stood, was. 원형은 standan. hringed-stefna=ringed prow.

33 īsiġ=icy, covered with ice. ūt-fūs=ready to set out. æbelinges=hero. fǣr=vessel.

34 ālēdon=lay down. 원형은 ālecgan. bā=then. lēofne=dear. bēoden=prince.

35 bēaga=ring. bryttan=distributor. bearm=bosom. scipes=ship.

36 mǣrne=famous. 원형은 mǣre. mæste=mast. bǣr=there. mādma=treasures. fela=many.

37 of=from. feorwegum=distant part. frætwa=ornaments. ġelǣded=brought. 원형은 ġelǣdan.

38 Ne=Nor. hȳrde=heard. 원형은 hȳran. cȳmlīcor=more beautifully. cȳmlīċe의 비교급. ċēol= ship. ġeġyrwan=adorn.

39 hildewǣpnum=war-weapon. heaðowǣdum=battle-dress, armour.

40 billum=sword. byrnum=coat-of-mail. 원형은 byrne. him=Scyld. læg=lay. 원형은 licgan.

41 mādma=treasure. mænigo=multitude. 원형은 meniġeo. mid=with. scoldon=had to. 원형은 sculan.

42 flōdes=flood. ǣht=possession, domain. feor=far. ġewītan=depart. 원형은 ġewītan.

43 Nalæs hī hine lǣssasn=Not at all less=much more. liotes의 한 예. Nalæs=Not at all. hī=they. hine=him. lǣssan=less. lācum=gift. tēodan=provided. 원형은 tēon.

44 bēodgestrēonum=people's treasure. bon=than. 비교적 드문 용법이다. bā=those. dydon= did. 원형은 dōn.

45 be=who. frumsceafte=beginning. onsendon=send away. 원형은 onsendan.

46 ǣnne=alone. 원형은 ān. ȳðe=wave. umborwesende=being a child. umbor=child. 시에서만 사용된다. wesende=wesan(=to be)의 현재분사.

47 7ā=Then. ġȳt=further, yet. him=for him. āsetton=erected. 원형은 āsettan. seġen=standard, banner. 원형은 seġn. gyldenne=golden.

48 hēah=high. hēafod=head. lēton=allowed. 원형은 lǣtan. holm=ocean. beran=bear.

49 ġēafon=gave. 원형은 ġiefan. gārsecg=spear-man=sea. ġēomor=mournful. sefa=heart.

50 murnende=mourn. 원형은 murnan. mōd=mind. cunnon=know. 원형은 cunnan.

51 secgan=say. tō=in. sōðe=truth. selerǣdende=counsellor in hall, hall-keeper

52 hæleð=hero. heofenum=heaven. 원형은 heofon. hwā=who. hlæste=freight. onfēng=received. 원형은 onfōn.

Then Scyld departed at the destined hour,
that powerful man sought the Lord's protection.
His own close companions carried him
down to the sea, as he, lord of the Danes,
had asked while he could still speak.
That well-loved man had ruled his land for many years.
There in harbour stood the ring-prowed ship,
the prince's vessel, icy, eager to sail ;
and then they laid their dear lord,
the giver of rings, deep within the ship
by the mast in majesty ; many treasures
and adornments from far and wide were gathered there.
I have never heard of a ship equipped
more handsomely with weapons and war-gear,
swords and corslets ; on his breast
lay countless treasures that were to travel far
with him into the waves' domain.
They gave him great ornaments, gifts
no less magnificent than those men had given him
who long before had sent him alone,
child as he was, across the stretch of the seas.
    Then high above his head they placed
a golden banner and let the waves bear him,
bequeathed him to the sea ; their hearts were grieving,
their minds mourning. Mighty men
beneath the heavens, rulers in the hall,
cannot say who received that cargo.

SCYLD SCEFING AND HIS LINEARITY (3)

Ðā wæs on burgum Bēowulf Scyldinga,
lēof lēodcyning, longe brāge
55 folcum gefrǣge ; — fæder ellor hwearf,
aldor of earde —, ob bæt him eft onwōc
hēah Healfdene ; hēold, benden lifde
gamol ond gūðrēouw, glæde Scyldingas.
Ðǣm fēower bearn forðgerīmed
60 in worold wōcun, weoroda rǣswan,
Heorogār, ond Hrōðgār ond Hālga til,
hrȳrde ic bæt ⋯ wæs Onelan cwēn,
Heaðo-Scilfingas healsgebedda.
7ā wæs Hrōðgāre herespēd gyfen,
65 wīges weorðmynd, bæt him his winemāgas
georne hȳrdon, oðð bæt sēo geogoð gewēox
magodriht micel. Him on mōd bearn,
bæt healreced hātan wolde,
medoærn micel men gewyrcean
70 bonne yldo bearn ǣfre gefrūnon,
ond bǣr on innan eall gedǣlan
geongum ond ealdum, swylc him God sealde
būton folcscare on feorum gumena.
Ðā ic wīde gefrægn weorc gebannan
75 manigre mǣgbe geond bisne middangeard,
folcstede frætwan. Him on fyrste gelomp,
ǣdre mid yldum, bæt hit wearð ealgearo,
healærna mǣst ; scōp him Heort naman
sē be his wordes geweald wīde hæfde.
80 Hē bēot ne ālēh, bēagas dǣlde,

sinc æt symle.　　Sele hlīfade

hēah ond horngēap ;　　heaðowylma bād,

lāðan līges ;　　ne wæs hit lenge bā gēn,

bæt se ecghete　　ābumswēoran

85　　æfter wælnīðe　　wæcnan scolde.

53　burgum=fortified place. Scyldinga=of the Scyldings.

54　lēof=dear. lēodcyning=king of a people. longe=long. brāge=time.

55　folcum ġefrǣġe=famous among peoples. folcum=people. ġefrǣġe=well-known. ellor= elsewhere. hwearf=turned. 원형은 hweorfan.

56　aldor=old. earde=land. Ob bæt=until. eft=again. onwōcu=was born to. 원형은 onwæcnan.

57　hēah=noble. hēold=ruled. 원형은 healdan. benden=while. lifde=lived. 원형은 libban.

58　gamol=aged. gūðrēouw=fierce in battle. 원형은 gūðrēow. glæde=gracious.

59　Ðǣm=to him. fēower=four. bearn=child. forðġerīmed=all told.

60　worold=world. wōcun=woke. 원형은 wæcnan. weoroda=band. rǣswan=leader.

61　til=good.

62　hrȳrde=heard. 원형은 hȳran. ⋯=빈칸에 Yrse라는 이름을 채워 넣은 원고도 있다. cwēn= queen.

63　Heaðo-Scilfingas=of the War-Schylfing. healsġebedda=bedfellow.

64　herespēd=success in battle. ġyfen(ġifan)=give.

65　wiġes=of war. weorðmynd=honor. winemāgas=friends and kinsmen. cf. wine(=friend)+m ǣġ(=kinsman).

66　ġeorne=readily. hȳrdon=obeyed. 원형은 hȳran. oðð bæt=until. ġeogoð=youthful company. gewēox=increased. 원형은 ġeweaxan.

67　magodriht=band of young retainers. miċel=large. Him on mōd bearn=came into his mind=occurred to him. mōd=mind. bearn=ran into. 원형은 beirnan.

68　healreċed=hall-building. hātan=command. wolde=wished. 원형은 willan.

69　medoærn=meadhall. miċel=great. ġewyrċean=construct.

70　bonne=than. yldo=men. 원형은 ylde. bearn=child. ǣfre=ever. ġefrūnon=learned. 원형은 ġefriġnan.

71　bǣr=there. on innan=inside. eall=all. ġedǣlan=distribute.

72　ġeongum=young. ealdum=old. swylċ=which. sealde=gave. 원형은 sellan.

73　būton=except. folcscare=folcscaru(=folk-share, public land)의 단수 여격. feorum=feorh (=life)의 복수 여격. gumena=guma(=man)의 복수 속격. 시에서만 사용된다.

74　Ðā=then. wīde=widely. ġefræġn=heard. 원형은 ġefriġnan. weorc=task. ġebannan=to order.

75　maniġre=many. 원형은 maniġ. mǣġbe=tribe. ġeond=over. middanġeard=earth.

76　folcstede=dwelling=place. frætwan=adorn. Him on fyrste ġelomp=to him in time it happened. on fyrste=in due time. ġelomp=happened. 원형은 ġelimpan.

77 ǣdre=early. yldum=men. wearð=became. 원형은 weorðan. ealġearo=quite ready.

78 healærna=hall-building. mǣst=greatest. scōp=created. 원형은 scyppan. him=for it. Heort=
Zealand에 있는 지명. naman=name.

79 wordes=of word. ġeweald=power. wīde=far and wide. hæfde=had. 원형은 habban.

80 bēot=boast, promise. ālēh=belied. 원형은 ālēogan. bēagas=rings. dǣlde=distributed. 원형
은 dǣlan.

81 sinc=treasure. symle=banquet. 원형은 symbel. Sele=hall. hlīfade=rose up, tower up. 원형
은 hlifian.

82 hēah=high. hornġēap=wide-gabled. heaðowylma=hostile surge=hostile flame. bād=awaited.
원형은 bīdan.

83 lāðan=hateful. līġes=flame. lenge=near at hand. ġēn=yet, still.

84 ecghete=sword-hatred. āþumswēoran=son-in-law and father-in-laws.

85 æfter=on account of. wælnīðe=moral enmity. wæcnan=arise. scolde=had to. 원형은 sculan.

When his royal father had travelled from the earth,

Beow of Denmark, a beloved king,

ruled long in the stronghold, famed

amongst men ; in time Healfdene the brave

was born to him ; who, so long as he lived,

grey-haired and redoutable, ruled the noble Danes.

Beow's son Healfdene, leader of men,

was favoured by fortune with four children :

Heorogar and Hrothgar and Halga the good ;

Yrse, the fourth, was Onela's queen,

the dear wife of that warlike Swedish king.

Hrothgar won honour in war,

glory in battle, and so ensured

his followers' support – young men

whose number multiplied into a mighty troop.

And he resolved to build a hall,

a large and noble feasting-hall

of whose splendours men would always speak,

and there to distribute as gifts to old and young

all the things that God had given him –

but not men's lives or the public land.

Then I heard that tribes without number, even

to the ends of the earth, were given orders

to decorate the hall. And in due course

(before very long) this greatest of halls

was completed. Hrothgar, whose very word was counted

far and wide as a command, called it Heorot.

He kept his promise, gave presents of rings

and treasure at the feasting. The hall towered high,

lofty and wide-gabled — fierce tongues of loathsome fire

had not yet attacked it, nor was the time yet near

when a mortal feud should flare between father —

and son-in-law, sparked off by deeds of deadly enmity.

(tr. Crossley-Holland)

THE TRAGEDY OF HILDEBURH (1)

      7ær wæs sang ond swēg   samod ætgædere
      fore Healfdenes   hildewīsan,
1065 gomenwudu grēted,   gid oft wrecen,
      ðonne healgamen   Hrōbgāres scop
      æfter medobence   mǣnan scolde,
      be Finnes eaferum,   ðā hīe se fǣr begeat,
      hæleð Healf-Dena,   Hnæf Scyldinga,
1070 in Frēswæle   feallan scolde.
      Nē hūru Hildeburh   herian borfte
      Ēotena trēowe ;   unsynnum wearð
      beloren lēofum   æt bām lindplegan,
      bearnum ond brōðrum ;   hīe on gebyrd hrunon,
1075 gāre wunde ;   7æt wæs gēomuru ides!
      Nalles hōlinga   Hōces dohtor
      meotodsceaft bemearn   sybðan morgen cōm,
      ðā hēo under swegle   gesēon meahte
      morborbealo māga.   7ær hēo ǣr mǣste hēold
1080 worolde wynne.   wīg ealle fornam
      Finnes begnas   nemne fēaum ānum,
      bæt hē ne mehte   on bǣm meðelstede
      wīg Hengeste   wiht gefeohtan,
      nē bā wēalāfe   wīge forbringan,
1085 bēodnes ðegne ;   ac hig him gebingo budon
      bæt hīe him ōðer flet   eal gerȳmdon,
      healle ond hēahsetl,   bæt hīe healfre geweald
      wið Ēotena bearn   āgan mōston ;
      ond æt feohgyftum   Folcwaldan sunu
1090 dōgra gehwylce   Dene weorbode,

Hengestes hēap   hringum wenede
efne swā swīðe,   sincgestrēonum
fǣttan goldes,   swā hē Frēsena cyn
on bēorsele   byldan wolde.

1063 sang=singing. swēġ=music. samod ætgædere=at the same time together. samod= unitedly. ætgædere=together.

1064 fore=before. Helfdenes hildewīsan=Healfdene's battle-leader=Hrothgar. 이것이 그가 아버 지(Healfdene) 생존시에 받았던 직함일 것이다. hildewīsan=leader in battle.

1065 gomenwudu=mirth-wood=joyful wood=lyre. cf. gomen=entertainment. grēted=(had been) plucked(touched). 원형은 grētan. ġid(ġiedd)=song, tale. wrecen=wrecan(=to recite, tell)의 과거분사.

1066 ðonne=when. healgamen=entertainment in hall. scop=poet.

1067 æfter=along. medobenċe=mead-benches. mǣnan=recite.

1068 be=about. 원고에는 없던 것을 채워 넣은 것이다. eaferum=eafera(=son)의 복수 여격. hīe= them. fær=sudden attack. beġeat=assailed. 원형은 beġietan.

1069 hæleð Healf-Dena, Hnæf Scyldinga=hero of the Half-Danes and of the Scyldings. Hnæf 는 Hildeburh의 Hildeburgh의 오빠이며 이들의 아버지는 Hoc이다. hæleð=hero. Healf=half.

1070 Frēswæle=Frisian battlefield. feallan=fall. scolde=had to.

1071 hūru=indeed. herian=praise. borfte=had occasion. 원형은 burfan.

1072 Ēotena=of the Jutes. trēowe=good faith, truth. unsynnum=guiltless. wearð=(she) was.

1073 beloren=deprived of. 여격과 함께 쓰인다. 원형은 belēosan. lēofum=beloved (ones). lindplegan=shield-play.

1074 bearnum ond brōðrum=of son and brother. bearn=son. brōðor=brother. on ġebyrd=in accordance with destiny (birth), what was fated at birth. hrunon=fell. 원형은 hrēosan.

1075 gāre=spear. wunde=wounded. ġēomuru=sad, grieving. 원형은 ġēomor. ides=woman, lady.

1076 Nalles=Not at all. 원형은 nealles. hōlinga=without cause. dohtor=daughter.

1077 meotodsceaft=decree of fate, death. bemearn=bewailed, mourned over. 원형은 bemurnan. syþðan=after. morgen=morning.

1078 sweġle=sky, heaven. ġesēon=see. meahte=could. 원형은 magan.

1079 morborbealo=deadly slaughter. māga=of kinsmen. bǣr hēo ǣr mǣste hēold=Where he (=Finn) had previously possessed. mǣste=greatest. 다음 줄의 wynne(=joy)를 수식한다. hēold=possessed. 원형은 healdan.

1080 wynne=joy. wīġ=battle. ealle=다음 줄의 bæġnas(=retainers)를 수식한다. fornam=carried off, took away. 원형은 forniman.

1081 nemne=except for. 여격과 함께 쓰인다. fēaum=a few. ānum=only.

1082 bæt=so that. hē=Finn. meðelstede=meeting-place. place of battle에 대한 대칭법(kenning).

1083 wīġ=battle. Hengeste=against Hengest. wiht=at all. ġefeohtan=win, fight to a finish.

1084 bā wēalāfe=the woe-remnant. 아마도 those left from the disaster, the survivors of the calamity의 뜻일 듯. wīġe=war. forbringan=dislodge from. 여격과 함께 쓰인다.

1085 bēodnes ðeġne=against Hengest, his prince's (Hnæf's) thane. bēoden=prince. ðeġn=retainer. hiġ=they (Hnæf and his followers). him=them (Frisians). 또 다른 해석은 hiġ=Frisians, him=Hengest or the survivors in general로 보는 것이다. ġebingo=truce, terms. budon= offered. 원형은 bēodan.

1086 ōðer=another. flet=hall, building. eal=complete. ġerȳmdon=would clear. 원형은 ġerȳman.

1087 hēahsetl=high seat (=throne). hīe=Hengest's men. healfre=of half (of it). 원형은 healf. ġeweald=control, authority.

1088 wið=with. Ēotna bearn=men of Jutes. bearn=son. 문맥으로 보아 Jutes인들 가운데는 덴마크이들 편에 가담한 사람들도 있었던 것 같다. āgan=possess. mōston=might, be allowed to.

1089 feohġyftum=treasure-giving. Folcwaldan sunu=Folcwald's son=Finn.

1090 dōgra ġehwylċe=on each of days=every day. dōgra=days. 원형은 dōgor. ġehwylċe=each. weorbode=would honor. weorbian의 가정법 과거 단수.

1091 hēap=company, troop. hringum=rings. wenede=wenian(=to treat, entertain)의 가정법 과거 단수. 여격과 함께 쓰인다.

1092 efne swā swīðe=even as strongly=to the same extent. efne=just. sincġestrēonum=with treasures.

1093 fǣttan=(of) ornamented, plated. Frēsena=of the Frisians. cyn=tribe.

1093-4 swā hē Frēsena cyn on bēorsele hyldan wolde=just as (to the same extent that) he would wish…. 덴마크 인들도 프리지아 인들과 마찬가지로 대우해야 한다는 조건이다.

1094 bēorsele=beer-hall, drinking-hall. 그러나 여기서 허용되는 음료는 sweet drink뿐이었다. hyldan=encourage. wolde=wished. 원형은 willan.

Then Hrothgar, leader in battle, was entertained
with music — harp and voice in harmony.
The strings were plucked, many a song rehearsed,
when it was the turn of Hrothgar's poet
to please men at the mead-bench, perform in the hall.
He sang of Finn's troop, victims of surprise attack,
and of how that Danish hero, Hnæf of the Scyldings,
was destined to die among the Frisian slain.

Hildeburh, indeed, could hardly recommend
the honour of the Jutes ; that innocent woman
lost her loved ones, son and brother,

in the shield-play ; they fell, as fate ordained,

stricken by spears ; and she was stricken with grief.

Not without cause did Hoc's daughter

mourn the shaft of fate, for in the light of morning

she saw that her kin lay slain under the sky,

the men who had been her endless pride

and joy. That encounter laid claim

to all but a few of Finn's thanes,

and he was unable to finish that fight

with Hnæf's retainer, with Hengest in the hall,

unable to dislodge the miserable survivors ;

indeed, terms for a truce were agreed :

that Finn should give up to them another hall,

with its high seat, in its entirety,

which the Danes should own in common with the Jutes ;

and that at the treasure-giving the son of Folcwalda

should honour the Danes day by day,

should distribute rings and gold-adorned gifts

to Hengest's band and his own people in equal measure.

THE TRAGEDY OF HILDEBURH (2)

1095 Ðā hīe getruwedon   on twā healfa
fæste frioðuwǣre.   Fin Hengeste
elne unflitme   āðum benemde
þæt hē þā wēalāfe   weotena dōme
ārum hēolde,   þæt ðǣr ǣnig mon

1100 wordum ne worcum   wǣre ne brǣce,
nē þurh inwitsearo   ǣfre ġemǣnden
ðēah hīe hira bēaggyfan   bana folgedon,
ðēodenlēase,   þā him swā gebearfod wæs ;
gyf þonne Frȳsna hwylc   frēcnen sprǣce

1105 ðæs morþorhetes   myndgiend wǣre,
þonne hit sweordes ecg   syððan scolde.

Ād wæs geæfned   ond icge gold
āhæfen of horde.   Here-Scyldinga
betst beadorinca   wæs on bǣl gearu.

1110 Æt þǣm āde wæs   ēþgesȳne
swātfāh syrce,   swȳn ealgylden,
eofer īrenheard,   æþeling manig
wundum āwyrded ;   sume on wæle crungon.
Hēt ðā Hildeburh   æt Hnæfes āde

1115 hire selfre sunu   sweoloðe befæstan,
bānfatu bærnan,   ond on bǣl dōn
ēame on eaxle.   Ides gnornode,
gēomrode giddum.   Gūðrinc āstāh ;
wand tō wolcnum   wælfȳra mǣst,

1120 hlynode for hlāwe ;   hafelan multon,
bengeato burston   ðonne blōd ætspranc,
lāðbite līces.   Līg ealle forswealg,

gǣsta gīfrost,   bāra ðe bǣr gūð fornam

bēga folces ;   wæs hira blǣd scacen.

1095 ġetruwedon=trusted in. 대격과 함께 사용된다. 원형은 ġetruwian. twā=two (both). healfa= sides.

1096 fæste=firm(ly). frioðuwǣre=peace-treaty.

1097 elne unflitme=with courage and without argument. unflitme는 여기에만 나타나는 단어인데 flit가 strife나 contention의 뜻이므로 without contention 정도의 뜻으로 해석할 수 있을 것이다. elne=ellen(=courage)의 단수 여격. āðum=oath. benemde=declared. 원형은 benemnan.

1098 wēalāfe=survivors of the disaster. weotena dōme=in (accordance with) the judgement of (his) counsellors. weotena=wita(=counsellor)의 복수 속격. dōme=judgement.

1099 ārum=honorably. cf. ār=honour. hēolde=would treat. 원형은 healdan. ǣniġ=any.

1100 wordum ne worcum=in (neither) words nor deeds. ne=neither. worc=deed. wǣre= agreement, treaty. brǣce=should break. 원형은 brēcan.

1101 nē=nor. inwitsearo=malicious intrigue. ǣfre=ever. ġemǣnden=should complain. 원형은 ġemǣnan.

1102 ðēah=though. bēaggyfan=ring-giver's. bana=slayer. folgedon=followed. 원형은 folgian.

1103 ðēodenlēase=princeless, lordless. bā him swā ġebearfod wæs=when(=since) (it) had been thus forced on them. bā=since. ġebearfod=forced, required. 원형은 ġebearfian.

1104 hwylċ=any of, a certain one. frēcnen sprǣċe=with some daring remark. frēcne=reckless.

1105 morborhetes=murderous hostility. myndgiend wǣre=should be reminding of=should bring to mind. 원형은 myndgdian. wǣre=should be. wesan(=to be)의 가정법 과거 단수.

1106 bonne=then. hit sweordes ecg syððan scolde=it should thereafter (be) the sword's edge= be a matter to be settled by the sword. syððan=thereafter. scolde=should be. 원형은 sculan.

1107 Ād=pyre. ġeæfned=made ready. 원형은 æfnan(=to make ready). icge=뜻이 분명치 않으며 splendid나 rich, mighty 정도의 뜻이었을 것으로 짐작된다.

1108 āhæfen=brought up. 원형은 āhebban. of=from. horde=treasury. Here-Scyldinga=of the army-Scyldings. 아마도 warlike Scyldings의 뜻일 듯. Here=army.

1109 betst=best. beadorinca=of warriors. on=for. bǣl=fire. ġearu=ready.

1110 Æt=on. ēbġesȳne=plain to see, easy to see.

1111 swātfāh=bloodstained. syrċe=mailcoat. swȳn=boar, swine. ealgylden=all-gilded.

1112 eofer=boar. 당시 앵글로-색슨족의 무기에는 수퇘지 형상을 새겨 넣은 경우가 많았다. īrenheard=iron-hard. æbeling=(a) nobleman. maniġ=many.

1113 wundum=wound. āwyrded=maimed. 행위자는 여격으로 나타낸다. 원형은 āwyrdan. sume=certain ones, some. 고대영어 특유의 억제된 표현이며 실제는 many의 뜻. on wæle=carnage(대학살). crungon=had fallen. 원형은 crincgan.

1114 Hēt=ordered. 원형은 hatan. æt=on.

1115 hire selfre sunu=the son of her herself=her own son. sweoloðe=flame, heat. befæstan= be committed to, entrusted. 여격과 함께 쓰인다.

1116 bānfatu=bone-vessels=body. bærnan=be burned. dōn=be consigned, put.

1117 ēame on eaxle=to uncle at shoulder=at his uncle's side. ēam=(maternal) uncle. on=by. eaxl=shoulder. Ides=lady. gnornode=mourned. 원형은 gnornian.

1118 ġēomrode=lamented. ġiddum=with songs. 원형은 ġiedd. Gūðrinc=warrior. āstāh=arose. 원형은 āstīgan. Hnæf의 시체는 장작 위에 놓여 있다.

1119 wand=curled. 원형은 windan. wolcum=skies. wælfyra=of funeral-fires. mǣst=greatest.

1120 hlynode=roared. 원형은 hlynian. for=before, in front of. hlāwe=mound. hafelan=heads. multon=melted. 원형은 meltan.

1121 bengeato=wound-gates. burston=broke out. 원형은 burstan. ætspranc=spurted out. 원형 은 ætspringan.

1122 lāðbite=hostile bites. līċes=body's. Līġ=fire. forswealg=swallowed up. 원형은 forswelgan.

1122-3 ealle…bāra=all of those.

1123 gǣsta=spirit. gīfrost=greediest, most eager. gūð=war. fornam=took away. 원형은 forniman.

1124 bēga folces=of the people of both (sides). bēga=of both. folces=of people. blǣd=glory, prosperity. scacen=departed. 원형은 sceacan.

Both sides pledged themselves to this peaceful
settlement. Finn swore Hengest solemn oaths
that he would respect the sad survivors
as his counsellors ordaiend, and that no man there
must violate the covenant with word or deed,
or complain about it, although they
would be serving the slayer of their lord
(as fate had forced those lordless men to do) ;
and he warned the Frisians that if, in provocation,
they should mention the murderous feud,
the sword's edge should settle things.
The funeral fire was prepared, glorious gold
was brought up from the hoard : the best of Scyldings,
that race of warriors, lay ready on the pyre.
Blood-stained corslets, and images of boars

(cast in iron and covered in gold)
were plentiful on that pyre, and likewise the bodies
of many retainers, ravaged by wounds ;
renowned men fell in that slaughter.
Then Hildeburh asked that her own son
be committed to the flames at her brother's funeral,
that his body be consumed on Hnæf's pyre.
That grief-stricken woman keened over his corpse,
sang doleful dirges. The warriors' voices
soared towards heaven. And so did the smoke
from the great funeral fire that roared
before the barrow ; heads sizzled,
wounds split open, blood burst out
from battle scars. The ravenous flames
swallowed those men whole, made no distinction
between Frisians and Danes ; the finest men departed.

THE TRAGEDY OF HILDEBURH (3)

1125   Gewiton him ðā wīgend   wīca nēosian,
freondum befeallen,   Frȳsland geseon,
hāmes ond hēaburh.   Hengest ðā gȳt
wælfāgne winter   wunode mid Finne
eal unhlitme.   Eard gemunde

1130   bēah be ne meahte   on mere drīfan
hringedstefnan ;   holm storme wēol,
won wið winde,   winter ȳbe beleac
īsgebinde,   obðæt ōber cōm
gēar in geardas   swā nū gȳt dēð,

1135   bā ðe syngāles   sēle bewitiað,
wuldortorhtan weder.   Ðā wæs winter scacen,
fæger foldan bearm.   Fundode wrecca,
gist of geardum ;   hē tō gyrnwræce
swīðor bohte   bonne tō sǣlāde,

1140   gif hē torngemōt   burhtēon mihte,
bæt hē Ēotena bearn   inne gemunde.
Swā hē ne forwyrnde   woroldrǣdenne
bonne him Hūnlāfing   hildelēoman,
billa sēlest,   on bearm dyde,

1145   bæs wǣron mid Ēotenum   ecge cūðe.
Swylce ferhðfrecan   Fin eft begeat
sweordbealo slīðen   æt his selfes hām,
sibðan grimne gripe   Gūðlāf ond Ōslāf
æfter sǣsīðe,   sorge, mǣndon,

1150   ætwiton wēana dǣl ;   ne meahte wǣfre mōd
forhabban in hrebre.   Ðā wæs heal hroden
fēonda fēorum,   swilce Fin slægen,

cyning on corbre,   ond sēo cwēn numen.

Scēotend Scyldinga   tō scypon feredon

1155   eal ingesteald   eorðcyninges,

swylce hīe æt Finnes hām   findan meahton

sigla, searogrimma.   Hīe on sǣlāde

drihtlice wīf   tō Denum feredon,

lǣddon tō lēodum.

1125 Gewiton=went. 원형은 ġewītan. him=동작의 동사와 함께 쓰인 재귀대명사. wīġend=warrior. wīca=dwellings. nēosian=seek out, find. 속격과 함께 쓰인다.

1126 frēondum=friend. befeallen=bereft of. 여격과 함께 쓰인다. 원형은 befeallan. ġesēon=see.

1127 hāmes=home. hēaburh=high stronghold. gȳt=still.

1128 wælfāgne winter=through (that) slaughter-stained winter. wunode=stayed. 원형은 wunian.

1129 eal=completely, utterly. unhlitme=다른 곳에 나타나지도 않으며 뜻도 분명치 않다. hlytm (=the casting of lots)를 어간으로 잡을 때 without lot, with misfortune, in disastrous plight 정도의 뜻으로 생각할 수 있다. Eard=homeland. ġemunde=remembered. 원형은 ġemunan.

1130 bēah=although. meahte=could, was able to. mere=sea. drīfan=drive.

1131 hringedstefnan=ring-prowed (ship). holm=ocean. storme=with storm. wēol=surged. 원형은 weallan.

1132 won=struggled. 원형은 winnan. ȳbe=waves. belēac=locked. 원형은 belūcan.

1133 īsġebinde=with icy bond. oþðæt=until. ōþer=a new. cōm=came. 원형은 cuman.

1133-4 ōþer cōm ġēar=ōþer gēar cōm. ġēar=year.

1134 in ġeardas=to (the) dwellings (of men). swā=as. nū=now. gȳt=still. dēð=does. 원형은 dōn.

1135 þā=those. syngāles=always, continually. sēle=seasons. 원형은 sǣl. bewitiað=observe. 원형은 bewitian.

1136 wuldortorhtan=gloriously bright. weder=weather.

1137 fæġer foldan bearm=(and) the lap of the earth (had grown) beautiful. fæġer=fair. foldan=earth. bearm=bosom. Funnode=strove to go. 원형은 fundian. wreċċa=the exile.

1138 ġist(gyst)=visitor, guest. of=from. ġeardum=dwellings. tō=about. ġyrnwræce=revenge for injury. 원형은 ġyrnwræcu.

1139 swīðor=more intensely. bohte=thought. 원형은 benċan. þonne=than. sǣlāde=sea-journey.

1140 ġif=whether. tornġemōt=hostile encounter. burhtēon=bring about. mihte=could. 원형은 magan.

1141 þæt hē Ēotena bearn inne gemunde=so that he might therein be mindful of···. Jutes족에 대한 복수의 필요성을 절제해서 표현한 것임. þæt=which. bearn=men. inne=inwardly. ġemunan=think about, be mindful of, remember.

1142   Swā=so. forwyrnde=denied. 원형은 forwyrnan. woroldrǣdenne=the way(condition) of the world=the way of vengeance.

1143   bonne=when. Hūnlāfing=덴마크 병사의 이름인 듯. hildelēoman=battle flame=gleaming sword.

1143-4   him…on bearm=into his lap. dyde=put, placed. 원형은 dōn.

1144   billa=of blades. sēlest=best.

1145   bæs…ecge=of which the edges=whose edges…. bæs=its. wǣron=were. 원형은 wesan. mid=among. ecge=edge. cūðe=known.

1146   Swylċe=thus, accordingly. ferhðfrecan=bold-spirited. eft=after, in turn. beġeat=assailed. 원형은 beġietan.

1147   sweordbealo=sword-death, death by sword. slīðen=cruel. hām=home.

1148   sibðan=when, after. grimne=savage, cruel. gripe=attack.

1149   sǣsīðe=sea-journey. sorge=grievance. mǣndon=bemoaned. 원형은 mǣnan.

1150   ætwiton=(and) blamed (on him). 원형은 ætwītan. wēana=sorrow, woe. dǣl=(their) portion, share. meahte=could. 원형은 magan. wǣfre mōd=enraged heart=Hengest's heart. wǣfre=restless. mōd=heart, spirit.

1151   forhabban=hold (itself) back. hrebre=breast. hroden=hrēodan(=adorn)의 과거분사.

1152   fēonda=enemy. fēorum=(with) lives. 원형은 feorh. swilċe=likewise. slæġen=(was) slain. 원형은 slēan.

1153   cyning=king. on=in. corbre=(his) troop. cwēn=queen. numen=taken. 원형은 niman.

1154   Scēotend=warriors, spearmen. scypon=ship. feredon=carried. 원형은 ferian.

1155   eal=all. inġesteald=household goods. eorðcyninges=king of the land.

1156   swylċe=such as. findan=find.

1157   sigla, searogrimma=(by way) of jewels (and) precious gems. siġla=jewels. searoġim= curious gems. sǣlāde=sea-voyage.

1158   drihtliċe=noble. wīf=woman. feredon=carried. 원형은 ferian.

1159   ſæddon=brought. 원형은 ſædan. lēodum=(her) people.

    Then those warriors, their friends lost to them,
    went to view their homes, revisit the stronghold
    and survey the Frisian land. But Hengest
    stayed with Finn, in utter dejection, all through
    that blood-stained winter. And he dreamed
    of his own country, but he was unable to steer
    his ship homeward, for the storm-beaten sea
    wrestled with the wind ; winter sheathed the waves

in ice — until once again spring made its sign
(as still it does) among the houses of men :
clear days, warm weather, in accordance as always
with the law of the seasons. Then winter was over,
the face of the earth was fair ; the exile
was anxious to leave that foreign people
and the Frisian land. And yet he brooded
more about vengeance than about a voyage,
and wondered whether he could bring about a clash
so as to repay the sons of the Jutes.
Thus Hengest did not shrink from the duty of vengeance
after Hunlafing had placed the flashing sword,
finest of all weapons, on his lap ;
this sword's edges had scarred many Jutes.
And so it was that cruel death by the sword later
cut down the brave warrior Finn in his own hall,
after Guthlaf and Oslaf, arrived from a sea-journey,
had fiercely complained of that first attack,
condemned the Frisians on many scores :
the Scyldings' restless spirits could no longer
be restrained. Then the hall ran red with the blood
of the enemy — Finn himself was slain,
the king with his troop, and Hildeburh was taken.
The Sylding warriors carried the king's
heirlooms down to their ship,
all the jewels and necklaces they discovered
at Finn's hall. They sailed over the sea-paths,
brought that noble lady back to Denmark
and her own people.

(tr. Crossley-Holland)

THE HAUNT OF GRENDEL AND HIS DAM

1345   Ic bæt londbūend,   lēode mīne.

selerǣdende   secgan hȳrde,

bæt hīe gesāwon   swylce twēgen

micle mearcstapan   mōras healdan,

ellorgǣstas.   Đǣra ōðer wæs,

1350   bæs be hīe gewislīcost   gewitan meahton,

idese onlīcnes ;   ōðer earmsceapen

on weres wæstmum   wrǣclāstas træd,

næfne hē wæs māra   bonne ǣnig man ōðer ;

bone on geardagum   Grendel nemdon

1355   foldbūende ;   nō hīe fæder cunnon,

hwæber him ǣnig wæs   ǣr ācenned

dyrna gāsta.   Hīe dȳgel lond

warigeað wulfhleobu,   windige næssas,

frēcne fengelād,   ðær fyrgenstrēam

1360   under næssa genipu   niber gewīteð,

flōd under foldan.   Nis bæt feor heonon

mīlgemearces,   bæt se mere standeð ;

ofer bǣm hongiað   hrinde bearwas,

wudu wyrtum fæst   wæter oferhelmað.

1365   7ær mæg nihta gehwǣm   nīðwundor sēon,

fȳr on flōde.   Nō ðæs frōd leofað

gumena bearna,   bæt bone grund wite.

Đēah be hǣðstapa   hundum geswenced,

heorot hornum trum   holtwudu sēcē,

1370   feorran geflȳmed,   ǣr hē feorh seleð,

aldor on ōfre,   ǣr hē in wille,

hafelan hȳdan ;   nis bæt hēoru stōw.

7onon ȳðgeblond   up āstīgeð

won tō wolcnum,　　ðonne wind styreþ
1375　lāð gewidru,　　oð ðæt lyft drysmaþ,
roderas rēotað.　　Nū is se rǣd gelang
eft æt þē ānum.　　Eard gīt ne const,
frēcne stōwe,　　ðǣr þū findan miht
sinnigne secg ;　　sēc ġif þū dyrre.
1380　Ic þē þā fǣhðe　　fēo lēaninge,
ealdgestrēonum,　　swā ic ǣr dyde,
wundnum golde,　　gyf þū on weg cymest.

1345　londbūend=country-dweller. lēode=people. londbūend와 lēode는 같은 내용을 표현을 달리
해서 나타내고 있는 경우이다.

1346　selerǣdende=hall-counsellor, hall-keepers. secgan=say. hȳrde=herd. 원형은 hȳran.

1347　gesāwon=saw. 원형은 ġesēon. swylċe=such. twēġen=two.

1348　micle=great. 원형은 miċel. mearcstapan=border-walker. mōras=moors. healdan=keep.

1349　ellorġǣstas=alien spirits, spirits from elsewhere. ðǣra=of whom. ōðer=one of the two.

1350　ðæs þe=in the (way) that, as. ġewislīcost=most certainly. 원형은 ġewislīċ. ġewitan=
make out, know. meahton=could. 원형은 magan.

1351　idese=of a woman. onlīcnes=likeness. ōðer=the other. earmsceapen=miserable creature.

1352　weres=man's. wæstmum=form. wrǣclāstas=tracks of exile, exile-paths. træd=trod. 원형
은 tredan.

1353　næfne=except. māra=greater. ōðer=besides.

1354　ðone=whom. ġeardagum=former days. nemdon=named. 원형은 nāman.

1355　foldbūende=country-dwellers, earth-dwellers. cunnon=know. 원형은 cunnan.

1356　hwæðer=whether. him=for him. ǣr=formerly. ācenned=begotten. 원형은 ācennan.

1357　dyrna=mysterious. gāsta=spirits, demons. dȳġel=secret, unknown.

1358　wariġeað[wariyaθ]=occupy. 원형은 warian. wulfhleobu=wolf slopes. 원형은 wulf-hlib.
windiġe=windy. næssas=headlands.

1359　frēcne=dread. fenġelād=path through the fen, fen-way. ðǣr=where. fyrġenstrēam=
mountain-stream, waterfall.

1360　næssa=cliffs'. ġenipu=darkness. niber=downwards. ġewīteð=goes away. 원형은 ġewītan.

1361　flōd=torrent. foldan=earth. Nis=is not. heonon=hence.

1362　mīlġemearces=mile-measures. mere=mere, lake.

1363　hongiað=hang. 원형은 hongian. hrinde=rimed, frosted, rimy. bearwas=groves. 원형은
bearo.

1364　wudu=wood. wyrtum=root. fæst=fixed. oferhelmað=overshadows. 원형은 oferhelmian.

1365　nihta=nights. ġehwǣm=each. 원형은 ġehwā. nīðwundor=horrible wonder. sēon=see.

1366 f̄yr=fire. flōde=water. ðæs=so, in that way. frōd=wise. leofað=lives. 원형은 libban.

1367 gumena=of men. bearna=children, sons. grund=bottom. wite=knows.

1368 Ðēah=though. hǣðstapa=heath-stalker, stag. hundum=hound. ġeswenċed=pressed. 원형은 swenċan.

1369 heorot=hart. hornum=antler. trum=strong. holtwudu=forest. holt와 wudu 모두 숲이라는 뜻이다. 이처럼 동의어를 나란히 묶어 합성어를 만드는 것은 pathway 등에서도 볼 수 있다. sēcē=seek. 원형은 sēċan.

1370 feorran=from afar. ġeflȳmed=pursued, chased. ġeflȳman. ̄ær=first. feorh=life. seleð=give up. 원형은 sellan.

1371 aldor=life. ōfre=bank, shore. ̄ær=before.

1372 hafelan=head. hȳdan=hide. Nis bæt hēoru stōw=That is not a pleasant place라는 것은 고대영어 시의 한 특징인 곡언법(litotes)의 한 예이다. Nis=is not. hēoru=pleasant. stōw=place.

1373 7onon=from there. ̄yðgeblond=surging water. up āstīgeð=climbs up. 원형은 āstīgan.

1374 won=dark. wolcnum=cloud. styreb=stirs. 원형은 styrian.

1375 lāð=hostile. ġewidru=storm. 원형은 ġewideru. oðbæt=until. lyft=air. drysmab=becomes misty, darkens. 원형은 drysmian.

1376 roderas=heavens, skies. 원형은 rodor. rēotað=weep. 원형은 rēotan. Nū=now. r̄æd=remedy. ġelang=dependent on, belonging to.

1377 eft=again. æt=with. ānum=alone. Eard=dwelling place, region. ġīt=yet. const=(thou) knowest. 원형은 cunnan.

1378 frēcne=perilous. stōwe=place. ðær=where. ġif=if. miht=may.

1379 sinniġne=sinful. secg=creature. sēc=seek. 원형은 sēċan. dyrre=dare. 원형은 durran.

1380 fǣhðe=audacity, violence. fēo=wealth, money. 원형은 fēoh. lēaninge=reward. 원형은 lēanian.

1381 ealdġestrēonum=ancient treasures. ̄ær=before.

1382 wundnum=twisted. gyf=if. on weġ=away, back. cymest=come 원형은 cuman.

    I have heard my people say,

men of this country, counsellors in the hall,

that they have seen two such beings,

equally monstrous, rangers of the fell-country,

rulers of the moors ; and these men assert

that so far as they can see one bears

a likeness to a woman ; grotesque though he was,

the other who trod the paths of exile looked like a man,

though greater in height and build than a goliath ;

he was christened *Grendel* by my people
many years ago ; men do not know if he
had a father, a fiend once begotten
by mysterious spirits. These two live
in a little-known country, wolf-slopes, windswept headlands,
perilous paths across the boggy moors, where a mountain stream
plunges under the mist-covered cliffs,
rushes through a fissure. It is not far from here,
if measured in miles, that the lake stands
shadowed by trees stiff with hoar-frost.
A wood, firmly-rooted, frowns over the water.
There, night after night, a fearful wonder may be seen –
fire on the water ; no man alive
is so wise as to know the nature of its depths.
Although the moor-stalker, the stag with strong horns,
when harried by hounds will make for the wood,
pursued from afar, he will succumb
to the hounds on the brink, rather than plunge in
and save his head. That is not a pleasant place.
When the wind arouses the wrath of the storm,
whipped waves rear up black from the lake,
reach for the skies, until the air becomes misty,
the heavens weep. Now, once again, help may be had
from you alone. As yet, you have not seen the haunt,
the perilous place where you may meet this most evel monster
face to face. Do you dare set eyes on it?
If you return unscathed, I will reward you
for your audacity, as I did before,
with ancient treasures and twisted gold.

(tr. Crossley-Holland)

The Slaying of Grendel's Mother (1)

      Æfter þǣm wordum   Weder-Gēata lēod
efste mid elne,   nalas andsware
bīdan wolde.   Brimwylm ofēng
1495   hilderince.   Ðā wæs hwīl dæges
ǣr hē þone grundwong   ongytan mehte.
Sōna þæt onfunde,   sē ðe flōda begong
heorogīfre behēold   hund missēra,
grim ond grǣdig,   þæt þǣr gumena sum
1500   ælwihta eard   ufan cunnode.
Grāp þā tōgēanes,   gūðrinc gefēng
atolan clommum.   Nō þȳ ǣr in gescōd
hālan līce ;   hring ūtan ymbbearh,
þæt hēo þone fyrdhom   ðurhfōn ne mihte,
1505   locene leoðosyrcan,   lāþan fingrum.
Bær þā sēo brimwylf,   þā hēo tō botme cōm,
hringa þengel   tō hofe sīnum
swā hē ne mihte,   nō hē þæs mōdig wæs,
wǣpna geweldan,   ac hine wundra þæs fela
1510   swencte on sunde,   sǣdēor monig
hildetūxum   heresyrcan bræc ;
ēhton āglǣcan.   Ðā se eorl ongeat
þæt hē in nīðsele   nāthwylcum wæs
þǣr him nǣnig wæter   wihte ne scebede,
1515   ne him for hrōfsele   hrīnan ne mehte
fǣrgripe flōdes ;   fȳrlēoht geseah,
blācne lēoman   beorhte scīnan.
      Ongeat þā se gōda   grundwyrgenne,
merewīf mihtig ;   mægenrǣs forgeaf

1520   hildebille,   hond sweng ne oftēah,

bæt hire on hafelan   hringmǣl āgōl

grǣdig gūðlēoð.   Ðā se gist onfand

bæt se beadolēma   bītan nolde,

aldre scebðan,   ac sēo ecg geswāc

1525   ðēodne æt bearfe.   Ðolode ǣr fela

hondgemōta,   helm oft gescær,

fǣges fyrdhrægl ;   ðā wæs forma sīð

dēorum mādme   bæt his dōm ālæg.

1492   Weder-Ġēata=of the Storm-Geats. Weder-Geats는 Beowulf가 속해있던 족속인 Gēatas의 다른 이름으로서 이들은 지금의 Sweden 남쪽에 살고 있었다. lēod=leader, chief.

1493   efste=hurried. 원형은 efstan. elne=courage. 원형은 ellen. nalas=not at all. andsware= answer. 원형 andswaru의 단수 속격.

1494   bīdan=wait for. 속격과 함께 쓰인다. Brimwylm=water-surging. ofēng=received. 원형은 onfōn. 여격과 함께 쓰인다.

1495   hilderince=battle warrior. hwīl dæġes=a period of the day. most of the day에 대한 곡언법의 한 경우이다. dæġes는 dæġ(dag)의 단수 속격.

1496   ǣr=before. grundwong=bottom. onġytan=make out, perceive. mehte=could. 원형은 magan.

1497   Sōna=at once. onfunde=discovered. 원형은 onfindan. sē ðe=he who. 남성이면서 Grendel's mother를 가리킨다. flōda=waters. 복수 속격형이다. begong=region, expanse.

1498   heoroġīfre=fiercely ravenous. behēold=(had) guarded. 원형은 behealdan. hund missēra= for a hundred half-years=fifty years. 오랜 세월을 나타내기 위한 표현. hund=hundred. missēre=half-year.

1499   grim=fierce. grǣdiġ=greedy. gumena=guma(=man)의 복수 속격. sum=a certain, someone. 복수 속격과 함께 쓰인다.

1500   ælwihta=alien creatures'. eard=abode. ufan=from above. cunnode=was probing. 원형은 cunnian.

1501   Grāp bā tōġēanes=(She) grabbed then towards (him)=made a grab for him. Grāp (=grabbed)의 원형은 grīpan. tōġēanes=towards. 여격과 함께 쓰인다. gūðrinc=battle-warrior. ġefēng=seized.

1502   atolan clommum=with (her) terrible clutches. atolan=terrible. clommum=clomm(=clutch) 의 복수 여격.

1502-3   Nō bȳ ǣr in gescōd hālan līċe=None the sooner did she hurt the healthy body within. bȳ ǣr=the sooner. in=within. ġescōd(=hurt)의 원형은 ġescebban.

1503   hālan=whole, healthy. līċe=body. hring=ring-armour. ūtan=on the outside. ymbbearh=

protected. 원형은 ymbbeorgan.

1504 bæt=so that. hēo=she. fyrdhom=war-garment. ðurhfōn=pierce, get through.

1505 locene leoðosyrcan=locked limb-corselet=mail-coat of interlocked rings. locen=linked. leoðosyrcan=body-shirt of mail. lāþan fingrum=with (her) loathsome fingers. lāþan= hostile.

1506 Bær=carried. 원형은 beran. brimwylf=water-wolf of the lake. botme=bottom.

1507 hringa bengel=the prince of rings. Beowulf의 쇠사슬 갑옷(mail coat)에 대한 언급인 듯. hringa=of rings. bengel=prince. hofe=dwelling. sīnum=her.

1508 swā=in such a way that. nō hē bæs mōdiġ=no matter how brave he was. bæs=however. mōdiġ=brave.

1509 wǣpna=weapon. ġeweldan=wield. 속격과 함께 쓰인다. ac=but. wundra=weird creatures. 원형은 wundor. bæs fela=so many. 복수 속격과 함께 쓰인다.

1510 swencte=harassed, pressed hard. 원형은 swenċan. sunde=swimming, water. sǣdēor= sea-beast. moniġ=many a.

1511 hildetūxum=with battle-tusks. heresyrcan=battle-coat. 원형은 heresyrċe. bræc=tore. 원형은 brecan.

1512 ēhton=(they) pursued. 원형은 ēhtan. āglǣcan=awe inspiring one=monster. eorl=nobleman. onġeat=perceived. 원형은 onġietan.

1513 nīðsele=strife-hall, enemy-hall. nāthwylcum=some sort of.

1514 nǣniġ=no. wihte=at all. re. scebede=might inju원형은 scebban.

1515 ne=nor. for=because of. hrōfsele=roofed hall. hrīnan=touch. 여격과 함께 쓰인다.

1516 fǣrgripe=sudden grip, snatch. flōdes=current. fȳrlēoht=fire-light. ġeseah=(he) saw. 원형은 ġesēon.

1517 blācne=glittering, shining. lēoman=radiance, gleam. beorhte=brightly. scīnan=shine.

1518 Onġeat=perceived. 원형은 onġytan. gōda=brave man. grundwyrġenne=cursed creature of the deep.

1519 merewīf=sea-woman. mæġenrǣs=mighty assault, violent blow. forġeaf=gave. 원형은 forġiefan.

1520 hildebille=with battle-sword. hond=hand. sweng=stroke, swing. oftēah=held back. 원형은 oftēon.

1521 hafelan=on her head. hringmǣl=ring-sword. 여기서 ring은 칼에 새겨진 장식의 모양을 나타낸다. ring-marked sword의 뜻. āgōl=sang out. 원형은 āgālan.

1522 grǣdiġ=greedy. gūðlēoð=battle-song. ġist=visitor. onfand=found. 원형은 onfindan.

1523 beadolēma=the battle light=gleaming sword. 1520행의 hildebille의 다른 표현. bītan=bite. nolde=would not.

1524 aldre=(her) life. 원형은 aldor. sceþðan=damage, harm. ac=but. ecg=edge. ġeswāc=failed. 여격과 함께 쓰인다. 원형은 ġeswīcan.

1525 ðēodne=prince. 단수 여격형이다. 원형은 bēoden. bearfe=need. Ðolode=(it had) endured. 원형은 ðolian. ǣr=previously. fela=many.

1526 hondġemōta=hand-to-hand encounters. 복수 속격형. helm=helmet. ġescær=(had) cut through. 원형은 ġescieran.

1527 fæġes=(a) doomed one's. fyrdhrægl=war-garment. forma=first. sīð=occasion, time.

1528 dēorum mādme=for the precious treasure=the sword. dēore=precious. mādme=treasure. 원형은 māþm. his=its. dōm=fame. ālæġ=failed. 원형은 ālicgan.

After these words the leader of the Geats

dived bravely from the bank, did not even

wait for an answer ; the seething water

received the warrior. A full day elapsed

before he could discern the bottom of the lake.

She who had guarded its length and breadth

for fifty years, vindictive, fiercely ravenous for blood,

soon realized that one of the race of men

was looking down into the monsters' lair.

Then she grasped him, clutched the Geat

in her ghastly claws ; and yet she did not

so much as scratch his skin ; his coat of mail

protected him ; she could not penetrate

the linked metal rings with her loathsome fingers.

Then the sea-wolf dived to the bottom-most depths,

swept the prince to the place where she lived,

so that he, for all his courage, could not

wield a weapon ; too many wondrous creatures

harassed him as he swam ; many sea-serpents

with savage tusks tried to bore through his corslet,

the monsters molested him. Then the hero saw

that he had entered some loathsome hall

in which there was no water to impede him,

a vaulted chamber where the flood rush

could not touch him. A light caught his eye,

a lurid flame flickering brightly.

Then the brave man saw the sea-monster,
fearsome, infernal ; he whirled his blade,
swung his arm with all his strength,
and the ring-hilted sword sang a greedy war-song
on the monster's head. Then that guest realized
that his gleaming blade could not bite into her flesh,
break open her bone-chamber ; its edge failed Beowulf
when he needed it ; yet it had endured
many a combat, sheared often through the helmet,
split the corslet of a fated man ; for the first time
that precious sword failed to live up to its name.

Eft wæs ānrǣd,　　nalas elnes læt

1530　mǣrða gemyndig,　　mǣg Hȳlāces.

Wearp ðā wundenmǣl　　wrǣttum gebunden

yrre ōretta　　þæt hit on eorðan læg,

stīð ond stȳlecg.　　Strenge getruwode,

mundgripe mægenes.　　Swā sceal man dōn

1535　þonne hē æt gūðe　　gegān benceð

longsumne lof ;　　nā ymb his līf cearað.

Gefēng þā be eaxle,　　nalas for fǣhðe mearn

Gūð-Gēta lēod,　　Grendles mōdor.

Brægd þā beadwe heard,　　þā hē gebolgen wæs,

1540　feorhgenīðlan,　　þæt hēo on flet gebēah.

Hēo him eft hrabe　　andlēan forgeald

grimman grāpum　　ond him tōgēannes fēng.

Oferwearp þā wērigmōd　　wigena strengest,

fēþecempa,　　þæt hē on fylle wearð.

1545　Ofsæt þā þone selegyst　　ond hyre seax getēah,

brād ond brūnecg,　　wolde hire bearn wrecan,

āngan eaferan.　　Him on eaxle læg

brēostnet brōden ;　　þæt gebearh fēore,

wið ord ond wið ecge　　ingang forstōd.

1550　Hæfde ðā forsīðod　　sunu Ecgbēowes

under gynne grund,　　Gēata cempa,

nemne him heaðobyrne　　help gefremede,

herenet hearde,　　ond hālig God

gewēold wīgsigor.　　Wītig Drihten,

1555　rodera rǣdend,　　hit on ryht gescēd

ȳðelīce　　sybðan hē eft āstōd.

1529 Eft=again. ānrǣd=resolute, determined. nalas=not at all. elnes=courage. 원형은 ellen. læt=slack, slow. 속격과 함께 쓰임.

1530 mǣrða=glorious deeds. 원형은 mǣrþu. ġemyndiġ=mindful of. 속격과 함께 쓰임. mǣġ= kinsman.

1531 Wearp=threw. 원형은 wearpan. wundenmǣl=sword with twisted patterns. wrǣttum= with ornaments. ġebunden=adorned.

1532 yrre=angry. ōretta=warriors. bæt=so that. læġ=lay. 원형은 licgan.

1533 stīð=sturdy, strong. stȳlecg=steel-edged. Strenge=strength. 원형은 strenġu. ġetruwode= trusted in. 여격과 함께 쓰인다. 원형은 ġetruwian.

1533-4 Strenge⋯mundgripe mæġenes=in (his own) strength⋯in the hand-grip of his might=the power of his hand-grip and his prowess in hand-to-hand combat.

1534 mundgripe=hand-grip. mæġenes=might. dōn=do.

1535 bonne=when. gūðe=war. ġegān=to gain. benċeð=intends. 원형은 benċan.

1536 longsumne=longlasting. lof=fame. nā=not at all. ymb=about. cearað=cares. 원형은 cearian.

1537 Gefēng=seized. 원형은 ġefōn. eaxle=shoulder. nalas=not at all. fǣhðe=hostility, violent act. 원형은 fǣhðu. mearn=felt sorrow. 원형은 murnan.

1538 Gūð-Ġēta=Battle-Geats. 복수 속격형. lēod=chief. mōdor=mother.

1539 Bræġd=flung. 원형은 breġdan. beadwe heard=(the man) hardy (=bold) in battle. beadu=battle. bā=now that. ġebolgen=enraged. 원형은 ġebolgen.

1540 feorhġenīðlan=life-enemy, mortal foe. flet=floor. ġebēah=fell. 원형은 ġebūgan.

1541 Hēo=she. eft=next, again. hrabe=quickly. andlēan=requital. forġeald=paid back. 원형은 forġyldan.

1542 grimman grāpum=with her cruel clutches. grim=fierce, cruel. grāp=grasp. him tōġēannes fēng=grabbed towards him=made a grab for him. him tōġēannes=towards him. fēng의 원 형은 fōn.

1543 Oferwearp=(she) overthrew. 원형은 oferweorpan. wēriġmōd=dispirited, weary. wiġena= of warriors. 원형은 wiġa.

1544 fēbecempa=foot-soldier. fylle wearð=was (brought) to a fall, 또는 took a fall. fylle=fall. weorðan=become, be.

1545 Ofsæt=(she) sat on. 대격과 함께 쓰인다. 원형은 ofsittan. seleġyst=hall guest. seax= sword. ġetēah=drew. 여격과 함께 쓰인다. 원형은 ġetēon.

1546 brād=broad. brūnecg=with bright edge. bearn=son. wrecan=avenge.

1547 āngan=only. eaferan=son, offspring. Him=Beowulf. eaxle=shoulder. læġ=lay. 원형은 licgan.

1548 brēostnet=corslet. brōden=woven. 원형은 breġdan. ġebearh=protected. 여격과 함께 쓰인 다. 원형은 ġebeorgan. fēore=life. 원형은 feorh.

1549 wið=against, by. ord=point. ingang=entry. forstōd=prevented. 원형은 forstandan.

1550 Hæfde ðā forsīðod=He would then have perished. Hæfde는 habban의 가정법 과거형.

forsīðod=came to the end. 원형은 forsīðian. sunu Ecgbēowes=Ecgtheow's son.

1551 ġynne=broad. grund=earth. cempa=warrior, champion.

1552 nemne=unless, if…not. heaðobyrne=battle-corslet. ġefremede=afforded, furnished. 원형은 ġefremman.

1553 herenet=battle-mesh. hearde=hard. hāliġ=holy.

1554 ġewēold=controlled. 원형은 ġewealdan. wīġsigor=victory in war. Wītiġ=wise. Drihten= Lord.

1555 rodera=heavens'. 원형은 rodor. rǣdend=ruler. on ryht=according to right (justice), rightly. ġescēd=decided. 원형은 ġescēadan.

1556 ȳðelīċe=easily. syþðan=when. eft=again. āstōd=stood up. 원형은 āstandan.

Then, resolute, Hygelac's kinsman took his courage

in both hands, trusted in his own strength.

Angrily the warrior hurled Hrunting away,

the damascened sword with serpent patterns on its hilt ;

tempered and steel-edged, it lay useless on the earth.

Beowulf trusted in his own strength,

the might of his hand. So must any man

who hopes to gain long-lasting fame

in battle ; he must risk his life, regardless.

Then the prince of the Geats seized the shoulder

of Grendel's mother - he did not mourn their feud ;

when they grappled, that brave man in his fury

flung his mortal foe to the ground.

Quickly she came back at him, locked him

in clinches and clutched at him fearsomely.

Then the greatest of warriors stumbled and fell.

She dropped on her hall-guest, drew her dagger,

broad and gleaming ; she wanted to avenge her son,

her only offspring. The woven corslet

that covered his shoulders saved Beowulf's life,

denied access to both point and edge.

Then the leader of the Geats, Ecgtheow's son,

would have died far under the wide earth
had not his corslet, his mighty chain-mail,
guarded him, and had not holy god
granted him victory ; the wise Lord,
Ruler of the Heavens, settled the issue
easily after the hero had scrambled to his feet.

THE SLAYING OF GRENDEL'S MOTHER (3)

Gesēah ðā on searwum   sigeēadig bil,
ealdsweord eotenisc,   ecgum b̄yhtig,
wigena weorðmynd ;   þæt wæs w̄æpna cyst,
1560   būton hit wæs māre   ðonne ̄ænig mon ōðer
tō beadulāce   ætberan meahte,
gōd ond geatolīc,   gīganta geweorc.
Hē gefēng þā fetelhilt   freca Scyldinga,
hrēoh ond heorogrim   hringm̄æl gebrægd,
1565   aldres orwēna,   yrringa slōh
þæt hire wið halse   heard grāpode,
bānhringas bræc,   bil eal ðurhwōd
fægne fl̄æschoman.   Hēo on flet gecrong.
Sweord wæs swātig,   secg weorce gefeh.
1570   Līxte se lēoma,   lēoht inne stōd,
efne swā of hefene   hādre scīneð
rodores candel.   Hē æfter recede wlāt,
hwearf þā be wealle,   w̄æpen hafenade
heard be hiltum   Higelāces ðegn,
1575   yrre ond ānr̄æd.   Næs sēo ecg fracod
hilderince   ac hē hraþe wolde
Grendle forgyldan   gūðr̄æsa fela
ðāra þe hē geworhte   tō West-Denum
oftor micle   ðonne on ̄ænne sīð,
1580   þonne hē Hrōðgāres   heorðgenēatas
slōh on sweofote,   sl̄æpende fræt
folces Denigea   f̄yft̄yne men
ond ōðer swylc   ūt offerede,
lāðlicu lāc.   Hē him þæs lēan forgeald,

1585　rēpe cempa,　　tō ðæs be on ræste geseah

　　　gūðwērigne　　Grendel licgan

　　　aldorlēasne,　　swā him ǣr gescōd

　　　hild æt Heorote.　　Hrā wīde sprong

　　　sybðan hē æfter dēaðe　　drepe brōwade,

1590　heorosweng heardne,　　ond hine bā hēafde becearf.

1557　Ġesēah=saw. 원형은 ġesēon. searwum=among (other) arms. 이들은 동굴 속 벽에 걸려 있었을 것이다. siġeēadiġ=victory-blessed. bil=sword.

1558　ealdsweord=ancient sword. eotenisc=gigantic, forged by giants. ecgum bȳhtig=firm in its edges.

1559　wiġena weorðmynd=a mark of distinction for warriors. wiġena=wiġa(=warrior)의 복수 속격. weorðmynd=esteem. wǣpna=weapon. cyst=choicest, best.

1560　būton=except that. māre=bigger.

1561　beadulāce=battle-play. ætberan=carry. meahte=would be able.

1562　gōd=noble, strong. ġeatolīc=splendid. gīganta ġeweorc=the handiwork of giants. gīganta=giant.

1563　gefēng=grasped. 원형은 ġefōn. fetelhilt=ornamented (ringed) sword-hilt. freca=bold man, warrior.

1564　hrēoh=fierce. heorogrim=deadly grim, deadly earnest. hringmǣl=ring-patterned sword. ġebræġd=drew. 원형은 ġebreġdan.

1565　aldres=of life. 원형은 aldor. orwēna=without hope. yrringa=angrily. slōh=struck. 원형은 slēan.

1566　bæt hire wið halse heard grāpode=so that it caught her hard on her neck. hales= hals(=neck)의 단수 여격. heard=hard. grāpode=caught. 원형은 grāpian.

1567　bānhringas=bone-rings. bræc=broke. 원형은 brēcan. bil=sword. eal=fully, entirely. ðurhwōd=went through. 원형은 ðurhwadan.

1568　fǣġne=doomed. 원형은 fǣġe. flǣschoman=house of flesh=body. flet=floor. ġecrong=fell (dead). 원형은 ġecrincgan.

1569　swātiġ=bloody. secg=man. weorce=deed. ġefeh=rejoiced in. 원형은 ġefēon.

1570　Līxte se lēoma=ray of light. 1517행에서 언급했던 그 빛임. Līxte=shone. 원형은 līxan. lēoma=gleam. lēoht inne=light within. 밝은 불빛 안에 더 밝은 빛이 있다는 뜻. stōd= appeared. 원형은 standan.

1571　efne=just. swā=as. hefene=heaven. 원형은 heofon. hādre=brightly. scīneð=shines. 원형은 scīnan.

1572　rodores=sky's. candel=candle. æfter=about, around. reċede=hall. wlāt=gazed. 원형은 wlītan.

1573 hwearf=moved. turned. 원형은 hweorfan. be=along. wealle=wall. wǣpen=weapon. hafenade= raised. 원형은 hafenian.

1574 heard=fierce. 앞줄의 wǣpen을 수식한다. be hiltum=by the hilt. ðeġn=thane.

1575 yrre=angry. ānrǣd=single-minded. fracod=useless.

1576 hilderince=warrior. ac=but. hraþe=quickly.

1577 forġyldan=pay back.

1577-8 gūðrǣsa fela ðāra be=for the many assaults which…. gūðrǣsa=attacks, assaults. fela= many. 동사의 목적어.

1578 ġeworhte=made, carried out. 원형은 ġewyrċan. tō=on. West-Denum=West-Dene(=Danes)의 복수 여격.

1579 oftor=more often. micle=much. ǣnne=one. sīð=occasion.

1580 heorðġenēatas=hearth-companions.

1581 slōh=killed. 원형은 slēan. sweofote=sleep. slǣpende=slǣpan(=to sleep)의 현재분사. frǣt= ate, devoured. 원형은 fretan.

1582 folces=people. fȳftȳne=fifteen.

1583 ōðer swylċ=other such=as many again=thirty altogether. ūt=out. offerede=carried out. 원형은 offerian.

1584 lāðlicu=loathsome, horrible. 원형은 lāðliċ. lāc=booty, plunder. Hē=다음 줄의 rēpe cempa, 즉 Beowulf. him þæs=for that. lēan=reward. forġeald=paid. 원형은 forġyldan.

1585 rēpe=fierce. cempa=warrior. tō ðæs þe=to that extent that, 또는 to such effect that. ræste=resting-place. ġeseah=saw. 원형은 ġesēon.

1586 gūðwēriġne=battle-weary, worn out from the fight. licgan=lay.

1587 aldorlēasne=lifeless. swā=so (much). ǣr=previously. ġescōd=(had) harmed, injured. 여격 과 함께 쓰인다. 원형은 ġescebðan.

1588 hild=fight. Hrā=corpse. wīde=widely. sprong=burst open, gaped. 원형은 springan.

1589 sybðan=when. hē=it. drepe=blow. brōwade=suffered. 원형은 brōwian.

1590 heorosweng=sword-stroke. hine þā hēafde beċearf=then deprived him of his head=he (Beowulf) cut off his head. hēafde=head. 원형은 hēafod. beċearf=cut off. 원형은 beċeorfan.

    Then Beowulf saw among weapons an invincible sword
wrought by the giants, massive and double-edged,
the joy of many warriors ; that sword was matchless,
well-tempered and adorned, forged in a finer age,
only it was so huge that no man but Beowulf
could hope to handle it in the quick of combat.
Ferocious in battle, the defender of the Scyldings

grasped the ringed hilt, swung the ornamented sword
despairing of his life – he struck such a savage blow
that the sharp blade slashed through her neck,
smashed the vertebrae ; it severed her head
from the fated body ; she fell at his feet.
The sword was bloodstained ; Beowulf rejoiced.

    A light gleamed ; the chamber was illuminated
as if the sky's bright candle were shining
from heaven. Hygelac's thane inspected
the vaulted room, then walked round the walls,
fierce and resolute, holding the weapon firmly
by the hilt. The sword was not too large
for the hero's grasp, but he was eager to avenge
at once all Grendel's atrocities,
all the many visits the monster had inflicted
on the West-Danes — which began with the time
he slew Hrothgar's sleeping hearth-companions,
devoured fifteen of the Danish warriors
even as they slept, and carried off as many more,
a monstrous prize. But the resolute warrior
had already repaid him to such a degree
that he now saw Grendel lying on his death-bed,
his life's-blood drained because of the wound
he sustained in battle at Heorot. Then Grendel's corpse,
received a savage blow at the hero's hands,
his body burst open : Beowulf lopped off his head.

(tr. Crossley-Holland)

참고문헌

김석산 (역). 1976. 『베오울프 外』. 서울 : 探究堂.

박영배. 1997. 『고대영어문법』. 서울 : 한국문화사.

Alexander, M. 1973. *Beowulf : A Verse Translation*. Penguin Books.

Alexander, M. 1995. *Beowulf*. Penguin Books.

Baker, P. S. 2003. *Introduction to Old English*. Blackwell Publishers.

Bolton, W. F. 1963. *An Old English Anthology*. London : Edward Arnold Publishers.

Bosworth, J., T. N. Toller, and A. Campbell. 1898, 1921. *An Anglo-Saxon Dictionary*. 2 vols. London : Oxford University Press.

Bradley, S. A. J. 1982. *Anglo-Saxon Poetry*. David Campbell Publishers.

Brook, G. L. 1964. *An Introduction to Old English*. Manchester : Manchester University Press. (문안나 역 『고대영어입문』 서울: 한국문화사)

Clark Hall, J. R. and H. D. Meritt. 1960. *A Concise Anglo-Saxon Dictionary*. Toronto : University of Toronto Press.

Crossley-Holland K. 1999. *The Anglo-Saxon World : An Anthology*. Oxford : University Press.

Diamond, R. E. 1970. *Old English : Grammar and Reader*. Detroit : Wayne State University Press.

Gordon, R. K. 1954. *Anglo-Saxon Poetry*. J. M. Dent & Sons.

Hamer, R. 1970. *A Choice of Anglo-Saxon Verse*. London : Faber and Faber.

Klaeber, F. 1950. *Beowulf and The Fight at Finnsburg*. Lexington, Massachusetts : Heath.

Marsden, R. 2004. *The Cambridge Old English Reader*. Cambridge : University Press.

Mitchell, B. 1995. *An Invitation to Old English and Anglo-Saxon England*. Oxford : Blackwell.

Mitchell, B. and F. C. Robinson. 2001^6. *A Guide to Old English*. Oxford : Blackwell.

Moore, S. and Knott, T. A. 1955. *The Elements of Old English.* Ann Arbor, Michigan : George Wahr.

Quirk, R. and C. L. Wrenn. 1958². *An Old English Grammar.* London : Methuen.

Rigg, A. G. 1968. *The English Language : A Historical Reader.* New York : Appleton-Century-Crofts.

Swanton, M. 1970. *The Dream of the Rood.* Manchester : Manchester University Press.

Swanton, M. 1975. *Anglo-Saxon Prose.* Totowa, N. J. Rowman and Littlefield.

Sweet, H. 1896. *The Student's Dictionary of Anglo-Saxon.* Oxford : Clarendon Press.

Sweet, H. 1953⁹. *Sweet's Anglo-Saxon Primer.* Revised by Norman Davis. Oxford : Clarendon Press.

Sweet, H. 1959¹⁴. *Sweet's Anglo-Saxon Reader in Prose and Verse.* Revised by C. T Onions. Oxford : Clarendon Press.

Treharne, E. 2004. *Old and Middle English c.890-c.1400 : An Anthology.* Oxford : Blackwell.

Wright, J. and E. M. Wright. 1923. *An Elementary Old English Grammar.* Oxford : Clarendon Press.

Old English

일러두기

고대영어는 모두 굵은 활자체로 표시하였다.

æ는 a 다음에 제시하였다.

þ/ð는 t 다음에 제시하였다.

접두사 ġe는 표제어 순서에서 무시되었다. 예를 들어 ġehelpan는 h항에 표시된다.

학습의 편의를 위하여 표제어로는 단어의 원형뿐만 아니라 흔히 쓰이는 굴절형도 제시하였다.

앞으로의 학습 편의를 위하여 본문의 단어 외에도 흔히 사용되는 단어도 모두 망라하였다.

변이형이 있는 경우에는 설명의 마지막에 제시하였다.

약자

adj	형용사 (adjective)
adv	부사 (adverb)
anom	(동사의) 불규칙형 (anomalous (verb))
comp	(형용사나 부사의) 비교급 (comparative (adjective or adverb))
conj	접속사 (conjunction)
dem	지시사 (demonstrative)
impers	비인칭 (동사) (impersonal (verb))
indecl	불변화형 (indeclinable)
indef art	부정관사 (indefinite article)
indef pron	부정대명사 (indefinite pronoun)
inf	부정사 (infinitive)
infl inf	굴절부정사 (inflected infinitive)
in phr	구에서 (in phrase(s))
instr	조격의 (instrumental)
interj	감탄사 (interjection)
interrog pron	의문대명사 (interrogative pronoun)
neg	부정어 (negative)

num	수사 (numeral)	
num adj	수 형용사 (numerical adjective)	
pers pron	인칭대명사 (personal pronoun)	
poss pron	소유대명사 (possessive pronoun)	
prep	전치사 (preposition)	
pron	대명사 (pronoun)	
pr n	고유명사 (proper noun)	
pt-pr	과거형 현재(동사) (preterite-present (verb))	
rflx	재귀(동사/대명사) (reflexive (verb or pronoun))	
sbj	가정법 (subjunctive)	
sup	(형용사나 부사의) 최상급 (superlative (adjective or adverb))	
<	굴절형	
see	변이형	

명사와 형용사

격 :   *n* 주격 (nominative)

        a 대격 (accusative)

        g 속격 (genitive)

        d 여격 (dative)

        i 도구격 (instrumental)

수 :   *s* 단수 (singular)

        p 복수 (plural)

성 :   *m* 남성 (masculine)

        n 중성 (neuter)

        f 여성 (feminine)

이들의 순서는 case-number-gender이다.

      예 : *gp*=genitive plural

          nsn=(adjective) in the nominative singular neuter

동사

변화형 :   *1~3*   약변화 동사

           I~VII   강변화 동사

           anom   불규칙동사 (anomalous)

           redp   반복동사 (reduplicating verb)

시제 :   *pr*   현재 (present)

	pt	과거 (preterite)
인칭 :	*1*	1인칭
	2	2인칭
	3	3인칭
수 :	*s*	단수 (singular)
	pl	복수 (plural)
법 :	*sbj*	가정법 (subjunctive)
	imp	명령법 (imperative)
분사 :	prp	현재분사 (present participle)
	pp	과거분사 (past participle)
	infl inf	굴절분사 (inflected infinitive)
문법상 :	*redp*	반복동사 (reduplicative)
	예 : *pr3s*	3인칭단수현재 (present tense, third-person singular)
	sbj pt1p	가정법1인칭복수과거 (subjunctive preterite first-person plural)
	imp s	단수 명령법 (imperative singular)

격지배 :	(+*a*)	대격지배 (with accusative)
	(+*g*)	속격지배 (with genitive)
	(+*d*)	여격지배 (with dative)
	(+*i*)	도구격지배 (with instrumental)
	(+*a/d*)	대격/여격지배 (with accusative or dative)

=*noun* 명사로 사용
=*adv* 부사로 사용

ā *adv* always, continuously, eternally, for ever

ābād < ābīdan

abbod *m* abbot abbodæ *ds*

Abēl *pr n* Abel Abēles *gs*

ābelġan *III* enrage ābolġen *pp*

ābēodan *II* declare, report ābēad *pt3s*, ābēod *imp*

āberan *IV* bear, carry ābær *pt3s*

ābīdan (+g) await, remain, suffer ābād *pt3s* ābīdon *pt3p*

ābiddan *V* pray, ask, obtain by asking ābædon *pt3p*

ābītan *I* bite, devour ābīte *sbj pr3s*

Abrahām *pr n* Abraham Abrahāmes *gs* Abrahāme *ds*

ābrǣce < ābrecan

ābrecan *IV* break, destroy, sack, violate ābrǣce *sbj pr3s* ābrece *sbj pr3s* ābrocen *pp*

ābrocen < ābrecen

ābūgan *II* bend, swerve, turn, submit

ābūtan *prep* (+a) around, about

ac *conj* but, nevertheless, however, and yet, moreover, because

ācennan *1* conceive, bring forth, give birth to ācenned *pp* ācende *pt3s* ācenned *pp*

āctrēo *n* oak tree

ācuman *IV* support

ācwæð < ācweðan

ācwellan *1* kill ācwealde *pt3s* ācwellanne *infl inf*

ācwenċan *1* quench, extinguish

ācweðan *V* speak, utter, declare ācwæð *pt3s* ācwið *pr3s*

ācȳban *1* make known, reveal acȳbeð *pr3s*

ād *m* funeral pyre, fire āde *ds*

Ādam *pr n* Adam Ādame *ds* Ādomes *gs*

ādīleġian *2* destroy ādȳlegod *pp*

ādl *f* sickness, disease ādle *as*

ādliġ *adj* ill, sick ādliġe *npm*

ādrēogan *II* practice, commit, carry on, endure ādrēogað *pr3p*

ādrīfan *I* drive away ādrifan *pt3p*

ādrūġian *2* dry up

ādȳdan *1* destroy ādȳdon *inf*

āfandian *2* find out, test, prove

afaran < eafera

āfaran *VI* travel, pass āfaren *pp*

āfeallan *VII* fall away, decay āfeallen *pp*

āfēdan *1* feed

āfeorsian *2* remove

afierran *1* depart

āfindan *III* find, discover

āflīeman *1* put to flight, drive into exile āflȳman

āflīgan *1* drive away

āflīman *1* put to flight, drive away āflīmed *pp*

āflȳman *see* āflīeman

after *see* æfter

āfȳlan *1* defile

āfyllan *1* strike down, slay ; fill āfylle *sbj pr3s*

āfyrhtan *1* frighten, terrify āfyrhte *pp npm*

āfȳsan *1* drive āfȳsed *pp*

āgālan *VI* sing āgōl *pt3s*

āgān *anom* go away āgāne *pp*

āgan *pt-pr* have, possess, owen, rule, control āgen *pr1s, pr3s* āhte *pt1s* nāge *sbj pr3s* nāh *pr1s* nāhte *pt1s*

āġeaf, āġeafon, āġefēð < āġiefan

āġēan *adv* again

āġēat < āġēotan

āgen *adj* own *nsm, dsn* āgene *asm, apm* āgenes *gsm* āgenne *asm* āgenre *dsf* āgenum *dsm, dsn, dpm*

āġēnlǣdan *1* lead back āgenlǣde *pr1s*

āġēotan *II* drain, empty, void, destroy āġēat *pt3s* āġēted *pp* āgotene *pp npm*

āġiefan *V* (+d) give, give up, render, deliver give back āġeaf *pt1s, pt3s* āġeafon *pt3p* āġefēð *pr3s* āġifan *inf* āġife *sbj pr3s* āġifen *pp* āġyfe *sbj pr1s* āġyfen *pp*

āġieldan *III* pay, yield ; pay for, atone for

āginnan *3* begin, proceed āgunnan *pt3p*

āglǣca *m* awe-inspiring one āglǣcan *np*

Agustinus *pr n* Auguistine *gs*

āġyf < āġiefan

āh < āgan

āhafen < āhebban

āhēawan *VII* cut away, hew āhēawen *pp*

āhebban *VI* raise, lift up, exalt, lift down, remove āhafen *pp* āhæfen *pp* āhebbað *pr3p* āhōf *pt1s, pt3s* āhōfon *pt3p*

āhebbian *II* ebb away āhebbad *pp*

āhefde < āhebban

āhieldan *1* incline, bend

āhōf, āhōfon < āhebban

āhōn *VII* hang, crucify āhengon *pt3p* āhongen *pp* āhōnne *infl inf*

āhrēosan *II* fall āhruron *pt3p*

āhte < āgan

āhte, āhtes < āwiht

āhwār *adv* anywhere

āhȳrian *2* hire

ālǣdan *1* bring, lead, carry off ālǣd *pp* ālǣde *sbj pr3s*

ālæġ < ālicgan

aldor *n* life, age, eternity aldre *ds* aldres *gs* ealdor *ns* ealdre *ds* āwa tō aldre for ever and ever on aldre ever, forever tō aldre to eternity, ever tō wīdan aldre for ever

aldor *see* ealdor

aldorlēas *see* ealdorlēas *adj* without a lord, lifeless, orphaned

ālecgan *1* lay down, put down ālēde *pt3s* ālēdon *pt3p*

ālēd, ālēdon < ālecgan

ālēogan *II* leave unfulfilled ālēoganne *infl inf* ālēoge *sbj pr3s*

ālicgan *V* fail, cease, lie down ālæġ *pt3s*

āliefan *1* allow, grant

āliehtan *1* light, illuminate

ālīesan *1* release, liberate, redeem ālīes *imp s*

ālīesend *m* redeemer

alle < eall

ālȳfan *1* grant, allow ālȳfed *pp*

ālȳsan *1* release, deliver *inf* ālȳse *sbj pr3s*

āmen *interj* amen (Lt < Hebrew *certainly*)

āmierran *1* destroy

āmyrran *1* (+g) disable, hinder, obstruct āmyrde *pt3s* āmyrred *pp*

ān *adj/indef art* one, a, singe, alone, only *nsm* āna *nsm* ānæs *gsm* āne *asf* ānnæ *adj asm* ānne *asm* ānræ *adj gsf* ānre *gsf* ānum *dsm, dpm* ǣnne *asm*

ān *pron/num* one, the one, a, an *nsm* āne *asf* ānne *asm* ānra *gpm* ānum *dsm*

āncenned *adj* only begotten *asm* āncennedan *dsm*

and *conj* and ond

anda *m* malice, envy, grudge, terror andan *as, ds*

andbīdian *2* await

andettan *1* confess

andġit *n* meaning, understanding, sense, knowledge, perception *ns* andġiete *ds* andġite *ds* andġyt *ns* andġyte *ds*

andġitfullīċe *adv* intelligibly, clearly andġitfullīcost *sup*

andġyt, andġyte *see* andġit

andlēan *n* reward, requital

andleofen *f* money, food andlifne *as* andlyfne *as*

andlīcness *f* likeness, resemblance

andswarian *1* answer, respond andswarode *pt3s* ondswarade *pt3s* ondswarede *pt3s* ondswaredon *pt3p* ondswarode *pt1s, pt3s* ondswarodon *pt3p*

andswaru *f* answer, reply andsware *as, gs* ondsware *as*

andweard *adj* present, actual andweardan *gsn* andwearde *asn, npm* andwerdan *gsn*

andwerde < andwyrdan

andwlita *m* form, face andwlitan *as, ds* anwlitan *as*

ġeandwyrdan *1* answer (+d) andwerde *pt3s* andwyrde *pt1s, pt3s* ġeondwyrdon pt3p

āne *adv* at once, at one time

anfēng < onfōn

anforht *adj* very afraid, terrified

ānga *adj* sole āngan *asm*

angel *m* fishhook

Angelcynn *pr n* the English people, England Angelcyn *as* Angelcynn *as* Angelcynne

anġinn *n* beginning, introduction, undertaking *ns* andġinne *ds* anġin *ns, as* anġinne *ds* anġyn *ns*

Angle *m pl* the English people

anġyn *see* anġinn

ānhaga *m* solitary one, loner *ns* ānhogan *asm*

ānhȳdiġ *adj* strong-minded, resolute *nsm*

āniman *IV* take away

ġeānlǣċan *1* unite, join together

ānlēpe *adj* single, solitary, private ānlēpne *asm* ānlīpie *npn*

anlīċ *adj* like

ānlīcnis *f* likeness, portrait, statue, image ānlīcnisse *ds, ac* ānlīcnissum *dp* onlīcnisse *ds*

ānlīpie *see* ānlēpe

ānmōd *adj* wholehearted, unanimous, resolute ānmōdre *dsf* onmōde *npm*

ānmōdlīċe *adv* unanimously

ānnæ, ānne < ān

ānrǣd *adj* single-minded, resolute, constant, agreed *nsm* ānrǣde *npm*

ānrǣdness *f* resolution, constancy, single-mindedness

ānre < ān

ansīen *f* face, countenance, form onsȳn *ns*

ansunde *adj* sound, intact *npf*

Antecrīst *pr n* Antichrist Antecrīstes *gs*

anweald *n* authority, rule, power

ānwealda *m* ruler, lord *ns*

anwlitan < andwlita

ġeanwyrde *adj* professed, known

Apollines *pr n* Apollo

Apollonius *pr n* Apollonius *ns* Apolloni (Lt vocative) Apollonium *as* Apolloniġe *ds* Apollonio *ds*

apostol *m* apostle *ns* apostola *gp* apostolas *np, ap*

apostoliċ *adj* apostolic apostoliċe *ns, as* apostolican *gs*

ār *f* oar āra *gp*

ār *m* a messenger *ns*

ār *f* grace, mercy, favor, benefit, pity, respect, estate *ns* āra *gp* āre *as, gs* ārum *dp*

ārās < ārīsan

ārǣdan *1* appoint, decree, determine, read *inf* ārǣd *pp* ārǣded *pp*

ārǣfnan *1* endure, carry out

ārǣran *1* raise up, erect, establish *inf* ārǣrde *pt3s, pp npm* ārǣrdon *pt3p* ārǣred *pp* ārǣredan *pp npm*

arc *m* ark arce *ds* arces *gs*

arċebiscop *m* archbishop *ns* arċebisceop *ns* arċebiscope *ds* arċebisopes *gs* ærċebiscepe *ds*

āreahte *see* āreċċan

āreċċan *1* relate, tell, render, translate āreċċcean *inf* āreċe *imp s* ārehte *pt3s*

āredian *2* prepare, find

ārēodian *2* redden, blush

ārfæsta *adj* merciful, kind, gracious

ārhwæt *adj* eager for glory ārhwate *npm*

ārian *2* (+d) honor ; spare, have mercy on

ārīsan *I* arise, spring up, originate, come to pass *inf* ārās *pt1s, pt3s* ārāsað *pr3p* ārīse *pr1s, pr3s* ārisen *pp* ārison *pt1p, pt3p* ārīst *pr3s* āryson *pt3p*

ārlēas *adj* impious, wicked ārlēasan *dsf*

arodlīċe *adv* quickly, readily, boldly

ārsmib *m* coppersmith

ārum *adv* honourably

ārweorb *adj* venerable

ārwurðe *adj* honorable *nsm* ārwurðost *sup nsm*

ārȳson < ārīsan

āsǣd, āsǣde < āsecgan

asca < æsc

āscēofan *II* push away, drive out āscūfan

āscian *1* ask, inquire āhsast *pr2s* āhsian *inf* āhsode *pt1s* āscade *pt3s* āxie *pr1s* āxode *pt3s* āxsa *imp s* āxsast *pr2s*

ġeāscian *2* learn (by asking), discover ġeāscodan *pt1p* ġeāscode *pt3s*

āscūfan *II* thrust

āsecgan *3* say, tell, express *inf* āsǣd *pp* āsǣde *pt3s*

āsendan *1* send forth āsende *pt3s*

āsettan *1* set down, place, put āsette *pt3s* āsetton *pt3p*

āsittan *V* run aground (of ship) āsǣton *pt3p* āseten *pp*

āsmēaġan *2* consider, think of, conceive, interpret

āspringan *III* spring forth

āspryttan *I* sprout, bring forth āspryt *pr3s*

assa *m* ass

āstāg, āstāh < āstīgan

āstandan *VI* stand up āstōd *pt3s*

āstīgan *I* ascend, mount, descend āstāg *pt3s* āstāh *pt1s* āstīge *sbj pr3s* āstīgende *prp nsm*

āstirian *1* stir, excite, move, remove *inf* āstyred *pp*

āstreahte *see* āstreċċan

āstreċċan *1* stretch ; prostrate oneself ; stretch out āstreċe *imp s* āstrehte *pt3s* āstreaht *pp*

āstyred < āstirian

āstyrian *see* āstirian

āswebban *1* put to sleep, put to death āswefede *pp npm*

āswefede < āswebban

ātēon *II* draw off, remove ātēah *pt3s* ātuge *sbj pt3s*

atol *adj* terrible, dire, monstrous *nsn, asn* atolan *asm, dpm* atolne *asm*

ātuge < ātēon

āð *m* oath *ns, as* aða *ds* aðe *ds*

āðbryċe *m* oath-breaking āðbrycas *ap*

āðum *m* son-in-law

ābumswēoras *m(pl)* son-in-law and father-in-laws ābumswēoran *dp*

āwa *adv* ever, always āwa tō aldre for ever and ever

āwearp < āweorpan

āweċċan *1* awake, awaken *inf* āwecb *pr3s* āwehte *pt3s* āwehton *pt3p*

āwēdan *1* go mad

āwendan *1* change, vary, translate *inf* āwend *pp* āwende *pt1s, pp npm* āwent *pr3s*

āweorpan *III* throw (away), cast down, reject āwearp *pt3s* āweorpe *imp s* āworpene *pp npm* āwurpan *inf*

āwestan *1* lay waste, ravage

āwierġan *1* curse, damn āwyrġed *pp*

āwiht *indef pron* aught, anything, nothing āhtes *gs* āwuht *as* (=adv at all) ōwiht *ns, as* ; *in phr* tō āhte at all, in any way

āworpene < āweorpan

āwrītan *I* write, write down, copy *inf* āwrāt *pt3s* āwriten *pp* āwritene *pp npf* āwritenne *pp asm* āwriton *pt3p* āwrytan *pp*

āwðer *adv* either āwðer oððe···oððe *either···or*

āwurpan < āweorpan

āwurtwalian *2* root up

āwyrdan *1* maim, destroy, damage, impair āwyrded *pp*

āwyrġed < āwierġan

āwyrtwalian *2* root up

ǣ *f* law, scripture *ns*

æcer *m* acre, field *as*

ǣdre *adv* early, swiftly, at once, forthwith

ǣfen *n* evening, vespers *as* ǣfenne *ds*

ǣfenglōmung *f* twilight

ġeæfenlǣcan *1* imitate

ǣfentīd *f* evening, evening-time ǣfentīde *as*

æfestfull *adj* envious

æfestian *2* be envious

æfestiġ *adj* envious

æfnan *1* make ready ġeæfned *pp*

ǣfre *adv* always, ever

æftan *adv* from behind, in the back

æfter *adv* after, afterwards, then, back

æfter *prep* (+a/d/i) after, following, according to, by means of, about, along æfter bām be after, according as æfter bon be after, when

ǣġ *n* egg ǣiġera *ns*

ǣġhwǣr *adv* everywhere, completely

ǣġhwylċ *adj* each, every *nsf* ǣġhwelċ *nsm* ǣġhwylċan *dsm*

ǣġhwylċ *pron* each, each one *nsm* ǣġhwylċne *asm* ǣġhwylċum *dsm*

ǣġ̌þer *adj* either, each ǣġðrum *dsm, dsn*

ǣġþer *conj* both ǣġðer, ǣġþer ġe···ġe both··· and ǣiġþer···ġe

ǣġþer *pron* each, either, both *nsm*

ǣht *f* property, possessions, ownership *as* ǣhta *as* ǣhtan *ap*

ǣiġra < ǣġ

ǣl *m* eel

ǣlċ *adj* each, every, any *nsm, asn* ǣlċæ *dsn* ǣlċe *asm, dsm* ǣlċes *gsm, gsn* ǣlchum *dsm* ǣlċne *asm* ǣlċra *gps* ǣlċcum *dsm, dsn*

ǣlċ *pron* each, everyone *nsm* ǣlċes gsm ǣlċre *asf*

ælde *mp* men, human beings ælda *gp* ældum *dp*

ǣlepūte *f* eel-pout

ælmesġeorn *adj* charitable

ælmesriht *n* right to alms

ǣlmesse *f* almsgiving, charity

ælmihtiġ *adj* almighty *nsm* ælmehtigan *gsm* ælmihtiga *nsm* ælmihtigan *dsm(=noun)* ælmigtiġne *asm* ælmihtigum *dsm*

ælne < eall

ælwiht *f* alien creature ælwihta *gp*

ġeǣmetiġan *2* empty, free, disengage ġeǣmetiġe *sbj pr2s*

ǣmtiġ *adj* empty *nsf*

ænde *see* ende

ǣniġ *adj* any *nsm, asn* ǣneġum *dsm, dpn* ǣġnes *gsm* ǣnġum *dsm* ǣniġ *asn* ǣniġe *asf* ǣniġne *asm* ǣniġre *dsf* ǣniġum *dsm* enġu *nsf*

ǣniġ *pron* any, anyone *nsm*

ǣnliċ *adj* unique, beautiful

ænne < ān

æppel *m* apple æppla *np*

æppelbǣre *adj* fruit-bearing

ǣr *adv* before, previously, formerly, already, early, soon *nō* bȳ ǣr none the sooner on ǣr beforehand

ǣr *conj* before, until ǣr ðǣm be, ǣr ðǣm ðe, ǣr ban, ǣr ban be, ǣrðon be before

ǣr *prep* (+d) before, until

ǣr *n* bronze, copper

ǣr *m* sea, wave ǣra *gp*

ǣrǣran *1* raise, build, build up,

ǣrċebiscepe < arċebiscop

ǣrdæġ *m* first dawn

ǣrende *n* message *as* ǣrænde *as*

ǣrendġewrit *n* letter *as*

ǣrendraca *m* messenger, minister ǣrenddracan *ap* ǣrendwrecum *dp*

ǣrest *adj* first ǣreste *nsf* æt ǣrestan *dsn* first of all

ǣrġewin *n* former struggle *as*

ǣrist *m/f/n* resurrection

ǣrnemerġen *m* early morning, day-break ǣrnemeriġen *ds*

ǣrost < ǣrest

ǣrur *adv* (comp of ǣr) earlier

ǣrwacol *adj* awake early

ǣs *n* carrion, food ǣses *gs*

æsc *m* ash(-spear), (ash-tree) warship *as* asca *gp*

æschere *m* army in ships

æstel *m* book-marker

ǣswic *m* offence, transgression ǣswicas *ap*

æt *prep* (+d) at, in, from, to, next to, with, by

ætberan *IV* bear away, carry

ætberstan *III* escape ætbærst *pt3s* ætberste *sbj pr3s*

ætbreġdan *III* take away

ætēowan *1* appear, show, reveal ætēowde *pt3s* ætēowdon *pt3p* ætēowed *pp* ætēowiað *pr3p* ætēowod *pp* ætȳwan *inf*

ætēowian *2* show, appear

ætforan *prep* (+d) before, in front of

ætgædere *adv* together, at the same time, united ætgædre

ætīewan *1* (+d) show

ætsomne *adv* together, united, at the same time ætsamne

ætspringan *III* spurt out ætspranc *pt3s*

ǣtterne *adj* poisonous, deadly ǣttern *nsm* ǣttrynne *asm*

ætwesan *V* be present

ætwindan *III* escape

ætwītan *1* censure, reproach, blame, impute ætwīten *pp* ætwīton *pt3p*

ætȳwan *see* ætēowan

æðelborennes *f* nobility

æaelboren *adj* nobly born, of noble birth

æbele *adj* noble *nsm, nsf* (=noun) æbelan *asm* æbelon *dsm*

ġeæbele *adj* inborn, natural

æbeling *m* atheling, prince, nobleman, lord *ns, as* æbelinga *gp* æbelingæ *ds* æbelinge *ds* æbelinges *gs*

æðellīċe *adv* excellently

ǣwbryċe *m* adultery ǣwbrycas *ap*

ǣwiscmōd *adj* ashamed, humiliated ǣwiscōd *npm*

baldlīċe *adv* boldly, rashly baldlīċe *sup*

bān *n* bone

bana *m* slayer, murderer banan *gs, ds* bonan *ds*

band < bindan

bānfæt *n* 'bone-vessels' body bānfatu *ap*

bānhring *m* 'bone-ring' vertebra bānhringas *ap*

ġebannan *VII* summon, command, proclaim

bār *m* boar

bāt *m* boat

babian *2* bathe *inf*

babu < bæb

bǣagas < bēag

bæc *n* back *as* ofer bæc backwards

bæcere *m* baker bæceras *np* ġebæd, ġebæd- *see*
ġebiddan

bǣl *n* fire, flame, funeral-pyre bǣle *ds*

bær, bǣr- *see* beran

bærnan *1* burn *inf* bærnað *pr.3p* bærndon *pt3p*

bærnett *n* burning, arson bærnette *ds*

ġebǣro *f* demeanor, behavior ġebǣrum *dp*

bǣron < beran

bæb *n* bath babu *np*

be *prep* (+d/i) about, according to, by, concerning,
with, along, near, beside, by, by means of,
through bæ, bī, be···twēonum between

bēacen *n* beacon, sign, portent *ns, as* bēacna *gp*
bēacne *ds*

ġebēad < ġebeodan

beadolēma *m* 'battle light' gleaming sword

beadorinc *m* warrior beadorinca *gp*

beadoweorc *n* warlike deed beadoweorca *gp*

beadu *f* battle, conflict, fighting beadowe *ds*
beaduwe *ds* beadwe *gs*

beadulāc *n* battle-play, battle beadulāce *ds*

bēag *m* ring, bracelet, treasure, valuables bǣgas
ap bēages *gs* bēagum *dp*

bealg < belgan

bearu *m* grove *ns* bearwe *ds* bearwas *np*
bearwum *dp*

bēag *m* ring, bracelet, treasure, valuables bǣagas
ap bēages *gs* beagum *dp*

bēahġifa *m* ring-giver, lord *ns* beaggyfan *gs*
bēahġifan

bēahġifu *f* ring-giving bēahġife *ds*

beald *adj* bold bealde *npm*

bealuware *mp* dweller in iniquity, evil men
bealuwara *gp*

bēam *m* tree, cross *ns* bēama *gp* bēame *ds*

bēancodd *m* bean-pod

bearm *m* bosom, lap, protection bearme *ds*

bearn *n* child, son, descendant *ns, as, np, ap*
bearna *gp* bearne *ds* bearnum *dp*

bearo *m* grove, wood *as* bearowe *ds* bearwas
np bearwe *ds* bearwum *dp*

bēatan *VII* beat, pound bēotan *pt3p* bēotun
pt3p

bebēad < bebēodan

bebēodan *I* command, bit, enjoin, commend,
assign (+d) bebēad *pt3s* bebēod *imp s*
bebēodende *prp nsm* bebīode *pr1s* beboden
pp bebudon *pt3p* bibēad *pt3s*

bebēolan *3* (+d) apply oneself

bebiriġed < bebyrġian

bebod *n* command, decree *as*

beboden, bebudon < bebēodan

bebyrġan *1* bury bebyrġed *pp*

bebyrġian *1* bury, inter bebiriġed *pp*

bēċ < bōc

bēċe *f* beech

beċeofan *III* deprive by cutting off beċearf *pt3s*

beclyppan *1* embrace

becōm, becōm- < becuman

becuman *IV* come, arrive, reach, meet with,
happen, overcome *inf* becōm *pt3s* becōman
pt3p becōmon *pt3p* becume *sbj pr3s* becumon
pt3p becwōm *pt3s*

bed < bedd

ġebed *n* prayer ġebedu *as*

bēdan *1* compel, constrain ġebēded *pp*

bedǣlan *1* deprive (+d) bedǣlden *pp npm* bidǣled
pp

bedd *n* bed, resting place bed *as* bedde *ds*
beddes *gs*

ġebēded < bēdan

bedelfan *III* bury bedealf *pt3s*

ġebedhūs *n* oratory, chapel

bediġlian *2* hide, conceal bediġlast *pr2s* bediġliað
pr3p

bedrīfan *I* drive, spatter bedrifenne *pp asm*

beebbian *2* leave by the ebb tide, strand
beebbade *pp*

beēode < begān

befæstan *1* entrust, commit, apply oneself (+d
to) *inf* befæste *sbj pr2s, sbj pr3s*

befeallan *VII* befall, happen to, bereave (+*d* of) befeallen *pp* befylð *pr3s*

befēolan *III* (+*d*) apply oneself *inf*

beflōwan *VII* flow round, surround beflōwen *pp*

befōn *II* clasp, encompass, enclose, include befangen *pp* befēað *pr3s* befēng *pt3s*

beforan *prep* (+*d*) before, in front of, in the presence of biforan

befrīnan *III* question, ask befrān *pt3s*

befylð < befeallan

bēga < bēġen

began < beġinnan

begān *anom* practice, carry out, surround beēode *pt3s* begǣst *pr2s*

begangan *VII* perform ; attend to ; practice

beġēat, beġēat- *see* beġietan

bēġen *dual pron/adj* both *npm, apm* bā *npf* bām *dpn* bēġa *gsn* bēġea *gpf*

beġeondan *prep* (+*d*) beyond begiondan

beġēotan *II* pour over, soak begoten *pp*

beġīeman *1* (+*g*) take care of, attend to

beġietan *V* come upon, acquire, get, seize, assail *inf* beġeat *pt3s* beġēatan *pt3p* beġēaton *pt3p* beġite *sbj pr3s* biġeat *pt3s*

begiondan *prep* (+*d*) beyond

begong *m* expanse, region

bēgra *see* bēġen

begrīnian *2* ensnare

behātan *VII* promise, vow behēt *pt3s* behētan *pt1p* behēte *sbj pt3s*

behēafdian *2* behead, decapitate behēafdod *pp*

behealdan *VII* behold, gaze on, watch over, guard, occupy *inf* behēold *pt1s* behēoldon *pt3p*

behēfe *adj* proper, necessary *nsf*

behelian *2* cover over, hide

behēt, behēt- *see* behātan

behionan *prep* (+*d*) on this side of

behrēowsian *2* repent begrēowsiað *pr3p*

behrīman *1* encrust with rime or frost behrīmed *pp*

behwyrfan *1* prepare *inf*

behȳdan *1* hide, conceal behȳdde *pp npm*

beirnan *III* run into

belēac < belūcan

belēosan *II* (+*d*) be deprived of, lose belēas *pt1s* beloren *pp*

ġebelgan *III* be *or* become enraged ġebolgen *pp*

belīefan *1* believe

belīfan *I* remain

belīðan *I* (+*g*) deprive of belidenne *pp*

belocen, belocenre < belūcan

belūcan *II* lock, close, surround, shut in, contain belēac *pt3s* belocen *pp* belocenre *pp dsf*

bemurnan *III* mourn over, bewail bemearn *pt3s*

benam < beniman

benǣman *1* (+*g*) take away, deprive of

benċ *f* bench

bend *m/f/n* bond

benemnan *1* name, declare benemde *pt3s*

benġeat *n* 'wound-gate' gash benġeato *np*

beniman *IV* take away from, deprive (of +*d*) benam *pt3s* benumen *pp* benumene *pp npn* binōm *pt3s*

benn *f* wound benne *np*

bennian *2* wound, injure ġebennad *pp*

benumen, benumene < beniman

bēo < bēon-wesan

bēod *m* table *as*

ġebēodan *II* offer, give, announce, proclaim ġebēad *pt3s* bēodab *pr3p* bēodeð *pr3s* ġeboden *pp* budon *pt3p*

bēodan *II* (+*d*) offer, command

bēon < bēon-wesan

bēon-wesan *anom* be, exist, become bēo *sbj pr1s, sbj pr3s, imp p* bēom *pr1s* bēon *inf, sbj pr3p* bēob *pr1p, imp p* bī *sbj pr3s* bīo *sbj pr3s, imp p* bīon *inf* bīoð *pr3p* bist *pr2s* bib *pr3s* byst *pr2s* byb *pr3s* eart *pr2s* eom *pr1s* is *pr3s* sī *sbj pr3s* sīe *sbj pr3s* sīen *sbj pr3p* siendon *pr3p* sig *sbj pr3s* sind *pr3p* sindon *pr3p* sint *pr3p* sīo *sbj pr3s* sȳ *sbj pr2s, sbj pr3s* syn *pr3p* sȳn *sbj pr3p* synd *pr1p, pr3p* syndan *pr3p* syndon *pr1p, pr3p* synt *pr3p* was *pt3s* wǣran *pt3p* wǣre *pt2s, sbj pt1s, sbj pt3s* wǣren *sbj pt3p* wǣron *pt3p* wǣrum *pt3p* wæs *pt1s, pt3s* wēre *sbj pt1s* wes *pt3s, imp s* wesan *inf* ys *pr3s* ; with *neg* nǣre *pt3s, sbj pt3s* nǣren *sbj pt3p* nǣron *pt3p* næs *pt1s, pt3s* nearon *pr3p* neom *pr1s* nis *pr3s* nys *pr3s*

beorg *m* hill, heap, barrow *as*

ġebeorg *n* protection, defence ġebeorge *ds* ġebeorh *ns*

ġebeorgan *III* (+d) protect, save, seek a cure for *inf* bearh *pr3s* ġebearh *pt3s* beorge *sbj pr3s*, beorh *imp s* burgon *pt3p*

beorht *adj* bright, gleaming, illustrious, radiant, beautiful *nsm, nsf, npn* beorhtan *asf, dsm dsf* beorhte *nsf* beorhtost *asm* beorhtra *gpm*

beorhte *adv* brightly

beorhtnes *f* brightness, clearness, splendor beorthnesse *ds*

beorn *m* man, warrior *ns, as* beorna *gp* beornas *np, as*

ġebēorscipe *m* feast, revels *ns, ds* bēorscipes *gs* ġebēorscipes *gs*

bēorsele *m* beer-hall, drinking-hall, banquet hall bēorselas *ap* bēorsele *ds*

bēot *n* boast, boastful speech, vow, threat *as*

bēotan, bēotun < bēatan

bēotian *2* vow bēotedan *pt1p* bēotode *pt3s*

bēotliċ *adj* arrogant, boastful, threatening

bēotung *f* threat bēotunge *as*

bēoð < bwon-wesan

bepǣċan *1* deceive, seduce bepǣhte *pp npm*

ġeberan *IV* bear, carry, bring, give birth to *inf* bǣr *pt3s* bǣre *sbj pt3s* bǣron *pt3p* berað *imp p* berenne *infl inf* bereb *pr3s* bēron *sbj 3p* bireð *pr3s* boren *pp* ġeborene *pp dsm* borenre *pp dsf* ġeborenum *pp dpm* (=noun one born in same family, brother) byreð *pr3s* ġebyreb *pr3s* byrð *pr3s*

berēafian *2* rob

berīdan *I* overtake berād *pt3s*

bern *n* barn

berōwan *irr* row round

berstan *III* burst, break, shatter bærst *pt3s* berstende *prp nsn* burston *pt3p*

berȳpan *1* plunder, rob berȳpte *pp npm, npn*

besārġian *2* lament, be sorry

bescieran *IV* cut off the hair of, shear

besenċan *1* sink, drown, submerge

besēon *V* look, have regard, look to, attend to besēah *pt3s* besēoh *imp s* bēsihb *pr3s*

besihb < besēon

besittan *IV* surround, occupy besǣton *pt3p*

beslaġen < beslēan

beslēan *VI* strike, take away by violence beslaġen *pp*

besorgian *2* be troubled about besorgab *pr3s*

bespǣċan *1* deceive, seduce bepǣhte *pp npm*

bestealcian *2* go stealthily, steal

bestelan *IV* steal away

bestēman *1* bedew, make wet, drench bestēmēd *pp*

bestȳman *1* make wet, bedew

bestȳpan *1* strip, plunder bestrȳpte *pp npn*

beswāc < beswīcan

beswīcan *I* deceive, betray beswāc *pt3s* beswīce *sbj pr3s* beswicen *pp* beswīcen *sbj pr3p* beswicene *pp npm, apm*

beswillan *1* soak, drench beswyled *pp*

beswingan *III* flog, beat beswuncgen

besyrwan *1* ensnare, deceive besyrwde *pp npm*

bet *comp* adv (<gōd) better

ġebētan *1* amend, atone for, compensate, pay compensation, make good, restore, satisfy bēt *pr3s* bētan *inf, sbj pr3p* ġebētan *sbj pr1p* bēte *sbj pr3s* ġebēte *sbj pr3s* bēttan *pt1p*

betǣċan *1* pursue, hunt ; entrust, commit, hand over, commend, offer betǣċe *pr1s* bðtǣċen *inf* betǣht *pp* betǣhte *pt3s*

betǣhte < betǣcan

betera *comp adj* (<gōd) better, superior *nsm* beteran *npm, apf* betere *nsn* betran *npm* betre *nsn*

betran < betera

betre < betera

betst *sup adj* (<gōd) best *nsm, nsn* betstan *gsm, gsf, isn, npm, dpm*

betweohx *see* betwux

betweonan *prep* (+d) between

betwih *see* betwux

betwux *prep* (+d/a) among, between, during betwix bǣm be while betweohx, betwih, betwyh

betȳnan *1* close, conclude betȳnde *pt3s* betȳnedum *pp dpf*

bebenċan *1* bring to mind, reflect on *inf*

beðian *2* bathe, warm, foment beðedon *pt3p*

beburfan *pt-pr need* beburfon *pr1p*

beweaxan *VII* overgrow beweaxne *pp npm*

bewerian *1* defend

bewindan *III* wrap, surround, envelop, coil about bewinde *sbj pr3s* bweunden *pp* bewendon *pt3p*

bewitian *2* watch, observe bewitiað *pr3p*

bewrēon *I* cover, hide bewriġen pp bewriġene, biwrāh *pt3s*

bī < be, bēon-wesan

bibēad < bebēodan

ġebicgan *1* buy, purchase ġebicge *sbj pr3s* bicgean *inf* bicgað *pr3p* ġebiġeð *pr3s* bohte *pt3s* ġebohte *pt3s* bohton *pt3p*

bīdan *I* (+g) remain, wait for, expect *inf* bād *pt3s* bīdað *pr3p* bīde *imp s*

ġebīdan *I* (+g) wait, remain, experience, endure, attain, reach *inf* ġebād *pt1s* ġebiden pp ġebidenne *pp* ġebīdeð *pr3s* ġebīdon *pt3p*

bidǣlan *1* (+d) deprive of, cut off from bidǣled *pp*

biddan *V* ask, ask for, demand, entreat, pray, beg (for +g) bæd *pt1s* bǣde *pt2s*, *sbj pt3s* bǣdon *pt3p* biddab *pr1p* biddæ *pr1s* bidde *pr1s* biddende *prp npm* biddeb *pr3s* bitt *pr3s*

ġebiddan *V* pray (*rflx* +d) ġebæd *pt1s* ġebǣde *sbj pt1s* ġebǣdon *pt1p* ġebiddab *pr3p*

bidrēosan *II* deprive bidroren *pp* bidrorene *pp npm*

bieldu *f* boldness, arrogance

bifian *2* shake, tremble inf bifode *pt1s*

bifōn *VII* surround, encase bifongen

biforan *see* beforan

big *see* be

ġebīġan *1* bend, turn, convert bīġdon *pt3p* ġebīġean *inf*

bīgang *m* worship, observance

biġeat < beġietan

bīgenġa *m* inhabitant, keeper

bīgengere *m* worker

biġleofa *m* food

bihrēosan *II* cover bihrorene *pp npm*

bilewit *adj* innocent, gentle, kind, sincere

bilewitne *asm* bilwitre *isn*

bilġesliht *n* sword-clash, battle billġeslehtes *gs*

bill *n* sword, blade *as* bil *as* billa *gp* bille *ds* billum *dp*

bilwitre < bilewit

ġebind *n* binding, mingling *as*

ġebindan *III* bind, fetter, hold fast, constrain, fasten, join *inf* bindað *pr3p* ġebindað *pr3p* binde *sbj pr3s* bindeð *pr3s* bond *pt3s* ġebond *pt3s* ġebunden *pp* ġebundene *pp npm*

binn *f* bin, manger

binnan *prep* (+d) within, in binon

binōm < beniman

bīo, bīoð < bēon-wesan

biriġ < burg

ġebiriġ < ġebyrian

biscepstōl *m* episcopal *see* biscepstōle *ds*

biscop *m* bishop *ns* bisceop *ds* bisceope *ds* biscep *ns*, *as* biscepas *np* biscepe *ds* biscepes *gs* biscopa *gp* biscopas *np* biscope *ds* biscopes *gs*

bisgo *f* toil, care, occupation *as* bisgum *dp*

bisgu *f* occupation, concern, care *as* bisgum *dp*

bismer *n/m* insult, ignominy, shame tō bismere with ignominy

bismerfull *adj* shameful

bismor *see* bysmor

bismorsprǣċ *f* blasphemy bismorsprǣċe *as*

ġebismrian *2* treat with ignominy, insult, mock

ġebīsnian *2* set an example, instruct by example

bist < bēon-wesan

bītan *I* bite, wound, cut, tear *inf* bītað *pr3p*

biter *adj* biting, sharp, bitter, fierce, grim, cruel *nsm* bitere *apm* biteres *gsm*, *gsn* (=noun) bitre *asf*, *npm* bitter *asf*

bib > bēon-wesan

biwāwan *VII* blow upon biwāune *pp npm*

biwrāg < bewrēon

blāc *adj* shining, bright, pale, black blāca *nsm* blācne *asm*

ġebland *n* commotion, turmoil

blandenfeax *adj* gray-haired

blāwan *VII* blow *inf*

blǣd *m* breath, spirit, life ; blessing, riches,

success, glory, splendor, fame *ns, as* blǣð *ns*
blēdum *dp*

blǣd *f* shoot, leaf, fruit, flower blǣda *np* blǣdum
dp

blēdan *1* bleed

blēdum < blǣd

blēo *n* color, hue blēon *dp* blēos *gs*

blētsian *2* bless

blētsung *f* blessing blētsunge *ds*

blind *adj* blind *nsm* blindum *dpm*

blindlīċe *adv* blindly

bliss *f* bliss, happiness, gladness, joy *ns* blis *ns*
blisse *as, gs, np*

blissian *2* be glad, make happy, please, rejoice
blissað *pr3s* ġeblissod *pp* blissode *pt3s*
blyssiġende *prp*

blīþe *adj* glad, cheerful, joyful, pleased, gracious
nsm, nsf, asn, dsn, isn, npm blīþra *comp nsm*
blīþran *comp npm*

blīþelīċe *adv* joyfully blȳðelīċe

blōd *n* blood *ns* blōde *ds*

blōdġyte *m* bloodshed *ns, as*

blōdiġ *adj* bloody, gory *asn* blōdiġne *asm*

bōc *f* book, deed, charter *ns, as* bēċ *gs, ds, np,
ap* bōca *gp* bōcon *dp* bōcum *dp* booc *ns*

bōcere *m* scholar, writer, scribe bōceras *np, as*
bōcerum *dp*

ġebōcian *2* grant by charter

Bōclæden *n* Book Latin

bōcræft *m* book-learning

boda *m* messenger bodan *np*

ġeboden < ġebēodan

bodian *2* proclaim, announce preach bodade *pt3s*
bodedon *pt3p* bodienne *infl inf* bodiġean *inf*
gebodod *pp*

bodiġ *m* body

bodung *f* message, preaching

boga *m* bow bogan *np*

ġebogen < būgan

ġebohte, bohton < ġebicgan

bolgen < ġebelgan

bond < bindan

booc < bōc

bord *n* shield *ns, as, ap* borda *gp* bordes *gs*
bordum *dp* borð *ns*

boren, ġeboren- *see* beran

bōsm *m* bosom, breast bōsme *ds*

bōt *f* remedy, relief, compensation, atonements *ns*
bōtð *ds* bōte *as, gs, ds*

botm *m* bottom botme *ds*

brād *adj* broad, wide, spacious, widespread *asn,
apn* brādan *gsn* brēde *asn* brēdne *asm*

brādnis *f* breadth, surface *ns* brēdnysse *as*

bræc < brecan

brǣcan, brǣce < brecan

ġebrǣd < ġebrēdan

brǣdan *1* spread *inf*

ġebrǣdan *1* bake, cook ġebrǣdne *pp asm*

brēac < brūcan

breahtm *m* sound of merriment, revelry
breahtma *gp*

brecan *IV* break, tear, force, transgress, breach,
violate *inf* brðc *pt3s* brǣcan *pt3p* brǣce *sbj
pr3s* brecað *pr3s* ġebroced *pp* brocen *pp*

ġebreġdan *III* draw, pull out, fling, weave, feign
brǣd *pt3s* ġebrǣd *pt3s* brǣġd *pt3s* ġebrǣġd
pt3s brōden *pp* bruġdon *pt3p*

brego *m* prince, chief, leader bregu *ns*

brēmbel *m* briar, bramble *ns* brēber *ns*

brēme *adj* famous, renowned

brēmel *m* bramble, brier brēmelas *ap*
brēmelum *dp*

brēost *n* (used in pl) breast, heart, mind
brēostum *dp*

brēostcearu *f* heart-care, sorrow, anxiety
brēostceare *as*

brēostcofa *m* heart(breast-enclosure)
brēostcofan *ds*

brēostnet *n* corslet

brēotan *II* break in pieces, hew down

brēr *m* briar, bramble, brērum *dp*

brīce *n* use, enjoyment, profit

bricg *f* bridge, causeway bricge *as*

bricgweard *m* guardian of the causeway
bricgweardas *ap*

bridd *m* young bird

brīdelbwang *m* rein

brim *n* sea, water *ns* brimu *ap*

brimfugol *m* seabird brimfuglas *ap*

brimlīðend *m* seafarer, Viking brimlīðendra *gp*

Brimman *m* seafarer, Viking

brimwylf *f* she-wolf of the sea or lake

brimwylm *m* water-surging, turbulent water

ġebringan *1* bring, lead, carry, present, produce, offer ġebrincð *pr3s* bringe *sbj pr3s* ġebringe *sbj pr3s* ġebringeð *pr3s* brōht *pp* brōhtan *pt3p* brōhte *pt3s* brōhton *pt3p* ġebrōhton *pt3p*

brocen < brecan

brōden < breġdan

ġebrōht, ġebrōht– *see* ġebringan

brob *n* broth, soup

brōþor *m* brother *ns* brōþer, brōðra *as* brōðru *np* brōþrum *dp* brōþur *ns*

ġebrōþor *m* brother, fellow-man ġebrōþer *np* ġebrōðra *np, ap* ġebrōþru *np* ġebrōþrum *dp*

brūcan *II* (+g/d) use, make use of, benefit from, enjoy, partake of, possess *inf* brēac *pt3s* brūcað *pr3p* brōcæn *sbj pr3p* brūce *sbj pr3s* brūcon *pt3p*

bruġdon < breġdan

brūnecg *adj* with bright edge, bright-bladed brūneccg *asn*

brycge < bricg

brȳcð < brūcan

brȳcst *see* brūcan

brȳd *f* bride, wife brȳde *ds*

brȳdguma *m* bridegroom

bryne *m* burning, fire, flame, heat *ns, as, ds*

Bryten *pr n* Britain Breotone *as* Brytene *as*

brytta *m* giver, dispenser bryttan *as*

Bryttas *pr n* the Britons *np, ap* Brettas *np* Brytta *gp* Bryttan *dp*

bryttian *2* divide out, distribute

Brytwylsc *adj* British

budon < ġebēodan

būend *m* dweller, inhabitant

bufan *adv* from above

bufan *prep* (+d) above

ġebūgan *II* bend, bow down, turn (away), withdraw, depart, sink, fall *inf* ġebēah *pt3s* ġebogen *pp* bugon *pt3p*

ġebund– *see* ġebindan

būne *f* goblet, drinking cup *ns* būnan *np*

būr *m* chamber, apartment *as* būre *ds*

burg *f* stronghold, fort, dwelling place, town, city biriġ *ds* burge *gs* burgum *dp* burh *ns, as* buruh *as* byri *ds* byriġ *ds, as*

burġġeat *n* city gate

burgon < beorgan

burgtūn *m* protecting hedge, fortified enclosure, habitation burgtūnas *np*

burston *see* berstan

burwaru *f* population, inhabitants burgwara *gp*

burhsittende *mp* town-dwellers burgsittendra *gp* burhsittende *np*

burh *see* burg

burhsittende *see* burgsittende

burh < burg

būrþēn *m* chamberlain, household officer būrþēne *ds*

būtan *conj* except, except that, except for, unless, but, only, as long as būton

butere *f* butter buteran *as*

buterġebwēor *n* butter-curd

buteric *m* leather bottle

būton *see* būtan

bycgan *1* buy bycge *pr1s* byġb *pr3s*

byldan *1* encourage, cheer

bylg *m* bellows

ġebyrd *n/f* destiny, birth

byrden *f* burden

byre *m* time, opportunity

ġebyreb < ġeberan

byrġan *1* bury *inf*

byrġen *f* tomb

ġebyrian *2 impers* be fitting, be appropriate, pertain to ġebiriġe *pr3s* ġebyrað *pr3s* ġebyriað *pr3p*

byriġan *1* taste byriġde *pt3s*

byrnan *III* burn birnendne *prp asm* byrnað *pr3p*

byrne *f* coat of mail, corselet *ns* byrnan *as, ap*

byrnwiġa *m* mailed warrior *ns* byrnwiġena *gp*

byrst *f* bristle

byrst *m* loss, injury *ns* byrsta *gp*

byrð < beran

byrþean *f* burden

byrþen *f* burden

ġebysenung *f* example, model

bysgod *adj* occupied

bysiġ *adj* busy bysiġe *npm*

bysmerian *2* mock, revile bysmeredon *pt3p* bysmorudun *pt3p*

bysmor *m* disgrace, shame, insult, derision *as* bismore *ds* bismre *ds* bysmara *gp* bysmore *ds*

ġebȳsnode see ġebīsnian

ġebysnungum < ġebysenung

byst, byþ < bēon-wesan

cāf *adj* bold, active cāfne *asm*

cald *adj* cold *asn* caldast sup *nsn*

cald *n* cold calde *is*

ġecamp *m* battle, combat campe *ds* ġecampe *ds*

campian *2* strive, fight campodon *pt3s* compedon *pt3p* compian *inf*

campstede *m* battlefield

candel *f* candle, light *ns* condel *ns*

cann, canst < cunnan

canōn *m* canon canōnes *gs*

Cantware *pr n* inhabitants of Kent

cāsere *m* emperor cāseras *np* cāseres *gs*

catt *m* cat

ċeald, ċealdost < cald

ċealf *n* calf

ċeallian *2* call, shout *inf*

ċēap *m* purchase, bargain, price *as* ċēape *ds* ċēapi *ds, is*

ċēapian *2* buy ġeċēapod *pp*

ċēapmann *m* merchant, trader

ceare < cearu

cearian *2* care, be anxious cearað *pr3s*

cearo *see* cearu

cearu *f* care, sorrow ceare *np, as* cearo *ns*

ġeċēas < ġeċēosan

ċeaster *f* town, city, stronghold ċeastra *ds, np* ċeastre *as*

ċeasterġewara *m* fellow citizen

ċeasterware *m pl* citizens

ċeasterwaru *f* citizens

ġeċēlan *1* cool

cempa *m* champion, soldier, warrior *ns* cempan *np*

cēne *adj* brave, keen, bold *nsm, npm* cēnra *gp* cēnre *comp nsf* cēnum *dpm*

cennan *1* beget, produce *inf*

ċēol *m* ship, keel ċēole *ds*

ċeorfan *III* carve, hew out curfon *pt3p*

ċeorl *m* man, peasant, commoner, freeman of lowest class, husband *ns, as* ċeorle *ds* ċeorles *gs*

ġeċēosan *II* choose, decide ġeċēas pt3s ġecoren *pp* ġecorenan *pp apm* (*noun*=chosen ones, disciples) ġecorenum *pp dpm* ġecuran *pt3p*

ċeosol *m* gravel, shingle ċeosle *ds*

cēpan *2* (+*g*) seize, attend to, look out for

ċerr *m* occasion, time ċerre *ds*

Chaldēas *pr n* the Chaldeans

ġeċīeġan *1* call out, shout, summon, name ġeċeġed pp ġeċīġ *imp s* ċīġe *sbj pr3s* ċiġġendra *prp gpm* cȳġdon *pt3p*

ċīepan *I* sell ċīepst *pr2s*

ċīepend *m* merchant, seller

ċierr *m* time, occasion ċierre *ds*

ġeċierran *1* turn, return, submit

ċiġġendra < ċīeġan

ċild *n* child *ns* ċilda *gp* ċildra *np* ċildum *dp*

ċildhād *m* childhood

ċildliċ *adj* childlike

cinges < cyning

cing, cing– *see* cyning

cinna < cynn

ċiriċe *f* church *ns* ċirċan *np, gs, ds* ċiriċan *gs* ċiriċean *gs, ds, np* ċyrċan *ds, np* ċyrċan *ds, np* ċyrċean *ds*

ċirran *1* turn, return ċirdon *pt3p*

clǣman *2* smear ; caulk

clǣne *adj* clean, pure *nsm, nsn, npm, apm*

clǣne *adv* utterly, completely

clǣnsian *2* purify, cleanse

cleofa *m* cellar

clēofan *II* split, cleave clufan *pt3p* clufon *pt3p*

cleofum < clif

clif *n* cliff, rock, crag cleofum *dp* clifum *dp*

clipian *2* call, summon, cry out clypiġende *prs pp* clipode *pt3s* clypode *pt3s* cleopode *pt3s*

clipung *f* calling

clomm *m* fetter, chain, grip, clutch clommas *np*

clomme *ds* clommum *dp*

clufan < clēofan

clypian *2* call, cry out, summon *inf* cliopodon
    pt3p clipode *pt3s* clypað *pr3s* clypode *pt3s*

clypodon *pt3p*

clyppan *1* embrace, clasp, cherish *inf* clyppað
    pr3p clyppe *sbj pr3s*

cnapa *m* boy *ns* cnappan *as*

ġecnāwan *VII* know, perceive, understand *inf*
    ġecnāwað *imp p* ġecnāwe *sbj pr3s*

cnēa < cnēow

cnear *m* small ship, galley *ns*

cnēo < cnēow

cnēomǣġ *m* kinsman, ancestor cnēomǣġum *dp*

ġecneordness *f* accomplishment

cnēow *n* knee *as* cnēa *gp* cnēo *as* cnēowa *ap*

cniht *m* youth, boy, servant *ns* cnihton *dp*

cnyssan *1* batter, press, urge cnyssasð *pr3p*

cōc *m* cook

coccel *m* tares, corn-cockle

cōlian *2* cool, grow cold cōlode *pt3s*

collenferhð *adj* bold-spirited, elated collenferhðe
    npf collenferð *nsm*

cōm, cōm- see cuman

compedon, compian < campian

compian *2* fight

con < cuman

condel see candel

ġecoren, ġecoren- see ġeċēosan

corn *n* corn, grain corna *gp*

corbor *n* troop, retinue, pomp corbre *ds*

costnung *f* temptation, trial

crabba *m* crab

cradolċild *n* child in the cradle, infant *np*

ġecrane < ġecrincgan

cræft *m* craft, trade, study, skill, cunning, power,
    strength *as* cræfta *gp* cræfte *ds* cræftes *gs*
    craæftum *dp*

Crēacas see Grēcas

crēad < crūdan

crēopan *2* creep

ġecrincgan *III* fall, fall dead, die in battle, perish
    inf ġecrane *pt3s* ġecrong *pt3s* cruncon *pt3p*
    crungon *pt3p* crungun *pt3p*

Crīst *pr n* Christ Chrīste *ds* Crīste *ds* Crīstes

gs Xrīste *ds*

crīsten *adj* Christian nsm crīstene *nsn*, *npm*
    crīstenes *gsn* crīstenra *gpm*, *gpn* crīstenre
    dsf crīstnæ *npf* crīstne *npm*

crīstendom *m* Christendom

ġecrong < ġecrincgan

crūdan *II* hasten, press on crēad *pt3s*

cruma *m* crumb cruman *ap*

cruncon, crung- see crincgan

cuǣdon < cweðan

cucu see cwic

culter *m* colter, knife cultre *ds*

cuma *m* guest, stranger cuman *ds*

cuman *IV* come, go *inf sbj pr3s* cōm *pt3s*
    cōman *pt3p* cōme *sbj pt3s* cōmon *pt3p*
    cōmun *pt3p* cumað *pr1p*, *pr3p*, *imp p* cume
    sbj pr3s cumen *sbj pr1p*, *pp* cumende *prp*
    asm cumon inf, *sbj pr3p* cwōm *pt3s* cwōman
    3p cwōme *sbj pt1s*, *sbj pt3s* cyme *sbj pr3s*
    cymeð *pr3s* cymst *pr2s* cymð *pr3s*

cumbolġehnāst *n* clash of standards
    cumbolġehnāstes *gs*

ġecunnad < cunnian

cunnan *pt-pr* know, know how to, be able, have
    the power to *inf* can *pr3s* cann *pr1s* canst
    pr2s con *pr1s* cunne *sbj pr3s* cunnen *sbj*
    pr3p cunnon *pr1p*, *pr3p* cūbe *pt1s*, *pt3s*
    cūðen *sbj pr3p* cūbon *pt1p*, *pt3p*

cunnian *2* (+g) try, put to the test, explore, find
    out, experience *inf* ġecunnad *pp* cunnade
    pt3s cunnað *pr3s* cunniġan *inf* cunniġe,
    cunnode *pt3s*

ġecuran < ġeċēosan

curfon < ċeorfan

cūð *adj* known, familiar *nsn* cūðe *npf* cūðra *gpn*

cūbe, cūðen, cūbon < cunnan

cwalu *f* death, murder cwale *ds*

cwæd, cwǣd-, cwæb < cweban

cweartern *m* prison

ġecwed- see ġecweban

cwellan *1* kill cwealde *sbj pt3s*

ġecwēman *1* please ġecwēmde *pt3s*

cwēn *f* woman, wife, queen, royal princess *ns*
    cwēnē *as* cwēnum *dp*

cwene *f* woman, wife cwenan *as* cwynan *ds*

ġecweban *V* say, speak, utter, declare, proclaim, call, propose, consider, regard *inf* cuǣdon *pt3p* cwæd *pt3s* cwǣdan *pt1p* cwǣde *pt2s, sbj pt3s* cwǣden *sbj pt3p* cwǣdon *pt3p* cwǣdun *pt3p* cwæb *pt1s, pt3s* ġecwæð *pt3s* ġecweden *pp npm* cwest *pr2s* cweb *pr3s* cwebab *pr1p* cwebe *pr1s, sbj pr1s, sbj pr1p* ġecweðen *pp* cwebende *prp nsm, npm* cwebenne *infl inf* cwyst *pr2s* cwyb *pr3s*

cwic *adj* living, alive (often=*noun*) *asn* cwicera *gpm, gpn* cwicra *gpm* cwicum *dsm, dpm*

cwide *m* remark, saying, statement, report

cwideġiedd *n* spoken utterance, speech cwideġiedda *gp*

ġecwidrǣden *f* agreement

cwielman *1* kill, murder, torment

cwīban *1* mourn, lament *inf* cwīðdon *pt3p*

cwōm, cwōman < cuman

ġecwylman *see* cwylmian

ġecwylman *1* kill

cwylmian *2* kill, murder cwylmde *pp npm*

cwynan < cwene

ġecȳdd, cȳdd- *see* ġecȳban

cȳf *f* tub, vat, cask

ġecȳġan *2* invoke, summon ġecȳġede *pp*

cȳġdon < cīeġan

ċyle *m* coolness, cold *ns* ciel

cymen *m* cumin cymenes *gs*

cyme, cym(e)b, cymst < cuman

cȳmlīċe *adv* beautifully, splendidly, nobly

cyn *see* cynn

cynecynn *n* royal line

cynedōm *m* kingdom

cynehelm *m* royal crown, diadem, garland *as*

cyneliċ *adj* kingly, royal, noble, public (building) *nsn* cyneliċan *apn* cyneliċes *gsm* cynelico *npn*

cynerīċe *n* kingdom, rule, sovereignty cynereċes *gs* kynerīċes *gs*

cyning *m* king, ruler *ns, as* cincges *gs* cing *ns, as* cinge *ds* cinges *gs* cyng *ns* cynge *ns, ds* cynges *gs* cyningce *ds* cynincges *gs* cyningas *np* cyningc *ns* cyninge *ds* cyninges *gs* kyning *ns* kyningas *np* kyninge *ds*

cynn *n* kin, race, stock, tribe, people, kind, gender *ns, as, ap* cinna *gp* cyn *as* cynna *gp* cynne *ds* cynnes *gs* kynnes *gs*

cȳpan *see* ċīepan

cȳpecniht *m* slave cȳpecnihtas *ap*

cȳpmann *m* merchant cȳpmenn *np*

ċyrċan, cyrċean < ċiriċe

ċyriċhata *m* opponent of the church ċyriċhatan *np*

ċyrm *m* cry, shout, uproar *ns*

cȳse *m* cheese *as*

cȳsġerunn *n* rennet

cyssan *1* kiss cysse *sbj pr3s* cyste *pt3s*

cyst *f* choice, the choicest, the best *ns*

cystiġ *adj* charitable. good, of good quality cystiġran *comp npm*

cystiġnes *f* bounty, munificence cystiġnessa *gp*

ġecȳban *1* announce, reveal, make known, proclaim, inform *inf* ġecȳdd *pp* cȳdde *pt3s* cȳddon *pt3p* cȳð *pr3s* cȳbað *pr3p, imp p* cȳðde *pt3s* cȳðdon *pt3p* cȳðe *pr1s, sbj pr3s* ġecȳðed *pp*

cȳðð *f* knowledge

cȳbbu *f* kinsfolk, home, native land cȳbbe *as, ds*

ġedafenian *2 impers* (+*d*) befit, be proper ġedafenað *pr3s* dafnað *pr3s* ġedafnode *sbj pt3s* ġedeofanode *pt3s*

ġedafenlīċ *adj* suitable, appropriate

dag- *see* dæġ

ġedāl *n* separation, break ġedāles *gs*

daroð *m* dart, spear daraða *gp*

dǣd *f* deed, act, action *ns* dǣda np, ap, gp dǣde *as, gs, ds* dǣdum *dp*

dǣdbōt *f* atonement, penance *ns* dǣdbōte *as* dǣtbōte *as*

dæġ *m* day, lifetime *ns, as ds,* daga *gp* dagas *np, ap* dagon *dp* dagum *dp* dæġe *ds* dæġes *gs* dæi *as* dæiġ *as, is*

dæġrǣd *n* daybreak, dawn

dæġhwāmlīċe *adv* daily

dæi, dæiġ *see* dæġ

dǣl *m* part, share, measure, extent, quantity, unit, word *ns, as* dǣlas *np, as, ap* dǣle *ds* dǣlum *dp*

ġedǣlan *1* share, deal out, distribute *inf* dǣlað
  pr3p dǣlænne *infl inf* ġedǣlde *pt3s* dǣlon *sbj*
  pt3p dǣlð *pr3s*

dænnede < dennian

dǣtbōte < dǣdbōt

dēad *adj* dead nsm dēade *nsn, npm* dēadne *asm*
  dēadra *gpm* dēadum *dsm*

dēaddæġ *m* day of death

dēah < dugan

dear, dearr < durran

dearnunge *adv* secretly

dēab *m* death ns, as dēabe ds dēabes gs

Defenas *pl* (people of) Devon Defenum *dp*

dehter < dohtor

delfan *III* dig delf *imp s*

dēma *m* judge, governor, ruler *ns* dēman gs

dēman *1* (+d) judge, adjudge, decide, ordain,
  decree *inf* dēmed *pp* ġedēmed *pp* dēmeð *pr3p*
  dōēmid *pp*

denu *f* valley, dale dena np

Denisc *adj* Danish Denisca *npf*

Deniscan *m pl* Danes Deniscena *gp*

dennian *2* stream(?) dænnede pt3s

dēofol *m* devil, the devil *ns, as* dēofle ds
  dēofles gs dēoflum *dp*

dēofol-ġield *n* idol

dēogol *adj* secret, hidden, mysterious dȳgel *asn*
  dīgelan *apm*

dēop *adj* deep, profound, solemn, great *nsfn, asn*
  dēopan *dsm, apn, asf*

dēope *adv* deeply, profoundly

dēoplīċe *adv* deeply

dēor *adj* bold, brave nsm dēorum *ipf*

dēor *n* wild beast, animal as dēora gp

dēore *adj* dear, precious, beloved, costly, valuable
  dēorost *sup nsn* dēorum *dsm* dȳre *nsm, apm*

dēore *adv* dearly, at great cost

ġedeorf *n* toil, labor

ġedeorfan *III* do laboriously, labor

dēorweorb *see* dēorwierbe

dēorwierbe *adj* valuable, precious dēorwirðe
  apm dēorwierbu *apn*

Dēor *pr n* Deor ns

deorc *adj* dark, gloomy deorcan *dpm*

deore *adj* dark, gloomy deorcan *dpm* dēorce

asn

dēore *adj* dear, precious, beloved, costly, valuable
  dēorost *sup nsn* dēorum *dsm* dȳre *nsm, apm*

dēore *adv* dearly, at great cost

ġedeorf *n* labor, toil ns, as

deorfan *III* labor deorfe *pr1s*

dēorwurðe *adj* valuable, precious, costly dēorwirðe
  apm dēorwurðan *gsm* dēorwurðre *dsf*
  dēorwyrðan *dsf* dēorwyrðe *asf*

Dēre *pl* inhabitants of Deira, Deirians

ġederian *2* (+d) injure, harm, do harm to *inf*
  derede *pt3s* ġederede *pt3s* dereð *pr3s*

dēst, ġedēb < ġedōn

dīacon *m* deacon, minister dīacones gs

diaconhād *m* deaconship diaconhāde *ds*

dīċ *m/f* ditch

dide < dōn

dīegol *adj* secret, hidden

dīepe *f* depth dīepan *as*

dīgelan < dēogol

ġedihtan *1* direct, compose, write *inf* ġedihte
  pt3s

dim *adj* dark, gloomy dimme *npf*

dimnes *f* dimness dimnesse *ds*

dō < dōn

dōēmid < dēman

dōgor *n* day dōgore *is* dōgra gp

dohte < dugan

dohtor *f* daughter ns, as, gs, ds dehter ds
  dohtra *np* dohtur *ns*

dol *adj* foolish *nsm*

dolg *n* wound, scar np dolh *ns*

dōm *m* decree, judgement, choice, glory, renown
  ns, as dōma gp dōmas np dōme ds dōmes
  gs dōmum *dp*

dōm(es)dæġ *m* Judgement day

dōmġeorn *adj* eager for glory dōmġeorne *npm*

dōmsetl *n* judgement-seat, tribunal dōmsetle *ds*

ġedōn *anom* do, act, perform, make, cause, treat,
  take, gain, put, bestow, consign dōn *inf* ġedōn
  inf dēst *pr2s* dēb *pr3s* ġedēb *pr3s* dide *pt3s*
  dō *pr1s, sbj pr3s, imp s* dōnne *infl inf* dōð
  pr3s, pr3p dydan *pt1p* dyde *pt1s, pt3s*
  ġedyde *pt3s* dydest *pt2s* dydon *pt1p, pt3p*

dorste < durran

dōð < dōn

draca *m* dragon, serpent *ns*

ġedrǣg *n* tumult, (noisy) company ġedreag (multitude) *as*

ġedreag *n* multitude, host *as*

drēam *m* joy, bliss, delight, happiness *ns* drēamas *np*, *ap* drēame *ds* drēames *gs* drēamum *dp*

ġedrēas < ġedrēosan

ġedreċċan *1* afflict, oppress ġedreċte *pt3p* ġedrehtan *pt3p*

drēfan *1* trouble, stir up, disturb, afflict drēfe *pr1s* ġedrēfde *pp* *npm* ġedrēfed *pp*

ġedrehtan < ġedreċċan

drenċ *m* drink *ns*

drenċan *1* drench, ply with drink drenċte *pt3s*

drēogan *II* suffer, undergo, endure *inf* drēag *pt3s* drēogað *pr3p* drēogeð *pr3s* drugon *pt2p*

drēoriġ *adj* sad, dejected *nsf* drēoriġne *asm*

drēoriġhlēor *adj* sad-faced *nsm*

ġedrēosan *II* decline, fail, fall, collapse, perish ġedrēas *pt3s* drēoseð *pr3s* ġedroren *pp* ġedrorene *pp* *npf*

drēorsele *m* dreary abode, hall of sorrow

drīfan *I* drive, expel *inf* drāf *pt3s* drīfað *pr3p* drīfe *pr1s*, *sbj pr3s*

drīġe *adj* dry drīġum *dpm*

driften *m* lord, the Lord, prince *ns*, *as* drihtne *ds* drihtnes *gs* dryhten *ns*, *as* dryhtne *ds* dryhtnes *gs*

driht *f* multitude, troop drihte *np*

drihten *m* lord, the Lord, prince *ns* drihtne *ds* drihtnes *gs* dryhten *ns* dryhtne *ds* dryhtnes *gs*

drihtliċ < dryhtliċ

drinc *m* drink

ġedrincan *III drink inf* ġedrincanne *infl inf* drinċþ *pr3s* drince *pr1s* drincst *pr2s* ġedruncen *pp* druncon *pt1p*

drohtnung *f* way of living drohtnunge *ds*

drugon < drēogan

ġedruncen, druncon < drincan

drȳcræt *m* sorcery, witchcraft

drȳġan *1* dry drȳġdon *pt3p*

drȳġe *adj* dry drȳġum *ds*

drȳġness *f* dryness

dryht *f* band of retainers

dryhtliċ *adj* lordly, noble, magnificent dihtliċ *nsn* drihtliċe *asn*

dryhten, dryhtnes *see* drihten

drysmian *2* grow dark drysmað *pr3s*

dugan *pt-pr* be of use, avail, thrive, be good dēah *pr3s* dohte *pt3s*

dugub *f* noble band (of warriors), troop, company, host ; prosperity, benefit *ns* dugeða *gp* dugebe *as*, *gs*, *ds* dugebum *dp*

dumb *adj* dumb, mute dumbe *npm*

dūn *f* hill, mountain, height dūna *np*

durran *pt-pr* dare dear *pr1s* dearr *pr1s* dorste *pt1s*, *pt3s* durre *sbj pr1s* durron *pr1p*

duru *f* door *ns*, *as*, *ap* dura *ds*, *ap* durum *dp*

dūst *n* dust *ns* dūste *ds*

ġedwǣrian *2* agree

dwellian *2* lead astray, deceive dwelode *pt3s*

ġedwolgod *m* false god

ġedwollīċe *adv* foolishly, heretically

dwolma *m* empty space, chaos

ġedwolsum *adj* misleading, confusing

ġedwyld *n* error, hersey *ns* ġedwylde *ds*

ġedyd– *see* ġedōn

dȳġel *adj* hidden, unknown

dyppan *1* dip

dȳre *adj* dear

dȳres *see* dēor

dyrne *adj* secret, hidden *nsf*, a*sm*

dysiġ *adj* ignorant, foolish *nsm* dysġra *gpm* (=*noun*) dysiġe *npm*(=*noun*)

dyrstiġ *adj* daring

dȳrwyrðe *adj* precious, costly

ēa *f* river, stream

ēac *adv* also, likewise, besides, moreover, even (often in adv phr ēac swilċe, welċe ēac, etc. likewise, in the same way)

ēac *prep* (+*d/i*) in addition to, plus

ēaca *m* increase ēacan *ds*

ēacen *adj* increased, augmented, pregnant

ēacian *see* ȳcan

ġeēacnung *f* child-bearing ġeēacnunga *ap*

ēadiġ *adj* blessed, happy, prosperous *nsm* ēadiga *nsm* ēadigan *asf* ēadiġe *apm*

ġeēadmēdan *1* humble, humiliate ġeēadmēte *pt3s*

eafera *m* son, heir, offspring, descendant afaran *np* eaferan *as* eafrum *dp* eaferum *dp*

ēage *n* eye *ns* ēagan *ds, np, ap* ēagna *gp* eagum *dp*

ēag-b̄yrel *n* window

eahta *num* eight

eahtoða *num adj* eighth

eal *see* eall

ēalā *interj* oh! ho! alas!

eald *adj* old, ancient, senior *nsm, nsf, npn* alde *ism* ealda *nsm* ealdan *asf, dsn, dsf, npm, apm* ealde *nsf, asn, npm, apm* ealdne *asm* ealdra *gpm* (=noun) *gpn* ealdum *dpm* yldestan *sup apm, dpm*

ealdġestrēon *n* old treasure

ealdor *m* leader, elder, prince, lord, master, chief, God *ns* aldor *ns* ealdras *np* ealdre *ds* ealdres *gs* ealdrum *dp*

ealdor *see also* aldor

ealdordōm *m* ealdormanry, office of ealdorman ealdordōme *ds*

ealdorlang *adj* life-long ealdorlangne *asm*

ealdorlēas *adj* without a lord, lifeless, orphaned

ealdorman *m* prince, ealdorman, nobleman, ruler *ns, as* aldormon *ns, as* aldormonnes *gs* ealdermen *ds* ealdormann *as* ealdormannes *gs* ealdormenn *ds* ealdormon *ns*

ealdorscipe *m* supremacy

ealdr- < ealdor

ealdra < eald

ealdre < aldor

Ealdseaxan *pr n* the Old Saxons, Old Saxony

eardstapa *m* wanderer

ealdsweord *n* ancient sword

ealġearo *adj* quite ready

ġeealgian *2* defend ealgodon *pt3p* ġealgean *inf*

ealgylden *see* eallgylden

eall *adj* all, every, each, the whole of *nsm, nsn, nsf, asn, npn, apn,* al *asf* ælne *asm* eal *nsf, npm, asn* ealla *npf* ealle *asf, npm, npf, apm,* apn, apf ealles *gsm, gsn* eallra *gpm, gpf* eallre *dsf* eallum *dsm, dsn, dpm, dpn, dpf* ealne *asm* ealra *gpm gpn*

eall *pron* all each, everything *nsn, asm, asn* alle *npm, apm* eal *nsn, asn, npn* eallan *dpm* eallæ *apf* eallæs *asn* ealle *asf, npm npn, apm, apn* ealles *gsn* eallon *dpm* eallra *gpn* eallum *dpm, dpn* ealra *gpm, gpn ; in phr* mid ealle altogether, fully, completely

eall *adv* all, fully, utterly, altogether eal

ealles *adv* fully, completely, quite

eallgylden *adj* all-golden ealgylden *nsn*

eallswā *conj/adv* just as, even as, likewise ealswā

eallunga *adv* altogether, entirely

eallwealda *n* the Almighty

ealneġ *adv* always

ēalond *n* island ēalondes *gs*

ealra < eall

ealswā *see* eallswā

ealu *n* ale

ēam *m* (maternal) uncle ēame *ds*

ēarn < ēare

eard *m* country, homeland, region, land, dwelling-place *as* earde *ds*

eardġeard *m* habitation, world *as*

eardian *2* live, dwell eardiende *prp nsm*

eardungstōw *f* place of settlement, habitation eardungstōwe *as, gs*

ēare *n* ear ēaran *np, ap*

earfobe *n* hardship, suffering. tribulation, misery earfeba *gp* earfoda *ap* earfoba *ap, gp* earfoðum *dp*

earfoðliċ *adj* full of hardship, laborious *nsn*

earm *adj* poor, wretched, miserable (=*often noun*) earman *gsf, dsf* earme *npm* earmra *gpm, gpn* earmum *dpm*

earm *m* arm *ns, as*

earmceariġ *adj* wretchedly anxious, care-worn *nsm*

earmlíċe *adv* miserably, wretchedly

earmsceapen *adj* wretched

earn *m* eagle

ġeearnian *2* earn, deserve, gain *inf* ġeearnab *pr3s* ġeearnedan *pt1p* ġeearnedon *pt3p* earnian *inf*

ġeearnung *f* deserving, desrts, merit, favor ġeearnunga *ap* earnungan *dp*

eart < bēon-wesan

ēast *adv* eastwards

ēastan *adv* from the east

Ēastengle *pr n* the East Anglians, East Anglia *np* Ēastengla *gp* Ēastenglum *dp*

ēasteð *n* river-bank ēasteðe *ds*

ēasteweard *adv* westward

ēastsǣ *m* eastern sea

Ēastseaxe *pr n* the East Saxons, Essex Ēastseaxan *np* Ēastseaxena *gp*

ēabe *adv* easily, readily

ēaðeliċ *adj* easy, weak, insignificant ēaðeliċre *comp*

ēabmōd *adj* humble, obedient, gentle *nsm*

eaxl *f* shoulder eaxle *ds* eaxlum *dp*

eaxleġespann *n* cross-beam eaxleġespanne *ds*

Ebrisc *adj* Hebrew Ebrisce *npm*

Ebriscġeðiode *m* the Hebrew language *ds*

ēċe *adj* eternal, endless, everlasting, perpetual *nsm, nsn, asn, apm* ēċan *asf, gsn, dsm, dsn, apn* ēċes *gsm* ēċne *asm* ēċcum *dpm, dpn*

ecg *f* edge, sword *ns* ecga *gp* ecge *as np* ecgum *dp*

ecghete *m* sword-hatred, hostility, war

ēċne < ēċe

ġeedcwician *2* revive, bring to life again

edor *m* building, dwelling ederas *np*

edwist *f* being, substance

ġeednīwian *2* renew, restore ġeednīnīwod *pp*

efeneald *adj* of equal age

ġeefenrǣċan *1* match, imitate

efenbēowa *m* fellow-servant

efne *adv* even, just, thus, now, only

efne *interj* behold, lo

efsian *2* cut the hair of

efstan *1* hurry efste *pt3s* efston *pr3p*

eft *adv* again, then again, back, after, afterwards, next, now

eftsīa *m* return

eġe *m* fear, dread, terror *as*

eġesa *m* awe, fear, terror, awesomeness, monstrous thing *ns* eġesan *np* eġsa *ns* eġsan *ds*

eġesful *adj* awful, awesome, dreadful, terrifying *nsm* eġefull *nsm* eġesfull *nsm* eġesfulle *npm*

egesian *2* terrify, frighten

eġesliċ *adj* fearful, dreadful *nsf, nsn* eġesliċe *nsf*

ēhtan *1* (+g) pursue, assail, persecute ēhte *sbj pr3s* ēhton *pt3p*

eiġlande < īġland

elcung *f* delay

ele *m* oil *ds*

ellen *n* strength, courage, fortitude, zeal *as* elne *ds* elnes *gs*

elles *adv* else, otherwise

ellor *adv* elsewhere

ellorgāst *m* alien spirit ellorgǣstas *ap*

elne < ellen

elbēodiġ *adj* foreign, hostile elbēodiġra *gpm* (=noun)

elbēodiġnes *f* residence in a foreign country

embe *see* ymbe

ende *m* end, conclusion, boundary, limit, district, region *ns, as* ænde *ds, is* endas *np*

endebyrdan *1* arrange, dispose ġeendebyrd *pp*

endelēas *adj* endless *nsm, nsf*

endemes *adv* together

ġeendian *2* end, finish, complete ġeendade *pt3s* ġeendað *pr3s* ġendedu *pp nsf* ġeendiað *pr3p* ġeendigan *inf* ġendod *pp* ġeendode *pt3s* ġeendodu *pp nsf*

endleofon *num* eleven

endleofta *adj* eleventh

ġeendung *f* end, death ġeendunge *as*

engel *m* angel *ns, as* engla *gp* englas *np ap* engles *gs* englum *dp*

Englisc *adj* English *nsm, asn, dsf* Engliscan *dsn* Engliscum *dsn*

Englisc *n* English (the language) *ns*

enġu < ǣniġ

ent *m* giant enta *gp* entas *np, ap*

ġeēod- *see* ġegān

eofer *m* boar, figure of boar on helmet eoferes *gs*

Eoforwiċċeastre *pr n* York

eom < bēon-wesan

eorðcyning *m* king of the land eorðcyninges *gs*

eorl *m* nobleman, warrior, hero, man *ns, as* eorla
gp eorlas *np, ap* eorle *ds* eorles *gs*

Eormanrīċ *pr n* Eormanric Eormanrīċes *gs*

eornost *f* earnestness *as*

eornostlīċe *adv* in truth, indeed

ēorodċist *f* troop, contingent ēorodċistum *dp*

eorðbūend *m* earth-dweller, inhabitant
eorðbūendra *gp*

eorbe *f* earth, world, ground, clay *ns* eorban *as,*
gs

eorbfæst *adj* firm in the earth

eorðscræf *n* earth-cave, grave eorðscræfe *ds*
eorðscrafu *ap*

eorðsele *m* earth-dwelling, barrow

eorðtilia *m* farmer, husbandman

eorbtilb *f* agriculture

eorðweġ *m* the earthly path eorðweġe *ds*

Ēote *pr n* the Jutes Ēotena *gp* Ēotenum *dp*

eotenisc *adj* gigantic, made by giants

ēoton < etan

ēow < ġē

ēower *poss pron* your *nsm* ēowere *npm* ēowre
npm, apm, apf ēowres *gsm* ēowrum *dsm*

erðan < eorbe

etan *V* eat, feed, provision oneself *inf* ǣt *pt3s*
ǣton *ptlp, pt3p* ete *prls, sbj pr3s* ġeeten *pp*
etenne *infl inf* etst *pr2s* ytst *pr2s*

ēbel *m* native land, home, country, territory *ns*
as ēðle *ds* ēðles *gs*

ēbgesȳne *adj* plain to see, easy to see

ēðle, ēðles < ēbel

ġecwidrǣden *f* agreement

fācen *n* treachery, evil, wickedness, crime fācn
as

fācenfull *adj* crafty, deceitful.

ġefadian *2* arrange, order, phrase *inf* fadode *pt3s*

fāgum < fāh

fāh *adj* hostile, guilty ; decorated, gleaming,
stained *nsm nsn* fāgum *dsm dp*

fala *see* fela

ġefaran *VI* set out, go, travel, advance, die *inf*
farað *prlp, pr3p, imp p* fare *sbj pr3s* faren

sbj pr3p ġefaren *pp* fareð *pr3s* færb *pr3s*
ġefōr *pt3s* fōran *ptlp* fōron *pt3p*

fandian *2* (+*g*) try, test, tempt

fanggene < fōn

faroð *m/n* current, sea

fatu < fæt

fæc *n* interval, period of time *as* fæce *ds*

fædde < f3dan

fæder *n* father, patriarch *ns, as, gs, ds* fðderas
np

fæderlīċe *adv* paternally

fǣġe *adj* fated, doomed to die *nsm, npm, apm*
fǣġean *dsm* fǣġes *gsm* fæġne *asm* fæġum
dpm, dpf

fæġen *adj* glad, joyful nsm

fæġer *adj* fair, beautiful, fine, pleasant, pleasing
nsm, nsn fæġera *gpm* fæġere *nsn npm*
fæġerum *dpm* fæġran *dsf* fæġre *ism*

fæġere *adv* fairly, agreeably, splendidly,
carefully, gently fæġre, fæġror *comp* fæġrost
sup

fæġnian *2* rejoice fæġniað *pr3s*

fǣhðu *f* feud, hostility, violence, revenge fǣhðe
as, ds

fæla *see* fela

fæmne *f* maid, wife, woman *ns* fæmnan *ds* fæmnum
dp fēmnan *as, gs*

fær *n* vessel, ship

fǣr *m* calamity, sudden danger, attack

færeld *n* journey, way, passage, movement
færelde *ds* færeldes *gs* færelte *ds* færeltes
gs

fǣrgripe *m* sudden attack, snatch

fǣringa *adv* suddenly, by chance

fǣeliċ *adj* sudden fǣrlīċum dsm

fǣrlīċe *adv* suddenly, quickly

fæst *adj* firm, fixed, constant, motionless, secure
nsm, nsf, asn fæste *npm, asf* fæstum *dsm*

fæstan *2* fast fæstende *prp*

fæste *adv* fast, firmly, securely, closely completely

fæstenbriċe *m* fast-breaking fæstenbrycas *np*

fæstende < fæstan

fæstness *f* firmness, firmament

ġefæstnian *2* establish, fasten, fix *inf* ġefæstnod
pp ġefæstnode *pp npm* ġefæstnodon *pt3p,*

pp, dpm

fæstnung *f* stability, permanence

fæt *n* vessel, cup *ns*

fǣtan *1* adorn fǣttan *pp, gsn*

fǣtels *m* pouch, sack

fætt *adj* fat

fǣtan *1* adorn fǣttan *pp gsn* (ornamented, plated)

fæbm *m* embrace, grasp, protection, keeping fæðme *ds* fæbmum *dp*

fēa *adj* few, a few *fēaum dpm* fēawe *apm* fēawum *dpm : see also* fēawa

fēa *adv* little, scarcely

ġefēa *m* joy ġefēan *ds*

ġefeah < ġefēon

feaht < feohtan

feala *see* fela

ġefeallan *VII* fall, fall in battle, die, fall to ruin *inf* fealleb *pr3s* fēol *pt3s* ġefēol *pt3s* fēoll *pt3s* ġefeoll *pt3s* fēollan *pt3p* fēollon *pt3p*

feallendlīċ *adj* unstable

fealu *adj* yellow, dusky, grey fealene *asm* fealwe *apm*

fēasceaft *adj* destitute, miserable, helpless, poor

fēawe, fēawum < fēa

ġefeċċan *2* fetch, bring, carry off *inf* ġefecgan *inf*

fēdan *1* feed, provision, nourish fǣdde *pt3s* fēdde *pt3s* fēdden *sbj pr3p* fēdeð *pr3s*

ġefeh < ġefēon

ġefehð < ġefōn

fela *adv* much feala

fela *indecl noun/pron* (*usually +gp*) ; *also adj* many, much, many things fæla, feala ; *in adv phr* swā fala as many bæs fela so msny

fēlahrōr *adj* very strong

felalēof *adj* much loved, very dear felalēofan *gsm*

felamōdiġ *adv* very brave

ġefēlan *1 feel inf* fēleb *pr3s* (+g)

feld *m* field, battlefield *ns* felda *ds*

fēleb < ġefēlan

fell *n* hide, skin

fēmnan < fǣmne

ġefēng, fēngon < ġefōn

feṅġelād *n* fen-way

feoh *n* money, price, wealth, goods, property, cattle *ns as* fēo *ds* fēos *gs* fioh *as*

feohġehāt *n* promise of money

feohġifre *adj* greedy for wealth, avaricious *nsm*

feoh-gift *f* rich gift

ġefeoht *n* battle, fight, fighting, war *as* ġefeohte *ds* ġefeohtum *dp*

feohtan *III* fight, attack *inf* fealht *pt3s* feohtende *prp npm* fiohte *sbj pr3s* fuhton *pt3p*

ġefeohtan *III* achieve (by fighting), win

feohte *f* fighting, battle

ġefēol < ġefeallan

fēole *f* file

fēolheard *adj* hard as a file fēolhearde *apn*

fēolian *2* file

ġefēoll, fēoll- *see* ġefeallan

ġefēon *V* (+g/i) *rejoice, exult* ġefeah *pt3s*

fēond *m* enemy, foe, devil *ns* fēonda *gp* fēondas *np ap* fēondum *dp* fȳnd *np, ap*

fēondrǣden *f* enmity frēondrǣdene *as*

feor *adj* far, far away (*from +d*) *nsn nsm* feorres *gsn*

feor *adv* far, far back, from long ago fyr *comp* fyrrest *sup* (*farthest*)

fēore, fēores, feorg < feorh

feorgbold *n* soul's dwelling, body *ns*

feorh *n* life, soul *as* fēore *ds* fēores *gs* feorg *ns* fēorum *dp* fiorh *as*

feorhġenīðla *m* life-enemy, mortal foe feorhġenīðlan *as*

feohġyft *f* treasure-giving, valuable gift

feorlen *adj* distant, remote

feorm *f* food

feorr < feor

feorweġ *m* distant part

fēos < feoh

fēower *num* four

feowertiġ *num* forty fēowertigum *dsm*

ġefēra *m* companion, comrade *ns* ġefēran *as, np, ap* ġefērana *gp* ġefērum *dp*

fēran *1* go, journey, set out, depart, proceed, run *inf* fērde *pt3s* fērdest *pt2s* fērdon *pt3p* fērende *prp, nsm* ġefēran *1* reach, attain, gain victory ġefērde *pt3s*

ġefērde < ġefēran

ferhðfreċ *adj* bold in spirit ferhðfrecan *asm*

ġeferian *2* carry, take, convey *inf* ferede *pt3s*
  feredon *pt3p* ġeferod *pp*

fersc *adj* fresh (water)

ferþ *n* heart, spirit, mind *ns* ferþe *ds*

ferðloca *m* breast, heart *ns* ferðlocan *as*

ġefērum < ġefēra

fēt < fōt

fēt < fēdan

fetelhilt *n* ornamented sword-hilt

feter *f* fetter feterum *dp*

ġefetrian *2* fetter feterum *dp*

ġefetian *2* fetch *sbj pr3s* ġefetiġe, fetiġan *inf*

fēþa *m* foot-troop, soldier fēþan *as*

fēþecempa *m* foot-warrior *ns*

feþer *f* feather feþra *as*

ġefexode *pp adj* haired, having hair

fīclēaf *n* fig-leaf *ap*

fierd *f* army, militia, campaign

fierlen *adj* distant

fierst *m/f* period, time

fierste < first

fīf *num* five fife *npm*

filiġian *2* follow (+d) filiġdon *pt3p*

findan *III* find, meet, devise, recover *inf* findað
  pr3p fintst *pr2s* funde *pt3s* funden *pp*
  fundene *pp npm* fundon *pt3p*

finger *m* finger *ns, as* fingra *gp* fingras *np*
  fingrum *dp*

fioh *see* feoh

fiohte < feohtan

fiorh < feorh

fiorm *f* use, benefit fiorme *as*

fīras *mp* men, people fīra *gp* fīrum *dp*

firmest < fyrmest

first *m* (space of) time, duration, period *as*
  fierste *ds* fyrst *as* fyrste *ds*

fisc *m* fish *as*

fiscere *m* fisherman fisceras *np*

fisc-cynn *n* race of fishes

fiscian, fixian *2* fish

fix *m* fish fixas *np*

flān *m* arrow flāna *gp* flānes *gs*

flǣsc *n* flesh *as*

flǣschoma *m* 'house of flesh' body

flǣscmete *m* meat, flesh

flǣscmettum *dp*

flaxe *f* flask, bottle

flēag, flēah < flēogan, flēon

flēam *m* flight, retreat *as* flēame *ds*

ġeflēmed < ġeflȳman

flēogan *II* fly *inf* flēag *pt3s* flēah *pt3s*
  flēoganne *infl inf* flēoged *pr3s* flugon *pt3p*

flēon *III* flee, run, avoid *inf* flēah *pt3s* flugon
  pt3p

flēotan *II* float, swim flēat *pt3s* flēotendra *prp*
  gpm (=*noun*)

flet *n* floor, dwelling, hall *as*

ġeflīeman *see* ġeflȳman

ġeflit *n* dispute, suit ġeflite *ds*

flōc *n* flounder

flōd *m* flowing water, sea, stream, flood-tide,
  tide *ns, as* flōda *gp* flōde *ds* flōdes *gs*

flōr *f* floor flōre *as*

flot *n* sea *as*

flota *m* ship, fleet, seaman, Viking flotan *as, ds,
  np, gp*

flothere *m* army from a fleet, army of pirates

flotman *m* seaman, Viking flotmen *np*

flōwan *VII* flow *inf* flōwende *prp, nsm*

flyht *m* flight

flȳma *m fugitive, exile* flȳman *as*

ġeflȳman *1* put to flight ġeflȳmed *pp*

flȳs *n* fur, sealskin flȳse *ds*

fnǣst *m* breath

fnēosan *1* sneeze

ġefō < ġefōn

fōda *m* food

ġefohtan < ġefeohtan

folc *n* people, tribe, nation, troop, army, crowd *ns
  as* folce *ds* folces *gs* folcum *dp*

folclagu *f* public law folclaga *np*

folcliċ *adj* popular, public, common

folclond *n* country folclondes *gs*

folcscaru *f* folkshare, public land folcscare *ds*

folcstede *m* dwelling-place, place of assembly,
  battlefield

foldbūend *m* earthdweller

folde *f* earth, ground, soil, land foldan *as, gs, ds*

folgað *m* office, employment

folgað *m* following, retinue, service, position *as*

folgian *2* (+d) follow *inf* folgie *sbj pr3s* folgedon *pt3p* folgodon *pt3p*

folm/folme *f* hand folman *ds, dp* folme *ds* folmum *dp*

ġefōn *VII* catch, seize, clutch, grasp, take, encounter (fōn tō +d succeed to, receive) fanggene *pp npm* fēng *pt1s, pt3s* ġefeng *pt3s* fēngon *pt3p*

for *prep* (+d/a/i) for, because of, before, in, in the face of, in the presence of, as, through for ðī *see* forðȳ : *for bǣm/ban/bon see* forbǣm

for *adv* very, too

ġefōr < ġefaran

foran *adv* beforehand, in front

fōran < faran

forbær < forberan

forbærnan *1* burn down, consume by fire forbǝrnde *pt3s* forbǝrndon *pt3p* forbærned *pp* forbærnedne *pp, asm*

forbēah < forbūgan

forbēodan *II* (person +d) forbid borbēodab *pr3p* forbēad *pt3s*

forberan *IV* forbear, bear, tolerate *inf* borbær *pt3s*

forbēodan *II* (+d) forbid

forbīġean *1* turn away

forbūgan *II* flee from forbēah *pt3s*

ford *m* ford forda *ds*

fordēman *1* damn, condemn fordēmde *pt3s* fordēmed *pp*

fordīlġian *2* blot out, destroy fordīlgode *pp npm*

fordōn *anom* do away with, destroy *inf* fordyde *pt3s* fordydon *pt3p*

fore *prep* (+d/a) for, on behalf of, before, in the presence of, because of

forealdian *2* grow old forealdod *pp* elderly

forealdod *adj* aged *pp of* forealdian(=grow old)

foresǣd *adj* aforesaid forsǣdan *dsn* forsǣde *nsf*

forescēawian *2* foresee, pre-ordain, appoint, provide

foresecgan *3* say before, se foresæġda the aforesaid

forespeca (*for* forespreca) *m* intercessor, advocate, sponsor *ns* forespecan *np*

forespreccen *adj* above-mentioned

forewerd *adj* early forewerdne *asm*

forfaran *VI* ruin, destroy, cause to perish, obstruct, blockade forfōre *pt3s*

forġīaf, forġeaf- *see* forġīefan

forġeald, forġelde < forġieldan

forġīefan *V* give, grant, release forġeaf *pt3s* forġēafan *pt3p* forġēafe *pt2s sbj ptls* forġēafen *pt3p* forġefe *sbj pt3s* forġiefene *pp npm* forġifen *pp* forġifene *pp npm* forġȳfan *inf* forġȳfe *sbj pr1s*

forġieldan *III* repay, requite, indemnify, reward forġeald *pt3s* forġelde *sbj pr3s* forgolden *pp* forġyldan *inf* forġylde *sbj pr3s* forġyldon *sbj pt3p*

forġīeman *1* neglect, despise

forġietan *V* (+g) forget forġitan *inf*

forġif- *see* forġīefan

forġitan < forġietan

forgolden < forġieldan

forgrindan *III* grind to pieces, destroy forgrunden *pp*

forġȳf- *see* forġīefan

foġyld- *see* forġieldan

forhabban *3* hold back, hinder

forheard *adj* exceedingly hard forheardne asm

forhēawan *VII* cut down, hack down forhēawen *pp*

forherġian *2* plunder, ravage, devastate forhereġeode *pp npf* forherġod *pp*

forht *adj* afraid, fearful *nsm*

forhtfull *adj* fearful, timid

forhtian *2* fear, be afraid, dread *sbj pr3p* forhtedon *sbj pt3p* forhtiab *pr3p* forhtiende *prp npm* forhtiġe *pr2p* forhtiġende *prp npm*

forhwan *conj* because

forhwega *adv* somewhere

forlǣtan *VII* let go, loose, abandon, neglect, leave, forsake *inf* forlǣt *imp s* forlǣte *sbj pr3s* forlǣten *pr3p, pp* forlǣtende *prp nsm* forlǣton *inf* forlēt *pt1s, pt3s* forlēte *pt2s* forlēton *pt3p*

forlēogan *II* lie, perjure oneself forlogen *pp*

forlogene *pp npm*

forlēosan *II* lose *inf* forlēas *pp npm* forlure *pt2s*

forlēt, forlēt- *see* forlǣtan

forliden *adj* shipwrecked

forlidennes *f* shipwreck forlidennesse *as*

forliġer *n* fornication

forlogen, forlogene < forlēogan

forloren, forlure < forlēosan

forma *sup adj* foremost, first forman *asm, dsm, dsn, dsf*

forniman *IV* take away, carry off, overcome, plunder, destroy fornam *pt3s* fornōm *pt3s* fornōman *pt3p* fornumene *pp npm, npn*

fornȳdan *1* force, compel fornȳdde *pp npf*

foroft *adv* very often

forsawene < forsēon

forsceamian *2* make ashamed

forscrincan *III* dry up, wither forscruncon *pt3p*

forsēon *V* despise, scorn, reject, renounce forsawene *pp npf* forsāwon *pt3p* forsihð *pr3s* forsīoð *pr3p*

forsīðian *2* journey disastrously, perish forsīðod *pp*

forspillan *1* destroy, kill forspilde *pt3s*

forstandan *VII* hinder, prevent ; *understand* forstōd *pt1s, pt3s*

forswelgan *III* swallow up, swallow down, devour *inf* forswealg *pt3s* forswelgen *sbj pr3p*

forswerian *VI* forswear, swear falsely forsworene *pp npm*

forsyngian *2* sin greatly forsyngod *pp* (ruined by sin, corrupt) forsyngodan *pp* dsf

forþ *adv* forth, forward, onwards, sway, henceforth, still

forbǣm *adv* (often written as two words) because, for, seeing that, inasmuch as forbām, for ðan, forbon, for bon, for bām be because forban be, for ðan be, for bǣm be

forðfēran *1 go forth, die* forðfērde *pt3s*

forðgān *anom* go forth, leave forðēodon *pt3p*

foraġeorn *adj* eager to advance, ambitious

forðġerīmed *adj* all told

forðġesceaft *f* preordination, eternal decree, future *ns*

forbolian *2* do without, lack

forbon *see* forbǣm

forbringan *II* dislodge from

forbrysmian *2* strangle, choke, suffocate forðrysmdon *pt3p*

forbtēah < forbtēon

forbtēon *II* bring forth, produce, exhibit

forðweġ *m* the onward path, the journey ahead forðweġe *ds*

forðȳ *adv/conj* therefore, because for ðī

forwandian *2* respect forwandiġendre *prp dsf* (respectful)

forwearð < forweorðan

forweorðan *III* fall to ruin, become ruined, deteriorate, perish *inf sbj pr1p* forwearð *pt3s* forwurdan *pt3p* forwurde *pr1s*

forweosan *I* perish, decay forweorone *pp apm*

forwiernan *1* restrain, refuse

forwundian *2* wound badly forwunded *pp* forwundod *pp*

forwurdan, forwurðe < forweorðan

forwyrde *n/f* destruction, ruin forwyrde *ds*

forwyrnan *1* deny, refuse forwyrnde *pt3s*

foryman *1* reduce to poverty forymde *pp npf*

fōt *m* foot *as* fēt *np ap* fōta *gp* fōtes *gs* fōtum *dp*

fōtmǣl *n* the space of a foot

fōtsæð *n* footprint, footstep fōtswaðum *dp*

fracod *adj* base, wicked, useless fracodes *gsm*

fram *adv* away from

fram *prep* (+d/i) from, of, since, concerning, on account of, by from

framian *2* avail, benefit

franca *m* spear, lance francan *as, ds*

ġefrǣġe *adj* well-known

ġefrǣġen, ġefræġn < ġefriġnan

frætwa *f(pl)* ornaments

frætwan *1* adorn, make beautiful

frēa *m* lord, master, the Lord *ns* frēan *as, gs, ds*

freca *m* bold man, warrior

frēċne *adj* dangerous, savage, bold *apm* (=*noun* savage ones, enemies) frēċnen *ds*

frēcness *see* frēcnys

frēċnys *f* harm, danger frēċnysse *as/ds*

frēfran *1* comfort, console *inf*

fremde *adj* foreign, strange (=*noun* foreigner, stranger) fremdan *ds* fremdum *dp*

fremfulnes *f* usefulness, benefit fremfulnesse *gs*

ġefremian *2* (+*d*) help, avail, do good, effect, accomplish *inf* ġefremod *pp* fremode *pt3s*

ġefremman *1* do, perform, provide *inf* ġefremed *pp* ġefremede *pt3s* fremedon *pt3p* ġefremedon *pt3p*

frēo *adj* free frēoh *nsm* frēum *dsm* frīġes *gsm* frīġne *asm* frīora *gpm* frīoum *dpm*

frēod *f* goodwill, friendship, peace frēode *as*

frēoh *adj* free

frēolsbriċe *m* non-observance of festivals frēolbricas *np*

frēomæġ *m* noble kinsman frēomǣġum *dp*

frēond *m* friend, relative, lover *ns* frēonda *gp* frēondas *np* frēonde *ds* frēondum *dp* frȳnd *np, ap*

frēondlēas *adj* friendless frēondlēasne *asm*

frēondlíce *adv* in a friendly manner, affectionately

frēoriġ *adj* frozen, chilled *nsm*

frēoriht *n* rights of free persons

Frēsisc *adj* Frisian

Frēswæl *n* Frisian battle-field Frēswæle *ds*

fretan *V* eat up, devour fræt *pt3s*

frēum < frēo

Frīesa *m* a Frisian

frīġ *f* affection, embrace, love *ns*

frīġes < frēo

friġnan *III* ask, question, inquire fræġn *pt1s* friġe *imp s* frīnan *inf* frīneþ *pr3s* frūne *sbj pt1s*

ġefriġnan *III* hear of, find out, learn (by asking) ġefræġen *pt1s* ġefræġn *pt1s* ġefruġnon *pt1p* ġefrūnon *pt3p*

frīġne < frēo

frīora, frīoum < frēo

frioðuwǣr *f* peace-treaty

frib *m* peace, refuge, (right of) sanctuary, protection *as* fribe *ds* fribes *gs*

frōd *adj* old, mature, wise, experienced *nsm* frōda *nsm* (=*noun*) frōdran *comp npm*

frōfor *f* consolation, joy, comfort, refuge frōfre

as frīġne < frēo *gs* frōfres *gs*

from *adj* strenuous, bold, brave

from *see* fram

fromsīþ *m* journey away, departure *ns*

fruma *m* origin, beginning fruman *as, ds*

frumsceaft *f* beginning, origin, creation

frūne, ġefrūnon < ġefriġnan

frȳnd < frēond

fugel *m* bird, fowl *ns* fugelas *np* fugles *gs* fuglum *dp*

fugelere *m* fowler, bird-catcher

fugol *m* bird

fugolcynn *n* race of birds

fuhton < feohtan

ful, fulan < full

fūl *adj* foul, disgusting *nsf* fūla *nsm* fōlan *asm* fūle *asm* (=*noun* vile people) *npm* fūlne *asm*

full *adj* full, filled (with), entire, completed, utter *nsf, asn,* ful *nsn, asn* fullan *asf, dsm* fulle *asf, npm* fulles *gsn* fulne *asm* fulre *comp nsn, dsf ; in phr* be fulan *fully, in full* be fullan

full *adv* fully, completely, very ful

fullgān *anom* perform, follow fullēodon *pt3p*

fullíce *adv* fully, completely, outright

fūllíce *adv* foully, shamefully fūllíce

fulluht *n/f* baptism as fulluhte *ds* fulwihte *as*

fulne, fulre < full

fultum *m* forces, troops, help, support *as* fultom *as* fultomes *gs* fultume *ds*

fultumian *2* help, support *inf*

fulwian *2* baptize ġefullod *pp*

funde, fund- < findan

fundian *2* be eager for, set out, come fundaþ *pr3s* fundode *pt3s*

furlang *n* furlong furlanga *gp*

furbon *see* furðum

furðor *adv* further, any more furður

furbra *adj* superior

furðum *adv* furthermore, moreover, even furbon

furbur *adv* further, forward furðor

fūs *adj* (+*g*) eager, ready hastening *asm* fūse *asn, npm* (=*noun*) fūsne *asm*

fȳftȳne *num* fifteen

fyl *see* fyll

fylde < fyllan

fylġan *1* follow, observe, attend to (+*d*) *inf* fylġean *inf*

fyll *m* fall, death, destruction fyl *as* fulle *ds*

ġefyllan *1* fill, fulfil, complete fyllan *inf* ġefyldæ *pp npf* fylde *pt3s* ġefyldon *pt3p* ġefylle *imp s* ġefylled *pp* ġefylede *pp npm* ġefyldð *pr3s*

ġefyllan *1* fell, strike down, kill *inf* ġefylled *pp*

ġefylsta *m* helper ġefylstan *ds*

fylstan *1* (+*d*) help, support *inf*

fȳlþ *f* foul sin fȳlþe *as*

ġefylð < ġefyllan

fȳnd < fēond

fyr < feor

fȳr *n* fire, hell-fire *ns as* fȳre *ds* fȳres *gs*

fyrdhom *m* war-garment, mail-coat

fyrdhræġl *n* war-garment, corset

fyrdian *2* go to war fyrdedon *pt3p*

fyrġenstrēam *m* mountain stream

fȳrlēoht *n* fire-light

fyrmest *sup adj* (<forma) foremost, first, chief *nsm* firmest *nsf* fyrmestan *npm*

ġefyrn *adv* formerly, long ago

fyrrest < feor

fȳrspearca *m* spark

fyrst *adj* first, foremost, front fyrestum *dpm*

fyrst *m* space off time fyrste *ds*

fyrst, fyrste *see* first

fyrwit *n* curiosity fyrwites *gs*

gā < gān

gād *f* goad

ġegaderian *2* collect, gather *inf* ġegaderode *pt1s, pt3s, sbj pt3s, pp npm* ġegaderodon *pt3p*

ġegaderung *f* gathering, company

gād-īsen *n* goad-iron, cattle-prod

gafol *n* tribute *as* gafle *ds* gafole *ds* gofol *as*

gāl *adj* wanton, wicked

galan *VI* sing *inf*

gālnys *f* lust, wantonness gālnysse *ds*

gamol *adj* aged, old, ancient

gamen *n* sport

gamenian *2* jest, joke gamenode *pt3s*

gān *anom* go, advance, proceed *inf, sbj pr1p*

ēodon *pt1p* ēode *pt1s, pt3s, sbj pt2s* ēodon *pt3p* gā *pr1s, sbj pr3s, imp s* gāþ *imp p* gǣþ *pr3s*

ġegān *anom* arrive at, reach, come to gain, overrun, conquer, occupy, win *inf*, pp ġeēodon *pt3p* ġegā *sbj pr3s*

gandang *VII* go, come, walk

gang *m* going, progress, motion, flow gange *ds* gonges *gs*

gang, ġegang- *see* ġegongan

gangan *see* gān

gangende *see* gān

ġegangan *redp* overrun

gār *m* spear, javelin *ns* gāras *ap* gāre *ds* gārum *dp*

gārmitting *f* spear-encounter gārmittinge *gs*

gārsecg *m* sea *ns*

gāst *m* ghost, spirit, soul, demon *ns, as* gāsta *gp* gāstae *ds* gāstas *np, ap* gāste *ds* gāstes *gs* gǣst *ns* gǣsta *gp* gǣstes *gs*

gāstliċ *adj* spiritual, ghostly, ghastly, awful. terrifying gāstlican *dsn* gāstliċe *asn* gāstlicum *dsn, dpm* gǣstliċ *nsn*

gāstlīe *adv* spiritually

gatu < ġeat

gāþ < gān

gǣlsa *m* pride, wantonness, luxury gǣlsan *as*

gærs *n* grass, herb

gǣst *see* gāst

gǣstliċ *see* gāstliċ

gǣþ < gān

ġe *conj* and ġe···ġe both···and

ġē *pers pron* ye, you *np* ēow *ap, dp* ēower *gp* (of you) īow *dp* ēower

ġēa *adv* yes ġē

ġeaf, ġeafan < giefan

ġealga *m* gallows, cross *ns* ġealgan *as*

ġealgtrēowe *n* gallows-tree

ġealgean *see* ġeealgian

ġeanwyrde *adj* known, confessed

ġēap *adj* deceitful, astute

ġēap *adj* curved, arched, broad *nsm*

ġēar *n* year *ns, ap* ġēara *gp* ġēare *ds* ġēarum *dp* ġēr *ns, as* ġēres *gs*

ġēara *adv* 'of yore', once, long ago ġēara *iū*

once long ago, years ago

ġearcian *2* prepare

ġeard *m* enclosure, dwelling ġeardas *ap* ġeardum *dp*

ġēardagas *mp* days of yore, former days ġēardagum *dp*

ġeare *see* ġearwe

ġearo *adj* ready, prepared *nsm, nsn* ġearuwe *npm*

ġearolīċe *adv* clearly

ġearu *see* ġearo

ġearuwe < ġearo

ġearwe *adv* readily, well ġeare

ġearwian *2* prepare, perform

ġeat *n* gate, door *as* gatu *ap*

Ġēatum *pr n* a Geat Ġēates *gs*

Ġēatas *pr n* Geats, Jutes Ġēatua *gp* Ġēatum *dp*

ġeatolic *adj* well-equipped, noble *nsn*

ġecneordness *f* accomplishment

ġecynd *n* origin, species, kind

ġedeorf *n* toil, labor

ġefērscipe *m* companionship

ġeġierela *m* garment

ġehæp *adj* fit, suitable

ġehiersum *adj* obedient

ġelǣred *adj* learned

ġelpan *III* boast, exult *inf* ġelpeð *pr3s*

ġeman *1* take heed ġēmde *pt3s*

ġēmde < ġīeman

ġēn *adv* still, yet, further

ġeō *adv* formerly, of old ġiū

ġeoc *f* yoke

ġeocian *2* yoke ġeġeoced *pp*

ġeogoð *f* youthful company

ġeogub *f* youth, youthfulness ġeogoð *ns* ġeogoðe *ds* ġeogube *ds* ġioguð *ns* iugobe *ds*

ġēomor *adj* troubled, sorrowful, sad, gloomy, mournful *nsm* ġēomorre *dsf* ġēomran *dsf* ġēomre *apm* ġēomuru *nsf*

ġēomormōd *adj* sad-hearted, despondent *nsm* ġēomormōdum *dsn*

ġēomrian *2* mourn, lament ġēomrode *pt3s*

ġeomrung *f* grief, lamentation

ġeond *prep* (+*a*) through, throughout, over, across ġiond, ġynbd

ġeondhweorfan *III* pass through, pervade ġeondhweorfeð *pr3s*

ġeondscēawian *2* survey, regard ġeondscēawað *pr3s*

ġeondbenċean *1* contemplate, mediate on ġeondbenċe *pr1s* ġeondbenċeð *pr3s*

ġeong *adj* young *nsm* ġeonge *npm* ġeongne *asm* ġiunge *npm* ġiungne *asm* iunga *nsm* iungan *dsm* (=noun) iunge *nsf* iungum *dpm, dpn*

ġeongan *see* gongan

ġeorn *adj* eager, zealous *nsm* ġiorne *npm*

ġeorne *adv* eagerly, readily, well, carefully, clearly. earnestly, keenly ġeornost *sup* ġiorne

ġeornlīċe *adv* eagerly, earnestly, carefully, closely ġeornlīcor *comp*

ġeotan *II* pour, gush

ġerǣde *n* trappings, accouterments

ġereord *n* food, feast

ġēsne *adj* (+*g*) empty, bereft of, deprived of, lacking *nsm, asm, npm*

ġestrēon *n* gain, possession

ġet *see* ġīet

ġeteald, ġetealde *see* ġetellan

ġetrȳwe *adj* true, faithful

ġewemmodlīċe *adv* corruptly

ġewislīċe *adv* certainly

ġewbǣrness *f* concord, peace, gentleness

ġid *see* ġiedd

ġiedd *n* song, poem, story, narrative, word, speech *ns* ġid *ns* ġiddum *dp* ġied *as*

ġiefan *V* give, grant, bestow, devote ġeaf *pt3s* ġeafan *pt3p* ġif *imp s* ġifan *inf* ġife *pr1s* ġyfeð *pr3s*

ġiefena < ġife

ġiefstōl *m* gift-throne ġiefstōlas *gs*

ġiefta *f pl* marriage, weddings

ġiefu *f* gift, grace

ġieldan *III* pay, repay, requite ġeald *pt3s, sbj pt3s* ġielde *sbj pr3s* guldan *pt3p* ġyldan *inf* ġyldað *pr1p* ġylde *sbj pr3s* ġyldon *inf*

ġielpes < ġylp

ġīeman *1* (+*g*) care for, take heed, take charge of, control *inf* ġēmde *pt3s* ġȳman *inf* ġȳmdon *pt3p* ġyme *sbj pr3s*

ġiestrandæġ *m* yesterday

ġiet, ġieta *see* ġyt

ġif *conj* if, whether, lest ġyf

ġif, ġifan *see* ġiefan

ġiernan *1* desire, covet with (+*g*)

ġiesthūs *n* guesthouse, inn

ġifend *m* giver ġifendes *gs*

ġifernes *f* greed, gluttony ġifernessa *ap*

ġīfre *adj* eager, avid, greedy *nsm* ġīfrost *sup* *nsm*

ġīfre *adj* eager, avid, greedy ġīfrost *sup nsm*

ġiefta *fp* marriage, wedding

ġifu *f* gift, favor, grace *ns* ġife *as, ds, ap* ġiefena *gp* ġyfena *gp*

ġīgant *m* giant ġīganta *gp*

ġim *m* gem, jewel *ns* ġimmas *np*

ġinn *adj* spacious, wide ġinnan *ism, dsf* ġynne *asm*

ġio- *see* ġeo-

ġioguð *f* young people, youth ġeoguðe *ds*

ġiond *see* ġeond

ġist *see* ġyst

ġistlībe *adj* hospitable

ġīt *see* ġyt

ġitsung *f* avarice, greediness (+*g for*) ġītsunga *ap* ġītsunge *as*

ġiunge, ġiungne < ġeong

glād < glēdan

glæd *adj* kind, gracious

glædlīċe *adv* joyfully

glæs *n* glass

glēaw *adj* wise, prudent, clear-sighted *nsm, nsf* glēawe *asf, nsf* (=*noun*) glēwra *com nsm*

glēawhȳdiġ *adj* thoughtful, prudent

glenġan *1* adorn ġeglænġde *pp asn* ġeglenġed *pp*

glīdan *I* glide glād *pt3s*

glīdan *I* glide glād *pt3s*

glīwstæf *m* melody, joy glīwstafum *dp* (=*adv* joyfully)

gnagan *II* gnaw

gnorn *adj* sad, troubled gnornra *comp nsm*

gnornian *2* mourn, lament, regret gnornað *pr3s* gnornode *pt3s*

god *n* god *ns, as* goda *gp* godas *np, ap* gode *ds* godum *dp*

God *m* God *ns as* Godæ *ds* Godæs *gs* Godd *as* Gode *ds* Godes *gs*

gōd *adj* good, excellent, favorable, worthy, virtuous, noble, generous *nsm* gōda *nsm* (=*noun*) gōdan *isn* gōde *asf, apm* gōdena *gpm* gōdne *asm* gōdra *gpn, gpf, comp gpm* gōdum *dsm, dpm, dpn, dpf* good *nsn, asn* goodan *apm*

gōd *n* benefit, property, possessions

godcund *adj* divine, religious, spiritual *asf* godcunda *nsm* godcundan *asm, asf, dsm, npm, dpf* godcunde *nsf* godcundra *gpm, gpf* godcundre *gsf, dsf* godcundum *dpm*

gōddǣd *f* good deed gōddǣda *ap* gōddǣdan dp

godfyrht *adj* god-fearing godfyrhte *ap*

gōdian *2* improve, enrich gōdiende *prp nsn* ġegōdod *pp*

gōdne < gōd

gōdnes *f* goodness, virtue gōndesse *ds*

gōdra < gōd

godspel *n* gospel, gospel-reading *ns, as* godspelles *gs*

gofol *see* gafol

gold *n* gold *ns as* goldæs *gs* golde *ds, is* goldes *gs*

goldhord *n* gold-hoard, treasure goldhorde *ds*

goldsmib *m* goldsmith

goldwine *m* lord(gold-friend)

gombe *f* tribute

gomen *n* entertainement gomene *ds*

gomenwudu *m* 'mirth-wood' lyre, harp

ġegongan *VII* go, advance, proceed, walk *inf* gang *imp s* gangan *inf* ġegangan *inf* gange *sbj pr1s, sbj pr2s, sbj pr3s* gangeð *pr3s* gangon *sub pr3p* geongan *inf* gonge *pr1s* gongende *prp nsm*

gonges < gang

good, good- *see* gōd

Gotan *pr n* (*mp*) the Goths Gotena *gp*

gram *adj* angry, fierce, hostile grame *npm* gramum *dpm* (=*noun* enemy)

grama *m* rage, anger graman *ds*

grāp *f* grasp, claw grāpum *dp*

grāp < grīpan

grǣdiġ *adj* greedy, fierce grǣdiġne *asm*

grǣġ *adj* grey grǣġe *asn*

ġegrǣmedan < ġegremian

Grēacas *pr n* the Greeks Crēacas *np* Grēcum *dp*

grēada *m* bosom

grēat *adj* great, huge grēate *npm*

ġegremian *2* enrage, incense, provoke ġegrǣmedan *pt3p* ġegremede *pp npm* ġegremod *pp* ġegremode *pp npm*

gremman *1* irritate

grēne *adj* green, uncooked *nsm* grēnne *asm* grēnum *dpn*

grēotan *II* weep, lament grēotende *prp npm*

ġegrētan *1* greet, address, approach, accost, touch *inf* grēt *pr3s* grēted *pp* grēteð *pr3s* grētte *pt3s* ġegrētte *pt3s* grētton *pt3p*

grim *adj* fierce, severe, cruel, angry *nsm* grimman *apm, dpf* grimme *npm, apf*

grimliċ *adj* cruel, terrible *nsn*

grimme *adv* fiercely, harshly

grīn *f/n* snare

grindan *III* grind, sharpen grindende *pp nsf* ġegrunden, ġegrudene *pp apm*

grīpan *I* seize, grab, take hold grāp *pt3s* grīpeð *pr3s*

gripe *m* grip, attack

grīstbitian *2* gnash the teeth, cough *inf*

gristbitung *f* gnashing of teeth

grið *n* truce, peace, sanctuary griðe *ds* griðes *gs*

griðlēas *adj* unprotected, violated griðlēase *npf*

grōwan *VII* grow

grund *m* ground, land, earth, region, bottom, abyss, depth *as* grundas *ap* grunde *is* grundes *gs*

ġegrund- *see* grindan

grundlēas *adj* fathomless, boundless grundlēase *apf*

grundwong *m* bottom, ground

grundwyrġen *f* cursed creature of the deep grundwyrgenne *as*

grymetian *2* roar, rage

guma *m* man *ns* guman *gs, np, gp* gumena *gp*

gūþ *f* battle, combat gōde *as* gōbe *gs, ds*

gūðhafoc *m* war-hawk

gūðlēoð *n* battle-song

gūðplega *m* battle-game, conflict

gūðrǣs *n* battle-storm, assault gūðrǣsa *gp*

gūðrēow *adj* fierce in battle

gūðrinc *m* warrior

gūðwēriġ *adj* battle-weary, worn out from the fight gūðwēriġne *asm*

gyden *f* goddess gydena *np*

ġyf *see* ġif

ġyfena < ġifu

ġyfeð < ġiefan

ġyld- *see* ġieldan

gylden *adj* golden

ġylp *m* boast, boasting, vaunting *ns* ġielpes *gs*

gylt *m* crime, sin *as*

gyltend *m* debtor, offender gyltendum *dp*

ġȳm- *see* ġieman

ġymm *m* gem, jewel, precious stone gimm

ġynd *see* ġeond

ġynne < ġinn

gyrdan *1* gird, encircle gyrde *pt3s*

ġyrnwrǣcu *f* revenge for injury ġyrnwrǣce *ds*

ġyrwan *1* prepare, adorn, dress ġeġerwed *pp* gierede *pt3s* ġeġyred *pp* ġyredon *pt3p* ġeġyrwed *pp* ġeġyryde *pp asp*

ġyst *m* guest, visitor, stranger ġist *ns* ġystas *np*

ġystrandæġ *adv* yesterday

ġȳt *adv* yet, further, still even, up to now ġēt, ġīet, ġīeta, ġīt, ġȳta *; in adv phr* bā ġȳt yet, will, further æāġȳt

Ⓗ

habban *3* have, possess, hold, keep, watch over, be subject to *inf* habbaþ *pr1p pr2p, pr3p* habbe *pr1s, sbj pr1p* hafast *pr2s* hafaþ *pr3s* hæbbe *pr1s, pr2p, sbj pr3s* hæbben *sbj pr3p* hæfdan *pt3p* hæfdæ *pt1s* hæfde *pt1s, pt3s, sbj pt3s* hæfdon *pt3p* hæfst *pr2s* hæfþ *pr3s* heafde *pt3s : with neg nabbaþ pr3p* nafaþ *pr3s* næbbe *pr1s, sbj pr3s* næfde *sbj pt1s* næfþ *pr3s* hacod *m* pike

hād *m* order, office, rank ; person, gender *ns* hāda *gp* dādas *np* hāde *ds* hēdum *dp*

hādbryċe *m* injuries to those in holy orders hādbrycas *ap*

ġehādian *2* consecrate, ordain ġehādod *pp* 3ehādode *pt3s pp npm* (=*noun* those in holy orders)

ġehādod *adj* ordained, in orders, clerical

hafab < habban

hafela *m* head hafelan *np, ds*

hafenian *2* raise, lift up hafenade *pt3s* hefenode *pt3s*

hafoc *m* hawk, falcon hafuc *ns*

hagolian *2* hail

hāl *adj* whole, sound, safe, uninjured *nsm, nsf, asn* hālan *dsn* hāle *npm*

hālga *m* holy person, saint hālgan *ds* hālgum *dp* hāliġra *gpm, gpf* hāliġre *dsf* ; *see also adj* hāliġ

ġehālgian *2* hallow, consecrate ġehālgod *pp*

hāliġ *adj* holy, divine, saintly *nsm asn* hālga *nsm* hālgan *asm, asf, gsm, gsn, gsm, npn, apn* hālgum *dpm, dpn* hāligan *asf, dsf* hāliġe *nsn, nsf, asn, asf, npm* ; *see also noun* hālga

hāliġdōm *m* sanctuary, relics hāliġdōmæ *ds*

hāliġnes *f* sanctuary

hālisn *2* heal

hals *m* neck *as* halse *ds* healse *ds*

hām *adv* home, homewards

hām *m* home, dwellings, abode *as, ds* hāmas *ap* hāme *ds*

hamor *m* hammer hamora *gp* homera *gp*

hāmweard *adv* homeward

hand *f* hand *ns, as* handa *dp, np, ap, gp* handon *dp* handum *dp* hond *ns* honda *ds, ap* hondum

handbred *m* palm of a hand handbredum *dp*

hangian *2* hang, depend on, be jointed to *inf* hongiað *pr3p*

hār *adj* hoary, old and grey *nsm* hāra *nsm* hāre *apf* hārne *asm*

hara *m* hare

hās *adj* hoarse *nsm*

hasewanpād *adj* dark-coated

hāt *adj* hot, fervent, intense, inspiring *nsm, nsn npf* hāta *nsm* hātan *asf, dsf* hātost *sup nsn* hātran *comp npm*

hāt *n* heat hāte *ds*

ġehātan *II* (1) order, command, summon, call, name (*often +inf*) hāt *imp s* hāte *pr1s* hāteb *pr3s* ġehātep *pr3s* heht, hēt *pt3s* hēte *sbj pt3s* hēton *pt3p* (2) call, be named hātan *inf* hātab *pr1p*, *pr3p* hāten *pp* ġehāten *pp* ġehātene *pp npm, npn* hāteb *pr3s* hātta *passive pt3s* hāttte *passive pr1s, pr3s* hēte *pt2s*

ġehātan *VII* promise, vow ġeheht *pt3s* ġehēt *pt1s, pt3s* ġehēton *pt3p*

hātheort *adj* passionate, impulsive

hāttan, hātte- < ġehātan

hǣ *see* hē

hǣbb- *see* habban

hǣfd-, fǣfst *see* habban

ġehǣftan *1* catch, shackle, fetter, hold captive *inf* ġehǣfte *pp* ġehǣfted *pp* ġehǣftne *pp asm*

hǣfb < habban

hæġl *m* hail *ns* haġle *ds*

hæġlfaru *f* hailstorm hæġlfare *as*

(ġē)hǣlan *1* heal, cure, save *inf* ġehǣl *imp s* ġehǣlde *pt3s, sbj pt3s* ġehǣled *pp* ġehǣlede *pp npm* hǣlb *pr3s*

hæle *m* man, warrior

hǣlend *m* savior *ns, as* hǣlende *ds* hǣlendes *gs* hǣlyn *as* hǣlynd *ns*

hǣleb *m* man, hero, warrior *ns, np, ap* hǣleba *gp* hǣlebum *dp*

hǣlfter *f* halter

hǣlo *f* safety, security, salvation *ns, ds*

ġehǣman *1* have intercourse with, copulate ġehǣ mde *pt3s*

hǣpse *f* hasp, fastening

hǣrfest *m* harvest time, autumn, fall *ns* hǣrfeste *ds*

hǣring *m* herring

hǣs *f* bidding, command hǣse *ds*

hǣto *f* heat hǣte *ds*

hǣben *adj* heathen (often=*noun*) hǣbenan *npm, asm* hǣbene *npm, npf, apm* hǣbenes *gsm* hǣbenra *gpm, gp* hǣbenum *dpm, dpf*

hǣbenġyld *n* idolatry, heathen sacrifice hǣbenġyld
as

hǣbenscype *m* heathenism, paganism, idolatry
hǣðenscipe as

hǣaennes *f* heathendom

hærfæste *m* autumn

hǣte *f* heat

hǣðena *m* heathen

hǣðstapa *m* heath-stalker

hē *pers pron* he, him, his *ns* hǣ *ns* hiene *as*
him *ds* hinæ *as* hine *as* his *gs* hym *ds* hyne
as hys *gs* ; *see also* sē

hēa *see* hēah

hēaburh *f* high stronghold

hēafde < habban

hēafod *n* head *ns, as, ap* hǣfde *ds* hēafde *ds*
hēafdum *dp*

hēafodmann *m* head man, captain hēafodmen
np hēafodmannum *dp*

hēah *adj* high, lofty, tall, deep, sublime,
illustrious, proud *nsm, nsn* hēa *nsf* hēage *npn*
hēagum *dpm* hēan *asm, dsm, dsn, dsf, apm,
dpn* hēanne *asm* hēhsta *sup nsm* hēhstan
gsm hēhste *nsn* hīeran *comp dsm* hȳhsta
sup nsm

hēahburg *f* capital

hēahsetl *n* hight seat, throne

heal *see* heall

healærn *n* hall-building, healærna *gp*

ġehealdan *VII* hold, possess, keep, maintain,
preserve, observe, guard, keep close, watch
over, control, rule, treat occupy *inf* healdanne
infl inf ġehealdanne *infl inf* healdab *pr3s*
ġehealdað *pr3p* healde *sbj pr3s* ġehealden *pp*
ġehealdene *pp npm* healdende *prp npm*
healdenne *infl inf* healdep *pr3p* ġehealdeb
pr3s hēold *pt1s, pr3s* hēodan *pt1p* hēolde
pt3s, sub pt3s ġehēolde hēoldon *pt3p* hīoldon
pt3p ġehīoldon *pt3p* hylt *imp s*

healf *adj* half healfne *asm* ōber healf
one-and-a-half *asn*

healf *f* half, side *as* healfe *as* healfre *gsf* healfa
ap

healgamen *n* hall entertainment

hēaliċ *adj* high, exalted, glorious hēaliċe *asf*

hēaliċne *asm* hēalicon *dsn* hēalicum *dpm*

heall *f* hall, palace heal *ns* healle *as, gs, ds*

ġehealp < ġehelpan

healreċed *n* hall-building

healsġebedda *m/f* dear bedfellow, consort,
spouse

hēan *adj* lowly, dejected, despised *nsm* hēanne
asm

hēddern *n* storehouse.

heslse < hals

hēan *adj* despised, dejected hēanne asm

hēan, hēanne < hēah

hēanliċ *adj* humiliating, shameful *nsn*

hēap *m* crowd, troop, company *as* hēape *ds*
hēapum *dp*

hēapmǣlum *adv* in troops, in droves

hearpere *m* harper

heard *adj* hard, strong, brave, fierce, stern, cruel,
bitter *nsm* (=noun +g) *nsf, asn* hearde *nsn,
npm* heardes *gsm, gsn* heardne *asm*
heardost *sup nsn* heardra *comp gpm* (=noun)
heardum *dpn* heordra *gpf*

hearde *adv* painfully, harshly, firmly heard

heardsēliġ *adj* ill-fortuned heardsǣliġne *asm*

hearpe *f* harp hearpan *as, gs, ds*

heaðobyrne *f* battle-corslet

heabolind *f* battle-shield (of linden wood)
heabolinde *ap*

heaðowǣd *f* battle-dress, armour heaðowǣdum
dp

heaðowylm *m* hostile flame

ġehēawan *VII* hew, cut down, hack, slay *inf*
ġehēawen *pp* hēaweb *pr3s* hēow *pt3s*
hēowan *pt3p* hēowon *pt3p*

hebban *VI* lift up, bear aloft *inf*

hēddern *n* storehouse

hefeliċ *adj* heavy

hefene < heofon

hefiġ *adj* heavy, dire, grievous *nsn* hefian *dsn*
hefiġran *comp npf*

heftiġtīeme *adj* burdensome

hēhfæder *m* God(=the high father)

hēhst- *see* hēah

ġehēht < ġehātan

hell *f* hell *ns* helle *as, gs*

hellewīte *n* hell-torment hellewītes *gs*

helm *m* helmet, protection, protector *ns, as* hellme *ds* helmas *ap* helmum

help *f* help helpe *as, ds*

ġehelpan *II* (+*g*/*d*) help *inf* helpe *sbj pr3s*

ġehende *adv* near, at hand

hēo *pers pron* she, her, hers *ns, as* hī *as* hīe *as* hiġ *as* hīo *ns* hiræ *ds* hire *gs* hyre *gs* ; *see also* sēo

hēo < hī

Heodeningas *pr n* the Heodenings Heodeninga *gp*

heofon *m* heaven *as* hefene *ds* heofenan *as* heofenas *ap* heofenes *gs* heofenum *dp* heofne *ds* heofnum *dp* heofona *gp* heofonan *dp* heofonas *np, ap* heofones *gs* heofonum *dp*

heofonliċ *adj* heavenly *nsf* heofenlican *apm* heofenlicum *dsn* heofonlecan *gsn, isn* heofonlican *gsn* heofonlīċe *asn* heofonliċne *asm*

ġehēold- *see* ġehealdan

heolstor *adj* dark, shadowy heolstran *dsm*

heolstor *n* darkness heolstre *ds*

heom (him) < hī

heonan *see* heonon

heonon *adv* hence, from here, henceforth heonan

heononforð *adv* henceforth, from here heonanforb

heora < hī

heorogrim *adj* deadly grim, ferocious

heorðwerod *n* hearth-troop, body of household retainers

hēore *adj* pleasant

heoroġīfre *adj* fiercely ravenous, greedy for slaughter

heorosweng *m* sword-stroke

heorot *m* stag

heort *m* hart, stag *as*

heorte *f* heart, will, courage *ns* heortan *as, gs, ds, ap* heortum *dp*

heorðġenēat *m* hearth-companion

hēow, hēow- *see* hēawan

hēr *adv* here, in this place, at this time

here *m* army, (invading) host ; war, devastation

ns, as, ds heres *gs* herġas *np* herġes *gs* heriġe *ds* heriġes *gs*

ġehēre < ġehȳran

heredon < herian

hereflȳm *m* fugitive from an army hereflēman *ap*

hereġeatu *f* war-equipment, heriot

herelāf *f* army remnant, survivors herelāfum *dp*

herenet *n* 'battle-mesh' corslet

herespēd *f* success in battle

heresyrċe *f* war corslet, mailcoat heresyrċan *as*

heretoga *m* leader of army, commander *ns* heretogan *np*

ġeherġian *2* ravage, plunder, harry, lay waste ġeherġodon *pt3p* ġeherġoden *pt3p* ġeherġod *pp*

herġung *f* harrowing, raving, pillage herġunge *ds*

herian *1* praise, glorify, extol *inf* hera *imp s* heredon *pt3p* heregian *inf* herġen *sbj pr3p* heriab *pr3p* heriġab *pr3p* heriġean *inf*

heriġe, heriġes < here

heriġean *see* herian

hērinne *adv* herein

ġehēt, ġehēt- see ġehātan

hete *m* hatred, malice

heteliċe *adv* terribly, violently

hetol *adj* hating, evil, hostile, savage hetole *npm* hetula *nsm*

hī *pers pron* they, them, their hēo *np* heom *dp* heora *gp* hī *np, ap* hīe *np, ap* hiġ *np, ap* him *dp* hiera *gp* hiora *gp* hira *gp* hȳ *np* hym *dp* hyra *gp*

hī < hēo

ġehicg- *see* ġehycgan

hider *adv* hither, here hieder

hīe < hī, hēo

hīeġ *n* hay

hīenan *1* humiliate ; strike down

hiene < hē

hiera < hī

hīeran *see* hȳran

hīeran < hēah

ġehīer- *see* ġehȳran

hierdebōc *f* shepherd's book

hierde *see* hyrde

hierdrǣden *f* guardianship

ġehīersum *adj* obedient

hīersumian *2* (+*d*) *obey* hīersumedon *pt3p*

ġehīersumnes *f* obedience

hiġ < hēo, hī

hiġ *n* hay hīġe *ds*

hiġe *m* mind, heart, courage, thought hyġe *ns*

hiġeb < hycgan

hiht *see* hyht

hild *f* battle, war *ns* hilda *gp* hilde *as, ds*

hildebil *n* battle-sword hildebille *ds*

hildelēoman *m* battle flame, sword hildelēoman *as*

hilderinc *m* warrior, hero *ns* hilderinca *gp* hilderincas *np* hilderince *ds*

hildetūx *m* battle-tusk hildetūxum *dp*

hildewǣpen *n* war-weapon hildewǣpnum *dp*

hildewīsa *m* leader in battle hildewīsan *ds*

him < hē, hit, hī

hinæ (hine) < hē

hindan *adv* from behind

hīo *see* hēo

ġehīoldon < ġehealdan

hiora, hira < hī

ġehīr- *see* ġehȳran

hiræ, hire < hēoh

hīred *m* family, household

his < hī, hit

hit *pers pron* it, its *ns, as* his *gs* hyt *ns, as*

hīw *n* form, fashion, appearance *ns* hīwe *ds*

hīwrǣden *f* family, household

hladan *VI* load, pile up blōd *pt3s*

hlāf *m* bread hlāfes *gs*

hlāford *m* lord, master, ruler *ns, as* hlāfordas *np* hlāfordæs *gs* hlāforde *ds* hlāfordes *gs*

hlāfordom *m* lordship

hlāw *m* mound, barrow hlāwe *ds* hlǣwe *ds*

hlǣder *f* ladder

hlǣfdiġe *f* lady hlǣfdiġan *ds*

hlæst *n* load, freight

ġehlæstan *1* load, deck ġehlæste *pp asf*

ġehlēapan *VII* leap onto, mount ġehlēop *pt3p*

hlehhan *VI* laugh, rejoice hlōh *pt3s*

hlēo *n* protector, lord *ns*

hlēobrian *2* sound, speak, proclaim hlēobrode *pt3s*

hliehhan *VI* laugh, exult hlōh *pt3s*

hlifian *2* rise up, tower hlifiġe *pr1s*

hlosnian *2* (+*g*) listen for hlosnode *pt3s*

hlūde *adv* loudly, aloud

hlȳdan *1* make a noise, shout

hlynian *2* roar, resound hlynode *pt3s*

ġehlystan *1* listen ġehlyston *pt3p*

hnāg < hnīgan

hnappian *2* sleep, nap, doze

hnīgan *I* bend down, bow hnāg *pt1s*

hō *see* hōh

hōcor *n* insult, derision hōcere *ds*

hōcorwyrde *adj* derisive, scornful *npm*

hof *n* dwelling, court hofe *ds* hofu *np*

hōh *m* heel hō *ds*

hōl *n* slander, malice *ns*

ġehola *m* companion, comrade

hold *adj* friendly, loyal, gracious *nsm* holdne *asm* holdost *sup asn* holdra *gpm*

hōlinga *adv* without cause, in vain

holm *m* ocean, sea, water *ns, as* holma *gp*

holmwudu *m* tree on the hill *as*

holt *n* wood, forest, copse holte *ds* holtes *gs*

holtwudu *m* forest, wood

homer *see* hamor

hōn *VII* hang, be hanged

hond, honda *see* hand

hondġemōt *n* hand-to-hand encounter, battle hondgemōta *gp*

hondplega *m* hand-to-hand combat hondplegan *gs*

hongiað *see* hangian

hangiað < hangian

hettend *m* enemy, persecutor

hord *n* hoard, treasure *as/ap* horde *ds*

hordcofa *m* treasure chamber, heart hordcofan *as*

horn *m* horn, gable hornas *ap*

hornġēap *adj* wide-gabled

hors *n* horse *as* horsa, horse *ds*

ġehorsian *2* provide with horses

horsweġ *m* bridle path, horseway horsweġe *ds*

hrā < hrǣw

hran *m* whale

hrabe *adv* quickly, soon, at once rabe, rabor
  comp

hræd *adj* quick, alert hræest *sup nsn*

hræding *f* haste hrædinge *ds*

hrædlīċe *adv* forthwith, quickly

hrædwyrde *adj* hasty of speech *nsm*

hræf(e)n *see* hrefn

hrēw *n* corpse, body *ns, np, ap* hrā *ns* hrǣ *ap*

hrēam *m* shouting, outcry, noise

hrēaw *adj* raw

hrefn *m* raven hræfen *ns*

hrēman *1* (+d) exult about *inf*

hrēmiġ *adj* (+g) exulting, boasting hrēmiġe *npm*

hremmas, hremn < hrefn

hreō *see* hreōh

hrēodan *II* adorn hroden *pp* ġehrodene *pp asf*

hreōh *adj* fierce, savage, distraught, troubled
  hrēo *nsm, asf*

hrēosan *II* fall, collapse, crumble *inf* hrēosende
  prp nsf ġehrorene *pp npm* hruran *pt3p*
  hruron *pt3p*

hrēowceariġ *adj* sorrowful, distressed *nsm*

hrēowlīċe *adv* cruelly, wretchedly

hrepian *2* touch hrepoden *sbj pt1p*

hrēran *1* move, stir *inf*

hreber *n* breast, heart, spirit hrebra *gp* hrebre
  as, ds

hrīeman *1* cry out, shout

hrīm *m* rime, frost *ns, as* hrīme *is*

hrīmċealde *adj* ice-cold

ġehrīnan *I* (+d) touch, reach ġehrān *pt3s*

hrinde *adj* rimy, frosted

hring *m* ring, ringed mail-coat ; circle, circular
  structure hringa *gp* hringas *ap* hringum *dp*

hringedstefna *m* ringed prow (ship) hringedstefnan
  as

hringmǣl *n* ring-marked sword

hrīb *f* snowstorm

hrīber *n* head of cattle, ox

hrōf *m* roof, sky, heavens *ns, as* hrōfas *np, ap*
  hrōfe *ds*

hronrād *f* sea(=whale road)

ġehrorene < hrēosan

hrōfsele *m* roofed hall

hruran < hrēosan

hrūse *f* earth hrūsan *as, gs*

hryre *m* ruin, fall, destruction, decay *as, gs, ds*

hrȳbiġ *adj* storm-eaten hrȳbġe *npm*

hū *adv* how

hū *conj* how

hueat *see* hwæt

hund *m* dog, hound *ns, as* hundum *dp*

hund *num* hundred

hungor *m* hunger, famine *ns, as* hunger *ns, as*
  hungre *ds*

hungriġ *adj* hungry

hundfeald *adj* hundredfold

hundtēontiġ *num* hundred

hungriġ *adj* hungry

hunta *m* huntsman huntan *np*

huntoa *m* hunting, game

huntung *f* hunting, game caught in hunting

hūru *adv* certainly, indeed, truly, especially

hūs *n* house, family *ns, as, np* hūse *ds*

hūsl *n* eucharist, host *as* hūsles *gs*

huxlīċe *adv* ignominiously, with insult

hwā, hwæt *indef/interrog pron* who, what, one,
  whoever, anyone, someone, something huaet
  nsn hwā *nsm* hwām *dsm* hwæne *asm* hwæt
  nsn, asn hwī *isn* (*see separate entry*) hwȳ
  isn (*see* hwī) ; *in adv/conj phr* (*isn*) for
  hwan *why* for hwon *why* tō hwon *as to
  what, why* ; *see also* swā swā

ġehwā *pron* (+g) each, every, everyone *nsm*
  ġehwām *dsm* ġehwǣne *asm* ġehwǣs *gsn*
  ġehwone *asm*

hwanon *adv* whence, from where hwonon

hwār *see* hwǣr

hwæl *m* whale hwæles *gs*

ġehwǣne < ġehwā

hwænne *adv* when, then hwonne

hwænne *conj* (the time) when, until (the time
  when) hwonne

hwǣr *adv* where, somewhere

hwǣr *conj* where hwār

ġehwǣr *adv* everywhere

ġehwæs < ġehwā

hwæt *adj* bold, brave, brisk, active *nsm*
  hwætran *comp npm*

hwæt *interj and adv* behold!, now, indeed

hwæt < hwā

hwǣte *m* wheat

hwætlīċe *adv* quickly

hwæþer *interrog adv* whether, which of two

hwæþer *conj* whether hweðer ðe or

hwæþer *pron* either, which (of two) *asm* hwæþerne *asm* hwæþrum *dsn*

hwæþere *adv* nevertheless, yet, still, but, and indeed hwæþre

hwelċ, hwelċ- *see* hwilċ

hwelp *m* whelp, the young of an animal *as*

hweorfan *III* turn, depart, journey, come, go, roam, move *inf* hwearf *pt3s* hweorfaþ *pr3p* hweorfende *prp* hweorfeþ *pr3s*

hwī *interrog adv/conj* (*isn of* hwæt) why hwȳ ; *in adv/conj phr* (why) for hwī, tū hwī, be hwȳ ; *see also* swā

hwider *adv* whither, in which direction

ġehwierfan *1* turn, change ġehwerfde *pt3s* ġehwyrfde *pt3s* ġehwyrfst *pr2s*

hwīl *f* time, while, period *ns* hwīle *as, ds* ; *in conj phr* þā hwīle þe *as while, as long as* þā hwȳle þe, þā wīlæ þæ ; *see also* hwīlum, lȳtel

hwilċ *adj* which, what kind of hwelċre *gsf, dsf* hwilċe *npm* hwylċ *nsf* hwilċe *asm, asf npm* hwylċum *dpn*

hwilċ *pron* (+*g*) which, any *nsm* hwelċere *dsf* hwylċ *nsm, nsn* wylċ *nsm*

ġehwilċ *adj* each, every, all ġehwilċe *npm* ġehwilċne *asm* ġehwylċ *nsm* ġehwylċum *dpm*

ġehwilċ *pron* (+*g*) each, any, some, whoever, whatever *nsm, nsf* ġehwelċum *dpm* ġehwilċum *dsm* ġehwylċ *nsm, asn* ġehwylċe *nsf, dsm, dsn, ism, isn* ġehwylċes *gsn* ; +ānra (*gp*) each one, every one : ġehwylċ *nsm* ġehwylċum *dsm* ġehwylċne *asm*

hwīlon *see* hwīlum

hwīlum *adv* at times, sometimes hwīlon

hwistlung *f* whistling

hwīt *adj* bright, radiant, white *nsm, nsn, asm* hwīte *npm* hwītes *gsn* hwītne *asm* hwītost *sup nsn* kwītum *dpm*

hwītnes *f* whiteness

hwon < hwā

ġehwone < ġehwā

hwonne *see* hwænne

hwonon *see* hwanon

hwȳ *see* hwī

ġehwylċ, ġehwylċ- *see* ġehwilċ

ġehycgan *3* think, consider, plot, determine, set one's mind (on), be mindful of, hope (for) *inf* hicgan *inf* hicgeaþ *imp p* ġehicgenne *infl inf* hiġeþ *pr3s* hycgaþ *imp p* hycge *sbj pr3s* hycgean *inf* hycgendne *prp asm*

hȳd *f* hide, skin hȳdum *dp* hȳþe *ds*

hȳdan *1* hide, hoard hȳdeþ *pr3s*

ġehȳdan *1* hide, bury ġehȳdde *pt3s*

hȳdiġ *adj* made of leather

ġehyġd *f* thought, intention, conception *ns*

hyġe *m* spirit, mind, heart, intention, reason, thought, courage, ambition, pride *ns* hiġe *ns, as, ds*

hȳgegeōmor *adj* sad at heart hygegeōmorne *asm*

hȳhst < hēah

hyht *f* hope, trust, joy, expectation, desire *ns* hiht *ns, as* hyhte *ds*

ġehyhtan *1* hope, trust

hyldan *1* bend, bow down

hylt < healdan

hȳnan *1* lay low, harm, fell, humiliate *inf* hȳþaþ *pr3p* hȳnde *pt3s* ġehȳnede *pp npf*

ġehȳran *1* hear, hear of, understand, serve, obey (+*d*) *inf* ġehēre *sbj pr3s* ġehierdum *pt3p* ġehīran *inf* ġehīrde *pt3s* hīrdon *pt3p* ġehȳr *imp s* ġehȳranne *infl inf* ġehȳrdan *pt3p* ġehȳrde *pt1s* hȳrdon *pt1p* ġehȳrdon *pt3p* ġehȳre *pr1s, sbj pr3s* ġehȳrenne *infl inf* ġehȳrest *pr2s* hȳreþ *pr3s* ġehyrst *pt2s* ġehȳrþ *pr3s*

hȳnð *f* humiliation, disgrace, damage, harm

hyrde *m* herdsman, shepherd, guardian, keeper *ns*

hyre < hēo

hȳrian *2* hire

hȳrling *m* hireling, hired servant

hyrnednebba *m* horny-beaked one *ns* hyrnednebban *as*

ġehȳrsum *adj* obedient, amenable

ġehȳrsumnes *f* obedience

hys (his) < hē, hit

hyse *m* warrior, youth *ns* hysas *np* hyssa *gp* hyssas *np* hysses *gs*

hyt *see* hit

hȳð *f* harbor

hȳbe < hȳd

iċ *pers pron* I, me, my *ns* ig, mǣ *ds* mē *as* (*often rflx*) meċ *as* mīn *gs ; see also poss pron* mīn

icge *adj* rich, splendid

īdel *adj* idle, vain, worthless, empty, desolate *nsm* īdelan *dpm* īdles *gsn* īdlu *npn*

īdelhende *adj* empty-handed

ides *f* woman, wife, lady idesa *np* idese *as, ds*

īeġland *n* island

ieldan *1* delay, be late

ielde *m pl* men

ieldran *mp* (*comp of* eald) elders, ancestors *np*

ieldu *f* age

ierfenuma *m* heir, successor

ierfeweardness *f* inheritance

iermðu *f* misery iermða *ap*

ierre *n* anger

ierre *adj* angry

ig *see* iċ

īġland *n* island ēġlond *ns* eiġlande *is* īġlande *ds*

īl *m* hedgehog

ilca *adj* same, like, very ilcan *asf, dsm, dsn, dsf, ism, isn* ilce *asn* ilcan *ism* ylcan *asm, gsm, dsm, dsn*

ilca *pron* same, the same ilcan *ism, isn* ilċe *nsn* ylca *nsm*

imbsǣton < ymbsittan

in *adv* in, inwards, inside, within

in *prep* (+a/d/i) in, into, on, within, at, among, during ; through

incundnes *f* inward conviction, sincerity incundnesse *ds*

indryhten *adj* noble, excellent

ingang *m* entrance, entry, penetration ingong *as* ingonge *ds*

inġesteald *n* household possessions *as*

inġebanc *m* inner thought, conscience *as*

inn *n* chamber, room inne *ds*

innanbordes *adv* within the country, at home

inne *adv* inside, within, inwardly, retained

ġeinnian *2* supply

inntō *see* intō

innweard *adj* internal, depths of

ġeinseġlian *2* seal

intinga *m* matter, cause, occasion intingan *as, ds*

intō *prep* (+d/a) into, to, against, in, for inntō

inwidda *m* malicious foe, villain, enemy

inwidhlemm *m* malicious wound inwidhlemmas *np*

inwitsearo *n* malicious intrigue

Iōuis *pr n* Jove Iōues *gs*

īow (ēow) < ġē

īrenheard *adj* iron-hard

irnan *III* run, hurry arn *pt3s* ærndon *pt3p* runon *pt3p*

is < bēon-wesan

īsenesmiþ *m* iron-smith

īsġebind *n* icy bond

īsiġ *adj* icy, covered with ice

iū *adv* formerly, of old, long ago

Iūdēas, Iūdēi *m pl* Jews

Iūno *pr n* Juno

kyning, kyning- *see* cyning

kynnes < cynn

lā *interj* lo! behold!

lāc *n* offering, sacrifice, booty *as, ap* lāce *ds* lācum *dp*

ġelāc *n* play, rolling, tumult *as*

lācnian *2* treat with medicine

lāf *f* what is left, remnant, legacy *ns* lāfan *dp* lāfe *as, gs, np* laga, lage < lagu

lāgen, lāgon < licgan

lagu *m* sea, water *ns, as*

lagu *f* law laga *np* lage *as, gs* lagum *dp*

lagulād *f* sea-way, sea lagulāde *ap*

lāgon < licgan

lagustrēam *m* water, river lagustrēamas *np*

lahbryċe *m* breach of law lahbrycas *ap*

lahlīce *adv* lawfully

lama *adj* lame, paralytic

ġelamp < ġelimpan

lamprede *f* lamprey

land *n* land, country, earth, region, realm *ns, as* landæs *gs* lande *ds* landes *gs* lond *as* londe *ds* londes *gs*

landbīgenga *m* peasant, native

landbūend *m* dweller in the land

landfruma *m* prince of the land, king

landlēode *m pl* people of a country

lang *adj* long, tall, long-lasting, long-coming *nsn* langa *nsm* lange *asf* lengran *comp gsn*

ġelang *adj* ready, dependent on

lange *adv* long, for a long time, far lencgest *sup* leng *comp* lengest *sup* longe

langlīċe *adv* for a long time

langob *m* longing, discontent langobe *ds* longab *as* longabes *gs*

langsum *adj* long, prolonged

langunghwīl *f* period of longing langunghwīla *gp*

lār *f* learning, teaching, instruction, doctrine, precept, advice, knowledge *ns* lāra *np ap* lāre *as, gs, ds*

lārcwide *m* precept, counsel lārcwidum *dp*

lārēow *m* teacher, master *ns* lārēowa *gp* lārēowas *np* lārēowe *ds* lārēowum *dp*

lāst *m* track, step *as* lāste *ds* lāstum *dp*

late *adv* late, slowly sīð ond late at last

lāttēow *m* leader, general, guide lādtēowas *np* lātēow *ns* lāttēowas *np*

lāþ *adj* hostile, hateful, loathsome, harmful, evil (*very often=noun* hostile one, enemy) *nsn, asm* laþan *gsn, dpm* laðe *npm* lāðestan *sup gsm, dpm* lāþne *asm* laðost *sup nsm, npm* lāþra *gpm* lāðran *comp asm, gsn, npm* lāþre *comp*

asn lāþum *dsn, dp*

lāðbite *m* hostile bite, wound

ġelaðian *2* invite, summon laðedon *pt3p* ġelaðod *pp* ġelaðode *pt3s*

lāðliċ *adj* horrible, repulsive laðlicu *apn*

lāðlicost *adv* (*sup of* lāðioce) in most wretched fashion

ġelæċċan *1* seize, take ġelæhte *pt3s*

læċe *m* physician *ns*

læċedom *m* a remedy, medicine læċedōmas *np*

læċehūs *n* hospital

ġelædan *1* lead, bring, take, derive *inf* læd *imp s* lædað *pr3p* lædde *pt3s* ġelædde *pt3s* læddon *pt3p* læde *pr1s* lædene *infl inf* lædeð *pr3s*

Læden, Lædene *see* Læden

lædene < lædan

Lædenware *mp* the Romans

læfan *1* leave, bequeath læfde *pt3s* læfdon *pt3p* lēfdon *pt1p*

læġ, lægum < licgan

ġelæhte < ġelæċċan

læn *n/f* loan *as* læne *ds*

læne *adj* transitory, fleeting, passing, temporary, temporal *nsm* lænan *dsn, apn* lænum *dsn*

ġelæran *1* teach, exhort, persuade (+d), instruct, guide, advise *inf* lærað *pr1p* lærde *pt3s* lærdon *pt3p* lære *sbj pr3s* ġelæred *pp* ġelærede *pp npm* (*learned*) ġelæredestan *pp sup spm* (most learned) læreð *pr3s*

ġelæred *adj* learned

læringmæġden *n* (girl) pupil

læs *adv* (*comp of* lyt) less

læs *indecl noun/pron* less, fewer *as* ; *in conj phr* by/bē læs(þe) (+*sbj*) lest, in case

læs *f* pasture

læst *adj* (*sup of* lytel) least, smallest læsta *nsm*

læst *adv* least

ġelæstan *1* perform, fulfil, achieve, support *inf* ġelæstanne *infl inf* ġelæste *pt3s* ġelæsted *pr3s*

læt *adj* slack, slow

lætan *VII* let, allow, cause to do, set, leave behind læt *pt3s, imp s* lætað *pr3p* læte *pr1s* lēt *pt3s* lētan *pt3p* lēton *pt3p*

ġelæte *n* junction (of roads) ġelætum *dp*

lǣwed *adj* unlearned, lay lǣwede *npm* (*noun* lay people) lǣwedum *dp*

le < lecgan

lēaf *n* leaf *np* lēafum *dp*

lēaf *f* leave, permission lēafe *as*

ġelēafa *m* belief, faith *ns* ġelēafan *as, gs, ds*

ġelēaffull *adj* believing, faithful ġelēaffullum *dsm*

leahtor *m* vice, sin, crime

ġelēanian *2* reward *inf*

lēan *n* reward, payment, requital lēana *ap* lēanes *gs* lēanum *dp*

lēas *adj* (+g) lacking, without, deprived of *nsm, nsn* lēase *npn*

lēasbreġd *n* cheating, trickeries lēasbreġdum *dp*

lēasung *f* falsehood, frivolity lēasunga *ap* lēasunge *gs*

lēat < lūtan

leax *m salmon ns*

lecgan *1* lay, set, place, apply, go le *imp s* lecgað *pr3p, imp p* lecge *sbj pr3s* lēdon *pt3p* leġde *pt3s* leġdun *pt3p* licge *sbj pr3s*

lēddon < lǣdan

Lēden *n* Latin (language) *ns, as* Lǣden *as* Lǣdene *ds* Lēdene *ds* Lēdenes *gs* Līden *ns* Lȳden *as* Lȳdene *ds*

lēdon < lecgan

lēfdon < lǣfan

leġ < lecgan

leġer *n* couch, grave *ap*

lehtrian *2* blame, revile lehtreð *pr3s*

lencgest < lange

ġelendan *1* go, land

leng, lengest < lange

lenge *adj* near at hand

lengran < lang

lengten *m* springtime

lēo *m/f* lion, lioness

lēod *m* man, chief, leader *ns*

lǣċehūs *n* hospital

lēoðcræftiġ *adj* song-skilled

lēoðcyning *m* king of a people

lēode *fp* people, nation *ap* lēoda *np, ap, gp* lēodum *dp*

lēodfruma *m* leader of people, lord *ns*

leoðosyrċe *f* corset, mail-coat leoðosyrċan *as*

lēof *adj* dear, beloved, agreeable, pleasing *nsm, nsf* (=*noun*) lēofa *nsm, nsf* lēofan *npm, dsm* lēofesta *sup nsm* lēofne *asm* (=*noun*) lēofost *sup npm* lēofostan *sup npm* lēofra *nsm* lēofran *comp asf* lēofre *comp nsn* lēof *in addressing persons,* sir, sire *ns*

leofab < libban

leofede, leofode, leofodon < libban

lēoht *adj* bright, radiant lēohtne *asm*

lēoht *n* light, daylight, the word *ns* lēohte *ds* lēohtes *gs*

lēohtfæt *n* lamp

lēoman *m* ray of light, gleam, radiance *ns* leoman *as*

ġeleornian *2* learn, study *inf* leornade *pt3s* ġeleornade *pt3s* leornion *sbj pr3p* ġeleornod *pp* ġeleornode *pt3s* leornodon *pt3p* ġeliornod *pp* ġeliornode *pt1p* ġeliornodon *pt3p*

leornung *f* learning, study leornunge *ds* liornunga *as*

lēoð *n* song, poem, poetry *as*

lēoðcræftiġ *adj* skilled in song *nsm*

lēt, lētan, lēton < lǣtan

leberhosu *f* leather gaiter

lǣwed *adj* unlearned, lay lǣwede *npm* (*noun* lay people) lǣwedum *dp*

libban *3* live, exist leofab *pr3s* leofede *pt3s* leofedon *pt3p* leofode *pt3s* leofodon *pt3p* libbe *sbj pr3s* libbendum *prp dpn* ġelifd *pp* lifde *pt3s* lifdon *pt3p* lifġe *sbj pr3s* lifġendra *prp gpm* (=*noun*) lifiab *pr3p* lifiendne *prp asm* lybban *inf* lybbe *pr1s* lyfdon *pt3p* lyfedan *pt3p* lyfiað *pr3p*

līċ *n* body, corpse *ns, as, ap* līċe *ds* līċes *gs*

ġelīċ *adj* (+d) like, similar to *nsn* ġeliċċast *sup npm* ġelīċe *asf, npm* ġelīċran *comp npm* ġelīċre *comp gsf*

ġelīċe *adv* equally, likewise, similarly

licgan *V* lie, lie down, lie dead, remain *inf* lāgon *pt3p* læġ *pt3s* lǣġe *sbj pt3s* lǣgon *pt3p* lǣgun *pt3p* leġ *pt3s* liġeð *pr3s* licgað *pr3p* licge *sbj pr3s* licgende *prp* līð *pr3s*

līċhama *m* body *ns* lēċaman *as* līċhaman *np, as, ap* līċhoma *ns* līċhoman *ds* līcian 2 impers (+d) please, be pleasing inf līcað pr3s līcode pt3s līcodon pt3p

ġelīċran < ġelīċ

lid n ship lides gs

lidman m seaman, Viking lidmanna gp lidmen np

ġelīefan I believe, trust in, allow, permit ġelīefe pr1s ġelīfde sub pt3s ġelīfst pr2s ġelȳfe pr1s ġelȳfeð pr3s ġelȳfab pr1p ġelȳfdon pt3p ġelȳfed pp ġelȳfendum prp dpm ġelȳfan

līefan see lȳfan

līeġ m/n flame, fire

līf n life ns, as, np līfe ds līfes gs ; in phr on līfe in life, when alive tō līfe alive

ġelifd, lifd see libban

ġelīfde < ġelȳfan

līffrēa m Lord of Life, God

lifġ-, lifi- see libban

līġ m flame, fire ns līġe ds

līhtan 1 alight, dismount līhte pt3s

līhting f lighting, illumination

lim n limb leomu ap limum dp

līm m bird-lime(새 잡는 끈끈이)

ġelimp n occurrence, event, fortune, circumstances as ġelimpum dp ġelymp as

ġelimpan III impers (+d) happen, be, befall, suit, turn out, belong (to) inf ġelamp pt3s limpeb pr3s limpb pr3s ġelimpb pr3s

limwēriġ adj weary in limb limwēriġne asm

lindplega m shield-play, battle lindplegan ds

lindwīġ n shield-army as

ġeliorn- see ġeleornian

liornung see leornung

lītl see lȳtel

lītling f infant, child

lið n joint, limb

līð < licgan

līðe adj gentle, mild nsm

līxan 1 shine, gleam līxte pt3s

loc n enclosure, fold loca ap

locene < lūcan

lof n praise, fame, glory ns, as

lofdǣd f praiseworthy deed lofdǣdum dp

loflāc n offering of prise, sacrifice

ġelōgian 2 place, fill ġelōgode pt3s

ġelōme adj frequent npn

ġelōme adv often, constantly

lond, lond- see land

londbūendum < landbūend

londryht n land-entitlement as

londstede m region, country ds

ġelong adj dependent on, belonging to

longab, longabes < langob

longe see lange

longian 2 impers (+a) afflict with longing longade pt3s

longsum adj long-lasting, enduring longsumne asm

loppestre f lobster

losian 2 be lost, fail, perish, escape inf losab pr3s losiġe sbj pr3s

lūcan II lock, join, link locene pp asf lucon pt3p

lufan < lufu

lufian 2 love, cherish, delight in inf lufast pr2s lufab pr3s, pr3p lufedon pt3p lufiad pt1p lufiab pr3p lufiġe pr1s lufiġean inf lufiġend prp (=noun lover) ġelufod pp lufode pt3s lufodon pt1p lufude pt3s

lufiend m lover

luflīċe adv lovingly, warmly, dearly

lufu f love, affection ns lufan as, gs, ds lufe as, ds lufun ds

lūs f louse lȳs np

lust m joy, ecstasy, desire, pleasure as lustum dp

lustbǣre adj desirable, pleasant

lūstian 2 hide

lustlīċe adv gladly, willingly

lūtan II bow, bend, stoop

lūtian 2 lie hidden

lybb- see libban

Lȳden, Lȳdene see Lēden

lȳfan 1 allow, grant līefað prlp lȳfde pt3s lȳfdest pt2s

ġelȳfan 1 believe, trust in, hope for, grant, concede inf ġelīefe pr1s ġelīfde sbj pt2s ġelīfst pr2s ġelȳfab pr1p ġelȳfdon pt3p ġelȳfe pr1s, sbj pr3s ġelȳfed pp ġelȳfendum prp dpm ġelȳfeb pr3s ġelȳfb pr3s ġelīefan

lyfdon, lyfedan < libban

lyft *f* air, mist, cloud *ns* lyfte *ds, ap* ; *in phr* on
  lyft *as* aloft, on high
lyre *m* loss, destruction *ds*
ɬysan *1* release, redeem, ransom
ɬyt *adv* little
ɬyt *indecl noun* (+*g*) little, few
lytegian *2* use guile, deceive
ɬytel *adj* little, small, petty (*often=noun*) *asn* lītle
  isn lītles *gsn* lītlum *dsn* ɬytelre *dsf* ɬytlan
  asm, asf ɬytle *asf, isn* ɬytlum *dsn* ; *in adv phr*
  lītle ̄ær *asn* a little while ago lītle hwīle *as*
  (for) a little while
ɬybre *adj* wicked, base *asm, asf* ɬybran *ds*
  (=*noun* unworthy person)

mā *indecl noun/comp adj* (*usually* +*g*) more *ns* ;
  in adv/conj phr b̄y mā more, the more bē mā
  be any more than þon mā be
mā *adv* more
ġemacian *2* make, form, do cause madedon *pt3p*
  maciað *pr3p* macode *pt3s* ġemacode *pt3s*
mādm- *see* mābm
mādma *see* mābum
māga, māgas < m ̄æġ
magan *pt-pr* be able, can, be competent, have
  power to, avail magan *pr1p, pr3p sbj pr3p*
  magon *pr1p, pr2p, pr3p* mæġ *pr1s, pr3s, sbj*
  pr3s mæġe *sbj pr1s, sbj pr2s, sbj pr3s*
  mæġen *sbj pr1p, sbj pr3p* meaht *sbj pr2s*
  meahte *pt1s, sbj pt1s pt3s, sbj pt3s* meahton
  pt3p, sbj pt3p mehte *pt3s, sbj pt3s* miht *pr2s*
  mihte *pt1s, pt3s, sbj pt3s* mihten *pt3p*
  mihton *pt1p, pt3p* muhton *sbj pt3p*
mago *m* male kinsman, young man
magodriht *f* band of young retainers
magon < magan
magobeġn m young retainer magobeġnas *np*
  magubeġnas *np*
magu m stomach magan *as*
man *impers pron* one, a person, someone,
  anyone, they mann, mon
man *see* mann
ġeman < ġēmunan

ġemana *m* community, common property
  ġemānan *ds*
mancus *m* mancus (a gold coin worth 30 silver
  pence) mancessa *gp* mancussa *gp* mancussum
  dp mandcussa *gp*
mancynn *n* humankind, mankind, people *ns*
  mancyn *ns, as* mancynne *ds* mancynnes *gs*
  moncynne *ds* moncynnes *gs* monncynnes
  gs
mānd ̄æda *f* evil deed mānd ̄æda *ap, gp*
maneġ- *see* maniġ
mānful *adj* full of evil, wicked mānfullan *npm,*
  apm (=*noun*)
manġere *m* trader, merchant manġeres *gs*
maniġ *adj* many *nsm* manega *npm, npf, apn, apf*
  maneġe *npm, npf, apf* maeġra *gpm* manegum
  dpf maniġe *npm* mæniġ *nsm* mæniġne *asm*
  monegum *dsm, dpn* moniġ *nsm, nsn, nsf*
  moniġe *npm* moniġra *gpm, gpf*
maniġ *pron* many, a multitude manega *npm*
  manegan *dpm* maneġe *npm, npf, apm, apf*
  manegum *dpm* maniġra *gpm* mæneġe *npf*
  mænegum *dpm* mæniġ *nsm* mæniġe *npm*
  moneġe *apf* monegum *dpm* moniġ *apn*
  moniġe *npm*
maniġeo < meniġu
maniġfeald *adj* manifold, numerous, abundant,
  various, diverse, complex maniġfealdum *dpf*
  mæniġfealdan *dsn* mæniġfealde *apf*
  mæniġfealdre *comp nsn* mæniġfealdum *dpm*
  meniġfælde *apf* meniġfældum *dpf* meniġfeald
  nsf
maniġfealdan *I* multiply, increase ġemaniġfealde
  pr1s
manlīċe *adv* manfully, nobly
mānlīċe *adv* wickedly
mann *m* person, man *ns, as* man *ns* manna *gp*
  mannes *gs* mannum *dp* mæn *ds* mænn *np,*
  ap men *ds, is, np, ap* menn *ds, np, ap* mon
  ns, as monn *as* monna *gp* monnes *gs*
  monnum *dp*
manneġ- *see* maniġ
mannr ̄ædenne *f* allegiance.
mansliht *m* manslaughter, murder manslihtum
  dp manslihtas *ap*

mansylen *f* selling of people mansylena *ap*

māra *ad* (*comp of* miċel, *often=noun +g*) more, greater, larger *nsn* māran *asm, asf, dsn, npn, apf* māre *nsm, nsn, nsf, asm, asn, isn*

Māria *pr n* Mary Mārian *as, gs, ds*

martyrdōm *m* a martyrdom martyrdōm *as*

māð < mīban

mabelian *2* speak, speak out, declare mabelode *pt3s*

mābum *m* treasure, precious thing mādma *gp* mādmas *ap* mādme *ds* māðma *gp* mābmum *dp*

mābbumġyfa *m* treasure-giver *ns*

mǣ (me) < iċ

ġemǣc *adj* suitable, well suited ġemǣcne *asm*

mǣċan < mēċe

ġemǣċċa *m* mate, husband

mǣden *n* maiden, virgin *ns* mǣdene *ds* mǣdenes *gs* mǣdenne *ds*

mǣġ kinsman, kin, parent *ns* māga *gp* mǣga *gp* mǣgas *np* mǣġe *ds* mǣgum *dp*

mǣġ, mǣġ- *see* magan

mǣġden *n* maiden

mǣġdenċild *n* female child

mǣġen *n* force, strength, power, army *ns, as* mǣġenes *gs* mǣġna *ap* mǣġnum *dp*

mǣġenrǣs *m* mighty assault, violent blow

mǣġrǣs *m* attack on kinsmen mǣġrǣsas *ap*

mǣġb f maiden, virgin, (unmarried) woman *ns, as, gs, np*

mǣġb *f* tribe, nation, race, generation kin mǣġða *gp* mǣġbe *ds* mǣġðum *dp*

mǣl *n* time, occasion, meal mǣla *ap, gp* mǣle *ds*

ġemǣlan *1* speak mǣlde *pt3s* ġemǣlde *pt3s*

mǣn < mann

ġemǣnan *1* complain of, lament, mention, relate, recite mǣnde *pt3s* ġemǣnden *sbj pt3p* mǣndon *pt3p* mǣneb *pr3s*

ġemǣne *adj* common (*to +d*), shared (*with +d*), in common, mutual, joint *nsm, nsn, npm, npn* ġemānan *dpm* ġemǣnum *dsm*

mǣneġe, mǣniġ, mǣniġe < maniġ

mǣniġe < meniġeo

mǣniġfeald, mǣniġfeald- *see* maniġfeald

mǣnn < mann

mǣre *adj* famous, renowned, great, illustrious, splendid *nsm, nsn, nsf, asf, npm* mǣran *gsf, dsm, dpm* mǣres *gsm* mǣrost *sup nsf* mǣrostan *sup apm* mǣrra *comp gpm*

mǣre < māra, mǣran

Mǣringas *pr n the* Mǣrings Mǣringa *gp*

mǣrbu *f* fame, renown, glory, glorious deed mǣrba *ap, gp* mǣrðe *as*

mæsse *f* mass, feast-day mæssan *as, ds*

mæsseprēost *m* (mass-)priest, clergyman *ns* mæsseprēostas *np* mæsseprēoste, mæsseprīoste *ds*

mǣst *adj* (*sup of* miċel) most, greatest *nsm* mǣstan *asm, asf, dsn* mǣste *asn, asf*

mǣst *adv* most, almost, mostly

mǣst *indecl noun* (*+g*) the most, the greatest, the greatest number *ns, as*

mæste *m* mast

mæstling *n* bronze

ġemǣtan *1* impers (*+d*) dream ġemǣtte *pt3s*

mǣte *adj* small, inferior, base *dsn* mǣtestan *sup npm* mǣtran *comp npm*

ġemǣte *adj* suitable for, fitted to (*+d*) *nsm, nsf*

mæx *n* net

mē < iċ

meahte < miht

meahtiġra < mihtiġ

mearcstapa *m* border-haunter mearcstapan *ap*

mearh *m* horse, steed *as* mēare *ds* mearg *ns*

mearn < murnan

mēċ < iċ

mēċe *m* sword, blade *as, ds, is* mǣċan *dp* mēċum *dp*

mēd *f* reward mēde *as, ds*

mēdder < mōdor

mēder < mōdor

medo *m* mead *as* meodo *ds*

medoærn *n* meadhall

medobenċ *f* mead-bench medobenċe *ds*

mehte < magan

melcan *see* melkan

melkan *III* milk melke *pr1s*

meltan *III* melt, dissolve, digest *inf* multon *pt3p*

men < mann

ġemengan *1* mix, mingle, blend ġemæġnde *pt3s* ġemeng *imp s* ġemenged *pp*

meniġeo *f* multitude, company *ns* mæniġe *ds* menġeo *ns*

meniġfeald- *see* maniġfeald-

meniġu *f* multitude menġeo *ns* mæniġe *ds* maniġeo *ds*

menn < mann

mennisc *adj* human, natural meniscre *dsf*

menniscnes *f* incarnation, humanness, human form menniscnesse *ds*

meodo *see* medo

meodoheall *f* mead-hall meoduhealle *ds*

meodosetl *n* mead-bench

meotod, meotud, meotudes < metod

meotodsceaft *f* decree of fate, death

mere *m* mere, lake, pool, sea *ns* meredēaða *gp*

mereflōd *m* sea-flood, ocean tide, ocean mereflōde *ds* mereflōdes *gs*

mereswīn *n* porpoise

merewēriġ *adj* sea-weary merewēriġes *gs* (=noun)

merewīf *n* sea-woman

meriġenliċ *adj* moning, of tomorrow meriġenliċere *ds*

ġemētan *1* meet, encounter, come upon, find ġem ætte *pt3s* ġemēteð *pr3s* ġemētte *pt1s* mētton *pt3p* ġemētton *pt3p*

mete *m* food *ns, as, ds* metta *gp* mettas *np* mettum *dp*

metod *m* creator, ordaining lord, God *ns* meotod *ns* meotodes *gs* metud *ns* metudes *gs* metod *ns* metode *ds* metodes *gs* metudes *gs*

ġemētte, ġemētton < ġemētan

mēðe *adj* worn out, dejected *nsm, npm*

meðelstede *m* meeting-place

miċċlum *adv* greatly, much

miċel *adj* big, great, much, intense *nsm, nsn, nsf, asn* (=noun much) micclum *dpm* (=noun many) miċelan *dpf* miċele *nsn, asf* miċelne *asm* miċelre *gsf, dsf* miclan *asm, dsm, dsn, dsf* miclum *dsm, dsn, dpn* myccla *nsm* mycclan *dsm* mycclum *dsn, dpf* myċel *nsm, nsn, nsf, asn* (=noun) myċele *asf* myċelre *dsf*

mycle *asf, dsn* myclum *dsm, dpm ; see also* māra *comp,* mǣst *sup,* micle *adv,* miclum *adv*

miċele *see* micle

micle *adv* much, greatly miccle

miclum *adv* much, greatly micclum, mycclum

mid *prep* (+d/a/i) with, amid, among, by, by means of, through mit *; in phr* mid bām bā *adv* with that, thereupon mid bām be *conj* when mid bȳ *adv* when mid bī ðe *conj* when mid bȳ ðe

middanġeard *m* middle-earth, earth, world *ns, as* middaneard *as* middanearde *ds* middanġearde *ds* middanġeardes *gs*

middæġ *m* midday, sext *as* middæġe *ds*

Middelengle *pr n* Middle Angles

midðīðe *conj* with

Mierċna < Myrċe

miht *f* might, power, strength, virtue, ability, authority, function *ns, as* meahte *as* mihta *gp* mihte *as, ap, ds* migtum *dp*

mihte < miht, magan

mihtiġ *adj* mighty, strong, powerful, important *nsm, asn* mihteġu *nsf* mihtiga *nsm* (=noun) mihtiġe *npm* mihtiġes *gsm* mihtiġra *comp nsm*

mihton < magan

mīl *f* mile mīla *gp*

milde *adj* mild, merciful, kind moldost *sup nsm*

mildheort *adj* merciful, compassionate mildheortan *dsm*

mildheortnes *f* loving-kindness, mercy *ns* mildheortnesse *ds*

mīlġemearc *n* distance in miles mīlġemearces *gs*

miltestre *f* harlot, prostitute

milts *f* mercy, favor miltsa *gp* miltse *as, gs*

ġemiltsian *2* pity, have compassion on miltsiġe *pr1s* ġemiltsiġend *prp*

mīn *poss pron* my, mine *nsm, nsn, nsf, asn, npm* mīnan *dsn* mīnæ *apm, dsf* mīnæn *dsm* mīnæs *gsm* mīne *asf, npm, npf, apm, apn, apf* mīnes *gsm, gsn* mēnnæ *dsm* mīnne *asm* mīnnum *dpm* mīnon *dsm* mīnra *gpm, gpf* mīnre *dsf* mīnum *dsm, dsn, dpm* mīræ, mīre *dsf ; see also* iċ

ġemindiġ *adj* mindful

Minerua *pr n* Minerva

mīnn- < mǣn

misdǣd *f* misdeed misdǣda *np, ap, gp* misdǣdan *dp* misdǣde *ds* misdǣdum *dp*

misfaran *VI* go wrong, err misfōr *pt3s*

mishȳran *1* (+*d*) not to listen to, disobey mishȳrde *pt3s*

misliċ *adj* various, diverse. manifold misleca *apf* misliċe *apm* mislicum *dpm, dpf* misliċe *apm, apn, apf*

mislīcian *2* displease

mislimpan *III impers* (+*d*) go wrong mislimpe *sbj pr3s*

missenlīċe *adv* variously, in various places

missēre *n* half-year missēra *gp*

misbynċan *1* appear incorrectly misbūhte *pt3s* misbūht *pp*

mit *see* mid

mitta *m* measure

mīban *I* hide, conceal, keep to oneself mǣð *pt3s* mībendne *prp asm*

mōd *n* heart, mind, spirit, will, courage, resolution *ns, as* mōde *ds, is* mōdes *gs* mīdum *dp*

mōdċeariġ *adj* sad at heart, anxious of mind *nsm*

mōdcearu *f* grief of heart, sorrow mōdceare *gs*

mōder *see* mōdor

mōdġebanc *m* purpose of mind *as*

mōdiġ *adj* spirited, brave, proud, heroic, arrogant, impetuous *nsm* mōdiġe *npm* mōdi *nsm* mōdiga *nsm* (=*noun*) mōdiġe *npm* mōdiġes *gs* (=*noun*) mōdiġre *gsf*

mōdor *f* mother *ns, as* mēdder *ds* mēdder *ds* mōder *ns* mōdor *ds*

mōdsefa *m* mind, spirit, heart *ns* mōdsefan *as*

molde *f* earth *ns* moldan *as, gs*

moldern *n* earth-house, tomb *as*

mon *see* man, mann

mōna *m* moon *ns* mōnan *as, gs, ds* mōne *ns*

mōnað *m* month *ap* mīnðas *ap* mōnðe *ds* mōnðes *gs*

moncynn, moncynnes < mancynn

mondryhten *m* lord, master *as*

moneġ- *see* maniġ

moniġ, moniġ- *see* maniġ

monn, monn- *see* mann

mōnð- *see* mōnað

monuc *see* munuc

mōr *m* moor, bog mōras *ap*

morgen *m* morning morgenne *ds*

morgenġiefe *f* gift from husband to wife on morning after wedding

morgentīd *f* morning-tide, morning

morb *n* violent deed, crime

morðdǣd *f* deadly deed, murder morðdǣda *ap*

morðor *n* violent crime, deadly evil, murder *as* morðer *as* morðra *gp* morðres *gs*

morborbealo *n* deadly slaughter

mōst, mōst- *see* mōtan

mōt *pt-pr* may

ġemōt *n* assembly, meeting, encounter *ns as* ġemōtes *gs*

mōtan *pt-pr* be able, may, be allowed to, must mōst *pr2s* mōste *pt3s, sbj pt1s, sbj pt3s* mōston *pt1p, sbj pt3p* mōt *pr1s, pr3s* mōtæ *sbj pr1s* mōte *sbj pr1s, sbj pr3s, sbj pr1p* mōten *sbj pr3p* mōton *pr1p, pr3p*

mōton < mōtan

muhton < magan

multon < meltan

ġemunan *pt-pr* think about, be mindful of, remember, consider (+*g*) ġeman *pr1s* ġemon *pr3s* ġemunde *pt1s pt3s, sbj pt3s* ġemunu *pr1s*

mundbyrd *f* protection, hope of protection *ns, as*

mundgripe *m* hand-grip

munt *m* mountain, hill

munuc *m* monk, nun *ns* monuc *ns* muneca *gp* munece *ds*

munucliċ *adj* monastic munucliċere *dsf*

murcnian *2* grumble, complain

murcnung *f* complaint, grief murcnunge *as*

murnan *III* care for, be anxious about, feel sorrow, mourn *inf* mearn *pt3s* murnað *pr3p* murnende *prp nsn* murnon *pt3p*

mūða *m* mouth (*of river*) mūðan *ds* mūðon *ds*

myccl-, myċel, mycl- *see* miċel

mycclum *see* miclum

myclian *2* increase

mylenscearp *adj* sharp from grinding mylenscearpan *dpm*

ġemynd *n* mind, memory, remembrance, commemoration *as* ġemynde *ds*

ġemyndgian *2* remember ġemyndgade *pt3s*

ġemyndiġ *adj* (+g) mindful (of), preoccupied, recollecting, intent on *nsm, nsf*

ġemynegian *2* remember, mention

mynetere *m* money-changer

mynster *n* church, monastery, minster, cathedral, nunnery *as* minster *as* minstres *gs* mynstær *ds* mynstere *ds* mynstre *ds* mynstres *gs* mynstrum *dp*

Myrċe *pr n* the Mercians *np* Merċna *gp* Mierċna *gp* Myrċon *dp*

myrhð *f* joy, mirth myrhða *ap*

nā *adv* no, not, not at all, never, by no means nō

nabbað < habban

nacod *adj* naked, bare *nsm* nacedan *asf*

nafað < habban

nāge (ne āge), nāh (ne āh) < āgan

nāht *indef pron* (+g) nothing *ns, as* nāuhte *ds* nōht *as*

nāhte (ne āhte) < āgan

nāhwæðer *conj* neither nāhwðer~ne neither~ nor

nalas, nales, nalles *see* nealles

ġenam < ġeniman

nama *m name, noun ns* naman *as, np ap*, namena *gp* namon *ds* noma *ns* noman *ds* nomum *dp*

ġenāman, ġenāmen < ġeniman

ġenamian *2* name, call, invoke namiað *pr3p* ġenamod *pp* nāmon *pt3p*

ġenamon < ġeniman

nān (ne ān) *adj* none, not one, not any, no *nsm, nsn, asn, apn* nēnan *dsn* nāne *asf* nānes *gsn* nānne *asm* nānre *dsf* nānum *dsm, dsn* nǣnne *asm*

nān *pron* none, not one, nothing *nsm, asn* nānne

asm nānum *dpm*

nānwiht *adv* not at all, nothing hāht, nōht

nānwiht *indef pron* (+g) nothing *ns* nāwihte *ds*

nānwuht *see* nānwiht

ġenāp < ġenīpan

nāt < witan

nāteshwōn *adv* not at all, in no way

nāthwylċ *adj* some, some sort of

nābor *adj/pron* neither *nsn, nsf* nāðres *gsn*

nābor *conj* neither nābor ne ··· ne neither ··· nor

nāuhte < nāht

nāwber *pron* neither nāwber ne~ne neither~ nor

nǣ *see* ne

nǣbbe (ne hæbbe), nǣbben (ne hæbben) < habban

nǣdl *f* needle

nǣdre *f* snake, serpent nǣdran *ds, as*

nǣfde (ne hæfde) < habban

nǣfne *conj* except that, unless

nǣfre *adv* never nēfre

nǣfb (ne hæfb) < habban

nǣġel *m* nail nǣġl

nǣġl *m* nail *ns* nǣġlum *dp* nǣiġlum *dp*

nǣġledcnearr *m* nailed ship

nǣniġ *pron* none, no one *nsm* nǣni *nsm* nǣngum *dsm* nǣnigum *dsm*

nǣnne < nān

nǣre (ne wǣre), nǣron (ne wǣron) < bēon-wesan

nǣs *adv* not, not at all

nǣs *m* earth, ground *as*

nǣs (ne wǣs) < bēon-wesan

nǣss *m* headland, promontory nǣssas *ap*

ne *conj* nor ne~ne neither~nor

nēah *adj* near, close (to +d) *nsf, nsn* ; *see also* nēahst

nēah *adv* near, nearly ; *see also* nēar

ġeneahhe *adv* in abundance, very often, constantly ġenehe

nēahst *sup adj* (<nēah) nearest, last nēhstan *dsm* ; *in adv phr* æt nēhstan at length, in the end, finally, next æt nȳhstan

nēahst *sup adv* (<nēah) (+d) nearest, next to

nēaxst, nēhste, nēxt

neaht, nahte < niht

nēaƚǣċan *see* nēalēċan

nēalēċan *1* draw near, approach *inf* nēaƚǣcte
  pt3s nēaƚǣcð *pr3s* nēaƚǣhte *pt3s* nēalehtan
  pt3p

nealles *adv* not, not at all, in no way nealas,
  nalæs, nales, nalles

nearolīċe *adv* briefly, summarily

nearon (ne+earon) < bēon-wesan

ġenēat *m* comrade, vassal

nēaxt *see* nēahst

nēde < nīed

nēfre *see* nǣfre

nēhċeaster *f* neighboring town nēhċeastra *gp*

nellan (ne willan) *anom* not to wish *inf* nele
  pr3s nellað *pr3p* nelle *pr1s*, *sbj pr3s* nelt
  pr2s noldan *pt3p* nolde *pt3s* noldon *pt1p*,
  pt3p

Nembroð *pr n* Nimbrod

ġenemnan *1* call, name, appoint *inf* nemnað *pr1p*
  nemneð, nemnde *pt3s* nemned *pp* ġenemned
  pp

nemne *conj* unless, except, if not nefne, nembe

nemnian *2* name, call ġenemnode *pp*

nembe *see* nemne

nēod *f* need, necessity

nēod *f* desire, zeal, earnestness

nēod, nēode *see* nȳd

nēodbearf *f* necessity, need

nēodbearf *adj* necessary

neom (ne eom) < bēon-wesan

neorxenawang *m* Paradise neorxenawanges *gs*
  neorxenawange *ds*

nēosian *2* (+g) seek out, find, go to

ġenerian *2* save, rescue ġenerede *pt3s* nerġende
  prp nsm ġenerode *pt3s*

nēten *see* nȳten

nett *n* net

nēxt *see* nēahst

nīdde, ġenīed < ġenȳdan

nīedbeðearf *adj* necessary, essential nīedbeðearfosta
  sup npf

nīetaen *n* beast, cattle nēten *ns* nytene *ds*
  nietenu *np*

niċ=ne iċ

nīed *f* necessity, hardship

nīed *f* need nēod, nēd

nīedunga *adv* of necessity

nīehst *adj sup of* nēah ; *in phr* æt nīehstan in
  the next place, thereupon

nierwan *1* curtail, restrict

nīeten *n* animal, cattle

nīew *adj* new

nigon *num* nine

nigontēoaa *num* nineteen.

nigoba *num adj* ninth nogoban *asf* nygoðan *asf*

niht *f* night *ns*, *as*, *ap* neaht *as* neahte *ds* nihta
  gp nihte *ds* nihtes *gs* (=*adv* at night)
  nihtum *dp*

nihthelm *m* cover of night

nihtscūa *m* shadow of night

ġeniman *IV* take, take away, grip, seize, bring,
  add *inf* nam *pt3s* ġenam *pt3s* nāman *pt3p*
  ġenāman *pt3p* ġenāmen *pt3p* nāmon *pt3p*
  ġenāmon *pt3p* ġenim *imp s* nimað *pr3p, imp*
  p nime *pr1s* ġenimeb *pr3s* nimst *pr2s*
  ġenom *pt3s* nōman *pt1p* ġenumen *pp*

ġenip *n* darkness, mist

ġenīpan *I* grow dark, darken nāp *pt3s* ġenāp
  pt3s nīpeð *pr3s*

nis (ne is) < bēon-wesan

niðer *see* nyber

nīðsele *m* enemy-hall, hostile hall

nīðwundor *n* baleful wonder

ġeniwad < nīwian

nīwe *adj* new *nsf, nsm, npf*

niwelness *f* chasm, abyss

ġenīwian *2* renew, restore ġenīwad *pp* ġenīwod
  pp

nō *see* nā

ġenōg *adj* enough, plenty of ġenōge *npm*

nōht *adv* not at all, not

nōhwæðer *conj* neither nōwðer

nold- *see* nellan

ġenom, nōman < ġeniman

noma, noman < nama

norð *adv* north

norban *adv* from the north

norðanweard *adj* northward

noradǣl *m* northern part, north

norðēastlang extending to the north-east

Norþhymbraland *n* Northmbria

Norðhymbre *pr n* the Northumbrians, Northumbria Norðhembra *gp* Norðhymbran *dp* Norðhymbron *dp*

notian *2* enjoy, use notab *pr3s*

notu *f* employment, use, advantage note *ds*

nōāðer *see* nōhwæder

nū *adv* now, just now, presently

nū *conj* now that, in as much as, since

ġenumen < ġeniman

nȳd *f* need, constraint, necessity, purpose *ns* nēde *as/ap ds* nēod *ns* nēode *ds*

ġenȳdan *1* compel, force, urge ġenēde *sbj pr3s* nīdde *pt3s* ġenīed *pp* nȳddon *pt3p*

nȳddon < nȳdan

nygoðan < nigoba

nȳhstan < nēahst

nyrwan *see* nierwan

nys (ne ys) < bēon-wesan

nyste (ne wyste) < witan

nyte (ne wite) < witan

nȳten *n* beast, animal, ox, cattle *as* nēten *ns* nȳtene *ds* nȳtenum *dp*

nyteness *f* ignorance

nyton=ne witon

nytt *f* use, benefit, service nyt *ns* nytte *ds*

nyttwyrðe *adj* useful

nytwyrbness *f* utility, use

nyber *adv* down, downwards niðer

ġeocian *2* yoke

odbæt *see* ob

of *prep* (+d) from, out of, away from ; about, concerning

ofær *see* ofer

ofdrǣdd *adj* afraid

ofdrǣdan *VII* fear, be afraid ofdrǣdde *pp npm, npf*

ofer *adv* over, after

ofer *prep* (+a) over, across, beyond, along, above, upon, through(out), after, against towards ofær

ōfer *m* edge, river-bank ōfre *ds*

oferbrǣdan *1* cover

ofercuman *IV* overcome *inf* ofercōman *pt3p* ofercumen *pp*

oferfierro *f* too great distance

ofergān *anom* go over, pass away oferēode *pt3s*

oferherġean *2* overrun, ravage, plunder, lay waste

oferhelmian *2* overshadow oferhelmað *pr3s*

oferhoga *m* despiser oferhogan *np*

oferhogian *2* despise oferhogað *pr3s*

ofermōd *adj* proud, overbearing ofermōda *nsm*

ofermōd *n* over-exuberance, excess of courage ofermōde *ds*

oferrǣdan *1* read through

ofersāwan *VII* sow over

oferseġlian *2* cross by sailing oferseġlode *pt3s*

oferweorpan *III* throw over, throw down oferwearp *pt3s*

oferwintran *1* live through the winter

offerian *2* carry off offerede *pt3s*

offrian *2* offer, sacrifice *inf* ġeoffrod *pp* offrode *pt3s* offrodon *pt3p*

offrung *f* offering, sacrifice offrunge *ds*

ofġiefan *V* abandon, give up ofġēafon *pt3p*

oflongian *2* seize with longing oflongad *pp*

ofost *f* haste, speed ofste *ds* ofstum *dp*

ofscēotan *II* shoot, pierce to death ofscēat *pt3s*

ofsittan *V* sit on ofsæt *pt3s*

ofslēan *VI* strike off, kill, slay, destroy *inf* ofslagen *pp* ofslæġen *pp* ofslæġene *pp npm* ofslǣhþ *pr3s* ofslēa *sbj pr3s* ofslēahþ *pr3s* ofsleġen *pp* ofslēhð *pr3s* ofslōg *pt3s* ofslōgon *pt3p* ofslōh *pt3s*

ofslōg, ofslōgon, ofslōh < ofslēan

ofsnīban *I* slaughter

ofspring *m* offspring, descendant(s) ofspringe *ds*

ofste, ostum < ofost

ofstician *2* pierce, stab, spear

oft *adv* often, frequently oftor *comp* oftost *sup adv* most often

oftēon *II* take away, withhold, hold back oftēah *pt3s*

oftor, oftost < oft

oftrǣdlīċe *adv* frequently

ofaynċan *1* displease, seem amiss, vex

ofþyrst *adj* thirsty

ofwundrod *adj* astonished

oll *n* contempt, scorn olle *ds*

on *prep* (+*d*/*a*/*i*) on, onto, in, into, to, at, against, during, among, amid, for, as, with according to

onǣlan *1* kindle, enflame onǣled *pp*

onbelǣdan *1* inflict upon onbelǣden *inf*

onbierġan *1* (+*g*) taste, eat

onbindan *II* unbind

onbyriġan *see* onbierġan

oncnāwan *VII* recognize, know, acknowledge, understand *inf* oncnāwe *pr1s* oncnēow *pt3s* oncnēowon *pt3p*

ond *see* and

ondrǣdan *VII* be afraind, dread (*often reflx*) ondrǣde *pr1s*, *pr3s* ondrǣdeþ *pr3s* ondrēd *pt1s* ondrēdon *pt3p*

ondswar- *see* andswar-

ondwaru *see* andwaru

ondweard *adj* present ondweardum *dpm*

ondwlita *see* andwlita

ġeondwyrdon < ġeandwyrdan

oneardian *2* inhabit oneardað *pr3p*

onfand < onfindan

onfēng, onfēng- < onfōn

onfindan *III* find out, discover, realize, perceive, experience *inf* onfand *pt3s* onfond *pt3s* onfunde *pt3s* onfunden *sbj pt3p* onfundon *pt3p*

onfōn *VII* (+*d*/*a*) receive, accept, take, undertake, undergo, sponsor onfēng *pt3s* onfēnge *pt3s, sbj pt3s* onfēngon *pt3p* onfongen *pp* onfongne *pp asf* onfōð *pr3p*

onfond < onfindan

onfong-, onfōð *see* onfōn

onfund- *see* onfindan

ongan < onginnan

onġēan *adv* again, back

onġēan *prep* (+*d*/*a*) against, opposite, facing, contrary to, towards onġēn

onġeat, onġeaton < onġietan

onġemang *prep* (+*d*) among, amidst

onġēn *see* onġēan

onġēton < onġietan

onġietan *V* know, perceive, understand, recognize, witness, experience *inf* onġeat *pt3s* onġēaton *pt3p* onġēton *pt3p* onġieten *pp* onġiotan *inf* onġitan *inf* onġite *pr1s* onġitenu *pp asf* onġytan *inf*

onġinnan *III* begin, precede, attempt, undertake ongan *pt1s* onġin *imp s* onġinnað *imp p* onġinnen *sbj pr3p* onġinst *pr2s* onġinð *pr3s* ongon *pt1s* ongunnon *pt3p* onġynnað *pr3p* onġynð *pr3s*

onġitan *see* onġietan

ongon, ongunnon, onġyn- *see* onġinnan

onġyrwan *1* unclothe, strip onġyrede *pt3s*

onġytan *see* onġietan

onherġian *2* harass onherġedon *pt3p*

onhwerfan *III* turn, change, reverse onhworfen *pp*

onlīcnes *see* anlīcnis

onlūcan *II* unlock *inf*

onlūtan *II* bend, bow *inf*

onlȳsan *1* free, redeem onlȳsde *pt3s*

onmiddan *prep* (+*d*) in the middle of

ondrǣdan *VII* be afraid, dread ondrǣde *pr1s* ondrǣtst *pr2s* ondrǣdea *pr3s* ondrēd *pt1s*

onmunan *pt-pr* (+*g*) pay attention to, care for onmunden *sbj pt3p*

onrǣs *m* attack

onsǣġe *adj* (+*d*) attacking, assailing *nsn*

onscyte *m* attack, calumny onscytan *dp*

onsendan *1* send forth, yield up *inf* onsende *pt3s* onsended *pp* onsedeð *pr3s*

onsnīþan *I* slaughter ofsnab *pt3s*

onstal *m* supply *as*

onstellan *1* establish, institute, set the example of onstealde *pt3s*

onuppan *prep* (+*d*) upon, above

onwǣcan *1* weaken, soften onwǣcen *sbj pr1p*

onwæcnan *VI* awake, be born onwæcneð *pr3s* onwōce *sbj pt3s*

onweald *m control, authority, power* (+*g* over) *as* onwald *as*

onweġ *adv* away

onwendan *1* change, overturn, upset, reverse, pervert, transgress against onwende *pt3s* onwended *pp* onwendeð *sbj pr3p*

onwōc *see* onwæcnan

onwrēon *I* disclose, reveal onwrēoh *imp s*

open *adj* open, clear *nsn* opene *npm* openum *dpn*

ġeopenian *2 open* ġeopenod *pp* ġeopenode *pt3s, pp npf*

openlīċe *adv* openly, plainly

ōr *n* beginning, origin *as*

ord *m* point, spear, vanguard *ns* orde *ds*

ōretta *m* warriors

orfcwealm *m* cattle-plague *ns*

orġelīċe *adv* proudly, insolently

ormǣte *adj* boundless

orsorg *adj* without anxiety, secure

orwēna *adj* without hope of, despairing

ostre *f* oyster

ob *conj* until op bæt until obbæt, odbæt

ob *prep* (+a) until, to, as far as, for

obberan *IV* bear away, carry off obbær *pt3s*

ōber *adj* other, another, second, next, one of two *nsm, nsn* ōbere *dsf* ōberne *asm* ōðerra *gpf* oðerre *dsf* ōðran *dpm* ōbre *asm, gsf, dsf, ism, npm, apm, apf* ōbres *gsn* ūðron *dsm* ōbrum *dsm, dpm, dpn, dpf* ; *see also* healf

ōber *pron* one, other, another *nsm, nsn, asm, asn, apn* ōbere *apm* oberne *asm* ōðran *dpm* ōbre *asf, npm, apf* ōbres *gsn* ōbrum *dsm, dpm* ; *in correl use* ōðer···ōðer the one···the other *nsm* ōðre···ōðre *dsn*

oðfæstan *1* set oðfæste *pp npm*

oðfeallan *VII* fall away, decay *inf* oðfeallenu *pp nsf*

oðlǣdan *1* lead away

ōbr- *see* ōber

oðrōwan *sv redp* row away

obbæt *see* ob

obbe *conj* or, or else, and aēththa, oððon, obbe ···obbe either···or ; *see also* āwðer

oðwindan *III* escape oðwand *pt3s*

ōwiht *see* āwiht

oxanhyrde *m* oxherd oxanhyrdas *np*

pāpa *m* pope pāpan *gs*

Paradīscus *m* Paradise Paradīsum *ds*

pæll *m* silk robe or hanging

Pehtas *pr n* the Picts Pehtum *dp*

pening *m* penny (silver coin about the size of American dime)

Pihtas *m* pl Picts

Pihtisc *n* Pictish (language)

pīn *f* torment, torture

pinne *f* leather flask, bottle

plantian *2* plant

plega *m* sport, entertainment plegan *ds*

plegian *2* entertain, play, contend plegodan *pt3p* plegode *pt3s*

pleōliċ *adj* dangerous

pliht *m* peril, danger

plihtliċ *adj* dangerous

prass *m* in battle array

prēost *m* priest prēostas *np*

pund *n* pound *as* punda *gp* pundum *dp*

prician *2* prick, pierce

purpure *f* purple robe

pusa *m* bag, scrip

rā *m* roebuck

rād < rīdan

ġerād *n* consideration, understanding, condition *as* ġerāda *as*

ġerādeġian *2* call to an account

radost < hraðe

ramm *m* ram

randas *m* shield randas *ap*

rānn *gp of* rā roebuck

rǣp *m* rope

ġerǣċan *1* reach, attain, obtain, strike *inf* ġerǣhte *pt3s*

rǣd *m* advice, counsel rǣda *gp* rǣdas *ap* rǣde *ds*

ġerād *n* reckoning, account, reason, judgement

rǣdan *1* read *inf* rǣdað *pr1p* rǣdde *pt3s* rǣde *pr1s* rǣdenne *infl inf* rǣt *pr3s* ġerǣdan *1* advise, guide, decree, determine ġerǣdde *pt3s* ġerǣdest *pt2s* rǣt *pr3s*

ġerǣdde < ġerǣdan

rǣdend *m* ruler

rǣding *f* reading

rǣġe *f* roe deer

rǣran *1* lift up, promote, commit *inf* rǣsde *pt3s*

rǣswa *m* prince, leader rǣswan *ds*

rǣste < rest

rǣt < rǣdan

rēad *adj* red rēada *nsm* rēadum *dsn*

rēaf *n* garment, clothing, armor *ns, as, ap* reafe *ds* rāafes *gs* rēafum *dp*

rēaflāc *n* robbery, plunder *ns, as, ap*

ġereaht, reaht- *see* (īe)reċċan

rēcan *see* reċċan

reċċan *1* (+g) care about, care for, be interested in, reck *inf* reċċað *pr3p* rēċe *pr1p* rōhtan *pt3p* rōhte *pt3s* rōhton *pt2p, pt3p*

ġereċċan *1* relate, explain, interpret, decide *inf* ġereaht *pp* reahte *pt3s* reahtan *pt1p* rehte *pt3s* ġerehte *pt3s* rehton *pt3p*

reċċelēas *adj* negligent, careless reċċelēase *npm*

ġereċednes *f* narrative

recene *adv* instantly, hastily, quickly ricene, rycene

ġerēfa *m* reeve, steward, officer, prefect *ns* ġerēfan *ds* ġerēfum *dp* ġerēua *ns*

rēġn *m* rain reġnes *gs* reġnum *dp*

regollīċe *adv* according to rule

ġerehte, rehton < ġereċċan

rēn *see* reġn

reord *f* speech, voice reorde *ds*

ġereord *f* speech, voice, language ġereorda *np* ġereorde *ds*

ġereord *n* food, feast

reordberend *m* speech-bearer, person *np* reordberendum *dp*

rēotan *II* weep rēotað *pr3p*

rēpe *adj* fierce, cruel, furious rēðne *asm* rēban *dsm* reðe *ap* rēbum *dpm*

ġererding *f* meal

rest *f* rest, resting place, bed rǣste *ds* reste *ds* ġerestan *1* rest *inf* (*find rest from* +g) rǣstan *inf* reste *pt3s, sbj pr3s* rested *pr3s* reston

pt3p

rēbe *adj* cruel, fierce, furious, raging rēðne *asm* rēaan *dsm* reðe *ap* rēaum *dpm*

ġerēua *see* ġerēfa

rēwet *n* rowing

rīċe *adj* (*often=noun*) powerful, mighty, great, noble rīca *nsm* rīcam *dsm* rīċne *asm* rīcost *sup nsm* rīcra *gpm*

rīċe *m* kingdom, real, authority, rule, power *ns, as, ds, is* rīċes *gs*

rīċelīċe *adv* sumptuously

ricene *see* recene

rīċetere *n* arrogance

rīċne < rīċe *adj*

rīcsian *2* reign, rule, prevail rīcsode *pt3s* rīxað *pr3s*

rīdan *I* ride, swing *inf* rād *pt3s* rīdeð *pr3s* rīdon *pt3p*

riftere *m* reaper

riht *adj* just, true, fitting, right, due *nsn, nsf* rihte *dsm* rihtne *asm* rihtre *dsf* ryht *nsn* ryhtoste *sup npm* ryhtre *comp nsn, asn*

riht *n* justice, right, what is right *as* rihte *ds* ryht *as* ryhte *ds* ryhtes *gs ; see also* rihte *adv*

ġeriht *n* what is right or direct, right, privilege ġerihta *np, ap, gp ; in phr* on ġerihte *ds* directly

rihte *adv* rightly, justly

rihtlīċe *adv* justly, properly

rihtne, rihtre < riht

rihtwīs *adj* just, righteous, upright rihtwīsan *npm, dpm* rihtwīsena *gpm* rihtwīsum *dpm*

rihtwīsnes *f* righteousness rihtwīsnesse *gs*

rīnan *1* rain rīnde *pt3s*

rinc *m* man, warrior rinca *gp* rincum *dp*

rīpan *I* reap

rīpere *m* reaper

rīptīma *m* time of reaping, harvest *ms* riptīman *ds*

ġerisene *n* what is seemly or decent ġerisena *gp*

rōd *f* cross *ns* rōde *as, ds*

roder- *see* rodor

rodor *m* sky, heaven, the heavens *as* rodera *gp*

roderas *ap* roderum *dp* roderes *gs*

rōf *adj* renowned, brave rōfe *npm* rōfra *gp*

rōht- *see* reċċan

Rōmāne *pl* Romans

Rōmanisc *adj* Roman Rōmanisces *gsn*

rose *f* rose

rōwan *VII* row hrēowan *pt3p*

rudu *f* redness, blush

rūn *f* consultation, secret council

rycene *see* recene

ryht *see* riht

ryhtre < riht

ġerȳman *1* clear, open, open a way for, make space for, extend rȳmde *pt3s* ġerȳmde *pt1s, pt3s* ġerȳmdon *pt3p, sbj pt3p* ġerȳmed *pp*

ryne *m* course, running rynum *dp*

rȳpere *m* robber, plunderer rȳpera *gp* rȳperas *np*

sacan *VI* fight, quarrel, contend sacað *pr3p*

sāċerd *m* priest *ns* sēcerda *gp* sāċerdas *np* sōcerd *ns*

saga *m* story, narrative sagan *ap*

saga < secgan

sāgol *m* rod, staff

sāh < sīgan

salowiġpād *adj* dark-coated salowiġpāda *nsm* saluwiġpādan *apm* (=*noun*)

samcwic *adj* half-alive

ġesamnian *2* assemble

same *adv* similarly swā same likewise

samod *adv* together, also, as well somod

sanct *m/f* saint sancta *gs* sanctan *ds* sancte *gs, ds*

sandċeosol *m* sand(gravel)

sang < singan, song

sang, sanga, sange < song

sār *adj* sore, painful, grievous *nsn* sārra *gpf*

sār *n* pain, wound, suffering, sorrow *as* sāre *ds*

sāre *adv* sorely, grievously

sārian *1* grieve, be sad sāriġes *prp npm*

sāriġ *adj* sorrowful sāriġes *gsn*

ġesārgian *2* wound ġesārgode *pp*

sārliċ *adj* sorrowful, grievous sārlicum *ds*

sārlīċe *adv* painfully, with grief

sārnes *f* grief, sorrow sārnesse *as*

sārra < sār

sāule, sāulum < sāwol

sāwan *VII* sow sāwenne *infl inf*

ġesāwe, ġesāwon < ġesēon

sāwere *m* sower

sāwol *f* soul, spirit, mind sāule *as, ds* sāulum *dp* sāwl *ns* sāwla *ap* sāwlæ *ds* sāwle *as, ds* sāwlum *dp* sāwul *ns*

sāwon < sēon

sǣ *m* sea *ns, as, ds* sǣm *dp* sǣs *gs*

sæċċ *f* strife, battle sæċċe *ds*

sǣcocc *m* cockle

sǣd *adj* (+g) sated with, weary of *nsm*

sǣd *n* seed sǣdes *gs*

ġesǣd- *see* ġesecgan

sǣdēor *n* sea-beast

sǣdere *m* sower

sǣdon < ġesecgan

sæġde, sæġdon, sæġest < secgan

sǣl *m* time, occasion, season ; prosperity, joy *ns* sǣlum *dp* sēle *ap*

sǣlād *f* sea-journey, voyage sǣlāde *ds*

sǣlīċ *adj* of the sea, marine

ġesǣliġ *adj* happy, blessed, favored, beneficial *nsm* ġesǣligan *asf* ġesǣliġe *npm*

ġesǣliġliċ *adj* blessed, happy ġesǣliġlica *npf*

ġesǣlþ *f* happiness, good fortune

sǣm < sǣ

sǣman *m* sailor, Viking sǣmanna *gp* sǣmannum *dp* sǣmæn *np* sǣmen *np*

ġesǣne < ġesȳne

sǣrima *m* sea-shore, coast sǣriman *ds*

sǣs < sǣ

ġesǣt, sǣt- *see* ġesittan

sǣsīð *m* sea-journey, voyage sǣsīðe *ds*

scacen < sceacan

scamfæst *adj* modest

scamu *f* shame, dishonor *ns* scome *ds* tō scame with ignominy

scandliċ *adj* shameful *nsn* scandliċe *npn* sceandlican *dpm*

scaða *m* criminal thief

ġescæphwīl *f* appointed time, fixed time (hour)

scæt, scætta < sceatt

sceacan *VI* hasten, hurry away, depart scacen *pp* scēoc *pt3s*

ġescead *n* distinction, reason

ġescēadan *VII* decide ġescēd *pt3s*

sceadu *f* shadow, darkness *ns* sceade *as*

scēaf < scūfan

scēafmǣlum *adv* sheaf by sheaf

sceaff *m* shaft, arrow, spear *ns* scefte *ds*

ġesceaft *n/f* creation, created, created thing, creature, establishment, disposition, destiny *ns* ġesceafta *np, ap, gp* ġesceafte *as* ġesceaftum *dp*

sceal, sceall, scealt < sculan

sceandlican < sandliċ

scēap *n* sheep *ap*

ġesceap *n* creation ġesceape *ds*

ġesceapen, ġesceapene < ġescieppan

scear *m* ploughshare sceare *ds*

sceard *adj* cut, bereft of scearde *npf*

scearn *n* dung, muck *as*

scearp *adj* sharp, acid scearpne *asm*

sceat *see* sceatt

scēat *m* corner, region, surface (of the earth) scāatas *ap* scēatum *dp*

sceatt *m* (sum of) money, property, tribute, sceat (a coin) scæt *ns, as* scætta *gp* sceat *as* sceattum *dp* scet *as*

scēat < scēotan

sceaba *m* enemy, ravager, criminal assassin sceaban *np*

scēawere *m* witness, spectator

scēawian *2 see*, behold, look at, inspect, examine scēawiað *imp p* scēawigan *inf* scēawode *pt1s, pt3s, sbj pt3s* scēawodon *pt1p*

ġescēawian *2* show ġescēawað *pr3s*

scēawung *f* seeing, examination. show, regard scēawunge *ds*

Scedeland *n* southern Scandinavian

scefte < sceaft

scendan *1* shame, insult scendað *pr3p*

sceold- *see* sculan

ġescēop < ġescieppan

scēotan *II* shoot, throw, hit, put in scēat *pt3s* scēotað *pr3p* scoten *pp*

scēos *pl of* scōh

sceota *m* trout

sceōwyrhta *m* shoemaker, leatherworker

sceppende < scyppend

ġescieran *IV* shear, split, cut through, strip ġescær *pt3s* scǣron *pt3p* scorene *pp npf*

scet < sceat

ġesceaaan *VI* (+d) injure, harm, destroy ġescēod *pt3s* sceaede *sbj pt3s* sceaaað *pr3p* sceaae *pr1s* ġescōd *pt3s*

ġescīe < ġescȳ

sciellfisc *m* shellish

ġescieppan *VI* create, shape, destine, assign ġesceappen *pp* ġesceapene *pp npm* scēop *pt3s* ġescēop *pt3s* ġescōp *pt3s*

scieppend *m* creator Scyppend *ns* Scyppendes *gs*

ġeschieran *IV* shear, split, cut through, strip ġescær *pt3s* scǣron *pt3p* scorene *pp npf*

scild *m* shield *as* scildas *np* scyld *ns* scylda *gp* scyldas *ap* scylde *ds*

scīma *m* light, radiance, splendor scīman *as*

scīnan *I* shine, flash, gleam *inf* scān *pt3s* scīnendan *prp dsf* scīnendum *dpm dpn* scīnon *pt3p* scȳneð *pt3s* scȳnð *pr3s*

scip *n* ship *as* scipa *ds* scipe *ds* scipu *np, ap* scype *ds* scypon *dp* scypum *dp*

scipflota *m* seaman, Viking scipflotan *np*

sciphere *m* ship-army, fleet

scīr *adj* clear, bright, gleaming *asn* scīre *apm* scīrne *asm*

scīrman *m* shireman

scīrmǣled *adj* brightly adorned

scīaan *I* cut

scōh *m* shoe

scoldan, scolde < sculan

scop *m* poet, singer

ġescōp < ġescieppan

scoten < scēotan

Scottas *m pl* the Irish, Scots

scotung *f* shooting, missile.

scridde < scrȳdan

scrīfan *I* prescribe, ordain, care about scrīfað *pr3p* scrīfe *sbj pr3s* scrīn *n* chest, shrine *as*

scrūd *n* clothing, dress, garment

scrȳdan *1* dress, clothe scrīdde *pt3s* ġescrȳd *pp* scrȳddon *pt3p*

scūfan *II* shove, thrust scēaf *pt3s*

sculan *pt-pr* have to, ought to, must, must needs, shall sceal *pr1s*, *pr3s* sceall *pr3s* scealt *pr2s* sceolan *pr3p* sceoldan *pt3p*, *sbj pt3p* sceolde *pt1s*, *sbj pt1s*, *pt3s*, *sbj pt3s* sceolden *sbj pt3p* sceoldon *pt1p*, *pt3p*, *sbj pt3p* sceolon *pr1p*, *pr3p* scoldan *pt1p* scolde *pt1s*, *pt3s*, *sbj pt3s* scolden *sbj pt3p* scoldon *pt3p*, *sbj pt3p* scolon *sbj pr3p* sculon *pr1p*, *pr3p* scylan *sbj pr1p* scyle *sbj pr1s*, *sbj pr3s*

ġescȳ *n* shoe, pair of shoes ġescīe *ap*

scylan < sculan

scyld < scild

scyle < sculan

scyndan *see* scendan

scȳneð, scȳnð < scīnan

scype, scypon < scip

scyppend *m* creator *ns*, *as* sceppende *ds* scyppendes *gs*

scypum < scip

Scyttisc *m* Scotch (language)

se, sēo, bæt *def art* the ; *demons pron/adj* that, those ; *pers pron* he, it, that, she, they, etc. *rel pron* who, which, that, what : se *nsm* sē *nsm* sēo *nsf* sīo *nsf* tæt *asn* thaem *dsf* thēm *dsn* bā *asf*, *npm*, *apm*, *apn*, *apf* bām *dsm*, *dsn*, *dpm* ban *ism*, *isn*, *dpm* bāra *gpm* bāre *gsf*, *dsf* bat *asn* bǣm *dsm*, *dsn* bæne *asm* bæra *gpn*, *gpf* bǣre *gsf*, *dsf* bæs *gsm*, *gsn* bæt *nsn*, *asn* be *nsm* bēre *dsf* bet *asn* bī *ism* bon *ism*, *isn* bonne *asm* bone *asm* bȳ *ism*, *isn* bys *gsm* ; *for phr with instr* bī/by, ban/bon *see* for, mā, mid, tō, wib

ġeseah < ġesēon

ġeseald, ġeseald- *see* ġesellan

sealt *adj* salt sealtum *dpf*

sealtere *m* salter sealteras *np*

sēamere *m* tailor

searo *n* war-gear, arms, things of value searowa *np* searwum *dp*

searoġim *m* curious gem, precious stone

searoġimma *gp* searoġimmas *ap*

sēab *m* pit sēabe *ds*

seax *n* knife, short sword *as* seaxes *gs*

sēċan *1* seek, seek out, approach, make for, visit, reach by seeking *inf* *pr1p* ġesēahte *pt3s* ġesǣcen *sbj pr3p* sēċað *pr1p*, *pr2p* ġesēċe *sbj pr1s*, *sbj pr3s* sēċean *inf* ġesēċean *inf* sēċende *prp npm* sēċenne *infl inf* sēċeð *pr3s* sōhtan *pt3p* sōhte *pt1s*, *pt3s* ġesōhte *pt3s* sōhton *pt3p* ġesōhtun *pt3p*

secg *m* man, retainer, warrior *ns* secga *gp* secgas *np*, *ap* secgum *dp*

ġesecgan *3* say, tell, declare, report, explain, ascribe *inf*, *sbj pr3p* saga *imp s* sǣd *pp* ġesǣd *pp* sǣdan *pt1p*, *pt3p* sǣde *pt3s* ġesǣde *pt3s* sǣdon *pt1p*, *pt3p* sægde *pt3s* sægdon *pt3p* sæġest *pr2s* secgað *pr1p*, *pr3p*, *imp p* secge *pr1s*, *sbj pr2s*, *sbj pr3s* secgeað *pr3p* seġe *imp s* seġeð *pr3s* seġst *pr2s* seġð *pr3s*

sefa *m* spirit, mind, heart sefan *as*

sēfte < sōfte

seġe < secgan

ġeseġen < ġesēon

seġn *m/n* sign, token, banner

sēl *adj comp* better

selcūð *adj* strange, novel

ġeselda *m* companion ġeseldan *ap*

seldan *adv* seldom

seldon *see* seldan

sele *m* hall *as*

sēle < sǣl

seledrēam *m* hall-joy seledrēamas *np*

seledrēoriġ *adj* sad for want of a hall

seleġyst *m* hall-guest, visitor

selerǣrend *m* hall-keeper selerǣdende *ap*

selesecg *m* hall-man, retainer selesecgas *ap*

sēlest *adj* best

self, self- *see* sylf

ġesellan *1* give, give up, surrender, supply, sell, restore *inf* ġesæld *pp* seald *pp* ġeseald *pp* sealdan *pt3p* sealde *pt1s*, *pt3s*, *sbj pt3s* ġesealde *pt3s*, *pp npm* sealdon *pt3p* ġesealdon *pt3p* sele *imp s* sellanne *infl inf* selle *sbj pr3s* ġeselle *sbj pr3s* sillan *inf* ġesille *sbj pr3s* silb *pr3s* syleð *pr3s* syllan *inf*, *sbj pr3p* syllanne *infl inf* syllað *pr3p* syllon *sbj pr3p* sylb *pr3s*

sēlra *adj* better

ġesēman *1* reconcile, bring to an agreement, attribute, arbitrate between sēman *inf* ġesēman *inf* sēmdan *pt3p*

sendan *1* send, cast *inf* sende *pt3s* sendon *pt3p*

ġesēne < ġesȳne

sēo < se (*pron*), sēon (*verb*)

sēoc *adj* sick, weak sēoce *nsf* sēocene *asm*

sēocnes *f* sickness sēocnysse *as*

seofan *num* seven seofene *npm* seofon

seof- *see* sylf

seofontēoða *adj* seventeenth

seolcen *adj* silken

seolfor *n* silver *ns* seolfre *ds* seolfres *gs* sylfor *as*

seolforsmib *m* silversmith

seolh *m* seal

sēon < sēo

ġesēon *V* look, see, observe, perceive *inf* ġesāwe *sbj pt1s*, *sbj pt3s* ġesāwon *pt3p* seah *pt3s* ġeseah *pt1s*, *pt3s* ġeseġen *pp* sēo *pr1s* ġesēo *pr1s* ġesēoð *pr2p*, *pr3p* ġesewen *pp* ġesīon *inf*

seonobend *f* sinew-bond, fetter seonobende *ap*

sēoban *II* boil, seethe, cook *inf* sēob *imp s* ġesoden *pp* ġesodene *pp apm*

ġeset *n* seat, habitation ġesetu *np*

ġeset < settan

setl *n* seat, throne, resting place setla *gp* setle *ds*

ġesetnes *f* law, decree, narrative ġesetnissa *ap* ġesetnissum *dp*

ġesettan *1* set, set up, set out, set down, put, place, settle, arrange, establish, make, compose *inf*, *pt3p* ġesætte *pt3s* ġeset *pt3s*, *pp* ġeseted *pp* seteð *pr3s* ġesett *pp* (appointed) ġesettanne *infl inf* settað *pr1p* sette *pr1s*, *pt3s* ġesette *pt3s*, *pp* ġesetton *pt3p*

ġesewen < ġesēon

sibb *f* peace, concord sib *ns* sibbe *as*

ġesibb *adj* related, close ġesib *ns* (=noun) ġesibban *ds* (=noun) ġesibbra *comp gpm*

sibleġer *n* incest sibleġeru *ap*

sibling *m* sibling, kinsman siblingum *ds*

siċċetung *f* sigh siċċetunge *as*

sīde *adv* widely ; *in phr* wīde ond sīde far and wide

sīe, sīen, sīendon > bēon-wesan

ġesīene *see* ġesȳne

sierwan *1* plot sierwe *sbj pr3s*

siex *num* six six

siexta *adj* sixth

siextiġfeald *adj* sixtyfold siextiġfealdne *as*

siġ < bēon-wesan

sīgan *I* sink, fall sāh *pt3s*

siġe *m* victory *as*

siġebēam *m* tree of victory *ns, as*

siġeēadiġ *adj* blessed with victory *asn*

siġefæst *adj* sure of victory, triumphant siġefæstran *comp npm*

siġle *n* jewel, brooch, neckless siġla *gp*

sigor *m* victory, triumph *as* sigora *gp* sigore *ds* sigores *gs* sigorum *dp*

ġesihð *f* sight, vision, presence ġesihðe *as, ds* ġesyhðe *as, ds*

silf, silfa, silfne < sylf

sillan, ġesille, silb < ġesellan

simle *adv* always, ever, continually

simble *see* symble

simle *see* symble

sīn *poss pron* his, its, her sīne *apm* sīnes *gsm* sīnne *asm* sīnre *dsf* sīnum *dsn*

sinc *n* treasure *ns, as* since *ds* sinces *gs*

sincan *III* sink

sincġestrēon *n* treasures, sincġestrēonum dp

sincbegu *f* receiving of treasure sincbege *as*

sind, sindon < bēon-wesan

singal *adj* continuous, everlasting

singan *III* sing, recite, chant, cry *inf* sang *pt1s*, *pt3s* sincge *pr1s* sing *imp s* singað *pr3p* singe *pr1s* singende *prp asm* singeð *pt3s* sungon *pt1p*, *pt3p* syngan *inf*

sinniġ *adj* sinful

sinsorg *f* constant sorrow sinsorgna *gp*

sint < bēon-wesan

sinu *f* sinew

sīo < bēon-wesan

siodo *m* custom, morality *as* siodu

siodu *see* siodo

siodðan *see* sibban

ġesīod < ġesēon

siobban *see* sibban

ġesittan *V* sit, dwell, remain, occupy *inf* sæt *pt3s*
ġesæt *pt3s* sǣte *sbj pt3s* sǣton *pt1p* sit *pr3s*,
pt3p sit *pr3s* sitt *pr3s* ġesittað *pr3p* sitte
pr1s sittende *prp npm*

sīb *adv* late, tardily *; in phr* sīð ond late at last

sīþ *m* journey, venture, experience, fate, time,
occasion, movement *ns, as* sīþas *ap* sīþe *ds*
sīðes *gs* sīþun *dp*

sīþian *2* travel, go *inf* sīþade *pt3s* sīþað *pr3s*
sīðe *sbj pr1s*

ġesīðð *m* travelling companion ġesīððe *ds*

sibban *adv* afterwards, after, later, then, next,
after that siodðan, siobban, sybban

sibban *conj* after, since, when, once sybban

sīwian *2* sew, stitch together sīwodon *pt3p*

sixtiġ, sixtigan < syxtiġ

slacian *2* delay, put off

slāpan *see* slǣpan

slāw *adj* slow, slothful

slæġen < slēan

slǣp *m* sleep *ns* slǣpe *ds* slēp *as*

slǣpan *VII* sleep, fall asleep slāpan *inf*
slǣpende *prp nsm* slǣpst *pr2s* slēpon *pt1p*,
pt3p

sleac *adj* stealthy

slēan *VI* strike, strike down, slay, slaughter,
erect *inf* slæġene *pp npm* slogan *pt3p* sloge
sbj pt3s slōgon *pt3p* slōh *pt3s*

ġeslēan *VI* strike, win (by fighting), conquer,
inflict *inf* ġeslæġene *pp npn* (forged)
ġesleġene *pp npm* ġeslōgan *pt3p* ġeslōgon
pt3p ġeslōh *pt3s*

slecg *f* sledge-hammer

sleġe *m* blow, stroke, slaughter, murder, killing

slēp *see* slǣp

slēpon < slǣpan

slīðen *adj* cruel, terrible, dire

ġeslōg-, ġeslōh *see* ġeslēan

smēaġan *1* ponder, think, mediate on, examine
smēade *pt3s* smēaġe *sbj pr3s* smēaġende
prp nsm smēað *pr3s*

smearcian *2* smile

smið *m* smith, craftsman smiþa *gp*

smiððe *f* smithy smibban *ds*

snāw *m* snow *ns, as* snāwe *ds*

snel *adj* bold, keen snelle *npm* snelra *gpm*

Snotingahām *pr n* Nottingham

snotor *adj* wise, clever, prudent, discerning *ns*
(=noun) snotera *comp nsm* snoteran *asf*
snotere *nsf* snoterost *sup nsm* snottor *nsm*
(=noun)

snotorwyrde *adj* wise of speech, plausible in
speech

sōcerd *see* sācerd

ġesoden, ġesodene < sēoþan

sōfte *adv* softly, easily, quietly sēfte *comp*

ġesōht- *see* ġesēċan

ġesomnia *2* assemble, join ġesamnod *pp*
ġesomnad *pp*

somod *adv* together (with), at the same time, as
well samod

sōna *adv* at once, directly, soon *; in phr* sōna
swā as soon as

song *m* song, singing *ns, as* sang *ns* sanga *gp*
sange *ds* songes *gs*

song < singan

sorg *f* sorrow, grief, trouble, care, grievance *ns*
sorga *gp* sorge *as* sorgum *dp* sorh *ns*

sorgceariġ *adv* anxious, sorrowing *nsm* (=noun)

sorgian *2* sorrow, grieve sorgiende *prp dsn*,
npm

sorglufu *f* sad love *ns*

sorh *see* sorg

sorhlēoð *n* song of sorrow, lament *as*

sōþ *adj* true, just, righteous *nsm* sōða *adj nsm*
sōðan *asm* sōðe *nsf* sōðne *asm* sōþra *com*
gpm sōþre *dsf* dōðum *dsm, dpn*

sōþ *n* truth *ns, as* sōðan *ds* sōþes *gs ; in phr* tō
sōþe *ds* as a truth, in truth

sōþlīċe *adv* truly, indeed, certainly, really

spadu *f* spade

spæc < sprecan

spǣċ < sprǣċ

sprǣcan < sprecan

spæra < spere

spǣtton < spittan

spearca *m* spark

specan *see* sprecan

spēd *f* success, means, power, opportunity *as* spēda *ap*

spell *n* narrative, tale, message, statement, homily *as* spelles *gs* spellum *dp*

spere *n* spear *ns* spæra *gp* speru *ap*

spillan *1* destroy, kill *inf*

spittan *V* spit spǣtton *pt3p*

spīwan *I* (+*d*) spew, vomit spāw *pt3s* spīwenne *infl inf*

spor *n* track, trail spore *ds*

ġespōwan *VII impers* (+*d*) avail, prosper, succeed spēow *pt3s* ġespēow *pt3s* ġespēwð *pr3s*

sprǣc < sprecan

sprǣċ *f* utterance, speech, language, point, suit, charge *ns* spǣċ *ns* sprǣca *ap* sprǣcan *gs* sprǣċe *as, gs, ds*

sprecan *V* speak, say, utter *inf* spæc *pt1s* spǣcan *pt3p* specan *inf* specað *pr1p* specenne *infl inf* spræc *pt3s* sprǣcon *pt3p* sprecab *pr1p* sprece *pr1s, sbj pr2s* sprecende *prp nsm* spriceð *pr3s* spricb *pr3s* sprycst *pr2s* spycð *pr3s*

sprenġan *1* sow

springan *III* jump, spring out, burst open, spread sprang *pt3s* sprong *pt3s*

spyrian *2* make a track, track, investigate spyrede *pt3s* spyriġean *inf*

spryttan *1* sprout, yield fruit

spurleðer *n* spur-strap

spycð < sprecan

spyriġean *I* follow, follow in the footsteps of

spyrte *f* wicker basket

ġestāh < ġestīgan

stalcung *f* stalking stalcunge *ds*

stalu *f* theft, stealing stala *ap* stale *np*

stān *m* stone, rock *ns, as* stānas *np* ntāne *ds*

ġestandan *VI* stand, be positioned, sit, stand up, arise, remain, last, occupy, be exist *inf* standab *pr3p* stande *pr1s* standende *pp asf* stǣnt *pr3s* stent *pr3s* stint *pr3s* stōd *pt1s, pt3s* stōdan *pt1p, pt3p* stōdon *pt1p, pt3p* ġestōdon *pt3p* stondan *inf* stondað *pr3p*

stonde *pr1s* stondeð *pr3s* stynt *pr3s*

stānhlib *n* rocky slope stānhleobu *ap* stānhlibe *ds*

stānwyrhta *m* stone-mason

ġestabelian *2* establish, restore, make stedfast ġestabelade *pt3s* ġestaðolian

staðol *m* fixed position, foundation, base, stem stabelum *dp* stabole *ds* staðulas *ap*

stǣdefæste < stedefæst

stǣfne, stæfnum < stefn

stælhere *m* predatory army stælherġum *dp*

stǣnen *adj* of stone

stǣniht *n* stony ground stǣnihte *ds*

stæð *n* shore, river-bank stæðe *ds*

ġesteal *n* structure, foundation

stede *m* place, position *as* styde

stedefæst *adj* steadfast, unyielding stǣdeæste *npm* (=*noun*) stedefæste *npm*

stefen *see* stefn

stefn *m* stem, root stefne *ds*

stefn *f* voice, sound *ns* stæfne *ds* stæfnum *dp* stefne *ds*

stefna *m* prow, stern stefnan *ds*

strǣl *m* arrow strǣlas *ap* strǣlum *dp*

stelan *IV* steal, rob stele *sbj pr3s* stelb *pr3s*

stemn *see* stefn

stent < standan

steorfa *m* pestilence *ns*

steorra *m* star *ns* steorrum *dp*

steppan *VI* step, go march, advance stōp *pt3s* stōpon *pt3p*

stician *2* stick, fix, stab, butcher sticiað *pr3p* sticode *pp npm*

stīepel *m* tower

ġestīeran *1* (+*d*(*pers*) +*g*(*thing*)) control, restrain, prevent *inf* ġestīreð *pr3s* ġestȳrde *pt3s*

stierċ *n* calf

ġestīgan *I* ascend, mount, descend, reach *inf* ġestāh *pt3s*

stillan < stille

stille *adj* silent, unmoving, fixed *nsm* stillan *dsm* stillu *npn*

stille *adv* still, quietly

ġestillan *1* stop, restrain

stilnes *f* peace, silence stilnesse *as*

stint < standan

ġestireð < ġestīeran

stiriġendlīċ *adj* moving

stīb *adj* hard, serve, strong, resolute *nsn* stīban *asf* stībe *apm*

stīðlīċe *adv* fiercely, loudly

stīðmōd *adj* resolute, stern-hearted stīðmōda *nsm*

stōd, stōdon < standan

stond- *see* standan

stōp, stōpon < steppan

storm *m* storm, tumult, turbulence *ns* stormas *np* storme *ds* stormum *dp*

stormsǣ *m* stormy sea

stōw *f* place, religious foundation *ns* stōwa *as*, *np*, *ap* stōwe *as*, *gs*, *ds* stōwum *dp*

strang *adj* strong, mighty, firm, bold, wilful, resolute *nsm* stranga *nsm* strangan *gsm* (=noun) strange *npm* strangestan *sup dpn* strangne *asm* strengest *sup nsm* strengra *comp nsm* strengran *comp gpm* strongum *dsm*

ġestranġian *2* strengthen

strǣl *m* arrow strǣlas *ap* strǣlum *dp*

strǣt *f* street, road

streċe *adj* severe, violent

strēdan *2* strew, scatter, sow

streng- *see* strang

strenġu *f* strength, power strenġe *ds*

strenþu *f* strength, power

ġestrēon *n* possession

strīc *n* sickness, contagion

ġestrīenan *1* beget, father ġestrīene *sjb pr3s* ġestrȳnde *pt3s*

strong *see* strang

strūdung *f* robbery strūdunga *ap*

strūtian *2* stand rigid, stiff

strȳnd *f* race, stock strȳnde *ds*

ġestrȳnde < ġestrīenan

styċċe *n* piece

styde *see* stede

stȳlecg adj steel-edged

stynt < standan

stȳpel *m* steeple, tower

ġestȳrde < ġestīeran

styrian *2* stir up, urge styrede *pt3s* styrode *pt3s*

sūl *see* sulh

sulh *f* plough sȳl *ds* sȳl

sum *adj* certain, a, an, some, about *nsm, nsn, nsf, asn* suman *dsm* sumæ *apf* sume *asf, npm, apm* sumne *asm* sumre *dsf* sumu *npn, apn* sumum *dsm*

sum *pron* one, a certain one, some one *nsm, nsn* sume *npm, npn*

sumor *m* summer *ns* sumera *ds* sumeres *gs*

sumorlang *adj* long as in summer sumorlangne *asm*

suna < sunu

sund *n* sea, water, swimming sunde *ds*

ġesund *adj* sound, safe, well, unharmed *nsm, nsf* ġesunde *npm* ġesundran *comp npm*

sundor *adv* apart

sune, sunena < sunu

Sunnandæġ *m* Sunday

sunne *f* sun *ns* sunnan *as*

sunu *m* son *ns, as, ds, ap* suna *ns, gs, ds, np, ap* sunum *dp*

sūþ *adv* south, southwards

sūðan *adv* from the south be sūðan south of

Sūðeseaxe *pl* (men of) Sussex

Sūðeseaxan *pr n* the South Saxons, Sussex *np*

sūðstæð *n* south coast sūðstæðe *ds*

swā *adv* so, such a, as, thus, likewise, in this fashion, in this respect, very swǣ ; *see also* bēah

swā *conj* as, just as, so, equivalent to, such that, when, although swǣ ; *see also* sōna

swā swā *adv/conj* (*joined or separated*) as, just as, just like, such as, just as though swǣ swǣ, swā…swā who(so)ever swā hwæt swā what (so)ever swā hwelċ swā who(so)ever

swāc < sīcan

swāt *m* blood swāte *gs*

swātfāh *adj* bloodstained

swātiġ *adj* bloody swātiġne *asm*

swāþbēah *see* bēah

swæċċ *m* flavor, taste

swǣġcræfte *see* swēġcræft

swǣs *adj* beloved, dear swǣsne *asm* swǣsra

comp gpm

swæð *n* track, trail

swētan *1* bleed *inf*

ġeswearc < sweorcan

sweart *adj* dark, black sweartan *nsm, asm, gsf, apm*

swefel *m* sulphur

swefn *n* dream *as* swefna *gp*

swēġ *n* sound, voice, noise, music *ns, as*

swēġing f sound

swēġcræft *m* musical skill *as* swēġcræfte *ds*

sweġel *n* sky, heaven sweġle *ds* sweġles *gs*

swelċ– *see* swilċ–

swelċe *adv* as if, as it were, as, like, likewise

swelċe ēac also, moreover

sweltan *III* die, perish *inf* swulton *pt3p* swylteþ *pr3s* swyltst *pr2s*

swenċan *1* harass, afflict, oppress swenċað *pr3s* ġeswenct *pp* swencte *pt3s* ġeswencte *pp apm*

sweng *m* blow, stroke *as* swenges *gs*

sweoloð *m/n* burning heat, flame sweoloðe *ds*

swēora *m* neck swēoran *as* swūra *ns* swūran *as, ds*

ġesweorcan *III* grow dark, despair ġeswearc *pt3s* ġesweorce *sbj pr3s* sweorceð *pr3s*

sweord *n* sword *ns, as* sweorda *gp* sweorde *ds, is* sweordes *gs* sweordum *dp* sword *ap* swurd *ns, as, ap* swurde *ds* swyrd *ap* swyrdum *dp*

sweordbealo *n* sword evil, death by sword

sweordbora *m* sword-bearer

sweoster *f* sister swistær *ds* swuster *ns, as* swustor *ns, gs* ġeswustra *ap* ġeswustrum *dp* swystær *ds* swyster *ds*

sweotol *adj* clear, evident, manifest

sweotole *adv* clearly, openly sweotolor *comp* sweotule

ġesweotolian *2* show, indicate

sweotolung *f* sign, manifestation

swerian *2* swear sweriġe *pr1s*

swīcan *I* deceive, be treacherous swīcað *pr3s*

ġeswīcan *I* cease (from +g), abandon, fail (+d) ġtswāc *pt3s*

swicdōm *m* deception, fraud, treachery swicdōmas

ap

swician *2* deceive, betray, fail swicode *pt3s*

ġeswīcan *I* cease

swicol *adj* false, deceitful, tricky swicolost *sup nsn*

swift *adj* swift, fast swiftne *asm* swiftust *sup nsn*

swiftlēre *m* slipper

swīge *f* silence, quiet *ns*

swīġian *2* to be silent, become quiet swīgað *pr3s* swīġende *prp nsm* swīgode *pt3s*

swilċ *adj* such, similar *apf* swilċere *dsf* swylċere *dsf* swylċcum *dsm*

swilċ *pron/rel* such, whichever, such as, like swilċan *dpn* swilċe *nsm* swylċ *nsn, asn* swylċe *npm* swylċne *asm* swylċcum *dpn*

swilċe *adv* likewise, also, thus, again, in addition to (*often in adv phr* ēac swilċe, swelċe ēac, *etc.* likewise, in the same way) swelċe, swylċe

swilċe *conj* as if, as though, just as, such that, such a swelċe, swylċe *; in phr* swylċe swā just as

swimman *III* swim swimmað *pr3p*

swīn *n* pig, boar, boar-image swīnes *gs* swȳn *ns*

ġeswinc *n* toil, hardship ġeswince *ds* ġeswincum *dp*

swincan *III* labor swinċe *pr1s*

swingan *III* beat, scourge *inf*

swingel *f* stroke, blow swincgla *ap*

swipu *f* whip, scourge

swistær *see* sweoster

swīþ *adj* mighty, strong, great swīðran *comp* right *asf* (=*noun* right hand) swīþe *asf* swīþre *comp nsf* swȳðran *comp asf* swȳðran *comp asf* swȳðre *comp nsf*

swīþe *adv* very, greatly, deeply, strongly, firmly, violently swīðe swīðe very greatly swīþor *comp* more, more firmly swīþost *sup* most of all, especially swīður *comp,* swȳþe, swȳþor *comp* swȳðost *; in instr phr* tō þan swīðe to such an extent that

swīðliċ *adj* violent, great, excessive swȳðlicum *dsf*

swībor < swīþe

swībost *adv* mostly, most strongly

swīðran < swīþ

swiðrian *2* become strong

swoncor *adj* slender, supple swoncre *apf*

sword *see* sweord

swulton < sweltan

swuncon < swincan

swungon < swingan

swūra, swūran < swēora

swurd, swurde *see* sweord

swuster, swustor *see* sweoster

ġeswustr- *see* sweoster

swutol *adj* clear, evident *nsn* swutele *npn*

swylċ, swylċ- *see* swilċ, swilċe

swyftlēre *m* slippers

swylteb, swyltst < sweltan

swȳn *see* swīn

swyrd, swyrdum *see* sweord

swyster *see* sweoster

swȳb- *see* swīb-

sȳ < bēon-wesasn

sȳferlīċe *adv* with purity, chastely

ġesyhðe < ġesihð

syl < sulh

sȳl < sulh

sȳlanscear *m* plowshare

syleð < ġesellan

sylf *adj* self, same seolfan *npm* sylfan *dsm, dpm*

sylf *pron* self, himself, herself, themselves, *etc*
self *nsm* selfe *npm* selfes *gsm* selfne *asm*
selfre *gsf* selfum *dsm* seolfes *gsm* seolfne
asm seolfra *gpm* silf *nsm, nsf* silfa *nsm*
silfne *asm* sylf *nsm, asn* sylfa *nsm* sylfe *asf,
npm, apm* sylfne *asm* sylfra *gpm* sylfre *gsf,
dsf* sylfum *dsm, dpm, dpn*

sylfor, sylfore < seolfor syll- *see* ġesellan

syll- *see* (ġe)sellan

sȳllan < sēl

syllic *adj* wonderful, marvellous *nsm* syllicre
comp asn

sylð < ġesellan

symbel *n* banquet, feast symbla *gp* symble *ds*
symle *ds*

symblan *1* feast, banquet symblað *pr3p*

symble *adv* always, ever, continuously simle,
symle, symlie

symle *see* symble

syn *see* synn

sȳn, synd, synd- < bēon-wesan

syndriġ *adj* special, private syndriġe *npm, apn*

ġesȳne *adj* visible, seen, evident, conspicuous
nsn, npf ġesǣne *nsn* ġesēne *nsn* ġesīene *npm*

syngāla *adv* always, continually syngāles

syngian *2* sin *sbj pr3p*

synn *f* sin *ns* sinna *ap* syn *as* synna *gp*
synnan *dp* synne *as, ds* synnum *dp*

synt < bēon-wesan

syrċe *f* mailshirt

sȳð *see* sīb

sybban *see* sibban

tācen *n* sign, portent, token, evidence tācn *ns*
tācne *ds* tācnum *dp*

tam *adj* tame

tāwian *2* afflict, ill-treat

tǣċan *1* teach, instruct, show, interpret, direct
inf, sbj pr3p tǣċe *pr1s, sbj pr2s* tǣċon *sbj
pr3p* tǣċb *pr3s*

tǣhte, tǣhton < tǣċan

ġetǣl *n* number, sequence, reckoning ġetǣle *ds*
ġetel *ns*

tǣlan *1* slander, wrong tǣleð *pr3s* tǣlst *pr2s*

tæt (bæt) < se

tē (ðē) < bū

tēah < tēon

tealt *adj* unstable, wavering tealte *npf*

tēam *m* family, progeny *ns*

tēar *m* tear, drop tēaras *np*

ġetellan *1* reckon, consider ġeteald *pp* ġetealde
pp npm

temian *2* tame, train

tēon *1* prepare, create, adorn tēode *pt3s*

ġetēon *II* drag, draw, bring, train, educate tēah
pt3s ġetēah *pt3s* ġetogen *pp* ġetugon *pt3p*

tēona *m* injury, hurt, wrong

tēonrǣden *f* humiliation

tēoaa *num* tenth

teran *IV* tear

than *see* bonne

tharf *see* bearf

thēm (bm) < se

tiċċen *n* kid

tīd *f* time, season, occasion, feast-day, hour, tense *ns*, *as* tīda *np*, *ap*, *gp* tīde *as*, *ds* tīdum *dp* tiid *as* ; *in phr* sumre tīde on a certain occasion tō sumre tīde at a certain time

tīeġan *1* tie

tīen *num* ten

tiġel *m* tile tiġelum *dp*

tiid *see* tīd

til *adj* good, brave, praiseworthy, useful *nsm* (=*noun* good man) tilne *asm* tilra *comp gpm*

tilia *m* farmer, farm laborer

tilian *2* till, cultivate, strive, labor, provide for (+d) *inf* (+g of thing) tilien *sbj pr1p*

tīma *m* time, opportunity tīman *ds*

timbran *1* build, construct timbredon *pt3p*

ġetimbrian *2* build ġetimbrode *pt3s* ġetimbrod *pp*

tin *n* tin

tintreġ *n* torment, punishment

tintreġian *2* torment, punish

tīr *m* fame, glory, honor tīres *gs* t̄yr *as*

Tīrisc *adj* Tyrian

tīaian *2* grant tīiaenne *infl inf*

tō *adv* too, too much

tō *prep* (+d/i/g) to, into, for, as, as to, in, of, with ; *with infl inf* to (do something), for (doing something) ; *in instr phr* tō ðī bæt in order that tō bon bæt to the extent that, until ; *see also* swīðe, bæs (*conj*)

tōbecuman *IV* arrive, come tōbecume *sbj pr*

tōberstan *III* burst open, break asunder, shatter tōbærst *pt3s* tōburston *pt3p*

tōbrecan *IV* break to pieces, destroy, violate, break open tōbræc *pt3s* tōbrocen *pp* tōbrocene *pp npn* tōbrocon *pp*

tōbrēden *III* (+d) shake off, tear to pieces, pull apart

tōbr̄ytan *1* crush

tōcnāwan *VII* understand, acknowledge

tōcyme *m* coming, arrival, advent *as*

tōdæġ *adv* today tōdæġe

tōd̄ælan *1* part, separate, share out tōd̄ælað *pr1p* tōd̄ælden *sbj pt3p* tōd̄ældon *pt3p* tōd̄æled *pp*

tōfaran *VI* go apart, disperse

tōfēran *1* be scattered, disperse tōfērdon *pt3p*

tōgædere *adv* together tōgædre

tōġēanes *prep* (+d) against, towards, at tōġenes

tōġeīeċan *I* increase, add to

tōġeīeht *pp* of tōġeīeċan added to

ġetogen < tēon

ġetoht *n* battle, conflict ġetohte *ds*

tōl *n* tool, implement

torbr̄ytan *I* crush tōrbr̄yt *pr3s*

tōmiddes *prep* amidst, among

torn *n* anger, misery, affliction *as*

torġemōt *n* hostile meetings *as*

tōteran *IV* tear to pieces

tōtw̄æman *1* divide, break up tōtw̄æmed *pp*

tōb *m* tooth *ns* tōðon *dp* tōbum *dp*

tōweorpan *III* cast down, destroy, put an end to tōwyrpð *pr3s*

tōwyrd *f* opportunity tōwyrde *as*

tredan *V* step on, trample trede *pr1s*

trēow *n* tree *as*, *np* trēowa *gp* trēowe *ds* trēowu *ap* trēowum *dp* trīo *ns*, *np*, *ap*, *gp* trīo *ns*, *np*, *ap*, *gp* trīow *ns* trīowa *gp* trīowum *dp*

trēow *f* tree *as*, *np* trēowa *gp* trēowe *ds* trēowu *ap* tēowum *dp* trīo *ns*, *np*, *ap*, *gp* trīowa *gp* trīowum *dp*

trēow *f* truth, faith, good faith *ns* trēowe *as*

ġetrēowan *1* believe in, trust ; exculpate oneself, clear oneself

ġetrēowe *adj* faithful, loyal, trustworthy ġetrēowestan *sup apm* ġetrēowra *comp npm* ġetr̄ywe *nsm*

ġetrēowb *f* truth, loyalty ġetrēowba *gp* ġetr̄ywða *np*, *ap*

tēowwyrhta *m* carpenter, wood-worker

treppe *f* trap

trīo, trīo- *see* trēow

trīowan, ġetrīowe < ġetrēowan

trum *adj* strong, firm, secure, vigorous *nsm* trumne *asm*

ġetruwian *2* trust, put trust in, confirm ġetruwedon *pt3p* ġetruwode *pt3s*

ġetrȳwða < ġetrēowþ

trym *n* piece, short length

trymian *1* arrange, draw up, exhort trymedon *pt3p* ġetrymed *pp*

ġetrymman *1* strengthen, comfort ġetrymmende *prp nsm*

trymmyng *f* strengthening, encouraging, confirmation tymmynge *ds*

ġetrȳwe *see* ġetrēowe

ġetrȳwða < ġetrēowþ

tū *see* bū

tūa < twēġen

tūcian *2* ill-treat, harass, afflict

tugon < tēon

tūn *m* enclosure, estate, manor, homestead, village tūnæ *ds* tūne *ds*

tunge *f* tongue *ns* tungan *as*

tungol *n* star, planet, constellation tungl *ap*

twā, twām < twēġen

twēġen *num* two, a pair *npm, apm* tūa *apn* twā *npn, apm, apn, apf* twām *dpm, dpn* twēġa *gpn* twēġea *gsm*

twelf *num* twelve twelfe *npm*

twēntiġ *num* twenty

twēon *II* (+*g*) doubt, hesitate (+*g*) twēode *pt3s*

twēon *m* doubt

twēonian *2* doubt

twēonum *see* be

tweowa *adv* twice

twīn *n* linen

twȳn < twēo

tȳde < tīd

ġetyhtan *1* train

tȳnan *1* enclose, shut

tyrwa *m* tar, pitch

bā *adv* then, at that time, after that time, thereupon, there

bā *conj* when, seeing that, now that, if, as, since, because, where bā bā (*often joined*) when

bā (*dem adj, pron*) < se

aafunge f consent, permission, accord aafiunga *ds* aafiungæ *ds* aafunga *ds* aafunge *as, ds*

bāġyt *see* ġyt

ġebāh < ġebicgan

bām < se

ban (bām, bon) < se

banc *m* thought, reflection, pleasure ; thanks (*for* +*g*) *as* bances *gs* bonc *ns*

banc (+*d*) thanks

ġebanc *m* thought, mind, purpose *as* ġebance *ds* ġeðonce *ds*

ġebancian *2* (+*d*(*person*)/+*g*(*for a thing*)) thank, give thanks to *inf* bancað *pr3s* ġebance *pr1s* banciað *pr3p* banciġende *prp nsm* bancode *pt3s*

bancful *adj* thankful

banon *adv* thereupon, after that ; thence, from there, out banonne, bonan

bār, bārtō *see* b̄ær, b̄ærtō

bāra < se

bāre < se

bæ, b̄æ *see* be, bē

bæġn, bæġne < beġn

b̄æm < se

bæne (bone) < se

bænne see bonne

b̄ær *adv* there, then, in that respect bār

b̄ær *conj* where, when, while bēr ; *often in conj phr* b̄ær b̄ær there where, where, wherever

b̄æræt *adv* thereat, there

b̄ære < se

b̄æron *adv* thereon, therein

b̄ærtō *adv* thereto, pertaining to (it), as well, for that (purpose) bārtō

bæs *adv* (*gs of* bðt) afterwards, in respect of that, to that degree, so, therefore ; *in phr* tō bæs so

bæs *conj* (*gs of* bæt) as, because, after ; *in phr* bæs be according to what, as, to the extent that tō ðæs be

bæs (*demons adj/pron*) < sē, bes

bæt *conj* that, so that, on condition that, because bet ; *see also* oð

bæt (*def art, demons pron*) < se

bætte(=bæt be) *conj* that

be *rel pr/conj* who, which, that, when, as, because be···be *either···or* be than ; *see* mā

bē (*instr of* se, **þæt**) *see* bȳ

bē (*pron*) < bū

bēah *adv* nevertheless, even so, yet, still, however swā bēah, swābēah

bēah *conj* though, although, even bēah be, bēh

bēahhwæbere *adv* yet, moreover

ġebeaht *n/f* advice, counsel, purpose *as* ġebeahte *ds*

ġebeahta *m* counsellor, adviser

ġebeahtend *m* counsellor

bearf *f* need, hardship, distress *ns* tharf *ns* bearfe *as*

bearf, bearft < burfan

bearfende *adj* (*prp of* burfan) in want, needy, wretched *asn* bearfendre *dsf*

ġebearfian *2* necessitate, force ġebearfod *pp*

bearle *adv* very hard, thoroughly, harshly, vigorously, violently, sorely, keenly

bēaw *m* custom, practice, disposition, virtue *ns* bēawa *gp* ðēawas *ap* ðēawum *dp*

beġen *m* thane, nobleman, retainer, warrior, follower bæġn *ns* beġen *ns, as* beġenas *np, ap* beġene *ds* bēġenes *gs* beġna *gp* beġnas *np, ap* beġne *ds* bēnan *dp*

beġnian *2* serve, minister to (+d) *inf* bēnian *inf* bēnode *pt3s*

beġnung *f* service, meal, first course ; retinue

bēh *see* beah

bēnan < beġn

ġebenċan *1* think, think of, consider, reflect, remember, intend, desire *inf* bæncb *pr3s* benċ *imp s* ġebenċ *imp s* benċab *pr2p, pr3p* benċe *sbj pr3s* benċean *inf* ġeðenċean *inf* benċeð *pr3s* ðenċð *pr3s* ġebōht *pp* bōhte *pt1s* ġebōhte *pt3s* bōhton *pt3p*

benden *conj* while, as long as

bengel *m* prince *as*

benian *2* stretch out, rack *inf*

bēnian *see* beġnian

bēning *f* divine service ðēninga *ap*

bēo *see* sēo

bēod *f* nation, people, tribe *ns* bēode *as, gs, ds, np* bēodum *dp* ðioda *np*

ġebēodan *1* join ġebēodde *pp npm*

bēodcyning *m* king of a people, monarch

bēode < bēod, bēowan

ġebēode *n* speech, language ġeðēoda *gp* ġebēode *ds* ġebēodes *gs* ġeðīode *as*

bēoden *m* lord, prince, ruler, the Lord bēodne *ds* bēodnes *gs* bēoðnes *gs*

bēodenlēas *adj* princeless, lordless ðēodenlēase *npm*

bēodġestrēon *n* people's treasure, great treasure

bēodscype *m* nation, discipline, law bēodscypes *gs* bēodscypum *dp*

bēodwita *m* learned man *ns*

bēof *m* criminal, thief *ns*

bēofa *m* thief

ġebēon *I/II* thrive, prosper *inf*

bēonde *adj* thriving, prosperous

bēos, beoss- *see* bes

bēostru *f* darkness, gloom

bēow *m* slave, servant bēowa *as, gp* bēowas *np, ap* bēowum *dp* ðīowa *gp*

bēowa *f* slave-woman *ns* ðēowan *ds*

bēowan *1* serve bēode *pt3s*

bēowdōm *m* slavery, servitude *as* bēowdōme *ds*

ġebēowian *2* be subject to, enslave, serve, follow (+d) ġebēowede *pp npm* bēowode *pt3s* ġebēowudð *pp*

bēodwita *m* learned

bēowot *n* servitude

bēr *see* bǣr

bes, bis, bēos *demons pron/adj* this, these bās *asf, npm, npn, apn* bæs *nsm* bēos *nsf* beosse *gsf* beossum *dsm* bes *nsm* bios *nsn* bīos *nsf* bis *nsm, nsn, nsf, asn* bīs *ism* bises *gsn* bisne *asm* bisre *gsf* bissa *gpn, gpf* bisse *dsf* bissere *dsf* bisses *gsn* bissum *dsm, dsn* bisum *dsn, dpm* bȳs *ism, isn* bysan *dsm, dsn* byses *gsm* bysne *asm* byson *dsm* byssa *gpm* bysse *dsf* bysses *gsn* bysson *dsn* byssum *dsn* bysum *dsn*

bet (bæt) < se, sēo, bæt

bī < se, sēo, bæt, bȳ

bicce *adj* thick, viscous *apm*

ġebicgan *V* receive, take, eat, drink ġebah *pt3s*

bider *adv* thither, there, to that place

bīn *poss pron* thy, thine, your, yours bīn *nsm*, *nsf, nsn* bīne *npm, asf* benes *gsn* bīnne *asm*, *asf* bīnre *gsf, dsf* bīnum *dpf* b̄yræ *dsf*

binc- *see* pynċan

bincg *see* bing

bing *n* thing, matter, event, case, circumstance, cause, act, property *ns, as, np, ap* bincg *as, np* binga *gp* bingan *dp* bingc *ap* binges *gs* bingum *dp*

bingian *2* pray, intercede (+*d*), supplicate ðingade *pt1s* bingiæ *sbj pr3s*

ġebinge *n* agreement, truce, terms

bingð < bynċan

ġebīode < ġeðēode

bios, bīos < bes

bīowa < bēow

bīowotdōm *m* service ðīowotdōmas *ap*

bis, bis-, biss- *see* bes

ġebōht *m* thought, mind, purpose *as* ġebōhtas *np* ġebōhte *ds*

ġebōht < ġebenċan

bōhte, bōhton < benċan

ġebolian *2* suffer, endure *inf* boledon *pt3p* boliað *pr1p* ġebolie *sub pr3s* bolien *sbj pr1p* boliġende *prp npm* ġebolod *pp* bolodan *pt3p* bolode *pt3s*

bon < se ; *see also* æfterm ēac, tō, wið

bon *see* bonne

bonan *see* banon

bonæ (bone) < se

bonc *see* banc

ġebonce < ġebanc

bone < se

bonne *adv* then, now, therefore, henceforth, rather, however, besides banne, bænne, bonnæ

bonne *conj* when, while, since, namely, yet

bonne *conj* (+*comp*) than than, bænne, bon

borfte, borfun < burfan

born thorn bornum *dp*

brāg *f* time period, season *ns* brāgum *dp* (=*adv* at times) ; *in phr* ealle brāge *as* continuously

bræd *m* thread

br̄æl *m* slave *ns as* br̄æla *gp* br̄æle *ds*

br̄ælfriht *n* rights of a slave

brēat *m* crowd, troop

brēo, brēora < brīe

bridda *num adj* third briddan *asm, gsf, dsm, dsf* bridde *nsf*

brīe *num* three *asm* brēo *nsn, npm, apn* brēora *gp, gpm* brī *npm* brīm *dpm, dpn* brīo *nsn* br̄y *npm, apm* br̄ym *dpm*

brīm < brīe

brymfæst *adj* glorious, illustrious, mighty brymfæstne *asm*

brīste *adv* boldly, confidently, resolutely

ġebrīstian *2* dare

brītiġ *num* thirty brītæġum *dpn* brīteġum *dpn* ðdritiġ, brittiġ

brītiġfeald *adj* thirtyfold brītiġfealdne *as*

ġebrōwian *2* suffer, endure *inf* brōwade *pt1s* brōwiġe *sbj pr3s* brōwiġenne *infl inf* brōwode *pt3s* ġebrōwode *pt3s*

brōwung *f* passion, suffering brōwunge *as, ds*

br̄y < brīe

brym *m* might, glory, majesty brymmas *np* brymme *ds* brymmes *gs* ðrymmum *dp*

br̄ym < brīe

br̄yb *f* might, host br̄ybe *np*

bū *pers pron* thou, thee, you *ns* tē *ds* tū *ns* b̄æ *ds* bē *as, ds* ; *see also* p ġē, *dual* ġit, *poss pron* bīn

ġebūht, būht- *see* bynċan

ġebungen *adj* (*pp of* bīon) excellent, distinguished *nsf*

burhbrūcan *2* enjoy fully

burfan *pt-pr* need, have occasion to, must bearf *pr3s* bearft *pr2s* borfte *pt3s* borftun *pt3p* burfe *pr1p, pr2s* burfon *pt3p* byrfen *sbj pr2p*

burh *adv* through

burh *prep* (+*a/d*) through, by, by means of, because of, on account of, in, into, beyond

burhbrūcan *2* enjoys fully

burhdrīfan *I* drive through, pierce *pt3p* burfdrifene *pp npm*

burhfōn *VI* penetrate

burhtēon *II* bring about, effect

burhwadan *VI* pass through burhwōd *pt3s*

burhwunian *2* remain, abide continuously burhwunað *pr3s* burhwunode *sbj pt3s*

bus *adv* thus, in this way, so buss

būsend *num* thousand *ns* būsendo *ap*

buss *see* bus

ġebwǣrlǣċan *1* agree, consent

ġebwǣrnyss *f* concord, peace

bȳ (*demons pron isn*) < se

bȳ *adv* therefore, for this reason ; *see also* for, tō

bȳ *adv* (+*comp*) the, by that bē ; *see also* lǣs

byder *see* bider

bȳfel *m* bush

bȳfþ *f* theft bȳfþe

bȳhtiġ *adj* firm, powerful

bylċ *pron, adj* such, of that sort

ġebyld *n/f* patience *ns as* ġebyldes *gs*

ġebyldiġ *adj* patient *nsm*

ġebyldigian *2* be patient

bynċan *1* impers (+*d*) seem, appear, think binċan *inf* binċæ *sbj pr3s* binċe *pr3s* binċð *pr2s, pr3s* bingð, ġebūht *pp* būhte *pt3s* ðūhton *pt3p* ðyncð *pr3s*

byrel *adj* pierced, perforated *nsm*

byrfen < burfan

byrl *n* hole, boring

byrl *adj* pierced, decayed rotted

ġebȳrstan *1 impers* (+*d*) thirst ġebǣyrsteð *pr3s*

bȳs, bys-, byss- *see* bes

bȳstro *f* darkness ðēostrum *dp* bȳstru *np* bȳstrum *dp*

bȳwan *1* urge, drive bȳwende *prp nsm*

Uēnus *pr n* Venus

ufan *adv* above, from above

ufeweard *adj* upper, topmost part of (*usually= noun*) *npn* ufeweardon *dsn* ufeweardum *dpm* ufonweardum *dpn*

ūhta *m* period before dawn, early morning ūhtan *ds* ūhtna *gp*

ūhtcearu *f* anxiety before dawn ūhtceare *as*

uhtsang *m* nocturns, matins

umbor *n* infant, child

umborwesend *adj* being a child

unbefohten *adj* without a fight, unfought unbefohtene *npm*

unc, uncer < wit

uncer poss pron dual our, of the two of us nsn uncerne asm

unclǣnes *f* uncleanness, impurity unclǣnesse *ds*

uncobu *f* disease ns

uncræft *m* evil practice, deceit uncræftan *dp*

undær *see* under

under prep (+*d/a*) under, beneath, covered by undær

underbeġinnan *III* undertake underbeġinne *infl inf*

undercyning *m* under-king, tributary king

underdelfan *III* dig under

underfōn *VII* receive, accept, assume, conduct underfēng *pr3s* underfēngan *ptlp* underfēngon *pt3p*

underġietan *V* perceive, understand underġeat *pt3s*

understandan *VI* understand, comprehend *inf* understandað *pr3p, imp p* understande *sbj pr3s* understandenne *infl inf* understondan *inf*

underntīd *f* terce, the third hour undertīde *as*

underbēodan *1* subject, devote underbēoded *pp*

unēaðe *adv* not easily, unwillingly

unēðelīċe *adj* inconveniently, awkwardly

unfæderelīċe *adv* in an unfatherly way, unlike a father

unflitme *adj* undisputed

unforcūð *adj* undisgraced, honorable *nsm*

unforht *adj* unafraid, fearless *nsm* unforhte *npm*

unformolsnod *adj* undecayed

unforscēawodlīċe *adv* unexpectedly, unawares, suddenly.

unforwandiendlīċe *adv* without bashfulness

unforworht *adj* uncondemned, innocent unforworhte *npm*

unġecnāwe *adj* unknown *npn*

unġecyndne *adj* alien, unnatural

unġelǣred *adj* uneducated, ignorant unġelǣredan *npm* unġelǣrede *npm* unġelǣredum *dp*

unġelīċ *adj* (+*d*) unlike, unalike, different

unġelimp *n* misfortune

unġemetlīċ *adj* immense, excessive, violent

unġesǣliġ *adj* unfortunate *nsn*

unġeawǣrnes *f* discord, conflict.

unġewuneliċ *adj* unusual, unfamiliar

unġiefe *f* evil gift

unġylde *n* excessive tax unġylda *np*

unhlitme *adv* involuntarily, disastrously

unhold *adj* faithless, hostile

unlagu *f* violation of law, unlawful act, injustice unlaga *ap*

unlīcð < unlūcan

unlūcan *II* unlock unlīcð *pr3s*

unmihtiġ *adj* powerless, weak unmihtiġare *comp nsn*

ġeunnan *pt-pr* (+d(*person*)/+g(*thing*)) grant, bestow, intercede an *pr3s* ann *pr1s* ġeunne *sbj pr3s*, *imp s* ūðe *pt3s* ġeūðe *pt3s* ūbon *sbj pt3p*

unnyt *adj* useless, unprofitable *nsn*

unoferswȳðed *adj* unconquerable, invincible unoferswȳðda *nsm*

unriht *n* injustice, wrong *as* unrihta *gp*

unrihtwīs *adj* unrighteous (*often used as noun*) unrihtwīsan *npm* unrihtwīsra *gpm* unrihtwīsum *dpm*

unrihtwīsnes *f* injustice, unrighteousness

unrīm *n* (+g) a countless number (of) *ns*

ġeunrōstsian *2* be sad, make sad

unrōt *adj* unhappy, dejected *nsm* unrōte *npm*

unryhtum < unriht

unscennan *1* unharness

unsidu *m* abuse, vice unsida *ap*

unsynnum *adv* without sins, guiltless

untīemende *adj* barren

untrymnes *f* infirmity, illness untrymnesse *ds* untrumnysse *ds*

unwæstm *m* crop failure unwæstma *gp*

unwealt *adj* steady

unweder *n* bad weather, storm unwedera *np*

unwittiġ *adj* innocent, simple, foolish

unwrītere *m* bad scribe, inaccurate copyist

ūp *adv* up, above, upwards, upstream, ashore, inland ūpp

ūpgang *m* rising, sunrise ūpgonge *ds*

ūpganga *m* passage to land, access ūpgangan *as*

uphēah *adj* high, lofty, tall uphēa *npf*

ūpp *see* ūp

uppan *prep* (+d) on, upon

uppe *adv* above, aloft

uppon *prep* (+d) on, upon, up to

ūre *poss adj* our *nsm, nsf, asn, dsf, dsn, npm, apn, apf* ūres *gsm gsn* ūrne *asm* ūrum *dsn, dpm* ; *see also pers pron* wē

urnon < irnan

ūs, ūsiċ < wē

ūt *adv* out, outside, abroad, publicly, forth, away

ūtan *adv* outside, from outside, from abroad

ūtanbordes *adv* outside the country, from abroad

ūtermere *m* outer sea, open sea

ūterra *adj, conj* outer

ūteweard *adj* outward, extreme

ūt-fūs *adj* ready to set out

uton *anom* (*pr1p* of wītan depart) (+inf) let us utan, utun, wutan, wuton

ūterra *adj* outer *comp* ȳtemeste *sup*

ūðe, ūbon < unnan

ūtweorpan *III* throw out

ūðwita *m* scholar, sage, authority ūðwitan *np* ūðwitena *gp*

wā *see* wēawālā *interj* (wā+lā) woe!, alas! (+d for)

wāc *adj* weak, slender, inferior wācne *asm* wācran *comp npm* (=*noun*)

wācian *2* weaken, be weak *inf* wācað *pr3s*

wadan *VI* go, advance, travel, traverse wōd *pt1s* wōdon *pt3p*

wālawā *interj* alas!

waldend *see* wealdend

wamb *f* stomach wambe *ds*

wan *indecl adj* (+g) wanting, lacking

wand < windan

wanden < wanian

wanhȳdiġ *adj* foolhardy, rash *nsm*

ġewanian *2* lessen, dwindle away, wane, curtail wanab *pr3s* wanedan *pt3p* wandean *pt3p* ġewanode *pp npn*

wann *adj* dark, black *nsf* wanna *nsm* won *nsn*

warian *2* hold, preoccupy warað *pr3s*

warnian 2 warn, caution *inf* warniġenne *infl inf*

waru f ware, article of merchandise

wæs < bēon-wesan

wāst, wāt < witan

ġewāt < ġewītan

wabum *m* wave wabema *gp*

wæċċan 2 be awake, watch wæċċende *prp npm* (=*adj* watchful, vigilant) wæċċendum *prp dpm* (=*noun* watchers)

wǣd f clothing, covering wǣdum *dp*

wǣdla *m* poor man

wǣdbrēċ *fp* breeches

wǣdla *adj* poor, barren, devoid of wǣdlan *asf*

wǣfersȳn f show, spectacle wǣfersȳne *ds*

wǣfre *adj* restless, wandering

wǣġ *m* water, wave, sea wǣgas *np* wǣġe *ds* wēgas *ap*

wægon < wegan

wæl *n* slaughter, carnage, the slain, battlefield *ns*, as walo *np* wæle *ds*

wælfāg *adj* slaughter-stained wælfāgne *asm*

wælfȳr *n* slaughter-fire, funeral-pyre wælfȳra *gp*

wælġifre *adj* greedy for carrion or slaughter bloodthirsty wælġifru *npn* wælġifrum *dp*

wælhrēow *adj* cruel, savage, bloodthirsty *nsm* wælhrēowe *apf*

wǣlhrēowlīċe *adv* cruelly, savagely

wǣlhrēownes f cruelty

wælnīð *m* deadly hate, hostility, moral enmity

wælrǣst f bed of slaughter, death in battle wælrǣste *as*

wælsleaht *m* slaughter-stroke, slaughter wælsleahta *gp* wælslihta *gp*

wælstōwe f place of slaughter, battle-filed wælstōwe *gs*

wælwulf *m* wolf of slaughter, (Viking) warrior wælwulfas *np*

wǣpen *n* weapon *ns as, np, ap* wǣpn *as* wǣpna *gp* wǣpne *ds* wǣpnes *gs* wǣpnum *dp*

wǣpenġewrixl *n* exchange of weapons, armed encounter wǣpnġewrixl *ns* wǣpenġewrixles *gs*

wǣre < wēr

wǣran, wǣre, wǣren < bēon-wesan

wærlīċe *adv* carefully, warily

wærod *see* werod

wǣron, wǣrun, wæs < bēon-wesan

wæstm *m* fruit, form, stature wæstmas *ap* wæstmum *dp*

wæstmbærnys f fertility

wæter *n* water, sea, river *ns, as* wætera *np, gp* wætere *ds, is* wæteru *np, ap* wæterum *dp* wætre *ds* wætres *gs*

wæterian 2 water

wæterscipe *m* piece of water, water

wæterbēote f torrent

wē *pers pron* we, us, ours *np* ūs *ap, dp* ūre *gp* ūsiċ *ap* ; *see also poss pron* ūre, *dual* wit

wēa *m* woe, misfortune, evil, harm, grief, misery, sin *ns* wā *ns* wēan *gs, ap* wēana *gp* ; *see also* wā, wālā

weal *see* weall

wēalāf f survivors of calamity, the woe-remnant

Wealas < Wealh

ġewealc *n* rolling, surging

weald *m* forest, wood walde *ds* wealde *ds*

ġeweald *n* control, use, power, dominion *as* ġewealde *ds*

ġewealdan *VII* (+*g*) wield, control, manage, possess, cause *inf* ġewealdest *pr2s* welt *pr3s* ġewēold *pt3s* wēoldan *pt3p*

wealdend *m* ruler, the Lord *ns* waldend *ns* wealdende *ds* wealdendes *gs*

Wēalh *m* foreigner, Welshman Wēalas *ap*

wealhstod *m* interpreter, translator *ns* wealhstodas *ap*

weall *m* wall, rampart *as* weal *ns* weallas *np*, *ap* wealle *ds* wealles *gs*

weallan *VII* well up, seethe, surge, boil, flow weallendan *prp asm* wēoll *pt3s* weōllon *pt3p*

wealsteal *m* place of walls, ruined site

wēana < wēa

weard *m* guard, watchman, guardian, protector, possessor *ns, as* wearde *as* weardas *np, ap*

weardian 2 possess, occupy, guard weardiað *pr3p*

wearg *m* felon, criminal

wearh *m* criminal wergas *ap*

wearp < weorpan

ġewearb, wearban < ġeweorban

wēabearf *f* woeful need wēabearfe *ds*

weardiġan *2 occupty* weardiað *pr:3p*

weaxan *VII* grow, increase, wax, be fruitful *inf* weaxe *imp p* weaxeð *pr:3s* wēox *pt1s, pt3s* wēoxon *pt3p*

wēdan *1* become mad, rage wēdde *pt3s*

wedbryċe *m* pledge-breaking wedbrycas *ap*

wedd *n* pledge, oath wed *as, np* wedde *ds, is* weddes *gs*

weder *n* weather, storm *ns, np* wederum *dp*

weġ *m* path, road, way, direction, course *ns, as* wega *gp* wegas *np, ap* weġe *ds ; in phr* on weġ *away* on wæġ

wegan *V* carry, bear wǣgon *pt3p* wēgon *pt3p* wēgas < wǣġ

wel *adv* well, fully, properly, effectively, quite, readily, indeed well

wela *m* prosperity, riches, happiness *ns* welan *as, ds*

ġeweldan *see* ġewieldan

welega < weliġ

ġewelhwǣr *adv* nearly everywhere

ġewelhwylċ *adj* nearly every ġewelhwylċan *dsm* ġewelhwylċan *dsm*

weliġ *adj* prosperous, well-to-do weliġne *asm*

well *see* wel

welt < wealdan

Wēlund *pr n* Weland *ns*

welwillended *adj* benevolent

welwillendnes *f* benevolence

welwillendnes *f* goodwill, kindness welwillendnesse *ds*

wēman *1* win over, entice

ġewemman *1* defile, profane, destroy

wēn *f* hope, expectation, belief wēna *np* wēnan *dp* wēnum *dp*

wēnan *1* think, believe, imagine, expect, suspect, hope *inf* wēnde *pt1s, pt3s* wēndon *pt3p* wēnē *pr1s, sbj pr3s* wēnst *pr2s*

wendan *1* turn, turn away, go, change translate *inf* wende *sbj pr1s* wenden *sbj pr1p, sbj pr3p* wendep *pr:3s* wendon *pt3p*

ġewendan *1* go, return, bring about *inf* ġewǣnde *pt3s* ġewǣndon *pt3p*

wēnde, wēndon < wēnan

wenian *2* accustom, entertain wenede *pt3s, sbj pt3s*

weofod *n* altar

ġewēold, wēoldan < ġewealdan

weoloc *m* whelk, murex

wēop, wēopon < wēpan

weorc *n* work, action, deed, task, achievement, affliction, pain, fortification *ns, as, np* weorca *gp* weorce *ds* weorcum *dp* weorkes *gs*

ġeweorc *n* work, labor, handwork, construction *ns, np* ġeweorce *ds*

weorod, weorode < werod

weorðmynd *f/n* honor, glory

weorpan *III* throw, fling, cast down, gush wearp *pt3s* weopan *inf* ġeweorpen *pp* wurpon *pt3p*

weorb *n* price weorðe *ds*

weorb- *see also* wurb-

weorban *III* become, be, come to, happen *; often=auxil vb* (is, will be, was, etc) *inf* uueorthae *sbj pr:3s* uuiurthit *pr:3s* wærd *pt3s* weard *pt3s* wearb *pt3s* wearban *inf* weorb *pr:3s* weorðað *pr:3p* weorbe *sbj pr:3s* weorðest *pr:2s* weorbeð *pr:2s* ġeworden *pp* wurdan *pt3p* wurde *pt3s, sbj pt3s* wurdon *pt3p* wurdun *pt3p* wurðan *sbj pr:3p* wurðe *sbj pr:3s* wurðeb *pr:3s* wyrð *pr:3s* wyrbeb *pr:3s*

ġeweorban *III* happen, come about, turn out *; impers* please *inf* ġewearð *pt3s* ġeweorðe *sbj pr:3s* ġeweorðeb *pr:3s* ġeweorden *pp* ġewurde *pt3s* ġewurden *pp* ġewurdon *pt3p* ġewurðan *inf* ġewurðe *sbj pr:3s* ġewyrð *pr:3s*

weorbfull *adj* worthy, honorable, glorious

ġeweorbian *2* honor, worship, exalt, enrich, reward, respect, obey *inf* ġewelðad *pp* ġeweorðade *pt3s* weorðað *pr:3s* weorðiað *pr:3p* ġeweorðod *pp* weorbode *sbj pt3s* ġeweorbode *pt3s, pp asn* wurðedon *pt3p* wurðian, wurðiab *pr1p, pr3p* wurðienne *infl inf* ġewurðod *pp* wurðode *pt3s* wurðodon *pt3p*

weorðlīċe *adv* splendidly *see* wurðlīċe

weorðmynt *f* esteem, honor, mark of honor *ns* weorðmynd *as* weorðmynde *as* wurðmynt ns wyrðmente *ds*

weoranesse *f* splendor, worth, estimation, honor

weorðscipe *m* dignity, honor.

weorþung *f* honor, veneration, worship, celebration weorþunge *ds*

weorud, weoruda *see* werod

weoruld, weorulde *see* woruld

weotena < wita

wēox, wēoxon < wēaxan

wēpan *VII* weep, bewail, mourn over *inf* wēop *pt3s* wēopon *pt3p* wēpēn *sbj pr3p*

wer *m* man, husband *ns, as* wera *gp* weras *np* were *ds* weres *gs* werum *dp*

wēr *f* covenant, pledge, treaty, agreement, protection wǣre *as* wērum *dp*

wēre < bēon-wesan

wereda, werede < werod

wergas < wearh

werian *1* protect, defend werede *pt3s* wereð *pr3s* weredon *pt3p*

ġewerian *1* defend, protect, make a (defensive) alliance ġeweredon *pt3p*

wēriġ *adj* weary, exhausted, wretched, sad *nsm, nsn* weriġe *npm* wēriġne *asm*

wēriġmōd *adj* weary, disheartened, dispirited

werod *n* company, band, host, army, multitude *ns, as* weorod *np* weorode *ds* weorud *ns* wereda *gp* werede *ds* weroda *gp* werode *ds* weruda *gp*

werod *adj* sweet

werod *pp of* werian

wes, wes- *see* bēon-wesan

westan *adv* from the west

westannorðan *adv* north-western

West-Dene *pr n* Danes West-Denum *dp*

wēste *adj* deserted, desolate, empty

wēsten *n* desert place, wasteland

westhealf *f* the western side

westm *see* wæstm

westsǣ *f* western sea

Westseaxe, -seaxan *pr n* West Saxons Wesseaxe *np* Wesseaxena *gp* Westseaxan *np* Westseaxna *gp*

wībed *n* altar wībedum *dp*

wiċ *n* dwelling-place, habitation, village *ns, as*

wīca *gp*

wiċċecræft *m* witchcraft

wīcian *2* dwell, encamp

wīcing *m* Viking *as* wīcinga *gp* wīcingas *ap* wīcinge *ds* wīcingum *dp*

wīd *adj* wide, broad, long wīdan *dsm, dsn ; in phr* tō wīdan aldre for ever

wīdcūa *adj* widely known

wīde *adv* wisely, spaciously, far afield, far and wide wīdost *sup* wīde ond sīde far and wide

ġewīde *adv* far apart ġewīdost *sup as* far apart as possible

ġewider *n* bad weather, storm ġewidru *ap*

widewe *f* widow

widuwe *f* widow widuwan *as, gs, ds* wydewan *np*

ġewieldan *1* get or have power over

ġewielf *see* ġewealdan

wierb < weorþan

wierbe *adj* worthy, honorable

wīf *n* woman *ns, np, ap* wīfa *gp* wīfæ *ds* wīfe *ds* wīfes *gs* wīfum *dp*

wīfhād *m* female sex

wīfhealf *f* female side in inheritance or descent

ġewīfian *2* take to wife, marry ġewīfode *pt3s*

wīfmann *m* woman wīfman *ns* wimmen *np*

wiġ *n* war, warfare, battle, fighting, strife, struggle *ns* wiġe *ds* wiġes *gs*

wiġa *m* warrior, fighter *ns* wiġan *as, np* wiġena *gp* wiġhena *gp*

wiġena < wiġa

wiġend *m* warrior wīġġend *as* wīġġendum *dp*

wiġheard *adj* war-hardened, fierce wiġheardne *asm*

wīġsigor *m* victory in war

wīġsmib *m* war-smith, warrior wīġsmibas *np*

wīhaga *m* battle-wall (of shields) wīhagan *as*

Wiht *pr n* Isle of Wight

wihte *adv* in any way, at all

ġewihte *n* weight *as*

wiites < wīte

wildēor *n* wild animal *ns* wildēora *gp*

wile < willan

wilġesīb *m* dear companion

willa *m* desire, purpose, determination, consent,

pleasure *ns* willan *as, gs, ds*

willan *anom* want, wish, will, intend, desire *;* also *auxil vb* will, shall *inf* wile *pr3s, sbj pr3s* willað *pr1p, pr3p* wille *pr1s, pr3s, pr1p, pr2p, sbj pr2s, sbj pr3s* willon *sbj pr2p* wilt *pr2s* wolde *pt1s, pt3s, sbj pt1s, sbj pt3s* woldest *pt2s* woldon *pt3p* wylæ *sbj pr3s* wyle *pr3s* wyllað *pr1p* wylle *pr1s, sbj pr2s, sbj pr3s, sbj pr2p ; for negative forms, see* nellan

ġewilnian *2* desire, yearn entreat ġewilniað *pr3p* ġewilnode *pt3s*

wilt < willan

wimmen < wīfmann

wīn *n* wine *ns, as* wīne *ds*

winas < wine

wind *m* wind *ns, as* winde *ds*

windan *III* wind, circle, fly, roll, curl, weave, brandish *inf* wand *pt3s* wundon *pt3p*

windiġ *adj* windy

wine *m* friend, lord *ns, as* winas *ap*

winedrihten *m* beloved lord, lord and friend winedryhtnes *gs*

winelēas *adj* friendless, lordless *nsm*

winemǣġ *m* beloved kinsman, near kinsman winemāgas *ap* winemǣga *gp* winemǣgum *dp*

winewincle *f* periwinkle

wīnġeard *m* vineyard, wine wīnġeardes *gs*

ġewinn *n* conflict, war, struggle, labor, hardship *as* ġewinne *ds*

ġewinna *m* adversary ġewinnan *ds*

winnan *III* struggle, suffer, contend, vie *inf* won *pt3s* wonn *pt1s* wunnon *pt3p*

ġewinnan *III* bring about, win, conquer *inf*

wīnsæl *n* wine-hall wīnsalo *np*

winstre *adj* left winstran *ds*

winsumum < wynsum

winter *m* winter *ns, as* wintra *gp* wintres *gp* wintrum *dp*

winterċeald *adj* wintry-cold winterċealde *asf*

winterċeariġ *adj* winter-sad

wintersetl *n* winter quarters

wiotan, wiotona < wita

wiotonne < witan

wirðe < wurþ

wīs *adj* wise, learned *nsm* wīsan *dsm* wīse *npm, apm* wīsra *comp gpm* (=*noun*)

ġewis *adj* aware, sure, certain, true *nsm* ġewissum *dsm*

wīsa *m* wise man, director, instructor

wīsan < wīse

wīsdōm *m* wisdom, knowledge, learning *ns, as* wīsdōme

wīse *adv* wisely

wīse *f* way, manner, idiom, fashion, matter wīsan *as, ds, ap* wīsum *dp*

wīsliċ *adj* wise, certain wīsliċne *asm* wīslicu *apn*

ġewīsliċe *adv* truly, carefully, precisely ġewīslīcor *comp* ġewislīcost *sup*

ġewissian *2* (+*d/a*) direct, guide ġewissode *pt3s*

ġewissum < ġewis

wissung *f* guidance, direction

wist *f* feast, feasting wiste *ds*

wist- *see* witan

ġewistfullian *2* feast

ġewistlǣcan *1* feast

wit *pron dual* we two *n* unc *a* uncer *g*

wita *m* wise man, counsellor, adviser, philosopher weotena *gp* wiotan *np* wiotona *gp* witan *np* witena *gp* witum *dp*

witan *pt-pr* know, understand, be aware of, be conscious of, feel, show *inf, pr1p* wāst *pr2s* wāt *pr1s, pr3s* wiotonne *infl inf* wistan *pt3p* wiste *pt1s, pt3s* wiston *pt3p* witanne *infl inf* wite *sbj pr2s* witon *pr3p* witun *pr1p ; with neg* nāst *pr2s* nāt *pr1s* nyste *pt3s*

ġewītan *I* set out, depart, go, pass away ġewāt *pt3s* ġewīt *pr3s* ġewitan *pt3p* ġewītað *pr3s* ġewiton *pt3p*

wīte *n* punishment, torment, penalty, fine *ns, as, ds* wiltes *gs* wīta *gp* wītu *np* wītum *dp*

wītega *m* wife man, prophet wītegan *np, as*

witena < wita

witenne < witan

wītiġ *adj* wise

wītnere *m* torturer

witodlīċe *adv* certainly, verily, truly

witon > wita, witan

wītu, wītum < wīte

wiþ *prep* (+*a/d/g/i*) to, towards, with, against, from, by, in return for uuib ; *in instr phr* wiþ bon be in the case that, on condition that

wiþerlēan *n* requital

wiðinnan *adv* within

wiðsacan *VI* forsake wiðsoce *sbj pt3s*

wiðstandan *VI* (+*d*) withstand, resist

wiðūtan *adv/prep* outside

wlanc *adj* proud, noble, bold, boastful, exulting in, presumptious *nsm*, *nsf* wlancan *dsn* wlance *npm*, *npf* wlancne *asm* wlonc *nsm*

wlāt < wlītan

wlætta *m* nausea, disgust, loathing wlættan *ds*

wlītan *I* look, gaze, see *inf* wlāt *pt3s*

wlite *m* face, appearance, countenance *ns*

wlitiġ *adj* splendid, beautiful wlitegan *gsf, dsn*

wlonc *see* wlanc

wōd *adj* mad

ġewōd, wōdon < ġewadan

wōdlīċe *adv* madly

wolcen *n* cloud(s), sky wolcna *gp* wolcne *ds* wolcnu *np* wolcnum *dp*

wolde, woldon < willan

wōlīċe *adv* perversely, wrongly

wōma *m* howling, terror

womm *m* stain, sin womme *ds* wommum *dp*

won *see* wann

wonn *adj* dark

wonn < winnan

wōp *m* weeping

word *n* word, command, speech, saying, utterance, verb *ns*, *as*, *np*, *ap* worda *gp* worde *ds* wordes *gs* wordon *dp* wordum *dp*

ġeworden, ġewordene < weorðan

ġeworht, ġeworht- *see* ġewyrċan

wōrian *2* crumble to pieces, decay wōriaþ *pr3p*

worn *m* crowd, swarm, multitude *as* wornum *dp*

woroldāre *f* worldly honor

woroldrǣden *f* worldly rule, the way of the world woroldrǣdenne *as*

woruld *f* world, age, eternity *ns*, *as* weoruld *as* weorulde *ds* worold *ns* worolde *gs*, *ds* woruld *as* worulda *gp* worulde *gs*

woruldafel *n* worldly strength, secular power woruldafelum *dp*

woruld-cræft *m* worldly occupation

woruldcund *adj* secular, worldly woruldcundra *gpm*

woruldhād *m* secular life

woruldman *m* man of the world, human being woruldmen *ap*

woruldþing *n* worldly affair woruldþincg *ap* woruldðinga *gp*

wracu *f* suffering, pain, enmity, vengeance wraca *as* wrace *as* wræce *as*

wrāð *adj* wrathful, angry, hostile, cruel *nsm* wraðra *gp* (=*noun* enemies)

wræc *n* misery, persecution, exile wræcc *ns* wræces *gs*

wræc, wrǣce < ġewrecan

wræcca *see* wrecca

wræclāst *m* path of exile *ns* wræclāstas *ap*

wræclīċe *adv* in exile, abroad

wræcsīþ *m* journey of misery, path of exile wræcsība *gp* wræcsības *ap* wræcsīðe *ds*

wrǣtt *f* work of art, ornament wrǣttum *dp*

wrecan *V* recite, tell wrece *pr1s* wrecen *pp*

ġewrecan *V* avenge wrecan *inf* ġewrecan *inf* wræc *pt3s* wrǣce *sbj pt3s* wrec *pt3s* ġewrec *imp s*

wreċċa *m* fugitive, exile, adventure, outcast *ns* wræċċa *ns* wreċċea *ns* wreċċena *gp* wreccum *dp*

wrēgan *1* accuse wrēgað *pr3p* wrēgdon *pt3p*

wreoton < wrītan

ġewrit *n* writing, letter, document, book, scripture *as* ġewrites *gs* ġewritu *ap* ġewritum *dp*

wrītan *I* write wreoton *pt3p* wrītaþ *pr1p* wrīte *sbj pr3s* ġewriten *pp*

wrītere *m* writer, scribe wrīteras *ap*

ġewritu < ġewrit

wrīðan *1* twist, bind, wrap

ġewroht- *see* ġewyrċan

wrōht *f* enmity, contention wrōhte *as*

wrōhtlācan *n* wrongful accusation, calumny

wudu *m* forest, wood, tree *ns* wuda *ds*

wuldor *n* wonder, glory, splendor, heaven *ns*, *as* wuldre *ds* wuldres *gs*

wuldor-fæder *m* father of glory

wuldortorht *adj* gloriously bright

wuldre, wuldres < wuldor

wuldrian *1* glorify

wulf *m* wolf *ns, as* wolfas *np* wulfum *dp*

wulfhlið *m* wolf-slope

wull *f* wool

ġewuna *m* custom, practice, rite ġewunan *ds*

wunade, wunað < wunian

wund *f* wound, wounding *ns* wunda *ap* wunde
   as, ap wundum *dp* wundun *dp*

wunden *adj* twisted, coiled *nsn*

wundenmǣl *n* sword with twisted patterns

wunder- *see* wundor-

ġewundian *2 wound* ġewundad *pp* ġewundod
   pp ġewundode *pt3s*

wundon < windan

wundor *n* marvel, miracle, wondrous thing,
   strange creature *ns, as* wundra *np gp* wundrum
   dp

wundorlic *adj* wonderful, remarkable *nsn*
   wunderlicre *gsf* wunderlicu *nsf* wunderlicum
   dsn, dpm wundorlican *asm*

wundrian *2* wonder, be astonished at wundrade
   pt1s wundrode *pt3s*

wundrum *adv* wondrously

ġewunelic *adj* common, customary *nsm*
   ġewunlic *nsn*

ġewunian *2* dwell, live, inhabit, remain, exist *inf*
   wunade *pt1s* ġewunade *pt3s* (was accustomed
   to) wunað *pr3s* wunedon *pt3p* wuniab *pr3p*
   ġewuniað *pr3p* wuniende *prp nsm, npm*
   wuniġan *inf* wuniġe *sbj pr3s* ġewuniġe *sbj*
   pr3s wuniġende *prp npm* wunode *pt3s*
   wunodon *pt3p*

ġewunlic *see* ġewunelic

wunnon < winnan

wunung *f* dwelling, abode wununge *gs*

ġewurd- < ġewelorban

wurdon *see* weorðan

wurm *n* snake, sword(?) wurman *dp*

wurpon < weorpan

wurð *adj* valued, dear, worth, worthy, deserving,
   entitled (to +*g*) wirðe *npf* wurðe *npf* wurðran
   comp npm wyrðæ *nsf npm* wyrðe *nsm nsf*
   wyrðes *gsn*

ġewurb- *see* ġeweorb-

wurðum < wurð

wūtan, wūton *see* ūton

wydewan < widuwe

wylæ, wyle < willan

wylfen *adj* wolfish, savage

wyllasð, wylle < willan

wyllspring *m* spring (of water)

wylst < wealdan

wylt < willan

wynlic *adj* pleasant wynlicran *comp apn*

wynn *f* joy, delight, pleasure, bliss *ns* syn *ns, as*
   wynne *ds* wynnum *dp* (=*adv* delightfully)

wynsum *adj* pleasant, delightful wynsumum *ds*
   wynsumo *nsf* wynsumu *npm*

ġewyrċan *1* do, make, prepare, perform, carry
   out, cause, wreak, bring about, achieve *inf*
   wirċean *inf* ġeworht *pp* worhtan *pt3p*
   worhte *pt3s* ġeworhte *pt3s pp npm*
   ġeworhtne *pp nsm, asm* worhton *pt3p*
   ġeworhton *pt3p* wrohtan *pt3p* ġewrohtan
   pt3p wyrċ *imp s* ġewyrað *pr3p* wyrċe *sbj*
   pr3s ġewyre *sbj pr3s* wyrċean *inf* wyreað
   pr3p wyrcð *pr3s*

wyrd *f* happening, event, fate, chance, destiny,
   Providence *ns, as* wyrda *gp* wyrde *ds, np*

wyrhta *m* worker, doer, maker *ns* wyrhtena *gp*

wyrm *m* worm, serpent, snake *ns* wurman *ds*
   wyrma *gp* wyrmum *dp*

wyrmlīċ *n* form of a serpent, snake pattern
   wyrmlīcum *dp*

wyrnan *1* (+*g*) withhold, be sparing of wyrnde
   pt3s wyrndon *pt3p*

wyrsa *adj* (*comp of* yfel) worse wyrsan *apf*
   wyrse *nsn*

wyrsian *2* grow worse, deteriorate wyrsedan
   pt3p

wyrt *f* herb, plant, vegetable wyrta *np* wyrtum
   dp

wyrtġemang *n* spices, perfume

wyrtruma *m* root wyrtruman *as*

ġewyrð < ġeweorban

wyrðmente < weorðmynd

wyrð- *see* wurð

wyrðode < weorbian

wȳscan *1* wish wȳscte *pt3s*

Xrīste < Crı̄st

ȳcan *1* increase, add to īhte *pt3s* ȳcað *pr3s* ȳce
  imp s
yfel *adj* bad, evil, wicked *nsn* yfelan *asf* (=*noun*
  evil creature) *dsn, npm* yfele *npm apm*
yfel *n* evil, harm, wickedness *as* yfela *gp* yfeles
  gs yflaes *gs*
yfelian *2* become bad, grow worse
ylde *m pl* men
ylde *m(pl)* men
yldestan < eald
yldo *f* age, old age
yldran, yldrena < eald
ylpesbān *n* ivory
ymb *prep* (+*a/d*) about, concerning, in respect of,
  after, around, near, at, over, towards, against
  embe, ymban, ymbe
ymbbeorgan *III* protect round about ymbbearh
  pt3s
ymbclyppan *1* embrace ymbclypte *pt3s*
ymbe *see* ymb
ymbfōn *redp* surround, encompass ymbfangen
  pp
ymbsittan *V* sit around, sit at table, surround,
  besiege imbsǣton *pt3p* ymbseten *pp*
  ymbsittendan *prp npm, apm*
ymbsittend *m* neighbor
ymbūtan *adv* round, around
yrgbo *f* cowardice yrġbo *as* yrhðe *as*
yrmb *f* misery, hardship, crime *ns* yrmba *ap, gp*
  yrmbe *as, ds*
yrre *adj* angry, enraged, fierce *nsm, npm*
yrre *n* anger *ns, as*
yrringa *adv* angrily
yrblinge *m* ploughman *ns* yrblingas *np*
ys < bēon-wesan
ȳterra *adj, conj* outer ȳtemest *sup* outermost,
  last
ȳtmæst *adj* last ȳtmæstan *apn*
ȳþ *f* wave ȳþa *gp* ȳþe *ap* yðum *dp*

ȳþan *1* lay waste ȳþde *pt3s*
ȳðelīċe *adv* easily
ȳðġeblond *n* surging water
ȳðiġan *2* flow, flood, surge